CONTEMPORARY
SOCIOLOGICAL THEORIES

harper ✦ torchbooks

A reference-list of Harper Torchbooks, classified
by subjects, is printed at the end of this volume.

CONTEMPORARY SOCIOLOGICAL THEORIES

THROUGH THE FIRST QUARTER OF
THE TWENTIETH CENTURY

PITIRIM SOROKIN

HARPER TORCHBOOKS
THE UNIVERSITY LIBRARY
HARPER & ROW, PUBLISHERS
NEW YORK, EVANSTON AND LONDON

To My Wife

CONTEMPORARY SOCIOLOGICAL THEORIES

ACKNOWLEDGMENT

F o r friendly criticism and stimulation the author is indebted to Professor F. Stuart Chapin. For encouragement, to the distinguished sociologists, Professors Franklin H. Giddings and Edward A. Ross. For help in the preparation of the manuscript he is obliged to Professors Ross L. Finney and Carl C. Zimmerman. For an effort to bring out a German edition of the book, to a prominent professor of the University of Berlin, Dr. R. Thurnwald, and Dr. H. Kasspohl. A readiness to render help requested on the part of the distinguished scholars of Europe and Russia, L. von Wiese in Germany, Gaston Richard in France, Corrado Gini in Italy, Adolfo Posada in Spain, Ivan Pavlov and E. V. Spectorsky in Russia, is gratefully acknowledged. The author offers his sincere thanks to the International Institute of Sociology, the International Institute of Sociology and Social Reforms, to the German and Ukrainian Sociological Societies, and to the Czecho-Slovakian Academy of Agriculture for the honor of membership granted to him. The Staff of the Library of the University of Minnesota, by its unfailing service, has greatly helped the composition of the book. Finally, and last but not least, to the students of the author's classes and seminars he is indebted for many a happy moment in mutual scientific work.

Minneapolis, October, 1927

EDITOR'S INTRODUCTION

S t u d e n t s of sociological theory are prone to fall into two contrasting types of error; either they accept speculative explanations of social phenomena with credulity, or they dismiss all theorizing as unscientific escapes from the hard reality of laborious research. Professor Sorokin's book is a sound antidote for both extremes.

By assembling quantitative data on social phenomena from an amazing variety of reputable sources, he confronts unfounded speculation with cold facts, and provides the student with tangible criteria for evaluating theory. By exhibiting time and again the recurrence of type theories, he shows how necessary it is for the research student to take pains to inform himself about the works of other students before plunging into fact-gathering and then drawing inferences which he naïvely considers are original with himself. In these two respects the present book is a substantial corrective for these most egregious forms of error often found in the works of contemporary social scientists.

The book is quite unique among works on social theory because of the enormous amount of factual and quantitative data assembled as the test of theories that various writers have expounded, and which so often are content to rest their validity on distinctions of a purely verbal sort. Professor Sorokin has no patience with what may be termed "substitute speech reactions."

If young students of sociology will read this book with care they will save themselves much wasted time in following theories that are mere "painful elaborations of the obvious," and incidentally discover how pure speculative theorizing leads unerringly to logical contradiction and fallacy.

Aside from the characteristics just mentioned, this book is a contribution to the scientific literature of sociology in that it deals primarily with contemporary theories. Earlier theoretical conceptions are considered only as it becomes necessary to link up the present with the past to preserve a balanced sense of historical perspective.

Serious students of the other social sciences, anthropology, economics, history and political science, will find this work a useful addition to their libraries, and a demonstration of the values and limitations of contemporary sociological theories. In this connection the work has real synthetic significance.

F. STUART CHAPIN

CONTENTS

Object of the book. Reasons for its writing and publication. Plan of the book and distribution of the materials. The classification of the schools of contemporary sociology. Some additional points.

1. Predecessors. 2. Contemporary social physics. 3. Contemporary social mechanics. 4. Contemporary social energetics. 5. Criticism. 6. Vilfredo Pareto and others. Pareto's conception of the relationship of a special science to sociology. What Pareto understands by scientific sociology. Quantitative description of the functional interdependence of social phenomena instead of one-sided causation. Pareto's concept of society and theory of factors. Pareto's conclusions concerning the residues and derivations. Pareto's conclusions concerning other elements in the form of a social system. 7. Criticism.

1. Biographical data and history of the school. 2. Methods of Le Play's school. 3. The sociological system. 4. Contributions of the school to social science. 5. Criticism and appreciation.

1. Predecessors. 2. Definition of geographical factors. 3. Fundamental propositions concerning the character conditioning of social phenomena by geographical factors. 4. Geographical conditions and distribution of human population on the earth. 5. Geographic conditions and the character of human dwellings, roads and means of transportation. 6. Geographical conditions and clothing. 7. Geographical conditions and food and drink. 8. Geographical conditions and economic life and organization: wealth, character of industries, busi-

INTRODUCTION

Object of the Book.—This book deals with the sociological theories of the last sixty or seventy years. Its objective is to survey the principal types of these theories and to find to what extent they are scientifically valid. All other approaches to a study of the theories, such as, for instance, why a certain theory is set forth by a certain author, or why it has become popular, or what is the personality of an author, are intentionally excluded. The reason is that the first task may be solved independently from the others. Moreover, it is impossible to embrace in one book all the possible approaches to the study of sociological thought. This book deals with the character and the validity of the theories, but does not deal with their authors. So much for this point.

Reasons for Its Writing and Publication.—In the opinion of the writer, the primary task of a scholar is to deal with facts rather than theories. If, however, disregarding this, he writes a book about other books, he does it because he has several reasons. In the first place we do not have any single book which gives a concise survey of all the principal sociological theories of the period mentioned. We have many an excellent monograph about a certain problem or a sociologist, but all such cover only a small part of the whole field.[1] We have several valuable works in the history of sociological thought,[2] but they pay inadequate attention to the last period of sociology. There are many valuable essays in the history of the sociology of a certain country for the last few decades,[3] but again, they cover only a part of the field.

---

[1] They are indicated further.

[2] See the text of the book.

[3] For America see Small, Albion, "Fifty Years of Sociology in the United States," *American Journal of Sociology*, May, 1916; Barnes, H. E., "American Psychological Sociology," *The Sociological Review* for 1922, 1924, 1925; Gillin, John L., Presidential Address in *Publications of the American Sociological Society*, Vol. XXI. For England, Barnes, H. E., "English Sociology," in *Publications of the American Sociological Society*, Vol. XXI. For Germany, Vierkandt, A., "Die Uberwindung des Positivismus in der deutschen Soziologie der Gegenwart," *Jahrbuch für Soziologie*, Vol. II; Barth. P., *Die Philosophie der Geschichte als*

Finally, even such valuable works as P. Barth's *Die Philosophie der Geschichte als Soziologie,* or F. Squillace's *Le dottrine sociologiche,* or M. Kovalevsky's *Contemporary Socielogists* (in Russian), or H. E. Barnes' *The New History and the Social Studies,* or papers of F. H. Hankins in H. E. Barnes' *The History and Prospects of the Social Sciences,* and of Charles A. Ellwood in E. C. Hayes' *Recent Developments in Social Sciences,* are either not translated into English, or are not up to date, or deal with the historical rather than the sociological aspect of the theories, or else they are too short to give a sufficient account of the principal schools in contemporary sociology. The situation is such that the writer has found difficulty in obtaining any book suitable as a text for the graduate students in his course in Contemporary Sociological Theories. Such a situation is the first excuse for the publication of the book.

In the second place, the field of sociology has grown to such an extent that, for a sociologist who is devoted to a study of a special sociological problem, it is extremely difficult to have an adequate knowledge of the whole field of the science. Being absorbed in his special study, he does not have time to go through the hundreds of various sources where information about the theories is given. Meanwhile, some approximate knowledge of the general situation in contemporary sociology is necessary for any sociologist. Not knowing that a certain theory has been developed long ago, or that a certain problem has been carefully studied by many predecessors, a sociologist may easily devote

---

Soziologie, Leipzig, 1922, Vol. II; VON WIESE, L., "German Sociology," *The Sociological Review,* Vol. XIX, No. 1; BRINKMANN, CARL, "German Sociology," *Publications of the American Sociological Society,* Vol. XXI. For Italy, MICHELS, ROBERT, "Elemente zur Soziologie in Italien," *Kölner Vierteljahrshefte für Soziologie,* III Jahrgang, 4 Heft, translated and published in *Revue International de Sociologie* and in *Suspilstvo,* Vol. III–IV. For France, see DUPRAT, G. L., "La psycho-sociologie en France," *Archiv für Geschichte der Philosophie und Soziologie,* Vol. XXX, Heft 1 and 2; FAUCOUNET, P., "Durkheim Sociological School," *The Sociological Review,* Vol. XIX, No. 1. For Russia, SOROKIN, P., "Die Russische Soziologie in Zwanzigsten Jahrhundert," *Jahrbuch für Soziologie,* Vol. II, translated and published in *Suspilstvo,* Vol. III–IV, and in an abbreviated form in *Publications of the American Sociological Society,* Vol. XXI; HECKER, J., *The Russian Sociology,* N. Y., 1915. For Czechoslovakia, BLÁHA, ARNOST, "Die zeitgenossische tschechische Soziologie," *Jahrbuch für Soziologie,* Vol. II. These works are only representative samples of the studies of this type.

his time and energy to the discovery of a new sociological America after it was discovered long ago. Instead of a comfortable crossing of the scientific Atlantic in the short period of time necessary for the study of what has been done before, such a sociologist has to undergo all the hardships of Columbus to find, only after his time and energy are wasted, that his discovery has been made long ago, and that his hardships have been useless. Such a finding is a tragedy for a scholar, and a waste of valuable ability for society and sociology. As a rule, explorers do not receive anything for such "discoveries." Meanwhile, if the energy and time had been given to the study of an unexplored part of the sociological field, sociology might have been enriched, and society would have received something from its scholar. This consideration is not a mere possibility, but a real situation which has happened many times. For this reason the books which give a general survey of the whole field of a certain science are not entirely useless.

In the third place, sociology has not suffered during the period mentioned from a lack of various theories. They have been produced in a great abundance, and have been appearing like mushrooms after rain. At the present moment the field of sociology is overcrowded by a multitude of various and contradictory systems. Every novitiate who enters the field is likely to be lost in it, and what is more important, such a novitiate has the greatest difficulty in discriminating between what in all these theories is valid and what is false. Therefore, one of the most urgent tasks of the contemporary sociologist is to separate what is really valid from that which is false or unproved in these theories. Such a separation is likely to be as necessary as the setting forth of a new hypothesis. Providing that it is done carefully, a critical analysis of the contemporary sociological theories may be of a real service to the science of sociology. This task is attempted in the book and is its primary purpose. A lack of space has not permitted me to criticize the theories in detail; nevertheless, the critical remarks are so developed as to suggest to a thoughtful reader the principal shortcomings of a theory or hypothesis. Not adding other reasons, the above excuses may be sufficient to explain why this book about other books has been written.

PLAN OF THE BOOK AND DISTRIBUTION OF THE MATERIALS.— The number of sociologists and sociological works for the period mentioned has become so great as to make impossible a substantial analysis of the contributions of all the individual sociologists in one volume. If such an attempt is undertaken, it is likely to result in a kind of a biographical dictionary with all its plusses and minuses. Among its minuses is liable to be a lack of a logical and coherent perspective of the whole field. This shortcoming is so serious as to make necessary some other method of survey which will be free from it. As we are not concerned with the biographies of sociologists, the best way seems to be this: to segregate all the important sociological theories into several classes or schools, and to analyze not so much the works of individual sociologists as the fundamental principles of the schools. Providing that in each school several of the most representative individual theories are given, that all the principal works are mentioned, and that all its principal generalizations and propositions are described, such a plan appears to be more plausible scientifically than any other one. It is more economical than the chronological and biographical plan of a dictionary. It is likely to give a more systematic and coherent knowledge of the field than a distribution of the materials on an incidental chronological basis, or on the data of the works of several individual sociologists picked up by a surveyor.

The above explains the logical construction of the book. It is in detail as follows: All the theories are divided into a few major schools, each one being subdivided into its varieties, and each variety being represented by several of the most typical works. At the beginning of each school, or its variety, a short paragraph about its predecessors is given to connect the present sociology with its past. A characterization of the principles of the school or theory is followed by a critical paragraph to show its fallacies or shortcomings. This plan, to be sure, has its own disadvantages, but they seem to be not so great as those of any other method.

THE CLASSIFICATION OF THE SCHOOLS OF CONTEMPORARY SOCIOLOGY.—The classification of the schools and their varieties in the book is as follows:

  I. Mechanistic School
        Social mechanics
        Social physics
        Social energetics
        Mathematical sociology of Pareto
 II. Synthetic and Geographic School of Le Play
III. Geographical School
 IV. Biological School
        Bio-organismic branch
        Racialist, Hereditarist and Selectionist branch
        Sociological Darwinism and Struggle for Existence theories
  V. Bio-Social School
        Demographic sociology
 VI. Bio-Psychological School
        Instinctivists' sociology
VII. Sociologistic School
        Neo-positivist branch
        Durkheim's branch
        Gumplowicz's branch
        Formal sociology
        Economic interpretation of history
VIII. Psychological School
        Behaviorists
        Instinctivists
        Introspectivists of various types
 IX. Psycho-Sociologistic School
        Various interpretations of social phenomena in terms of culture, religion, law, public opinion, folkways, and other "psycho-social factors"
        Experimental studies of a correlation between various psycho-social phenomena

It goes without saying that this classification is quite conditional. It has a significance only as far as it helps to distribute a vast material into relatively few classes. It may, however, be replaced by any other classification if it happens to serve an investigator's purposes better. In other words, the classification is to be regarded as purely technical rather than something principal and dogmatic.

SOME ADDITIONAL POINTS.—The impossibility of surveying separately all the numerous individual theories makes some subjectivism inevitable in the choice of which theories are to be taken as representative and which are to be merely mentioned. It is probable that, in spite of the writer's desire to be impartial, some amount of subjectivism has slipped into the book. Nevertheless, the writer hopes that the amount is not very great. Probably almost all the competent sociologists would agree that the theories taken as representative for a certain school or its variety are really typical, and have been set forth earlier than many other similar theories.

There is, however, one point which may meet with disagreement on the part of sociologists. This point is that the writer has given relatively less attention to the textbook type of sociological works than to the monographic investigations; and to the speculative and "philosophical" works rather than to the factual, quantitative, and special studies. This has been done deliberately and the writer takes full responsibility for it. The very nature of a textbook forces its author to fill it with commonplaces which are but a popularization of the results obtained by monographic studies. There are a few exceptions, and they are noted in the book; but the rule remains and explains the writer's standpoint. As to the speculative systems of social philosophy, we must discriminate those "social philosophies" which have given a deep insight into the nature of social phenomena from those which have been a mere "word-polishing." The speculations of the first type deserve the greatest attention; the speculations of the second type must be passed by.

Finally, there is no need to stress the great importance of the factual and "inductive" studies. To them, primarily, belongs the credit of a real promotion of sociology as a science. They represent the only basis for deciding whether a certain philosophical generalization is valid or not. Through such studies we are given relatively accurate sociological correlations and causal formulas, and in such studies mainly lies the hope of a further perfecting of sociology as a science. Hence the attention given to them throughout the book. Their results are used to test the validity of the general sociological theories. Their conclusions are utilized for the demonstration of an inadequacy in a theory. Their data are laid down to show the existence or non-existence of a correlation in a certain field. In addition, a special chapter is added where the principal studies of this type are surveyed. It is certain that not all of the studies are mentioned, but probably no important type is omitted.

The next point to be mentioned is this: The book deals exclusively with those sociological theories which face the facts, that is, which try to describe and analyze social phenomena as they are. All the theories which try to preach what ought to be, in what way the social world should be changed, and what ought to be done for this purpose, are omitted. The reason is that as far as such theories are busy not with what was, is, and will be, but with what ought to be, or ought not to be, they are out of science. Although valuable from a practical standpoint, they belong to a field beyond that of science.

Last, but not least, almost all the important sociological theories are criticized in this book. The writer wants to stress the fact that his criticism of a theory does not mean at all that he does not appreciate it, or does not have respect for its author. The opposite conclusion is true. This should be borne in mind to understand the writer's real attitude. His criticism is due to the very nature of the science,—it appeared with criticism, has grown with criticism, and lives with criticism. If we care to promote sociology as a science, a critical attitude must be displayed by all sociologists as regards any sociological theory, without any exception whatsoever. Being grateful and reverent to all the builders of sociology, the best way in which we may be faithful to them is to separate what is true and what is false in the large mental heritage left by them. Otherwise, instead of a scientific sociology we will have a pseudo-scientific complimentary art, having nothing in common with a real science.

CONTEMPORARY
SOCIOLOGICAL THEORIES

CHAPTER I

THE MECHANISTIC SCHOOL

In this school may be classified all sociological theories
which interpret social phenomena in the terminology and concepts
of physics, chemistry, and mechanics. Its various branches exhibit some differences of detail; one branch gives preference to
the interpretation *modo geometrico,* another, *modo mechanico et
physico,* still another, *modo energetico,* and, finally, another, *modo
mathematico.* These differences will be elaborated in some detail
as we proceed; but they do not annul the general similarity that
pervades all branches of this school, which for the sake of brevity
may be designated in the following discussion as "The Mechanistic School."

I. PREDECESSORS

The essential elements of the mechanistic interpretation of
man's nature, behavior, and social activities were set forth long
ago. Since the mechanistic school views all social phenomena as
mere variations of physical phenomena, its essential characteristic
is a monistic conception of the universe as a whole, including
the universal application of all natural law, or unity of all its
laws. For this reason potentially all the monistic conceptions of
the world, and especially the materialistic monism, contained one
of the substantial elements of the mechanistic school. As is well
known, the monistic philosophies in their materialistic, as well as
their idealistic varieties, are very old. We find them in the remotest past. Thales' statement that "the essence of all things in
the universe is water," or Anaximenes' theory that "the essence"
is air, or the materialistic and atomistic monism of Empedocles,
Leucippus, Democritus, Anaxagoras, and Lucretius are representative samples of that monistic interpretation of the universe in
which psychical and social phenomena were viewed as mere variations of material phenomena; more than that, psychical and social

3

phenomena were interpreted in a strictly mechanistic way by these Greek philosophers, especially in the theories of materialistic atomism. Similar theories existed also in ancient India and China. Another element of the mechanistic interpretation of social phenomena, that was known also to the past, is the application of mathematics to their interpretation and a belief in the universality of quantitative regularities, or laws, in the dynamics of social, as of all other, processes. These elements were strongly emphasized by Pythagoras and his school, as well as by the atomistic philosophers mentioned above. Further, both elements of the mechanistic sociology are found in the theories of the Epicureans and the Stoics. Cicero stresses their presence in the theory of Epicurus.[1] Seneca and certain other Stoics, with their rather materialistic monism, regarded even time, virtue, and evil as "things," and even as sensual or physical things.[2]

Generally speaking, in the periods of conspicuous progress in the physical and mathematical sciences, their conclusions have been carried over into the field of social phenomena; and, as a result, have called forth a mechanistic interpretation in that field also. This explains why "the mechanistic sociology" became a dominant type of interpretation for social phenomena in the seventeenth century. This was the conspicuous century for creative work in physics, mechanics, and mathematics. As Professor E. Spektorsky rightly declares, it was not the centuries of the Renaissance, nor even the eighteenth (which actually produced but little in these fields), but the seventeenth century which was the most productive epoch in the progress of physical and mathematical sciences.[3] To support this statement it is enough to mention

---

[1] "*In physicis plurimum posuit,*" says he about the teaching of Epicurus. See CICERO, *De finibus bonorum et malorum,* Lib. I, chap. VI, XIX, and *passim.*

[2] See *Stoicorum veterum fragmenta.* Collegit J. ab. Arnim, Volumen III, Lipsiae, 1903, pp. 20 ff; Seneca, *Epistola,* 117; "*placet nostris quod bonum est corpus esse,*" writes Seneca to his correspondents.

[3] See the excellent work of SPEKTORSKY, E., *The Problems of Social Physics in the Seventeenth Century,* Vol. I, Warsaw, 1910, Vol. II, Kiev, 1917; in Russian *Problema sozialnoy physiki v XVII Stoletii.* This work is probably the best for the study of social physics of the seventeenth century. I am indebted to Professor Spektorsky for kindly sending me the only copy of his work which he himself could obtain. The work is so valuable for the history of social, political. and ethical thought, that it ought to be translated to make it available for the foreign specialists.

the names of Newton, Galileo, Copernicus, Descartes, Leibnitz, Pascal, Huygens, Kepler, Francis Bacon, R. Boyle, and Leeuwenhoek, though many others might be added.

The extraordinary progress of physics, mechanics, and mathematics during this century called forth an extraordinary effort to interpret social phenomena, in the same way that mechanics had so successfully interpreted physical phenomena. As a result we have "The Social Physics" of the seventeenth century, which, at least in its plan and aspirations, has not been surpassed by all the mechanistic theories of the nineteenth and twentieth centuries. More than that, in their efforts to create a social mechanics the thinkers of the seventeenth century laid down those principles of psychology, of the social and political sciences, which at the present moment are regarded by many as something that has been quite recently discovered.[4] The essential characteristics of the social physics of the seventeenth century may be summed up as follows: First, in contrast with the preceding thinkers the social theorists of the seventeenth century (Hobbes, Spinoza, Descartes, Weigel, Leibnitz, and others) abandoned anthropomorphism, teleologism, moralism, and hierarchism in their study of man's nature, mentality, behavior, and social phenomena. Second, they began to study social and psychic phenomena as a physicist studies physical phenomena, rationally but objectively. Man was re-

[4] Such for instance is the behavioristic school in psychology. Its aspiration to study man's behavior and mentality without any reference to "inner psychical experience," that is, to study them as a kind of mechanistic phenomena, is nothing but a modification of the mechanistic and quantitative psychology of the seventeenth century (Descartes, Leibnitz, Spinoza, Malebranche, and others), which viewed man as an automaton, and tried to study the psychical processes as physical ones, measuring and interpreting them in terms of physical mechanics. See SPEKTORSKY, Vol. I, pp. 81 ff., 339 ff.; Vol. II, p. 408. The same is true of their efforts to be objective in their methods, and to study social and psychical phenomena as specialists in physics study theirs and so be free from any ethical, religious, and other considerations. It is true also of their efforts to measure everything in a strictly scientific way. In sociology and social psychology recent theories of conation (L. Ward) or theories of "instinctive" interpretation of social and behavioristic facts, or such theories as Thomas's "four wishes," or Ratzenhofer's and A. Small's "sixfold interests" (declared by Small to be "the latest word of sociology"), or many other varieties of this type of "interpretations," all were formulated by Hobbes, Spinoza, Weigel, Malebranche, G. Grotius, Descartes, Leibnitz, J. Am. Komensky, and others. See SPEKTORSKY, *ibid.*, Vol. II, pp. 411–422, and *passim*. The same must be said of Pareto's or Tarde's "monadologies."

garded as a physical object—a kind of machine [5] or physical automaton. His life and action were regarded "as a regular functioning of the human machinery; his death, as a wreck of it." "There was not admitted any vitalistic force." Descartes and Hobbes compared death with the stopping of a watch mechanism.[6] The human soul is interpreted as a movement as regular as any motion studied in mechanics. *"Vita motus est perpetuus,"* says Hobbes. *"Notre nature est dans le mouvement,"* wrote Pascal. "Human life is nothing but a circulation of blood and circulation of thoughts and desires," explains Malebranche. Where there is movement there is inertia, according to mechanics; and inertia is to be recognized also in human society and psychical movement. It is manifested in a human being's tendency to preserve himself and to look after his own interests. *"Suum esse conservare, suum sibi utile quaerere,"* says Spinoza. This is a universal law of nature, and it is the law of human nature also. Viewing the human soul in this mechanical way, the physicists of the seventeenth century tried to analyze it into its components, as a mechanism may be disassembled into its parts. The corresponding components of the human soul were found in a series of primary "tendencies," or "conations" (self-preservation, gravitation to or repulsion from other human beings, etc.) or "affections," or "appetites." Classifying them (six principal affections, according to Descartes, or three, according to Spinoza), they regarded a human being as an embodiment of these components, and human activity as a result of these conations (gravitation or repulsion or relationship). Their mutual gravi-

---

[5] *"Hominis corpus quatenus machinamentum quoddam . . . machinamentum humani corporis,"* wrote Descartes. *"L'on peut fort bien comparer les nerfs de la (humaine) machine aux tuyaux des machines de ces fontaines, ses muscles et ses tendons aux autres divers engins et ressorts. . . . De plus, la respiration et autres telles actions . . . sont comme les mouvements d'une horloge,"* and so on. *Renati Des Cartes Meditationes de prima philosophia,* Meditatio sexta, p. 43 of the Amsterdam edit., 1685; his "l'Homme," in *Oeuvres,* Cousin, IV, pp. 347-348. *"Quid est cor nisi elastrum, quid nervi nisi chordae, articuli nisi . . . rotulae,"* wrote Hobbes, *Leviathan,* Introductio, Opera, III, 1. *"Le corps de l'animal est une machine en même temps hydraulique, pneumatique et pyrobolique . . . une Espèce d'un Automate Naturel, qui surpasse infiniment les Automates artificiels,"* says Leibnitz. See SPEKTORSKY, *op. cit., passim.*

[6] "The body of a living man differs from that of a dead man only as much as a watch or any other automaton when they are wound up differ from the same watch or automaton when they are broken." DESCARTES, "Les passions de l'ame," Art. VI, *Oeuvres,* Cousin, IV, 41. SPEKTORSKY, *op. cit.,* Vol. II, p. 410.

tation or repulsion results in a regularity of human activity and of psychical processes which, being similar to the regularity of physical movement, could be interpreted by the principles of mechanics. In this way they set forth "the mechanics of psychical processes" and of "human activity." Thus a human soul was interpreted as "a kind of astronomical system" in which different processes go on with the same regularity as in an astronomical system interpreted by mechanics. The "human individual was regarded as a kind of astronomical system of affections or other psychical elements bound together by mutual attraction or repulsion." [7]

From this it was easy to pass to the construction of "a social mechanics" or of "a mechanistic interpretation of society." "Society was regarded as a new astronomical system whose elements were human beings, bound together by mutual attraction or repulsion, like the atoms of physical substance." Finally, the mutual relationship of societies and of states was viewed again as a new system of balanced oppositions whose elements themselves were human groups. Thus we have gradually enlarging series of gravitations and repulsions (of man, society, groups of societies) which, according to Spinoza, did not constitute any specific realm in the kingdom of nature, but easily entered, as a part, into the mechanistic kingdom of the universe without a break in its mechanistic structure (Spektorsky, Vol. II, p. 422). The scheme of the social order may thus be seen to be in three parts, as follows:

1. The *human being:* an astronomical system composed of the attraction and repulsion of conations;
2. *Society:* an astronomical system composed of the attraction and repulsion of individuals; and
3. *Mankind:* an astronomical system composed of the attraction and repulsion of groups.

From the above it is clear that any supernaturalism, indeterminism, any freedom of the will, were expelled from the sociological theories of these social physicists. They viewed all these phenomena as a result of the natural play of natural causes. Their purpose was to study these phenomena as a system of relationship,

---

[7] SPEKTORSKY, Vol. II, pp. 411–422.

to measure these relations and to give the results of such a study in the forms of the laws of social mechanics.

Hence, the mathematical method of their studies. Of any science they demanded that it be a science of mathematical type. *Generalem quandam esse debere scientiam, . . . eamdemque . . . Mathesim universalem nominari* (Descartes) is the motto of their method. "Without mathematics human beings would live as the animals and beasts," Weigel declared. "All truths are discovered only through measurement," said Malebranche. Hence their geometrical and mathematical method. Hence their conception that the truth is nothing but quantitatively described relationship. Hence their attempts to create "Pantometrika," "Psychometrika," "Ethicometrika," "Sociometrika"; in brief, a universal quantitative science of relations applied to the study of all phenomena, including psychical, ethical, political, and social ones. (See Spektorsky, Vol. I, pp. 328 ff.) *"Mens, mensura, quies, motus, positura, figura sunt cum materia cunctarum exordia rerum."* Such was their motto. H. Grotius interpreted the phenomena of law *"sicut Mathematici figuras a corporibus semotas considerant";* Leibnitz explained juridical relations in *modo geometrico,* with charts and diagrams; Weigel and Puffendorff drew a series of circles of human actions *"ad analogiam systematis Copernicaei." "In societate inter homines nihil fere agitur quod a numerorum et mensurae scientia non dependeat,"* claimed Richard Cumberland.[8] Politics was interpreted *"per magnitudinem, figuram et motum."* This is not all. In order that these declarations and aspirations be realised the attempt became necessary to build "social mechanics" factually. And we see indeed some attempts to do this. The conceptions of space, time, gravitation, inertia, and force or power are the fundamental principles by which physical mechanics succeeded in interpreting the motion of physical objects, beginning with that of atoms and ending with that of the planets, stars, and systems of the universe. The social physicists of the seventeenth century tried to do the same as the physicists themselves. In the first place they constructed the conception *of a moral or social space* in which social, and moral, and political movements go on. It was a kind of space

---

[8] See CUMBERLAND, RICHARD, *Disquisitio philosophica de legibus naturae,* 1671.

analogous to physical space, and superposed upon it. To the *position* of a material object in physical space, there corresponded, in social space, the conception of *status*, as of sex, age, occupation, freedom, religion, citizenship, and so on. In this way they constructed a system of social coördinates which defined the position of man in this moral space as exactly as the system of geometrical coördinates defines the position of a material object in physical space.[9] Physical mechanics explains the motions, also, of physical objects by the principles of inertia and gravitation. Similarly, social mechanics regarded the social processes as a result of the gravitation and inertia of human beings or groups. In physical mechanics any physical system is regarded as an equilibrium. In the same way, any society or group or state was regarded by the social physicists as a system of equilibrium of centrifugal and centripetal forces. A series of political institutions was interpreted as a system of counter-balances. The social and political organization of a society, and the phenomena of power and authority were interpreted as resultants of the pressures of "social atoms" (individuals) and "social molecules" (groups). In this way these social theorists created "social statics" or a theory of social equilibrium, analogous to "statics" in physical mechanics.

They also laid down the elements of social dynamics. In mechanics motion or change is a function of space and time. Time also plays its rôle in the social mechanics of the seventeenth century; for these thinkers conceived the idea, not only of a status in moral space, but in moral time as well. This led them to constructions *in respectu ad durationem* and even to the theory of a specific *status quandicativus* with a specific "moral time." Historical and social events were viewed as motions or movements and time as a coefficient of motion. *"Tempus nihil aliud est quam magnitudo motus,"* wrote Leibnitz. Any process came to be understood as a kind of mechanically moving object. "Time was depicted by a geometrical line; historical processes began to be illustrated by various curves, and an individual's life history, by a curve as of a falling body. Straight lines, parabolas, and spiral curves began to be used to describe these processes." In

[9] Compare Sorokin, P., *Social Mobility*, Chap. I.

brief, the physicists were the real initiators in the social, as well as in many other fields of science.[10]   From the above it follows that the plan of social mechanics outlined by the thinkers of the seventeenth century was grand and magnificent indeed.[11]   If they did not succeed in realizing it more or less satisfactorily, it was not the fault of lack of effort, but that of the complexity of the problems studied.   In spite of many failures and childish statements, their effort to create a social physics yielded as a by-product a series of valuable contributions to the social and psychological sciences, contributions which at the present moment are being rediscovered as something quite new and unknown to the past.

Furthermore, the mechanistic interpretation of social phenomena now in vogue is nothing but a repetition, with slight modifications of the principles laid down by the great thinkers of the seventeenth century, often, however, without any reference to their names or works.   It is true that some of the methods and conclusions of these earlier thinkers have been further developed in the biological, psychological, statistical, and sociological works of the eighteenth and first half of the nineteenth centuries.   This has been the case with W. Petty's seventeenth century study of

---

[10] See SPEKTORSKY, Vol. I, *passim*, and pp. 328–554; Vol. II, *passim*, and pp. 450–628.

[11] Especially interesting and imposing was the *Pantometrika* of a forgotten thinker, Edhard Weigel. He perhaps more consistently than any other tried to create the universal quantitative science, "*Mathesis universae.*" On this problem Weigel worked for a long time and with great persistence. Its importance grew in his opinion, as his efforts continued. He tried to solve the problem in various ways. Finally he was broken under its burden. He became almost a maniac and began to see everywhere only figures, figures, and figures. According to his conception the universal mathematics, or *Pantometrika*, was to be a specific science of quantity, as opposed to quality. It ought to be because without quantitative knowledge there is no real knowledge applied, he contended, to any field of phenomena. Any causal relation, indeed, any relationship whatsoever, may be measured. Real scientific determinism is a quantitative determinism. In this way all objects are resolved into quantity. The quantities studied in *Pantometrika* were to be three kinds: physical, moral, and terminological. Under moral quantities Weigel subsumed economic value, social dignity, prestige, power, social achievements, services, crimes and so on. All of these phenomena were to be measured. Real moral philosophers or jurisconsults were to be mathematicians. These ideas he tried to develop in detail in a series of works: *Idea Matheseos Universynopsis*, etc., 1669; *Universi Corporis pansophici Prodromus de gradibus humanae cognitionis*, etc., Jenae, 1672; *Corporis Pansophici Pantologia*, etc. About Weigel, see SPEKTORSKY, Vol. I, pp. 488-563.

social and moral phenomena,[12] and with that century's deterministic and objective study of such phenomena irrespective of any religious or moral evaluation. Such later development was carried forward in ethics and psychology by Jeremy Bentham's "moral arithmetic," by Herbart's studies in "mechanistic psychology," and by others in the field of statistics. But the same cannot be said for the "social mechanics" of the seventeenth century, in the narrower sense of that term. Almost all attempts in that field which were made in the eighteenth and first half of the nineteenth centuries were but variations of the social physics of the seventeenth century.

Along the lines of social physics of the seventeenth century George Berkeley (1685-1753) constructed his theory of moral attraction and social stability.[13] According to his "social physics," physical gravitation has its analogue. The centrifugal forces are manifest in the form of egoism, which drives persons apart; while the social instincts correspond to the centripetal forces, because they draw persons together. Society is stable when the centripetal forces are greater than the centrifugal. The rôle of physical mass in social mechanics is played by the population; the rôle of physical distance, by the homogeneity or heterogeneity of individuals.[14] In brief, Berkeley's theory of moral attraction is a mere variation of the theories of the seventeenth century.

The same must be said of the majority of the mechanistic theories in sociology of the eighteenth [15] and of the beginning of the nineteenth centuries. Some of the Encyclopedists may be included here. Saint-Simon's attempts to interpret social phenomena in the light of Newton's law of gravitation and system of mechanics did not add anything essentially new to the social physics of the seventeenth century. Later on F. M. Ch. Fourier, among his many theories, made a sketch of the mechanistic inter-

[12] PETTY, W., *Several Essays in Political Arithmetics*, 1699.
[13] See BERKELEY, G., *The Principles of Moral Attraction*, Works, Fraser edition, Vol. IV.
[14] Compare E. Bogardus' conception of "social distance," and F. H. Giddings' theory of the social rôle of "the consciousness of kind."
[15] See, for instance, LORD KAME, *Sketches of the History of Man*, 4 vols., 1788; DUNBAR, JAMES, *Essay on the History of Mankind in Rude and Cultivated Ages*, 1780; *vide* HUTH, H., *Soziale und individualistische Auffassung im 18 Jahrhundert*, 1907.

pretation of history; but, like many of his other theories, it was not systematically developed and was set forth in a somewhat erratic and extravagant form. Finally, Auguste Comte and A. Quetelet both show the influence of the seventeenth century's social physics, especially in the terminology which they employ. "Social statics" and "social dynamics" are the principal parts of sociology, according to Comte; while Quetelet even uses the term "social physics" as the title of his work. It should be distinctly stated, however, that this use of an earlier terminology is misleading, for their interpretations of social phenomena were far from being the mechanistic interpretation of the seventeenth century. Since the second half of the nineteenth century this has begun to show decided symptoms of revival. Since that time there have appeared several works which, though pretending to be a new interpretation of social phenomena, have, as a matter of fact, moved along the general plan of social physics in the seventeenth century. Let us now turn to a survey and analysis of these recent recapitulations and developments. Modern representatives of this school of sociology are: H. C. Carey, Voronoff, E. Solvay, L. Winiarsky, A. P. y Barcelo, Haret, W. Ostwald, W. Bechtereff, Edgeworth, F. Carli, A. Bentley, T. N. Carver, Alfred J. Lötka, and finally V. Pareto, not to mention other names.[16] Their works may be divided into four or five principal branches: the branch of social physics (Carey); of social mechan-

---

[16] Of other works in which the authors claim to interpret social phenomena according to the laws of physics and mechanics, but actually fail to do so, may be mentioned the following: PLANTA, J. C., *Die Wissenschaft des Staates oder die Lehre vom Lebensorganismus*, Chur, 1852; ZACHARIA, K. S., *Vierzig Bücher vom Staate*, 7 vols., 1839–43; MISMER, *Principes sociologiques*, 1880; DE MARINIS, *Sistema di Sociologia*, Torino, 1901; FISKE, J., *Outlines of Cosmic Philosophy*, Lond., 1874; BAGEHOT, W., *Physics and Politics*, N. Y., 1884. Simmel and the formal school in sociology use extensively geometrical analogies and forms; but trait is purely incidental to their theories; therefore they have only the remotest relation to the "mechanistic" interpretation of social phenomena. (See "The Formal School" in this book.) Somewhat more mechanistic or energetistic to some extent are the interpretations of economic and juridical phenomena given by HELM, G., *Die Lehre von der Energy*, pp. 72 ff., Leipzig, 1887, and by BOZI, A., *Die Weltanschauung der Jurisprudenz*, pp. 108 ff. A comparatively good (though a little elementary and out of date) characterization of the mechanistic school is given in F. Squillace's *Le dottrine sociologiche*, Roma, 1902, Chap. I; and Petre Trisca's *Prolégomènes à une Mécanique Sociale*, Vol. II, Paris, Alcan. 1922; in G. Solomon's introduction to Bousquet's *Grundriss der Soziologie Paretos*. 1926.

ics (Barcelo, Haret, Lötka) ; the social energetics (E. Solvay, W. Bechtereff, W. Ostwald, T. N. Carver, L. Winiarsky) ; and finally of mathematico-functional "pure sociology" (Pareto, Carli).

2. CONTEMPORARY SOCIAL PHYSICS

H. C. Carey's *Principles of Social Science* [17] is one of the most conspicuous attempts in the second half of the nineteenth century at a physical interpretation of social phenomena. At the very beginning of the first volume of the *Principles* we find his emphatic declaration that "the laws which govern matter in all its forms, whether that of coal, clay, iron, pebble stones, trees, oxen, horses, or men" are the same.[18] Hence, the mechanistic monism which permeates his sociological and economic theories. In harmony with Carey's general "mechanistic" attitude are his theories that "man is the molecule of society" ; [19] that association is only a variety of "the great law of molecular gravitation" ; [20] that "man tends of necessity to gravitate towards his fellowman," "that gravitation is here (in human societies), as everywhere else in the material world, in the direct ratio of the mass (of cities), and in the inverse ratio of the distance" ; [21] centralization and decentralization of a State and of a population in the cities is nothing but a variety of centripetal and centrifugal forces working according to the laws of physical mechanics.[22] As in physics, the greater the difference of the temperature of two bodies the more intense is the process of the transmitting heat in the form of motion from one body to another ; in a similar way, the

[17] H. C. Carey was born in 1793 and died in 1879. The first volume of his *Principles* was published in 1858 (Philadelphia, Lippincott Co.), earlier than H. Spencer's *First Principles* (1862), *Principles of Biology* (1864), *Principles of Sociology* (1876) or *Principles of Ethics* (1879).

[18] *Principles*, Vol. I, 1858, p. 62; compare his *The Unity of Law*, Chap. IV, and pp. 127 ff., Philadelphia, 1872.

[19] *Principles*, Vol. I, p. 41.

[20] *Ibid.*, p. 42.

[21] *Ibid.*, pp. 42–43.

[22] By the way, Carey was also one of the earliest representatives of the sociologistic school. (See the chapter about this school.) Like August Comte and the sociologistic school he contends that psychology is to be based on sociology and psychological phenomena are to be explained through social conditions, but not contrariwise. See *Principles*, Vol. I, Chap. II.

greater the differences between individuals or groups the greater is the power of association and commerce between them.

Among purely agricultural communities association scarcely exists; whereas, it is found in a high degree where the farmer, the lawyer, the merchant, the carpenter, the weaver, etc., are seen constituting portions of the community.[23]

Progress for Carey is a motion. "Motion comes with heat, and heat results from association." [24]

Here are other samples of Carey's mechanistic interpretation of social and economic phenomena.

From the indestructibility of matter, as the physical premise, it obviously follows that what we term production and consumption are mere transformation of substance. Whether fossil coal is converted into heat, smoke, and ashes; corn into hogs' flesh; corn, pork, turnips, and mutton into human muscle and brain; the uniform phenomenon is alteration of matter in its quality merely, without increase or diminution of its quantity. In every transition of matter from one condition to another, force is employed, or, as we say, consumed, and force is also evolved or produced. . . Economic value is nothing but a kind of inertia; utility, an equivalent of mechanical momentum.

Consumption of a product is "nothing else than its passage from a state of inertness to one of activity." [25] Commerce is "a change of matter in place"; "production, mechanical and chemical changes in the form of matter." [26]

Such interpretations of social and economic phenomena involving comparisons of these phenomena with physical ones, and especially of man with various mechanisms, go on throughout all Carey's works. While the so-called organismic school in sociology drew analogies between social and organic phenomena, the mechanistic school compares social processes with physical mechanisms. In this respect Carey's works are representative

---

[23] *Ibid.*, p. 199. In this theory Carey much earlier than Simmel or Durkheim indicated the solidaristic or cohesive rôle of the social division of labor and, in a developed form, laid down the central idea of Durkheim's work. And yet, his name is not mentioned among the predecessors of Simmel and Durkheim.

[24] *Ibid.*, p. 61.

[25] The *Unity of Law*, pp. 127 ff.

[26] See *Principles*, Vols. I, II, III, *passim*.

of the latter; and the above gives a general idea of his method of interpreting social and economic facts. Carey's own summary of his principles of social science is clear and comprehensive. It is given at the end of the third volume of his *Principles* and in abbreviated form it runs as follows :[27]

Fundamental Physical Laws	*Corresponding Social Forms of these Laws*

The simple laws which govern matter in all its forms, and which are common to physical and social science, may be briefly stated thus:

1. All particles of m a t t e r gravitate towards each other, the attraction being in direct ratio of the mass, and the inverse one of the distance.	1. Man becomes subjected to the great law of molecular gravitation in the direct ratio of the mass, and in the inverse one of the distance. [Phenomena of association and concentration of the population.]
2. All matter is subjected to the action of the centripetal and the centrifugal forces, the one tending to the production of local centres of action, the other to the destruction of such centres, and the production of a great central mass, obedient to but a single law.	2. Local centres attract man in one direction, while great cities, centres of the world, attract him in the other.
3. The more perfect the balance of these opposing forces, the more uniform and steady is the movement of the various bodies, and the more harmonious the action of the system in which they are embraced.	3. The more perfect the balance of these opposing forces, the greater is the tendency towards the development of local individualities, and towards the extension of association throughout the interior of communities, with constant increase of the power of production, in the value and freedom of man, in the growth of capital, in the equity of distribution, and in the tendency towards harmony and peace.

[27] *Principles*, Vol. III, pp. 466–468, Philadelphia, 1867. For the sake of clearness I put his physical and social laws in two parallel columns.

4. The more intense the action of those forces, the more rapid is the motion, and the greater the power.

Heat is a cause of motion and force, motion being, in its turn, a cause of heat and force.

The more heat and motion produced, the greater is the tendency towards acceleration in the motion and the force . . . towards decomposition of masses, and individualization of the particles, of which they are composed.

The g r e a t e r the tendency towards individualization, t h e more instant are the combinations, and the greater the force obtained.

The more rapid the motion, the greater the tendency of matter to rise in the scale of form [from inorganic to o r g a n i c world, and finally to man].

4. The greater is that motion and force, the more does man become subjected to the law of gravitation (association).

The more intense becomes the heat, the more rapid is the societary motion, and greater the force exerted.

Individuality is developed in the ratio of the diversity of the modes of employment, and consequently diversity in the demand that is made for the production of human power.

The greater the diversity, the greater is man's power to control and direct the great forces of nature, the larger the number of persons who can draw support from any given space, and the more perfect the development of the latent powers of both earth and man.

Such are the essential physical laws and their social manifestation. The above is sufficient to characterize the essentials of Carey's social physics and its similarity to the principles of the social physics of the seventeenth century.

3. CONTEMPORARY SOCIAL MECHANICS

Probably the most typical samples of a transfer and direct application of the laws of physical mechanics to an interpretation of social phenomena are the works of Voronoff, Haret, Alfred Lŏtka and Antonio Portuondo y Barcelo.[28]   All these

---

[28] VORONOFF, *Foundations of Sociology*, Russ., 1909; HARET, *Mécanique sociale*, 1910; BARCELO, A., *Essais de mécanique sociale*, Paris, 1925; previously part of it was published in *Revue Intern. de Sociologie*, 1915; LŎTKA, ALFRED J., *Elements of Physical Biology*, Baltimore, 1925. Considerably different is the position of R. de la Grasserie who tried to create a Cosmic Sociology. In his theory of universal interaction and its varieties there is very little from mechanics. See DE LA GRASSERIE, R., *De la cosmosociologie*, Paris, Giard and Brière.

authors start their discussion with an indication that "the body of human individuals, with all its organs and material elements, composes a system which is subjected to the laws of physical mechanics," like any other material system; and that, "in spite of man's desire to escape from the law of gravitation and from all other laws of mechanics, he cannot do it" (Barcelo). "The laws of the chemical dynamics of a structural system . . . will be precisely those laws . . . which govern the evolution of a system comprising living organisms." [29] From such rather obvious premises these writers infer that "if the principles and the laws of social mechanics are applicable to all forms of force, they evidently are also applicable to man and to those psychical forces that are styled social." Having indicated these reasons, these writers proceed in a true mechanistic fashion to transfer the conceptions and terminology of mechanics into the field of social phenomena, and to give us such mechanistic interpretations as the following: According to Voronoff, association and coöperation are "addition and multiplication of forces"; war and social struggle, "subtraction of forces"; social organization, "an equilibrium of forces"; degeneration and decay, "disintegration of forces"; law and judicial phenomena, "co-relation of forces," and so on.[30]

Similar though somewhat more complex are the mechanistic interpretations of Haret and Barcelo. In their works the translation of the non-mechanistic language of social science into that of mechanics goes on in the following way: The individual is transformed into a material point, and his social environment into "a field of forces," (*champ de force*). As soon as this is done, there is no difficulty in applying the formulas of mechanics to **social** phenomena; all that is necessary is to copy these formulas, inserting the word individual instead of material point, and the term social group instead of a physical system or a field of forces. Proceeding in this way, both writers give us a series of formulas of social mechanics like the following: "An increase of kinetic energy of an individual is equivalent to a decrease of his potential energy." "The total energy of an individual in his field of forces remains constant throughout all its modifica-

[29] LŌTKA, *op. cit.*, p. 16.
[30] See VORONOFF, *Osnovanija soziologii, passim.*

tions." [31]   "The total energy of a social group in regard to its action (*quant à une action*) at a moment of time (T_1) is equivalent to that total energy of the group which it had at an initial moment (T_0) plus the total amount of work which during this period of time (T_1-T_0) has been done by all forces exterior to the group which have influenced individuals or elements of the group," and so on.[32]   To complete the identity of social with physical mechanics these thinkers, especially Barcelo, supply a considerable number of mathematical formulas both simple and complex which they have extracted from the subject matter of mechanics.   Such are the essential traits of this type of the mechanistic school in sociology.[33]

4. CONTEMPORARY SOCIAL ENERGETICS

Different varieties of this branch of mechanistic theory are represented by the works of E. Solvay, the founder of the Solvay Institute in Belgium; by those of W. Ostwald, great chemist and theorizer of energetics; in the *Collective Reflexology* of a prominent Russian psychologist, W. Bechtereff (1857–), and in *The Economy of Human Energy* by a distinguished American economist, T. N. Carver (1865–).   Let us briefly glance at the framework of their energetistic interpretations.

The least serious and the least valuable of these works is Bechtereff's *Collective Reflexology*.[34]   Although Bechtereff has published several earlier investigations of recognized value, the second part of this book is of questionable scientific worth.   The explanation is probably to be found in the abnormal conditions of the Russian Revolution, under which this work was produced. Having declared that "the laws of super-organic, that is, of social, phenomena are the same as the laws of inorganic and organic phenomena," into his interpretation of social phenomena he simply

---

[31] "*L'energie total de l'individu dans son champ se conserve constante à travers toutes ses modifications.*"

[32] See HARET, *op. cit.*, Preface and *passim*; BARCELO, *op. cit.*, *passim*.

[33] Much more elaborate are the formulas of Lötka.   Several chapters of his book are really valuable and contribute something beyond a mere transfer of the formulas of mechanics into the social field.

[34] BECHTEREFF, W., *Kollektivnaija Reflexologia*, Russ., Petrograd, 1921; Part II, pp. 221–420.

imports all the laws of physics, mechanics, chemistry, and biology that he can find. We have a total of twenty-three such laws governing social phenomena; the law of the preservation of energy; of the proportionality of the ratio of motion to motive force; of gravitation; of repulsion; of the equality of action with counter-action; of similarity or homology; of rhythm; of inertia; of continuity of movement and change; of entropy; of relativity; of evolution; of differentiation; of reproduction; of elective generalization; of historical sequence; of economy; of adaptation; of interaction; of compensation; of dependable relationship and of individuality.

In order to show what is meant by each of these "laws" in the field of social phenomena two or three illustrations may be given. The law of the preservation of energy means "that each person is an accumulator of energy," that "the spiritual personality of man never disappears completely," that "a social group, having created its culture, does not die spiritually." [35]   Such is the essence of this law. The law of the proportionality of the rate of motion with the moving force is illustrated by such facts as the following, that "an addition of reinforcements to an army facilitates a more rapid achievement of the military purpose in proportion to the additional force"; or that "the development of a religious movement is reinforced through the performance of religious ceremonies," and so on.[36]   The law of homology means that "social organization everywhere proceeds according to the same plan"; that "the historical development of the civilizations of all peoples has been going on along the same general plan." [37] The law of inertia is manifested in the existence of conservatism, tradition, habit, prestige, authority, and the like.[38]   The law of relativity consists in the fact that everything in social life is relative; for example, "a theory of constitutional government may appear radical in an absolute monarchy, while the same theory may seem very conservative in a democratic country." [39]   These

[35] *Ibid.*, pp. 225–230.
[36] *Ibid.*, pp. 314–319.
[37] *Ibid.*, pp. 270–282.
[38] *Ibid.*, pp. 292–307.
[39] *Ibid.*, pp. 230–2.

samples are sufficient to indicate the general character of Bechtereff's "law of social energetics."

The social energetics of E. Solvay does not need a detailed
characterization because its essential traits, with the exception
of Solvay's "positive politics," are reproduced in W. Ostwald's
work. It is enough to say that, according to Solvay, "social phenomena are nothing but a combination of three factors: organic,
psychic and inorganic, the last of which plays an especially important and primary rôle." Life is nothing but the phenomena
of the transformation of energy. Consequently, social life is
also nothing but "energetistic phenomena." For these reasons
the general laws of energetistic mechanics are applicable to social
phenomena. Sociology is social physics or social energetics. The
primary task of sociology is "to reduce the totality of biological
and social phenomena to fundamental physico-chemical actions
and reactions." [40]   Accordingly man and society are viewed as
"energetistic apparatuses"; man's life and society's history, as
processes of the transformation of energy, subject to the laws
of energetistic mechanics, and especially to the laws of the least
effort and realization of maximum energy. Production, consumption, distribution and a series of other phenomena are interpreted
in the same way. All this culminates in his "Scientific Positive
Politics of Energetics," in which many liberal programs of social
and political reconstruction are suggested.

According to W. Ostwald (1853–   ), "energetics can give to
social sciences (*Kulturwissenschaften*) several fundamental principles, but it cannot give all the principles needed by social
sciences." [41]   Pursuant to this thesis, Ostwald offers his energetistic interpretation of social phenomena. It may be summed up
as follows:

1. Any event, or any social or historical change in the last

---

[40] SOLVAY, É., "Formules d'introduction à l'énergetique physio et psycho-
sociologique,'' pp. 53 ff.,213 ff., in *Questions d'énergetique sociale*, Institut Solvay,
Bruxelles. See there *passim*. A systematic analysis of Solvay's "social energetics" is given by the Director of the Sociological Institut of Solvay, G. Barnich,
in his *"Essai de politique positive basée sur l'énergetique social de Solvay,"* Bruxelles,
1919, *passim* and pp. 1–186.

[41] OSTWALD, W., *Energetische Grundlagen der Kulturwissenschaften*, Vorvort,
Leipzig, 1909. See also OSTWALD, W., *Die Energien*, Leipzig, 1908.

analysis is nothing but a transformation of energy. (Lectures
1 and 2)

2. From the energetistic point of view the creation of culture
is nothing but a transformation of crude (*rohe*) energy into useful energy (*Nutzenergy*). The greater the coefficient of useful
energy obtained in such a transformation, the greater is the
progress of culture. A primitive lamp, for example, which transforms chemical energy into light energy, gives only about three
per cent of useful energy, while a more perfect lamp gives
fifteen or more per cent. For this reason, we may say that
the substitution of this better lamp for the less perfect is
progress. (Lecture 2)

3. Man is an apparatus for the transformation of all other
forms of energy.

4. Adaptation is nothing but the best possible utilization of
crude energy and its transformation into useful energy. The
higher the percentage of useful energy obtained in this way, the
better is the adaptation. (Lectures 5-7)

5. Society, as a totality of individuals working together for
a common purpose, is an arrangement for the better utilization
and more perfect transformation of crude into useful energy.
Where there is no order and no regulation of mutual relations,
but a disorderly struggle, there is a useless waste of energy, and
its perfect transformation is impossible. Through its order society makes possible the better transformation of energy. Only
in so far as society serves this purpose is its existence justified.
When, instead, it hinders rather than helps in obtaining this result
it loses the very purpose of its existence. (Lecture 8)

6. The functions of language, law, commerce, trade, production, punishment, state, government and other cultural phenomena
can be expressed in the same terms. They all facilitate a better
utilization of crude energy and prevent its useless waste. In the
primitive stages of culture this purpose was achieved imperfectly,
since the methods of its achievement were rude. The principal
means of maintaining order were violence and coercion which
led to an enormous waste of energy. However, with the progress
of culture the methods of social control became less expensive.
(Lectures 9-11)

7. The value and justification of any state consists in a better and better utilization of energy for the benefit of all its members; and only in so far as this purpose is served by a state is its existence justified. (Lecture 12)

8. Wealth and money are but concentrated forms of useful energy. Their accumulation serves the same purpose. The justification of private property consists in its facilitation of this purpose. When it ceases to do that, it loses its reason for existence. (Lecture 13)

9. Science is the most fundamental means of the utilization of energy. For this reason it is the basis of civilization; "the best blood and the deepest root of any culture." Great inventors and scientists are to be appreciated because they serve this purpose. Hence the great value of education, of schools, and of all institutions for the accumulation, enrichment, and diffusion of science. Hence also the necessity for conditions like freedom of thought and investigation without which this purpose could not be served successfully. (Lecture 14)

Such are the skeleton and principal considerations of W. Ostwald's energetistic interpretation of social phenomena.

Similar is the interpretation of civilization and social processes given by T. N. Carver in his interesting book about human energy.[42] The life of an individual and the history of a group are viewed by him as a transformation of "the largest possible sum of solar energy into human energy." The social process is a transformation of energy and its redistribution; civilization is nothing but an accumulation of this transformed energy; and progress, its better and better utilization. Especial attention is given by this author to an energetistic interpretation of "economic phenomena." Here he does not limit his task to a mere statement of general principles, but attempts to develop a detailed, sometimes even quantitative, analysis of basic economic phenomena from the above point of view. The book, in general, is

---

[42] CARVER, T. N., *The Economy of Human Energy*, 1924. To this school belongs further N. L. SIMS' *Society and its Surplus*, N. Y. 1924. In the preface and at the beginning of the book Professor Sims very emphatically sets forth an energetistic point of view. In his analysis of various social phenomena he fails, however, to carry on his energetistic *"desiderata"* and gives a long survey of social evolution and social processes in which the energetistic point of view is very little in evidence.

better than many of the works mentioned above, and some of Carver's theories are really valuable.

Let us next briefly outline L. Winiarsky's "mechanistic and energetistic interpretations." [43]

1. For Winiarsky, "a social aggregate is nothing but a system of points, *i.e.*, individuals, who are in a perpetual movement of approaching or withdrawing from one another."

2. "The primary cause of these movements is attraction."

3. Like chemical affinity this attraction is elective and proceeds along certain lines and in a certain direction, namely, toward a maximum of pleasure and a minimum of resistance. The phenomena of social attraction, or social interaction, have accordingly a purely mechanical basis, though this mechanical attraction has a more complex character among human beings than among inorganic things, and is overgrown, so to speak, by psychical phenomena. Our choice of friends and enemies is an example of this principle.

4. Nevertheless, psychical phenomena themselves are nothing but a modification of biological energy, which, in turn, is a form of physico-chemical energy. For this reason, our choice itself is subjected to the above laws of mechanics, as is shown by pure political economy.[44] The attraction between male and female is another instance of the same principle. As the basis of this attraction is the "gravitation" or "chemical affinity" of the spermatozoa and the ovum. It manifests itself in the reciprocal desires of the young man and the girl, which they themselves do

[43] See WINIARSKY, L., "La Méthod mathématique dans la sociologie et dans l'économie," *La revue socialiste*, 1894, Vol. XX, pp. 716–730; "Essai d'une nouvelle interprétation de phénomènes sociologiques," *ibid.*, Vol. XXIV, 1896, pp. 430–454; "L'equilibrio sociale," *Rivista Italiana di sociologia*, Sept., 1899; "Deux théories d'équilibre economique," *Revue internationale de sociologie*, 1896, pp. 904–930; "Essai sur le mécanique sociale," *Revue philosophique*, Vol. XLV, 1898, pp. 351–386; "L'équilibre esthetique," *ibid.*, Vol. XLVII, 1899, pp. 569–605; "L'énergie sociale et ses mensurations," *ibid.*, Vol. XLIX, 1900, pp. 113–134, 256–287. The last three articles are the most important. About Winiarsky see GROPPALI, A., "Essai récent de sociologie pure," *Revue intern. sociologie*, 1900, pp. 425–442, 487–519; SQUILLACE, *op. cit.*, pp. 107–119; TRISCA, PETRE, *op. cit.*, Vol. II. Like his predecessors, Winiarsky names Herbart, Weber and Fechner, Delboeuf, Edgeworth, Gossen, Walras, Jevons, Pareto, as having tried to apply mathematical method to the study of psychical and economic phenomena. As indicated in our previous discussion, this list of Winiarsky's predecessors might well have been lengthened by the addition of several dozen names at least.

[44] *L'énergie sociale*, pp. 113–115.

not always recognize as arising from this deeper drive. It is subject to the same law of maximum pleasure. When this attraction, which is really sexual, is not satisfied, then, according to the law of the transformation of energy, it is sublimated into other psychical phenomena, such as coquetry, ornamentation, and other means of sexual attraction, which in turn give rise to æsthetic phenomena, the fine arts, and poetry.[45] The same is true of other basic forms of gravitation or attraction such as food attraction. In this way the psychical phenomena are interpreted as a form of biological energy which in its turn is nothing but a form of physico-chemical energy. Thus "psychical and physical phenomena are reduced to the same laws of mechanics." [46]

5. Energy has various forms, and may be transformed from one to another as, for example, from potential to kinetic, and *vice versa*. Life is a specific form of physico-chemical energy. Organisms generally, and the human organism especially, are an embodiment of energy, and mechanisms for its transformation.

6. The transformation of energy by an organism proceeds through the processes of alimentation and reproduction. In the field of vital phenomena the general law of mechanical attraction manifests itself in the form of the sex and food attractions. Love and hunger are, so to speak, primary drives of organisms generally, and of human beings particularly, determining their mutual attraction and repellence. Human beings seek, first of all, the satisfaction of these needs. It is under the influence of these needs that they enter into contacts of various kinds with one another. This basic fact accounts for the origin of all the various social phenomena, and for all the more complex forms of the transformation of energy by social groups.[47]

7. "As a bullet, when it encounters an obstacle, transforms its energy of motion into an inner energy of heat, light or electricity; so the crude movement of human masses that is driven by sex and hunger, when it encounters an obstacle in the natural environment or other groups which prevents the direct satisfaction of those needs, likewise transmutes the energy of hunger

---

[45] *L'équilibre esthetique*, pp. 569–573.
[46] *L'énergie sociale*, pp. 114–116.
[47] *Essai sur le mécanique sociale*, pp. 351–386.

and sex into economic, political, juridical, moral, æsthetic, religious or intellectual form. In this way vital energy is transformed into psychical and social."[48] This theory of how the energy of hunger and love originated and how they are transformed into complex psycho-social phenomena, Winiarsky, furthermore, developed in great detail.

8. These processes of the transformation of energy proceed, moreover, according to the basic laws of thermodynamics. First the amount of energy in all these transformations remains constant. Second, the same laws of thermodynamics explain this social phenomena of change, differentiation, equalization, domination and historical progression generally. If the intensity of thermal energy in two physical systems is not equal there results transference of energy from one system to another and the greater the difference the more intensive is the process. This radiation of energy always proceeds from the system with a greater intensity to that with a lower intensity of thermal energy. In this sense the process of radiation is non-reversible. On the other hand, as radiation proceeds, the difference in the energy-intensity of the two systems becomes less and less until both systems become equal. This is the reversible aspect of the thermodynamic processes. Thus they take place only when there is inequality of energy, but proceeding tend to equality or entropy. Now the same basic laws operate in the field of psycho-social phenomena also, according to Winiarsky. The unequal amount and intensity of energy with which different individuals and groups are charged, account for all social and historical events. These are nothing but manifestations of the radiation of energy from individual to individual and from group to group. If energy had been equal in all individuals the whole drama of human history would not have taken place. Instead there would forever have been dead equilibrium. Only where there exists an inequality of force-intensity there is motion, change, life, or history.[49] Similarly, unequal distribution of energy among indi-

[48] *L'énergie sociale*, p. 120. From this and from the article *L'équilibre esthetique*, one has to conclude that Winiarsky laid down the essentials of the Freudian theory considerably earlier than it was done by Freud.

[49] This idea was developed by K. Leontieff much earlier than by Winiarsky. It constituted the basic principle in Leontieff's criticism of the equalitarian and

viduals and groups is responsible for all such social phenomena as inequality, differentiation, stratification, domination and the like.

As in thermodynamics the process of thermal energy equalization proceeds from the body with the higher temperature to that with the lower, so the individuals or social groups with the greater psycho-social energy radiate their energy to the individuals or groups with less. From which it follows that all phenomena of social differentiation, such as inequality, exploitation, domination, class distinction, and caste stratification, are but manifestations of the general phenomena of energy-radiation from systems of higher to those of lower energy. But as in physics the transference of heat leads to its gradual equalization in all the bodies concerned, so, in the social process, the corresponding transference leads to the rise and growth of social equality. "Such is the explanation of the progress of liberty and the disappearance of monopoly and other privilege in all fields of social phenomena." The greater the inequality the more intensive will be this process of equalization. Liberal, socialist, communist, and equalitarian

socialistic movements. "The upward evolution of an organism or of a society always displays the phenomena of differentiation. Its disintegration, on the other hand, always displays a fusion of what before was separate and different. This fusion leads to a weakened cohesion of the organism's or society's parts, which results at last in its destruction." Hence Leontieff's "three periods in the life-cycle of any society"; the initial period of simplicity, then a period of blooming complexity and differentiation, and finally a period of equalitarian disintegration and decay. In the history of modern Europe the first of these periods lasted until about the ninth century, while society was still simple. The second period corresponds to the climax of European civilization between the ninth and the seventeenth centuries. "But since the eighteenth century Europe has entered upon a period of fusion and equalization. Its greatness lasted only a thousand years. The fact that in the nineteenth century it is setting up equality as an ideal means only that it is exhausted and is tending again toward an undifferentiated simplicity. But before it can reach that it is doomed to fall apart and give place to other societies. All that is really great, fine and durable has been created, not, indeed, by universal liberty and equality, but instead by differences in rights, social positions and educational opportunities—but in a society united under a supreme and sacred authority." The equalitarian movement betrays a tendency toward the simplicity of a corpse and the equilibrium of death. However, Leontieff was not the first to set forth this theory, for similar ideas had already been expounded by Danilevsky as early in the century as 1869. Thus were O. Spengler's theories anticipated by half a century. Indeed, in all its essential characteristics Spengler's work is a mere repetition of the social speculations of Leontieff and Danilevsky. See LEONTIEFF, K., *Bysantinism and Slaves*, Russ., 1873; DANILEVSKY, *Russia and Europe*, 1869, 2nd ed., 1871. See also BERDIAIEFF, *Philosophy of Inequality*, Russ., 1923.

movements are all forms of this basic law of social thermo-dynamics. "Even in a primitive group, order, power, law and social control spontaneously appear; simply because the energy arising from its inequalities passes in the form of domination from a higher to a lower point, but never inversely. Since the radiation of energy proceeds in this way, there is a tendency toward the equalization of differing intensities; and this goes on until an equilibrium is reached in which there are no such differences; whereupon, according to the laws of thermodynamics, all transformation stops." [50]

9. From this, Winiarsky logically concludes that, in the future, the state of social entropy,—a dead and immovable equilibrium, —will come in some way into the history of mankind, as it has in the history of the whole universe. Equalization of individuals, classes, castes, races, and so on, proceeds now with a great intensity. We are already at the beginning of the long process of social entropy, which is conspicuously manifested by the influence of socialistic and equalitarian movements (*Ibid.,* pp. 129-133).

10. From the above he infers that the object of social science is to study this energetistic system of men and objects, subjected to the laws of mechanics in their activities and relationship. In order that this study may be really scientific, it has to be not alone qualitative, but also quantitative. Corresponding phenomena must be measured. To be able to do so, social science must have a unit of measurement, such as money, which is the measure for economic energy. Therefore, money (or price units) may serve as a unit for the measurement of all the social transformations of energy. The reasons are as follows:

"Biological energy is the central motor of social phenomena. Passing through a series of transformations in the forms of polit-ical, juridical, moral, æsthetical, intellectual, and religious phe-nomena; it eventually arrives at economic energy, which, being measured through money (gold), serves for the measurement of biological energy itself. Economic energy plays there the same rôle as heat energy in mechanics." Comparing the social utility (which is a general form of bio-social energy) of a material, or its immaterial value, with the social utility of gold, we may obtain

[50] *L'énergie sociale,* pp. 124–127.

an index of the intensity and the amount of energy in the social object; comparing it with the indices of other objects expressed in the same gold value we may obtain some of the approximate quantitative data necessary for the creation of quantitative "social mechanics." "Gold is a general social equivalent, an incarnation and personification of bio-social energy. At the same time it is a general transformer: the greater part of material and immaterial values may be produced through corresponding money expenditures." This furnishes the possibility of making them measurable in units of the same money. It is up to the future energetics to realize these quantitative social mechanics.[51]

Such is the essence of Winiarsky's theory of social energetics or mechanics. The above gives an idea of the principal varieties of the contemporary schools of social physics and social energetics, or mechanics.[52] Postponing for a moment an analysis of

[51] *L'énergie sociale*, pp. 262-287.

[52] The theories which refute any psychological interpretation of social phenomena and any use of "subjective" terms, and which use such terms as "social pressure" or "pressures of social groups" or "energies of social activity" and so on, remain undiscussed. According to their intentions, they show also an inclination to a "mechanistic" or "energetistic" interpretation of social facts; but, in their realization of this intention, they usually fail to carry it on. *The Process of Government* and *Relativity in Man and Society* by Arthur F. Bentley, may serve as conspicuous examples of the works of this kind. Being rather justified in his criticism of various psychological explanations of social phenomena, A. Bentley (see his *The Process of Government*, 1908, pp. 7-8, 17-18, 35-37, 50 and *sbsqnt.* and *passim*), in his constructive plan, fails to carry on his objectivism and physicism into his interpretation of social phenomena. He finally reduces his "pressures" to the "interests," and, in this way, reintroduces into sociological interpretation the same "psychical and subjective factors" which he had so vigorously attacked in the first part of his work. The same is true in regard to his new work, *Relativity in Man and Society*, 1926. Besides not making a quite successful application of the mathematical theory of relativity to social science, Bentley's "reforming" of sociology in this book is purely terminological, rather than factual. For any serious partisan of objectivism in sociology, it is impossible to accept Ratzenhofer's "interests," or Simmel's "forms" or Durkheim's "social mind" and "collective representations," as basic explanatory principles of an objective social science. It is evident that these principles are purely subjective, and are of the same nature as H. Spencer's "affections" and A. Small's "interests," which are so strongly criticized by Bentley himself. In spite of this, as though forgetting his own criticism, Bentley strongly praises these theories in his new book and by this, he once more shows that his "objectivism" is purely terminological. With still greater reason this may be said of several other theories which criticize "psychologism" and "subjectivism" in sociology; pleading for an "objective sociology," and abundantly using expressions like "social pressure." The majority of them, however, are "subjective," "speculative," and "psychological" through and through. Their "social pressures" remain undefined, even to the authors themselves. As soon as they start to

V. Pareto's works, which deserve much greater attention, let us briefly discuss the scientific value of the above theories.

5. CRITICISM

There is no doubt that the plans of either social physics, social energetics, or of social mechanics, such as are laid down by the above authors, are tempting. Indeed, what may be more magnificent than a social mechanics which, by a series of mathematical formulas, unveils all the mysteries of the most mysterious drama of human history! What may be more scientific than a discipline which successfully shows that all complex phenomena of human behavior, of social relationship, and of social processes, are but a mere variety of physical phenomena subjected to the same laws and accurately described by them! What may be more fascinating and more tempting than such a theory! And yet, when we take the above theories and soberly try to analyze their contributions, we are greatly disappointed. Frankly, I think that all the above theories have contributed but little to the scientific understanding of social phenomena. I believe that they give only a series of superficial analogies; and that when they attempt to reduce social phenomena to the physical, they disfigure and misinterpret not only the social phenomena, but the laws of physics, mechanics, energetics, and logic as well. I am aware of the severity of this criticism, and yet it appears to me quite justified. My reasons are as follows:

A. In the first place, *the theories trangress the basic logical law of the necessity for adequacy in a logical subject and a logical predicate in a logical judgment.* If I say, "A human being is an animal with two eyes," my judgment is in some respects true, because human beings have two eyes; but from the standpoint of logical adequacy it is quite wrong, because not only human beings, but many other animals, have two eyes also. The logical

---

"interpret something," the "subjectivism" and "psychologism," which they pitilessly banished before, are at once reintroduced under slightly changed names, such as "psycho-social environment," "psycho-social factors," and so on. As a result, such works do not have the positive qualities of either a purely psychological interpretation, or even of purely objective, mechanistic, or behavioristic interpretations; while they do have the shortcomings of both. Their intention to build an objective sociology remains in fact a mere "*pia desideria.*"

predicate, "animal with two eyes," is referred here to the class: "human being," which is much narrower than the class of animals which really has two eyes. Hence, the logical inadequacy of the judgment. If, on the other hand, I say, "A human being is an animal which shaves his whiskers," my judgment will be again inadequate, because there are human beings who do not have whiskers (females) and who do not shave them. Here the logical predicate is referred to a logical subject which is in fact much broader than is indicated in the judgment. These examples show two kinds of logical inadequacy in judgments: one, where the logical predicate is referred to a logical subject which, in fact, is much narrower; and another, where it is really a much broader class than the classes (logical subjects) to which the predicate's characteristic are attached in the judgments. All such judgments are unscientific, and the most common shortcomings of various hypotheses and theories consist in just these two kinds of inadequacies; all the improved and more scientific generalizations have consisted merely in the substitution of a more adequate for a less adequate logical statement. Copernicus' theory is better than Ptolemy's because it is more adequate. Newton's laws of mechanics are better than those of Kepler for the same reason.

Not all concepts and theories which may be unreproachable from some standpoint, have a real scientific value. For instance about such classes of phenomena as "ten-cent cigars" or "dogs with long tails and short necks," it would be possible to make so many "true statements" that their exposition would fill many volumes. About "ten-cent cigars" it would be possible to state that they are subjected to the law of gravitation, that they fall down according to such and such laws of mechanics, that their size may enlarge according to such and such laws or physics, and so on. Furthermore, it would be possible to make a series of "true statements" concerning their chemical composition. Additional volumes of our imaginary science on "ten-cent cigars" could be filled by truths of a biological and botanical character. Similar voluminous "sciences" could be created about "dogs with long tails and short necks," about "pewter soldiers," and so on and so forth. But such "sciences" would be nothing but a mockery of, or a parody of, a real science.

These are conspicuous examples of how scientific theories ought not to be made, rightly says Petrajitzky.[53]

Their unscientific character consists in their logical inadequacy, in that their statements (logical predicates) are referred to the inappropriate,—in this case to classes of logical subjects which are too narrow,—while these statements (logical predicates) ought, in fact, to be referred to much broader classes of logical subjects. For example, the statements of inertia, gravitation, and so on in our pseudo-science, are made only about cigars, specifically, "ten-cent cigars"; while they in fact ought to be applied to all material objects, that is, to an incomparably broader class of phenomena. Such pseudo-scientific theories are only misleading, because they create the supposition that the characteristics given to a class of objects represent only their specific traits,—something which belongs only to them, and to nothing else.[54]

As there is no limit to the creation of such classes, and as the capacity of the human memory is limited, an abundance of such theories and "sciences" would become a greater burden for us than their absence. [55]

The same, with a corresponding modification, may be said of the theories in which the logical predicate (the characteristics) is ascribed to a much larger class of phenomena than that to which it really belongs. Such are, for instance, the judgments · "All organisms have two hands," "All human beings are Roman Catholics," "All Americans are blonds," "All professors are geniuses," "All monarchs are cruel," and so on.

The above makes clear what I mean by the "logical inadequacy" of a judgment or theory. Now it is easy to see why the above energetistic or mechanistic theories are inadequate. In the first place, they are a variation of the above pseudo-scientific theory of "ten-cent cigars." The laws of physical mechanics do not say

[53] See a brilliant analysis of this principle of the logical adequacy of the logical subject and predicate in PETRAJITZKY, L., *Introduction to the Theory of Law and Morals*, (Russ., *Vedenie v teoriju prava i nravstvennosty*), St. Petersburg, 1907, *passim*. See also TSCHUPROFF, A. A., *Essays in the Theory of Statistics*, (Russ., *Ocherki po teorii statistiki*), St. Petersburg, 1909, *passim*.

[54] PETRAJITZSKY, L., *op cit.*, pp. 72–77, *passim*.

[55] TSCHUPROFF, A., *op. cit.*, pp. 1–20, and *passim*.

that they are applied to all material bodies with the exception of human bodies. They are applied to human bodies and to all other social things of a physical character also. Therefore, there is no reason to insist on, and to create, a special theory of "social gravitation," or "social inertia," or a "law of social entropy," or any special law of physical mechanics. The "mechanists" try to break with violence into a room whose doors are open. The laws of physics, mechanics, and chemistry are applied to all social objects of a physical character, and there is no reason to make a noise about creating a "human physics," a "human gravitation" or a "human chemistry." Such attempts are nothing but efforts to create a "physics, chemistry, and mechanics of dogs with long tails and short necks." In this respect the theories discussed are inadequate, and therefore defective.

But one form of inadequacy in a theory is usually followed by another form, and this we see in the mechanistic theories. Trying to interpret man and social phenomena in the light of the principles of mechanics or general energetics, they disregard a series of the specific characteristics of social phenomena, which belong only to the human world, and which do not belong to other physical, chemical, or energetic phenomena. As a result of the school's "equalization" of social and physical phenomena, the theories ascribe to physical phenomena a series of human characteristics (anthropomorphism), and take off from social phenomena a series of their specific traits. Because of this, the laws of mechanics are disfigured, their "nature" is made "anthropomorphic" and the essentials of social phenomena are passed over, without even touching them.

It may be true that social instinct is nothing but a variety of physical gravitation, yet, can we say that each phenomenon of gravitation, for instance, of the earth and the moon, is a "social instinct"? It may be true, as Voronoff says, that the "social phenomena of association and coöperation are nothing but those of the addition and multiplication of forces"; but does this mean that each case of addition and multiplication of forces studied by mechanics is a social phenomenon of coöperation and association? Evidently not. If not, then what is the difference between social coöperation and association, and between other cases of addition and multiplication of forces studied by mechanics? We do not find any answer to the question in the above theories. It may be true that war and social struggle are the phenomena of "subtraction of forces," but does this mean that each case of subtraction of forces studied by mechanics is war and social struggle? If the phenomena of law are those of "co-relation and coördination of forces," then what is the difference between this "coördination of forces" and the coördination of forces A and B which are at the ends of a lever? In spite of the fact that the second case is also "coördination of forces," it is by no means a phenomenon of law. We are told by the energetists that the dissipation of heat through radiation, and the phenomenon of crime are both phenomena of wasted energy. Does this, however, mean that all dissipation of heat, and every waste of energy is "crime"? W. Ostwald may be right in saying that language, law, commerce, state, culture, government and other social phenomena are nothing but transformations of a rude energy into a useful one. Does this, however, signify that each case of such a transformation, studied by physical mechanics, composes the phenomena of language, law, government, and so on? Evidently not. If not, what is the difference between the transformation of the energy of sun-heat, or in that of the mechanical motion of wind and in these cases of cultural phenomena? It may be that wealth and money are nothing but concentrated useful energy. Does it follow from this that any concentrated energy (for instance, the energy of a volcano) is money and wealth?

The above shows the other side of the logical inadequacy of the criticised theories. They study social phenomena only as purely physical manifestations. All that is specific in social facts, and all that differentiates them from an inorganic substance, is factually excluded from the study. Human beings are simply transformed into a mere physical mass; facts of social life, human conduct, heroism, crime, love, hatred, struggle, coöperation, organization, ethics, religion, arts, literature, and so on,—all these are transformed into a mere "physical mass," and a study is made of its transformation and its "motion." In this way all that is specific in social phenomena is lost, being passed over and left without any analysis. This means that social physics and energetics are useless, because they do not study social phenomena as something specifically different from "physical mass" and "its motion." They are useless also because human beings, as a physical mass, are studied by physics, chemistry and mechanics; and there is no reason for the existence of a social physics and mechanics which would do the same.

This conclusion would remain valid even if it could be shown that human beings and their interrelations are a mere combination of electrons. Even in this case, the "human" combination of electrons would remain a specific combination, differing from any combination in an inorganic or organic body, and necessitating a separate study.[56] Thus the monism of the discussed theories leads to a double fallacy: it disregards all the specific characteristics in social phenomena; and, at the same time, ascribes to general physical phenomena some of the characteristics which do not belong to them, but rather, only to the kingdom of man and social phenomena. This is the fundamental shortcoming of these theories.

B. The above is well corroborated by the factual generalizations given by social physicists, mechanists, and energetists. Take, for instance, Carey's law of social gravitation. At first glance it appears to be something valuable, but merely a superficial analysis would show its complete fallacy at once. The factual study of the growth and decay of cities does not corroborate the statements. Cities do not "attract" the human molecules in direct ratio to the mass or in the inverse ratio of the distance. Any statistician who would predict the rate of growth (or of decrease in the size) of a city on the basis of this law, would be doomed to failure. The law does not at all explain why some places, uninhabited before, become the abode of a rapidly growing city, at one period; nor why this city stops growing and declines at another period. In brief, the law is rather useless for an explanation of the real facts of the concentration and dispersion of population. It is evident also that Carey's other "identifications" of the physical and social laws do not amount to anything

---

[56] See a detailed discussion of this in SOROKIN, *System of Sociology*, Vol. I, pp. 7–10.

beyond curious analogies whose scientific value is nil. They do not, and cannot, explain anything in the real movement of social processes.

Bechtereff's "laws" are nothing but a caricature of scientific law, in which the meanings of the laws of physics and chemistry, as well as of social facts, are disfigured. The conclusion must be similar concerning the theories of Solvay, Ostwald, Haret, Barcelo, Winiarsky, and others. So far as they only repeat the statements of physics, mechanics, and chemistry, they represent a useless and somewhat misleading duplication of the truths of these scientific disciplines. As far as they try to identify physical and mechanical laws with social ones, they give only fallacious analogies which do not, and cannot, explain anything in the field of "social mechanics." To say that the "primary cause of the movement of individuals is attraction," is to say something which can either be proved or disproved. To say that the universal phenomenon of gravitation assumes the forms of food and sex attraction in the social field, is meaningless or fallacious analogy. If the analogy were well founded, we would have to expect that sex and food attraction would be in the direct ratio of the mass, and in the inverse ratio of the distance (of food or sex). Obviously there is no reason for such an absurd statement, and the analogy is, therefore, baseless. To identify an equalitarian movement (which is besides, depicted wrongly) with the phenomenon of entropy, or the phenomenon of social differentiation with that of thermodynamics, signifies no more than a curious and useless analogy; an analogy which explains nothing in the phenomena of equalization or differentiation in their appearance and change. Let some one try to "explain" by means of this analogy either the origin and development of a caste-régime, or the "democratic movement" in any country at any time. Such an investigator will see at once that Winiarsky's thermodynamic principles do not work at all, giving no help to the understanding of these processes and their development. Take any of the generalizations of the school and try to apply them in an explanation of any social phenomena. The results will be the same for they neither work nor explain anything. A number of the representatives of the school insist on a quantitative study of social phenomena, but not one of them has produced a single quantitative formula, or given a coefficient of correlation between two or more social processes. It is true that they copied and put into their articles several formulas of physical mechanics, but alas, they themselves do not know how to apply them, nor how to use them in regard to social facts. Since no unit for the measurement of "social forces" has been found as yet, all these formulas are to be regarded as a mere exercise in the copying of mechanical formulas, nothing more. The fictitious character of all these formulas is shown by Winiarsky himself. After all his sweeping statements and formulas, when he comes to the problem of the measurement of social phenomena, all that he can offer is a statistical study and statistical comparison of various social phenomena, in spite of all his principles and formulas of social mechanics. This is a convincing manifestation of the inapplicability of these formulas and principles.

Finally, let us take the behavior of individuals, A, B, C, D. Can we explain the immense variety of their actions through the principle of physical mechanics, through that of inertia, gravitation, or by means of the principles of levers of the first and of the second orders, and so on? Do they help us to understand why A becomes a hermit, B marries, C dies on a battlefield, D writes a poem, and so on? Do these principles throw a light on the religious, political, æsthetical, and other social phenomena? Can they explain why the history of one people has developed in one way, and that of another in quite a different manner? It is sufficient merely to put these questions in order to see that we are still very far from being able to reduce social phenomena and their mechanics to the simple laws of physical mechanics. For this reason we should be modest in our desire to make such a reduction. We cannot set forth daring but utopian pretensions. Under the existing circumstances, such pretensions are rather comical and childish.[57]

The above is sufficient to show the fallacies of the school. In spite of its tempting character, it has not produced anything really scientific, after the social physics of the seventeenth century. Only in an indirect way has it served social science, especially through

[57] SOROKIN, *ibid.*, p. 8.

the social physics of the seventeenth century. This service has consisted in the school's insistence on the quantitative and causal study of the social facts; and in its premature, but suggestive pretensions to view the social processes "mechanically." This has influenced social science and facilitated quantitative and causal studies of social phenomena. Apart from this service, contemporary social mechanics, physics, and energetics do not amount to anything conspicuously valuable. Only a further and a great progress of social science may give a real basis for future social mechanics, but it will probably be radically different from the present "social mechanics" as a mere transfer of the conception and laws of physical mechanics into the field of social phenomena.

6. VILFREDO PARETO [58] AND OTHERS

PARETO'S CONCEPTION OF THE RELATIONSHIP OF A SPECIAL SCIENCE TO SOCIOLOGY

Earlier than Winiarsky and many other representatives of social mechanics, Pareto, following the works of Gossen, Walras, Jevons, Cournot, and Edgeworth, laid down his theory of a "pure economics," or other pure social science, which corresponds to "rational mechanics" and of its relationship to sociology.

In rational mechanics, two kinds of motions are studied; the real and the virtual. The former are those which really take place; the second are those which are to follow under certain circumstances, indicated in a hypothesis, which will help us to understand the characteristics of the real motions. . . . A study of the real movements would be almost exclusively descriptive; while a study of the virtual movements would be essentially theoretical. The former may be synthetic; the latter, analytic. The human intellect cannot fruitfully study various phenomena at the same time; we must consider them one after another. From this follows an absolute necessity for isolating, more or less arbitrarily, the various parts of a phenomenon and studying them separately in order that they may later be re-united into one bunch to obtain a synthetic concept of a real phenomenon. . . . Pure political economy corresponds to rational mechanics.

Like it, pure political economy has to simplify the complex

[58] Born in Paris, in 1848, of Italian parents. Died in 1923. Professor of Economics and Sociology at the University of Lausanne, Switzerland. See Pareto's biography in PANTALEONI, M., "In occasione della morta di Pareto," *Giornale degli Econimisti*, Nos. 1-2, 1924.

reality and to take the simplest isolated conditions and the simplest *homo-œconomicus* (the virtual economic phenomena) to make their analytical study possible.   In such a study, human beings must be regarded as mere hedonistic molecules, as in rational mechanics the complex solid bodies are regarded as mere material points.   When such a study is made there comes the synthetic stage in which all the analytical data of pure economics and of other pure sciences are to be united to explain the real and complex social phenomena.   Though man always remains *homo-œconomicus,* he is in reality, something much more complex than a hedonistic molecule.   We must take into consideration his affections, instincts, prejudices and so on.   In order to explain the real complex economic phenomena, we must take into consideration all the important factors which we disregard in our "pure economics," but which in reality exist and influence "pure economic phenomena."   The one science which uses the conclusions of pure economics and of other pure social sciences, making a synthesis of their data, is sociology.   Thus, as pure economics begins to take more and more into consideration all the important human traits, and proceeds its synthetic way, it begins to turn more and more into sociology, as the synthetic science of a real man and of real social phenomena.[59]

The same is true in regard to any special pure science.   This has been exactly the way in which Pareto, from a "pure economist" became a sociologist.   Like the methods of rational mechanics, those of pure economics are essentially mathematical.   Mathematical or functional also are the methods of synthetic social science, as the science which studies mutual dependence of various social phenomena.   (See more about this point.)   This gives an idea about Pareto's "pure economics" and of other "pure social sciences"; and of their relation to sociology.   These ideas were brilliantly realized by Pareto in his treatises on economics.[60]

[59] PARETO, V., "Il compito della sociologia fra le scienze sociali," *Rivista Italiana di sociologia,* July, 1897; "I problemi della sociologia," *ibid.,* 1899; "Un applicazione di teorie sociologiche," *ibid.,* 1900; *Traté de sociologie génerale,* Vol. II, Paris, 1919, §§ 2009–2024.

[60] See PARETO, V., *Cours d'économie politique,* 1896–97, Lausanne; *Les systèmes socialistes,* Paris, 1902–3; *Manuale di economia politica,* Milano, 1906; and a long series of Pareto's articles published in the leading Italian, French, and Swiss economic and sociological Journals.

They gave him a well-deserved fame and the leadership in the field of mathematical economics, greatly influencing Winiarsky and other partisans of the mechanistic school in sociology. In this way, Pareto became the originator of this school in contemporary sociology, so I shall discuss his theory in this chapter.

I do not mean to suggest by this, however, that Pareto's sociology is in any way similar to the primitive "social mechanics" criticized above. Pareto was too original and too serious a thinker to satisfy himself with the above somewhat childish "mechanical analogies." Proceeding from purely analytical economics to a more and more synthetic study of the real (complex) social phenomena, he remained a "mechanisticist" only as far as the "mechanistic method" means, according to K. Pearson, the most accurate and the shortest description of a studied phenomenon. In all other respects Pareto's sociology has very little in common with the above "mechanistic theories." A summary of Pareto's sociological conceptions is given in his two large volumes, *Trattato di sociologia generale,* which was published in Italian in 1915-16, (translated into French in 1917-19); and in his *Les systèmes socialistes,* which two are the most important of all his sociological works. *Trattato* is not a textbook. It has nothing in common with the usual type of "The Principles," "The Foundations," and the "General Sociologies." Pareto's treatise is the product of an original and outstanding scientific mind. It has been said to be as original and important as Vico's and Machiavelli's treatises.[61] If such an estimation may be accepted, the outstanding value of Pareto's works is beyond doubt. Beyond doubt also is Pareto's great influence on Italian and French economic and sociological thought, and also on political thought

[61] See R. Michels' quoted paper about Italian sociology and Pareto's works in *Kölner Vierteljahrshefte für Soziologie,* July–August, 1924; the same in *Revue intern. de Sociologie,* 1924, pp. 518–530; BOUSQUET, G. H., "V. Pareto," *Revue intern. de Sociologie,* 1924, pp. 113–117; BOUSQUET, *Grundriss der Soziologie Paretos,* 1926; CARLI, F., "Paretos soziologisches System und der Behaviorismus," *Kölner Vierteljahrshefte für Soziologie,* IV. Jahrgang, 3 u. 4 Heft; GINO BORGATTA, *L'Opera sociologica e le feste guibilari di V. Pareto,* Torino, 1917; *Jubilé du V. Pareto,* Lausanne, 1920, (publ. by the University of Lausanne, where Pareto was professor); a special number of *Giornale degli Economisti,* Nos. 1–2, 1924, dedicated to Pareto and composed of the papers of R. Michels, M. Pantaleoni, E. Barone, G. del Vecchio, R. Benini, E. Ciccotti, and of other prominent economists and sociologists.

and practice in Italy. As is known, the ideology of the Italian
Fascism has taken a great deal from the theories of Pareto. The
outstanding character of his theories is well witnessed also by
those socialist and anti-Fascist writers who have styled him the
"Karl Marx of Bourgeoisie." So much about Pareto's general
characteristics. Let us now turn to his *Trattato*. Like almost all
writers about Pareto, I must give warning. His *Trattato* is so
poorly written, and the material is so carelessly arranged, that
in a brief summary it is impossible to give any adequate idea of
Pareto's work.[62] It must be read and studied in the original.
Even the best analysis will be only a shadow of the work itself.[63]
All that I can do here is to give such a shadow of the leading
ideas of Pareto's theory.

WHAT PARETO UNDERSTANDS BY SCIENTIFIC SOCIOLOGY

By scientific sociology Pareto means a "logico-experimental
science" based exclusively on the observation of and experimentation with, the facts. No reasoning, no speculation, no moralization, nothing which goes beyond the facts, or does not describe
their uniformities or qualities can compose an element or a theory
of logico-experimental sociology. In other words, no *a priori*
element or principle is to enter in, or to be admitted to, sociology.
The propositions and statements of such a sociology are nothing
but a description of the facts and their uniformities. As such,
they never are absolute, but relative, being subject to change as
soon as new facts show their inaccuracy. The categories of
"necessity," "inevitability," "absolute truth," or "absolute determinism," and so on, are out of such a science. Its propositions
are only more or less probable, being based on the principle of,

---

[62] Bousquet rightly says: "*Trattato est aussi mal rédigé que possible. . . ·
L'abondance des preuves experimentales nuit à la clarté de démonstration, les sujets
sont abordés sans aucun esprit de suite, et le lecteur ne comprend pas où il va.*" *Op. cit.,*
p. 116. Comp. BARONE, E., *Giornale d. Economisti,* 1924, p. 22. There is a
short compendium of Pareto's Treatise by Farina; but even it does not give an
adequate idea of Pareto's work.

[63] In this respect Pareto's work reminds one of the works of another outstanding sociologist and economist, Max Weber. In spite of quite different starting
points and terminology, the methodological conclusions of both authors (in the
field of sociology) are very similar. Since the most important sociological work
of M. Weber concerns the problem of religion, it will be more convenient to discuss his sociology in the chapters on the sociology of religion.

and being measured according to, the theory of probability. Nothing that is beyond observation or experimentation may become the object of such a science. About such problems, logico-experimental sociology can say nothing. No entity, no absolute principle, no absolute value, no moral evaluation—nothing that lies beyond observation and experimental verification may become a component of a "logico-experimental sociology."

Up to this time, almost all sociological theories have not been such logico-experimental propositions. To this or that degree they have always been dogmatic, metaphysical, non-logico-experimental, absolute and "moralizing." They usually trespass the boundaries of facts, observation, experimentation, and even of logic. From this standpoint, August Comte's or Herbert Spencer's "sociologies" are almost as unscientific as those theological and religious theories which they criticize. Under other names, these and other sociologies, have introduced into their theories the same "superfactual and super-experimental entities" (moral evaluation, dogmatism, "religion of Progress and Evolution," religion of "Positivism," and so on) which are nothing but the super-observational and superfactual "entities" and "absolutes" of the criticized religious doctrines, only slightly changed verbally. Sociological theories of the "Religion of Mankind," the "Religion of Solidarity," or of "Democracy"; the concepts of "Progress," "Socialism," "Evolution," "Brotherhood," "Liberty," "Justice," "Equality," and so on; theories which preach what ought to be and what ought not to be; theories which evaluate what is good and what is bad; and various "laws" of evolution and development,—all such theories and propositions, so abundantly scattered throughout contemporary social and sociological thought, are as unscientific as any "theology," because they are nothing but a modification of it. Like it, they are not based on facts or observation nor do they describe the characteristics and uniformities of the facts, but dogmatically command what ought to be, or postulate some entities which lie beyond observation and experimentation.[64]

Such, in brief, is Pareto's conception of the logico-experimental science of sociology. It is easy to see that this conception of

[64] See PARETO, V., *Traité de sociologie générale*, Vol. I, pp. 1–64, Paris, 1917.

science is similar to that of A. Cournot, E. Mach, R. Avenarius, H. Poincaré, A. Rey, P. Duhem, K. Pearson, A. Tschuproff, F. Enriques, partly to that of H. Vaihinger, and M. Weber,[65] and to that of some other prominent representatives and theorizers of contemporary science. This does not mean that Pareto denies any usefulness in the non-logico-experimental theories and beliefs; but on the contrary, he, more than anybody else, insists on the fact that "the non-scientific" (or the non-logico-experimental theories) are very often useful and necessary for the existence of a society, while the logico-experimental theories may often be socially harmful. In this way Pareto separates the categories of Truth and Usefulness. If, nevertheless, he pitilessly expels all the non-logico-experimental propositions from the field of science, he does it only to avoid a mixture of science with other forms of social thought.

QUANTITATIVE DESCRIPTION OF THE FUNCTIONAL INTERDEPENDENCE OF SOCIAL PHENOMENA INSTEAD OF ONE-SIDED CAUSATION

The next important part of Pareto's methodology is his criticism of the concept of one-sided causation in its application to the study of social phenomena. The concept of a "cause" and "effect" supposes a relationship of one-sided dependence between two or more phenomena. Factually, such a relationship is almost never given in the relationship of various social phenomena. As a rule they are mutually dependent. If, for instance, the qualities of the members of a society influence its social organization, the latter also influences the former. For this reason, the conception of a one-sided relationship of a cause and effect could not be applied to a scientific study of social phenomena. When it is applied, it shows the fallacy of either a "simplicist" theory or of a "cinematographic" one. By the fallacy of a "simplicist theory," I mean the following: Let us take a society. Its character and equilibrium are composed of, and are dependent on, geo-

---

[65] From a quite different standpoint Max Weber also comes to the conclusion that sociological regularities are nothing but *"Erwartungschancen"* or typical probability-expectations. See WEBER, M., *Wirtschaft und Gesellschaft, Grundriss der Sozialökonomik*, III. 1921–22, p. 14; *Gesammelte Aufsätze zur Wissenschaftslehre*, 1922, pp. 420, 444 ff.

graphical environment; (A) economic situation; (B) political constitution; (C) religion; (D) ethics and knowledge; (E) and so on. All these variables mutually depend on, and mutually influence, one another. Through this interaction they permanently change the character of a society and its equilibrium. We have then a mutual dependence of these "variables," and a dynamic equilibrium of a society, which may pass permanently from one state:

A, B, C, D, E...................... to another
A', B', C', D', E'......................
A", B", C", D", E".................. and so on

Now a "simplicist" theorizer takes an element A, as a cause, and tries to view B, C, D and E, as its "effects." [66] Some other simplicists may take B, or C, or D, as a "cause" and try to view the other elements as effects. In this way we receive, and we indeed have, plenty of various contradictory theories which all represent a simplicist type of sociological theory, (all of them being one-sided theories which try to explain the whole social life through a geographic, racial, economic, political, or any other factor). As a result of such a procedure, the theory is inevitably one-sided; its generalizations, inadequate; its diagnoses, false; and its formulas, fallacious; to say nothing of the useless fights between various simplicist theories which are caused.

The following is meant by the fallacy of a "cinematographic" theory. The sociologists observe and describe the transition of A into A', A" and so on; the transition of B into B', B" . . .; and of C into C', C" . . . just as we are shown picture after picture in a motion picture drama. This transition is described by these cinematographic theories under the name of evolution. By this description they limit their task, and think that every-

[66] For instance, F. de Coulanges says, "the domestic religion taught man to appropriate land and guaranteed his rights of property." Pareto shows how fallacious is this statement, and how the concept of a cause (instead of a mutual dependence) is responsible for the fallacy. PARETO, *ibid.*, Vol. I, pp. 254–255. In the same way he gives a series of similar "causal theories" of August Comte, Herbert Spencer, H. S. Maine, Duruy, J. S. Mill, and so on, and convincingly shows their fallacious character due to the same reason. *Ibid.*, §§ 256 ff. For the same reason he is right in saying that the majority of various anthropological and ethnographic "explanations" are defective.

thing in the way of a scientific study is completed. The fallacy of such theories, even when their schemes of an "evolution" are accurate (which is rare) is in their superficiality. They do not, and cannot, give any generalization beyond a purely empirical, "historical description." They cannot supply us with "formulas of uniformities," and do not give any analysis of the phenomena.[67]

In order to avoid either of these fallacies, sociology has to deal with the concept of a functional relationship between social phenomena instead of a one-sided causal relationship. Conceptions of "cause" and "effect" must be superseded by those of a "variable" and "function." In a purely methodological way it is necessary in the beginning to isolate a definite "variable" which is always present as a component of social phenomena and then to study its "functional relationship" to the other phenomena B, C, D, E. The same must be done in regard to the "other variables" B, C, D, E. When this stage is finished, a series of the obtained "formulas" of functional correlation should be introduced for the study of the complex series of interdependent social phenomena, A, B, C, D. . . .[68] In this synthetic stage of the study, our primary attention should be given to those social relationships which are relatively constant. We must observe their fluctuations in time and space and the interdependence and correlation of these oscillations. We must grasp the repeated uniformities in their complex variation and change, describing them qualitatively, and measuring them quantitatively. All that is unique, or quite irregular, non-repeated, or "incidental," we must leave, at least for a time, until we have at our disposal the formulas for the series of the most important "uniformities" and their quantitative indices. *De minimis non curat praetor.* In this way we will obtain a series of "successive approximations" to the complex reality. Contrary to those of the simplicist theorists, these "successive approximations" will be about accurate.[69] They will also differ from those of the cinematographic theories,

---

[67] PARETO, *ibid.,* § 2023. Comp. BARONE, E., "L'opera di V. Pareto e il progresso della scienza," *Giornale d. Economisti,* 1924, pp. 22–24.

[68] Comp. WEBER, M., *Gesammelte Aufsätze zur Religionssoziologie,* Tübingen, 1922, Vol. I, pp. 21–22, 82, 183, 238, and *passim.*

[69] Compare with M. Weber's corresponding theory of the purpose of sociological generalization. See further about M. Weber.

in that they will give us an insight into the functional relationship of the phenomena and formulas of uniformities, and the
indices of correlations, which approximately describe the most
fundamental social processes.   Thus these points of Pareto's
methodology may be summed up as follows:

A. A conception of mutual dependence instead of one-
   sided dependence.
B. A conception of functional relationship instead of that
   of cause-effect.
C. A study of the constant elements of a social system instead of its unique, incidental, and quite irregular
   components
D. A study of the uniformities and correlations in the
   fluctuation (in space and time) of these constant
   elements.
E. A quantitative measurement of the uniformities, their
   fluctuation, and their correlation, instead of a purely
   qualitative description.
F. Following this method, we will obtain a series of
   formulas which represent a successive approximation
   to the extremely complex social reality and its
   dynamics.[70]

Again, it is easy to see that these methodological propositions
are practically identical with those of H. Poincaré, E. Mach,
Duhem, K. Pearson, and other noted methodologists of science.
They are also in complete agreement with a quite recent trend
in the interpretation of causal relation, determinism, and so on in
natural sciences.   These concepts are more and more losing their
metaphysical flavor of "inevitableness" and "necessity," being
transformed into the theories of functional relations, which are
based on the principles of probability. In accordance with Pareto's
principles also is the recent development of the quantitative studies
of social phenomena, of mathematical statistics, and of the mathematical theory of correlation (including partial correlation), and a

---

[70] PARETO, *op. cit.*, Vol. I, pp. XIII–XVI; §§ 96, 99, 138, 254–255, 267, and
passim; Vol. II, §§ 1731–1732, 1767, 1861, 2061, 2080, 2088–2104, 2336, and
passim.   Pareto's criticism of the "causal" theories of the most prominent
authorities is highly instructive.

trend to perfection in the mathematical theories of variables, and so on.

Now let us see briefly how this plan has been carried on by Pareto. His subsequent propositions, backed by a long and elaborate inductive analysis of the facts and mathematical formulas, may be outlined here only schematically. Those who are anxious to study Pareto's corroborations should turn to his work, where nearly two thousand pages are filled by corresponding proofs.

PARETO'S CONCEPT OF SOCIETY

Some sociologists depict society as an organism; some others, as a mere totality of individuals, while still others use the term mechanism. Accordingly, we have sociological organicists, realists, nominalists, and mechanisticists. Pareto remains rather out of all these schools. For him an existing social group is a mere "social system" which, as long as it exists, is in a state of equilibrium; that is, in a state in which the forces which try to disrupt the social system are successfully counterbalanced by the integrating forces. Following the path of other social physicists, Pareto, for the sake of simplifying the study, views society as a system of human molecules which are in a complex mutual relationship.[71]

PARETO'S THEORY OF FACTORS

The concrete forms of a social system are many and various. Then what are the factors responsible for a certain form of it? "A form of society is determined by all the elements which influence it: the form in its turn reacting on these elements." All these elements, or factors, may be divided into three classes: "(1) soil, climate, flora, fauna, geologic conditions and so on; (2) other elements exterior to the given society at a given time; such as other societies which are exterior to a given society

---

[71] PARETO, op. cit., Vol. II, pp. 1306–1316, §§ 2060 ff. Notice here Pareto's mathematical formula of social equilibrium. Not very different from Pareto's concept of social equilibrium is that of F. Carli. "Social equilibrium," says Carli, "is a totality of the internal rhythms (between the elements of a social system) and the interno-external, which develop in a non-contradictory manner. In other words it is a totality of the correlated internal and interno-external variations which go on either being constant or varying in a uniform manner." CARLI, F., L'Equilibrio delle Nazioni, Bologna, 1920, p. 34.

spacially, and the consequences of the preceding stages of the society exterior to its given stage in time;" (3) the inner elements of a social system; such as race, the character of the residues and feelings, interests, ideologies and other qualities of the human molecules which compose a given social system.[72]

This shows that in this respect, Pareto is a pluralist. These elements, as a rule, are mutually dependent. "In order to explain completely a given social form, it would be necessary to know all these numerous elements quantitatively; their effects, their combinations, their correlations." Unfortunately, at the present time such a knowledge is impossible. In order to make it possible we will have to simplify the situation, to take only some of the more important elements, disregarding, at least for a time, the less important ones. Only when each of these important elements and their combinations has been studied thoroughly and quantitatively will a complete sociological synthesis be possible. Meanwhile, we must satisfy ourselves with a simplified study of the social system and of the most important factors of its equilibrium.[73]

THE ELEMENTS OR FACTORS STUDIED BY PARETO

Of the above numerous factors or elements, Pareto studies thoroughly some specific ones, namely: (1) "residues" (reminiscent of Allport's "prepotent reflexes," or psychiatrists' "complexes"); (2) "derivations" (speech-reactions, ideologies); (3) economic factors; (4) heterogeneity of human beings and social groups; (5) social mobility and circulation of élites. It is understood that Pareto does not think that these elements exhaust all the important factors responsible for the form of a social system. Many other factors are important but these are not studied by Pareto for the reason that a thorough study of even the above five elements is exceedingly complex and difficult. Other sociologists will have to make a careful and quantitative study of additional factors. This explains the character of Pareto's "Treatise in Sociology." It is a kind of monographic study of the above mentioned five elements in a social system. In other words,

---

[72] PARETO, *op. cit.*, Vol. II, § 2060.
[73] *Ibid.*, §§ 2061–2066.

Pareto simplifies methodologically a real social system, assuming that it is composed only of these five elements; and in this way tries to construct a rough theory which is to be an approximate image of a real and much more complex social system. Having no space here to follow Pareto's long and painstaking analysis of the forms, the correlations, and combinations, the fluctuations, the indices, and the effects of each of these five elements, all that I can do is to give only dogmatically some of his principal conclusions.

PARETO'S CONCLUSIONS CONCERNING THE RESIDUES AND DERIVATIONS

1. Among other elements, the equilibrium of a social system depends upon the characteristics of its human molecules, particularly on their forms of behavior, or their actions. Human actions depend greatly on the character of their "drives." Among these "drives," the especially important are those which are relatively constant. Pareto calls them "residues." His residue is not an instinct, nor is it exactly a "sentiment." It is one of the relatively constant "drives" existing among the members of any society, regardless of the question as to whether their constancy is due to instinct or to something else. "Residues" are related to what Allport styles "prepotent reflexes," L. Petrajitzky, "emotions," and what many psychologists style "complexes," as "an inferiority complex," or what A. L. Lowell calls "dispositions." In the final analysis they are based on instincts, but contrary to them, their manifestation is not "rigid," but varies greatly, assuming the most different, even opposite, forms. For instance, the sexual residue, contrary to the sex-instinct, may manifest itself not only in the actions of copulation (the proper form of satisfaction and manifestation of the sex-instinct), but also in sexual asceticism, in the mutilation of the sex-organs, and in the ascetic slandering of sex-appetite and sexual life. The same may be said of other "residues" in their interrelation to instincts.[74] "The residues are the manifestation of instincts and sentiments as the

[74] See Pareto's detailed analysis of the residues in the quoted work, Vol. I, Chap. VI, §§ 842 ff; Vol. II, Chap. XI.

elevation of mercury in a thermometer is the manifestation of a rise in the temperature." [75]

There are six principal classes of residues, each of which is divided into a series of subclasses. The classes are as follows: (1) *Residues of Combinations:* These are the drives to make physical and mental combinations of various things generally, of opposite things, of like with like, of rare things with exceptional events, and so on; (2) *Residues of the Persistence of Aggregates:* The drives to keep the persistence of man's relations to other men and to places; of the living to the dead; and the persistence of abstractions, of symbols, of personified concepts, and so on; (3) *Residues (or Needs) of the Manifestation of Sentiments Through Exterior Acts:* Religious exaltation, political agitation, and so on; (4) *Residues in Regard to Sociability:* Drives which compose particular societies and factions; imposing a uniformity on the members of an aggregate, such as neo-phobia, pity, cruelty, asceticism, drive for popularity, inferiority and superiority complexes, and so on; (5) *Residues of the Integrity of Personality:* Drives which preserve one's personality against alteration, the drive for equality, and so on; (6) *Sexual Residues.*[76]

On first approach, this classification may appear very incongruous, and yet, when one studies its reasons, and its analysis, it loses a great deal of this incongruity. These residues are found in any society and, in this sense, they are constant elements of any social system. However, their distribution among various individuals and groups is not identical. There are individuals (and groups) with greatly developed residues of Combinations, but with few weak residues of the Persistence of the Aggregate; and there are individuals and groups with the opposite distribution. Within the same society, in the course of time, and through various circumstances, the distribution of the residues among its human molecules may be greatly changed. When this happens, the social system changes its form.

2. The character of the residues determines the character of

[75] *Ibid.*, § 875.
[76] *Ibid.*, § 888. See §§ 889–1396, and §§ 1687–2059, devoted to an analysis of these residues.

human actions. They are to some extent *a manifestation of the residues.* Among human beings, this manifestation assumes two principal forms: *actions not followed by speech-reactions or by conscious subjective processes* such as instinctive and automatic actions, (Scheme: A, [residue] leads to B, [act]); and *actions followed by speech-reactions and ideologies,* or conscientious psychical processes, theories, motivations, justifications, representations of purposes, intentions, "beautification," and other explicit and implicit speech-reactions. The scheme is: A (residue) leads simultaneously to $\begin{cases} \text{B (act)} \\ \text{C (speech-reactions).} \end{cases}$ All these speech-reactions and ideologies, Pareto calls "derivations." This leads to his "sociology of ideas and ideologies," or to a "sociology of human speech-reactions."

3. Some authors have properly remarked that, in this respect, Pareto is near to K. Marx. Like Marx, he does not assign much importance to "derivations" or "ideologies." For him they are but a manifestation of the residues. The residues are "the father of ideologies." The "derivations" are a kind of weathercock which turns according to the direction of the wind of the residues. Their influence is not nil, but it is much less than many think. They are much more variable and flexible than the residues. The same residue may give an origin to, or may be veiled under, different "derivations," and *vice versa.* Sometimes various residues may be "wrapped" up in similar "derivations." The following examples may illustrate this. A residue in the form of the horror of manslaughter is manifested in the following derivations:

> "Don't kill because you will go to hell."
> "Don't kill because it is forbidden by God."
> "Don't kill because it is immoral."
> "Don't kill because it is inhuman, or against Law, Progress, and Justice."
> "Don't kill!"

These derivations are only "veils" which hide the real agent hindering the act of killing, which is the corresponding residue.

According to the circumstances, the residue may give origin to these and to many other "ideologies." In spite of many differences, all the ideologies are practically nothing but various "dresses" for the same residue.

The speech-reactions of an orthodox Catholic who does not admit religious tolerance, and those of an ardent communist who violently assails "intolerance," are quite different. Their residues are, however, the same; a drive to impose on all others their own standard of conduct and beliefs. The speech-reactions of many ascetics in regard to sex are the most critical, but the very fact that they talk so much about sex, and so bitterly assail it, is an indication that the residue of these "derivations" is the same as that of the "obscene speech-reactions" of a profligate person.

4. Since action and derivations are so dependent on the residues, there follows from this a series of very important conclusions concerning the residues and dynamics of ideologies. First, residues often contradict each other within the same man. Hence, our behavior and our actions are, in greater part, also self-contradictory and illogical. Defining "logical actions" as those in which the intended subjective purpose of an action coincides with its objective result, Pareto, more than any one else, shows that a greater part of our actions are non-logical. Carried on by a complex play of the residues, we perform an immense number of actions which are non-logical, or in which the subjective purpose of the action (ideology) happens to be quite different from its objective result. Only in the field of logico-experimental behavior, in the field of scientific performances, do they coincide. Apart from it, and in but a few other cases, human behavior is essentially non-logical and contradictory, because our residues are often mutually contradictory. Our actions are inconsistent from a logical standpoint because our residues are in a dynamic state, wherein the dominant residue at a given moment may be quickly succeeded by another different one. Under the influence of the former, we behave ourselves in one way; under the influence of the latter, in quite a different manner. In brief, Pareto's analysis of the correlation between the dynamics of the residue and that of action, and conclusions concerning the non-logical actions of

human beings, represent, possibly, an unsurpassed analysis of human behavior.[77]

5. With still greater reason, the above may be said of Pareto's theory concerning the nature of the derivations (ideologies). Since the relationship of the residues is so complex and often contradictory, it is to be expected that human derivations (ideologies and speeches) are rarely logical and accurate from a logico-experimental standpoint. An immensely greater part of them, including the political, religious, sociological, economic, and what-not "theories" are non-logical, inconsistent, self-contradictory, or pseudo-scientific. They do not describe accurately the studied facts, but represent a mere "motivation," "justification," "beautification," "rationalization," "moralization," or "idealization" of a kind of behavior to which we are driven by our residues. The residues changing, our "pseudo-scientific" theories change also. One residue giving way to another opposite one, our theory "A is B," gives way to that of "A is non-B." Hence, the logic of human reasoning in the majority of the cases is far from being logical. An ideology is accepted or non-accepted in the majority of cases, not so much because it is true or false, but because of its agreement or disagreement with our residues. This explains the influence of newspaper propaganda, of fiery speeches, and of all kinds of utterances which influence our emotions and senti-ments. Instead of scientific proof, they use the authority of purely verbal pseudo-proofs, which appeal to our proclivities. In spite of this, such derivations are often even more convincing than scientific proofs, if the derivations are in agreement with the dominant residues. Hence, if we wish to change the opinions and ideologies of a man or a group, the best way is to change their residues. The residues being changed or destroyed, the corresponding derivations (ideologies) will also be changed (*Ibid.*, Ch. XI). From this standpoint, the sociology of Comte with its ideals (derivations) of Positivism, Progress, and Re-ligion of Mankind, is as unscientific as the rudest fetishistic belief. The theories of Progress, Solidarity, Democracy, Justice,

---

[77] PARETO, *op. cit.*, Chap. II. Compare LOWELL, A. L., *Public Opinion in War and Peace, passim* and Chaps. I–III. President Lowell in his special analysis comes to conclusions very similar to Pareto's statements.

Socialism, Nationalism, Patriotism, Internationalism, and so forth, are the same non-logical derivations, only differing in form from primitive magical and religious beliefs which they assail. Almost all the ardent fighters of prejudices and superstitions are but a variety of the same superstitions and similar to the dogmatic minds whom they fight. Considering consecutively all of the most prominent contemporary social thinkers, like Comte, Spencer, H. Sumner Maine, not to mention a legion of various "ideologists," Pareto convincingly shows the inconsistency, self-contradiction, fallacy, and illogicity of their statements, while he indicates the residues responsible for this "pseudo-scientism." More than anyone else, he has shown the "pseudo-scientific nature" of the "Gods (concepts) of Progress," "Evolution," "Democracy," "Solidarity," "Justice," "Law," "Natural Rights," "Morals," and so on. For him these "scientific" concepts and theories are as fallacious as any of the rudest superstitions. They are the same non-logical derivations, only "dressed" according to the fashion of the day. That is the whole difference. Therefore, like some of the behaviorists, Pareto views "derivations" as "minor reactions" in our behavior. He indicates the impossibility of basing any scientific conclusion about a man, group, or epoch on the corresponding speech-reactions only. For him they are only a kind of very misleading thermometer indicating what residues are behind them.

The above is sufficient to give an idea as to why Pareto does not pay much attention to the "derivations." A long part of his work is devoted to a study of the fluctuations of the derivations in correlation with the fluctuation of the residues. Although the residues fluctuate also, the tempo and the amplitude of their fluctuation is much slower and limited than that of the derivations. They are especially variable and changeable. Further, Pareto shows that, in spite of the difference of the derivations in their concrete forms among various people and times, the principal classes of residues wrapped in the ideologies are relatively constant. To a superficial observer, there is an immense difference between a savage who deifies his fetish or king, and an atheistic socialist of the present time; and yet both of them have the same residue of "deification." The only difference is that the savage deifies some fetish and, for a corroboration of his belief, makes reference to a "magic code"; while an atheist deifies K. Marx, Lenin, or Rousseau, and for corroboration of his statement quotes Marx's "Capital," Rousseau's "Discourse," or what not. In the past the residue of obedience was manifested principally in a subordination to the kings, priests, and nobility. Now these are slandered, but the residue remains and manifests itself in an obedience to the demagogues, leaders of labor unions, captains of industry, and so forth. The "dresses" are different, but the residue is the same. The residue for imposing uniformity on the members of a society has been manifested in the past in religious intolerance, in a persecution of attacks on private property, divorces, short skirts, and so on. Now we are tolerant in this respect, but instead we have an intolerance toward drinking (prohibition), and toward any criticism of the actions of reformers and the followers of the "Religion of Humanity," "Progress," and so on. Derivations have changed, but the residues remain. The above conception of Pareto does not mean, however, that all these derivations are absolutely inefficient or socially harmful. They have some efficiency, though not so great as many think. Further, in opposition to all those who think that every truth is useful, while every superstition is harmful, Pareto stresses the point that the real situation is different. Many prejudices (derivations) have happened to be useful in keeping the integrity of a social system; while many truths have facilitated its disintegration. In other words, a derivation (myth, legend, ardent belief, or superstition which beautifies the reality, inspiring enthusiasm) may be useful for a group; and, on the other hand, a naked truth may often be disastrous. In this point Pareto comes to conclusions similar to those of Machiavelli, J. Frazer, G. Le Bon, G. Sorel [78] and others. In their own way, superstitions and illusions are as vital for a society as the logico-experimental truths. The above gives the most general outline of Pareto's leading ideas in this respect. Briefly summarized, the material in the book con-

[78] See, for instance, FRAZER, J. G., *Psyche's Task*, Lond., 1913; SOREL, G. *Reflection on Violence*, pp. 133 ff, N. Y. 1912; Sorel's theory of the usefulness of myths.

sists of painstaking analyses of the influence of the residues on derivations; of the residues on residues; the influence of environment on the residues; of the derivations on derivations; of the derivations on the residues; and the fluctuation and diffusion of both the residues and the derivations. I am compelled to omit this material because of lack of space.

6. Among other points of Pareto's theory of residues there should be mentioned his statement that the above six classes of residues are distributed unequally among various individuals, social classes, and social groups. There are individuals and groups with many and strong residues of the first class (the Residues of Combinations); and there are other individuals and groups with numerous and strong residues of the second class (of the Persistence of Aggregates). The same is true in regard to the other classes of the residues. This is important in the sense that the character of the predominant residue shapes the human personality of an individual or a group greatly. It puts a conspicuous stamp on them, and determines to a great extent either the behavior of an individual, or the character of the social organization of a group. Among these classes of residues, some of the especially important are those of the first and the second class. On their bases Pareto outlines his hypothesis of two principal *social types* of individuals: that of the *speculators* and that of the *rentiers*. To the first type belong all those who have strong and numerous residues of combination. They are the combiners, entrepreneurs, and machinators, who are always contemplating some new combination (financial and business schemes, inventions, political and diplomatic reconstructions, or something else). Whatever the field of their combinations is they always have a new combination. In this respect they are reformers and reconstructers. They do not have psychological conservatism. Often they are unmoral and dishonest, being too plastic in all respects. The *rentiers* are those whose predominant residue is that of the persistence of the aggregate. For this reason, they psychologically represent the type of the conservative, those who do not care for innovations or for new combinations; but who try to save, preserve, and maintain that which already exists. They are the people with a strong sense of duty, with a narrow but

determined will, and with decisiveness in their actions. They may be found among the "narrow-minded," determined leaders of any movement. They are rigid in their behavior and often fanatical.

In this sense, these are the eternal types found in any society. When the first type, or the speculators, is predominant in a government (common among democratic and plutocratic governments), the upper classes show an ability for combination. Through this power, they temporarily promote the economic welfare of a society. They successfully deceive the governed masses through various humanitarian and democratic machinations, promises, and so on. Naturally they are corrupted. The corruption and machination sooner or later bring disastrous results, which causes the upper classes to be eventually superseded by the opposite type, or the *rentiers*. In this way, the alternation of the types has happened many times in the history of various countries, and is going on at this time. According to the author, the majority of any pre-war democratic governments is composed of the plutocratic parliamentary machinators or corrupted "speculators." They have an ability for combination but at the same time they are so corrupted, and become so soft-hearted and "humanitarian," that they are superseded by people of the type of *rentiers* (regardless of whether such a substitution is good or bad).[79]   Events seem to have considerably corroborated Pareto's expectation.[80]

PARETO'S CONCLUSIONS CONCERNING OTHER ELEMENTS IN THE FORM OF A SOCIAL SYSTEM

In a less detailed way, Pareto also studies other important elements of the factors of social equilibrium: the economic factors or interests, the heterogeneity of human beings, and the social stratification and circulation of the élites.

Economic Interests.—We can scarcely question that "individuals and groups are pushed by instinct and reason to appropriate useful or agreeable material values, and to seek for honors

---

[79] See Chap. XIII, where an analysis is made of some experimental studies of personality types analogous to the types of Pareto.
[80] See about this theory, PARETO, *op. cit.*, Vol. II, Chap. XII.

and esteem," or in other words, that they have "interests." The totality of such interests plays a considerable part in determining social equilibrium. Their complex reality cannot be explained completely by economics, but requires a synthetic sociological study. On the other hand, sociology cannot explain the complex social reality, unless it takes into consideration the propositions of pure economics as a special science, which studies them in an isolated way, and under simplified conditions. The economic interpretation of history is right so far as it insists on the important rôle of economic factors in social phenomena. But it is wrong in so far as it tries to explain them only through this factor, or makes it a "cause," while other factors are made mere "effects." To this extent the theory is a mere variety of the above simplicist theory. (See also the chapter upon the Economic School.)

Social Heterogeneity.—The next important and constant element or factor in a social system is the heterogeneity of the individuals. It is again an eternal fact and an unquestioned one. Physically, morally, and intellectually, individuals are heterogeneous. From this heterogeneity, the phenomena of social stratification and social inequality originate. These also are eternal and constant elements of any social system. In connection with this part of his theory, Pareto develops his sharp criticism of the theories of equality, democracy, self-government, and so on. All corresponding ideologies are mere derivations not corresponding to the facts at all. There never has been any social or political system in which equality or real democracy has been realised. What is styled democracy is rather plutocracy; the control of the governed people principally through deceit, machination, and combination, and by demagogues, capitalists, hypocrites, and cynical persons. Another important type of government is that of rude coercion, which controls through the application of physical compulsion. One may be as good or bad as another. Whatever devices are used, the basic fact of the heterogeneity of individuals will produce social inequality and stratification. In ideologies there may be used such epithets as democracy, equality, and other high-sounding phrases. They cannot, however, annul the facts of stratification exhibited in all societies and groups.

Circulation of the Élites.—The existence of social stratification means that in every society there are, roughly speaking, two principal strata: the lower and the upper classes. The distribution of the residues among them is different, and they differ in many other respects. Since there is a stratification, there must be also a circulation or shifting of individuals from the lower to the upper classes, and from the upper to the lower classes. Its intensiveness varies from society to society and from time to time, but, in some degree, it exists even in a caste society. One of its permanent causes is that any existing aristocracy is, sooner or later, doomed to disappear. "History is a cemetery of the aristocracies." The vacuum created by a dying out of the aristocracy must be filled; and the filling is accomplished through the climbing of the fitted members of the lower classes to the upper social positions. In this way within every society goes on a constant process of circulation of the élites. Studying some of its details, Pareto shows the principal methods through which aristocracy or plutocracy tries to keep its position. Such methods are: extermination, imprisonment, bribery, corruption, and the elevation of the possible and dangerous leaders from the lower classes. Here again this "K. Marx of Bourgeoisie" sets forth theories similar to those of the most radical revolutionary syndicalists and anarchists. On the other hand, contrary to the "soft-hearted ideologists of a liberal humanitarianism," he claims that a "liberal" opinion about the inefficiency of physical and cruel measures for the maintenance of the privileged aristocratic positions is wrong. Together with Sorel, he states that by the proper application of a vigorous force and cruel coercion, arisocracy can maintain and prolong its existence; and that, contrary to popular opinion, such cruel aristocracies have existed for a longer time than the meek "humanitarian aristocracies." For this reason, Pareto prophesies the downfall of the present parliamentary, soft-hearted, and pacifist plutocracies of the democratic countries; and the ascent of a new, rough, virile, and militaristic aristocracy from the lower classes.[81] Such a cycle has happened many times and will happen again in the future.

[81] This has been realized by Fascism, which offered to Pareto a place among its ideological leaders.

Having outlined these constant elements of a social system, Pareto proceeds to correlate them with each other, with the residues, the derivations, and with a series of other phenomena.[82]

PARETO'S CYCLICAL CONCEPTION OF SOCIAL CHANGE

Studying the oscillations of various phenomena, Pareto gives a series of cyclical theories for various social processes. A "linear conception" of social change remains strange to him. He shows the fallacies of all "historical tendencies," "historical laws of evolution," and of "linear theories of the stages of progress." What is factually given in history is only the fluctuations and oscillations of various lengths of time, and of various velocities. The existence of any perpetual "linear" evolution of a society or social institutions has not been proved.

Such, in brief, is a simplified skeleton of the principal ideas of Pareto's sociology. As I have mentioned, this can give only a remote idea of Pareto's book. Its value lies, perhaps, not so much in the character of his general theory, as in a series of research monographs, whose combination it represents. An abundance of mathematical formulas, diagrams, and a long series of historical and factual corroborations, plus a poor arrangement of the materials, makes an adequate summary of the work in a brief form exceedingly difficult. Nevertheless, some idea of it has probably been given in the above.

7. CRITICISM

In the opinion of the writer, the leading ideas of Pareto's sociology are to be recognized as sound and promising. Though almost all of these ideas were set forth before Pareto, he has succeeded in developing and systematizing them. His conception of sociology in its relationship to special social sciences is much better than a great many other corresponding theories. His theory of the mutual dependence of various social phenomena, and of functional and quantitative methods of their study, is in agreement with the present tendency in natural and social sciences. His analysis of human behavior, of the rôle of the residues and

[82] PARETO, *op. cit.*. Chaps. XII–XIII.

derivations, and of the non-logical "logic" of human actions, is again likely to be true. His somewhat sharp and "ironical" utterances concerning the non-scientific character of a great many "sociological" theories are to be recognized as valid. His idea of successive approximations, and of the necessity for concen. trating our attention on relatively constant elements of the social system, appears valuable also to me. Finally, his theory of the heterogeneity of human individuals, of social stratification, of the circulation of the élites, and his criticism of the "sweet" ideologies of Progress, Democracy, Solidarity, and so on have been corroborated and developed by many other authors. Part of this has been done independently, and part under Pareto's influence.[83]

Side by side with these valuable characteristics, Pareto's theories have some serious shortcomings. In the first place, his concept of the residue remains somewhat unclearly defined, and,

---

[83] The theory of the heterogeneity of individuals and groups, as we shall see further, has been developed by a great many biologists and sociologists of the racial and anthropological school (Gobineau, F. Galton, H. Chamberlain, K. Pearson, O. Ammon, V. de Lapouge and all the eugenists and hereditarists. See the chapter about the Racial and Anthropological School). The same authors, and many others, developed the above ideas of the social circulation of the élites. Under Pareto's influence, the theories of circulation and of social equilibrium were developed by M. KOLABINSKA, *La circulation des élites en France,* Lausanne, 1912; SENSINI, G., "Teoria dell'equilibrio di composizione delle classi sociali," *Rivista Italiana di Sociologia,* Sept., Oct., 1913. See also SENSINI, *La teoria della Rendita* and BOVEN, P., *Les applications mathématique à l'économie politique,* Lausanne, 1912; CARLI, F., *op. cit.* Finally, the writer in his study of social mobility, found many of Pareto's ideas suggestive. See SOROKIN, *Social Mobility.* See there other references concerning social circulation and stratification. Theories similar to Pareto's leading ideas about democracy, solidarity, inevitability of social stratification, the plutocratic and oligarchic character of a democratic or equalitarian régime, the rôle of violence in history, the dying out of aristocracy, and so on; some earlier, some later, some independently, and some under the influence of Pareto have been developed by a series of prominent authors. See DANILEVSKY, and LEONTIEFF, *op. cit.,* LE BON, G., *The Crowd,* especially his *Psychology of Socialism;* MOSCA, G., *Elementi di scienza politica,* 1895; OSTROGORSKY, M., *La démocratie et les parties politiques,* Paris, 1912; MICHELS, R., *Sociologia del partito politico moderno* (transl. into French, English, German); MAINE, HENRY S., *Popular Government,* Lond., 1896; SOREL, G., *Reflections on Violence;* KROPOTKIN, P., *A Rebel's Speeches* (Rechi buntovtschika), Russ., 1919, *passim;* the works of theorizers of the revolutionary syndicalism like Lagardelle, and others; BRYCE, J., especially his *Modern Democracies,* N. Y., 1921; LOWELL, A. L., *Public Opinion in War and Peace;* LIPPMANN, W., *Public Opinion,* N. Y., 1922; and especially his *Phantom-Public,* 1925. As to Pareto's theory of the cyclical concept of social processes, see the paragraph about Cyclical Conception in this book.

in its essence, it is "subjective," in the sense that it is taken as a kind of an inner "drive" (sentiment, instinct) which could not be objectively studied and measured. Like many other psychologists, Pareto "puts" these "residues" into a man, and later on deduces from them whatever he likes. For this reason, all the objections applied to similar psychological interpretations (see the chapter about the Psychological School) as a variety of "animistic conceptions," [84] must be applied to Pareto's method and theory. It is true that Pareto went much further in such a study than almost all psychologists, and yet he could not completely avoid the inadequacy of such a method. From this it follows that such inner "drives" are almost impossible to study objectively and quantitatively. In spite of Pareto's inclination to such a quantitative study, he did not factually give a real quantitative investigation of his residues. This explains also why Pareto's classification of the residues appears to be considerably arbitrary and questionable, naturally influencing many of his deductions and conclusions in the same way.

In the second place, it is hard for me to discriminate his "residues" from his "interests," as economic factors. The boundary line between them is very dark and poorly drawn. For this reason it becomes difficult to determine just exactly what is the degree of influence exerted by each of these factors in determining social equilibrium.

In the third place, Pareto himself many times stresses the fact that the same residue may be wrapped into the most different derivations, and that, for this reason, it is always very uncertain exactly what residue is the source of a certain derivation. This very fact makes questionable Pareto's many reductions of the certain derivations to the certain residues. His conclusions may and may not be true. Because of this we are often at sea, and do not know the real relations of the residues with the derivations.

[84] A primitive man puts into, or behind the given phenomena, various "spirits," and through their activities explains all concrete phenomena, beginning with the thunderstorm and ending with birth, death, and other conspicuous facts in human life. The psychologists, instead of the old-fashioned "spirits" or "mysterious supernatural powers," put into man "emotions," "wishes," "ideas," "residues" and what not; and through their influence try to interpret human and social phenomena as a "manifestation" of their activity. It is easy to see that the procedure in both cases, is essentially the same,—animistic. The only difference is in that of the terminology.

In the fourth place, Pareto's theory of social circulation is too general and inadequate. It needs many corrections and much development.

These remarks show the most important weak points of Pareto's theory. However, they do not annul his valuable contributions to the methodology of social science, to the sociology of human speech-reactions and ideologies, or to the whole concept of social phenomena. His work is possibly the best continuation of the plan of social physics developed by the thinkers of the seventeenth century. Pareto tries to carry on this plan, throwing aside its weak points and promoting what is valuable in this magnificent contemplation. If the other contemporary mechanistic and energetistic theories mentioned above have factually added very little to the theories of the seventeenth century, in Pareto's works they reappear again with all their brilliancy and fascination. Pareto's studies show that, properly taken, the social physics of the seventeenth century is not a mere dream of a bold human mind, but may be developed into a real scientific sociology which will probably not be able to disentangle all the "mysteries" of human behavior and human history, but may clarify, to some degree, the more important of them.

A series of other mentioned studies which proceed along the lines of Pareto's principles, and which have already given some valuable results, seem to warrant such an expectation, and stimulate the cultivating of "the mechanistic and quantitative investigations of social systems," as has been outlined by Pareto.

CHAPTER II

FRÉDÉRIC LE PLAY'S SCHOOL

T H E name of Frédéric Le Play deserves to be put among the few names of the most prominent masters of social science. He and his pupils have created a really scientific method of the study and analysis of social phenomena; they elaborated one of the best systems of social science; and, finally, they formulated several important sociological generalizations. In all these contribu- tions Le Play and his continuators have displayed a conspicuous scientific insight, a brilliant talent for scientific analysis and syn- thesis, and an originality of thought. As a result, they compose a real school in sociology with very definite methods and prin- ciples.

I. BIOGRAPHICAL DATA AND HISTORY OF THE SCHOOL

Pierre Frédéric Guillaumme Le Play was born April 11th, 1806, in a French village between the port Honfleur and the forest of Brotonne. His father, who died in 1811 when Frédéric was still a child, held an unimportant position in the revenue service. His mother was a woman of strong character with pro- found religious convictions. The early years of Le Play were spent in a village under conditions of hardship and need. From 1811 to 1815, he stayed in Paris in the family of his father's sister. Here the boy received his first intellectual education. In 1815 Le Play had to return to his native village, where he stayed the next seven years attending the Collége du Havre. In 1825 he entered the École Polytechnique and in 1827, the École des Mines. In 1829, he and his friend, Jean Reynaud, made a scien- tific trip to Germany. During the time of this study they walked about 4000 miles. He graduated with a brilliant record from the School of Mines in 1832 and then became co-editor of the

Annales des mines; in 1835, the head of the Government Committee on Mining Statistics; and in 1840, professor of Metallurgy and sub-director of the School of Mines.   During the next few years, as a recognised authority in mining, he was invited by different countries to direct the improvement and re-organization of the mining industry.   One of these countries was Russia, where he organized and directed a group of mines in the Urals employing 45,000 men.   These foreign positions gave him an opportunity to visit and to study thoroughly all of the European and some of the Asiatic countries.   In 1855 he published his famous *Les ouvriers européens,* the result of his scientific study for more than a score of years.   In 1856 he founded "The International Society for Practical Studies in Social Economy." Branches were established in many countries.   Its activity was manifested in the publication of many family monographs which composed the series *Les ouvriers des deux mondes.*   In 1864 he published two volumes of *La réforme sociale en France,* and in 1870, *L'organisation du travail.*   In 1867 he became a Senator in the French Assembly.   In 1872 he founded the "Union of Social Peace" to study social questions according to the methods of natural science.   In 1881 he began to publish *La réforme sociale,* a fortnightly publication of joint scientific and practical interest.   In the same year he published his *Constitution essentielle.*   His death occurred in 1882.[1]   Outstanding characteristics of Le Play's personality are: a great sincerity, a great honesty, a deep religious feeling, and a mind well trained in natural sciences.   The outstanding characteristics of his environment are: his origin from a humble family; his life among country people; the events of the great French Revolution, and the revolutions of 1830, 1848, and 1870-71; and, finally, his extensive travelling throughout Europe and Asia.   The social upheavals and their disastrous results stimulated his interest in a study of social phenomena and also his desire to find a scientific method

---

[1] For his biography see HERBERTSON, DOROTHY, "Le Play and Social Science," *The Sociological Review,* Vol. XII, pp. 36 ff., 108 ff; Vol. XIII, pp. 46 ff; DE CURZON, EMM., *Frédéric Le Play,* Paris, 1899; DEMOLINS, E., "Nos deux premiers maîtres," *Société Intern. de Science Sociale; l'Origine, le But, et l'Organisation de la Société, Brochure de propagande,* Paris, Bureaux de la Science Sociale; many data are given in the works of Le Play himself and in those of his pupils.

to improve social conditions. His intense moral and religious nature gave great sincerity to this desire. His talent and excellent training in natural sciences made it easy for him to discover and apply scientific methods to a study of social facts.

The work, begun by Le Play, attracted many pupils and collaborators. After his death, they continued his work and introduced some substantial improvements in his methods, as well as in his statements and theories. Among these pupils and collaborators, the most prominent were Henri de Tourville (1843-1903), Edmond Demolins (1852-1907), Robert Pinot, Paul de Rousiers, Vidal de la Blache,—although V. de la Blache does not belong to Le Play's school, his works influenced to a considerable degree the geographical part of the school's sociological system,—and many others. They founded the "Société Internationale de Science Sociale," and its review, *La science sociale*. This valuable scientific publication has included many important sociological studies and monographs. Later on, a portion of these studies was published in book form. Among these publications probably the most important are: H. de Tourville, *The Growth of Modern Nations*, (Engl. tr., N. Y., Longmans, Green & Co., 1907); E. Demolins, *Comment la route crée le type social*, two vols.; *Anglo-Saxon Superiority: To What Is It Due?* (Engl. tr., London, 1898), *Les Français d'aujourd'hui; L'éducation nouvelle;* P. de Rousiers, *La vie americaine; La question ouvrière en Angleterre;* and J. B. M. Vignes, *La science sociale d'après les principes de Le Play*, two vols., Paris, 1897. A short exposition of the principles and methods of the school is given in a special *Brochure de propagande: Société Intern. de Science Sociale; L'Origine, le But et l'Organisation de la Société*, Paris.[2] Recently the English Sociological Society has begun to study and to promote the principles of the Le Play school.[3] As a result we have a great revival of interest in this school and new studies of a similar nature. Although Le Play has now been dead almost half a century his influence does not show any symptoms of weakening or decay. It is still very vital and is likely to con-

---

[2] One of the papers of this book, DE ROUSIERS, P., *La science sociale*, is translated and published in the *Annals of the American Academy of Political and Social Science*, Vol. IV, 1893-94, pp. 620-646.

[3] See *The Sociological Review*, Vols. XI, XII, XIII.

tinue so. Let us now turn to a study of the characteristics of this school.[4]

The contributions of Le Play's school to social science consist first, in the creation of a definite method of analysis of social facts; second, in the composition of a definite sociological system and the formulation of a series of sociological generalizations; and, third, in the setting forth of many practical propositions for improvement of social conditions (applied sociology). Let us briefly survey each of these contributions.

At the beginning of his social studies, Le Play realized that the principal obstacle to the scientific study of social phenomena consisted in the lack of a real scientific method which might be used conveniently for the analysis of social phenomena. Before the time of Le Play it was understood that social science must be based upon the observation of social facts and their inductive analysis. But it was uncertain how social phenomena should be observed and what facts were the most important in the immense amount of material. Le Play fully realized that in order to be able to observe an enormous multitude and variety of social facts scientifically, an investigator had to have a simple and definite unit of social phenomena, whose study, like that of the atom in physics and chemistry, or of a simple cell in biology, would give all the essentials of the more complex social facts. Thus, the first problem to be solved was the problem of an elementary and basic social unit. The second problem consisted in finding a method for the quantitative measurement of different components or elements of the unit. The mathematical mind of Le Play understood that without quantitative measurement the study was doomed to be vague and uncertain, and the results of doubtful value. The first of these problems was solved by taking *the family for the elementary and basic social unit;* and the second, by using *the family budget as the quantitative expression of family life and, correspondingly, a basis for a*

----

[4] I do not give Le Play's predecessors. Being synthetical in its character, Le Play's theory has to be regarded as a continuation of the works of all social thinkers who contributed to all the principal sociological schools. The names of these thinkers are given in the subsequent chapters of this book.

quantitative analysis of social facts. The reasons for these selections were numerous. The family is the simplest and the most elementary form of society. In various forms it exists in all societies and at all times because of the helplessness of the new-born babies. The family is the group which takes care of them. It is an institution which procures the means of subsistence for its members. It is the first social environment which surrounds, trains, and educates these new-born children. Through this environment it shapes them as the members of a society. All of the elementary social and political interrelations exist in the family. It is the one group which exists among all peoples, and, indeed, many peoples do not have any more complex social organization. In short the family is the universal and simplest model of society and contains all of its essential characteristics.[5] On the other hand, the family budget reflects the entire life, organization, and functions of the family. By analyzing carefully all items of family income and of its expenditures, we obtain a quantitative expression of the whole family life, its organization and functions.[6] Such were the starting points of the method of analysis of a social system introduced by Le Play. This, however, was no more than the starting point. Le Play fully understood that the organization and functions of any family are conditioned by many factors. In the first place, one of the fundamental functions of the family is obtaining means of subsistence for its members; consequently family organization is determined by the methods of obtaining the means of subsistence—*work.* But these methods again are determined by the environment in which the family lives, by *place,* and primarily by geographical *place,* because the character of the *place* determines the *work* through which the families obtain their means of sub-

---

[5] See in the *Brochure de propagande*, DEMOLINS, E., "Comment on analyse," pp. 74–77; PINOT, R., "La classification des espèces de la famille," *passim;* VIGNES, *op. cit.,* Vol. I, Chaps. I–II; LE PLAY, *Ouvriers européens,* Vol. I, *passim; La réforme sociale en France,* 1866, Vol. I, Chap. III.

[6] See LE PLAY, *Ouvriers européens,* second edit., Vol. I, pp. 224–228. "All the acts which constitute the life of a workingman's family result more or less directly in an income or an outlay"; "observer possesses a complete knowledge of a family when he has analysed all the items which are found on the debit and the credit side of the domestic accounts and where he has obtained an exact correspondence between the two tables."

sistence. Thus we have the famous formula of Le Play: *Place, Work, and People, (Family)*. In this way the social unit (*family*) is connected with geographical *environment* and *work*. But that is not all. In so-called compound societies there are many social groups and institutions larger and more complex than the family. If family type determines their character, they, in their turn, influence the family type. Hence, it was necessary to continue the analysis of the social system beyond the family institution and to proceed to the analysis of neighborhood, county, province, state and other larger social groups, within which the family exists. Thus, Le Play connected the family with all the essential conditions which in their totality compose the system of a given society. Beginning with the family, his system of analysis embraced the *geographical location* of the family and of a corresponding society; the *work* or *economic organization of the family and of a corresponding society;* and *the whole social and political institutions* of a given society. In other words, almost all the essential factors and constituents of a social group were included in this analysis. At the same time, by an analysis of the family budget, he found a very convenient method of quantitative analysis of corresponding phenomena. Thus after long and systematic work, Le Play elaborated his method of the study of a social system which he emphasized in his "Workingmen of Europe" and which he used for his famous family monographs published in this fundamental work.[7] There is no need to say that this pioneer work, done by Le Play, found a great many followers. His system of analysis of family budgets, with slight variations, is used by economists of the present time. He, himself, used this method to make a number of brilliant analyses of social systems. His own monographs about various types of families and corresponding societies are still the most accurate and unrivalled examples of studies of social phenomena and types.

His followers, however, found that the method of Le Play had some defects. In the first place, Le Play's scheme of analysis of social systems was relatively inadequately developed in that part which concerns the organizations and institutions which are beyond, or larger and more complex than, the family. The

---

[7] See the nomenclature and its items in the volumes. *Les ouvriers européens.*

monographic method of Le Play "did not grasp society as a whole; it allowed facts of great importance to escape, so that a conscientious disciple could perform his task with exactness and yet fail to see the underlying causes of the prosperity or of the wretchedness of the country where his observations were made." In the second place, the family budget method "deals only with phenomena which can be expressed in dollars and cents." Here again are shortcomings even in regard to the study of the family itself, because "it is not true that all the acts which constitute the life of a family result *always*, even indirectly, in an income or in an outlay. For instance, the essential function of the family, the education of the children, cannot be expressed in figures." The same is true concerning the history and the origin of the family. Further, "the budget never gives more than one of the elements which should enter into a proper appreciation of them, that is the money value. The others are overlooked."[8] Furthermore, Le Play, in connection with the same quantitative method, emphasized the procuring of means of subsistence as the primary function of the family and somewhat underestimated the functions of the training and education of its children. This led Le Play to an overestimation of the methods of the transmission of property in the family from father to children and, on this basis, led to an unsatisfactory classification of fundamental types of families.[9]

These defects influenced his most prominent followers to revise, modify and perfect his method. This work has been done by Henri de Tourville, by Demolins, de Rousiers, Pinot and some others. As a result we have the so-called *La nomenclature de la science sociale* which preserves all the essential characteristics of the Le Play method but in a modified and improved form. Let us glance at this *Nomenclature* which represents a very careful and systematic scheme for the analysis and study of social systems and organizations. E. Demolins is correct in saying that "the *Nomenclature* is an extraordinary accurate and convenient instru-

[8] DE ROUSIERS, P., "La science sociale," *Annals of the American Academy of Political and Social Science*, Vol. IV, pp. 135–141.

[9] See PINOT, R., "La classification des espèces de la famille établie par Le Play, est-elle exacte?" in *Société Intern. de Science Sociale, Brochure de Propagande,* pp. 44–64.

ment of social dissection. It supplies a kind of a sieve which permits us to sift all elements of a social type and to classify them, according to their qualities, within a series of twenty-five divisions." [10] In this *Nomenclature* the family is still the starting point of the analysis, (social unit) but its characteristics, its relations to its total environment and the environment itself are grasped in such a systematic and exhaustive way that, having studied a typical family or a group of families through all of the twenty-five divisions, an investigator easily grasps the whole type of a society, its organization, conditions, composition and factors. The *Nomenclature* leads an investigator from the simplest to the most complex phenomena. These twenty-five fundamental divisions, each subdivided into many sub-divisions, are as follows:

I. *Place of the Family* (physical geography of family, or society): Soil; sub-soil; configuration of surface; rivers, streams, distribution of water; climate; plant environment, steppes, forests, and so on; animal environment of the earth and the waters.

II. *Work or Labor of the Family:* 1. Simple collection of the gifts of the place (picking up of natural products, fishing, hunting); 2. extraction of the necessary products (cultivation and agriculture, mining, etc.); 3. fabrication: by hands, with the help of animal energy, with that of wind, waterfalls, fire, coal and oil; 4. transportation: through carriers, by boat, using steam energy, electricity, etc.

III. *Property of the Family:* Composition of its values, forms of possession, subvention and transmission; land property and its character; property forms and institutions in the community.

IV. *Movable Property:* Cattle and animals; instruments and tools of work; furniture; personal (slaves, etc.).

V. *Salary and Wages:* Their objects; amount; forms, etc.

VI. *Savings:* Objects; character; amount; forms.

VII. *Family:* Type: patriarchal, pseudo-patriarchal, particularist, unstable; father, mother, children, their number, apti-

---

[10] DEMOLINS, E., "Comment on analyse et comment on classe les types sociaux," in *Société Intern. de Science Sociale, Brochure de Propagande*, p. 76.

tudes; married children; emigrants from family; single; servants; old members; sick and disabled members.

VIII. *Standard of Living or Modes of Material Existence of Family:* Food; home; dress; hygiene; recreation.

IX. *Phases of Family Existence:* Origin of the father and the mother; important events: births, education and training, celebrations and festivities, enterprises, alliances and marriages, establishment of heir, replacements and departures, adoptions, donations and inheritances, etc.; perturbations: accidents and sicknesses, returnings, deaths, unemployments, debts, bad conduct, condemnations and chastisements, public service, social calamities and other perturbations.

X. *Le Patronage* (protection and bosses): Patriarch; foreman; bosses; corporations.

XI. *Commerce:* Shopkeepers; merchants; commercial substitutions.

XII. *Intellectual Culture:* Intellectual culture resulting from the conditions of life; liberal arts and their agents: teacher, instructor, physician, scholar, artist, man of letters, lawyer; corporations of arts and professions.

XIII. *Religion:* Private cult; public religious cult; religious corporations; relations of dissenters.

XIV. *Neighborhood:* Next neighbor families; extended neighborhood; diversity and relations of neighborhood.

XV. *Corporations:* Corporations of communal interests; corporations of social welfare.

XVI. *The Parish:* The parish divisions; parish property; parish duties, authorities and control.

XVII. *Unions of the Parishes:* Their diversity; their property and funds, services and duties, participants and agencies, authorities, control and federation.

XVIII. *The City:* Its ecology and geography; its property, interests, services, duties, participants, agencies and authorities, activity and control.

XIX. *Provincial Divisions*

XX. *The Province*

XXI. *The State*

XXII. *The Expansion of the Society:* Emigration; invasion; colonization.

XXIII. *Foreign Societies:* Ways and avenues of contact; emigration and immigration; competition.

XXIV. *History of the Society:* Historical origin of the present situation; historical variation of the society; comparison with the previous local societies.

XXV. *Rank of the Society:* Actual rôle of the society in the world; reforms; the future of the society.[11]

Such in brief is the *Nomenclature,* as a method of analysis and synthesis of society. In its essence it combines all relevant factors which affect social life and organization, and combines them in a logical, systematic and causal way. The division *place* takes into account what is known under "geographic factors and environment." Divisions II, III, IV, V, and VI take into account what is known as "economic factors." In this way *place* and *labor* determine the type of a family. Divisions VII, VIII, IX, indicate all the essential traits of family organization and functioning. Beginning with division X we go beyond the family and, through family relationships with the larger social bodies, enter the super-family social environment: its institutions and groups. By proceeding from the simple to the more complex groups, we reach step by step the largest and finally the ultimate social body: mankind. We must recognize that the *Nomenclature* takes into consideration almost all essential factors of human behavior and of social processes and organization. Differing from the majority of sociological systems it is free from one-sidedness. It has all that is valuable in the statements of the geographical school in sociology; it gives full attention to economic conditions; it pays extraordinary attention to the family itself as a social factor; it appreciates adequately the rôle of contact and of interaction; that of religion, law, arts and sciences; the influence of the composition and character of all social groups; and the rôle of race and heredity. But that is not all. All divisions of the *Nomenclature* are not mechanically combined in a haphazard way, but, on the

[11] See DEMOLINS, *op. cit.,* Appendix; DE ROUSIERS, *op. cit.,* pp. 63 f.

contrary, they show a remarkable logic and causal sequence. This sequence does not decide which of the factors is of more and which is of less importance, but it shows how and in what way they condition each other. *Place,* especially in regard to the simple societies, determines the methods of procuring the means of subsistence—*labor,* forms of property and other receipts of the family; these conditions determine the type of family organization and functioning; this determines the type of people who come out of such family; and this, again, conditions the type of superfamily organizations and institutions. In a modified form, which takes into consideration the history of a society of which the family is a unit, the same sequence may be applied to a complex society. Finally, like a botanical classification of plants, the *Nomenclature* is at the same time, a systematization of social groups based on a genetic principle. [12] In brief, the *Nomenclature* is really a great contribution to the method of social science.

3. THE SOCIOLOGICAL SYSTEM AND THE PRINCIPAL CONTRIBUTIONS OF THE LE PLAY SCHOOL

Using the above method numerous followers of Le Play have made many monographic analyses of the social systems of different peoples. Unveiling the factors responsible for the historical destiny and the character of the social organizations of a given society, the analyses have yielded several important sociological generalizations. Let us give samples of how these investigators answer the problem: Why the historical destiny and organization of a given society have been such as they are and what factors are responsible for their character.

After this we shall enumerate the principal generalizations of the school. As an example I will summarize Demolins' study of the peoples of the steppes. The first part of the analysis is a detailed description of the climate and geographical conditions of the steppes of Central Asia and Oriental Europe (analysis of *place*). The principal product of this region is grass. Hence, "exclusive presence of grass determines a uniform mode of labor:

---

[12] The genetic or evolutionary character of the *Nomenclature* is especially stressed in the indicated work of M. Vignes, and in DEMOLINS, *Comment la route crée le type social,* Vols. I, II, *passim.*

pastoral art." [13] "We find indeed in this part of the earth numerous groups of shepherds." Of the animals, the most important here is the horse. "The steppes are exclusively well adapted to horses, and it is the horse which adapts the steppes to man." "Without horses the pastoral mode of life would be impossible." [14] In the steppes horses are an exclusive means of transportation and migration. Horses give the shepherds their principal food in the form of "horse-milk," or *koumys*—the food which is exclusively pleasant, rich with all the important elements of nourishment, and easy of preparation. For these and many other reasons the horse plays an extraordinarily important rôle in the life of the pastoral peoples.[15] Thus, through such a character of the steppes the peoples who inhabit them can exist almost exclusively through a mere *collection* of the gifts of nature without being obliged to "cultivate" the necessities and to transform them in any considerable proportion.

Fabrication in such groups is limited to the preparation of a few objects of food, shelter, hygiene, and of recreation. The character and qualities of these objects are also determined by the steppes. In a like manner the forms and the technique of fabrication (*labor*) are determined by the steppes. Food is prepared from milk and meat only. Its preparation and provision do not demand either a strenuous effort or the existence of special classes of butchers or milkmen. The operations are easily conducted by single families. The character of the dwelling is likewise determined by the same factor. Nomadic life urges them to have dwellings which may be taken down and moved in few minutes. Hence pastoral tents or *yourtas* are made from the skins of the animals. Fuel and the few objects of furniture have the same movable character adapted to the mode of life as determined by geographical conditions. The same may be said of cloth. The mode of life (out of doors) does not demand any specific forms of recreation. There yet remains the necessity for self-protection which is satisfied by the fabrication of a few weapons. These are easily prepared within each family.

[13] DEMOLINS, *Comment la route crée le type social*, Librairie de Paris, Vol. I, p. 9.
[14] *Ibid.*, p. 11.
[15] See pp. 11–22.

Motor power necessary for all this is almost exclusively human energy. The principal machine is the human hand. This does not require any organization besides the family. It may be seen that all the necessities may be produced within the family. This fact makes any organization larger than a family unnecessary. Thus, *the steppes determine the character of labor and production and put on them the stamp of production in a family-community.*

The steppes put similar marks on the *character of the property and the family-type* of the nomads. There is no reason for an appropriation of the land. A nomad family has to move as soon as grass in a given place is consumed; therefore "for the nomads it is more necessary to have a free passage and a free migration throughout the steppes than an exclusive right of ownership of limited portions of the land." [16] "As the grass grows spontaneously and no labor is spent for its cultivation, it is natural that the land remains common property; private property appears only when land requires cultivation to yield the necessary products. The necessity of this work is the origin of the institution of private property." [17] By determining the organization of work, the steppes determine the character of common property among the shepherds. Community of *Labor* and *Property,* in its turn, puts a stamp of community or communism on the *Family* of the steppes people. It is the patriarchal family with the father or the patriarch at its head and with all children except married daughters rallied around him. The patriarch exerts supreme power over all members of the family. Everything, except insignificant objects, is the common property of the family. In this way, *the type of patriarchal family has been produced on, and through the steppes.* [18]

The effects of such a patriarchal family on its young generation are definite: Since everything is in common, since an individual is only a kind of "a cell" in the family community and the family acts as a whole in every kind of a transaction, it is natural that such a family organization suppresses the individual initiative of its children and incessantly trains them to rely not upon them-

[16] DEMOLINS, *Comment la route crée le type social,* Librairie de Paris, Vol. I, pp. 59 ff.

[17] *Ibid.,* pp. 59 ff.

[18] *Ibid.,* p. 60–63.

selves but on the family, and on traditions and on customs transmitted from generation to generation. The offspring of such a family are naturally conservative; their attention is turned to the past, not to the future; they are guided exclusively by the customs and habits of their fathers and forefathers and not by their own initiative.

The self-sufficiency of the family in the steppes makes unnecessary any permanent aggregation or integration of families into a larger social body, political group or economic organization. Families of the steppes are situated side by side without any permanent cohesion or integration into a larger unit. Among the nomads of the steppes there does not exist any permanent state or government. The only larger form of aggregation is the grouping in the form of *caravans,* and this is very temporary. The caravan is a superfamily under the personal and temporary authority of the caravan leader or chief.[19] This authority appears because of the necessity of a chief to guide the caravan, to keep order without which it is doomed to perish, and to establish good relations with the populations along the way.[20] Under such conditions the "caravan is an armed troop which has a chief and procures its own supplies." It may be turned into an army very easily by an increase of its power, an efficient chief and the presence of a country to be invaded. Hence, the great invasions of Attila, Genghis Khan, Tamerlane, and those of China by the nomadic Mongols and many others which originated in the steppes represented nothing more than the great caravans of the steppe nomads turned into an army. Formed from the whole people including all women and children, able to flee easily in case of defeat, and plundering the countries in their way, such caravans exhibited great power. But the same conditions of caravan organization explain why all empires established by such invaders have been unstable and shortlived. With the death of their talented leader, such empires quickly disintegrated because of a lack of any other basis for their integration.[21]

[19] DEMOLINS, *Comment la route crée le type social,* Librarie de Paris, Vol. I, Chap. III.
[20] *Ibid., pp.* 72–76.
[21] DEMOLINS, *Comment la route crée le type social,* Vol. I, p. 80 ff.

Such in brief is the analysis and explanation of the social system of the steppe peoples. Beginning with *place* the author has shown consecutively how the steppes created this social type. "Steppes determine the pastoral art practiced by its inhabitants, communism (*Communauté*) of labor and of property, the patriarchal family, the limited character of fabrication and of commerce, the character of arts, the public cult, public authorities and so on." [22]   Each of these characteristics is conditioned by others and finally by the character of the steppes.

Through peaceful migration and invasion these steppe peoples spread throughout the world and at the same time spread the principal characteristics of their social system, especially the patriarchal type of family. One wave of these nomads moved to the north and reached the area of the *tundras*. Being unable to turn back they had to stay there under geographical conditions (*place*) quite different from those of the steppe [23] (much colder climate, absence of horses, presence of reindeer, scarcity of food, fishing and some hunting as the only sources of existence, and so on).[24]   This different environment caused a considerable transformation in the social system of the steppe people now settled on the tundras. The Eskimos and the Lapps illustrate this. Their forefathers came from the steppes, but under new conditions they and their offspring had to make a decided change. Long ago a branch of the people of the tundras probably crossed Bering Straits and came to America. Here, according to the character of the area through which they had to pass and in which they had to stay, (the way of the Savannas, the way of the Rocky Mountains to the south, and the way of the lakes to the southeast) they were transformed again and finally formed the principal types of American Indians, the hunters of the prairies and the hunters of the forests with their typical social institutions and types of families. The conditions of the prairies with their bisons shaped the organization of the new inhabitants into the clans of the hunters (the Indians of the prairies). The patriarchal type of family still survived, but it was somewhat weakened. Another

[22] *Ibid.*, p. 195.

[23] DEMOLINS, *Comment la route crée le type social*, Vol. I. (See the causes of this, pp. 114 ff.)

[24] *Ibid.* (See the details, pp. 117 ff.)

type was produced by those who went and "settled" in the region of the Rocky Mountains (the Indians of the mountains). The third type was formed by those who principally inhabited the region of the Great Lakes (the Indians of the lakes-region). Finally, a different and the most miserable type of society was formed by those who were driven to the forests of South America (South American Indians). Here, as well as in the forests of Central Africa, the conditions of forest-life led to the dispersion of the large clans, the reformation into small groups, and to a substitution of the *"unstable"* family for the patriarchal type. Hunting in the forests caused a change from the large patriarchal family into a simple group composed of a hunter and his wife. The children at early maturity left their parents in order to procure their own means of subsistence because the forest-conditions did not permit food for a large group of men living together. In this way a type of the "unstable" family was developed—a type without long history or any traditions; a type without any esteem of the young generation for the old people and the patriarch. Under such conditions it was impossible to inculcate into the young generation either community of property, or the conservative traditionalism of the patriarchal family. The forest hunting produced only isolated, savage, beast-like individuals. Such, in brief, is the origin of the *"unstable"* type of family. As the patriarchal type was originated in the Asiatic steppes, so the *"unstable" type was produced by the forests of South America and Africa.*[25]

Especial attention has been given by the school to tracing the origin, causes and history of the *particularist type of family* and of *the particularist type of society.* This work was done principally by Henri de Tourville. According to de Tourville, the formation of the particularist type of man, family, and society was as follows: A group of the patriarchal type, under the leadership of Odin,—a caravan leader and warrior,—started from the region of Don, in the southeastern part of present Russia, and moved to Scandinavia. Here the peculiar environment of the western part of Scandinavia gradually transformed them and their descendants from the patriarchal into the particularist type.

[25] DEMOLINS, *Comment la route crée le type social,* Vol. I, Chap. IV.

The fiords and the scarcity of fertile land in Norway forced them to turn to fishing as the principal method of obtaining their means of subsistence. As a means of transportation in the fiords boats were developed which could carry husband and wife and perhaps a few of the children. Having settled at a fiord, such a family had "the narrow and scattered pieces of land suitable for cultivation, the perpendicular banks favorable to fishing, and sheltered waters favorable to navigation in small boats." [26] Such conditions did not permit the children of these families to stay with their parents and thus to form the large patriarchal type. A large family could not obtain the necessary means of subsistence at the same place. This forced the adult children to separate from their parents and to go by boat to another place and to live independently. The patriarchal family (and other social institutions of the patriarchal type) were broken down under the pressure of the specific geographical environment of the western slope of Scandinavia. "Each adult son was obliged to look for some habitable nook in the recesses of that rocky land, and *to accustom himself to do without the help which is afforded by the association of individuals, and to depend on that self-help which is acquired by the personal development of an estate.*" [27] In this way the environment developed a self-reliance, initiative, and independence, —the characteristics of the particularist type of men, — among the fishers and cultivators of Western Scandinavia. Thus was shaped a new type of men, and a new, particularist type of family, "founded on the ability of the individual to create a home for himself." [28]

As soon as this most important revolution in the type of men and of family was accomplished, many modifications took place in the sphere of public life and social institutions. First "public life was abolished; private life, which was all-sufficient to itself, triumphed absolutely." "The small boat and seacoast fishing enabled each individual emigrant to live alone, to do without a community, even without a neighbor and a master." Further it

[26] DE TOURVILLE, H., *The Growth of Modern Nations, A History of the Particularist Form of Society*, p. 49, N. Y., 1907; see there a detailed analysis of the geographical conditions of Scandinavia and the history of the migration of Odin and the Odinids, Chaps. I, II, III.

[27] *Ibid.*, pp. 68–69; see all of Chap. IV.

[28] *Ibid.*, p. 70.

led to the substitution of direct ownership of the land (small farms or estates) for the system of the patriarchal community.[29] Association with other men did not disappear, but, in place of the enforced association of the patriarchal community, free social organization was substituted and "only where it was absolutely necessary." This led to the establishment of contractual associations, to the elections of leaders or public authorities, to independence and to self-government, the conspicuous characteristics of the particularist society. Different from the society with an unstable family (created in the forests), the fishermen and farmers of Scandinavia created associations. Different from the patriarchal type of society, their associations became voluntary, based entirely on covenant and agreement, and in addition they were created only when and where they were necessary and desirable. In this way the particularist type of family created self-governing social and political bodies, with elected authorities, restricted in power, instead of the forced, autocratic and traditionalist authorities of a patriarchal society. In brief, the particularist type of family led to what is now styled the real democratic and free society.[30] Thus, Scandinavia was that "world laboratory where and only where the particularist type of men, family and society was shaped and created." [31] Such was its origin.

After he has developed his thesis thus far, de Tourville further traces the diffusion and historical destinies of the particularist type of men and of social organization. Later some members of this particularist society migrated and settled as agriculturists on the plains of Saxony. They did not migrate in mass but purely as individuals. On these Saxon plains they modified their social organization somewhat, but the new organization was still primarily of the particularist type.[32] From this center in the plains of Saxony, the particularist type of society spread throughout all of Europe. Some individuals known as the "Franks" migrated to the west. At first they acted as agents and officials of the Roman emperors, and of the Merovingian and Carlovingian

[29] *Ibid.*, pp. 71–72.
[30] *Ibid.*, pp. 74 ff.
[31] *Ibid.*, pp. 38–39.
[32] *Ibid.*, Chap. V.

kings. However, they soon acquired land and estates, settled down and began to fight for their independence and for their particularist principles. In this struggle they were successful in coping with the growing autocracy of the Merovingian and Carlovingian kings and warriors and obtained their independence and immunity. In addition they helped to liberate other social classes from the interference of the monarchical authorities, and undermined the régime of military and patriarchal organization introduced by Rome and later maintained by the Merovingians and the Carlovingians. What is known as feudalism and its victory in the ninth century was in essence nothing but the struggle and the victory of the particularist over the patriarchal type of men. The particularist Saxons and Franks defeated their antagonists who were headed by the Merovingians and Carlovingians.[33] Thus we have a very original and positive interpretation of feudalism. The valuable achievements of feudalism in its period of growth, according to de Tourville, were: a great decrease of militarism and warfare; the emancipation of the serfs; the establishment and expansion of liberty and self-government; a great progress in agriculture; a harmony and solidarity of the social classes; an extraordinary development of free association; an increase of voluntary enterprises, and so on.[34] Later, owing to an unfortunate combination of historical conditions, the particularist type of men, family, and society were overpowered in Europe and replaced partly by the patriarchal and partly by the unstable types.[35] Another stream of the particularist migrants from the Saxon plain and Scandinavia went to England. Here they settled and step by step established themselves in spite of many obstacles. The particularist settlers gave the English social organization particularist characteristics. In a rather peaceful way they predominated over the Celts, and later on, in succession, over the Angles, the Danes, and the Norman conquerors. In this way the Saxons in England triumphed over all other populations of the British Isles. They shaped English society according to the particularist tradition and created its institutions and

[33] *Ibid.*, Chaps. VIII to XIII.
[34] *Ibid.*, Chap. XII.
[35] *Ibid.* (See analysis in Chap. XVIII and subsequent.)

history.   Still later, a part of them emigrated from England to America, Australia, New Zealand and elsewhere and created these other great particularist societies.[36]   Such in brief is the origin, development, expansion, and the history of the particularist type of family and society.

In a similar way the members of this school have studied, analyzed and explained the factors, the forces, the formation, and the underlying characteristics of other types of societies and social organizations.[37]

The above gives an idea how the followers of the Le Play school apply the *Nomenclature* for an analysis of a social system; how they correlate one class of social phenomena with another; and how they classify different types of societies, families and institutions.   They never deal with abstractions or pure speculation.   With the *Nomenclature* as a guide, they plunge into the dark and incomprehensible sea of history and methodically, patiently, and carefully try to unravel its riddles.   One who reads their works may disagree with their opinions, but he never feels that the investigators were amusing themselves with mere verbosity.   A pulsation of intensive, systematic and original, vivid and interesting scientific thought is felt on every page of the best works of the school.

4. CONTRIBUTIONS OF THE SCHOOL TO SOCIAL SCIENCE

We can now enumerate briefly the principal contributions of this school to social science.   The first contribution is the method of the school.   It consists in viewing the family as the social unit; in a quantitative approach to the study of social phenomena; and in the creation of the *Nomenclature* as a guide for sociological analysis.   The second contribution consists of the family monographs and of the studies of family budgets started by Le Play and his followers.   The third contribution is represented by generalizations concerning the influence of geographic environment

[36] *Ibid.*, Chaps. XIII–XVII, XXVIII–XXX; DEMOLINS, *Anglo-Saxon Superiority: To What Is It Due?*, pp. i–xl, London, 1898.

[37] See DEMOLINS, *Comment la route crée le type social*, Vols. I, II, *passim;* DEMOLINS, *Les Français d'aujourd'hui*, Vols. I, II; and all volumes of *La science sociale* where many monographs have been published; see also the bibliography given in DEMOLINS, *Comment la route crée le type social.*

on various sides of social life and institutions. It is certain (see further, the Geographical School) that this influence was known and studied long before Le Play and his school. The Le Play school, for its part, increased our knowledge in this field, and showed very clearly the influence, the correlation, and the avenues of influence of *place* on social processes and organization. The general standpoint of the school in this respect is well illustrated by the following quotation:

On this planet, there exists an infinite variety of populations; what cause created this variety? The common answer is: *race*. But the racial factor does not explain anything because we have, as yet, to explain what produces racial variety itself. Race is not the cause but the result. The primary and decisive cause of the diversity of peoples and races is *the road which has been followed by the peoples*. It is the road (environment) which created race and social type. It has not been an indifferent matter for a people which road they followed: that of the Grand Asiatic Steppes, or of the Tundras of Siberia, or the American Savannas or African Forests, (or the Arabian Deserts and so on). Unconsciously and fatally these roads fashioned either the Tartar-Mongol type, Eskimos-Lapps, the Red-Skinned, or the Negro. . . In Europe the Scandinavian type, the Anglo-Saxon, the French, the German, the Greek, the Italian, and the Spanish are also the result of the roads through which their ancestors passed before arrival at the present habitat. Modify one or another of these roads and through that you will change the social type and race.[38]

This led the school to formulate many correlations between *place* and different characteristics of social organization. Among them the most important are:

A. Correlations between *place* and the forms of labor, such as:
      Steppe and shepherdship
      Tundras and fishing and hunting
      Sea coast and fishing
      Forest and hunting
      Plain and agriculture

B. Correlations between *place* and the forms of Property, such as:
      Steppe and common property of the family

[38] DEMOLINS, *Comment la route crée le type social*, Vol. I, Preface.

Tundras and common property of the family
Fiords and individual property

C. Correlations between *place* and the Type of Family, such as:
Steppe and patriarchal family
Tundras and weakened patriarchal family
Forest and unstable family
Fiords and particularist family

D. Correlations between *place* and Superfamily Institutions and Associations:
Steppe and the caravans and invasions
Fiords and contractual associations, and so on

E. Correlations between *place* and many social processes and phenomena, such as: migration, forms of arts and religion, wars, and so on [39]

In general the school has contributed to the study of the influence of geographical environment on social type probably no less than any other group of social geographers.

The fourth contribution of the school consists in an elucidation of the interdependence of various sides of a social type as indicated in the *Nomenclature*. Examples are the correlations established between the forms of Labor and that of Property; [40] between the forms of Property and the types of Family; between the Family types and the types of Superfamily organization, and so on.

The fifth, and probably the most important contribution of the school, consists in its classification of the fundamental types of the family, in an elucidation of their origin, in the description of the social functions of the family, and finally in an exhibition

---

[39] See the correlations in the above quoted works of Le Play, de Tourville, Demolins, de Rousiers, Pinot.

[40] Examples: Private property grows parallel to an increase of labor necessary for production or cultivation of the necessities. It is almost absent among the pastoral nomads, who live on through a simple collection of the gifts of nature and do not invest any special labor for cultivation of the soil. A family occupies a place only for a short moment and, after a consumption of its grass, moves to a new one. Among the semi-nomad people, like Bashkirs, who begin to cultivate land, "the duration of labor increases. This is accompanied by prolongation of the appropriation of the land and by a progress of the institution of private property." Later on, among more complex types of society, it is necessary to invest a greater and greater amount of labor to get the means of subsistence; the simple collection of the gifts of nature is more and more superseded by the necessity of their fabrication. Correspondingly, the institution of individual property grows more and more. See DEMOLINS, *Comment*, Vol. II, pp. 21–28.

of the family's enormous importance for the whole social organization and historical destiny of a group.

I have already outlined the origin and the characteristics of the three fundamental types of family. Let us discuss in greater detail other family problems. According to the school, the principal social functions of the family are: the production of human beings, the securing of means of subsistence for its members; and especially the social and economic education of the young generation. These functions have been performed by all types of family regardless of its concrete form. In this sense the family has been and is the primary, the most important, and the most effective social institution.[41] "Every day society is submitted to a terrible invasion: within it a multitude of small barbarians are born. They would quickly overthrow the whole social order and all the institutions of society, if they were not well disciplined and educated. This education is made absolutely necessary and difficult by the fact that a new-born child is un-social." He does not know the laws of society and the necessary forms of conduct which make social life possible. He does not inherit such tendencies. He even refuses to follow them spontaneously. He does not know how to get the means of subsistence. He does not wish to enter any social group and to conform to its rules. Hence, the necessity for his education, training, and instruction without which he can neither adapt himself to social life nor help make social life and the continuity of the social group possible. "This education is the fundamental function of the Family. No other institution can substitute for it in this respect."[42]

The family has been the first and the most important factory in which biological human beings have been transformed into social individuals. It is the sculptor which shapes racial traits out of "human clay" and gives this clay its most decisive and desirable characteristics. The family education determines the type of social organization.[43]

---

[41] See PINOT, R., *op. cit., passim.*

[42] *Ibid.*, p. 58.

[43] Compare COOLEY, CH. H., *Social Organization*, Chap. III. See further chapter about Sociologistic School and recent studies of the correlations between family characteristics and the traits of its members.

"Every family brings up its children according to the conditions and necessities of the place and the group among which it exists." According to the character of education which the family gives to its young generation, it is possible to distinguish three or four fundamental types of families. They are as follows:

The Patriarchal Family.—"It moulds the young generation so that the children remain together in peace under the authority of the head of the family, causes them to sacrifice all their individual efforts for the Family-community and to depend entirely on this family organization. Within it the individual is annihilated and completely absorbed by the community." [44] "This type of family is common among the less progressive populations of the East. There, children do not rely on themselves for their establishment, but on the family community, which will keep them or welcome them back if per chance they have left home and failed. Under these conditions little personal instruction is needed, and only a minimum amount of instruction is given, the family, sometimes helped by the priest, is sufficient to impart it." [45] The societies with this type of family are conservative, stagnant, and retarded.

A modification of this type of family is the *Quasi-Patriarchal* type or stock-family (*fausse famille-souche*) whose members sometimes may go away, but permanently keep their contact with the paternal family, send it all their money, and sacrifice everything for it. They even become celibates if it is necessary and sooner or later usually return back to it. Individual initiative is developed a little more in such a family than in a pure patriarchal type; nevertheless, in essence it has all the characteristics of the patriarchal type. [46]

The second principal type is the *unstable family.* "It does not fit its young generation for anything special; neither does it unfit them for anything general. It brings up its children without imparting respect for authority and traditions, as does the patriarchal family, and at the same time, it does not fit them for originality, or for the independent production of new ideas, as does the particularist type of family. Within such a family, the quality of subordination, as well as of initiative, are equally

[44] PINOT, *op. cit.*, 63.
[45] DEMOLINS, *Anglo-Saxon Superiority*, p. 77.
[46] PINOT, *op. cit.*, p. 63.

absent, and the individual who in reality has not received any education or training and who is not capable of doing anything, becomes a prey of States and Governments." [47]   The societies which have this type of family represent "A Communistic State Formation."   There the large public community takes the place of the dissolved family community; here the young people rely principally on the State for establishment in life, such as through the many appointments in the army or the different services which the State distributes.   Most of the nations of Western Europe, notably France and Germany, belong to this type.   To obtain these appointments, examinations have to be passed.   In order to keep away the bulk of the applicants, the examinations are made stiffer and more difficult."   In such a society, the official bureaucracy rules, the interference of the Government is great, and its machinery is centralized.   Prussian military and bureaucratic society and, its natural development, the State socialistic organization, is the natural form of a society with such a type of a family.[48]

The third type is the *Particularist Family*.   "It enables its young people to manage their own business or affairs independently and to establish themselves in a definite field of activity. It develops a great deal of individual initiative.   Thanks to it, the value of the individual is highly appreciated.   The individual is the organizer and master of all private and public groupings in this type of a society.   Here we have the triumph of the individual over the state.[49]   The Scandinavian and the English-speaking nations are the best examples of this type of family and society.   Here "the individual prevails over the community, private life over public life, and in consequence, the useful profession over the liberal and administrative professions."   Here the individual relies neither on the family nor on the state for his establishment.   The state disposes but few appointments, because public powers are not centralized and only a very few officials are employed.   Here the individual relies principally on his own energy and resources to succeed in an independent career.   The chief aim of education (in the family and outside of it) in such a

[47] PINOT, *op. cit.*, p. 64.
[48] DEMOLINS, *op. cit.*, p. 77.
[49] PINOT, p. 63.

state of society, must therefore be to develop these individual qualities and to form practical men.[50] Demolins and de Rousiers have shown in detail the differences in training and education of the young people in the family and the schools of Germany and France as examples of a state communistic formation with an unstable family at its bottom, and in the family and the schools of England and America as examples of particularist societies with the particularist type of family at its bottom.[51] In a particularist family (of the Anglo-Saxon and the Scandinavian type) "the parents do not consider their children as property, nor that the children are a mere continuation of themselves. They have no greater anxiety than to hasten the emancipation of their children. They treat their children from infancy as mature persons. Because of this treatment they develop responsible and original personalities. Parents educate their children to meet future necessities. They also endeavour to increase, as much as possible, the strength, energy, and physical development of their children. The children are initiated very early into the practice of material, everyday acts. As a rule, parents have their boys taught some manual trade. There is little display of parental authority. The boys know that their parents will not be responsible for their situation in life." As a result out of such a family come strong and energetic individuals who know what they want, are imbued with corresponding knowledge and experience, and are accustomed to have their rights and to take their responsibilities.[52] The system of education outside of the family in a particularist society is only a continuation of the principles of the family education. It is permeated with the same characteristics and is quite different from the school-system in the "Communistic State Type of Societies" (in Germany and France).[53]

As a result of such an organization, "young men, made physically strong, accustomed to material facts, trained to rely on themselves and to look upon life as a battle, bring a superabundance of youthful strength to cope with the difficulties of exist-

---

[50] DEMOLINS, *ibid.*, pp. XIII, 78–79.
[51] See DEMOLINS, *Anglo-Saxon Superiority, passim;* DE ROUSIERS, *La Vie Americaine, passim;* DE TOURVILLE, *op. cit., passim.*
[52] DEMOLINS, pp. 95 ff.
[53] See *ibid.*, Chaps. I–III.

ence; they enjoy these difficulties, expect them, and triumph over them." Here lies the secret of Anglo-Saxon superiority and power. Here is the source of the miracles which have been performed by this people.

Anglo-Saxon superiority! Although we do not all acknowledge it, we all have to bear it, and we all dread it. We cannot go one step in the world without coming across *L'Anglais.* The Anglo-Saxon has supplanted us (the French) in North America, in India, and in Egypt. He rules America, by Canada and the United States; Africa, by Egypt and the Cape; Asia, by India and Burmah; Austral Asia, by Australia and New Zealand; Europe, and the whole world, by his trade and industries and by his policy. The Anglo-Saxon is now at the head of the most active, the most progressive, and the most overflowing civilization (*Ibid.,* pp. xxvii-xxx). And now compare, and decide, and judge. I have tried to show the hidden springs which enable that race to threaten and invade the older and more decrepit societies (p. 103).

The above shows the correlation which exists between the type of family and the whole social organization and its historical destinies. As we have seen, the Le Play school has shown how each of these types of family has originated, in what kind of environment and under what conditions. The above also gives an idea of the tremendous influence of the family on the whole social organization and institutions. Various leaders of the school have formulated many other correlations which cannot be given here.[54]

As yet there has been no sociological school which shows the functions, the classification, and the social importance of the family as clearly as the Le Play school, with the exception of Confucius and the Confucianist school in China. This school may be paralleled with the Le Play school in an understanding of the decisive influence of the family institution. But Confucianism pleaded for the patriarchal family while the Le Play school pleads for the particularist type.

The sixth contribution of the school consists in a series of studies of an applied character in which it has tried to indicate

---

[54] See the quoted works. One of these correlations is that real democracy and self-government are possible only among the people of the particularist type with a particularist family.

many measures for the practical reconstruction of society. Among these measures some have a specific character while some others are general and applicable to all societies at all times. The above theory of the particularist type of family may serve as an example of the specific suggestions of the school. In it the school sensed the highest of family and of social organization; and as a result tried to propagate this form throughout the world, especially in France. To achieve this purpose it endeavored to remodel the unstable French family into the particularist type and to change the system of French education. With this intention, Demolins and others opened their own school, *L'École des Roches,* in which they organized the curriculum according to particularist principles.[55] On the other hand, they severely criticized, and with reason, the existing system of school education in France and Germany. Conforming to the same particularist ideal, they interpreted socialism as a mere modification of the patriarchal social type, with all its negative traits, but lacking its positive qualities.[56] For the same reason they opposed an expansion of state interference at the cost of voluntary private activity and all measures which lead to a decrease of individual initiative and independence. In this respect their position is similar to that of H. Spencer. On the other hand, conforming to the same particularist ideal, they decisively opposed any artificial or hereditary aristocracy. They demanded that all positions be opened to free competition. They severely criticized absentee-owners of land, saying that if landlords had lost their influence it was due to the fact that they no longer performed their social duties.

Le Play's *Universal Constitution of Mankind* is an example of the school's general applied sociology. In this work he endeavored to discover inductively the conditions necessary for a prosperous existence of any society. He summed up the principles which he had previously developed in the works: *La réforme social en France* and *L'organisation du travail.* Here again Le Play reminds us of Confucius. Both were conservative. Neither

---

[55] See DEMOLINS, *L'éducation nouvelle,* Librairie de Paris, year is not indicated. *Anglo-Saxon Superiority,* Part I.

[56] See DEMOLINS, *Anglo-Saxon Superiority,* pp. 236–277; *Le socialism dévant la science sociale.* These works are one of the most original and thoughtful interpretations of socialism.

pretended to discover new principles but assumed that proper principles had already been discovered through the past experience of peoples and generations. "I am only a transmitter, not a maker, believing in and loving the ancient," said Confucius. Similarly, Le Play said, "Concerning the fundamental principles of social science there is nothing to be invented, in this science the new is but what has been forgotten." [57] He stressed the fact that neither his method of observation, nor his theories and principles, nor finally his applied sociology were discovered by him; they had already existed in the social sciences of long ago. This modesty is really characteristic of Le Play. In regard to the conditions necessary for the successful existence of a society he said:

Since the revelation of the Ten Commandments and their sublime interpretation by Christ, the human mind has not discovered more useful principles. Nations which practice these principles are progressing and those which are not, declining. . . Solution of the social problem does not require an invention of new principles.[58] . . An innumerable number of the thinkers who have analyzed the virtues and vices of man did not add anything new to the decalogues of Moses and to the teachings of Christ. [59]

Correspondingly his system of social constitution is simple and definite. Among the fundamental conditions necessary for the prosperous existence of any society are: a sincere belief in God and religion; the existence of the authority of the parents; the existence of a sovereign government and of loyalty toward it; the firm institution of private property; the practice of solidarity and honesty in the interrelations of individuals and classes; mutual help and coöperation and other principles found in the majority of ethical and religious systems. In his works already mentioned [60] he analyzed each of these conditions, and showed why they were necessary for the existence of a society and what should be the details of organization of the religion, of the family, of labor, of private property, of government and of other social

[57] See DE CURZON, op. cit., pp. 3–5, 21–23, 44, 54 ff.
[58] LE PLAY, La paix sociale, p. 31.
[59] LE PLAY, La réforme sociale, Vol. I, p. 12, 1866.
[60] See Constitution essentielle, passim; La réforme sociale en France, passim; see also DE CURZON, op. cit., passim.

institutions. On the basis of observation, he found that the above conditions had been present in all societies in the periods of their well-being, prosperity and happiness, and were absent in the periods of decay, demoralization and disintegration. It is clear that his plan of social reconstruction is opposed to those which are in vogue at the present time. Instead of advocating class hatred, Le Play pleaded for class solidarity; instead of atheism and materialism, religion; instead of revolution, reform; instead of egotism, altruism; instead of profit, sacrifice; instead of rights and privileges, he stressed more duty; instead of destruction of the existing institutions, their slow and careful remodeling. Such in brief are the method, the principles, the contributions and the reforms offered by Le Play and his continuators.

5. CRITICISM AND APPRECIATION

I have already given my appreciation of the school. Le Play deserves to be put on the level with such masters of social science as Comte and Spencer.[61] The aggregate contribution to sociology of the Le Play school is scarcely less than that of any other contemporary school of sociology.[62]

However, side by side with its positive qualities it has several serious shortcomings. In the first place, the *Nomenclature* and the principles of the school can by no means embrace and solve all problems of sociology. They cover only a part of the field. For instance, they do not touch and do not explain such fundamental social processes as wars, enrichment and impoverishment, appearance and disintegration of religion, growth or decrease of population, and social antagonisms. Equally they do not touch and do not explain many problems of social organization. In brief, the system of the Le Play school covers only a part and not the whole of the field of sociology.

---

[61] S. H. Swinny has already expressed the same idea. See SWINNY, S. H., "Sociology; Its Successes and Its Failures," *The Sociological Review*, Vol. XI, No. 1, 1919, p. 3; see also SWINNY, "The Sociological Schools of Comte and Le Play," *ibid.*, Vol. XIII, No. 2, April, 1921.

[62] It is curious to note the opinion of P. Barth, who in the last edition of his *Die Philosophie der Geshichte als Soziologie* styles Le Play as a romantic and finds his system a mere theory of "social economics from the standpoint of family-law." BARTH, *op. cit.*, pp. 727–732, Leipzig, 1922. From a speculative social philosopher, like Barth, such an appreciation is to be expected.

In the second place, though the school is free from a narrow-minded dogmatism, nevertheless, some of its statements appear to be somewhat one-sided. Take, for example, the statement of Demolins concerning the factors of geographical environment and race. If it is futile to try to explain varieties of peoples and social types through the racial factor only and to ignore environment agencies completely, it is equally futile to make the opposite mistake, as the Le Play school partially does. The factor of race and heredity is almost completely ignored by the school. Without it we cannot explain why, for instance, some of the individuals of the steppes of Central Asia started in one direction; some others, another; and the rest remained there. How can we account for such differences through *place* only? Further, the appearance of the leaders of the caravans, as well as the other forms of social differentiation and stratification, are also unaccountable through the factor of environment alone because the leaders and the led, the influential and the non-influential individuals were in the same environment. More than that. We read in Demolins' book:

When we study the origin of culture we are first struck by the appearance of two categories of family; on the one hand are the foreseeing families, capable of working in view of remote effects; on the other hand, there are families and individuals who are capable of acting only under the pressure of immediate necessity or in view of immediate satisfaction. In this way, there are formed two distinct classes: the superior and the inferior. Thus appears inequality among men. [63]

It is evident that such social differentiation cannot be accounted for by *place* because all of these families lived in the same geographical conditions. Demolins does not try at all to explain such a fact. It is highly probable this differentiation is due to inherited and racial differences of individuals. So much concerning this one-sidedness.[64] To the credit of the school, however, it must be said that unlike many social geographers, it does

---

[63] DEMOLINS, *Comment la route*, Vol. II, pp. 12-13.

[64] See other "geographical" fallacies of the school in the chapter about the Geographical School in sociology. The criticism of the one-sided "geographism" given there also concerns the Le Play school.

not pretend to make the factor of geographical environment omnipotent: it recognizes that among more complex societies the direct influence of geographic environment tends to decrease and is superseded by other factors.[65]

The next shortcoming of the school seems to consist in an inadequate geographic explanation of the origin of different types of family. Its theory may contain a considerable portion of truth. But is it enough to say that the patriarchal family was produced by steppes; the unstable, by forests; the particularist, by the fiords of Western Scandinavia? Let us take for example the theory of the origin of the particularist family in the fiords of Scandinavia. According to the school, there and only there the particularist type of family originated. Responsible geographical factors for such a production were those conditions which forced the people of Scandinavia to live in small separate families and to permit their children to go away as soon as they matured. However, such geographical circumstances existed in many other places. Also, the forest conditions, which, according to the school, produced the unstable family, were similar in some respects: they forced the people to live in small separate families and to permit the adult children to leave the parental family. Why did these conditions not produce the particularist type of family? Therefore the explanation of the origin of the particularist type through the geographical conditions of the fiords is not sufficient and is not quite convincing. Also the statement that this type was produced only in the fiords sounds like an exclusively one-sided statement which is not sufficiently corroborated. This insufficiency is still greater when we are told that the descendants of Odin, who lived in the same fiords, in some mysterious way were not transformed into the particularist type, but preserved the militant type of warriors; and for many centuries continued to supply military leaders for the Danes, the Normans, the Franks, the Saxons, the Goths and so on. If the geographical conditions of the fiords were responsible for the transformation of the patriarchal type into the particularist, then the descendants of Odin should have undergone the same transformation. Since they did not change but remained what they

[65] See DEMOLINS, *Comment la route*, Vol. I, pp. 196–197.

were before coming to the fiords, then the geographical factors evidently are not enough to explain the transformation. It may be that the origin of the particularist type was due not only to the fiords but to other factors as well. The same may be said of the origin of other types of family and societies. Evidently this theory of the school is still nothing but a tentative hypothesis.

Even if we grant that the environment theory of the Le Play school [66] is satisfactory in regard to the origin of the types of family and man, we have a new problem concerning the destinies of each type. Are the acquired characteristics of each type of men biologically inherited or not? The school is silent on this point. Meanwhile whether or not we admit the theory of an inheritance or of a non-inheritance of such traits, in both cases the theories of the school are unsatisfactory. If the acquired traits of men of each type are not inherited, then it is incomprehensible, why, for instance, in England, in spite of the identity of the environment, the descendants of the Saxons have maintained throughout centuries the particularist characteristics, while the descendants of the Celts and the Danes and the Normans, who lived in the same place, did not acquire the same particularist characteristics. (See de Tourville, Chaps. XIII-XVII.) If the decisive factor is the environment and the corresponding acquired traits are not inherited, then all who have stayed in the same geographical environment for many generations should have acquired similar traits, regardless of the race. And yet, de Tourville, as well as Demolins, stresses that up to this time in England the particularist type is represented only by the descendants of the Saxons and that the Celtic and other elements in the English population do not belong to this type at all. It is clear that such a fact could not be accounted for or reconciled with the statement that "the road creates a social type." If the corresponding traits are inherited, then how is it possible that "the inherited patriarchal type" could be transformed into the particularist one, and how is it possible that the particularist type of the early Franks was transformed into the "state-communistic type" while the descendants of the Anglo-Saxons did not undergo such a change? In the writings of the

[66] See DE TOURVILLE, *op. cit., passim.*

school we do not find any answer to these questions. They avoid it. And therefore their theory does not and cannot dissipate the mystery of the origin and development of each of their principal types.

The next weak point is the appreciation of different types and their rôle. We have seen that the particularist type is destined to be powerful and dominating and that in it lies the secret of the expansion of the Anglo-Saxon domination. If this is so, then why was this type conquered in Europe? Why could it not keep the dominating position which, according to the school, it held during the ninth and tenth centuries? Why was it overpowered by the state-communist type? This diversity of the historical destinies of the particularist type in Europe and in Scandinavia or in England is not unveiled by the school at all. It forces us to an inference, that the particularist type is not necessarily always the conqueror. The school probably somewhat overestimates the power and the strength of this type and underestimates the positive qualities of other types. This is the more probable because history shows that great and durable empires and brilliant civilizations have been created by the peoples of ancient Egypt, Babylonia, Assyria, Greece, Rome, China, India, and ancient Peru, who were conspicuously the peoples of a statecommunist or the patriarchal type. And the history of France or Germany for the last century does not show that the people of a state-communist type are incapable either of creating the highest forms of civilization or of being powerful in the struggle for existence. Take further the Jewish people. Their family organization still has many characteristics of the patriarchal type. And yet these people display an extraordinary vitality and energy.

Further, for the above reasons it is also possible to question whether the school does not exaggerate the influence of familyorganization on the types of men, social institutions, and historical destinies of a society. It seems to be probable that there is some exaggeration in the statements of the school. It has not demonstrated that men of each of its types are necessarily the product of family education only and are not due to racial or hereditary factors. The school's statements do not give definite corroboration of its pretensions, and still remain on the level of a probable but not proved hypothesis. If this is so, then the very heart of the theory of the school that Anglo-Saxon superiority is due to the particularist type of the Anglo-Saxon family, may also be questioned. With the same probability one may contend that it is due to the racial factor and that the particularist type itself is nothing but a manifestation of corresponding innate qualities of individuals or groups.

Thus we come to the conclusion that the theory of the school contains only a part of the truth, and does not sustain all the sweeping generalizations advanced. Many of its hypotheses still remain only guesses. Finally, one may partially agree with the system of applied sociology depicted by the school. But again, it is not sufficient: granting that the Ten Commandments include all the essential conditions necessary for the well-being of a society, we see that they are not always obeyed, and are often transgressed. At the present moment we see that the existing religion is weakening and the attacks against property are increasing. Under such conditions it is not sufficient to indicate the Commandments in order to create a real applied sociology. Is it not necessary to find some means of making these principles effective? Is it not necessary to invent some measures which will make people follow these Commandments? By this I want to say that the applied program of the school is not sufficient and does not remove the necessity for discovering scientific measures which, at least, would make the Commandments efficient and effective.

Such in brief are the principal shortcomings of the school. They may be summed up as follows: First, the system and the program of the school do not cover the whole field of social phenomena and social problems; second, the school underestimates the factor of heredity and race and overestimates the factor of geographical environment; and third, many problems, analyzed by the school, among them the origin of the types of family and the correlation of the types with the social system and historical destinies of a corresponding society, are not quite sufficiently explained. Finally, the applied program is ineffective.

These shortcomings of the school should not prevent us from recognizing its great contributions, its scientific character, its originality, and its stimulating influence.   At the present moment when the particularist type of family and society is undergoing a crisis and is menaced by another, especially the state-communist type, the works of the school are especially valuable from the theoretical, as well as from the practical standpoint.

CHAPTER III

GEOGRAPHICAL SCHOOL

I. PREDECESSORS

A L M O S T since the beginning of man's history it has been known that the characteristics, behavior, social organization, social processes, and historical destinies of a society depend upon the geographical environment. In attempting to write the history of the geographical school, one's difficulty consists not so much in indicating the thinkers who have pointed out the influence of the geographical environment as it does in indicating those who have not mentioned it. Lord Kame in 1788 wrote about "the endless number of writers who ascribe supreme efficacy to climate." [1] The most ancient records of the thought of the East, which have reached us, contain several statements of this kind. The ancient astrological beliefs in their essence are nothing but an embodiment of the idea that man's destinies are ruled by stars and by other geographical conditions. The people's proverbs and "weather lore" of the past are permeated by the same idea. They contain many statements concerning the influence of various geographical conditions on physical and psychical traits of men, and on social and historical events. Hundreds of individual thinkers, whose names and ideas are preserved in history, have indicated in some form this or that effect of geographical factors. The thinkers of ancient India and Persia; the priests and the physicians of ancient Egypt; the astrologers of different countries; the Jewish prophets; Confucius, Lao-Tse, Mencius, and other sages of ancient China; Hippocrates, Plato, Aristotle, Thucydides, Xenophon, Herodotus, Strabo, Polybius, Eratosthenes, Varro, Vitruvius, Vegetius, Paul the Deacon, Servius, Cicero, Florus, Sallustius, Lucretius, Seneca, and almost all the prominent philosophers, historians, poets, and writers of ancient Greece and Rome; many of the Church Fathers, like St. Augustine, and Tertullian; many

[1] See LORD KAME, *Sketches of the History of Man*, 4 vols., 1788.

mediæval thinkers, like Giovanni Villani, St. Thomas Aquinas, Michelangelo, Machiavelli, Ibn-Khaldun and Jean Bodin; all these and many others have mentioned the conditioning rôle of various geographical factors. Later on, the effects of geographical agencies were stressed by Richard Mead, John Arbuthnot, Bernhardus Varenius, Sir John Chardin, J. B. Vico, Lord Kame, W. Temple, Lenglet du Fresnoy, Turgot, Cuvier, Herder, and Montesquieu. In the nineteenth and the twentieth centuries a great multitude of historians, social philosophers, economists, geographers, political scientists, sociologists, anthropologists and ethnographers, biologists and men of medical science made many contributions in this field. The names of Lamarck, Karl Ritter, Arnold Henry Guyot, Johann Georg Kohl, Alexander von Humboldt, K. E. von Baer, Oscar Peschel, H. T. Buckle, F. Le Play, H. de Tourville, E. Demolin, L. Metchnikoff, P. Lavrov, Mackinder, A. Kirchoff, F. Ratzel, Ch. Comte, P. Mougeolle, A. Matteuzzi, É. Reclus; and finally, the names of P. Vidal de la Blache, Jean Bruhnes, C. Vallaux, E. Huntington, E. G. Dexter, E. Ch. Semple, Morcelli, Lehman, Shyten, H. L. Moore, and Beveridge, are a very few representatives of a great multitude of people who have tried to emphasize various effects of geographical conditions on man's behavior and psychology, and on social organization, social processes and the historical destinies of a group.[2]

As a result of the work of this multitude of authors there scarcely is any physical or psychical trait in man, any characteristic in the social organization of a group, any social process or historical event, which has not been accounted for through geographical factors by this or that partizan of this school. Distribution of the population on the surface of the earth, the density of population, racial differences, the character of economic, polit-

---

[2] See the history of the geographical school in the works: KOLLER, A. H., *The Theory of Environment*, The Collegiate Press, 1918; THOMAS, F., *The Environmental Basis of Society*, 1925; BARNES, H. E., *The New History and the Social Studies*, Chap. II, N. Y. 1925; BARTH, P., *Die Philosophie der Geschichte als Soziologie*, 1922, pp. 544–555; see the literature and the references in VALLAUX, C., *La mer*, Paris, 1908, appendix "Bibliographie." All these and many similar works, however, are far from being exhaustive. They are incomplete even in regard to the thinkers of the Western countries and they completely ignore the Eastern thinkers and writers of the present, as well as of the past. The best first-hand source, for theories of the ancient East, is the series of fifty volumes of *"The Sacred Books of the East"* published under the editorship of F. M. Müller.

ical, and social organization, the progress and decay of nations, the character of religious ideas and beliefs, the forms of the family and of marriage, health, fertility, intelligence, crimes, suicide, cultural achievements, the number of men of genius, the traits of literature, poetry, and civilization, the movement of economic and social life, in brief, almost all social phenomena have been attributed to geographical influences. At the beginning of a study of these theories one is impressed by their brilliancy and originality; continuing the study one is perplexed and bewildered by their contradiction and vagueness; and finally he is lost in the sea of these theories not knowing what in them is valid, and what is wrong or doubtful. This explains why the primary need in this field at the present moment consists not so much in a formulation of a new geographical theory or of a new "correlation" between geographical factors and social phenomena as in a most rigorous analysis and shifting of what is valid and what is childish in these numerous hypotheses.

Such a shifting is the purpose of this chapter. The lack of space does not permit me to make the shifting quite exhaustive. For this reason I have to omit all purely speculative "geographical theories" and concentrate my attention only on those which are factual and more mature from the scientific point of view. The results of their scrutiny, however, may be applied, with still greater reasons, to all the less elaborated, the less scientific or more metaphysical "geographical conjectures, hypotheses and generalizations."

2. DEFINITION OF GEOGRAPHICAL FACTORS

In order to avoid vagueness in our analysis of the influence of geographical environment, we must state that by this concept we mean all cosmic conditions and phenomena which exist independent of man's activity, which are not created by man, and which change and vary through their own spontaneity, independent of man's existence and activity. In other words, if we take the total environment of a man or that of a social group, and subtract from it all environmental agencies directly or indirectly created or changed through man's existence and activity, we will have left approximately what is known as geographical

environment. "Natural" climate, temperature, soil, relief of surface, distribution of water and water courses, natural flora and
fauna, natural changes of seasons and geophysical processes, the
phenomena of gravitation, storms, earthquakes, sea-currents and
so on, as far as they exist and change regardless of man's existence and activity, are examples of geographical agencies in the
above sense of the word. On the other hand, all phenomena and
conditions, whose existence and variation are direct or indirect
results of man's existence and activity, compose the agencies of
anthropo-social, but not geographical, environment. Cultivated
fields, forests and gardens, artificial channels, artificial modification of natural relief of the surface of the earth, or artificial climate, and soil and sub-soil, all such phenomena are excluded from
the geographical or "natural" agencies in the proper sense of the
word.

Now let us turn to our analysis of the correlations established
between geographical agencies and social phenomena.

3. FUNDAMENTAL PROPOSITIONS CONCERNING THE CHARACTER OF CONDITIONING OF SOCIAL PHENOMENA BY GEOGRAPHICAL FACTORS

There is no doubt that the totality of geographic conditions
determines, to some extent, human behavior, social organization
and social processes. But what is the nature of this conditioning? Is it direct or indirect? Is it rigid and inflexible? Is it
possible to formulate definite and general correlations of geographic conditions with social phenomena? In order not to be
lost in the sea of complex geographic influences, let us formulate
at once some fundamental propositions which outline the nature
of these influences and which will guide us in our analysis. These
propositions are as follows:

1. *The conditioning rôle of geographical agencies (B) may be
direct and indirect: direct when they directly determine a definite
series of social phenomena (A) according to the formula:
$A = f(B)$; indirect when they condition a definite series of
social phenomena, not because they influence them directly, but
because they influence some other phenomena (C) or (D) which
in their turn condition the series A. In this case the formula of*

indirect conditioning is: $C = f\ (B)$; *therefore* $A = f\ (C)$. If A were not dependent on C, then the geographical factors would not have conditioned A at all. It is clear that indirect conditioning may consist sometimes of a long series of links of functional relations: B may condition C; C, the phenomena D; D, that of E; and only E may condition A. It is evident that, other conditions being equal, the longer is such a series of indirect relations and the more numerous are the middle members (C, D, E, F,) of such a series between A and B, the more remote becomes their interrelation and the less definite is the correlation between A and B. In such cases the geographical agencies may exert some influence, but it becomes so strongly neutralized and modified by interference of the "middle agencies" between A and B, that the correlation between them becomes intangible, or entirely indefinite. Since it is intangible, and unable to be described in a definite formula, it is practically equal to an absence of such correlation. In analyzing the conditioning rôle of geographical agencies we must always discriminate between its direct and indirect forms.

2. *According to the above, the conditioning influence of geographical agencies is not equally rigid and direct in regard to different categories of social phenomena.* While some of them exhibit a close and noticeable direct correlation with geographical agencies, some others do not show such a correlation at all. In this respect the hypothesis of J. Bruhnes, which in essence is identical with the Le Play school's *Nomenclature* series, appears to me as relatively valid. He states that those forms of human activity and corresponding social phenomena which pertain to the satisfaction of the primary necessities of man, such as alimentation, shelter for sleep, clothing and a few others, are in a more direct relation with geographical conditions than other human activities and social phenomena which are of different character. Correspondingly, he indicates six series of social phenomena where the correlation with geographic agencies is closer than in other fields of social facts. These six series are: human habitation (inhabited areas, the character of houses and constructions), the direction and the character of roads, cultivation of plants and breeding of animals, exploitation of minerals and devastation in

plant and animal life. All that lies beyond these "six essential facts," such as forms of family and of political and social organization, the character of religions, the character of laws, of literature, of science, etc., exhibit less, if any, correlation with geographical factors.[3] In its essentials this hypothesis seems to be valid.

3. *In the field of social phenomena where the correlation is noticeable it rarely has a rigid character. The determinism of geographical factors as far as we can grasp is almost always relative.* J. Bruhnes expresses the same idea in the following way: "Between the facts of the physical order there are sometimes relations of causality; between facts of human geography (geographical conditions and social phenomena) there are usually only *relations of connection.* To force, so to speak, the bond which connects phenomena with each other is scientifically false; and there will be great need of the spirit of criticism which will enable one to see clearly the many cases where connection is accidental and not causal." [4]

This non-rigidity or relativity of geographical conditioning manifests itself in many forms. First, though in many cases geographical factors determine whether such and such social phenomena (*e.g.,* the mining industry or the fact of the inhabitation of a definite area by men) *may or may not take place* in a definite location; nevertheless, *geographical possibility does not mean that such a phenomenon really occurs in this location.* For instance, in spite of the rich natural resources of the place, the mining industry may not exist there owing to lack of non-geographical factors. In this way, geographical conditioning in the absolute form becomes null and void. It is not rigid. The same relativity of geographical determinism exhibits itself in cases in which geographical conditions determine that "such a phenomenon may not take place at any given location" as, for instance, cultivation of plants in a desert or in an extraordinarily dry area. And yet, we know that due to artificial irrigation such things happen. This means that the geographical impossibility of a phe-

[3] BRUHNES, J., *Human Geography,* Chaps. I–II, Rand McNally Co., N. Y. Compare with the Le Play school *Nomenclature.*
[4] BRUHNES, J., *Human Geography,* p. 593; compare DE LA BLACHE, P. V., *Principles of Human Geography,* N. Y., 1926.

nomenon does not prevent it. This is another illustration of the
non-rigidity of geographical conditioning. Expectations based
on geographical conditions exclusively in many cases may not be
justified.

Second, the non-rigidity of geographical determinism shows
itself further in the possibility of *many and various social forms
within the same geographical area.* Like an abode, geographical
conditions may, in a relative degree, determine whether the place
is suitable for human habitation or for the construction of a
building. But whether the corresponding society will assume the
forms of a primitive tribe, or those of a complex civilized society;
whether the building will be a primitive hut, or pyramid, or castle,
or palace of parliament, or commercial skyscraper; these things
are not determined by geographical agencies. Almost always a
large field of choice is left. What takes place depends not so
much on the geographical as upon the non-geographical factors.
The same idea is expressed by C. Vallaux in the words that "the
influence of geographical factors is negative but not positive;
they often may hinder a phenomenon but they do not determine
what will be." [5]

4. From the above it follows that the formulation of definite
and general correlations between geographical and social phenomena is greatly hindered by this non-rigidity and indirectness of
geographical determinism. It is still more strongly handicapped
by the neutralization of the effects of one geographical agency
by another, and by neutralization of the effects of all geographical agencies by the non-geographical factors. *And the more
complex are the forms of civilization, the less noticeable, the less
definite and the less tangible is the correlation between geographical conditions and social phenomena.* This does not mean that
in such societies geographical agencies stop working, but that
their effects are more and more neutralized by other agencies.
Therefore, they become less tangible, less noticeable, and more
difficult to observe, grasp and generalize. For these reasons, *it is
to be expected that the attempts to establish such correlations
may give at best only some tentative and very approximate
hypothesis which may be applied to some societies and times and*

[5] VALLAUX, C., *Le sol et l'état*, p. 106, Paris, 1911.

rarely may pretend to be valid in regard to all societies and all times. Furthermore, it is to be expected that among many alleged correlations many will be fallacious, not to mention those which, being purely speculative, cannot pretend to be scientific at all.

Such, in brief, are the guiding principles and the general conclusions concerning geographical theories. On the following pages we shall see their validity. Let us now turn to the analysis of the principal correlations which have been formulated by different authors. We shall begin with the correlations in the field of Bruhnes' "essential facts" because they may be more definite and conspicuous.

4. GEOGRAPHICAL CONDITIONS AND DISTRIBUTION OF HUMAN POPULATION ON THE EARTH

The field of social phenomena where the influence of geographical factors is to be expected, is in the location of human population and its density. It seems evident that geographical areas which, according to their climate, soil, relief of surface, distribution of water, flora and fauna, are more convenient for human habitation and for satisfaction of human primary necessities, are to be more densely inhabited than the area less convenient in this respect.

This proposition, however, is evident only in appearance because which geographical conditions are "convenient" yet remains to be found. Besides, the conditions convenient for a primitive society may be quite inconvenient for an industrial society; the geographic environment convenient in one respect, *e.g.,* in climate, may be quite inconvenient in another respect, *e.g.,* poor in water, in minerals, in soils, etc. Therefore, this and similar propositions of the geographers, at the very best, may claim only a limited—local and temporary—significance. This may be seen from the following discussion.

It is claimed that in spite of human migrations and the fluctuation of the density of population of different areas "the general distribution of the larger human masses seems subject to a fixity, of course relative, and yet a fixity that is certain and surprising. The Siberian *tundras,* the Saharan *hamadas,* or the

Amazon forest are almost devoid of men." [6]   The same is true in regard to arctic regions and other places of similar inconvenience.   A series of other data tend to show the same correlation.   This may be seen from the data on the following page.[7]

Temperature, amount of rainfall, altitude are the geographical agencies; therefore, the correlation of these conditions with the density of the population shown by the tables tends to testify in favor of the influence of these factors on the distribution of the population on the earth.   However, on the other hand, a series of other facts testify that the correlations shown by these data are in no way universal and constant.   We cannot say that everywhere the most densely populated areas have a temperature of from 50 to 55 degrees, a rainfall of from 40 to 50 inches, and an altitude of below 100 meters, as it is shown in these tables. Due to a different combination of various geographical conditions, and especially to the interference of the non-geographical factors, the boundaries between the inhabited and uninhabited areas are changing and the above points of optimum are very different for different places, societies, and times.   Many places uninhabited in the past become inhabited at the present moment, and *vice versa,* in spite of the absence of noticeable change in the geographical environment of these places.   Through irrigation many deserts are transformed into inhabited areas.   Through activity of civilized men many uninhabited prairies, forests, and similar places of America, Russia, and Asia are improved and become the habitat of man.   If, as we shall see further, Mougeolle's, S. C. GilFillan's, and Stefansson's theory of "the Coldward or the Northward Course of Civilization," [8] is very questionable, nevertheless, it gives plenty of facts which show that great uninhabited areas of the North in the course of time have become inhabited densely, and have been transformed into centers of civilization.   These and a great many similar facts indicate that the boundaries between the inhabited and uninhabited

[6] BRUHNES, *Human Geography*, p. 47.

[7] VON MAYR, G., *Statistik und Gesellschaftslehre*, B. II, 1897, p. 51.   See other similar data in BRUHNES, *op. cit.*, pp. 186 ff; RATZEL, F., *Anthropogeographie*, 1891, Vol. II, pp. 210 ff.

[8] See GILFILLAN, S. C., "The Coldward Course of Progress," *Political Science Quarterly*, 1920, pp. 393-410.   STEFANSSON, *The Northward Course of Empire*.

Density of the Population in the United States per Square Mile (1890)	Average Temperature (Fahrenheit)	Density of the Population in the United States per Square Mile (1890)	Average Rainfall (Inches)	Density of the Population in Europe per Square Kilometre	The Altitude
4.69	under 40 degrees	0.8	under 10	334	below 100 meters
12.51	from 40 to 45 degrees	1.8	from 10 to 20	216	from 100 to 200 meters
28.61	from 45 to 50 degrees	8.1	from 20 to 30	134	from 200 to 300 meters
31.02	from 50 to 55 degrees	43.1	from 30 to 40	69	from 300 to 400 meters
22.78	from 55 to 60 degrees	59.0	from 40 to 50	79	from 400 to 500 meters
17.89	from 60 to 65 degrees	25.1	from 50 to 60	34	from 500 to 600 meters
14.16	from 65 to 70 degrees	18.1	from 60 to 70	53	from 600 to 700 meters
7.49	from 70 to 75 degrees	4.1	over 70	43	from 700 to 800 meters
3.59	above 75 degrees			44	from 800 to 900 meters
				23	from 900 to 1000 meters
				18	from 1000 to 1100 meters
				1.3	from 1100 to 1200 meters
				0.8	from 1200 to 1300 meters
				0.0	from 1300 to 1400 meters
				0.0	above 1400 meters

areas are moving; consequently, geographical determinism in this respect is non-rigid and very relative. The same is true in regard to the optimum point of altitude, temperature, and rainfall. While for Europe, according to the above table, the most densely populated zone of altitude is below 100 meters, and places above 1400 meters are almost uninhabited, for the tropical regions, and for Abyssinia, Arabia, Central and South America, and for many other places, the most densely populated zones of altitude are above 1500 meters.[9]

Shifting of the most densely populated zones in the course of time from one altitude to another, in spite of an absence of a noticeable change in geographical conditions, is a still more conspicuous and unquestionable illustration. P. Mougeolle even formulated a general "law of altitude," according to which, with the development of civilization, the most densely inhabited areas and cities are descending from the zones of high altitude (mountains and plateaus) to those of lower altitudes (plains).[10] Even though this "law," as a general formula, is questionable, the shifting of the zones of density of population in regard to altitude is proved by Mougeolle beyond a doubt. This illustration shows how relative the geographical determinism is in this field; how different and shifting are the geographical points of optimum in regard to the distribution of the population of the earth; how "local" and "temporary" are all generalizations and correlations in this field; and how impossible it is to construct the map of the density of the population of different areas exclusively on the basis of the geographical conditions.

What has been said concerning altitude may be said in regard to "points of optimum" temperature and rainfall in their interrelations with the density of population. They are also shifting in time and space. They vary for different places, times, and societies. For these reasons this analysis of the correlation between geographical conditions and the density of the population seems to corroborate completely the fundamental propositions stated above.

[9] See the data in BRUHNES, *Human Geography*, pp. 186–196.
[10] See MOUGEOLLE, P., *Les problèmes de l'histoire*, pp. 97–106, Paris, 1886; MOUGEOLLE, P., *Statique des civilisations*. Paris, 1883, *passim*.

5. GEOGRAPHIC CONDITIONS AND THE CHARACTER OF HUMAN DWELLINGS, ROADS AND MEANS OF TRANSPORTATION

It is evident that the character of human habitations or houses more than many other social phenomena must depend on geographic conditions. In its material (wood, stone, brick, fur, etc.) and in its form, shape, and architectural type, it is influenced by geographic conditions. In the places rich with forests wooden houses predominate, while where woods are scarce some other materials must be used. The same is true of the architectural type and shape, and the site of the dwelling. To some extent this expectation is warranted by the facts. But again this extent is rather moderate. In the opinion of one of the best "human geographers" it is estimated as follows: "If geography is far from explaining everything in the house, at least the human habitation cannot be completely understood without an appeal to geography." [11] This estimate of geographical influences in this field does not ascribe very much to them, and an innumerable series of facts may be indicated to show that "geographical conditions are far from explaining everything in the house." Places the most different in geographical respects often show remarkable similarities in types of dwellings. A conspicuous example of this is given by the United States of America, where over an immense area with the most different climate and other conditions, one sees practically similar types of houses in the East and the West, in the North and the South. The variations in houses in different parts of the country rarely surpass those between different houses of the same city or neighborhood. On the other hand, it is enough to compare the types of dwellings in similar geographical conditions, e.g., those in the prairies of America and in the prairies (steppes) of Russia, in the seashore regions (e.g., New York, Trieste, Almeria or Algeria), to see the greatest differences among them, in spite of a similarity of geographic conditions. The same is true in regard to the primitive peoples. "The Hopi and Navajo Indians have both occupied, for a long period, the same part of northwestern Arizona. . . . Though the

[11] BRUHNES, *Human Geography*, p. 94. See also Chap. III.

same building material is available," nevertheless, "the Hopi construct the well-known terraced sandstone houses with a rectangular cell as the architectural unit, while the Navajo dwell in conical earth-covered huts."[12] Add to this the changes in dwellings of the same area in the course of time. Without any noticeable change in the geographic conditions of the area, the dominant type of dwelling, often within some thirty or forty years, changes considerably.

It is useless to insist on these evident facts. They can only mean that geographical determinism in this field is loose and relative. Its effects sometimes may be completely obliterated by a play of other factors. If the human habitation cannot be understood completely without an appeal to geography, every attempt to account for it by geography alone is hopeless and fallacious. All that has been said of human habitation may be applied to the direction and character of roads, and generally to the means of transportation.[13]

6. GEOGRAPHICAL CONDITIONS AND CLOTHING

This category of social phenomena also has a correlation with geographical conditions, though less noticeable than that of dwellings and roads. Clothing in the colder regions or seasons is somewhat thicker and warmer than in warmer regions or seasons. But this is almost the only way in which the influence of geographical agencies manifests itself. Immensely numerous differences and variations in the clothing of different societies, groups, and times seem to be conditioned by other than geographical agencies. The extravagances of fashion, the yearly changes in men's and women's clothes, the different uniforms of various social groups (soldiers, priests, monks, officials, and so on), the different costumes of various peoples and especially through historical times; these and thousands of similar phenomena seem to have nothing to do with the geographical factors. The indirect influences are slight and unnoticeable.

---

[12] LOWIE, R. H., *Culture and Ethnology*, pp. 49–65, N. Y., 1917.
[13] See an able analysis in BRUHNES, *op. cit.*, pp. 110 ff.; VALLAUX, C., *La mer*, Paris, 1908, *passim*.

7. GEOGRAPHICAL CONDITIONS AND FOOD AND DRINK

There is also some dependence between the flora and fauna of a geographic environment and the quantity and the quality of food and drink of a society. The seashore people eat more fish than a people who inhabit an area without waters rich with fish. A society situated in a fruit-bearing area eats more fruit than those in areas where the trees are absent or cannot be cultivated. Such correlations may be found in many places. But these are neither general, nor always noticeable. Even among relatively primitive tribes it is easy to see that the principal forms of food are often similar among tribes situated in essentially different environments, and different among tribes of similar environments. Here are a few cases of the many collected by F. P. Armitage.

Principal kinds of food and corresponding peoples

   Rice: Oraons, S. Indians, Chinese, Koreans, Mundas, Japanese, Looshais, N. Aragans, Tonkingese, Laosians, Siamese
   Wheat, Millet or Oats, plus Cattle or Fish: Kabardians of the plain and mountains, Armenians, Albanians, Tadjiks, Turkomans, Norwegians, Finns, Livs, Kirghiians, Scots
   Fish plus Flesh: Eskimos, Dogribs, Chinooks, Kootenayans, Comanches, Blackfeet, Crows, Crees, Charruas, Macobys
   Flesh plus Maize: Sioux, Pawnees, Ojibwas, Lenguas, Machicuys, Iroquois, Algonquin, Muskohogian, Concapah, Yakui, Mohaves, Navajos, Yumas, Pimas, Papagos, Opatas, Mayas, Mexicans, Tepehuans [14]

In each "food-group" we see peoples who live in the most different geographical environment. The same "independence of food" from geographical factor is still more conspicuous in complex societies. In spite of the most different geographical conditions of the United States of America food is substantially the same. Furthermore, "the people of western Europe consume large quantities of coffee, tea, and cocoa, while cow's milk from European mountain pastures is consumed by the inhabitants of Shanghai and South Africa. Increased facilities of transporta-

[14] ARMITAGE, F. P., *Diet and Race*, pp. 30–32, London, 1922.

tion tend more and more to intermingle all human foods." On the other hand, the food of different social classes dwelling in the same geographical environment, in the same city, often differs, quantitatively and qualitatively, much more than the food of peoples living in the most different geographical conditions.

An idea of this difference is given by the following table, one of many similar. In Russia the food of different classes of the peasantry before the Revolution was as follows: [15]

The Classes of the Peasantry with a Yearly Income	Number of Calories Consumed in the Form of Per Cent of the Total		
	Vegetative Food in Per Cent	Animal Products in Per Cent	Number of Calories
Up to 100 rubles...........	81.3	18.7	3,230
From 100 to 150 rubles......	75.6	24.4	4,139
From 150 to 200 rubles......	72.5	27.5	5,072
200 and over..............	69.0	31.0	5,760

If we take the quantity and the quality of food of different social classes of the Russian society, the difference will be still greater. The same is true of different classes of other societies.[16] The difference in food of different social classes of the same society cannot be accounted for through geographical conditions. The same is true in regard to the differences between the food of the Russian, the English, the Chinese and the American societies, as a whole. The same may be said for "trends" in food habits such as in France, where in the period from 1840 to 1895 the consumption of bread, wine and potatoes per head of the population increased by 50 per cent; that of meat, cheese, and cider, by 200 per cent; that of sugar and coffee by 400 per cent.[17] All such changes and differences and trends seem to have nothing to

[15] KLEPIKOV, S., *Pitanie Russkago Krestianina*, 1920, pp. 13 ff.

[16] See a great many data for different countries in WEBB, A., *The New Dictionary of Statistics*, pp. 156–165, 273–289, London, 1911; GROTJAHN, A., "Über Wandlungen in d. Volksernährung," *Schmoller's Staats und Sozialwissenschaftliche Forschungen*, Bd. XX, Heft. 2, Leipzig, 1920, pp. 58–64; SLOSSE et WAXWEILER, E., *Recherches sur le travail humain dans l'industry*, 1910. PERVUSHIN "Potreblenie," in *Granat's Encyclopedia*, Vol. 33 (Russ.).

[17] D'AVENEL, G., *Le mécanism de la vie moderne*, p. 157, Paris, 1908.

do with geographic factors.   Meanwhile, they compose the most substantial phenomena in this field of geographical determinism.

8. GEOGRAPHICAL CONDITIONS AND ECONOMIC LIFE AND ORGANIZATION

A. *Geographical Conditions and Wealth.*—We have numerous theories of the geographical conditioning of economic phenomena. The first group of these theories tries to show that geographic conditions have determined almost completely the amount of wealth produced and owned by a society, especially during the earlier stages of social life.   "Of all the results which are produced among a people by climate, (food) and soil, the accumulation of wealth is the earliest, and in many respects the most important . . . and the history of wealth in its earliest stages will be found to depend entirely on soil and climate." [18]

Such is the essence of these theories in Buckle's formulation. There is no doubt that there is a part truth in the statement. But only a part.   Even in regard to many primitive tribes the above proposition is fallacious, not to speak of its fallacy in regard to complex societies.   In the first place the phenomenon of wealth itself is not something static but something that varies strongly in its nature, according to the social circumstances. Which of the products of a geographic environment become economically valuable, depends not only on the nature of these products but also on the character of a society.   Oil, naphtha, even coal and iron ore, or an abundance of water-falls have no economic value for a society which does not know how to utilize them.   A territory rich with these products is very unfavorable for the accumulation of wealth by a primitive tribe of hunters or tillers; and the same territory is very favorable for the enrichment of a modern industrial society.   The same geographic environment may have great economic value for a people who know how to exploit it; and it may have no value for a people who do not have this knowledge, and *vice versa:* quite different geographical regions may have similar economic value for different peoples.   This means that there is no such thing as a

---

[18] BUCKLE, H. T., *Introduction to the History of Civilization of England*, new and revised edition by J. M. Robertson, pp. 24–28, and Chap. II, London, N. Y.

geographic environment valuable in itself, under all circumstances, for all societies, regardless of their character. For these reasons Buckle's proposition needs a serious limitation. In the second place, the assumption that all brilliant and wealthy civilizations of earlier times have happened in an exclusively "favorable" natural environment, is also questionable. The geographical conditions of Sparta, or Athens, or even ancient Egypt may be styled as "rich" and fertile only in a very relative sense. If there were no accommodations made by the inhabitants, the natural environment of these societies is to be recognized as rather "poor." And yet, this did not hinder the production and accumulation of great wealth. On the other hand, in spite of the richness of the natural resources of America, its pre-European inhabitants did not accumulate great wealth.[19] In the third place, the assumption that primitive tribes who live within the same geographical environment are equally wealthy is also not accurate. Among other authors, R. H. Lowie and R. Thurnwald have shown this in regard to the Hopi and the Navajo Indians, and in regard to a series of other tribes.[20] In the fourth place, the average per capita wealth of contemporary societies and corresponding differences in this respect cannot be accounted for through the hypothesis. The same is true in regard to the fluctuations of impoverishment and prosperity during the course of time within a population which lives in the same geographic environment. The natural resources of Russia are scarcely poorer than those of any other country; and yet, the per capita wealth of its population is one of the lowest. The Indians and the Americans inhabit the same territory; and yet the former were poor, the latter were and are rich. Bruhnes gives a long series of facts which show the accumulation of considerable wealth and economic prosperity among populations in a very hostile natural environment, and *vice versa.*[21] These reasons are enough to show the one-sidedness

[19] See further the classical criticism of these theories given by Gobineau. His objections are valid in essence up to this time. Some of Buckle's fallacies in this respect are justly indicated and checked by Robertson in his editorial remarks and footnotes in the above edition of Buckle's book.

[20] See LOWIE, R. H., *Culture and Ethnology*, pp. 48 ff., N. Y., 1917; THURN-WALD, R., "Die Gestaltung der Wirtschaftsentwicklung aus ihren Anfängen heraus," in *Erinngerungsgabe für Max Weber*, Vol. I, pp. 273–336, Münich, 1923.

[21] See BRUHNES, *op. cit.*, Chap. VIII, and pp. 593 ff. See his discussion.

of the theories under discussion. There is some truth in the theories because, under given conditions of a society the character of natural resources may facilitate or hinder an accumulation of wealth, but this is only one factor among many, and it is scarcely more important than many other non-geographical agencies.[22]

B. *Geographical Conditions and the Character of Industries of a Society.*—A second series of the geographical theories tries to show the existence of a close correlation between geographical conditions and economic or industrial activities of a given society. Practically every textbook in economic or industrial geography, and almost every textbook in history, emphasizes the great conditioning rôle of geographical factors in this respect.[23]   Place determines the method of obtaining the means of subsistence of a society or the character of its economic activities. We have seen how Le Play's formula shows the determining rôle of geographical conditions. In a similar way it is traced by a crowd of historians and economic geographers. It is evident that a society whose territory does not include coal or other valuable minerals and metals cannot be expected to develop the mining industry. It is clear also that a territory with infertile soil cannot be expected to produce a society whose principal industry is agriculture. This means that there is some truth in all these theories. But again, the correlation between geographic environment and the industrial activities of a society is often overestimated. Though in many cases it is tangible, in most of the others it is very loose and even indefinite.

It is hard to agree with the claim of Demolins and other geog-

[22] The fundamental source of the fallacies of the geographers is their disregard of social environment and of hereditary differences of human beings. In this respect Buckle's complete disregard of inherent differences, expressed in his note on page 22, is typical for many geographers. If a one-sided geographical theory of the production of wealth is very defective, still more defective is a geographical theory of the distribution of wealth, which is also typically outlined by Buckle. It is so fallacious that it does not need even to be criticized. See BUCKLE, *op. cit.*, pp. 28 ff.

[23] See as example SEMPLE, ELLEN CH., *American History and Its Geographic Conditions*, 1903; SEMPLE, *Influences of Geog. Environment*, 1911; SMITH, J. R., *Industrial and Commercial Geography*, 1913; WHITBECK, R. H., and FINCH, V. C., *Economic Geography*, 1924; HUNTINGTON, E., and WILLIAMS, F. E., *Business Geography*, 1922; WHITBECK, R. H., *Industrial Geography*, 1924; see other literature cited in these books.

raphers that a mere knowledge of the geographical conditions of a given territory is sufficient to enable us to forecast the character of the industries or the principal economic activities of the population of such a territory. The conditions of the steppes of Russia and American prairies is similar in many respects; and yet the economic activities of the nomadic and half-nomadic population of the Russian steppes and those of the American prairies are different. The population of the mountains of Switzerland, the Basques of the Pyrenees, and the Tibetans, live in similar mountainous conditions; and yet the industries through which they get their means of subsistence are different. The Bushmen and the Herrero dwell in the same deserts, but hunting is the basic industry of the former and cattle-breeding of the latter.[24] Many Indian tribes lived in areas where the soil was fertile and very favorable for the development of agriculture; and yet it almost did not exist at all among them. On the other hand, in the Western Carpathians, which are much less favorable for the development of agriculture, it is greatly developed and 88 per cent of the ground is cultivated, while in the Eastern Carpathians where land is more fertile, cultivation is less developed and only 13 per cent of the land is tilled.[25] On Majorca, especially on the great western sierras of the island, in spite of the most unfavorable conditions, the people "have accomplished and are still accomplishing the miraculous feat of developing irrigated gardens of their *huertas*." [26] *Post factum,* we are prone to believe historians when they say that "the development of navigation by the Phœnicians was due to the favorable sea-shore environment." In fact these and a great many similar explanations are misleading. In the case of the Phœnicians, the real situation was as follows:

It will be difficult to find any less hospitable regions in the Mediterranean than the little corner of the Syrian shore where are situated the ports of Tyre and Sidon, famous in antiquity. The situations are unfavorable in themselves, and very often a heavy swell from the open sea makes it difficult to enter or to leave the port, and yet,

[24] See THURNWALD, R., *Die Gestaltung der Wirtschaftsentwicklung aus ihren Anfängen heraus*, Münich, 1923.
[25] BRUHNES, *Human Geography*, p. 525.
[26] *Ibid.*, p. 594.

the Phœnicians were a people of navigators and colonists. Why? Because their commercial ingenuity made up for the unkindness of nature. [27]

The same is true of a great many other *post factum* geographical interpretations of the industrial activities of different peoples given in the courses of history. From the fact that the Greeks, or the Phœnicians became navigators and developed a great maritime commerce they concluded that the geographical position was responsible for it.[28] In fact in these and in many other cases the geographical environments were far from being favorable. Besides plenty of peoples have lived in a much more favorable environment for the development of navigation and failed to do so.[29] Such discrepancies between geographical conditions and the character of the industrial activities of a population are so numerous that the above statement of the geographers loses its general character and eventually means only indefinite geographical determinism. The final proofs are those changes of the industrial activities of a population which sometimes occur in a short period of time. For instance, in the United States during the last thirty years, the percentage of males engaged in agriculture decreased from 50 to 35 of all males gainfully employed. This is a very serious change in the industrial activities of the population. Neither can it be accounted for through geographic conditions. In essence they are now exactly the same as thirty years ago. The following table shows the number of workers engaged in certain specified occupations in the United States per million of the population.[30]

The table shows very serious changes in occupational activities of the population within the period of seventy years. These changes cannot be accounted for through geographical conditions.

[27] BRUHNES, *op. cit.*, p. 595; DUBOIS, MARCEL, *La crise maritime*, p. 25.

[28] See a more detailed analysis as to the extent of Greek geographical environment which was favorable for maritime navigation in VALLAUX, *La mer*, paragraph 7.

[29] See many facts in BRUHNES, *op. cit.*, Chap. VIII, and pp. 594 ff. See also Vallaux's criticism of corresponding geographical theories of K. Ritter and F. Ratzel and the convincing and abundant factual material given to show the inadequacy of all one-sided geographical theories of this kind. VALLAUX, C., *La mer*, pp. 27 ff., and Chap. II; VALLAUX, *Le sol et l'état*, pp. 152 ff., and *passim.*

[30] JONES, M. Z., "Trend of Occupations in the Population," *Monthly Labor Review*, May, 1925.

Occupation	Number of Workers per Million of Population of the United States							
	1850	1860	1870	1880	1890	1900	1910	1920
Farmers...........	103,097	79,809	77,320	84,318	83,904	74,606	64,231	57,550
Wheelwrights......	1,323	1,040	543	311	204	178	41	35
Brick and stone masons and plasterers	2,733	.....	.....	.....	.....	.....	.....	1,676
Physicians and surgeons...........	1,757	1,751	1,618	1,708	1,665	1,737	1,643	1,372
Clergymen........	1,157	1,194	1,138	1,290	1,401	1,469	1,283	1,204
Plumbers..........	81	.....	.....	.....	.....	.....	.....	1,956
Clerical...........	4,369	.....	.....	.....	.....	.....	.....	41,246
Chauffeurs........	.....	.....	.....	.....	.....	.....	498	2,697

According to Petrenz, in Leipzig, during the period from 1751 to 1890, 349 new occupations appeared and 115 of those previously existing disappeared.[31] It is difficult to explain these changes by the influence of geographical factors. These and thousands of similar examples show that the industrial activities of a society change, and sometimes radically, in the same geographical environment. This is further proof of the one-sidedness of Demolins' claim, and the exaggerated character of the corresponding geographical theories.

The geographical conditions of America or Russia within the next two hundred years probably will change very little; and yet who can foresee or predict what will be the principal industries of these countries at that time? We probably would not be far from the truth if we said they would be very different from the present. Any new invention, any considerable change of the racial composition of the population or of the social organization and interrelations of a society with other societies calls forth serious and substantial modifications of its industrial activities.[32]

[31] PETRENZ, O., *Die Entwicklung der Arbeitsteilung in Leipziger Gewerbem,* p. 89, Leipzig, 1901.

[32] Even the nature of geographical conditions is changed by complex societies. The nature of the geographical conditions of the United States is now, after great progress by science, quite different from that before. What is now regarded as a very favorable nature (rich with oil, coal, iron) in the past was regarded as very unfavorable, and *vice versa.*

In regard to complex society especially, there is no possibility of any close correlation between physical environment and industrial activities.

C. *Geographical Conditions and Business Cycles and the Rhythm of Economic Life.*—The third group of geographical theories consists of those attempting to establish a correlation between geographical conditions and the waves of prosperity and impoverishment, business revivals and depressions. The theories claim that the economic life of a society ultimately is determined by geographical agencies. Plato often said that great geographical processes like earthquakes or inundations were responsible for the decay of prosperity and of the civilizations of many societies. A great many other authors have stressed the parallelism between dynamics in climate and economic cycles in the life of different societies.

At the present time we have several studies of this kind. As examples of such studies, we may mention the sun-spot theory of business cycles of W. Stanley Jevons, published in 1875;[33] the same theory slightly modified by H. Stanley Jevons;[34] the theory of W. H. Shaw, concerning the correlation between the periodicity of wheat yields and climatic changes;[35] Brückner's theory of the correlation of climatic changes with the fluctuation of the economic life of a society;[36] H. H. Clayton's theory of the commercial panics in the United States and their correlation with periods of deficient rainfall in the Ohio Valley;[37] a similar theory of W. H. Beveridge;[38] and finally the meteorological theory of business cycles developed by E. Huntington (1876–)[39] and

[33] JEVONS, W. S., *Investigations in Currency and Finance*, 1884, pp. 194–243.

[34] JEVONS, H. S., "The Causes of Unemployment," *The Contemporary Review*, 1909, pp. 165–189.

[35] SHAW, W. N., "An Apparent Periodicity in the Yield of Wheat," etc., *Proceedings of the Royal Society*, Series A, Vol. LXXVIII (1906), pp. 69–76.

[36] BRÜCKNER, "Der Einfluss d. Klimaschwankungen auf die Ernteerträge und Getreidepreise in Europa," *Geographische Zeitschrift*, Vol. I, 1895, pp. 39–51, 100–108.

[37] CLAYTON, H. H., "The Influence of Rainfall on Commerce and Politics," *Popular Science Monthly*, Dec., 1901.

[38] BEVERIDGE, W. H., "British Exports and the Barometer," *The Economic Journal*, March, 1920; "Weather and Harvest Cycles," *The Economic Journal*, 1921, pp. 429–449.

[39] HUNTINGTON, E., *World Power and Evolution*, 1919, Chaps. II, III, IV.

especially by H. L. Moore (1869–   ).[40] There are several other works of this kind but they need not be mentioned because they add very little, if anything, to the data and the statements of the works indicated. The theory of W. S. Jevons and partly that of H. S. Jevons are now unsupportable in their concrete form.[41] All of the other theories are similar in character. Because the most elaborate and the most scientific appear to be those of Beveridge and Moore, my analysis is therefore limited to a discussion of these two authors and to a brief analysis of a somewhat different hypothesis of Huntington.

The essence of Dr. H. L. Moore's elaborate theory is as follows:

The weather conditions represented by the rainfall in the central part of the United States, and probably in other continental areas, pass through cycles of approximately thirty-three years and eight years in duration, causing like cycles in the yield per acre of the crops; these cycles of crops constitute the natural, material current which drags upon the surface the lagging, rhythmically changing values and prices with which the economist is more immediately concerned. [42]

According to his mathematical analysis, the correlation between the fluctuation of crops and an index of the mean effective rainfall in the Ohio Valley during the critical periods of the crops (July-August) is $r = .584$.[43] Having shown this correlation, Moore proceeds to find a further correlation between the fluctuation of the crops and the business cycle. His theory is as follows:

The rhythmically varying yield per acre of the crops is the cause of economic cycles; when the yield increases, the volume of trade, the activity of industry, and the amount of employment increase; the demand for producers' goods rises; the demand curves for agricultural commodities rise; with the ultimate result of a rise of general

[40] MOORE, H. L., *Economic Cycles; Their Law and Cause*, N. Y., 1914; *Generating Economic Cycles*, N. Y., 1923.

[41] W. C. Mitchell says this theory "scarcely affords a convincing explanation of business cycles." MITCHELL, *Business Cycles*, 1913, p. 19.

[42] MOORE, H. L., *op. cit.*, p. 149.

[43] MOORE, H. L., *op. cit.*, p. 53.

prices. The contrary changes would follow upon a fall in the yield per acre of the crops.

The theory is supported by the author's painstaking analysis of the fluctuations of the business-barometer (measured through pig-iron production) and those of crop production. The coefficient of correlation between them is $r=.718$, with a lag in the cycles of pig-iron production of one or two years. The coefficient of correlation between the fluctuations of crops and the movement of general prices is still higher (with a lag of about four years) : here $r=.800$.[44]   Such is the essence of this theory.

Beveridge's theory of business cycles is similar to that of Moore. The only differences are in the data, methods, and some of the conclusions. The essentials of his theory and argumentation are as follows : Wheat prices in western and central Europe, during the period from 1500 to 1869, appear to show that in the fluctuation of prices there is a major periodicity of 30.6 years or 15 years one way and 15 the other, and a minor fluctuation of 15.2 or 15.4 years. With a lag of one year this periodicity corresponds, in his opinion, to the periodicity in crops due to fluctuations of the weather. Other factors influenced the fluctuation of prices, but the most fundamental was the weather. "The chart (of prices) must be accepted as essentially a reflection of harvest success and harvest failure." In his first article he claimed that the periodicity of 15.2 or 15.4 years in the fluctuation of prices corresponded to a similar periodicity of weather conditions due to sun spots. In his second paper, in answer to some objections presented by the secretary of the Royal Meteorological Society, W. W. Bryant, Beveridge gave a more complex interpretation. He agreed that the periodicity of the sun spots was not 15 but about 11 years. He admitted that "a cycle of 15.3 years had not been found in any meteorological record." However, he claimed that weather fluctuations showed periodicities of 4.38 or 4.77, 8.34 years. Besides, there was the periodicity of 4.37 years in rainfall. The period of 15.3 or of 30.6 years could be divided correspondingly into the periods of 4.38, 4.77, 8.34, 4.37 years which were similar to the fluctuations of meteorological phenomena. In his further analysis he indicates that besides the periodicities of

[44] MOORE, H. L., *op. cit.*, pp. 147 ff.

15 and 30 years in the movement of prices there were periods of 4.38, 5.11, 2.74, 3.71, 34.992, 48, 74-75, and 271 years.[45]

Such are the essentials of Beveridge's theory. The meteorological theories are similar to those of Moore and Beveridge, but less elaborate and based on less data. The theory of Huntington is somewhat different. He tries to establish the influence of climatic conditions on economic life not so much through the medium of harvests, conditioned by the weather, as through the medium of the health of the population which is affected by climatic agencies. His principal thesis is that climate and its fluctuations cause fluctuations in health and the efficiency of physical and mental work; fluctuations in health and in work efficiency lead to corresponding fluctuations of business and economic conditions of a society. He tries to corroborate this contention with many data, among which the most important are those which show the parallelism of the death rate and the business depressions or revivals in Connecticut, New York, Massachusetts and Chicago in the period from 1870 to 1910. "A high death rate (as an index of health) regularly precedes hard times, while a low death rate precedes prosperity. Health is a cause far more than an effect (of business prosperity). Health in its turn is determined by the weather." Such in brief is the essence of Huntington's theory.[46]

Now let us briefly discuss to what extent the above theories are valid. We will admit at the start that many dynamical processes in the geographical environment of a society influence, and sometimes very seriously, dynamics of economic life. Earthquakes, like the recent one in Japan or many others, or the drying-up of an area, or its inundation, and similar natural processes may disorganize or even imperil the economic life of a society. However, such catastrophic changes in geographical environment are relatively very rare and often of short duration. Therefore in a long life of a society they do not count much in the non-catastrophic fluctuations of economic processes.

In the second place, it is scarcely possible to deny a conditioning rôle to climatic and geographic agencies in determining the

[45] BEVERIDGE, *Weather and Harvest Cycles, passim.*
[46] HUNTINGTON, E., *World Power and Evolution,* pp. 29–31, and Chaps. III, IV.

quantity and quality of harvest, and through it, especially in agricultural countries, of fluctuations of the business cycle. However, though human control in this field is still limited, nevertheless, interference of the other non-geographical agencies, like agricultural knowledge, human energy, care, and so on, and also the expansion of trade and commerce, now and in the past, have been limiting and neutralizing to a considerable extent the effects of geographical influences. Besides, in any wide area geographical factors rarely are identical; if favorable in one place they are unfavorable in another, and in this way they, themselves, may neutralize their own effects to an extent which renders them incapable of seriously influencing the whole economic life of a society. Nevertheless, we must still recognize to some extent the conditioning rôle of geographical factors in the dynamics of economic life.

But does this mean that this conditioning is so great and so decisive that such phenomena as business cycles and movements of prices must reflect it regularly, as the above theories claim? Can we say that this correlation is so close that it may be traced in the business cycles of an industrialized society? It is hard to answer this question definitely. Nevertheless the reasons for a negative answer are almost as strong as for a positive one. The weakest points of theories such as those of Beveridge are as follows: First, they claim that a definite periodicity of weather conditions (or of sun spots) exists and with this periodicity attempt to correlate corresponding fluctuations in business. Even granting that such a periodicity exists, we are somewhat embarrassed by its diversity as reported by different authors of this school. According to Moore these periods are of 8 and 33 years of length; according to Beveridge they are 4.37, 5.1, 11.12, 8.34, 15.3, 30.6 and other years of length; according to Jevons, both W. S. and H. S., they are 10.44, 3.7, 7 and 11 years; according to W. N. Shaw, 2.75 and 3.67 years; according to Brückner, 35 years, and so on. This discordance in the length of weather periodicities among the proponents of this theory of economic cycles makes a definite, and more or less general, periodicity in weather conditions somewhat uncertain and raises the question as to whether the above periods are really existing or have arisen as a result of arithmetical and mathematical manipulations of the authors.

Some of them, like Professor Moore, have obtained their periods from a computation of a real amount of rainfall in the Ohio Valley [47] but some others, like Beveridge, deduced the periodicity in weather fluctuation from that of the fluctuation of wheat prices. Besides, the lengths of the periods of Beveridge's theory are so various and different that the very fact of their existence amounts almost to an absence of any definite periodicity: to say that there are periods of 2, 3, 4, 5, 7, 11, 15 and so on years practically means that there are no periods. Thus the first defect of all these theories vitiates their starting point and suggests their tentative and uncertain character. Their second defect results from the fact that the periodicity of the sun spots or of weather fluctuations is also uncertain. Though Sir Arthur Shuster's theory of the eleven-year periods of the sun spots is popular, nevertheless, this period represents only an approximate average of various figures ranging from 16 to 6 years between the maximum periods of the sun spots in the years from 1750 to 1906.[48] As any series of figures may give some average, this eleven-year period is rather fictitious and not a real periodicity of the sun-spot maximums. Furthermore several other meteorologists have indicated the existence of different periodicities of the sun spots and weather fluctuations. This discordance of the meteorologists indicates the uncertainty of the very fact of the existence of any periodicity in these fields. And some of the prominent specialists in the field of meteorology probably are not far from the truth when they deny decidedly the existence of any definite periodicity in the fluctuation of the sun spots or weather conditions. An example of this is the paper "Weather and Cyclical Fluctuations," by Walter W. Bryant, honorary secretary of the Royal Meteorological Society. In his criticism of Beveridge's theory he indicates that there is no definite periodicity either in the sun spots, in the effects of the tide-raising efficiency of the moon, or in the weather fluctuations.

[47] Though even this is seriously questioned. See WRIGHT, PH. G., "Moore's Economic Cycles," *Quarterly Journal of Economics*, Vol. XXIX, pp. 631–641.

[48] The sun-spot maximums happened in the years: 1750, 1761, 1770, 1778, 1804, 1817, 1830, 1837, 1848, 1860, 1871, 1883, 1893, 1906. The sun-spot minimum periods give a similar series.

"Accepting the barometer data I have examined those from 1873 to 1904 (for India and other places) and from 1873 to 1903 for North America, each being a homogeneous series. The barometer figures show no evidence of any period such as fifteen and one-third years" (claimed definitely by Beveridge in his first paper).

As to the periodicity of the sun spots, says Bryant, Professor Kimura has analyzed them from 1750 to 1911, found their curve, and made a prediction of their movement up to 1950. "But the actual figures disagreed with the prediction of the first year and became worse and worse year by year." The conclusion of the author is that in view of the absence of any definite periodicity in meteorological conditions "it does not seem likely that the time has yet come for long-range forecasting to become a practical factor in the regulation of the world's food supply." [49] The validity of these objections has been recognized, partly explicitly and partly implicitly, by Beveridge in his second paper. He is much less decisive in his statement, and practically gives up his theory of the fifteen years' periodicity in the fluctuation of weather conditions. Instead, he indicates numerous different periodicities in the fluctuation of prices, but fails to show corresponding periods in the fluctuation of the weather. Finally, he concludes, "There is hardly any enterprize more deluding or more desperate than the search for weather cycles. The gold we gather turns incessantly to ashes, but the 15.3 year cycle seems to have the ring of true metal." [50]

This is practically a confession to the invalidity of his own theory, which is still more weakened because his prediction of an exceptionally poor harvest for the years 1923, 1924, 1925 seems not to have been corroborated.[51]

---

[49] BRYANT, W., "The Weather and Cyclical Fluctuations," *The Economic Review*, 1921, pp. 46–49. See also WARD, R. DE C., *Climate Considered Especially in Relation to Man*, pp. 356 ff., Chap. XI, N. Y., 1918. "The results of investigations of the sun spot periodicity and of periodic oscillations of (climate) have not been satisfactory. In some cases the relation to sun spot periodicity is open to debate; in others the results are contradictory." Such is a brief summary of the situation of the problem. *Ibid.*, pp. 356–357.

[50] BEVERIDGE, *op. cit.*, p. 449.

[51] Still more questionable are the attempts to correlate the periods of the sunspot maximums with revolutions and social upheavals or psychical pandemics (theory of a Russian, Professor Chijevsky, published in 1922); the sun spots with

This means that the corner stone of the meteorological theories of business cycles, the existence of a definite periodicity in the sun spots or in the weather fluctuations, is not certain at all. Naturally still less valid is a theoretical scheme erected on such an uncertain foundation. And the discordance of the theories about the length of the periodicities is a further corroboration of this uncertainty. Lack of correlation between business cycles and the alleged cycles in weather conditions, as soon as they are definitely proclaimed, is further evidence of the inconclusive character of all these theories. To avoid such contradictions the authors try, through division and subdivision of their periods, to patch up their theories, but such efforts are far from being successful. Some of them, again in disagreement with one another, try to achieve the alleged parallelism of business and weather fluctuations through the use of different lags such as one, two, three, four or five years, according to the demands of the theory. It is evident that such mathematical manipulations as the subdivision of the alleged periodicities and the use of elastic "lags" which shorten and lengthen according to the requirements of the problem, can make correlations where none exist. Furthermore, the data which are carefully analyzed, like those of Professor Moore, are nevertheless too local to form a basis for world-wide generalizations, and for the claim that "the rhythmically varying yield per acre of the crops is *the cause* of economic cycles." It may be one of the causes, but it certainly is not *the* cause. Finally, the correlation of the years of business revivals and depressions with the years of good and bad harvests does not even support the idea of a mutual relationship between business fluctuations and crops.

There are many cases in which increased yields accompanied increased prosperity or in which poor crops and depressions went together. But the correlation between volume of production and business conditions is far less perfect for wheat than for minerals (pig-iron and coal). The years of 1899 for America, 1895 for

---

epidemics (Sardeaux), with religious upheavals, and so on. This skepticism, however, does not hinder one from welcoming the newly organized French Society of Scientific Astrology, whose purpose it is to study scientifically the problem of meteorological influences on social life. Something valuable may come out of such a study.

Britain, 1897 for France, and 1907 for Germany were the years of poor crops and, at the same time, of prosperity for each of these countries. The years of 1908 for America, 1902 for Britain, 1903 for France and 1902 for Germany were years of good crops, and at the same time of business depression. Good crops tend to bring prosperity (in an agricultural country) and poor crops depression in the seasons which follow. But the numerous exceptions to this rule show that other factors often overbalance the effects of the harvests.

Besides, growth in production of wheat and pig-iron and coal is also far from being parallel.[52]

These considerations [53] seem to be sufficient for the conclusions that any close correlation between weather conditions and economic fluctuations is not proved as yet; that the theories of the parallel periodicities without lags still need to be proved; and that even where the parallelism is found it is necessary to show further that it is not incidental. Some influence of geographical factors in the field of economic phenomena must be recognized, but it is so complex and so strongly modified by other factors that it is very "loose" (except in catastrophes) and is scarcely possible of description in a definite mathematical formula.

Huntington's variety of the meteorological theories of business fluctuations, we shall see further, exaggerates enormously the influence of climate upon health and efficiency. Therefore, its corner stone is not valid, not to mention many possible objections to his method and data. His whole theory is still more questionable than the above theories. A criticism of his correlation between climate and health will be given further so that we shall not discuss his theory here.[54]

---

[52] MITCHELL, W., *Business Cycles*, pp. 237–239, 452–453.

[53] See other objections to these theories in *L'année sociologique*, pp. 806–811, 1923–24, and in special studies of business cycles and economic fluctuations. As an additional reason against the correlation it may be mentioned that the correlation between sun-spot number and tree growth which is expected to be much higher than that between sun-spot number and economic conditions, is only +0.1212. "The relationship is by no means so intimate as many writers imply." HARRIS, J. ARTHUR, "The Correlation Between Sun-Spot Number and Tree Growth," *Monthly Weather Review*, Jan., 1926, 54: 13–14.

[54] Sometimes the influence of meteorological conditions upon business fluctuations is seen in the so-called "seasonal fluctuation of business." Even such authors as A. Hansen, who seem to be far from partisans of the meteorological theory of business cycles, writes: "The seasonal fluctuations are those which are

Thus it seems that even in the field of economic phenomena, where a greater and more direct influence of geographical conditions is to be expected, it is neither so omnipotent as to overweigh the influence of other factors, nor so decisive as to be manifest in rigid correlations, nor so general as to account for differences in economic processes and organization within different social groups and within the same group at different times. If it is fallacious to deny any rôle to geographical factors in this field, it is no less fallacious to overestimate the rôle as many geographers and other scholars have done.

9. GEOGRAPHICAL ENVIRONMENT AND RACE

The position of many geographers on this question is expressed typically by Buckle in the following statement:

I cordially subscribe to the remark of one of the greatest thinkers of our time, who says of the supposed differences of race, "Of all

---

due to the influence of the seasons, summer and winter, harvest and seed time."
I am afraid there is a curious substitution of the meaning of words. There are some short-time fluctuations ("seasonal") and still they may be due to other than geographical or meteorological conditions. From the fact of their existence it does not follow at all that the responsible factors are meteorological. Only when such short-time fluctuations within the year show that they repeat regularly from year to year approximately in the same climatic periods or in the same months, is such a regularity evidence in favor of climatic factors. Meanwhile, if not all, then at least a great number of such "seasonal fluctuations" do not show any such regularity. For instance, Hansen's data of railroad earnings show that the months of maximum earnings in different years were quite different: December, July, and October in 1902, April and July in 1903, February, November and December in 1904, December and November in 1905; February and January in 1906, April and May in 1907, November and December in 1908. This means that they occur in different months in different years, and in periods of quite different weather (*e.g.*, in December and July) in the same year. The same is true of the months of minimum earnings. According to the simple rules of inductive logic such a "seasonal" fluctuation is pretty definite testimony that fluctuations have nothing to do with the seasons as climate or meteorological phenomena; that the agencies responsible for fluctuations are to be looked for somewhere else than in the field of climatic conditions; and that, finally, the fluctuations are rather irregular to be styled "seasonal" in the proper sense of the word. Other tables and data given by Professor Hansen in his careful study, invariably, and even more conspicuously, show the above irregular characteristics of the so-called "seasonal" fluctuations of "investment composite," of "banking composite," and so on. See HANSEN, A. H., *Cycles of Prosperity and Depression in the United States, Great Britain and Germany*, pp. 15–16, 19, 27, 31, 32–33, 42, 58–59, Madison, 1921. The above remarks apply to a great many other economic and non-economic "seasonal fluctuations." Apparently the "seasonal fluctuations" are simply "short-time" fluctuations whose factors are to be found somewhere else than in climatic or meteorological conditions.

the vulgar modes of escaping from the consideration of the effect of social and moral influences on the human mind, the most vulgar is that of attributing the diversities of conduct and character to inherent and natural differences" (Mill's *Principles of Political Economy*, Vol. 1, p. 390). Ordinary writers are constantly falling into the error of assuming the existence of this difference. But while such original distinctions of race are altogether hypothetical, the discrepancies which are caused by differences of climate, food, and soil are capable of a satisfactory explanation. [55]

After this Buckle proceeds to show how geographical agencies have produced the most substantial differences among various societies, in bodies, in minds, in social organization, and in historical destinies. For him, as for many others, especially earlier geographers, racial differences, either in a greater part or entirely, have been due to differences in environment, and especially in geographical conditions. In this extreme form the theory may scarcely be sustained by any serious geographer of the present, but in a somewhat milder form it is supported by a great many partizans of this school. One of the best examples is Dr. Ellen Churchill Semple's *Influences of Geographic Environment, On the Basis of Ratzel's System of Anthropo-Geography* (N. Y., 1911). In this volume a long series of physical characteristics of man are attributed to the direct and indirect influences of geographic environment (differentiation of human races under the influence of different geographical environments, differences in stature, in pigmentation, in thickness of skin, in the character of hair, in size of chest, and so on).[56] Following many of her predecessors, and especially Ritter and Ratzel, the author, in a somewhat milder form, tries to show by several examples the validity of her principal correlations. Many other authors in a more technical and more competent, but in a narrower form, support the same thesis of a correlation between geography and racial characteristics in the zoölogical sense of the term. As examples of such theories I may mention those of J. A. Allen,

[55] BUCKLE, H. T., *Introduction to the History of Civilization in England*, New and Revised Edition by J. M. Robertson, p. 22, London, Routledge.
[56] See SEMPLE, *op. cit.*, Chap. II and *passim*.

W. Ridgeway, A. Keith, F. Boas, and others.[57] To what extent are all these claims valid? Are they corroborated by the facts or are they still in the stage of purely tentative hypotheses? Let us discriminate briefly between the valid and invalid portions of these claims. In the first place, the assumption of many of these authors of the so-called monogenic theory of human origin and of a later differentiation of mankind into different races under the influence of different environments, is a mere guess. This, as well as the opposite or polygenic hypothesis, is and probably will remain a mere guess, which cannot be proved or disproved.[58] For this reason this argument of the geographers and environmentalists in favor of their theory cannot have any scientific value.[59]

There is another point which greatly weakens the position of the geographers in this field. Racial characteristics in a proper sense of the word are those which are inherited. The assumption that such characteristics may be altered by the geographic environment and, being altered, become hereditary traits, supposes the possibility of the inheritance of acquired traits. This, as it is known, is a presumption which is still denied by the majority of the biologists. Therefore the theory of the alteration of racial traits through direct influences of geographic factors at the very best is based on a very uncertain and questionable foundation. Until the theory of inheritance of acquired traits is proved we cannot admit the possibility of a modification of racial, that is, of hereditary traits under the direct influence of geographic conditions. Alteration of these traits through amalgamation and similar factors, does not belong in the category of geographical

---

[57] See ALLEN, J. A., "The Influence of Physical Conditions in the Genesis of the Species," *Smithsonian Annual Report for 1905*, Wash., 1906; RIDGEWAY, W., "The Application of the Zoölogical Laws to Man," *Nature*, Vol. LXXVIII, 1908; KEITH, A., "On Certain Factors Concerned in the Evolution of Human Races," *Journal of the Royal Anthropological Institute*, Lond., 1916, Vol. XLVI; and KEITH, A., "La differenciation de l'humanité en types raciaux," *Revue generale des sciences*, Paris, 1919, 30me année. Dr. Franz Boas has stressed, not so much the influence of geography as environment in general and especially social environment upon the bodily characteristics of man. See BOAS, F., *The Mind of Primitive Man*, 1911; *Changes in Bodily Form of Descendants of Immigrants*, Wash., 1911.

[58] See SERGI, G., *Le origine umane*, Torino, 1913; DIXON, R. B., *The Racial History of Man*, pp. 503 ff., New York, 1923.

[59] E. Ch. Semple, like many other environmentalists, writes without any serious reason that "the unity of the human species is clearly established."

determinism and for this reason cannot be used as an argument in favor of their theories.

In the third place, almost all serious theories which advocate the possibility of the modification of racial characteristics through geographical agencies recognize that this is possible only in a long course of time; hundreds and thousands of years are necessary for a given racial type to be considerably changed under the direct influence of geographic factors.[60] If this is so it means that geographic environment works so slowly that it is practically of no significance as an explanation of racial modifications in the course of the history of a population which rarely goes back beyond two or three thousands of years. It is of still less importance for an explanation of the biological changes of a population and of its historical destinies for a shorter period of time computed by tens of years. It is true that we have some very valuable attempts to prove the possibility of a modification of racial characteristics within a short period of time. Among such attempts Professor Boas' study of the bodily changes in American immigrants and R. M. Fleming's study are possibly the best. But Dr. Franz Boas ascribes the modifying rôle not so much to the geographic as to the social environment. Besides, his conclusions have been met with such strong criticism on the part of the prominent specialists, and their objections are so serious, that at the very best the results of Boas' study are to be taken as inconclusive.[61]

[60] See MORSELLI, "Le razze umane e il sentimento di superiorita etnica," *Rivista Italiana di Sociologia*, 1911, pp. 331 ff. "Racial traits may change under permanent influence of environment, but hundreds and even thousands of years are necessary for such a transformation. I do not know any single case of transformation of a race within one or two generations except the cases due to an amalgamation. The environment of a race cannot modify quickly its physical and psychical characteristics. As to the educational factor, it is absurd to expect it can change a race in a short period of time. It is true that we see at the present a rapid change of the characteristics of a people, but scientific observation shows that such changes are of a psycho-social, but not a racial nature." See also DIXON, *op. cit.*, pp. 479 ff., and *passim;* DE LAPOUGE, V., *Les seléctions sociales*, pp. 65 ff.

[61] See BOAS, FRANZ, "Changes in Bodily Forms of Descendants of Immigrants," *Senate Documents*, Vol. LXIV, Washington, 1911; Miss R. M. Fleming's paper in *Man*, Vol. XXII, pp. 69–72. Among critical analyses of these works see especially SERGI, G., "Influenza dell' ambiente sui caratteri fisici dell'uomo," *Rivista Italiana di sociologia*, 1912, pp. 16–24; FLEURE, H. J. and JAMES, T. C., "Geographical Distribution of Anthropological Types in Wales," *Journal of the*

In connection with the progress in the study of the rôle of glands, especially the ductless glands, in the formation of man's body and physiological processes, we have a series of attempts to explain through the alteration of gland activity by geographic environment, the changes in the racial characteristics of man. An example of such attempts is the theory of Sir Arthur Keith.[62] At the present moment, there is no doubt that many body traits, stature, form of cranium, weight, and so on, may be altered through modifications of the structure and of the functions of glands and especially of the ductless glands. But the point is that these glands, as a rule, are influenced almost exclusively through chemical ingredients consumed principally in the forms of food and drink (it is evident that surgical or medical modification of glands did not play any rôle in the past, and even now they are quite insignificant means applying only to a very few individuals). This explains why a great many geographers, even before the discovery of the rôle of glands, pointed out that food was the most efficient geographical agency in the modification of physical and mental traits of a racial group.[63] I do not object to many facts of this kind, but nevertheless serious reservations must be made against their use as arguments in favor of the geographical hypothesis.[64]

In the first place, not all kinds of food may be important in

---

Royal Anthropological Institute, pp. 37–42, Vol. XLVI, 1916; PEARSON, K. and TIPPETT, L. H. C., "On Stability of the Cephalic Indices Within the Race," Biometrika, pp. 118–138, Vol. XVI, 1924. C. Gini indicated several shortcomings in the statistical method used by F. Boas. General conclusions of the critics are typically represented by the following statement of Pearson and Tippett: "Dealing with a large amount of data, we are unable to find any change of real significance in the cephalic indices for school children from 5 to 20 years old. The cephalic index is remarkably stable. Having regard to the fact that extraordinary environmental differences in this country appear to make no significant change in the shape of the head, it is very difficult to accept Professor Boas' view that the child born to Jewish parents in Europe differs in head shape from the child born to the same parents after their arrival in America. The cephalic index of the Jews is much the same in the most diverse environment in Europe, and we do not believe that anything but hybridization or long selective action, can change the type."

[62] See his works already cited. However, he strongly stresses the relative unchangeableness of racial traits.

[63] See e.g., Buckle's discussion of the problem, op. cit., Chap. II, passim; SEMPLE, E., op. cit., Chap. II.

[64] See a further chapter about food as a social factor. See also the quoted book of Armitage, though he exaggerates the effects of food upon race.

this respect. Only food and drink which are lacking in definite types of vitamines or contain definite ingredients may exert noticeable effects on glands and through these on the anatomical and physiological characteristics of the population. Such deficient food is either a rare phenomenon (because the ordinary diet of different peoples generally contains all the necessary ingredients) or it is almost equally common among different racial groups and for this reason, with few exceptions, cannot account for their bodily and other differences.

In the second place, what is more important, the geographers put food and drink among geographic agencies as though the food and drink (alcohol, wine, beer, etc.) are entirely determined for every society by its geographical conditions. We have seen that even for a relatively primitive society such a correlation between its geographic conditions and the character of its food is far from being definite and rigid. In regard to more advanced and complex societies this correlation is so insignificant that there is almost no serious reason for such a claim. What and how much society eats and drinks is determined not only and, in many cases, not so much by the geographic, as by other factors. Therefore, to include all the effects of the quantity and the quality of food and drink on the population as the effects of geographic conditions is fallacious. We must discount a great many cases of such modifications of bodily traits through the agency of food as arguments for geographic conditioning. If this is done, very few of the modifications due to food may be classed as geographic factors. For the same reason Keith's gland theory of the modification of races cannot be used as corroborative evidence of the geographic theory of race determination.

In the fourth place the geographic theory of race determination is far from being corroborated by factual observation. If its claim of rigid correlation between the kind of geographic environment and the character of races were true, we should expect the existence of correlations between stature, pigmentation, cephalic and nasal indices and so on, on the one hand, and definite geographic conditions, on the other. Corresponding studies and measurements do not fulfill this expectation. For instance, the studies of Mendès-Côrrea, D. N. Anoutchin, B. A. Gould, Brocà,

Boudin, P. Topinard, R. Livi, J. Bertillon, G. Retzius, J. H. Baxter, Ch. B. Davenport, A. G. Love, and of several others did not find any correlation even between stature (a trait which is much more dependent upon environment and especially upon food than many real racial characteristics) and geographic environment or latitude, or altitude, or longitude, or geological conditions, or flora and fauna, or even the character of food and of other geographical conditions of society.[65]

The same is true in regard to the character and the length of the feet and arms, the pigmentation, dolichocephaly and brachycephaly, and the color of hair and eyes and body. The attempts to correlate these characteristics with a definite geographical environment or its components have not yielded any positive results. "Thus it is not sufficient to talk of environment in explanation of evolution: it is necessary also to take into consideration inner conditions of equilibrium of an organism and organic correlations." [66] Such results are unfavorable for the validity of the geographic theories. The geographers, however, may object that migrations and race-blending naturally led to a disappearance of

[65] See GOULD, B. A., *Investigations in the Military and Anthropologic Statistics of American Soldiers*, pp. 131–132, N. Y., 1869; MENDÈS-CÔRREA, A. A., "Le milieu geographique et la race," *Scientia*, 1921, 30: 371–80; see his data and references; see also MITCHELL, P., *Le Darwinisme et la guerre*, Paris, 1916, pp. 67 ff.; "it is impossible to establish a correlation between pigmentation of hair and eyes and an environmental factor of any kind," p. 69; ANOUTCHIN, D. N., *Geographical Distribution of the Stature of the Male Population of Russia* (in Russia), St. Petersburg, 1889, RETZIUS, G., and FÜRST, C. M., *Anthropologia, suecica*, p. 60, Stockholm, 1902; LIVI, R., *Antropometria militare*, Vol. I., pp. 48–49, Roma, 1896; BROCÀ, "Récherches sur l'ethnologie de la France," *Mémoirs de la Societé d' Anthropologie de Paris*, 1866. As a matter of fact not a single large anthropometric measurement of the population of various countries has discovered the discussed correlation or has accounted for the distribution of various physical traits in the population through geographic conditions. The same is true of the recent measurement of the American Army. See *Army Anthropology* by CHARLES B. DAVENPORT and A. G. LOVE, Washington, 1921, *passim*.

[66] *Ibid.*, p. 380. "There is almost no reason to suppose that the cephalic index is under a direct influence of an environment, it appears to be a hereditary character of a race," concludes such a prominent zoölogist as P. Ch. Mitchell. See his *Le Darwinisme et la guerre*, pp. 67 ff. Not convincing is also a recent attempt to correlate man's nasal index with climatic conditions. The nasal indices of various races which for thousands of years dwell in the same climate remain different and the nasal index of the same race whose members dwell in different climates remain essentially the same. These facts make the correlation very questionable. *Vide* THOMSON, A. and BUXTON, D., "Man's Nasal Index in Relation to Certain Climatic Conditions," *Journal of the Royal Anthropological Institute*, Vol. LIII, 1923.

the correlations between geographic conditions and racial characteristics of a population at the present time.   Through migrations
and blending, racial groups with definite characteristics, shaped
by their geographic environment in the past, have been dispersed
throughout the most different areas and naturally do not exhibit
any correlations.   Unfortunately for the geographers, such correlations are difficult to establish even for the past.   Whatever
may be the basis of the race classification, one fact seems to be
certain; each racial type from "immemorial times" happens to
have been dispersed and living in the most different areas.   If
for instance we take the eight fundamental racial types, according
to the classification of Professor Dixon, each of these types
seems to have been distributed in the south and the north, among
the most different geographic conditions.[67]   In other words, we
cannot find, even in the past, a period in which we would certainly have had a principal racial type confined within a definite
uniform geographic environment.   This means that even for the
past such correlation between geographic conditions and a definite
racial type seems not to have been found.[68]   This makes the
validity of the theory still less convincing.   Finally, we do not
have any single case in which we have observed a change of racial
characteristics under a different environment.   The Nordic whites
have been living in tropical regions for generations, and still
remain white in spite of the different climate.   They do not show
any sign of transformation in the direction of the black races.
"We can observe no difference in skin color between the American negro and his kinsman in Africa; the one is as black as the

[67] See DIXON, op. cit., passim, and chapter, "General Conclusions," pp. 475 ff.
Instead of Dixon's classification we may take others, and the wide geographic
dispersion of all the principal types remains the same.   See for instance, HADDON,
A. C., The Races of Man; SERGI, G., Hominidae, 1911; DENIKER, J., The Races of
Man, 1900.
[68] There are plenty of guesses concerning the place of origin of many racial
types and from which they spread.   But these hypotheses are mere guesses; they
are contradictory; they also show that each type has lived in the most different
areas and remained unchanged, in spite of quite different geographical conditions
(contrariwise it would have been impossible to say that the Proto-Negroid type
inhabited Europe if the skulls and skeletons found there were changed); finally,
the theories which admit hypothetically a modification of a type under the influence of different environments (e.g., depigmentation of black race in the region
of Baltic sea) are mostly guesses and require time computed by "millennia."
See DIXON, op. cit., pp. 479 ff.

other, although the American negro is no longer living in tropics." [69]   All we have are changes of some non-hereditary or non-racial traits.   Such changes may take place under the direct influence of geographic environment, but they have nothing to do with a direct change of racial characteristics.

The above seems to be sufficient to show that the claims of the geographers are greatly exaggerated; that in regard to a change of real racial characteristics under the direct influence of geographic environment, their theory is very questionable as yet and not proved.

All that remains as relatively valid from these theories is as follows: First, some somatic and physiological characteristics of a population which are not hereditary may be changed under different geographic conditions.   Second, in the course of millennia racial traits may be changed through geographic factors, but this is not yet proved, and if it were proved, it can help very little in deciphering the great changes in the biologic composition of the population which have taken place in the historical eras and much shorter periods of time.   Third, many somatic changes, due to environmental agencies, cannot be ascribed to geographical agencies, but should be ascribed rather to other than geographic factors.   Fourth, geographic agencies seem to be able to influence the racial composition of the population only indirectly through natural selection.   After they are changed, these conditions may facilitate survival of one type of human beings and be favorable to increased mortality of another type.[70]   In this indirect way, working through the medium of selection, geographic factors seem to be efficient.   But even in this indirect way, in view of the fact that social environment is more effective in many cases, the efficiency of geographic factors working through selection may be easily overestimated.

10. GEOGRAPHICAL CONDITIONS AND HEALTH

In the preceding paragraphs I touched the phenomena whose dependence on geographical conditions is relatively the most conspicuous.   I have not denied this dependence but have shown

[69] DIXON, *op. cit.*, p. 480.
[70] See the chapter, "Anthropo-Racial and Selectionist School."

that the correlation is very loose and very relative and tends to be obliterated in proceeding from the less to the more complex forms of society. Let us now turn to the more complex phenomena of human health, energy, behavior and psychology. In this field we have hundreds of geographical theories which attempt to prove the rigid dependence on geographical factors. Hundreds of pages would be necessary to outline and to scrutinize the thousands of "correlations" which have been formulated in this field. As a lack of space does not permit such a task, I shall proceed in a different way: I shall analyze the most elaborated "geographical theories" in this field and shall try to show to what extent they are valid. The results of such an analysis, with still greater reason, may be applied to all less elaborated "geographical generalizations." As a starting point for such an analysis I shall take the works of Professor E. Huntington (1876–   ), which are some of the best in this field. If his principal ideas are very old, his corroborations and discussions are new and more inductive and factual than those of many of his predecessors. The analysis of these works, by the way, will give us an opportunity to mention and to discuss the results of many other studies in the field covered by Huntington. In his principal sociological works: *Civilization and Climate, World Power and Evolution* and *The Character of Races,* Dr. Huntington has tried to show that climate is one of the most important factors influencing civilization. He tries to prove this by establishing a series of correlations between climate and health; between climate and energy and the efficiency of labor; between climate and mental processes as: intelligence, genius, and willpower; and, finally between climate and the character, growth, and decay of civilizations. In order to determine to what extent his fundamental idea of the conditioning of civilization by climate is true, we must, at least very briefly, scrutinize the validity of his minor correlations between climate and health, energy and other mental processes.

Climate and Health.—It is a very old idea that climate influences human health. In its essence the validity of the idea can scarcely be denied, especially in regard to extreme climates. But in this general form it is vague and meaningless. To become more definite the theory must answer, at least, the following questions: Does climate influence human health through temperature, or through humidity, or through variability or through some other elements? What is the optimum point of climate for the most favorable human health in all respects? Is such an optimum point the same for all human beings or does it vary from man to man, and from group to group?

Long before the work of Huntington a series of works were published which tried to answer these questions on the bases of statistical and experimental investigations.[71] Some of these authors have tried even to formulate some general laws. In regard to the death rate, which Huntington takes as the index of health, Moser formulated three "laws" nearly a century ago: first, monthly curves of the death rate and temperature go together, the average and extreme points of both phenomena paralleling each other; second, the lower average temperatures are accompanied by the higher death rates, and *vice versa;* third, a rise of temperature above normal in the winter reduces, and in the summer, increases the death rate while a decrease of temperature below normal in winter and in summer has correspondingly opposite results.[72] Huntington does not add any substantially new ideas to those of his predecessors except that he supplies new data for the corroboration of the climatic influences on health, and attempts to point out the most favorable ("the ideal") climate for all human beings at all times. This "ideal climate" is that with an average temperature of about 64° F., of about 80° humidity and a relatively variable one.[73] In this respect he follows (in regard to temperature) the theory of Dexter.[74] In regard to the statistical data, supplied by Huntington, one must

[71] See, *e.g.*, MOSER, L., *Die Gesetze der Lebensdauer*, Berlin, 1839; CASPER, J. L., "Der Einfluss der Witterung auf Gesundheit und Leben des Menschen" in *Denkwürdigkeite zur medizinische Statistik*, Berlin, 1846; GISI, W., *Die Bevölkerungsstatistik der Schweiz. Eidgen*, Aarau, 1868; and FORRY, *The Climate of the U. S. and its Endemic Influences*, N. Y., 1842. See further the well-known works in the statistics of population of G. von Mayr, É. Levasseur, J. E. Wappäus, H. Westergaard, Oettingen, A. Newsholme and others where the fluctuations of death, birth, and marriage rates according to seasons and temperature are discussed and analyzed. See also their references.

[72] MOSER, *op. cit.*, pp. 242 ff.

[73] See *World Power*, pp. 71 ff., 85, 98–99; *Civilization and Climate*, pp. 14–15.

[74] See DEXTER, *Weather Influences*, p. 75, N. Y., 1904.

confess that they compose an impressive series of figures and curves which appear very convincing. And yet, a more detailed analysis of the data makes them much less conclusive. I would have to go too far astray from my purpose, if I were to scrutinize them one by one in detail. Instead of this I can only briefly indicate the principal objections to the conclusive validity of Huntington's results.

A. In the first place, although the death rate is one of the important criteria of health, it by no means is unique and adequate, especially when it is applied to countries of a different character. For instance, Huntington, without hesitation, on the bases of different mortality rates of different countries, concludes that countries like Russia or Serbia have poorer health than many European countries.[75]   Meanwhile the question is much more complex.   Countries with high birth rates, as a general rule, have a high death rate and those with low birth rates have low death rates.[76]   High birth rate is a criterion of the vitality of a people no less important than the death rate.[77]   Historical examples like Rome and Greece with their low birth rate at the period of decline, testify that a low birth rate is likely to be a symptom of the decreasing vitality of a people. Therefore, the countries, which from the standpoint of death rate are very healthy, from the standpoint of their birth rate may occupy an opposite rank.   In the second place, studies of death rates of different age groups in the countries with low mortality rates like England, Germany, and France, and in the countries with high mortality rates like Russia, Hungary, and Bulgaria or Serbia, have shown that the age groups above 30 and 32 years in the

[75] See HUNTINGTON, *The Character of Races*, pp. 231 ff., Fig. no. 13, N. Y. 1924.

[76] See recent figures in YULE, H. U., "The Growth of Population," *Journal of the Royal Statistical Society*, 1925, pp. 31–33. The correlation between both rates is + .81, 1901–10, for 22 countries; between their fluctuations, + .70 or + .75.

[77] For this reason it is comprehensible why the most prominent statisticians use different formulas for measuring the "vitality" of people. The principal of them are: $D/\sqrt{B}$ (Sundbärg); (D = death; B = birth); B/D (Brown, Wernicke); $\frac{100\ B}{D}$ (R. Pearl, J. S. Sweeney); and D^2/B (Rubin). Though even these formulas are far from being an adequate "vital index," they undoubtedly are better than Huntington's criterion. See RUBIN, M., "A Measure of Civilization," *Journal of the Royal Statistical Society*, Vol. LX, 1897; PEARL, R., "The Vitality of the People of America," *American Journal of Hygiene*, 1921; SWEENEY, J. S., *The Natural Increase of Mankind*, Chap. I, Baltimore, 1926.

countries with high mortality rates have mortality rates lower than the same age groups in England, in spite of the more hygienic conditions in this last country.[78]   This means, that even according to Huntington's own criterion, these more mature age groups in the countries with high mortality rates (due principally to an abundant proportion of children) must be recognized as healthier than the same age groups in the countries with low death rates (due principally to a low birth rate and therefore to a low child mortality).   This also means that if we take as a criterion of health the death rate of the younger age groups, the different countries will rank one way; and if we take the death rates of the age groups above thirty years, their ranks will be quite different, if not opposite.   In the third place, though the mortality rate of Russia is much higher than that of Germany or France, yet its population, on the basis of recent statistics, (before the Revolution) was proved to be better and healthier than the population of practically all other European countries with much lower mortality: in the years from 1890 to 1894, out of 772,000 Russian recruits only 1.8 per cent were entirely unsuitable while in Germany this per cent was 6.2; in Russia the proportion of suitable recruits was 35 per cent higher than in Germany and in the majority of other European countries, though the Russian requirements in regard to health were somewhat higher than in those other European countries.[79]   This shows again how inadequate a criterion of health is the general death rate.   Its inadequacy becomes still greater if we take into consideration that in Germany (and the same phenomenon has been

[78] See SCHALLMAYER, W., "Eugenik, Lebenshaltung und Auslèse," *Zeitschrif für Sozialwissenschaft*, Bd. XI, Hefts 5–8, 1908; PRINZING, FR., "Kulturelle Entwicklung und Absterbeordnung," *Archiv für Rassen und Gesellschafts Biologie*, Bd. 7, 1910, pp. 579–605; RÜDIN, E., *Uber Zusammenhang zwischen Geisteskrankheit und Kultur, ibid.*, pp. 722–748.   See also MACDONEL, W. R., "On the Expectation of Life in Ancient Rome," etc., *Biometrika*, Vol. IX, 1913.

[79] See SCHALLMAYER, *op. cit.;* CLAASSEN, W., "Die Abnehmende Kriegstüchtigkeit," etc., *Archiv für Rassen und Gesellschaft Biologie*, Vol. VI, 1909, pp. 73–77; CLAASSEN, W., "Die Einfluss von Fruchtbarkeit," etc., *ibid.*, pp. 482–492; see also his other paper, *ibid.*, pp. 129–132.   The reason for this phenomenon is that, due to the high death rate among the children, all weaklings are eliminated in Russia and only strong people survive to the age of 21 and above, while in countries with a low birth rate and a low mortality a much greater per cent of the weaklings survive.   This explains the lower death rate of the age groups above 30 years in the less civilized countries.

shown in other European countries), between the end of the nine-teenth century and the time of the World War the death rate was declining while the per cent of biologically defective people among the population and recruits was rather increasing.[80]   A series of similar facts could be given, but the above show how condi-tional and relative and inadequate is the criterion of health chosen by Huntington.[81]   For these reasons, at the very best, Hunting-ton's data show only the dependence of the death rate, and not that of health, on climate.

B. Furthermore, many of Huntington's data on the fluctuation of the death rate concern not the aggregate death rate but that from influenza and pneumonia.[82]   It is evident that deaths from influenza and pneumonia are more dependent on the weather than other forms of death; therefore it is rather fallacious to make the movement of the death rate from pneumonia typical for that of the aggregate death rate.[83]

C. Furthermore Huntington treats the seasonal and yearly movement of the death rate rather roughly: [84] If there appears even a remote parallelism between the fluctuations of the death rate and temperature or humidity, he contends that the fluctua-tion of the death rate is the result of that of climate.   However we know how doubtful such a method is.   E. Durkheim in his analysis of the factors of suicide has shown convincingly how un-reliable such conclusions are even in the field where the parallel-ism between the fluctuations of climate and suicide is much more

[80] See the figures in the papers of Claassen, Schallmayer, and Prinzing. Also see, for England, *Report Upon the Physical Examination of Men of Military Age by National Service Medical Boards*, London, Febr., 1920.   In France this phe-nomenon is still more conspicuous.

[81] Later on we shall see how this inadequate health criterion of Huntington makes many of his theories questionable.   Among them his attempt to explain the differences in death rates of different countries through the influence of climate is especially fallacious. See his *The Character of Races*, Figs. 12 and 13, pp. 231 ff.

[82] See HUNTINGTON, *Civilization and Climate*, Chaps. VIII and IX, New Haven, 1924.

[83] The movement of deaths from influenza, pneumonia, and tuberculosis is not identical with the monthly movement of all causes. See WHIPPLE, G. CH., *Vital Statistics*, N. Y., 1923, Tables 58, 86, 92, 96, Fig. 72, and others; *Public Health Reports*, Vol. XXXVI, pp. 1498–1501.

[84] In this respect I agree with Dr. Hexter who says that "he doubts Dr. Hunt-ington's method.   Dr. Huntington has utilized the graphic method of comparison. This method is liable to lead to false conclusions." HEXTER, M. B., *Social Consequences of Business Cycles*, p. 169, 1925.

striking.[85]   A. Binet found that the appetite of pupils (in form of the amount of bread consumed) varied "seasonally."   If he had followed Huntington's method, he would have accounted for the fluctuation through climatic factors.   Fortunately Binet does not follow this "rough" method, and in the process of analysis he shows that the responsible factor is not climate but intellectual school work.[86]   For serious reasons we may question the validity of the causal connection between many curves of the death rate and climatic factors which Huntington attempts by his "rough" method.   The fact that both curves in selected cases are parallel to some extent is not sufficient to prove their interrelations are causally or functionally connected.   This is somewhat corroborated by the data of Huntington himself.   In the first place, several of his curves intended to show the parallelism (positive or negative) of fluctuations of the death rate and climate causes (*e.g.,* Figure 7, p. 62, in *World Power and Climate*), show such a "loose parallelism" that only by considerable leniency is it possible to say that the curves prove anything.

D. At the basis of Huntington's theory lies the questionable presumption that short-time fluctuations of the death rate ("seasonal fluctuations") are due to climatic—"seasonal"—factors. As I indicated above, such a presumption is not necessarily correct.   Only when these "seasonal" fluctuations parallel climatic fluctuations, from year to year; when they rise or fall uniformly with uniform fluctuations of temperature; and when identical temperature movements at various times and in various countries are followed by identical movements of the death rate; only then is it possible to account for such "seasonal" fluctuations of the death rate through meteorological factors.   When such characteristics are absent we have no reason to suppose that the meteorological factors are responsible for such "seasonal" fluctuations. Meanwhile the data concerning the "seasonal" fluctuations of the death rate do not show the above characteristics.   All they show is the existence of short-time fluctuations whose factors are to

---

[85] See the classical criticism of such procedures in DURKHEIM, E., *Le suicide,* Chap. III, *passim,* Paris, 1912.   See further his discussion of the correlation between suicide and geographical factors.

[86] BINET, A., "Consommation du pain," *L'année psychologique,* 1897, Vol. IV, pp. 337–355.

be yet explained. The meteorological factors alone can account for very little of these fluctuations. Take, for instance, the months of the maximum death rate within a year or a series of years. In the same area they are different according to the various authors, and different in different years, and fall at quite different seasons with different meteorological conditions. For instance, according to Huntington, such months for Massachusetts are February or March; but according to Dr. Hexter, they are December and March.[87] According to Professor Whipple, in New York in 1910, the maximum months were March, April, and July; but in 1920, February and March.[88]   According to Dr. Falk, for the registration area of the United States in 1919 the maximum month was January.[89] This irregularity of the months of maximum death rate only suggests that the death rate fluctuates within a year, but it does not permit us to conclude that the fluctuation is "seasonal" and due to "meteorological factors." This suggestion is further corroborated by the data for "seasonal" fluctuations of the death rates in various countries. If these fluctuations were due to meteorological conditions we should expect that the months of a maximum death rate in the countries with a similar climate would be the same or nearly so; while in the countries with quite different climates they would be considerably different. Is such an expectation corroborated by the data? I am afraid it is not. For instance, the month of maximum death rate in the years from 1889-93 was January in Belgium, Prussia, Wurtemberg, Austria, Sweden, Buenos Aires and Scotland. Note the same month in countries with quite different climatic conditions. On the other hand, in European Russia it was August, in France, March; in Bavaria, March; in Italy, February; in Saxony, August; in Bulgaria, December; in Uruguay, December; and in Serbia, March. Note again the difference in the month of maximum deaths between Serbia and Bulgaria, or Bavaria and Saxony whose geographic conditions are far more similar than, for example, the conditions of Sweden and Buenos Aires. These data appear to marshal against the meteorological theory. The same characteristics are shown by the months of minimum death

[87] See HEXTER, M. B., *Social Consequences of Business Cycles.* pp. 55 ff., 1925.
[88] WHIPPLE, G. CH., *Vital Statistics*, Tables 58, 86, 1923.
[89] FALK, I. S., *Principles of Vital Statistics*, p. 183, 1923.

rate in these countries. June was such a month for Italy, Bulgaria and Massachusetts; July, for France, Rumania and Serbia; September, for Austria, Scotland, Norway, Sweden and Finland; October, for Belgium, Prussia, Bavaria, Wurtemberg, European Russia, Denmark, and Buenos Aires; November, for Saxony; May, for Rhode Island and Uruguay.[90] This shows that the month of the minimum death rate, e.g., October, was the same for countries with the most different climate; and vice versa, countries with a somewhat similar climate had different months of minimum death rate. That is not all, however. The monthly death rates in different years for the same country show that the curves are different from year to year, and the months of maximum, as well as of minimum death rate, shift: one year such a month is January, another, February or March, or July or December.[91] Such shifting is difficult to account for through climatic factors. It indicates that the "seasonal" fluctuation is very irregular and possibly many other factors must be considered. Further, if climate were such a decisive factor in the "seasonal" fluctuation of the death rate we should expect that the death rate of the months which are similar in climate would be somewhat similar, while the months with quite different climatic conditions would be different. The figures, however, do not fully corroborate this expectation. It is certain that the climate of August and December in Italy differs more than November and December, and yet the death rates of August and December are almost identical while those of November and December differ considerably. The death rate in December and April in Wurtemberg is almost the same (1058 and 1056) in spite of a great contrast in climate, while the death rates in December and November and December and January are considerably different (1058 for December, 902 for November, and 1141 for January), though climatic conditions of these months are more similar than those of December and April.[92] The statistics of the "seasonal" fluctuation of the

[90] See VON MAYR, Statistik und Gesselschaftslehre, Vol. II, p. 212, Freiburg, 1897.
[91] Compare, e.g., "Seasonal Distribution of Mortality in Massachusetts for 1910 and 1920," in WHIPPLE, op. cit., pp. 266 and 358; they show a very considerable difference. The same is true of almost any other country.
[92] VON MAYR, op. cit., p. 212. For Massachusetts, in 1910 the death rates in July, April, February and January are practically equal, while those of August and September (103 and 98) or April and May (107 and 97) differ greatly in

death rate in every country show these "miraculous" fluctuations:
evidently they do not agree with the climatic hypothesis. One
more fact is to be noted: The "seasonal" fluctuations of the death
rate show that their "seasonal" curves are different for different
age groups: from 0 to 1 year, from 10 to 20, from 30 to 40, and
so on. Each of the age groups of the same population has its own
months of maximum and of minimum death rate.[93] Further,
there are also conspicuous differences in the "seasonal" death
curve for different occupational, economic, sex, even religious
classes. These differences suggest still stronger that the so-called
"seasonal" fluctuation of the death rate is not "seasonal" at all in
the sense that it is conditioned by seasonal climate, but that it is
only an irregular fluctuation in time whose factors remain as yet
to be found. This brief discussion is enough to show that Dr.
Huntington simplifies the situation too much; that his hypothesis
cannot account for much of the real character of these "seasonal"
fluctuations; and that from these irregular fluctuations he infers
too rashly that climatic agencies are the most responsible factors.[94]

E. Huntington further says that in regard to health "humidity
is of great importance" (*World Power*, p. 84). However, the
studies, statistical and experimental, of numerous other authors,[95]

---

spite of more similar weather in these months than in July, January and April.
See WHIPPLE, Table 36.

[93] See the figures for the age groups of Hessen, Oldenburg, Lubeck, Baden
and Berlin in VON MAYR, *op. cit.*, p. 213.

[94] There is no need to say that if these "seasonal" fluctuations cannot be
accounted for through climatic factors, still less can they account for the trends
in the curve of the death rate, *e.g.*, a decrease of death rate in the Western countries during the last three decades; nor for the differences in the death rate
among different societies (*e.g.*, why Slavic countries as Russia, Serbia, and
Bulgaria, have a death rate higher than a great many Western countries); nor
for the sudden extraordinary changes of the death rate in the same society (*e.g.*,
a three- or four-fold increase in the death rate of Russia in the years of 1919–
1921); nor for a difference in the death rate of various occupational, economic,
religious, national, and other social groups which live in the same place and
under the same climatic conditions. Since any climatic explanation of these
substantial facts of the death rate is impossible, and since even the seasonal
fluctuations cannot be entirely accounted for through climatic factors, we must
conclude that Dr. Huntington has overestimated their importance and that his
correlations to that extent are questionable.

[95] See *e.g.*, STECHER, L. IDA, *The Effects of Humidity on Nervousness and General
Efficiency*, N. Y., The Science Press, 1916. See the description of other experiments in this volume. The experimental investigations of the New York State
Ventilation Commission did not find any noticeable effects of humidity upon
health; similar results came from the careful study of the Committee on the

either did not find any noticeable effects of humidity on health or on the death rate, or to the contrary, found the opposite effects from those of Huntington. For these reasons the conclusions of Huntington remain, at the best, inconclusive.

F. If we take the results of what Huntington styles "a most conclusive study of the general effects of the weather upon health," they exhibit rather an embarrassing "correlation." The author took the monthly deaths from 1900 to 1915 inclusive in thirty-three cities of the United States with a population of over 100,000. These same sixteen months were divided into two groups according to their temperature: the eight warmest and the eight coldest, and the difference in the death rates of these two groups was computed. The results are as follows:

The eight warmest Januaries in New York averaged 6.0° F. warmer than eight coldest, and had fewer deaths by 0.6 per cent. In February the excess of temperature in the eight warmest months amounted to 6.5° and their death rate was 4.1 per cent less than that of the cooler months. In March the corresponding figures were 6.4° and 9.7 per cent; in April 3.8° and 4.5 per cent; in May, on the contrary, an excess of 3.5° in temperature was accompanied by a death rate 1.5 per cent greater in the warm months than in the cool months, while in July, although the eight warm months averaged only 2.8° above the eight cooler months the excess in their death rate rose to 14.2 per cent.[96]

I am inclined to think that these data prove either too much or too little; on the one hand it is too much to have an increase of the death rate by 30 or 14.2 per cent on account of differences in

---

Atmosphere and Man of the National Research Council of the U. S., and of the Metropolitan and the New York Life Insurance Companies. The results of those investigations which found some effects (Greenberg, Besson, Huntington, W. E. Watt, Goldsbury, P. W. and H. M. Smith) either concern a specific form of death from diseases of the respiratory organs where the correlation is likely to exist, or are discordant and often contradictory to each other. See HUNTINGTON, *Civilization and Climate*, Chaps. VIII and IX; BESSON, L., "Relations entre les elements meteorologique et la mortalité," *Annales des services techniques d'hygiene de la Ville de Paris*, 1921; WATT, W. E., *Open Air*, Chicago, 1910; GOLDSBURY, P. W., "Humidity and Health," *Boston Medical and Surgical Journal*, September, 1911.

[96] *Civilization and Climate*, p. 205. In *World Power* Huntington gives more detailed data for the months of March and July from which it follows that "a difference of 7° F. in the average temperature of July is accompanied by a difference of nearly 30 per cent in the number of deaths." *World Power*, pp. 60–61.

temperature of 7° F. or 2.8° F.; on the other hand it is too little that in some months (Januaries) the difference of 6° F. produced only 0.6 per cent difference in the death rate. It appears to one who is not a specialist in mathematical methods that these inconsistencies reduce the significance of the correlation. This conclusion is still further corroborated by the fact that in some cities storms, or a rise of temperature in the winter, were found to be beneficial for health, while in other cities (Chicago, Denver, Pittsburgh) this effect is absent; that some cities like New York are "unusually regular in their responses to the weather" while in other cities, like Cleveland and San Francisco, "departures from the normal (climate) produce relatively little effects." [97]   Add to this the fact that all these data are not absolute but are "departures in percentages from the normals," and that "the normals are the estimated numbers of deaths that each place would have experienced per month in any given year if the number of deaths changed regularly in response to the growth of the city and the improvements in medical practice"; further, the great difficulty in making such estimates objectively (the author does not say how he measured "the growth of the city and improvements in medical practice") and the inevitableness of some degree of subjectivity in such complex estimations; add finally that the data were smoothed; when all this is considered the significance of the data appear quite doubtful.   If they prove anything it is only that the death rate varies at different rates in different months and in different cities and that very much of the causes of such fluctuations yet remains to be found.   These objections are made on the bases of the data given in the book.   If now we make a comparison in space and time of the death-rate variation of different places and times and seasons, we may easily see that the results are very discordant and contradictory.   It is not possible to say that everywhere and for all time the death rate is the lowest in the climate with a temperature of about 64° F., and with a considerable but not an excessive humidity, as Huntington believes he has established.[98]   I believe that Dr. Huntington has overestimated the significance of his results.

[97] *Civilization and Climate*, pp. 205 ff.
[98] Even the data on death rates in different seasons given by Huntington show that the maximum death rate in New York City falls not in the month whose

These brief remarks show that the greatest certainty in regard to the influence of climate upon death rate is that excessive temperature, or humidity or storms are likely to be harmful to health and to increase the death rate. But the space between the two excessive points too warm or cold, too dry or humid, and so on, is large, and the limits of excess seem to be different for different peoples; besides, these factors may be neutralized by the interference of different social factors. For these reasons, even in regard to an excessive climate, there is a great deal of uncertainty.[99] The attempts to prove a very much closer correlation within the excessive limits between variations of climatic agencies and the death rate, in spite of the abundant material of Dr. E. Huntington, are inconclusive, not to mention the fact that death rates are inadequate criteria of health. Let us now pass to the second fundamental correlation which Huntington tries to establish.

II. CLIMATE AND HUMAN ENERGY AND EFFICIENCY

The next fundamental correlation which Huntington attempts to prove is that climatic agencies such as temperature, storminess, humidity, and light have a strong influence on human energy and

---

average temperature deviates the greatest degree from 64° F. as is the case for December, November, January and February, but in other months (July); on the other hand, the minimum death rate is not in June or August, whose average temperature is the nearest to 64° F., but in November and October. Verification of the theory of "the ideal climate" by the data of death rates of different countries in different seasons does not furnish corroboration of the theory of Huntington. The fact remains that the death rate is not lowest in the months nearest this "ideal climate" and is not the highest in the months which differ most from this "ideal climate." Furthermore, the people do not seem to choose their habitation in an agreement with the ideal climate of Huntington. The table of the density of population in the United States, according to the zones of average temperature, shows that the most densely populated zones have an average temperature from 45° to 55° F.; the next place belongs to the zone with the temperature between 55° to 60° F.; only third place is given to the zone with a temperature from 60° to 65°, which being the nearest to the ideal temperature of Huntington, ought to be inhabited the most densely. See the table on page 108.

[99] Professor R. Ward quite correctly stresses the complex and therefore indefinite character of the influences of climate upon health. Numerous "studies (in this field) have often led to very contradictory conclusions. Rules, previously determined as the result of careful investigation, often break down in a most perplexing way." He also stresses the fact that many alleged effects of climate on health are in fact due to factors other than climate. See WARD, R., *op. cit.*, Chap. VII.

efficiency. He finds the best outside temperature for efficient physical work is about 64° F. (about 70° at midday, and 55° at night); for mental work it is about 38° or 40° F.; and that humidity also influences the efficiency of work, excessive dryness or dampness being harmful while a relative humidity of about 80 per cent is a facilitating condition. Changes in climate (storms, wind, temperature, and so on), when they are not too great, are favorable; while too great changes or constant climatic conditions are unfavorable. Light alone seems not to have an important effect on efficiency. These are the principal conclusions obtained by Huntington,[100] and all are based on numerous data.[101] Let us glance at the validity of Huntington's correlations. His first argument is that the efficiency of the farmer of the southern part of the United States, measured by the amount of improved land and the value of farm products, is less than that of the farmers of the northern parts (*Civilization and Climate,* p. 38 ff.). The argument might be questioned; so many factors affect the amount of improved land or the value of farm products that it is rather strange how such a careful investigator as Dr. Huntington can even use such data as a proof of the effects of climate on efficiency. He has made a fundamental statistical fallacy in that he tried to solve a problem of multiple correlation by the use of inadequate methods of gross correlation. He has completely ignored many principles of economics which deal with the combinations of factors of production, of market price and valuations of real property. A second factor is the neglect of allowances for types of soil and drainage. Many of the farms in the southern states (comparison A) are swampy land and this affects the averages. A third neglected factor is that of rainfall. Rainfall in the southern states, with its consequent erosion of the lighter soils in the east as well as the heavier soils in the piedmont and mountain territories, forbids the clearing of land in a great many cases. If Professor Huntington knew the extreme difficulty of even securing straight roads under the enormous erosion of southern

[100] See *World Power,* pp. 71, 85 ff., 98–99, Chaps. V and VI; *Civilization and Climate,* pp. 14–15, Chap. VI, and *passim.*

[101] See also BUCKLE, H. T., *Introduction to the History of Civilization in England,* Chap. II. Buckle and his predecessors developed correlations similar to those of Huntington.

rains he would not cite the absence of cleared land as an evidence of the effect of climate upon the energy of southerners. A further factor is that of the type of farming connected with types (chemical) of soils. Much of the area in the eastern parts of the north furnish milk for the cities. The soil is heavy and possesses sufficient lime for pastures. Farmers can use it for grazing and at the same time it passes for cleared land under the census classification. In the eastern parts of the south much of the soil is acid and will not support the ordinary lime-requiring grasses. Neither is it needed for grazing. His comparison B is mainly between a portion of the great cornbelt and the forest regions of the Lake States, on the one hand, and the mountain and southern coastal plain states, on the other. Differences in climate and farming systems affect the need for farm improvements and building and machinery. To explain all these differences by the effects of climate on energy is liable to be extremely fallacious.[102] On page 39 Huntington gives figures which show that regardless of any climatic changes the value of the total farm property of the southerners has increased between 1900 and 1920 from 28 to 64 per cent in its per cent of the value of northern farms. Does this not refute the validity of the climatic factor in this case? Between 1900 and 1920 the average value of the southern negroes' farms increased almost twice (from 11 to 20 per cent), while that of the northern negroes' increased from 59 to 74 only. Will climate explain this? In this case I think that a plain real estate dealer may supply us with a more scientific explanation of these contrasts in the value of the southern and northern farms, and in their changes and fluctuations, than the hypothesis of Dr. Huntington.[103]

[102] For a verification of these statements I am indebted to Professor Carl Zimmerman.

[103] Using Huntington's method it is possible to claim that the southern climate is more favorable for efficiency because, in the periods from 1900 to 1920, the large cities situated along the line from Superior to Galveston show a greater per cent of growth of population the farther south the city. Mr. Frank Hayes kindly supplied me with data which show the following per cents of increase of population of these cities from 1900 to 1920: Superior and Duluth, 65 per cent; St. Paul and Minneapolis, 88 per cent; Des Moines, Iowa, 104 per cent; Kansas City, 145; Dallas and Fort Worth, 283; and Houston and Galveston, 123 per cent. Following Huntington's method it is possible to infer that the southern climate is more favorable to efficiency of work than the northern climate. It is not necessary to add that such an inference is as fallacious as those of Huntington.

Other corroborations given by the author in Chapters II and III of his book appear of no more validity to me. They are either statements based on quite incidental, fragmentary, and questionable observations or data which testify against the author's hypothesis (death rates in Panama and other cities, sexual licentiousness of white men with tropical natives, and so on). The data concerning the seasonal fluctuations, of efficiency of work of factory operatives and students, and so on, which Huntington gives in Chapters IV, V, and VI, of his *Civilization and Climate* have an incomparably greater scientific significance. However, even their significance is far from being convincing or conclusive. My principal reasons for this statement are as follows: In the first place, Huntington's "inductive" method is too "rough." He noticed that the efficiency of several hundred workers was low in December and January; that it rose from February to June; declined in July and August; and rose again and reached the maximum in October and November. On the basis of this fact he made a few dogmatic remarks that such fluctuations could not be caused by other than climatic factors,—and concludes that it must be entirely due to climatic agencies. (See Chap. IV.) Such a procedure is far from being inductive.[104] In the second place, looking at the curves from different years and different factories (Figures I and II, pp. 84, 93-94) I see only a remote parallelism between them, and in some cases there is even no parallelism at all (*e.g.,* curves G and H in Figure 8, p. 124). In the third place, Huntington's curves testify against his fundamental statement that the optimum point of temperature for physical work is about 64° F. His Figure I shows that the maximum of efficiency of the operatives for all years was in October and November when the temperature was between 40° and 55° F. but not in June or September when the average temperature was about 64° F. In the fourth place, Huntington mentions only a very few investigations of this kind. Meanwhile there exist considerable numbers of such studies, including, among them, several carried on

---

[104] As an example of this "correlation" we may take the figures on page 117 of his book. The difference in severity of heat between 1910 and 1912 is only two points (50 and 52); while the difference in deficiency of work is 50 points. I am afraid that such proofs prove too much.

with exclusive carefulness.[105]   Comparison of the results obtained by these studies with those of Huntington, shows: There is no uniformity in the influence of the seasons upon the efficiency of working people; in some industries and factories efficiency declines in the summer; and in others situated in similar climatic conditions, it increases.   For instance, the seasonal curve of an output in five tin plate factories, studied by Dr. Vernon, is opposite to Huntington; besides, the curves of each of the five factories are considerably dissimilar.[106]   The same is true in regard to other seasons.

It is rather fallacious to try to find a uniform influence of temperature or of seasons upon all workers, of all ages, of both sexes, and so on, as is done by Huntington.   Careful analyses of Bernays, Weber, Bienkowsky, Schmitz, Vernon, May, Smith, and the Industrial Fatigue Research Board, show that different categories of operatives in the same factory are reacting differently to climate.   In Bernay's study, for instance, the efficiency of work of the male operatives under 40 years of age declines in the spring, while that of the operatives above this age increases, though generally the differences between the efficiencies of different seasons are very slight.   In a similar way, the efficiencies of the male and female operatives, of the qualified and unqualified, single and married, urban and rural-born, are affected differently by spring.   The same is true in regard to other seasons.[107]   These works disclosed further the existence of a much more conspicuous and more regular fluctuation of efficiency of work within the hours of a working day, and within the days of a week.   To see in these, as well as in the "seasonal" fluctuations, the direct effects of climate, or to account for them principally through climatic

[105] See for instance, WEBER, MAX, "Zur Psychophysik der Industriellen Arbeit," *Archiv für Sozialwissenschaft*, Bd. 28; BERNAYS, MARIE, "Untersuchungen uber die Schwankungen der Arbeitsintensitat," etc., in *Schriften des Vereins für Sozialpolitik*, Bd. 135, Dritter Teil, Leipzig, 1912; BERNAYS, MARIE, "Gladbacher Spinnerei und Weberei" in the same *Schriften*, Bd. 133, Leipzig, 1910; SCHMITZ, WALTER, "Regelung der Arbeitszeit und Intensitat der Arbeit," in *Archiv für exacte Wirtschaftsforschung*, Bd. 3, Heft 2; *The Reports of Industrial Fatigue Board*, Nos. 1–22; WILSON, D. R., "On Some Recent Contributions to the Study of Industrial Fatigue," *Journal Royal Statistical Society*, July, 1923.

[106] See VERNON, "The Influence of Hours of Work and of Ventilation on Output in Tinplate Manufacture," *Industrial Fatigue Research Board*, Report No. 1.

[107] BERNAYS, "Gladbacher Spinnerei," pp. 397 ff.; see here figures and data. See also the above works of M. Weber and others.

agencies or to ignore the non-climatic factors is impossible. In the light of these results, the sweeping conclusions inferred by Huntington from his data, can pretend in no way to be conclusive. This conclusion is reinforced by the results of a series of experimental studies of the influence of different climatic factors upon several physiological processes and physical activities of man. The net result of these various studies is discordant and contradictory. For instance, the growth of weight of 1200 tubercular patients at Saranac Lake, given in *Civilization and Climate* (Figure 2a, curve A), is opposite to the seasonal curve of growth of weight of 130 boys in Copenhagen, studied by Malling-Hansen[108] and that of several thousand children in Boston; the results obtained by Dr. Winifred Hall and G. Stanley Hall, concerning the same question, differ somewhat from the results of both preceding studies.[109] Similar discordance came from the results of the studies of fluctuations of muscular strength in connection with the fluctuation of climatic agencies. Two experimental studies of Schuyten yielded results considerably different; [110] both of these results are different from Porter's and from those obtained by Lehman and Pedersen; [111] and then all are somewhat different (according to months) from the results yielded by the study of A. H. Peaks and L. L. Kuhnes.[112] Besides, in Peaks' study two groups of the children tested have shown seasonal fluctuations of strength not quite identical.[113] The experimental work of L. J. Stecher concerning the influence of humidity on various muscular performances yielded no definite results. "We find no evidence that average performance (of hand steadiness, aiming, tapping) are adversely affected by dryness." [114] Similarly no re-

[108] MALLING-HANSEN, *Perioden im Gewicht der Kinder und in der Sonnenwärme*, Copenhagen, 1886, Fragment III, A and B; PORTER, W. T., "The Seasonal Variations in the Growth of Boston School Children," *American Journal of Physiology*, May, 1920. Huntington gives figures not seeing that they decidedly contradict his curve of seasonal health. Compare *Civilization and Climate*, pp. 154 and 158.

[109] See PEAKS, ARCH. H., *Periodic Variations in Efficiency*, Baltimore, 1921, p. 7.

[110] See SCHUYTEN, M. C., "Über Wachstum der Muskelkraft bei Schulern während des Schuljahres," *Zeitschrift für Psychologie*, Bd. 23, p. 101 and *passim*.

[111] LEHMAN, A. and PEDERSEN, R. N., "Das Wetter und unsere Arbeit," *Archiv für gesamte Psychologie*, Bd. X, 1907, *passim*, and pp. 53–55.

[112] PEAKS, *op. cit.*, *passim* and pp. 32, 91; KUHNES, L. L., *Variations in Muscular Energy*, an unpublished thesis for Ph.D. at N. Y. University, 1915.

[113] See PEAKS, *op. cit.*, p. 32, Tables for A and B divisions

[114] STECHER, *op. cit.*, p. 43 and *passim*.

sults of temperature (68°, 75° and 85°) on strength were found in the experiments of the New York State Commission on Ventilation. The authors' theories as to the character of the effects of various climatic agencies are still more discordant. Besides, the studies show that the fluctuations of the strength of people of different ages and sex have a different and often an opposite character in the same season and under the influence of the same climatic change. Finally, when all these different curves of the fluctuation of strength in different months are confronted with the different curves of the fluctuation of efficiency of factory operatives in the same months, they are far from being parallel or coincident.

We shall not discuss the results of the studies of the fluctuations of respiration or the amount of hæmoglobin in the blood or of the growth in stature at different seasons. The results are of the same character as those of the fluctuations of strength and weight. Thus we must conclude that Huntington has not proved the case for "seasonal" curves of energy and that his theory of "the ideal climate" (for physical efficiency) is also questionable.

12. CLIMATE AND MENTAL EFFICIENCY

Let us now analyze the validity of the theories of Huntington and his predecessors concerning the influence of climatic agencies on mental work. The essence of Huntington's theory about this is that "mental work resembles physical but with interesting differences": the optimum outside temperature for mental work is about 39° F. instead of 64° F.; further, "when the temperature falls greatly, mental work seems to suffer more than physical, and declines as much as when there is no change. It receives a little stimulus from a slight warming of the air, but appears to be adversely affected when the air becomes warm rapidly" (*Civilization and Climate,* p. 142, also pp. 14-15).

The principal corroboration of this theory consists in the curve of mental efficiency based on the marks received by 240 students in mathematics at West Point in 1909-12; of 220 students in English at Annapolis in 1912-13; and of 1300 students in mathematics at Annapolis in 1907-13. The efficiency of typewriting of three children and a few data taken from some other investiga-

tions are also included. The proof of the theory consists in the
fact that the curves of efficiency of the students fluctuate with
seasons and in a somewhat similar manner: they rise from September to November, decline from November to December; rise
again from January or February to March or April, and then
decline again. (See Figures 3 and 8 in *Civilization and Climate,*
pp. 105, 124.) From these data and from the curve which shows
that the marks are the highest in the days with a temperature of
about 40° F., and some references to a few results obtained by
other authors, Huntington concludes that his theory is proved,
and besides, that physical and mental efficiency are of a similar
nature with the exception of the differences mentioned above.
This "proof" is far from convincing. Putting aside the question
as to the validity of his method of estimation of mental efficiency
on the basis of marks, especially when the marks are smoothed
and somewhat modified in different ways,—on the basis of the
data itself we are entitled to make the following preliminary criticisms. In the first place, the curves of seasonal efficiency of
manual and mental work given in his Figures 3 and 8 do not
permit the contention that seasonal fluctuations of both efficiencies
are parallel. Beginning with the temperature of 39° F., mental
efficiency begins to decrease while the physical efficiency increases
up to 60° and 65° F. There is little parallelism here. In the
second place, the efficiency curves of the work of the students and
of the three children, given in Figure 8 (curves 9 and 1), do not
show any parallelism. Curve 9 shows that the optimum point of
efficiency is not 39° but 67° F. In the third place, this appears to
be another pseudo-induction in which a mere fluctuation of efficiency is attributed to climatic causes without any serious attempt
at a functional analysis of the causes of the fluctuation. It is
evident that marks of the students depend on many non-climatic
factors and that, at least, some analysis of these factors should
have been made. Now let us consider the data outside of Huntington's book. Do they agree with his conclusions? Are they
similar? Is there any basis of definite conclusions as to the influence of climatic agencies on mental processes? Let us briefly
survey the situation.

E. G. Dexter's study of clerical errors and of the ability to discriminate gave results different from those of Huntington: the curve of clerical errors shows that they are the least numerous not at 39° but at 58° F.; and only an excessive heat of above 77° F. seems to be followed by an increase of errors. The curve discrimination does not show any noticeable correlation with fluctuations of temperature. Both mental processes showed quite an opposite fluctuation in correlation with barometric conditions. Low barometric readings are followed by few clerical errors but, on the other hand, the rapidity of discrimination is high under high barometrical conditions. His data concerning the influence of humidity, winds, and fair or clouded weather upon the curve of clerical errors and discrimination differ from Huntington's and from one another.[115] The results of other studies of the dependence of mental processes upon climatic agencies are different and often contradictory. Two studies of Schuyten concerning the influence of seasons upon attention yielded discordant results, which are also different from Huntington's curves.[116] Lobsien's studies of the seasonal fluctuation of primary memory have shown a fluctuation in different seasons heterogeneous with all the above curves.[117] The Lehman and Pedersen study of the influence of temperature, light, barometric pressure, and seasons upon mental work of addition and on memory (*Gedächtnisleistungen*) found that first, each of these agencies affects the efficiency of these different psychical processes differently; second, that for addition the optimum temperature is different for two individuals studied; third, the optimum point for one is 44.6° F., (7° C.) and for another is 50° F. (10° C.). Both points are different from the optimum of 39° F. in the study of Huntington; and fourth, the movements of the curves of addition and of temperature do not show any resemblance to the seasonal fluctuations of Huntington's mental efficiency curve. This study found results quite different from Huntington's on the optimum temperature for mental

---

[115] DEXTER, E. G., *op. cit.*, Figures 19, 20, 21, 22, 50; Chap. XIII.

[116] SCHUYTEN, M. C., "Influence des variations de la temperature atmospherique sur l'attention voluntaire des élèves," *Bulletin de l'academie royal des sciences, de lettres de Belgique*, Vol. XXXII, Brussels, 1906.

[117] LOBSIEN, M., "Schwankungen der Psychische Kapazität," *Pedago. Psychologie*, Bd. 5, 1902. LOBSIEN, M., "Experim. Untersuchungen über Gedächtnissenwicklung bei Schulkindern," *Zeitschrift für Psychologie der Sinnesorgane,* Bd. 27, 1901.

work.[118]   Further, Peaks' experimental study of memory has shown that the seasonal fluctuation is different for two groups studied. The fluctuations of both groups are far from being identical with the curves of Huntington.[119] On the other hand, Hines's study of the efficiency of pupils in various temperature conditions has shown that the optimum point of the classroom temperature for mental work is between 65° and 70° F., and that temperature at, and below 60° F., is very harmful to mental work.[120] Furthermore, contrary to Huntington's theory, the experimental study of the influence of humidity on efficiency of mental work, performed by Stecher, did not find any noticeable effects.[121] The experiments of Thorndike and McCall, Bass, and the New York State Commission on Ventilation [122] find that different conditions of the air in regard to temperature, humidity and the degree of the carbon dioxide show no effect on mental work, the rate of improvement of mental functions, accuracy of judgment or upon the choice of alternatives. There is no use to continue the enumeration of the results of other and similar experimental and statistical studies. Later on I shall discuss some of Huntington's other "proofs" of his claim. For the present, the above gives a sufficient basis for the following conclusions: first, various studies of the influence of climatic agencies upon mental work have shown either no effects or effects which are very discordant and contradictory; second, these results are by no means identical or similar to the principal statements of Huntington; third, his own data are somewhat contradictory; fourth, this discordance of results does not give any solid basis for definite generalizations about the influence of climate upon mental work; fifth, still less does it permit sweeping generalizations concerning the decisive influence of

[118] LEHMAN and PEDERSEN, *op. cit.*, pp. 94–104 and *passim*.

[119] PEAKS, *op. cit.*, Chap. III.

[120] HINES, L. N., "Effect of School Room Temperature on the Work of Pupils," *The Psychological Clinic*, Vol. VIII, 1909.

[121] STECHER, *op. cit.*, *passim*, and Chap. VIII.

[122] THORNDIKE, E. L., *Ventilation in Relation to Mental Work*, Teachers College, Columbia University Contributions to Education, N. Y., 1916; BASS, "Experiment in School Room Ventilation with Reduced Air Supply," *Transactions American Society Heat and Ventil. Engineers*, 1913, Vol. XIX, p. 328; THORNDIKE, RUGER, McCALL, "The Effects of Outside Air and Recirculated Air upon the Intellectual Achievement and Improvements of School Pupils," *School and Society*, 1916, 3, 679.

climate upon the origin, progress, and decay of civilizations and upon their character; and sixth, the conclusion about the influence of climatic agencies upon mental functions has been inferred from the mere existence of a fluctuation of these functions in different periods of a year.   Such an inference from the fact of fluctuation to the climatic factors as causes is not valid.   As there are regular and more conspicuous monthly, weekly, and diurnal fluctuations of mental efficiency which have very little to do with climatic agencies,[123] the existence of "seasonal" fluctuations is not necessarily due to climatic factors and cannot serve as evidence in favor of their conditioning rôle.   This is enough to prove that the second fundamental premise of the sweeping sociological generalizations of Huntington is not proved.   The same, as we have seen, may be said about his first fundamental premise concerning the correlation of climate and health and efficiency of physical work.   Now before we proceed to an analysis of the broadest sociological generalizations of Huntington and others in this field, let us briefly discuss other, somewhat narrower, correlations which students have attempted to establish between geographical factors and various social phenomena.   An analysis of their validity will help greatly in the decision as to the validity of the broadest generalizations.

13. CLIMATE AND SUICIDE

A series of investigators, such as De Guerry, Legoyt, A. Wagner, L. Bodio, A. Leffingwell, Morselli, Krose, Gaedeken, Dexter, G. von Mayr,[124] to mention only a few, have shown that there is a

[123] About these diurnal, weekly and monthly fluctuations see PEAKS, *Periodic Variations in Efficiency;* the works of M. Bernays, Max Weber, Stecher, Kuhnes; LOMBARD, W. P., "Some Influences Affecting the Power of Voluntary Muscular Contraction," *Journal of Physiology,* Vol. XIII, 1892; KRAEPELIN, E., "Zur Hygiene der Arbeit," *Zeitschrift für Psychiatrie,* Vol. XXV, 1898; CHRISTOPHER, W. S., *Report on Child Study Investigations,* Chicago, 1898-9; MARSH, H. D., "The Diurnal Course of Efficiency," *Columbia University Contribution to Philosophy and Psychology,* Vol. XIV, 1906; and GATES, A., *Diurnal Variations in Memory and Association,* Univ. of California Press, 1916.

[124] See DE GUERRY, *Statistique morale de la France,* Paris, 1835; WAGNER, A., *Die Gesetzmassigkeit,* etc., Vol. I, pp. 128 ff., Hamburg, 1864; MORSELLI, *Il suicido,* Milan, 1879; DEXTER, *op. cit.,* Chap. XI; VON MAYR, *Statistik und Gesellschaftslehre,* Tübingen, 1917, pp. 281-291; KROSE, H. A., *Die Ursachen der Selbstmordhaufigkeit,* pp. 4 ff., Freiburg, 1906; MINER, J. R., "Suicide and its Relation to Climatic and Other Climatic Factors," *American Journal of Hygiene,* 1922; JACQUART, C. J., *Le suicide,* p. 99 ff., Bruxelles, 1908; GAEDEKEN, P.,

clearly cut and definite "seasonal" fluctuation of suicide in some European and in some non-European countries. The maximum of suicide in all European countries is in the summer. The maximum is in June or May; the next place belongs to the spring; next one to the fall, and the minimum comes in the winter.[125] The studies have disclosed also that there are weekly and diurnal periodicities in the movement of suicide. Besides, they have shown that the frequency of distribution of suicide in space also shows regularity: in Europe, for instance, the average number of suicides, according to the latitude, is as follows:

Latitude	Number of Suicides per Million of Population
From 36 to 43 degrees of latitude..................	21.1
From 43 to 50 degrees of latitude..................	93.3
From 50 to 55 degrees of latitude..................	172.5
More than 55 degrees of latitude...................	88.1[126]

From these facts many of the investigators have inferred that the movement of suicide is strongly and directly conditioned by climatic factors. Some have laid it to fluctuations of temperature, others to fluctuations of light and pressure, and others to a combination of all these and other climatic agencies. Such conclusions seem natural. And yet, more serious analyses of all these phenomena, first by Durkheim, and later by Krose and Jacquart, have shown that at the very best the influence of climatic factors, if such an influence generally exists, is very indirect and insignificant; that the climatic hypothesis cannot explain either the fluctuations or the suicide rate in the course of time; in different countries and societies; or between city and country districts; among the single, married and divorced; or sudden increases or decreases in the same society; or even the character of the diurnal, weekly, monthly and "seasonal" fluctuations of this phenomenon. Durkheim has shown that the factor responsible for suicide is not climate but an increase or decrease of the social

"Contribution statist. à la réaction des organisme," etc., *Archive d'anthropologie criminelle*, Lyon et Paris, Vol. XXIX, 1909, pp. 81 ff.; and LEFFINGWELL, A., *Illegitimacy*, London, 1892, pp. 21 ff. In these works other literature and statistical data are referred to.

[125] By the way the suicide rate is also one of the criteria of vitality. The seasonal fluctuation of this phenomenon is considerably different from Huntington's curves of death rate or reversed health rate.

[126] DURKHEIM, E., *Le suicide*, p. 83. Paris, 1912.

isolation of the members of a society. He has convincingly exhibited how this and some other social factors condition all the above fluctuations of suicides, including also the "seasonal" ones. His hypothesis reconciles with the statistical data of suicides; his analysis of the phenomenon is less mystical than the climatic theory; and his theory gives a more plausible explanation of the facts.[127] Hence we must conclude that the correlation of suicides and climatic conditions is not proved, as yet; and even if it exists, which is questionable, it is not direct and primary.

14. CLIMATE AND INSANITY

Many authors, such as Leffingwell, Norbury, Huntington, Dexter, Watt, and others have tried to establish a correlation between climatic agencies and the fluctuations of insanity or of general mental diseases.[128] The principal basis of such a contention is also the existence of "seasonal" fluctuations in the number of people who are admitted to asylums. Some of these authors contend that the phenomena of insanity and suicide are closely correlated. After Durkheim's study of suicides we must admit if such a correlation exists, which is questionable, at any rate it is pretty remote.[129] Further, it is possible to contend, with a reasonable degree of certainty, that, if climatic agencies condition the movement of insanity, their rôle at any rate is not primary but secondary. This inference follows from the fact that neither the distribution of insanity among different societies, nor the fluctua-

[127] See the brilliant analysis of the climatic theories of suicide in Durkheim, Le suicide, Chap. III. As I mentioned before, this case especially illustrates how difficult it is to solve the problem of "causation" of social phenomena; how easily one may make the mistake of "*post hoc ergo propter hoc*," and how unscientific it is to make an inference from the mere fact of the fluctuation of some phenomena in time or space to the first and most conspicuous condition as the "cause," in this case, to the climatic factors. See also J. R. Miner's study which shows no influence of climate on the fluctuation of suicides.

[128] See Leffingwell, *op. cit.*, pp. 98 ff.; Norbury, F. P., "Seasonal Curves in Mental Disorders," *Medical Journal and Record*, Vol. CIX, 1924; Huntington, *Civilization and Climate*, pp. 155 ff., 225; Dexter, *op. cit.*, Chap. IX; Watt, Wm. E., *Open Air*, 1910.

[129] See Durkheim, *op. cit.*, Chap. I. While males have a higher percentage of suicide, females are higher in insanity; while Jews have a higher percentage of insanity than Protestants or Roman Catholics, in regard to suicide the situation is reversed. The seasonal curves are not quite parallel either. Evidently, if there were a close correlation between these phenomena these and many similar discordances could not have taken place.

tions of the insanity curve from year to year within the same society, nor the different rates of insanity in different classes, sexes, religious and race groups of the same society and under the same climatic conditions, can be accounted for through climatic factors.   In other words, the most substantial differences and changes in the insanity rate are the results of non-climatic factors.

The question as to whether climatic agencies play some secondary rôle in the increase and decrease of the insanity rate is less certain.   As I have indicated, the only basis for a positive answer to this question is the prevalence of "seasonal" fluctuations of insanity.   Here, as well as in all "seasonal" fluctuations of social phenomena, the very fact of "seasonal" fluctuations does not mean anything if it is not somewhat similar from year to year.   Without such a regularity it is meaningless.   Even if there is such a regularity, it does not necessarily mean that it is caused by climatic factors.   Now is there such a regularity in the "seasonal" fluctuations of insanity, from year to year?   Furthermore is there a regularity in the sense that the seasonal movement of the insanity curve in similar climatic conditions is similar?   As to the first question, the answer is that the regularity is very relative: for instance, the monthly curve of the number of lunatics admitted into asylums in Scotland during the years from 1865 to 1874, shows that from March to April the number of lunatics decreased, while during the years from 1880 to 1887 it increased in April; the fluctuations of the number of lunatics from April to May is also opposite in both periods; the same differences are true in regard to fluctuations from May to June, from June to July, from August to September, and from September to October.[130]   Likewise, the months of the maximum and the minimum insanity rate shift from March to June and July in different years within the same population and are different for places of similar climatic conditions, and sometimes are the same for places with quite different climates.[131]   This means that the "seasonal" regularity of fluctuations of insanity rates is somewhat irregular.

[130] See LEFFINGWELL, A., *op. cit.*, Appendix, p. 157.
[131] Compare the data in DEXTER, *op. cit.*, p. 170; LEFFINGWELL, *op. cit.*, p. 157; HUNTINGTON, *Civilization and Climate*, p. 156; DURKHEIM, *op. cit.*, p. 89.

All that remains is that during one half of a year (and the months which compose this half depend considerably upon the investi-gator) the insanity rate is somewhat higher than in the other half: for Europe and America we may say either the winter and spring months have a rate somewhat higher than the summer and fall months or that the spring and summer months are somewhat higher than the fall and winter months. From these remarks one may see how little remains of these "seasonal" fluctuations of insanity. Its correlation approaches close to a chance-fluctua-tion because some probability always exists. Finally, if in these "seasonal" fluctuations of the insanity rate something more than mere chance exists, the partizans of the climatic factors must show that, namely, the climatic and not other factors is responsible, and why and how climatic agencies condition such fluctuations. All we have in this respect are but discordant guesses. In their attempts to explain the nature of climate, the authors mention "irritating temperature," "exasperating dryness" or "barometric pressure," "excessive humidity," "fatigue of nerves" (which is something different from climate), or more honestly style this unknown influence as "mysterious" (Leffingwell and many others). No serious attempt to define what temperature or de-grees of light or dryness are favorable to insanity or to verify these hypotheses inductively, is found in the works of "the cli-matists." We may conclude that the correlation between insanity and climate is not proved as yet, and if in the corresponding theories there is some truth, it cannot mean more than a slight degree of partial correlation. Even this statement may be questioned.

15. CLIMATE AND CRIME

All that has been said of the alleged influence of climate upon suicide or insanity may be said also of its relationship to crime. The existence of an influence is accepted by many criminologists on the basis of "seasonal" fluctuations of crimes against prop-erty and persons. These fluctuations, and the reverse character of the "seasonal" fluctuation of the number of crimes against property and those against persons, are regarded as sufficient proof of the influence of climatic agencies upon crime.[132]   In regard to this correlation it is possible to make the following statements:

First, the frequency and fluctuations of crimes (against property, as well as against persons) in various countries and in various parts of the same country, in urban and rural districts, and among different social strata and groups (economic, occupational, religious, racial, cultural, national), are such that, except in part, they cannot be accounted for through the influence of climatic conditions at all.   This means, that at the best, climatic agencies exert only secondary and indirect influences.   The substantial traits of the movement of crime are determined by other factors.

Second, the same may be said about fluctuations of crime within the same or different societies in time, as from year to year.   Extraordinary increases or decreases of crime in a definite year or in a series of years, as a rule, are due to other than climatic agencies.   Indirectly, in agricultural countries, climatic agencies, through conditioning the crops, may play a considerable rôle but only through poverty or prosperity.   These are the direct causes and not climatic factors.

Third, the above statements mean that the medium of climatic agencies may play a part only in a limited field of "seasonal" fluctuation of crime.   Even in this field their possible influence may be indirect only in the sense that men become more or less "criminal" not because the temperature is higher or the humidity is lower or the sunlight is less bright, but because the direct factors of criminality such as poor crops or out-of-doors social life are partly influenced by climatic conditions.   It may be that some forms of crime, *e.g.,* sexual crimes, are directly stimulated by climatic factors, but even this is not proved conclusively.

Fourth, even in this limited sense the influence of climatic

[132] The corresponding literature is immense.   The correlation has been emphasized in the works of A. Moreau de Jonnès, Ad. Quetelet, Oettingen, Levasseur, Lombroso, E. Ferri, Leffingwell, B. Foldes, H. Kurella, Lacassagne, Guerry, Jentsch, Aschaffenburg, Dexter, P. Gaedeken, J. L. de Lanessan, and in many general texts of criminology like M. Parmelee's *Criminology*, and J. L. Gillin's *Criminology and Penology*, Chap. V., though Gillin is rightly cautious in this respect.   See the literature in von Mayr, G., *Statistik und Gesellschaftslehre*, Bd. III, pp. 614–615; and in the texts of Gillin and Parmelee.   See the statistical data especially in von Mayr's work, pp. 600–615.

agencies is still somewhat questionable. We are prone to find a regularity where there is the slightest pretext: It is accepted as proved that important and regular "seasonal" fluctuations of crime exist. Meanwhile the real situation is considerably different. In the first place, tables generalized too much mask the fact that the movements of both crimes against property and persons are different and often opposite in various places of similar climatic conditions.[133] In the second place, the regularity of the "seasonal" fluctuations of crime is somewhat exaggerated: it is sufficient to look attentively at the monthly figures of crime against property or persons from year to year to see that their movement from month to month is far from being uniform in "ups" and "downs" for different years. For instance, in Belgium, in 1910, the number of crimes against persons in February was less than in January, and in 1911, it was greater than in January. The same is true in regard to other crimes, and other months, and other countries.[134] This means that the regularity of the "seasonal" fluctuation of crime is far from being definite. This is also corroborated by the fact that the months of maximum and of minimum crime often shift from one to another in the same country in different years; that they sometimes are different for the countries of almost similar climatic conditions, and identical for the countries of different climates; that in some southern countries the "seasonal" curve of crime often has quite a different character (not the opposite, which could be explained by differences in temperature, but a very dissimilar character); and that in a more detailed form different kinds of crimes against property, as well as against persons, exhibit much more complex and much less regular and uniform fluctuations than we are led to believe on the basis of a few general and one-sided figures.[135] These and many other considerations are enough to

[133] As only one out of many examples of this kind I may indicate the seasonal curve of homicides in Seattle: The number of homicides there has been the lowest in the warmest months (May, June, July) and the highest in the coldest months, (December, January, February). See SCHMIDT, C. F., "A Study of Homicides in Seattle, 1914 to 1924," *Social Forces*, June, 1926, p. 751.

[134] See the figures of Belgium in VON MAYR, *op. cit.*, p. 610.

[135] These facts may be seen even in the figures that are given in von Mayr's work, in spite of von Mayr's own theory, see pp. 609 ff.; a great many "climatic fallacies and pretensions" in an interpretation of factors of crime have already been dissipated by many criminologists, beginning with G. Tarde, and ending

show that the so-called regularity of the "seasonal" fluctuations of crime is a "loose" statement. The factors are to be discovered yet. Finally, if we try to find out why, how, and in what way climatic agencies condition crimes our results are practically nothing but indefinite dogmatic repetitions of contradictory allusions to the "weakening" or "irritating" influence of temperature or air or humidity or wind and so on. And often the same author on one page ascribes an "irritating" character to one climatic condition, while on another page of the work he lays it to quite different climatic agencies (because there the movement of crime is different and cannot be explained by the first reason).[136] The corresponding "explanations" are so vague that we do not know, of temperature or humidity or barometric pressure, which facilitates and which hinders crime. The situation remains almost mysterious and hopeless. These remarks are enough to show that if there exists any correlation between climatic agencies and crime it is of secondary importance and still needs to be tested. Some indirect influence of these factors appears probable but it is somewhat intangible. At any rate the principal fluctuations of crime in space and time are not due to climatic factors.

16. CLIMATE AND BIRTH, DEATH, AND MARRIAGE RATES

I shall not discuss at all the curious but rather fantastic geographical theories in this field, like Jenkin's theory of a correlation between Jupiter and the death rate, but I shall limit my criticism to the more reasonable hypotheses. The preceding conclusions may be applied as well to the fluctuations of death, birth and marriage rates in space and in time and to the "seasonal" fluctuations especially.[137] An attentive study of the corresponding

with the works of N. Colajanni, Bonger, van Kan, Gernet, Charychov, and of many other criminologists of the so-called sociological school. See van Kan, J., *Les causes économiques de la criminalité;* Tarde, G., *La criminalité comparée,* and *Penal Philosophy;* Colajanni, N., *La sociologia criminale;* Gernet, M., *Crime and its Prevention,* (Russ.) and *Juvenile Delinquents,* (Russ.); Charychov, *Factors of Crime* (Russ.); Bonger, W. A., *Criminality and Economic Conditions;* Thomas, D., *Social Aspects of the Business Cycle,* London, 1925.

[136] These traits may be seen even in the books of such modern "climatists" as M. Parmelee; read attentively pages 43–53 of his *Criminology.*

[137] See the statistical data in Oettingen, A., *Die Moralstatistik,* 1882, chapters devoted to an analysis of death, birth and marriage rates; Levasseur, E., *La population Française,* Vol. II, Paris, 1891; von Mayr, G., *Statistik und Gesell-*

statistical data shows that the principal fluctuations in space and time of the rates of these vital processes cannot be accounted for through climatic factors. The same is true in regard to "trends" in these phenomena. Practically the only field where the influence of climate may be admitted is that of the so-called "seasonal" fluctuations. But even here, as far as the complex Western societies are concerned, the direct influence of climatic conditions is very uncertain and questionable. The "seasonal" curves of these processes are even less definite and regular than in many of the processes discussed above. For instance, the birth rate or correspondingly the number of conceptions has two high peaks: the birth rate in February and March and in September and October; the conception rate in January and December and in May and July. These are in the most different climatic conditions. The same is true in regard to the yearly periods of the minimum conception and birth rates.[138] On the other hand, the "seasonal" fluctuations of the birth rates of different social groups, for instance, Protestants and Catholics, who live in the same area, under the same climatic conditions, show considerable difference. Such "seasonal" fluctuations of birth rates testify that they are conditioned by factors different from climate. In the second place, the "seasonal" fluctuation of these vital processes is far from being regular and is therefore far from being "seasonal" in the proper sense of the word. They seem to be mere fluctuations whose causes are yet to be discovered. In the third place, in the course of time these fluctuations become more and more indefinite and less and less "seasonal." For these reasons it is possible to contend that even the so-called "seasonal" fluctuations of these processes do not definitely prove the direct and important influence of climatic factors. Among primitive tribes, and among the non-domesticated animals, sexual life and conceptions have a definite seasonal character. It is well known that the non-domesticated animals have a definite period of rutting. Only during such periods do they perform and physiologically can perform sexual functions. Westermarck, Wagner,

---

schaftslehre, Vol. II; and the parts on the population statistics in the works of Wappäus, H. Westergaard and others.

[138] See also WHITE, R. C., "The Human Pairing Season in America," American Journal of Sociology, Vol. XXXII, pp. 800–805.

B. Spencer and Gillen, Oldfield, Bonwick, Mannhardt and many
other investigators have shown that among primitive peoples and
the forefathers of the Romans, the Greeks, and contemporary
European populations there has been and is a kind of a remnant
of this phenomenon of rutting manifested in the conspicuous intensiveness of sexual life at certain periods of the year.[139]   But
even such a definite seasonal location of sexual life seems not
to have been due to climatic conditions directly but to other factors
and especially to the factor of alimentation.   The two most plausible hypotheses offered for an explanation of the rutting of animals,
the theory of Leuckart, and that of Westermarck, both stress the
rôle of food and only the indirect influence of climate as a factor
conditioning food-abundance.   According to Leuckart, the rutting
period coincides with the period of the most abundant food; according to Westermarck the rutting periods are those when a species can procure the food and other necessities for offspring at the
moment of its birth.   On the other hand the rôle of the food-factor
is accentuated by the fact that our domesticated animals, who are
put in a condition where their food is secured throughout the
whole year, mate also throughout a whole year.[140]   This shows
that among animals even the direct factor of "seasonal" fluctuations of conception and of sexual life is not so much climate as
food.[141]   Climatic conditions play only an indirect rôle, as far as
they condition the seasons of abundant and of scarce food.   For
this reason it is comprehensible why the "seasonal" fluctuations of
conceptions and births among primitive peoples are more definite

[139] See WESTERMARCK, E., *History of Human Marriage*, Chaps. I, II; WAGNER,
Handwörterbuch der Physiologie, the article of Leuckart, Bd. IV, p. 862; GRUEN-
HAGEN, *Lehrbuch d. Physiologie*, 1885-7, Bd. III, p. 528. MANNHARDT, *Walde
und Feldkulte*, Berlin, 1875, Bd. I, Chap. V; KHARUSIN, *Ethnography*, Volume:
Family and Kinship, (Russ.), pp. 50 ff,; OLDFIELD, "The Aborigines of Australia,"
Transactions of Ethnological Society, New Series, Vol. III, p. 230; BONWICK, *Daily
Life and Origin of the Tasmanians*, p. 178, Lond., 1870; FRAZER, J. G., *The Golden
Bough*, Vol. III, pp. 230 ff., Lond., 1890; ELLIS, H., *Studies in the Psychology of
Sex*, Vol. I, pp. 85 ff., Philadelphia, 1910.

[140] See GAGEMAN, *Physiology of Domesticated Animals*, (Russ.) 1908, pp. 232-
233; HEAPE, W., "The Sexual Season of Mammals," *Quarterly Journal Microsc.
Science*, Vol. LXIV, 1900, p. 12; MARSHALL, F. H., *Physiology of Reproduction*,
pp. 57 ff., Lond., 1910; DARWIN, CH., *Variations of Animals and Plants under
Domestication*, Vol. II, p. 90, Lond., 1885.

[141] See reference below.   See also the paper of A. MEYERSON, in *American Review*,
January-February, 1924, and PELL, C. E., *The Law of Births and Deaths*. Lond.,
1921.   These writers discuss the rôle of the food factor in fertility.

than among cultural peoples whose supply of food and other necessities has become almost independent of seasons.[142]

This discussion is enough to show that at the best the rôle of climatic factors in these vital processes is only indirect, and in civilized societies it is so strongly neutralized by other non-climatic factors that the influence of the climate becomes almost intangible. It is impossible to establish the correlation between climate and vital processes in any more definite form. This statement applies also to the movement of the death, and especially of the marriage rate within Western societies.[143]

[142] It is also questionable whether such phenomena as sexual maturity among human beings is influenced by climate. Some data which show that in tropical regions the age of menstruation is lower (12.9 years) than in the cold regions (16.5 years) (according to Engelman) are far from being general. In the United States, for instance, no influence of climate upon menstruation has been detected. Among the Eskimo the age is at about thirteen years, which is almost as low as in the tropics. Furthermore, a series of studies have shown that it is influenced by racial factors. In Hungary it fluctuates from stock to stock such as from 13–14 among the Slavs to 16 or 17 among the Styrians. It is often lower for the upper strata and higher for the lower classes. In America such a correlation has been found. These and similar data make us believe that if climate influences the sexual maturity age this influence is far from direct, or definite or even tangible. See the data in ENGELMAN, G. J., "First Age of Menstruation in the North American Continent," *Transaction of American Gynecological Society*, 1901, pp. 87 ff.; KRIEGER, E., *Die Menstruation*, pp. 17 ff., 52 ff., Berlin, 1869; KELLY, H. A., *Medical Gynecology*, pp. 83 ff., Lond., 1912; RASERI, "Inchiesta della Societe Anthropol." in *Annali di Statistica*, serie II, Vol. VI, 1881; MARRO, A., *La Puberta*, Torino, 1900.

[143] The above statements concerning the irregularity of the so-called seasonal fluctuations of death, marriage, and mortality rates, and the impossibility of accounting for these fluctuations mainly through climatic factors are also corroborated by a very careful study of these processes by M. B. Hexter and D. S. Thomas. Though Dr. Hexter himself writes the following indefinite statement: "much evidence exists to show that the birth-rate (and marriage and mortality rates) is highly influenced by the seasons, even among civilized men," nevertheless, his data bring out the fallacies of so-called seasonal fluctuations. The seasonal movement of the birth rate of Boston from 1900 to 1921 shows that the months of maximum are March, December and July, and the months of minimum are April, November and September. This means that the maxima occur in the most different climatic conditions. The same is true of the months of minimum. In addition, November and December, which do not differ noticeably in climatic conditions, exhibit the greatest contrast in regard to the birth rate. If climatic conditions were responsible for a seasonal fluctuation of birth rates we should expect that months which have approximately similar climatic conditions would have similar birth rates. Since this is not the case, according to all laws of inductive logic, we cannot explain the "seasonal" fluctuations through climate. Further, monthly data for the years from 1900 to 1921 show that monthly fluctuations are considerably dissimilar from year to year. The points of minimum and maximum shift from month to month in different years. The same is true in regard to the movement of marriages, deaths, and divorces. This

17. GEOGRAPHIC CONDITIONS AND RELIGION, ART, AND LITERATURE

It is to be expected that geographical environment will be in some way reflected in the products of the imaginative work of man, in his arts, literature, music, painting, architecture, and beliefs. This expectation, especially for relatively primitive and isolated groups who have dwelt in the same geographical environment for a long time, seems to be corroborated to some extent. However, this extent is negligible. What seems to be proved is only that the art, the literature, and the beliefs of a people are somewhat "colored" with the images, figures, and forms most often taken from the geographical environment in which such a people live. Among many writings of those who have spoken of such "colorings" of religious beliefs by the "colors" of the local geographical environment, the short paper of R. H. Whitbeck is possibly the best. His paper shows that many peoples usually symbolize their friendly gods by such geographic agencies as under the existing conditions are beneficial to the society, while they picture unfriendly gods by harmful geographic phenomena. The Satan of Egypt was the Thyphon, that of India was Vritra, the serpent, and the evil deities of ancient Norway were the frost giants or mountains. Likewise, the ideas of different peoples concerning paradise and hell show the same "coloration." Paradise for the American Indian is a hunting ground abundant in game; for the desert Arabian it is an oasis containing trees, streams of water and an abundance of cool and refreshing shade; and for the ancient Norse it is a warm and sunny place. On the other hand, hell usually is depicted as a place in which are embodied the geographical conditions from which the population suffers: cold in the north, heat in the tropics, and so on. Whit-

---

is enough to suggest that these fluctuations are far from being "seasonal" in the proper sense of the word and cannot be accounted for through the influence of climate or other geographical factors. See HEXTER, M. B., *Social Consequences of Business Cycles, passim*, and pp. 20 ff., 55 ff., 70 ff., Boston and N. Y., 1925. See also WHIPPLE, G. CH., *Vital Statistics*, p. 306, N. Y., 1919, where Professor Whipple gives the "seasonal" movement of the death rate in 1910 which yields a "seasonal" curve of the death rate different from the curve of Hexter. Dr. Falk's curve of the death rate for the United States Registration Area in 1919 shows a somewhat different curve from that of Hexter and Whipple. See FALK, I. S., *Principles of Vital Statistics*, 1923, p. 183.

beck indicates further that when peoples change their territory and live in quite a different environment, their images of gods and their other beliefs undergo a corresponding modification. For instance when the Aryans entered India their chief deity was Dyaus (sky), and Indra, the rain-giver, was of minor rank. Later on, in view of the great importance of rain in India, the chief deity became Indra while Dyaus was demoted to a second-rank god. The same author and several others further show that many other religious images and beliefs are colored in a similar way.[144]

Similar correlations may be observed in folklore, in songs, fairy tales, poems and other literary products of different peoples during the earlier stages of their history. The character of the geographic environment which forms the background, the kinds of trees, plants and animals which are depicted, and the general scenery of the *Thousand and One Nights* or the *Iliad* and *Odyssey,* or the Norse *Edda,* or the Hindu *Mahabharata* are quite different from each other and each is marked by the characteristics typical of the locality in which its creator lived. Many authors have discussed such correlations. H. Taine tried to explain the difference between the Flamand and the Florentine schools of painters through differences in the geographic conditions of Italy and the Netherlands. Eug. Veron, Aug. Matteuzzi, Ch. Letourneau, Mme. de Stael and many others have attempted to show similar correlations between geographic conditions and architecture, painting, literature, music, etc.[145]

The above correlation in "coloration" of the products of art, literature, and religion, is admitted. At the same time I must

[144] See WHITBECK, R. H., "The Influence of Geographical Environment upon Religious Belief," *The Geographical Review*, Vol. V, 1918, pp. 316–324; see other references here. To the credit of the author it must be said that he does not force his correlation and frankly says that "many factors combine to mold a people's religious beliefs. Geographical environment necessarily is one of these, sometimes a conspicuous influence, and sometimes perceptible only in minor ways." *Ibid.*, p. 317. See similar theories and correlations in MOUGEOLLE, *Les problèmes de l'histoire*, pp. 374 ff.; DUPUIS, *Origine de tous les cultes*, IX; the paper of L. Drapeyron in *Revue de geographie*, 1-er *partie*, 1-er année; SEMPLE, E., *op. cit.*, Chap. II; PESCHEL, O., *The Races of Man*, pp. 314–318, N. Y., 1894.

[145] See TAINE, H., *Philosophie de l'art*, III; VERNON, EUG., *L'esthétique;* especially MATTEUZZI, AUG., *Les facteurs de l'évolution des peuples*, pp. 52 ff., 211 ff., Paris, 1900; LETOURNEAU, CH., *L'évolution littéraire dans les diverses races humaines*, Paris, 1894.

condition the statement by showing that even for a relatively early stage, the correlation is far from being rigid and universal, and that it is likely to become less and less tangible as we proceed to later stages of more complex and more mobile societies; and finally, that a great many geographers and authors have greatly exaggerated the influence of geographic conditions in this field. The validity of the first and the second propositions is proved by the fact of the existence of similar or identical beliefs, symbols, myths, legends, fairy tales, architectural types, music and so on among peoples who inhabit very different areas and live under different longitudes, latitudes, and altitudes. It is also true that peoples who are in the same geographical conditions often have quite different beliefs, tastes, and standards in art and literature. Consider the areas of the expansion of Christianity, Buddhism, Mohammedanism, Confucianism or any great religion. The followers of each of the religions are found among different geographic conditions and climates. This means, that in spite of geographic differences, all have essentially similar beliefs. If there are differences, they are due not so much to geographic as to cultural dissimilarities of social groups. Take the dynamic history of mythology: it shows that similar myths have expanded among peoples with unlike geographical conditions.[146] The same is true in regard to Gothic architectural style, or to Empire, or to imitations of antique styles. Are not the compositions of Beethoven, Grieg, Verdi, Rossini, Tschaikovsky or of any great composer played in all latitudes and longitudes? Is not the same true in regard to the works of the great masters in poetry, painting, literature and sculpture?

On the other hand, consider the population of the same place, *e.g.,* of a big city of the past or of the present. Do we not find the people there with very different religious beliefs, æsthetic tastes, and literary standards, in spite of the identity of their geographic environment? Both of these categories of facts are so evident, so certain, so common in the past and in the present, that there scarcely is any need of further proof that the correlation we are discussing is relative, loose and even imperceptible.

---

[146] See *e.g.,* FRAZER, J. G., *The Golden Bough, passim,* and Part IV. *Adonis, Attis, Osiris,* London, 1907; see also MACKENZIE, D. A., *Migration of Symbols,* N. Y., 1926.

From these statements it is easy to see the fallacy in doctrines such as the following: "Social institutions and religious ideas are no less (than physical characteristics) the product of environment. We might just as well ask the Ethiopian to change his skin as to change radically his social and religious ideas. It has been shown by experience that Christianity can make but little headway amongst many peoples in Africa or Asia where on the other hand Mohammedanism has made and is steadily making progress. This is probably due to the fact that Mohammedanism is a religion evolved . . . in latitudes bordering on the aboriginal races of Africa and Asia" (Ridgway). If the author had taken into consideration the mere fact that Mohammedanism, as well as Christianity, has spread among people who live in both warm and cold climates, in plains and on mountains, under varying geographical conditions, he would not make such rash generalizations. Further, if he had taken into consideration that the culture complex of the peoples in Asia was more congenial to the culture complex of Mohammedanism, this additional reason would cause him to refrain from making climate the main factor in the expansion of Mohammedanism and Christianity. Furthermore, sometimes populations change suddenly within a few years from one religion into another, (spreading of Christianity within the Roman Empire and its conquests in Gallia, Ireland, and Britain; its introduction into Russia by the order of the government; similar expansions of Buddhism, Mohammedanism, and so on) and sometimes, as rapidly back into the previous one. Thus we have ample evidence that great changes in religion have been taking place within the same geographic habitat and without any changes in conditions. This is sufficient to show that such changes in the religion of a population are not correlated with geographic factors.

Here is another example of such fallacious reasoning: Abercromby found [147] that the area of expansion of the Mohammedan religion in Asia and in Africa coincided with the area in which the mean annual rainfall was below ten inches. Hence he concluded that the amount of rainfall was a vital factor in the ex-

[147] See ABERCROMBY, JOHN, *Seas and Skies in Many Latitudes*, pp. 42–43., Lond.; WARD, R. DeCOURCY, *Climate Considered Especially in Relation to Man*, pp. 258–259, N. Y., 1918.

pansion of Mohammedanism or Christianity. A study of the areas of Mohammedanism in Europe and in Asia (India) shows the fallacy of this theory. A correlation between deserts and monotheism set forth by E. Renan is likewise invalid.

The next example of this bad logic is found in H. Taine. He explained the difference between the Florentine and the Flemish schools in painting by their geographical environment. When, however, he found that two schools were similar in many respects, he saved his theory by the statement that their geographical environment was similar! He adjusted the facts to meet the case.

Matteuzzi claimed that geographic differences in northern and southern Europe manifested themselves in the fields of the literature and music of these peoples. He claimed that northern people had less imagination and fantasy, and less ability for deductive generalizations than the southern people. On the other hand, the southern people were more musical.[148] These and other "generalizations" of the author show a great deal of imagination but are utterly fallacious from the standpoint of science. It is only necessary to recall such imaginative and fantastic creations of the northern peoples as the Finnish epic *Kalevala;* the series of Russian epical poems, fairy tales and legends; *Edda* of the Norse; the epics connected with King Arthur; the *Nibelungenlied;* or the epic about Roland, to see the fallacy of the "generalization." It is necessary to forget the names of Bach, Beethoven, Mozart, Chopin, Wagner, Rimsky-Korsakov, Grieg, Brahms, Tschaikovsky, Musorgsky, and thousands of other great composers of the north to assert that the Italians are more musical. It is possible to claim that southern Europeans have greater powers of deduction and generalization [149] only after forgetting such names as Descartes, Kant, Copernicus, Newton, Darwin, Leibnitz, Pasteur, Claude Bernard, Lamarck, Lobachevsky, H. Spencer, and others.

I could fill hundreds of pages with examples of such false generalizations.[150] But there is scarcely any need of it. In their

---

[148] See MATTEUZZI, *op. cit.*, pp. 52 ff., 211 ff.

[149] See a sound criticism of these theories in KOVALEVSKY, M., *Sovremennya Soziologi*, St. Petersb., 1905, Chap. IX.

[150] We have here the same unhappy use of the method of "illustration" which is a real plague in the social sciences. Instead of a systematic verification of a

scientific value they are similar to the most unfortunate correlations between climate and social phenomena made by Montesquieu.[151]   But what could be overlooked in the writings of the great author of *The Spirit of the Law* on account of the lack of factual material in his time, cannot be excused in these modern authors.   Their theories may be interesting, sometimes even suggestive, but unfortunately at the first scientific scrutiny they fall like a house of cards.[152]

18. GEOGRAPHIC CONDITIONS AND SOCIAL AND POLITICAL ORGANIZATION OF SOCIETY

We have seen that the Le Play school tried to explain the principal types of the family through differences in the habitats of peoples.   Since Montesquieu, several writers, in a similar way, have accounted for such characteristics of the family as monogamy, polygamy or polyandry through geographic environment Several authors, like Ritter and Ratzel and their followers, have gone further and tried to account for the size of a body politic, the form of its organization, its peaceful or military character, the optimism or pessimism of the people, the progressiveness or backwardness, the love for freedom or for subordination, and hundreds of other characteristics, through these geographic influences.   Are these and many similar statements valid?

I have already indicated the shortcomings of the theory of the origin of different types of families given by the Le Play school. It may explain a part of the evolution of each type, but not very much.   Attempts to correlate forms of marriage and varieties

---

hypothesis, the authors use one or a few fragmentary cases favorable to their conclusion and victoriously declare that it is "proved." Such a method of proving is utterly anti-scientific in its nature.

[151] Montesquieu formulated a great many correlations between geographic conditions and various social phenomena, slavery and freedom, polygamy and polyandry, monarchy and republic, Protestantism and Catholicism, and so on. At the present we consider a great many of these correlations doubtful.

[152] I have no desire to discuss here theories like M. Müller's theory of the origin of religion and its evolution, in which he emphasizes the rôle of geographic conditions, and especially of magnificent natural phenomena, like thunderstorms, in the beginning of beliefs in God, supernatural beings, and so on. This does not directly concern my topic; besides it has been criticized by many authors, such as E. Durkheim, so my criticism is unnecessary. See DURKHEIM, *Elementary Forms of Religious Life*, N. Y., 1915, chapters devoted to the criticism of M. Müller's and Revill's theories of naturism.

of the family with geographic environment have not been successful. Try to correlate monogamy, polygamy, polyandry, endogamy, exogamy, or duration of marriage with climate, altitude,
latitude, longitude or any component of geographic environment.
It becomes evident at once that such a correlation does not exist.
All these are found in vastly different geographic conditions.[153]
The statement applies also to many other characteristics of the
family.   One of the best authorities in the field of family evolution, J. Mazzarella, after his study of the area of diffusion and
the causes of the matriarchate, the ambilian form of marriage,
polygamy, and so on, concludes: "These institutions do not depend (directly or tangibly) on geographic causes because they are
found among peoples quite different from the standpoint of geographic conditions" (from the arctic to the tropics, from the
islands to the mountains, from the deserts and plains to the forest
regions).[154]   This becomes more evident when one takes into
consideration that in the same area, and sometimes in a period
of time too short for any serious change of geographic environment, the family institution undergoes radical modifications.   In
the same geographic area we often see family institutions of
different types, according to the population.   The same family
or marriage type (polygamy or monogamy) is found in areas
with great contrasts in geography.   Many geographers have attempted to establish other correlations between geographic and
social phenomena.   Here are several typical examples:

*Correlation Number 1: Geographic conditions determine the
size of a body politic and political, racial, national, and cultural
frontiers.   Areas separated by mountains or seas have separate
political, racial, national, and cultural groups, while populations
situated on large plains form a large body politic.   The same
correlation is claimed in regard to race, language, and culture.*

---

[153] See the catalogue of corresponding peoples in WESTERMARCK, E., *The
History of Human Marriage*, Lond., 1921, Vol. II, Chaps. XVIII, XIX, XX;
Vol. III, Chaps. XXVII, XXVIII, XXIX, and *passim*.   Here again the authors
usually "prove" their claims through the method of "illustration."   The most
favorable illustration of polyandry caused by geographical condition is Tibet.
Even such sociologists as Simmel use this "proof."

[154] See the excellent studies of MAZZARELLA, J., *Les types sociaux et le droit*, pp.
179–180, and *passim*, Paris, 1908; *La Condizione guiridica del marito nella famiglia
matriarchale*, Catania, 1899.

Selected illustrations are given to corroborate the statements.[155]
We shall test the proposition by looking at the contradictory facts
of the past, as well as of the present. Neither the Ural, nor the
Altai, nor the Himalaya, nor the Carpathian and other mountains
have hindered the Russian, the Chinese, the Austrian, the Swiss,
the American, or the British Imperial bodies politic from expanding on both sides of the mountains or over the seas. In the past,
the Roman, Egyptian, Assyrian, Chinese, Turkish and Persian
Empires, as well as those of Alexander the Great and of Genghis
Khan have spread in a similar fashion. On the other hand, "separate nationalities may exist within regions which seem to be
marked by physical nature for political unity" and "the map of
Europe affords very few natural boundaries"; beyond a few
cases "there is hardly a mile of political frontier in Europe which
is natural in any valid sense—that is to say, a well marked physical obstacle interposed between peoples differing in race and
language." [156] During a thousand years or even during a century
geographic conditions remain practically the same while political
bodies and cultural areas usually change very considerably, even
radically. The absence of any correlation between the habitat of
the principal races and the geographic environment has been
shown. These fundamental series of facts show the fallacy of
the proposition. If a relationship exists, it is not rigid, perma-

---

[155] See RATZEL, F., *Politische Geographie*, Chaps. XII to XV, 1903; SEMPLE, E.,
op. cit., Chap. II; GEORGE, H. B., *The Relations of Geography and History*, pp. 11
ff., Chap. III, Oxford, 1901.

[156] GEORGE, H., *op. cit.*, pp. 66, 70. Here and in Chapter VI the author considerably disproves his own statements given in Chapters I and II. See a detailed
analysis and the conclusion that geographic conditions do not perceptibly determine the size of a body politic in VALLAUX, *Le sol et l'état*, Chap. IV. Vallaux
tries to save something of this correlation by offering the following modification:
"The body politic does not depend upon climate or the relief of habitat, or the
possibility of expansion in space, or the position. However, from the standpoint
of the place where it originates, it depends on the degree of the character of
(geographic) differentiation grouped within this place. There is a permanent
tendency to form an autonomous state in the most differentiated geographic
areas; and activities of a state, formed in such a region, urge it to expand towards
the areas which are less differentiated." *Ibid.*, pp. 202 ff. This somewhat obscure
proposition is further complicated by an indefinite subdivision of active and
passive geographic differentiation and by a series of subtle discriminations which
are indefinite and unconvincing. The facts which are used to support the proposition are so contradictory and illogical that it cannot be accepted as proved.
See *ibid.*, Chap. VI.

nent, or universal. It may be an indefinite shadow with a very vague connection but surely not a tangible correlation.

Correlation Number 2: Ratzel's famous correlation between geographical space and several social characteristics of large and small political bodies is of a similar nature. The essence of this theory is as follows:[157] The population of the states with large territories, because of the vastness of the abode, possesses a spirit of expansion and militarism, an optimism and youthfulness, and a psychology of growth. Within such social bodies there are much less racial and social conflicts than in those with a small territory. In the political units with small spaces (abodes) the populations are more pessimistic, arrive earlier at a mature spirit of nationalism, have a psychology marked by the spirit of locality, are stagnant, and lack virility. Such is a part of Ratzel's theory of space or Raum.[158] Everybody who knows a little history may easily see the fallacious character of the theory. It is hard to find more optimism in the populations of Russia or China compared with those of Switzerland or of the Netherlands. It is still harder to believe that within such vast political bodies as China, the previous Austria-Hungary, or Turkey, there has been less racial, national, and social conflicts and struggles than in Denmark, or Switzerland, or Norway. The small Balkan states have aspirations for expansion and militarism at least as intense as those of large bodies politic. In brief, the facts completely contradict this famous theory.[159]

[157] See RATZEL, *Politische Geographie*, Chaps. XII to XV.

[158] In a modified form the same theory is set forth by Simmel, without mentioning the name of Ratzel. See SIMMEL, *Soziologie*, Chap. IX, pp. 614–708.

[159] See the detailed and careful criticism in VALLAUX, *Le sol et l'état*, Chap. V. There are plenty of other theories which try to establish correlations between the character of geographic environment and optimistic or pessimistic moods of societies. For instance, Sir Archibald Geikie in his *Scottish Reminiscences* claims that the grim character of the Scot is due to "the gloomy valleys," cloudiness, and the inclement winter of Scotland. Draper contends that differences in climate are responsible for differences in moods of the populations of the northern and southern states of the United States. Letourneau attempts to explain the mysterious and melancholy character of the literature of the peoples of northern Europe through their gloomy geographic environment, long winters, long nights, vast forests and so on. Such correlations are very numerous. There is no need to say that they cannot be taken seriously. The very fact of a predominant mood ascribed by the authors to a given population is very questionable. They have not even tried to show why, for instance, they think that the character of the Scots is more grim than that of the Russians or the Chinese, or of any other people. The real situation in this respect is probably much more complex: the national character, being

Correlation Number 3: Matteuzzi, probably better than any other geographer, has tried to show how geographical conditions were responsible for the political organization of ancient Egypt, Assyria, Persia, Greece, Rome and so on. Here is a sample of his "explanations."

In Egypt, a centralized political despotism was due to the plains of the Nile and the Nile's irregular overflows. Every district needed water and tried to abduce it upon its territory. In this way many conflicts between the districts arose and the weaker ones suffered.

In order to protect the rights of the weaker districts and to coördinate the system of distribution of the water of the Nile among the districts, Ancient Egypt had to create a political power which would be able to control the matter. In this way the Nile determined not only the physical but the political structure of Egypt also.

Through the same factor he explains the appearance of castes in Egypt. In a similar way, irregular overflowings of the Tigris and the Euphrates were responsible for the centralization of power in the hands of one despot in Assyria and Chaldea.

In Persia there are no rivers through which to explain the unlimited Persian monarchy combined with the system of satraps. Therefore Matteuzzi makes the Persian mountains responsible for the Persian political system. In Phœnicia, the republican system was due to the character of the seashore and mountains which facilitated an isolation of the parts. In Greece, the political organization was due to the sea, the soil, and the mountains. As, however, this combination is a mere repetition of the previous geographic factors, so the author admits the influence of cultural imitation in Greece. There is no need to continue the list of Matteuzzi's explanations.[160] It is scarcely necessary to criti-

---

grim or melancholy in one respect, is likely to be very joyful in other respects. If even the statements of a predominant character of a people were true it would be necessary to prove that it is due to the geographic environment and not to other factors. Such attempts have never been made seriously. For these reasons all such theories are journalistic speculations and nothing more.

[160] MATTEUZZI, *Les facteurs de l'évolution des peuples*, pp. 45 ff., and *passim*. Theories similar to Matteuzzi's are so common that they may be found in the majority of the textbooks of sociology. There they are given as something beyond doubt. The example of the Nile as responsible for the creation of the Egyptian political organization has become traditional "proof."

cize these theories.   Matteuzzi's characteristics of the political régimes in many countries are inaccurate.   For instance, his description of the Persian political organization is erroneous; several historians, and especially Pizzi, have drawn quite a different picture of the political institutions of Persia compared with that of Matteuzzi.[161]   This is also true of several other countries. This fact alone makes Matteuzzi's conclusions questionable.   Further, the invalidity of the theory appears from the fact that similar results—despotic political régimes in Egypt, Chaldea, and Persia,—are ascribed to quite different geographic factors.   In Egypt and Chaldea the political régimes were attributed to fertile plains and overflowing rivers; and in Persia, to mountains and deserts.   The same applies to the republican régimes in Phœnicia, Greece, and Rome.   If the laws of inductive logic have any value it is certain that Matteuzzi is not inductive.   Furthermore, a brief survey of history and geography shows that similar political régimes, e.g., unlimited monarchies or republics, have existed under various geographical conditions and vice versa.   In the same geographic environment we find the Samoans and the Maoris with an aristocratic and feudal system and the Papuans with scarcely any chiefs and with a system of communal partnership.[162]   The lack of the correlation becomes especially conspicuous when we consider the evolution of a political régime within the same geographical area.   During the history of Athens, Rome, or of any European country the political system has changed several times while the geographic environment has remained practically unchanged.   These changes give ample proof that the correlation between the two series of phenomena does not exist in any important degree.   Thus Matteuzzi's hypothesis and hundreds of similar theories are doubtful.[163]

Correlations Number 4 and 5: Among other fashionable geographic theories two hypotheses must be mentioned: one the so-called *Equatorial Drift,* and the other the so-called *Northward Trend of Civilization.*   The essence of the theory of equatorial

[161] See Pizzi, "Le instituzione politiche degl' Irani," *Rivista Italiana di Sociologia,* 1902, March–June.

[162] See the facts in Thurnwald, R., *op. cit.*

[163] See a detailed criticism of Matteuzzi's theory in Kovalevsky, M., *Sovremennya Soziologi,* Chap. IX.

drift is that peoples living at ease in the warm lowlands have been overrun by hardier races bred in the more rigorous climates of farther north or of higher altitudes.[164] Even the fact of the existence of such a drift as far as it is a permanent and perpetual tendency is doubtful. The only corroboration of this hypothesis is a series of facts like the conquest of India by the Aryans, that of China by the Mongols and Manchus, and of Greece and Rome by the barbarians, or the southward movement of the Toltecs and the Aztecs in Mexico, and the northward pressure of the Kaffirs and the Patagonians. On the basis of such one-sided and fragmentary data it is hardly possible to claim the existence of such a drift. These facts may be confronted by more numerous instances of peoples, who, though located in southern areas, have conquered peoples of the north. The consolidation of the Summerian and the Accadian Empires was started from the South (Ur, Lagash, Uruk), and extended far north, up to the Mediterranean. The first consolidation of Egypt was made from the south (with a center at Hieraconpolis) and extended by conquests to the north. During the second dynasty north or lower Egypt secured the upper hand, but during the third dynasty southern Egypt was again victorious. Later on, such victories of southern and northern Egypt with a corresponding shifting of the metropolis (Memphis, Hieraconpolis, Thebais) were repeated many times, not to mention conquests of many northern peoples by the Egyptians. The conquest of Greece and Rome by the northern barbarians is frequently used as an argument. The records of history tell us of hundreds of conquests and long dominations over these northern peoples by the Greeks and the Romans. Is it not true also that the conquests of Athens and Rome expanded not only toward the south but toward the north? Did not the Arabs conquer many peoples situated far north of Mecca and Medina? Did not the struggles of southern and northern China lead sometimes to the domination of the south over the north? Did not the conquests of Genghis Khan, or Tamerlane or the Turks extend over an enormous area to the

---

[164] WARD, R., *Climate*, p. 234–235; before Ward the theory was set forth by many geographers, beginning (in modern times) with Montesquieu; see MONTESQUIEU, *Spirit of Laws*, Vol. I, pp. 238 ff., 284 ff., Lond., 1894. See also VALLAUX, *Le sol et l' état*, pp. 41 ff.

north? Is not the same true even in regard to the great migration of the peoples at the beginning of the Middle Ages when a wave of the Asiatic peoples moved from the south to the north subjugating and destroying all that lay in their way? In the history of Europe, Spaniards have not been always beaten by the northern Europeans. Military or cultural success has not always belonged to the peoples situated on the north. I have recalled a few of these elementary facts, which may be multiplied *ad libitum,* only because they are forgotten by the partizans of the Equatorial Drift theory. These show its fallacy.[165]

The theory of the northward course of civilization consists in a claim that "the leadership in world civilization is inseparably linked with climate and that with advance in culture it has been transferred toward colder lands, and when extant culture has declined, leadership usually has retreated southward," and "that the part of civilization's banner has led steadily northward while culture was advancing and *vice versa.*" [166] Corroboration of the theory consists in a historical indication that "civilization began in Egypt and Summeria, hot countries, then the leadership

[165] A part of this same theory is the idea, widely accepted, that the tropical and sub-tropical climates are responsible for the production of an impotent, idle and non-virile type of people who are as a result, destined to be dominated by the virile populations bred in northern climates. To discuss the value of this theory we must agree as to what is meant by the terms *tropical* and *sub-tropical.* When climatologists speak of these regions they refer to the area 40° or 45° north latitude to 40° or 45° south latitude. This includes most of the civilizations of ancient times, as well as Japan and the southern portions of the United States. One who knows a little history can hardly agree that these populations are necessarily impotent. If they are non-virile at the present time and have been conquered by northern peoples, this has not always been so and may not continue in the future. Due to its great numerical preponderance, the population of the more temperate zones naturally could have conquered small social groups situated in the tropics. Finally we see a very definite reawakening and great increase in activity among various social groups in Asia, India, Africa, Arabia, who have always been supposed to be destitute of force and capacity. This is an additional repudiation of the theory. In spite of its popularity it is likely to be fallacious. For a verification of these statements take the historical atlases of these countries, see where they are situated, study the character of their climate and environment, (for instance, in WARD, R., *Climate,* Chaps. I to VII) study their history and then what I have said just now will be clear. About the reawakening of these societies see PRINCE, A. E., "Europe and the Renaissance of Islam," *The Yale Review,* April, 1926; also history of Japan in the 19th century.

[166] GILFILLAN, S. C., "The Coldward Course of Progress," *Political Science Quarterly,* Vol. XXXV, 1920, pp. 393, 399; see also the book by Stefansson. Earlier, the theory, in a slightly different form, was set forth by P. Mougeolle, in his *Statique des civilisations,* 1883.

was assumed by Babylonia, Crete, Phœnicia, Assyria, etc., tending always toward the north. . . Four southward movements may be noted, all of which coincide with declines of civilization. Thus, on the break-up of the Roman Empire, civilization centered in Carthage and Alexandria, as well as Constantinople, and presently in Damascus and Bagdad; then gradually it moved northward through the Middle Ages, passing the Roman high level about 1350 and attaining regions colder than ever before. On the diagram . . . it is shown how the centers of civilization moved further from the cities mentioned to Venice, Milan, Antwerp, London, Paris, Berlin, New York, Chicago, Winnipeg, and Petrograd." Recently "Scandinavia has shown great cultural activity, as if preparing to lead the world. Russia is rousing herself from a sleep of ages. In 2000 the most virile architecture will perhaps be found (not in Berlin but) in Detroit and Copenhagen, in 2100 in Montreal, Christiania and Memel." The author further claims that "also within each nation civilization has moved coldward in progressing. The Greek civilization began in Crete and ended in Constantinople. The leadership of Italy passed from Sicily through Rome to Milan, and that of Spain from Cadiz to Madrid and Barcelona." There are some exceptions but, according to the author, they only prove the rule. Such is the essence and proof of this clearly cut theory. The cause of all this is climate.

No doubt the theory is interesting and appealing, especially to the peoples who live in the north and have not achieved world leadership yet. However, one may doubt whether the time will come when the Lapps and the Eskimos will lead the world. Speaking seriously, the theory represents speculation backed by a one-sided and a defective selection of historical facts. The only true one in the theory is the statement that with the progress of civilization and with the growth of population, the area inhabited by men expands to the south and north, and many unfavorable places, inaccessible for less cultural peoples, become inhabited. Beyond this all three contentions of the theory are questionable. There are no definite and clear criteria of the rank of a civilization and of its progress and regress. Naturally such vagueness makes it possible for an author to arrange the regions and the periods in any desirable form and hierarchy. Further, the use of the size of the leading cities as an adequate criterion of civilization may be questioned. On this basis we cannot say anything definite of the civilizations of Summeria, Accadia, ancient Egypt, or even Greece and Rome, because the data are either lacking or are uncertain. Aside from these considerations, which are enough to invalidate the theory, it is easy to prove the defective character of its three claims.

In order to prove the contention that in a period of decline the leadership of civilization shifts to the south, the author points to the shifting of authority in Egypt from the Lower to the Middle or from north to south. Meanwhile the historians of ancient Egypt say that the period of Middle Egypt with Thebae as the capital, and especially during the eighteenth and nineteenth dynasties was the climax of the Egyptian civilization rather than the period of its decline. On the other hand, in the period of the decline of ancient Egypt, its center shifted not to the south but to the north (Saïs and Alexandria). Still more fantastic is the author's distribution of Summeria, Accadia, Babylonia, Chaldea and Bagdad from the standpoint of their temperature, their comparative cultural level, and the progress and regress of civilization. (See his diagram on page 395.) His claim that "on the break-up of the Roman Empire civilization," the leadership shifted again to the south, to Carthage, Alexandria, and Constantinople is almost as bad. In the first place Constantinople has the same latitude as Rome and its average temperature is colder by 4° F. In the second place, if Carthage and several other African and Asiatic cities showed some progression in the period of the decline of the Roman Empire, a similar gain was shown by northern cities such as Milan, Lyon, Trier, Ravenna, Tarraco and so on. They also increased greatly and gained in size, population, wealth, splendor, and cultural significance. In the history of Greece we find that the period of the decline of Greek culture was followed by a shifting of the political center of Greece not toward the south but rather toward the north. It went from Sparta and Athens to Bœotia and Macedonia. In these, as well as in many similar cases, we see only a shifting of the center of culture or of political influence to some other place when an existing center begins to decline. Further, such cases as the appearance of quite new cultures, the Arabic culture for example, cannot be regarded as a progress or a regress in comparison with the Roman culture because they are quite heterogeneous.

The second doubtful contention of the author is that leadership in civilization steadily shifts to the north in the course of history. This theory is based principally upon the data of the nineteenth and the twentieth centuries. Is it not true that even during this recent period a series of new great powers—like Japan, Australia, Latin America, and South Africa,—have appeared? Is it not also true that in America, during the last few decades, California has grown more rapidly than the majority of the northern states? Finally do we not see a re-awakening of the majority of the Asiatic and the old African societies (China, India, Arabia, even Turkey), after centuries of sleeping? These and many similar facts only indicate that the centers of civilization are shifting in the course of time, and that the areas of civilization are expanding with the achievements of man. And that is all. If man began to pass over both poles, he also began to fly, to conquer, and to settle tropical forests, deserts, and other places uninhabited or slightly inhabited before. Besides, it is rather useless to talk about the leadership in civilization generally because of the vagueness of the concept. If we take leadership in material technique it undoubtedly has belonged, during the last two centuries, to the peoples of central or northern Europe; but before that it belonged to the Arabian, the Asiatic, the African, or possibly even to some American peoples. In the field of religion, Europe never has been a leader; even Christianity and Mohammedanism, not to mention Confucianism, Buddhism, Hinduism, Tao-ism or Judaism, originated outside of Europe. In the field of philosophy and ethics, or even arts Europe scarcely has surpassed Asia and Egypt. I will not continue this line of thought. This is rather sufficient to show the inadequate character of the theory. All the facts given in corroboration may be easily confronted with facts of an opposite kind.

The above analysis of the representative correlations between geographical conditions and various phases of political and social organization shows that there may be some connection between them; but the relation is so indefinite that its existence may be questioned seriously. An attentive scrutiny of these sweeping geographical hypotheses shows more fallacies than scientifically proved statements.

19. CLIMATE AND GENIUS AND THE EVOLUTION OF CIVILIZATIONS

Among several theories dealing with this problem probably the best is that of Dr. E. Huntington. For that reason I shall discuss mainly his hypothesis. Objections to this theory apply more fully to other, less elaborated generalizations.

Huntington's theory of the relationship between climate and genius and the progress or the decay of civilizations is a logical inference from his three minor hypotheses, namely: that climate is a decisive factor in health; that it determines physical and mental efficiency; and that climate continually changes in time. From these premises he concludes that climate determines the growth and decay of civilizations, its distribution on the earth, and the historical destinies of nations. Since a civilization is the result of the energy, efficiency, intelligence, and genius of the population, and since these qualities are determined by climate, *ergo:* climate is the factor in the progress or regress of civilizations.

If these three premises are valid, the conclusion is true and *vice versa*. In the first part of this chapter I have attempted to show that the first and second premises are far from being valid. The author gives the third premise outstanding importance by saying that "a large part of the reasoning of this book stands or falls with the hypothesis of climatic pulsations in historic times." [167] Nevertheless this hypothesis is even more questionable than the first two. A perusal of meteorological records shows that climate has not changed to a very great extent in historical times.[168] A series of prominent specialists in climate say that "popular (and Huntington's) belief in climatic changes are untrustworthy." Huntington's theory of the pulsation of climate is based on the study of the "big tree" rings in California. This method and the deductions made from it about the pulsation of climate have been

---

[167] *Civilization and Climate*, p. 7.
[168] See WARD, R., *op. cit.*, Chap. XI.

challenged seriously by the specialists.[169]   In the third place, if we grant that pulsation of climate in California is accurately reflected in the "big tree" rings, it does not follow that in other places of the earth climate has been pulsating in the same way as in California.   Fourthly, Huntington's method of computing the character of climatic changes and their exact periods in Ancient Greece or Rome or in any other historical country, is pure speculation, based on nothing.   Besides, his own hypothesis is very elastic and he modifies it according to the circumstances.[170]   This is sufficient to show the great extent to which the third premise is questionable and uncertain.   Thus all three foundations upon which Huntington has built the ponderous structure of his sweeping generalizations are not sound.   This fact is sufficient to vitiate his conclusions and to make them extremely doubtful.   However, let us glance at the additional proofs and at some of the details of his philosophy.   The proofs are given in the form of maps which show the distribution of climate on the earth and in Europe; the distribution of health rates in Europe; the distribution of civilization on the earth and in Europe; and the distribution of eminent men in Europe.   All these maps, according to Huntington, show "a remarkable similarity."   Health is high in the countries where the climate approaches the ideal suggested by Huntington; civilization is high in the same countries and low in those with poor climate and poor health; and the number of eminent men parallels the distribution of climate and health.   Further, in the past, Rome and various other countries grew and made progress during periods when their climate was near to the Huntington "ideal," and declined when their climate changed unfavorably. Shifting of the centers of civilization in the process of history has paralleled the moving of favorable climatic zones.   Thus everything shows a remarkable confirmation of Huntington's hypothesis.   "Apparently climate influences health and energy, and these in turn influence civilization." [171]   The author thinks that the hypothesis explains even a great many other characteristics of

[169] *Ibid.*, p. 350 ff.

[170] Compare *e.g.*, *Civilization and Climate*, Chap. XIV; *World Power and Evolution*, Chap. VIII; *The Character of Races*, Fig. 15.

[171] See *Civilization and Climate*, Chaps. X to XVIII; *World Power and Evolution*, Chaps. VIII to XIII; *The Character of Races*, Ch. XV.

various peoples and their historical destinies. On this basis, Dr. Huntington interprets the history of Greece, Rome, Turkey, Germany and of many other countries.

Although these maps and generalizations are very interesting, I fear that they are very questionable. We have already discussed the validity of their basic premises. Since the correlations between the "ideal" climate and health and efficiency are not corroborated, maps constructed on these bases are even more questionable. The most questionable hypotheses of all are those drawn from questionable maps based on still more questionable hypotheses. Besides, what scientific value has a map (see Figs. 22, 43, 44, in *Civilization and Climate*) where the zones of favorable or unfavorable climate are such that half of Europe and three-quarters of Asia are shown as having an identical climate (the area extending from 25° to 70° of latitude and from 30° to 180° of longitude)? In fact, in this vast area, there are the most varied types of climate; and many parts of it more closely approximate the climate of unfavored zones than that of the favored regions. This applies to each of the five climatic zones into which Huntington divided the surface of the earth. It is possible to show a "remarkable similarity and coincidence" between anything and any contention by using this method.

The other maps of the distribution of health, climate, and genius are no better. I already have shown the inadequacy of death rates as a criterion of the health of various countries. I also have shown that even the correlation between "seasonal" fluctuations of death rates and of climate has not been proved as yet. However, Dr. Huntington is not embarrassed by all these complications. He takes the death rates of various countries and puts them on the map in such a way that vast areas with very different rates appear identical, and *vice versa*. On the basis of this questionable procedure he points out the "remarkable coincidence with other maps." (See Maps nos. 10, 11, 12 and 13 in *The Character of Races.*) It is still more remarkable that the author admits some small "exceptions" to the rule such as the similarity of the climates of Japan and Korea (which contradict in regard to health and to rank of civilizations); or the relatively small number of eminent men in Belgium which contradicts its favorable climate and its place on the map of civilization. Another contradiction appears in comparing the map of civilization, where the indices of the civilizations of England and Scotland are 100 and 98, with the map of the number of geniuses, where a decidedly reverse relation is found. If it were possible to put all Russia (one-sixth of the earth) in one climatic zone, and in one mortality or civilization zone, then why pay any attention to the small "exceptions"? Why not make the maps identical so that the relationship appears absolute? If large differences may be obliterated, why not all of them?

However, there is more. Even if we grant that the maps are accurate we may ask what are the proofs that differences in health, civilization, and in production of genius are due to variations in climate, as Dr. Huntington claims.[172] There is no proof except the map of climate inadequately constructed on a questionable basis. If it were accurate the correlation would not prove that the relationship were causal. Many other factors might explain the relationship or coincidence.

Let us go further. Let us grant that all of the shortcomings of the theory which we have already pointed out do not exist. Instead let us ask what would have been the map of the distribution of civilization, health, and genius in different countries, if Dr. Huntington had taken the period of 100 or 200 B.C. instead of that following A.D. 1600. We can say with certainty that the highest index of civilization and the number of men of genius for that period would have been the countries around the Mediterranean, and in Asia. At present these countries have a very low index. The countries around the Baltic Sea, England, and northern Europe which now have the highest indices would then have had the lowest index. The reason is simple. At that moment the populations of central and northern Europe were barbarian while those of Rome, Greece, northern Africa, China, India, and of many other Asiatic regions were the brilliant civilizations. Even if the maps were constructed for the period of 1840 the indices of such countries as Japan would be quite different. The same

[172] His claim is so strong that he is certain that "the regions around the North Sea would probably *always* excel eastern and southern Europe" in production of men of genius because of their different climates. *The Character of Races*, p. 233.

can be said of numerous other phenomena which Huntington tries to explain through his climatic hypothesis. Why, for instance, do various countries, which remain in the same geographic environment, make rapid progress and outdistance peoples that were once superior to them and then afterwards decline themselves? Sometimes such transformations happen in relatively short periods such as one or two centuries.

Dr. Huntington meets these contradictions by his hypothesis of the shifting of climatic zones and of the pulsation of climate. This theory, as we have pointed out, is not recognized as proved by the climatologists. I have tried to find climatic changes during the last fourteen hundred years in the area of England and northern and southern Europe, which would explain the waning rôle of the southern peoples and the increasing rôle of those of the north. I did not find any satisfactory answer. Furthermore, in Japan during the period from 1845 to 1890 there was no noticeable change in climate; and yet during this period the country changed from a poorly known and backward barbarian society into a world empire. The Japanese indices of health, civilization, and genius have changed considerably since 1845. The reader who tries to find an answer to this question in the works of Huntington (including the joint work with Fisher, on *Climatic Changes,* New Haven, 1922) seeks in vain. Grant that climatic zones shift in historical periods. It is further necessary to show that their shifting and the changes in the leadership in civilization have been parallel; that any country in which the climate moves away from Huntington's ideal decays; that any country in which climate moves closer to the ideal progresses; and that all these processes occur exactly in the same periods. Only when these parallelisms are shown may the hypothesis approach validity. Such a proof is not found in Huntington's works. Here is a sample of his climatic interpretation of Rome's decay.

From 450 to 250 B.C. the climate (of Rome) was probably decidedly more stimulating than in any part of Italy today. . . That period ended in a great decline in rainfall and storminess. Then by 220 or 210 it had apparently fallen to about the present level. For a hundred years nearly the same conditions prevailed, and for a century and a half the climate returned to a condition as favorable as in 240 B.C.[173]

A reader of these lines may think Dr. Huntington has at his disposal there the detailed record of the Meteorological Bureau of Ancient Rome, or at least some certain historical records which permit a definite characterization of the climatic changes. Unfortunately, the reader is wrong. Dr. Huntington does not have such meteorological records because they do not exist; nor has he a single line of proof from the historical testimony of the contemporaries; nor even a quotation from some reliable historian of Rome. The quotations he gives from Dr. W. Simkhovich concern only the character of the soil; and, besides, Simkhovich's theory of the exhaustion of the soil is objected to by more competent historians of Rome.[174]   All that Dr. Huntington has are the data concerning the growth of "the big tree rings" in California, on which he constructs a diagram of climatic pulsation in historic times. This task and the climatic deductions based on it are challenged by the climatologists. On the basis of this very hypothetical diagram which cannot give even the approximate rainfall, or fluctuations of temperature and storminess for California, alone, Dr. Huntington, after considerably modifying the diagram, (see it on page 188, *World Power,*) drew detailed conclusions concerning Roman climate with an apparent accuracy for periods as short as ten years. The accuracy of his weather predictions may be envied by many meteorologists trying to predict changes in contemporary weather. It is obvious that Dr. Huntington's theory of the pulsation of climate in Rome, in its essence, is nothing but a mere speculation adapted to the course of Roman history. The periods of the growth of Rome are characterized as the periods of good climate and *vice versa.* He does not deduce the character of historical processes from the established climatic data; but, on the contrary, deduces climatic data from the character of the historical processes. He concludes "there is a remarkable parallelism" between climatic and historical pulsations. Further, if changes of climate took place in Rome, it

[173] *World Power and Evolution*, pp. 190 and 192.
[174] See ROSTOWTZEFF, M., *The Social and Economic History of the Roman Empire*, p. 495 and Chap. VIII, Oxford, 1926.

would be necessary to show that these changes were so great as to call forth the decay of Rome, and that they were much greater than the differences between the climates of England, Japan and Scandinavia. Huntington recognizes the climate of these places as invigorating and facilitating to the progress of civilization. Nothing of such a test has been done by Huntington. And it could not be done.

If these tests are not sufficient others might be used. For instance, it would be much more accurate to test the correlation of climate and genius by taking the exact place of birth of men of genius given in studies by Ellis, Odin, or of E. L. Clarke, J. McKeen Cattell, J. Philiptschenko, F. Maas, C. Castle, Charles H. Cooley, S. Nearing, S. Fisher, myself and others. In all of these studies the necessary data concerning birthplaces and the time of birth of these men are given. By obtaining the necessary climatic data, correlations could be made which would easily test the climatic hypothesis.

I shall give but one more argument. We know well that different social classes living in the same climate produce different proportions of men of genius.[175] We know also that the number of outstanding men in the same country from decade to decade or from century to century, or from region to region fluctuates; for instance there is the conspicuous increase of the proportion of the leading American scientists and captains of industry coming from the Middle and the Far West during the last two or three decades; these and hundreds of similar facts can hardly be reconciled with Huntington's theory.

We shall go no further. There may be some correlation between genius and civilization and climate but most of it remains to be discovered. Dr. Huntington's work in spite of the talent and energy he displays, cannot be recognized as conclusive.

The same conclusions apply to many other theories of this kind. We shall leave them without analysis.[176] May I add in conclu-

[175] See a number of these studies in my book, *Social Mobility*, Chap. XII.

[176] I have not given any analysis of such books as KELSEY, C., *The Physical Basis of Society*, TEGGART, F. J., *The Processes of History*, New Haven, 1918, or MACKINDER, H. J., *Democratic Ideals and Reality*, Lond., 1919, or SHALER, N. S., *Man and the Earth*, and several other books simply because they, being too general, do not add anything new either to the geographical theory or to its criticism. Recently published, G. Taylor's *Environment and Race* is even more speculative than Huntington's works.

sion, that in spite of the fact that I have been very severe with Dr. Huntington in the preceding pages, I have the greatest respect for him and for his valuable attempts to build sociological theory on a sound objective basis. We must credit the school with many interesting and suggestive theories; and with several correlations, which are, at least, partly true. Any analysis of social phenomena, which does not take into consideration geographical factors, is incomplete. We are grateful to the school for these valuable contributions. This, however, does not oblige us to accept its fallacious theories, its fictitious correlations, or finally, its overestimation of the rôle of geographical environment. We must separate the wheat from the chaff. After this "sifting" is made the remainder enters the storehouse of sociological principles.

CHAPTER IV

BIOLOGICAL INTERPRETATION OF SOCIAL PHENOMENA

Bio-Organismic School

I. PRINCIPAL TYPES OF BIOLOGICAL THEORIES IN SOCIOLOGY

THE human being is an organism and, as such, is subject to what are known as biological laws. This is the reason why many theories of both the past and the present have tried to interpret social phenomena as a variety of life phenomena. The extraordinary progress of biology during the last seventy years has given an additional impetus to biological interpretations in sociology. Hence, the contemporary biological theories in social science. These are numerous and vary in their concrete forms, but nevertheless, it is possible to group them in a relatively few fundamental classes. The principal concepts of the post-Darwinian biology are: organism, heredity, selection, variation, adaptation, struggle for existence, and the inherited drives (reflexes, instincts, unconditioned responses) of an organism. Correspondingly we have: 1. *The Bio-Organismic Interpretation of Social Phenomena;* 2. *The Anthropo-Racial School,* which interprets social phenomena in the terms of heredity, selection, and variation through selection; 3. *The Darwinian School of the Struggle for Existence,* which emphasizes the rôle of this factor; and 4. *The Instinctivist School,* which views human behavior and social processes as a manifestation of various inherited or instinctive drives. Besides these, there are many "mixed" theories, which in their analysis of social facts, combine biological factors with the non-biological ones. These may be classed among the biological, as well as among the other sections of sociology. For the sake of convenience in this section, we shall discuss only the first three schools. The "instinctivist" sociological theories will be analyzed in the section of psychological sociology. The reason for this is that they have been discussed principally by psychologists and are closely interwoven with other psychological interpretations. As to the "mixed" theories, they will be scattered throughout various sections of the book. Only one of these mixed theories—that of the *Demographic School*—is to be put within the biological section. It will be understood, however, that such an arrangement is purely conventional and a mere matter of convenience for the sake of orientation in the field of numerous sociological theories. What is important is the proper analysis of the theories rather than their placing within this or that conventional section. Let us now turn to the principal biological schools in contemporary sociology.

2. BIO-ORGANISMIC SCHOOL AND ITS RELATION TO OTHER ORGANIC THEORIES

The first principal school of biological sociology is represented by the bio-organismic theories. The term "bio-organismic" needs some explanation. Among the fundamental conceptions of society it is possible to discriminate four principal types: first, the *mechanistic* conception of society, as a kind of a machine system; second, the *nominalistic or atomistic conception* which sees in society nothing but individuals, and does not recognize in it any superindividual reality; third, an *organic conception,* which views society as a living unity, recognizing its superindividual reality, its "natural" origin and spontaneous existence; fourth, a *functional conception* which does not care at all whether society is a mechanism or organism, natural or artificial, but which tries to view it as a system of interrelated individuals (synthesis of the sociological realism and nominalism). This system does not provide any reality beyond that of its members, but at the same time, it is different from that reality of the same individuals in their mutual isolation. The functional conception tries to ascertain the forms, the character, the uniformities (functional analysis) in fluctuation, variation, evolution of the relationships of the individuals who compose a social system, of the relationships of the groups of a system, and the relationships of one social system to other social systems.

Among these four conceptions, the organic has been the most

popular.   Its characteristics belong to practically all varieties of
the organic theory of a society.   These varieties may be divided
into three principal subclasses: 1. *Philosophical Organicism,* which
contends only that society is a living unity, that it has superindividual reality, that it lives according to "natural" laws, and that it
originated spontaneously.   Philosophical organicism is often not
concerned at all by any comparison of society with a biological
organism, or with a "psychological entity" like "collective soul,"
"public opinion," "social mind" or anything of the sort.   It has
significance mostly as a conception opposite to the atomistic or
nominalistic and mechanistic conceptions of society.   Contrary
to the former, it recognizes the super- or transindividual reality of
society; and in opposition to the latter, it refuses to view society
as an inanimate mechanism controlled only by exterior forces, and
especially as an artificial mechanism created by man in the way
of social contract or intentional volition.   2. The second form of
the organic conception of a society is represented by *Psycho-Social
Organicism.*   Psycho-social organic theories have the above general characteristics of philosophical organicism.   Sometimes the
boundary line between them is almost intangible and philosophical
organicism imperceptibly passes into a psycho-social organicism.[1]
But the less "refined" psycho-social theories of organicism often
go further.   To the characteristics of philosophical organicism
they add the contentions that society is a superindividual organism of ideas, representations, minds, and volitions; that the social
mind, or social volition, or social "self," or "social opinion" exists
as a reality *sui generis* beyond the reality of minds, volitions,
opinions and representations of its members; and that in this
same sense society is a kind of spiritual personality—a real social
or group mind.   Correspondingly in these theories there is often
given a psychological personification of the social group, together
with many analogies between the individual and the social mind.
The theories represent a type of the psycho-social interpretation

[1]As an example of such a "refined" organic theory which stands somewhere between the philosophical and the psycho-social organicism, the conception of Th.
Litt, developed in his *Individuum und Gemeinschaft,* Leipzig-Berlin, 1919, may
serve. See *passim* and pp. 6–7, 12, 17–18, 29–30, 102–105.   Still more "refined'
is C. Gini's "New Organicism" brilliantly set forth in his "*Il neo-organic smo,*"
Catania, 1927.   Practically it is almost identical with the functional conception
of society.

of sociological realism. They are represented by the Sociologistic School. (See the chapter about this school.) 3. The third fundamental variety of the organic interpretations of society is given by *Bio-Organismic Theories of Society*. Sharing all the principles of the philosophical organicism, biological organicism claims that society is nothing but a specific variety of *biological* organism. In its nature, functioning, origin, development, variation,—in brief, in its whole life-process, it exhibits the characteristics similar to those of any organism, is subject to the same biological laws; and like an organism, it has not only psychosocial, but physical reality. In their essence these theories represent an extreme type of sociological realism. We must not mix the bio-organismic theories with philosophical and psycho-social organic conceptions of society. They differ greatly from each other. The above shows also that while bio-organismic theories belong to the biological school in sociology, the other branches of the organic conception do not. In this chapter I am going to discuss only the bio-organismic theories. Psycho-social organicism will be discussed in the chapter on the sociologistic school. Philosophical organicism does not need a special discussion in sociology: its place is in philosophical treatises.

3. PREDECESSORS

Various samples of the above three types of the organic conception of society are as old as are the most ancient sources of social thought known to us. The comparison of a society, particularly of a state in its social classes, institutions, and social processes, with an organism, especially with man or with his body and soul, or with the parts of his body and bodily processes, may be found in the ancient Hindu, Chinese, Greek, and Roman philosophical and social thought. Here are samples. In the ancient Sacred Books of India, four principal castes are depicted as created from the mouth, the arms, the thighs, and the feet of the Lord.[2] The king's power is pictured as composed of eternal particles of Indra, of the Wind, of the Sun, and so on.[3] Punish-

---

[2] See, for example, "Laws of Manu," *Sacred Books of the East*, Vol. XXV, I: 31: example, Oxford, 1886.

[3] *Ibid.*, VI: 4.

ment is compared with the son of the Lord and with a creature "with a black hue and red eyes." [4]   Social initiation is regarded as the second birth,[5] and so forth.   In the works of Plato, organic analogies are rather common.   "In the individuals there are the same principles and habits which there are in the State: (1) spirit of passion, typical of the Northern peoples, (2) love of knowledge and wisdom, typical of the Greeks; and love of money, typical of the Phœnicians."   Similar analogies in the properties of a body and society are numerous in Plato's works.[6]   The same is true of Aristotle.   In his "Politics" we find comparisons of the soul and the body with the upper and the lower classes; of the reason's control over affections, of the master's control over slaves; of the harmony within man with that within a body politic, and so forth.   In the famous Agrippa's Fable, the analogies are pushed to their limit.   In works of Cicero, Seneca, Florus, T. Livy, and other Roman and Greek historians, comparisons of the life-cycle of a man with that of a society, which, like man, passes through childhood, maturity, and old age; of the birth and death of both, and so on, are again very numerous.   They sometimes are carefully developed into a systematic theory.   (See the chapter about cyclical conception of social change.)   Side by side with this, we find "the natural origin" of a society, its development according to the laws of nature, especially according to the same laws which govern a development of an organism; the superindividual reality of a society, and its "organic" character; all indicated by various ancient Hindu, Chinese, Greek and Roman writers.[7]

The history of mediæval thought shows that, in spite of its predominant nominalism, "under the influence of the allegories of the Bible and the patterns set forth by Greek and Roman writers, the comparison of mankind and social groups to an ani-

[4] *Ibid.*, VII: 25, 14.

[5] *Ibid.*, II: 148, 169–170.

[6] Plato, *The Republic*, tr. by Jowett, N. Y., 1874, pp. 435–436, 462, 557 and others.

[7] See the survey and the "organic" citations from Aristotle, Cicero, Livy, Seneca, St. Paul and others in VON KRIEKEN, A. TH., *Ueber die sogennante organische Staatstheorie*, Leipzig, 1873; pp. 19–26, TOWNE, E. T., *Die Auffassung der Gesellschaft als Organismus*, pp. 15–24, Halle, 1903; BARKER, E., *The Political Thought of Plato and Aristotle*, pp. 127, 138–139, 276–281, N. Y., 1906.

mate body was generally adopted and stressed." [8] This reminds one of the organic analogies used by writers in the dispute between the secular and the ecclesiastical powers; of John Salisbury's *The Policraticus;* of the works of Nicolas of Cues, and of other thinkers of the Middle Ages, including even such rather nominalistic philosophers as Saint Thomas Aquinas. Further theories of Machiavelli, Campanella, Guicciardini and others, claimed that the State, like a man, passes through the cycles of childhood, maturity, and old age, and that, like an organism, it experiences the periods of vigor and sickness.[9]

Later on, in spite of the social physicism of the theories of the seventeenth century, and the atomistic and individualistic character of the theories of the eighteenth century, organic analogies and various organic conceptions continued to be used even by the social physicists and individualists. The difference between these theories and a real organicism is principally that the mechanists of the seventeenth century compared society and state with "artificial man." Pascal's famous comparison of society with a man; Hobbes' *Leviathan,* with its detailed organismic analogies; and similar comparisons used by Fortescue, Althusius, G. Grotius, J. Bodin and others may be contrasted with the physiocratic conception of the economic organization of a society as a "natural, living unity," but they are all samples of the organic conceptions of that time.[10] The end of the eighteenth and the beginning of the nineteenth centuries were marked by a conspicuous reaction of social thought against the atomistic, individualistic, and mechanistic conceptions of the preceding period. This reaction assumed the form of a revival of various organic interpretations. Contractual theories of society, theories of its artificial nature, and sociological atomism theories all lost credit. Their place was

[8] VON GIERKE, OTTO, *Political Theories of the Middle Age,* tr. by F. Maitland, Cambridge, 1900, notes, pp. 103–104, 112, 122 ff.

[9] See for this period, VON GIERKE, *op. cit., passim;* VON KRIEKEN, *op. cit.;* TOWNEY, *op. cit.;* GUMPLOWICZ, L., *Geschichte der Staatstheorien,* Part II, Innsbruck, 1926; JANET, P., *Histoire de la science politique,* Paris, 1887; DUNNING, W., *Political Theories, Ancient and Mediæval,* N. Y., 1902.

[10] See about this period, COKER, F. W., *Organismic Theories of the State,* pp. 14–16, N. Y., 1910; DUNNING, W., *Political Theories from Luther to Montesquieu,* N. Y., 1913; JANET, *op. cit.;* DENIS, "Die Physiokratische Schule und die erste Darstellung der Wirtschaftsgesellschaft als Organismus," *Zeitschrift für Wirtschaftsgeschichte,* VI, 1897.

occupied by the theories of De Bonald, J. de Maistre, E. Burke, Adam Müller, Herder, Lessing, Fichte, I. Kant, Shelling, H. Leo, Hegel, and of others, in which various characteristics of organic conception were laid down.[11]

Since that time, the three above types of organic conceptions,— philosophic, socio-psychological, and biological, have been again and again laid down by a great many authors. K. C. Krause, H. Ahrens, F. J. Schmitthenner, G. Waitz, F. A. Trendelenbourg, Saint-Simon, Auguste Comte, J. v. Görres, C. Th. Welcker, F. and Th. Rohmer, K. Volgraff, F. J. Stahl, and to a certain extent Lorenz v. Stein, A. Lasson, Otto Gierke, K. S. Zacharia, C. Frantz, J. K. Bluntschli, and finally H. Spencer, have, in this or that way, developed various organic interpretations of state, society, and social phenomena.[12]   The great progress of biology and the theory of evolution in the second half of the nineteenth century gave an especially strong impetus to the development of the bio-organismic theories in sociology.   In this way we come to the contemporary bio-organismic interpretations of social phenomena.   Let us turn to them.

4. CONTEMPORARY BIO-ORGANISMIC THEORIES IN SOCIOLOGY

The most prominent representatives of this current of sociological thought are: P. Lilienfeld, (a Russian of German stock, 1829-1903),[13] A. Schäffle (a German professor and statesman, 1831-1903),[14] R. Worms, (a French professor, permanent secre-

[11] Concerning that period see COKER, *op. cit.*, pp. 16–31; MOULINÉE, H., *De Bonald*, Paris, 1915; DE MAISTRE, J., "Considérations sur la France," "Soirées de Saint-Petersbourg," in his *Oeuvres complete*, Lyon, 1891–2, Vols. I–V; MERRIAM, C. E., *History of the Theory of Sovereignty since Rousseau*, N. Y., 1900; MICHEL, H., *L'idée de l'état*, Paris, 1898; BURKE, E., "Reflections on the Revolution in France," in *Works*, Bohn's ed., Vol. II; SALOMON, G., "Die Organische Staats-und Gesellschaftslehre," in WORMS, R., *Die Soziologie*, pp. 111–124, Karlsruhe, 1926.

[12] About this period see COKER, *op. cit.*, pp. 31–139.   See there the works of these authors and other references.   See also HAFF, K., *Institutionen der Personlichkeitslehre und des Körperschaftsrechts*, 1918; MOULINÉE, *op. cit.*, KAUFMANN, *Über den Begriff des Organismus in der Staatslehre des 19 Jahrhunderts*, Heidelberg, 1908.

[13] Principal works of P. Lilienfeld are: *Gedanken über die Socialwissenschaft der Zukunft*, 5 vols., Mitau, 1873–81, Berlin, 1901; *La pathologie sociale*, Paris, 1896; *Zur Verteidigung der Organischen Methode in der Soziologie*, Berlin, 1898; "La methode graphique," and "L'évolution des formes politiques" in *Annales de l'institut. intern. de sociologie*, 1896.

[14] The most important work in this respect is Schäffle's *Bau und Leben des socialen Körpers*, 1875–6, 3rd ed., 1896, 2 vols.

tary of the International Institute of Sociology and editor of the
Revue international de sociologie, 1869-1926) [15] and J. Novicow
(a Russian, 1849-1912).[16] To these names a series of others
may be added who, in a somewhat milder form, have professed
the same bio-organismic principles. Such a one is A. Fouillée
(a prominent French philosopher, psychologist, and sociologist,
1838-1912) who tried to reconcile the organismic and the contractual theories in the form of an interpretation of a society
as "a contractual organism." [17] More recently there appeared a
series of works which continued to maintain all the essential
principles of the bio-organismic interpretation. Such, for instance, are the works of La Ferriére,[18] Kjellén,[19] M. Roberts,[20]
and of several others.[21]

In view of the considerable similarity of the basic principles
of all these authors, of the well-known character of their theories,
and of the questionable value of their conclusions to the science
of sociology, we may survey all these theories summarily, without
a special analysis of the interpretations of each. Proceeding in
this way, we may sum up their basic principles in the following
manner: First, the society or social group is a special kind of an
organism in a biological sense of the word. Second, being an
organism, society resembles, in its essential characteristics, the
constitution and the functions of a biological organism. Third,
as an organism, society is subjected to the same biological laws
as those by which a biological organism functions and lives.
Fourth, sociology is a science which is to be based primarily upon

---

[15] For Worms' organicism, the most enlightening works of Worms are: *Organisme et société,* 1896; *Philosophie des sciences sociales,* 3 vols., Paris, 1903-7,
2nd ed., 1913-20; *La sociologie, sa nature, son contenue, ses attaches,* Paris, 1921.

[16] Of Novicow's works the important in this respect are: *Conscience et volonté
sociale,* Paris, 1897; *Les luttes entre sociétés humaines et leur phases successives,*
Paris, 1896; *La théorie organique des sociétés, defense de l'organicisme,* Paris, 1899;
La critique de Darwinism sociale, Paris, 1910.

[17] Of the numerous works of Fouillée, see his *La science sociale contemporaine,*
1880, 4th ed., Paris, 1904.

[18] See LA FERRIÉRE, *La loi du progrès en biologie et en sociologie,* 1915, Paris; see
also his "L'organisme sociale," *Revue international de sociologie,* 1915, Nos. 5-6.

[19] See KJELLÉN, *Der Staat als Lebensform,* 1917.

[20] See ROBERTS, M., *Malignancy and Evolution,* Lond., 1926.

[21] Besides the sociologists, several biologists have set forth a bio-organismic
theory. See HERTWIG, O., *Die Lehre vom Organismus und ihre Beziehung zur
Socialwissenschaft,* Berlin, 1899; *Allgemeine Biologie,* Jena, 1906.

biology. Such are the essential characteristics of the bio-organismic conception of society.

"What is a society?" asked Spencer, and answers: "Society is an organism." After this he indicates that the social and the biological organisms are similar in the following important respects: both have phenomena of growth; in the process of growth both exhibit differentiation in structure and functions; in both there exists an interdependence of their parts; both are composed of units (cells and individuals); destruction of an organism or of a society does not always mean the destruction of the units of which they are composed; both have a special sustaining (alimentary) system, a special distributive system (vascular and circulatory system in an organism and arteries of commerce in a society) and a special regulating system (nervous system in an organism and governmental system in a society). Side by side with these similarities there are, however, three important dissimilarities. First, an organism is symmetrical while society is asymmetrical; second, an organism is a concrete aggregate while society is a discrete one; third, in an organism, consciousness is concentrated in the nervous system, while in a society it is diffused throughout the whole aggregate so that society does not have a special social sensorium.[22] Following this plan, H. Spencer analyzes in detail society's characteristics, functions, systems, and processes.

P. Lilienfeld's views are as follows: "Human society, like natural organisms, is a real entity (*ein reales Wesen*). It is nothing but a continuation of Nature, a higher manifestation of the same forces which lie at the basis of all natural phenomena." Representing "a system of mutual relationship and interaction of human beings," it has the same characteristics as a biological organism in its functions of multiplication, growth, differentiation, sickness, death, regeneration, integration of parts, cohesion, purposivity, spirituality, structural perfectibility and the storing or capitalization of energy. In these characteristics the biological and the

---

[22] SPENCER, H., *The Principles of Sociology*, Vol. I, Part II, N. Y., 1910; *The Inductions of Sociology, passim*, and pp. 447–462.

social organisms are similar, and both differ from an inorganic body.[23]

"The biological organism is a united mass of a living substance which is capable of preserving itself under certain exterior conditions." The same is true in regard to an ants' hill and to human society. Using M. Verworn's classification of organisms, Lilienfeld indicates that there are five principal classes: the cell, tissue (complex of cells), organ (complex of tissues), person (complex of organs), and state or society (complex of persons). Thus society is only the highest form of an organism. Like an organism it is a living unity, absorbing the ingredients of its environment, and having the process of metabolism. Its individuals are as dependent on the whole society as a cell in an organism; and like it, society has its nervous system and its reflexes. Within it, besides its members, there is a material substance which corresponds to the "intercellular substance or space" in an organism. The principal difference between a social and a biological organism is that society is somewhat less integrated than an organism.[24] But, again, in this respect there are three degrees of organisms: plants which lack an ability to move in their parts and in their whole; animal organisms which have an ability to move as a whole; and social organisms, which can move in their whole, as well as in their parts (individuals). Thus, this difference means only that the social organism is the highest class of organism, and nothing more.[25] Some have raised the objection that in an organism the cells cannot move freely, or belong at the same time to several organisms, or even shift from one organism to another; while in a society individuals can move, can belong to several societies, and can shift from one society to another. To this, Lilienfeld answers that a greater mobility of individuals in an organism means only that it is an organism of a higher class. Wandering cells are also in an organism, some of them passing even from one organ to another (spermatozoids). Another objection is that, contrary to an organism, society does not exhibit the phases of birth and death. Lilienfeld meets this by

[23] LILIENFELD, *Die Menschliche Gesellschaft als realer Organismus*, Vol. I, pp. 1, 34 ff., 58–68, Mitau, 1873.

[24] LILIENFELD, *Zur Vertidigung*, pp. 9–12, 15, 21 and *passim*.

[25] *La pathologie sociale*, Ch. I, and pp. 307 ff.

indicating that, like an organism, one society often gives birth to another, and that societies may die. The objection that society differs from an organism in that it is asymmetrical, the author meets by a statement that social hierarchy is a specific kind of a symmetry in the social body. The objection that an individual has a "self" and a specific integrated consciousness, while a society does not, is met by an indication that individual conscious-ness or self is also mosaical, and that it represents an ever-chang-ing process similar to the public mind and the governmental ac-tivity in a society. Other objections and analogies ascribed to the organismic theories are declared by Lilienfeld childish. They be-long not to the organismic theory, but to its critics, who unfairly ridicule the theory and ascribe to it the analogies which do not belong to it.[26] The general conclusion of Lilienfeld is that *"nihil est in societate quod non prius fuerit in natura."* Sociology is to be based on biology and has to apply all its laws to the scientific interpretation of social phenomena. Without the organismic prin-ciples a scientific sociology is impossible, and *Sociologus nemo, nisi biologus.*[27]

The theory of Schäffle is moderate, especially in the second edition of his work, where he even stresses conspicuously the difference between a society and organism; but it is still bio-organismic in its realization. The leading principles of his soci-ology are similar to the above; for his "social morphology" is characteristic of Schäffle's fivefold classification of "social tissues," which are homological to corresponding tissues in an organism. Such social phenomena as the army, police, clothing, roofs, safes and fortresses are nothing but "a protective social tissue," which corresponds to the epidermal tissue of animals. Various technical and practical social arrangements are as noth-ing but the muscular social tissues which correspond either to the cross-striped-voluntary or to the smooth-involuntary-muscles of an organism. Educational and intellectual institutions of a society correspond to the nervous system.[28] Having studied the

[26] *Zur Vertidigung,* pp. 48–57.

[27] *Ibid.,* pp. 9, 31, 56–57; *La pathologie sociale,* Chap. I; *Die Menschliche Gesell-schaft,* pp. 398–399.

[28] See SCHÄFFLE, *Bau und Leben des socialen Körpers,* 1896, Vol. I, Books II–IV, pp. 111–175, and *passim.*

tissues, he proceeds to study the social organs made up of these social tissues. Schäffle studies the state from this organismic standpoint.

More conspicuous is the biological organicism in the theory of J. Novicow. Like Lilienfeld, in spite of a crushing criticism of the theory at the International Congress of Sociologists, he still insists that the criticism did not set forth any destructive objection against bio-organicism as a theory, which claims that the laws of biology are "equally applicable to cells, to aggregates of cells, to plants or animals, and to the aggregates of individuals styled society." "Since society is composed of living creatures, it can be but a living creature." He further answers the principal objections set forth against the organismic theories. In an organism, as well as in a society, the struggle goes on not only with heterogeneous bodies, but between various parts of each of them also. The difference between the concreteness of an organism and of a society is very relative because our conception of space is very subjective. To a creature millions of times less than a man, a man's body would appear as a whole continent with oceans, seas, mountains and so on. That is, it would appear quite a discrete thing. On the other hand, to a creature millions of times greater than man, many societies would appear quite a concrete body. Finally, spacial discreteness or concreteness is not important for an organism; what is important is the functional interaction and interdependence of its parts, regardless of their spacial nearness. From this standpoint, interdependence of England and New Zealand is no less than the parts of an organism. Furthermore, he ridicules the objection that the members of a society can live autonomically while there has not been any isolated foot which would go and live alone. "A sprout of a plant may be transplanted, but a man's head could not be 'ingrafted' into another body. Does this mean that man is not an organism?" asks Novicow.[29]

He further proceeds to develop his theory of social volition and consciousness, as they exist apart from individual volitions and consciousness. Contrary to the other organicists who see the

[29] *Conscience et volonté sociales*, pp. 1–9. See also his paper in *Annales de l'institut intern. de sociologie*, Vol. IV.

organ of such social sensorium in government, Novicow sees it in the élite of a society, in its intellectual aristocracy. The members of such an élite are "real, sensitive cells of a society," they are "real starters" (*le véritable moteur*) of all social actions. Through their production of ideas and sentiments they (like receptors in the nervous system) transmit the stimuli to "the effectors" (government, etc.), and in this way perform the rôle of a social nervous system. "Every social action is carried on through persuasion. This persuasion is a volition which originates in the brain of an élite and is transmitted to other brains." Such, in brief, is the organ and the mechanism of social consciousness and social volition.[30]

R. Worms, in his monograph: *Society and Organism,* showed himself an extreme bio-organicist. Later on, however, he recognized many shortcomings of the extreme organismic theories,[31] though the fundamentals of bio-organismic conception he supported throughout his life. He states that in origin, structure, and functions, society is analogous to organism. His analysis of the similarities and the dissimilarities of society and organism he sums up in the following way: "We must conclude," he says, "that though there exist unquestionable differences between the societies and the organisms, they are not so important as to separate them radically from each other." [32]

It is practically useless to continue a detailed survey of the character and the contents of a great many other bio-organismic works. It is enough to say that in the way of analogies there has been displayed a real ingenuity in inventing the most startling comparisons, which try to define even the sex of various social organisms (for instance Bluntschli thought that the state is a masculine organism while the Church is a feminine one),[33] and in finding the social homologues to the heart, circulation of blood, stomach, lungs, arms, hair, head, and what not. At the same

---

[30] *Conscience et volonté sociales,* pp. 43–44, 51 ff., 69–74, 97–102, 137 and *passim.*

[31] See his acknowledgment of this in WORMS' *Philosophie des sciences sociales,* Vol. I, 1913, pp. 47–48; also his *Les principes biologiques de l'évolution sociale,* Paris, 1910.

[32] *Philosophie des sciences sociales,* p. 55. See Chap. III.

[33] See BLUNTSCHLI, J. K., *Lehre vom modernen Staat,* Vol. I, p. 23, Stuttgart, 1875; *Gesammelte kleine Schriften,* p. 284, Nordlingen, 1879. Generally speaking, Bluntschli's work is perhaps one of the most logical and conspicuous examples of bio-organismic theories.

time, in regard to "bio-organicism," the theories vary from an extreme biologism to a mild, rather bio-psychological, interpretation of society, including even such conceptions as Fouillée's "contractual organism." Let us now discuss briefly to what extent these theories may be recognized as valuable from the scientific standpoint.[34]

5. CRITICISM

In bio-organismic theories we must strongly discriminate between two different classes of statements. The first class is composed of the statements that sociology has to be based on biology; that the principles of biology are to be taken into consideration in an interpretation of social phenomena; that human society is not entirely an artificial creation; and that it represents a kind of a living unity different from a mere sum of the isolated individuals. These principles could scarcely be questioned. They are valid. They are shared, moreover, not only by the bio-organismic school, but by a great many other sociological schools. In this sense they do not compose a monopoly of the bio-organismic theories, or their specific characteristics.

Quite different should be our conclusion in regard to the second set of the bio-organismic conceptions. This set is composed of the conclusions inferred from the above general principles. Since

[34] In view of the enormous amount of literature devoted to the criticism of the bio-organismic theories, there is no necessity to make my criticism detailed. Of this literature, see *Annales de l'inst. intern. de sociol.*, Vol. IV, which contains the papers of Lilienfeld and Novicow as the proponents of the bio-organismic theories; and the papers of G. Tarde, L. Stein, and other critics of bio-organicism. See also the quoted papers of Coker, Salomon, and others. In addition *vide* GIDDINGS, F., *Principles of Sociology*, Book IV, Chap. IV, N. Y., 1896; BARTH, P., *op. cit.*, pp. 306–424; DUPRAT, *Science sociale et démocratie*, 1900, pp. 59, 68 ff.; HAFF, K., "Kritik der Genossenschaftstheorie," *Jahrbuch für Soziologie*, B. II, pp. 277–299; BARNES, H. E., "Representative Biological Theories of Society," *Sociol. Review*, Vol. XVII, 1925; LITT, TH., *Individuum und Gemeinschaft*, 1924; GUMPLOWICZ, L., *Gesch. d. Staatstheorien*, pp. 396 ff.; WILLOUGHBY, *The Nature of the State*, pp. 32–38, N. Y., 1896; LEROY-BEAULIEU, *L'état moderne et ses functions*, Paris, 1890, Book I, Chap. IV; KISTIAKOWSKI, B., *Gesellschaft und Einzelwesen*, Berlin, 1899; STEINMETZ, R., "Die organische sozialphilosophie," *Zeitschrift für Sozialwiss.*, 1898; SMALL, A., and VINCENT, *Introduction to the Study of Society*, 1894; PATTEN, S., "The Failure of Biological Sociology," *Annales of the Amer. Acad. Polit. Social Sciences*, Vol. IV, 1896; MIKHAILOVSKY, N. K., *What Is Progress?*, (Russ.), *Darwinism and Social Sciences, Analogical Method in Social Sciences*, in *Works of Mikhailovsky*, Russ., Vol. I; KAREEFF, N., *Introduction to the Study of Sociology*, Russ., Chap. IV, 1907.

biological laws are applicable to human beings, they conclude that all human society is an organism. Since human society like any organism is composed of living individuals, they infer that society ought to be similar to an organism in society's structure, organs, and functions. Hence, the analogies of the school. These propositions compose their specific characteristics. By it, the school differs from many others which share the statements of the above first class, but refuse to accept the conclusions of the second class. It is true that the bio-organismic sociologists, being confronted with severe criticism, have many times stressed the point that their organismic analogies do not compose an important part of their theories, being, in fact, nothing but an illustration of their principles, a mere *façon de parler*, no more.[35] And yet, contrary to these declarations, they have continued to use these analogies over and over, filling with them hundreds of pages of their works, and to use them as the principal argument of their contentions. Besides, if we take off these analogies and the identification of society with an organism from these theories, there remains very little in them. Their originality and specific nature disappear; and, through that, disappears the school itself. In this case it dissolves among a great many other theories which in various ways profess the first set of the principles. For these reasons, the second set of the statements is to be taken as the

[35] For instance H. Spencer emphatically protested against an interpretation of his analogies in any other than an "illustrative" sense. "I have used the analogies elaborated, but as a scaffolding to help in building up a coherent body of sociological inductions. Now let us drop this alleged parallelism between individual organization and social organization. Let us take away the scaffolding: the inductions will stand by themselves." . . . "This emphatic repudiation of the belief that there is any special analogy between the social organism and the human organism, I have a motive for making" (in view of a misrepresentation of Spencer's conceptions). See SPENCER, H., *The Principles of Sociology*, Vol. I, N. Y., 1910, p. 270, and the foot-note on p. 592. See also pp. 214–223. Even such an extreme organicist as P. Lilienfeld no less emphatically protests against various comical analogies and their unfair interpretation. See his *Zur Verteidigung der organischen Methode in Soziologie*, pp. 22–28, Berlin, 1898; the same is true of J. Novicow. See NOVICOW, *Conscience et volonté sociale*, Paris, 1897; on page 9, he writes: "Certainly social organisms are entirely different from biological organisms. . . There is no morphological resemblance between them. It is childish to try to establish any similarity of this kind." A. Schäffle, in the second edition of his *"Bau und Leben des Sozialen Körpers,"* 1881, p. VIII, dropped the analogies of the first edition to avoid their misinterpretation. A similar thing was done by R. Worms. See WORMS, *Philosophie des sciences sociales*, Vol. I, pp. 47–52, Paris, 1913; *Soziologie*, German tr., 1926, p. 37. The same is true of other prominent organicists in sociology.

"*differentia specifica*" of the bio-organismic theories. They stand and fall with these principles. If they are true, the school remains; if they are wrong, the school falls down.

It is easy to show the fallacy of these principles. Since man is an organism, the laws of biology are applicable to him, but from this it does not follow at all that human society is a biological organism. The rules of arithmetical addition or multiplication are equally applicable to an arithmetical computation of men, cattle, stones, and what not. Does it follow from that that man is a cow, or that a cow is a stone, or that all these objects are identical? The laws of mechanics or chemistry are equally applicable to man, stone, or plant. Does it follow from this that a man, a plant, and a stone are the same things? In a similar way, from the supposition that the laws of biology are applicable to man, it does not follow at all that man is a cow, or a plant, and still less is it possible to infer that the human society is an organism. In other words, the applicability of some rules or formulas of uniformities (laws) to various objects, does not mean an identity of the nature of these objects.

We may agree also that human society is composed of a living substance, that is, of human beings. But it is fallacious to infer from this that human societies are but biological organisms. In the final analysis, either a stone, an animal, a plant, or a man is composed of atoms or electrons. Does this mean that stones, plants, animals, and men are identical things, and can be identified with one another in their structure, organs, or functions; or that they could be interpreted with the same principles in their composition and activity? We may agree that human society is a kind of a unity in which its members are interdependent upon each other. It is, however, fallacious to conclude from this that human society is an organism, because an organism is also a kind of unity. The solar system, an automobile, a plant, an animal, a river, or a man, all represent a kind of a unity with interdependent parts. Does it follow from this that human society is the same unity as the solar system, a car, a plant, a river; or that all these objects are identical?

As a unity, human society may disintegrate, the human being may die, a stone may be broken into pieces, or a river may dry up. In all these cases, each of these unities disappears. Is it possible to infer from this that the various processes of the disappearance of each unity are identical, and that for this reason the corresponding phenomena (objects) are identical also? Evidently not. Meanwhile, the bio-organismic analogies of a similarity of the organismic processes with the social (though both show the phenomena of growth, sickness, multiplication, differentiation and so on) represent just such a reasoning and such an inference. If a logician needs an excellent illustration of a fallacy in analogical reasoning, he cannot have a better example than the bio-organismic analogical methods. The above is enough to make clear their "organic" fallacy. It is needless to make a detailed criticism of their organic analogies. Their weakness has been ridiculed and criticized more than enough. There is no need to repeat these well based objections.

One point, however, is to be mentioned. This is the practical inferences made by various bio-organicists from their bio-organismic premises. Some of them used their analogies as an argument in favor of monarchy, administrative centralization, absolutism, or socialism, as a form of the greatest integration of social organism (*e.g.*, Bluntschli). Some others, for instance Spencer, used them to support decentralization, individualism, liberalism, and a restriction of governmental interference. This shows, in the first place, the vagueness of logical content of these bio-organismic principles, which, being the same, permit persons to make quite opposite inferences. It shows also the unscientific nature of these "applied" inferences. In their essence, they are nothing but Pareto's "derivations," "ideologies" which are intended not so much to describe the reality, as it is, as to supply a "justification," "beautification," or "motivation" of the various "appetites," "aspirations," and "desires" (residues) of their authors. Being such, they are neither scientific, nor non-scientific, but extra-scientific and outside the path of science.[36]

[36] The modern variety of such ideologies is given in the form of various theories of solidarity; beginning with Fouillée's "contractual organism" and ending with L. Bourgeois' "solidarity," O. Spann's "universalismus," Th. Litt's "Lebens einheit," the nationalistic "patriotism," socialistic "collectivism," the ideologies of the Catholico-monarchical movement, represented by *L'action française*, Fascism's theories of syndicalism, and so on. All these "ideologies" are based on an "organic" conception of a society, either in its philosophical, or psycho-

As to the practical value of the bio-organismic analogies, they may have some "pedagogical" worth in supplying "concrete images" which help to visualize the abstract and complex "structure" of a social system, but this value is limited. Besides, through the misuse of analogies, their value is greatly overweighted by their scientific fallacies. Therefore, G. Tarde's severe conclusion about the bio-organismic theories seems to be right in essence.

The conception of social organism has been somewhat useful only

sociologistic, or bio-organismic forms. From the theoretical premises of these organic doctrines, each of these ideologies infers an applied political program to be carried on, and a series of practical social, political, and moral propositions This "what ought to be done" is outlined by each of these ideological movements according to the tastes, desires, and inclinations of their authors. Each of them, however, tries to "base," or to "justify" and to "prove" his practical program with the organic principles. After the above, it must be clear that all these different "ideologies" are nothing but "derivations" in Pareto's sense, and all of them are unscientific, which does not hinder their being socially useful or harmful, because scientific truth and social usefulness or harmfulness are in different categories, and are far from being always coincident. Samples of these "ideologies" are given in the following works: MAURRAS, CH., *Romanticisme et révolutions*, Paris, 1912; DELAFOSSE, J., *Théorie de l'ordre*, 1901; COTTIN, P., *Positivisme et anarchy*, 1908. These "ideologies" represent "the monarchical, clerical, or traditionalist aspirations" embodied in the group of *L'action française*. Ideology of Fascism represents also a variety of this type. See also the quoted work of Moulinée, which shows well its connections with various organic doctrines. The group of the "humanitarian," "liberal," the "positivistic" and the somewhat "pinkish" "ideologies" of solidarity, based also on organic premises, is well represented by Fouillée's "contractual organism" (which reminds one of "wooden iron") in his quoted work and in his *La propriété sociale et démocratie* (1884) and *Eléments sociologiques de la morale*, 1905; by BOURGEOIS, L., *La solidarité*, 1897; *Essai d'une philosophie de la solidarité*, 1902; by BOUGLÉ, C., *Le solidarisme*, 1907; HAURIOU, M., *La science sociale traditionelle;* by GIDE, CH., *Essai d'une philosophie de la solidarité, 1902*. In America, corresponding "practical ideologies" are inserted into the "psycho-organic" sociological treatises, and a great many textbooks in sociology and social sciences, which "preach" the doctrine of solidarity with the help of "organic"—principally psycho-organic—doctrines. Corresponding Syndicalist, Communist, and Socialist ideologies of solidarity, based also on a variety of the organic doctrines, may be found in abundance in the works of K. Marx, and the Marxian socialists; in the works of "the humanitarian socialists" like the Fabian socialists in England; and in the journalistic works of authors like H. G. Wells, and this type of "ideologists;" others in the works of ideologists of revolutionary syndicalism, like Lagardelle, Sorel, G. Griffuhels, Berth, and so on. Finally, the ideologies of the contemporary "Guild-Socialism" are to be mentioned also, as a conspicuous example of these "applied doctrines" based on one of the organic conceptions of a society. All these theories are, in their greater part, neither scientific, nor non-scientific, but extra-scientific ideologies lying outside of science. This statement concerns all such ideologies regardless as to whether they are based on "philosophical," "bio-organismic" or "psycho-sociologistic" organicism.

for naturalists to whom it suggested the cell-theory, physical division of labor, and other clear and important ideas. But if it is useful to sociologize biology, it is harmful to biologize sociology. . . Bio-organicism is not only fallacious, but it is dangerous. If I do not see its contributions, I do excellently see fallacies which it supports. The fallacy of a creation of a sociological ontology, of the building up of various metaphysical entities, as real things, or of the permanent use of terms like "social principle," "the soul of a crowd" and other vague concepts of a biological metaphysics; this is, possibly, the worst kind of all metaphysics. [37]

As a matter of fact, all these analogies and comparisons have added little, if anything, valuable toward an understanding of social phenomena. They have not disclosed any new correlation, any new uniformity, or any new formula of a factual relationship of various elements of a social system. For these reasons we must refuse to follow the bio-organismic school in this respect. Dropping this part of bio-organicism, we have derived from it a series of statements of the first type mentioned above. As was stated, these are likely to be valid, but they are not a monopoly of this school. We may say that society represents a kind of system, or a kind of unity, but this is not identical to the unity of an organism.[38] We may say that the social group is a reality

---

[37] TARDE, G., "La théorie organique des sociétés," *Annales institut international de sociologie*, Vol. IV, pp. 238–239. Not without reason also Duprat ironically says of the bio-organismic theories: "*Mentalisez d'abord un organism; remplacez la cellule purement biologique, qui n'est qu'une abstraction, par une synthèse d'atomes psychiques ou de monades; superposez à la vie la conscience; puis socialisez ce que vous venez de mentalisez ainsi; donnez à chaque élément psycho-physiologique une tendance à la vie en commun, à l'association, donnez à l'aggrégat un gouvernement, une sorte de monarchie avec l'âme, dont la sensibilité, l'intelligence, la volonté seront les ministres. . . . Qu'y aura donc gagné la science? Ne resultera-t-il pas une plus grande obscurité encore de ces analogies parfois forcées?* DUPRAT, *op. cit.*, pp. 59, 68–69.

[38] Whether we style the unity of a social system "mechanical," or "organic," or "psychic," it is a matter of terminology and is not important in itself. What is important is how we describe its characteristics and the functional relations which we may discover among various components of a social system, and between the social system and its environment. From this functional standpoint, the only important thing is accuracy in the description of the properties and components of a social system and of their functional relationship and regularities. If this task is performed properly, the adjectives "mechanical," "organismic," and "psychic" add very little to our knowledge of social phenomena. If the task is not performed at all, the adjectives are likely to be useless and misleading. In this case they may give only a purely superficial and terminological knowledge of the phenomena and, owing to a vague meaning of the words, "mechanical,"

of a *sui generis* different from that of its members taken in a state of mutual isolation. But society does not exist independently, and we must not forget the reality of interacting individuals who compose a given social system. We may say that the laws of biology are to be taken into consideration in an interpretation of social phenomena; but this does not mean that a social system is a biological organism. We may agree that a social system is shaped and controlled not entirely by the forces exterior to it; but this is true in regard to any unity, whether it is a "mechanical," an organic, or a social one. We may agree that society is not an artificial system created intentionally by man; but this is true of the solar system, of organisms, and of a great many other "organic," "mechanical," and "psychic" unities, which have come into an existence spontaneously. It is true that social institutions are a product of a great many forces and of a long series of trials and errors, and should not be regarded as something purely "incidental," which may be easily changed at once; but this again is true of a great many other non-social unities.

After this consideration of the characteristics of the bio-organismic school, let us turn to some of the special theories which directly or indirectly are connected with it, and which try to apply its fundamental principles to an interpretation of a series of important social phenomena. Among such theories the most important are those which try to interpret the phenomena of social differentiation, of social adaptation, and of the social struggle for life. Let us glance at them.

"organic" and so on, they are likely to lead to a series of misconceptions, not to mention an endless and sterile dispute originated by such a vague meaning of the words. For this reason, I think that a scientific study of the phenomena should concentrate its attention on the above factual analysis and description of a social system, and should pay less attention to the business of word-polishing; using "mechanical," "organic," "psycho-social," "atomistic," "universalistic" and so on. Unfortunately, a great many sociologists have been busy principally with this word-polishing. Even in the quite recent sociological studies of O. Spann, Th. Litt, C. Brinkmann, A. Vierkandt, K. Breysig, W. Sauer, and others, too much space has been devoted to the "word-polishing," and too little to factual analysis of the phenomena and their functional relations. I regard this as a heritage of the philosophical stage of sociology which is to be passed over, and the sooner it is left behind, the better.

6. BIOLOGICAL AND SOCIAL DIFFERENTIATION

H. Spencer, Karl Baer, Ernst Haeckel and other biologists indicated that the perfection of an organism varies directly as the degree of its complexity, differentiation, and integration. The greater the differentiation between the organs and the morphological structure of an organism, the greater the division of functions between its organs, causing its parts to be integrated that much more closely with a corresponding loss in their autonomy; the more perfect an organism is, the higher place it occupies in the evolutionary "ladder of life," and the more advanced it is in the evolutionary process. Such is the biological criterion of the perfectibility of an organism, given in Spencer's formula of evolution or progress, which we find in Baer's and Haeckel's classification of organisms.[39] This formula naturally called forth a series of sociological theories whose business was to answer the problem as to whether or not the formula could be applied to societies. If society is a biological organism, the formula should be applicable to it. In this case, the more a society is differentiated and integrated, the more it is centralized, the less freedom its members have, and the greater is the division of social labor; the more perfect and progressive and advanced the society should be, and *vice versa*. In a disguised or explicit, a rough or a mild form, such conclusions have really been made, especially in regard to social differentiation and integration as the criteria of social progress. Examples of this are given in H. Spencer's works and in those of a "psycho-social" organicist, E. Durkheim, wherein there are many other theories. In their classification of social types and their place in the evolutionary series, in their formula of progress, and in their estimation of the rôle of the social division of labor, both of these authors did practically nothing but apply the above criteria of a perfect organism to society. According to them social evolution and progress consisted essentially in an increase of social differentiation and

---

[39] See H. Spencer's formula of evolution or progress in his *First Principles*, p. 396, N. Y. 1895; its application to social phenomena in Spencer's essay about *Progress*, and in his *Principles of Sociology*, Vol. I, Part II, Chaps. X–XII, and *passim*. See HAECKEL, E., *Prinzipien der Generellen Morphologie*, 1906, pp. 106 ff.

integration; in an increase of social division of labor; and in a transition from the state of "an indefinite, incoherent homogeneity to a definite coherent heterogeneity." [40]

On the part of the "individualists," such inferences naturally called forth a bitter criticism of the organismic theories, as well as of their political and practical conclusions. The best samples of such theories are given in the works of A. Lalande, N. K. Mikhailovsky, L. Winiarsky, G. Palante, G. Tarde, P. Lavroff, [41] N. Kareef, to mention only a few names.

In the first place, these authors, and among them especially N. K. Mikhailovsky and A. Lalande, have shown that the very terms, "more perfect" and "less perfect" in an application to organisms are not permissible because the terms are the judgments of evaluation and as such, they cannot be used in objective biologic science.

---

[40] See indicated chapter in the works of H. Spencer. See DURKHEIM, E., *Les régles de la méthode sociologiques*, Paris, 1904, pages devoted to an outline of social morphology and to a classification of social types; see also his *De la division du travail social*, Paris, 1893, *passim*. See about Durkheim's sociology the chapter "Sociologistic School" in this book. It is necessary to note, however, that in other parts of Spencer's works, especially in his theory of the militant and industrial type of society, in his criticism of socialism, governmental interference, and "State-Slavery," Spencer, like many other social thinkers, radically changes his attitude and practically drops his formula of evolution, as well as his bio-organismic theory. If the formula of evolution and progress is valid, and if society is an organism, the greater social centralization, governmental regulation, and social division of labor, while the lesser is individual autonomy, the more perfect and progressive the society is to be. Such in fact are Spencer's statements developed in the first volume of his *Principles of Sociology*, in his essay about *Progress*, and in his *First Principles*. But when he begins to discuss the above problems, he quite illogically changes his attitude and develops the theories radically contradictory to the basic principles of his bio-organic theory and his formula of evolution or progress. Similar inconsistencies are found in the theories of Durkheim, too. I do not mention here a series of much more extreme political inferences drawn from the above biological criteria of perfection of organism, and intended to justify political absolutism, centralization, caste-system and so on, on the basis of these criteria. The works of the bio-organicists of the past and of the mentioned contemporary political ideologists (Maurras, Delafosse, P. Cottin, ideologists of the Fascism, of Syndicalism, Socialism and Communism) give various types of similar inferences and "justification." They are rich also with the inconsistencies of their "ideologies" and their basic principles.

[41] See LALANDE, A., *La dissolution opposée à l'évolutions dans les sciences physiques et morales*, Paris, 1899; PALANTE, G., *Combat pour l'individu*, Paris, 1904; *Antinomies entre l'individu et société*, Paris, 1913; WINIARKSY, L., "Essai d'une nouvelle interprétation de phénomènes sociologiques," *Revue socialiste*, 1896; MIKHAILOVSKY, N. K., *What is Progress? Darwinism and Social Sciences, Struggle for Individuality*, in his *Works*, Russ.; see about Mikhailovsky's, Kareef's and Lavroff's theories in HECKER, J., *Russian Sociology*, pp. 85–204, N. Y., 1916.

Biology may classify and describe the species and the characteristics of the organisms, and may show their genealogies, but it cannot evaluate them and range them as "more and less perfect." Such an evaluation would be nothing but an introduction of anthropomorphism and a subjective concept of perfection into biology. In the second place, they indicated that Spencer's explanation of the objective science of evolution (the instability of the homogeneous) is inadequate; for it is not the homogeneous which is unstable, but, on the contrary, the heterogeneous. In the third place, they indicated that, from the standpoint of vitality and immortality, the most vital and really immortal organisms are not those which are differentiated and complex, but the simplest ones. Contrary to fragile and mortal complex organisms, they are ineradicable, the most vital, imperishable, and immortal. This has been indicated by the authors to show the subjectivity of the above criteria of biological perfection. In the fourth place, the authors indicated that society is not a biological organism; therefore, if the biological formula of perfection were even valid, it could not be applied to society. In the fifth place, they stressed that the social application of the formula made by Spencer is also wrong. Properly used, it has to be applied not to society, but to an individual. In this case it would mean that the more differentiated the organs and the functions of an individual are, the greater is the division of labor among his organs; and the more perfect he is, the more many-sided is his personality. Such are the characteristics of the men of genius; such are the properties of a really Great Man, and such are the indispensable conditions for human happiness and for the progress of human beings. Consequently, the more perfect society is that which gives the greatest opportunity for a realization of such an ideal of individualism. Spencer's, Durkheim's, and other organicists' differentiated and integrated theories of society do not give any chance to develop the individual. If society progresses in its differentiation and integration, "what happens at the same time to the actual individual,—the member of society? Does he experience the same process of development as the type of organic process?" Thus asks Mikhailovsky and answers, "No."

While society becomes more and more differentiated and hetero-geneous, the individual—a member of it—proceeds the opposite way of transformation: he becomes more and more onesided, homo-geneous, narrowminded and specialised. Such a "progress" of society tends to turn an individual into a "mere digit of the foot" of the society. Understand, then, that in such a progress the individual regresses. If we contemplate only this aspect of the matter, society is the worst enemy of man, for it strives to transform the individual into a mere organ of itself.

From this standpoint what Spencer and Durkheim regard as social progress (an increase of social differentiation), is to be styled rather social regress.

In the homogeneous mass of primitive society the individuals were heterogeneous. . . . They were complete bearers of their culture; they were manysided personalities. . . . But with the transition of society from the homogeneous to heterogeneous, there began the destruction of this full personality of individuals and its transition from the heterogeneous to homogeneous.[42]

Thus, if the formula of perfection were applicable, it would have to be applied to an individual, but not to a society. Being applied to an individual, it gives quite a different evaluation of an undifferentiated and differentiated society, of the division of labor, of specialization and so on, than does the evaluation given by Spencer, Durkheim, and other bio- and psycho-sociological organicists.

Such, in brief, are these two principal streams of sociological thought originated by, or under the influence of, the biological formula of the perfection of an organism in its application to the phenomena of social differentiation.

7. CRITICAL REMARKS

The above criticism of the bio-organismic school makes un-necessary a detailed criticism of the application of the principle of physiological differentiation to a society. Since we recognized the fallacious character of the principles of the bio-organismic

---

[42] MIKHAILOVSKY, *Works*, Vol. I, pp. 29 ff., 149 ff., 461 ff., 573 and *passim*, St. Petersbourg, 1896; WINIARSKY, *op. cit.*, pp. 309–310, 312 ff.; see also the mentioned works of Palante, Lalande, and others.

school and the impossibility of identifying society and organisms it follows that the formula of the biological perfection of an organism could not be transported into sociology and applied to a society. If it were applicable to this field at all it had to be applied rather to the individuals than to a group. In this respect Mikhailovsky, Winiarsky and other critics of the theory seem to be right. Besides, as some of them mentioned, the category of a "more perfect" and a "less perfect" organism is a subjective evaluation, but not a statement of a matter of fact. For this reason, these terms and others like "superior and inferior" organisms are illegal within the field of biology itself. In a similar way, there is no possibility of identifying the concepts of "evolution," which is a "colorless" concept in the sense of evaluation, and means only a development of the phenomenon in the course of time (and space) regardless as to whether it tends to a better or to a worse condition. Scientifically illegal is also the concept of "progress," which is a finalist and evaluative term. For this reason, Spencer's and similar identifications of these two terms are to be regarded as fallacious. If even social evolution had really consisted in an increase of social differentiation and integration, this would not have meant that such a process is necessarily progress.[43] More of the above objections of the anti-organicists indicate other weak points of the discussed analogy. Properly taken, it represents nothing but "an ideology" in which some data of biology are taken to justify some subjective aspirations of the authors. As such they are outside of science, and the fewer of their number found in sociology, the better it will be for the science.

[43] See SOROKIN, "The Category of 'Ought to Be' in Social Science," *Juridichesky Vestnik*, 1917, Russ.; "Fundamental Problems of Progress," *Novyija Idei v soziologii*, Vol. III, Russ.; "Is Any Normative Science Possible?" in SOROKIN, *Crime and Punishment*, 1914, Introduction, Russ.

CHAPTER V

ANTHROPO-RACIAL, SELECTIONIST, AND HEREDITARIST SCHOOL

U N D E R this school I am going to discuss the principal theories which give an exclusive importance to the factor of race, heredity and selection in determining human behavior, the social processes, organization, and the historical destiny of a social system. The theories compose a second branch of the biological school of sociology.

I. PREDECESSORS

The factors of race, selection, and of heredity were known long ago. In *The Sacred Books of the East* we find many statements which stress their rôle. In the practices of ancient societies, "blood," "race," and "selection" were given an exclusive importance, determining the social status, both of individuals and of groups. The ancient social stratification of castes and classes, of the aristocracy and slaves, of the plebeians and the patricians, and of the noble and the humble, was based principally on "blood" and "race." Accordingly, ancient societies practiced very extensively what is now styled "eugenics." Following are a few of the many examples found in the source literature of these societies.

In the *Sacred Books of India* we find the theory that the different castes were created out of different parts of the body of Brahma, and that they are innately different; consequently, any mixture of blood, or cross-marriage, or even any contact of the members of different races is the greatest crime, and the social status of every individual is entirely determined by the "blood" of his parents. There are also a great many purely eugenic prescriptions aimed to keep the purity of the blood, to facilitate the procreation of the best elements in the population, and to check that of the unhealthy.[1] In other words, eugenics was well known and widely practiced in ancient societies.

"Twice-born men (of the higher castes) who, in their folly, wed wives of the low caste, soon degrade their families and their children to the state of Sûdras." "He who weds a Sûdra woman becomes an outcast" (with whom any contact becomes impossible). "A Brahmana who takes a Sûdra wife to his bed will (after death) sink into hell; if he begets a child by her he will lose the rank of a Brahmana" (be automatically excluded from the upper caste). The manes and the gods will not eat the offerings of that man. "For him who drinks the moisture of a Sûdra's lips, who is tainted by her breath, and who begets a son by her, no expiation is prescribed." (Such a sin is unforgivable.) Further, it is prescribed that one should avoid taking a wife from the families in which no male children are born, where there are hemorrhoids, phthisis, weakness of digestion, epilepsy, leprosy; when a maiden has red eyes, and so on. "In the blameless marriages, blameless children are born to men; in the blameable marriages, blameable offspring. One should avoid the blameable marriages." [2] Such are a few of the many eugenic prescriptions long ago practiced in ancient India.

In the Bible also we find many endogamic rules aimed to preserve the purity of blood or race among the Jews.

A bastard shall not enter into the assembly of Jehovah; even to the tenth generations shall none of his enter into the assembly of Jehovah. [3]

Ye shall not give your daughters unto their [Gentile] sons, nor take their daughters for your sons, or for yourselves.[4]

Transgression of this is styled by Ezra as "mingling of the holy seeds with the people of the land," and is strongly prohibited.[5]

In the *Odyssey* and *Iliad* there are also many places which stress the importance of blood purity:

[1] See *Laws of Manu*, Chaps. I, II, III, IV; *Apastamba*, Prasna I, II; *Gautama*, Chap. X; *Narâda*, XII; *The Institutes of Vishnu*, II, III, in *The Sacred Books of the East.*

[2] *Laws of Manu*, II, 6-42. See other indicated *Sacred Books of India.*

[3] Deuteronomy, xxiii : 2.

[4] Nehemiah, xiii : 25; also xiii : 3, where it is said that "they separated from Israel all the mixed multitude."

[5] Ezra, ix : 2. See also Deuteronomy, vii : 3; Exodus, xxxiv : 16.

Taste ye food and be glad and thereafter we will ask what men ye are; for the blood of your parents is not lost in you but ye are of the line of men that are sceptred kings, the fosterlings of Zeus; for no churl could beget sons like you.

Such are the words addressed to the strangers exclusively on the basis of their appearance.[6] As to the great thinkers of Greece, like Plato and Aristotle, they quite clearly realized the innate inequality of men, and consequently, of races. Plato's guardians are to be selected from men who are naturally suitable for this class, while the members of other classes are composed of the people naturally fit for their lower social standing.[7] Aristotle stresses the fact that there are inborn slaves and inborn masters.[8] The same may be said of a great many ancient thinkers. Everywhere the factors of "blood," "race," "heredity" and "selection" were known, were taken into consideration, and were put into practice in various efficient forms.

Since that time up to the nineteenth century, there have been few prominent social thinkers who have not, in some way, touched these problems. "All through the history of political theory we have seen distinctions of race presented as the causes of and sufficient explanations of distinctions in institutions and power." [9] At the end of the eighteenth, and at the beginning of the nineteenth centuries, a series of philologists, historians, and social thinkers,—Sir William Jones, F. Schlegel, T. Young, J. G. Rhode,

[6] *Odyssey* IV, 60. Cf. I, 222, 411; *Iliad*, XIV, 126.

[7] Plato, *The Republic*, tr. by Jowett, pp. 191–198, N. Y. 1874.

[8] "It is from natural causes that some beings command and others obey: for a being who is endowed with a mind capable of reflection and forethought is by nature the superior and governor, whereas he whose excellence is merely corporeal is formed to be a slave; whence it follows that the different state of master and slave is equally advantageous to both." On account of the same natural or innate difference, "it is as proper for the Greeks to govern the barbarians, as if a barbarian and a slave were by nature one."—Aristotle, *Politics*, tr. by W. Ellis, Dutton Co., Chap. II, Chap. XIII and *passim*.

[9] DUNNING, W., *A History of Political Theory from Rousseau to Spencer*, p. 311, N. Y., 1920. See a history of these theories in the works: SCHALLMAYER, W., *Vererbung und Auslese in Lebenslauf der Völker*, 2nd ed., pp. 142 ff.; SIMAR, TH., *Étude critique sur la formation de la doctrine des races au XVIIe siècle et son expansion au XIXe siècle*, Bruxelles, 1922; HANKINS, F. H., *The Racial Basis of Civilization*, Part I, N. Y., 1926. See also the works about Gobineau and Chamberlain, indicated further, which contain a historical review of their predecessors. However, all these works give either a quite fragmentary survey or mix the racial theories with those which emphasize nationality, patriotism, or superiority of a people, regardless of their race.

J. V. Klaproth, A. Kuhn, J. Grimm, F. A. Pott, F. Müller, and many others, —started the theory of Aryanism, and later on, of Teutonism and Nordicism. Though some of them understood that the Aryans were a linguistic group, nevertheless they often mixed the Aryan people with the Aryan race, and in this way facilitated an appearance of a purely racial interpretation of history. The most famous and the most influential among such theories happened to be the racial theory of Gobineau. His work could be regarded as the corner stone of numerous similar theories set forth after him.[10] Among relatively recent theories which compose the anthropo-racial school in sociology, the most important are: 1. The racial theories of Gobineau and Chamberlain; 2. The "hereditarist" school of Francis Galton and K. Pearson; 3. The selectionist theories of V. de Lapouge and Otto Ammon. Besides these, there are many other monographs which emphasize the principles set forth by these authors. They will be mentioned further. We shall begin our survey with these three groups of theories. After that we shall briefly mention other works of the school, trying to see which of their generalizations are valid, and which are not.

2. HISTORICO-PHILOSOPHICAL BRANCH OF THE SCHOOL

Arthur de Gobineau [11] (1816-1882).—Count Gobineau's racial interpretation of history is given in the four volumes of his *Essai sur l'inégalité des races humaines* (Paris, 1853, 1855).[12] The essentials of his theory are as follows: For a starting point,

---

[10] It is rather curious to read the statement of K. Pearson that before Darwin there was no possibility of either an organic conception of society, or a proper understanding of the rôle of heredity, race-struggle, and selection. There is no doubt that all these factors were understood well, and if one compares many sociological statements of Gobineau with those of Pearson, he will see a great similarity between them, in spite of the fact that Gobineau's work was published before Darwin's and Galton's works.

[11] About Gobineau, his life, his theory, and predecessors, see LANGE, M., *Le Comte A. de Gobineau*, Strassburg, 1924; HONE, J. M., "Arthur, Count of Gobineau, Race Mystic," *Contemp. Rev.*, 1913, pp. 94–103; DREYFUS, R., *La vie et les propheties du Comte de Gobineau*, Paris, 1905; SELLIÈRE, E., *Le Comte de Gobineau*, Paris, 1903; SCHEMANN, L., *Gobineau, eine Biographie*, 2 vols. Strassburg, 1913–16; HANKINS, *op. cit.*, Chaps. II, III.

[12] There is an English translation of the first volume of Gobineau's work by A. Collins, *The Inequality of Human Races*, N. Y., 1914.

Gobineau takes the problem of the development and decay of societies. What are the causes of such phenomena? What factors determine either an upward movement of society and civilization or their decay? With a great erudition for his time, he takes the existing hypotheses one after another and shows their inadequacy. Having characterized society in a manner "more or less perfect from the political, and quite complete from the social point of view, as a union of men who live under the direction of similar ideas and who have identical instincts," [13] Gobineau shows that neither religious fanaticism, nor corruption and licentiousness, nor luxury leads necessarily to decay, as many authors thought. The Aztec Empire was religiously fanatical and was accustomed even to sacrifice human beings to their gods; yet this did not lead to its decay, but rather facilitated a long historical existence of this society. The upper classes of Greece, Rome, Persia, Venice, Genoa, England, and Russia lived in luxury for many centuries, yet this did not lead to their decay. The same may be said of corruption. The earliest ascending stages of ancient Rome, Sparta, and many other societies were far from being virtuous and honest. The early Romans were cruel and pitiless; the Spartans and Phœnicians used to rob, plunder, rape, and lie. They exhibited the greatest corruption; yet this did not hinder these societies from rising and prospering. "It is not in virtue that we find the cause of their vigour at the earliest stages of their history." On the other hand, in the period of decay, many societies exhibit an increase of humanitarianism, softening of mores, a decrease of cruelty, corruption, and brutality, and yet this does not stop their decay. Finally, throughout the history of France and other countries there has been much fluctuation in the amount of corruption, with nothing showing a drift toward decay in the more corrupt periods. For these reasons it is evident that corruption cannot account for decay. Similarly, religious decay is not a sufficient cause to explain it. Persia, Tyre, Carthage and Judea fell down when their religion was very intensive. Even in Greece and Rome, religion, especially among the masses of the population, was quite strong in the period of decay. These and

[13] GOBINEAU, *Essai sur l'inégalité des races humaines*, Vol. I, pp. 11–12.

similar inductions show that "it is impossible to explain a people's ruin through their irreligion." [14]

Neither do the merits of a government influence the historical longevity of societies.   Bad governments may be classified as those which are foreign, and those which are imposed by foreign, degenerate, and class-selfish governments.   China had, for thousands of years, a foreign (the Mongol) government, and yet, in spite of this fact, China exists and has often shown great social progress.   England was conquered by the foreign Normans, and yet this did not ruin England.   Furthermore, we know that societies with a degenerated, or class-selfish government have continued to exist in spite of these conditions.   These, and similar historical inductions testify that national decay cannot be accounted for through the character of the government.[15]   In this way Gobineau shows the insufficiency of all these theories.   This does not mean that he does not attribute any influence to these factors.   He does, but only as to their facilitating the condition brought about.   These phenomena may lead to decay only when they are a manifestation of some deeper cause.

After clearing the ground, Gobineau offers his own theory.   It consists of the statement that the fundamental factor of the progress or decay of a society is *the racial factor*.

> Going from one induction to another I came to the conclusion that ethnical (racial) problems dominate all other problems of history.   It is the key to them; and inequality of races is sufficient to explain the entire enchainment of the destinies of peoples. [16]

Understanding by the decay or degeneration of a nation the fact "that the people do not have as much inner valour as they had before," the cause of such a degeneration is that "the people do not have the same blood in their veins any more because through successive cross-marriages, its value has been changed, and they have not been able to preserve the race of their founders."   Correspondingly, "a people and their civilization dies out when the people's fundamental racial constitution is changed or engulfed among other races to the degree that it ceases to exert the necessary influence."   As soon as such conditions are given, the mortal

[14] *Ibid.*, Chap. II.   [15] *Ibid.*, Chap. III.   [16] *Ibid.*, p. viii.

hour of a society and of its civilization is struck.[17]   The purity
of a race, if the race is talented, is the condition absolutely necessary for preventing the decay of the society and of its civilization.
Such a people is potentially immortal.   If they are conquered by
an invader, they, like the Chinese under the Mongols, or the
Hindus under the Englishmen, can avoid decay, can preserve their
civilization, and, sooner or later, will restore their independence.
On the other hand, racial mixture leads to degeneration, even
though the society has the most brilliant culture created by its
ancestors.   So it happened with the Greeks and the Romans.   They
could not maintain the purity of their race in the later stages of
their history, and therefore, in spite of a wonderful culture they
decayed.[18]

This leads Gobineau to his second proposition about the *inequality of human races*.   They *are* unequal.   *There are the superior and the inferior races*.   The former are capable of progress;
the latter are hopeless.   Civilization and culture have been created
by the superior races exclusively, and each type of culture is nothing but a manifestation of racial qualities.   To corroborate this
statement, Gobineau gives a long series of proofs.   The inequality
of races is proved by the fact that up to the present time there are
many races, which in spite of many thousand years of existence
still remain at the most primitive stages of culture.   They have
not been able to create anything valuable, or to progress in spite
of the different environments in which they have been existing.
Their creative sterility is due to their racial inferiority rather than
to the environmental factors.   "The majority of races are forever
incapable of being civilized" and "no environmental agency can
fertilize their organic sterility."   Such is the statement of the
author.   This naturally leads him to a criticism of various theories
which have tried to account for racial differences and differences
in cultural development through environmental factors, especially
through their geographic environment.   "The progress or stagnation of a people does not depend upon geographic conditions,"
says Gobineau.   Partizans of this theory used to say that people
placed in a favorable geographic environment progress, while the
people who stay among unfavorable geographic conditions are

[17] *Ibid.*, pp. 39–40.   [18] *Ibid.*, p. 53.

stagnant. The author states that history does not corroborate such a theory. The environment of America was very favorable, and yet the aboriginal races of America, —except three races of South America, —could not create any great civilization, but remained in the primitive stages. On the other hand, the environment of Egypt, or Athens, or Sparta, or Assyria, was far from being favorable. It was poor and unfertile until artificial irrigation and other measures were created. And yet, in spite of the unfavorable conditions, these races, thanks to their inner genius, modified their natural environment, and created brilliant civilizations. The same independence of culture from the environment is shown by the fact that we find the progressive peoples under the most different geographical environments. The same is true in regard to stagnant races. Finally, the absence of any close correlation between the character of the races and that of geographic environment is witnessed by the fact that, in the same environment in one period there exists a brilliant civilization, and in another period, it disappears, being superseded by a stagnant and incapable people. If geographic conditions were responsible for the progress or stagnation of a people, such things could not take place. Going in this inductive way and giving one fact after another, Gobineau skilfully shows that "geographical theories" cannot give any satisfactory explanation of the racial and cultural differences of peoples.[19]

The next criticism of the author is directed against the theories which try to account for the differences of various peoples by social environment, —that is, through the character of the social and political institutions. Gobineau indicates that these theories are wrong also. In the first place, because institutions and laws themselves are only manifestations of racial traits, not their causes. They are created by the people according to their inner qualities, but the people do not create these qualities. The institutions do not fall from the heaven as something ready-made. Neither do they exist before the existence of the peoples with their inner qualities. When laws or institutions, quite heterogeneous to the racial instincts of a people, are compulsorily introduced by a foreign nation, or by a conqueror, or by a radical reformer, they

[19] Gobineau, *Essai sur l'inégalité*, Chap. VI.

usually do not have any success, but remain on paper, representing a mere decoration. Sometimes, when a race cannot resist such innovations, it dies, like many primitive people who have been unable to adapt themselves to such a heterogeneous culture. Even a pure imitation of a foreign culture or institutions is possible only when, in the veins of an imitating race, there is a part of the blood of the people whom they imitate. The negroes of America can imitate some superficial cultural traits of the white race only because in their veins there is already a considerable part of the white blood. The author gives again a long series of facts of this kind, and concludes that the discussed theories cannot give any satisfactory explanation of the differences brought about in various peoples through the social environment.[20] From this viewpoint he analyzes in a detailed form the rôle of religion, and especially the rôle of Christianity, in order to show that even this environmental factor cannot explain the differences of various peoples. Though Christianity is accepted by different peoples, teaching them all the same ideas, nevertheless it is forced to leave the institutions of these peoples untouched in their essence. The Eskimo Christian remains Eskimo; the Chinese Christian remains Chinese; the South American native remains what he was; and all these different Christians remain different from one another in spite of the identity of their religion. This shows that unless religion is a direct manifestation of racial instincts (in which case it cannot be universal and cosmopolitan) it cannot change the racial qualities and explain the differences of the races.[21]

After this critical part, Gobineau outlines his theory of the origin, inequality, and social rôle of the racial factor. The three volumes of his work are practically devoted to the development of this theory. Its essence is as follows: Besides the above arguments, the fact of racial inequality is corroborated by, and is partially due to, the probable heterogeneous origin of different races. In this way, he was one of the first authors who set forth the theory of the heterogeneous origin of different races,—the theory stressed later on by Gumplowicz and many anthropologists. Since different races sprang from different sources, it is natural that they are, and must be, different, especially in the early stages

[20] *Ibid.*, Chap. V.   [21] *Ibid.*, Chap. VII.

of their history, when they were purer than they now are. In spite of a long course of history, and a great mixture of blood, even now the races are still different anatomically, physiologically, and psychologically. Such differences are permanent and could not be obliterated by any environmental factors. Only cross-marriage or mixture of blood may change racial characteristics.

At the beginning of human history there existed three pure, principal races: the white, the yellow, and the black. All other racial varieties have been nothing but a mixture of these fundamental races. Of them the most talented and creative was the white race, especially its Aryan branch. In its pure form this race has performed real miracles. It has been practically the creator of all the ten principal civilizations known in the history of mankind. Six of them, namely,—the Hindu, the Egyptian, the Assyrian, the Greek, the Roman, and the Teuton civilizations, were created by the Aryans, who represent the highest branch of the white race. The remaining four civilizations,— the Chinese, Mexican, Peruvian, and Maya, were founded and created by other branches of the white race, mixed with outside races. This white race expanded and conquered other races, but, at the same time, amalgamated with them. From this amalgamation came different racial groups and corresponding civilizations, but the more the amalgamation progressed the more the white race lost its precious qualities, and the more its various branches (like the Greek or the Roman) degenerated. At the time of Jesus Christ the first and the most brilliant part of the history of mankind had been completed. At that time the amalgamation of races had already reached a considerable proportion. Since this period, and up to the present time, it has been progressing, with some fluctuations. The result of such race-blending is a tendency to decay, which has been shown in the history of the last few centuries. It expresses itself in many forms, and one of these is the progress of egalitarian ideas, democratic movements, and the blending of cultures, which, however, does not show anything of that brightness and genius which stamped the previous great civilizations created by relatively pure races. The future prospects drawn by Gobineau are naturally not very hopeful,— blood-mixture having already progressed so far that the process can scarcely be stopped, it is likely to progress more and more.

After the age of the gods, when the Aryan race was absolutely pure; and the age of heroes when race-blending was slight in form and number, it began, during the age of nobles, to slowly progress. After this age, race-mixture advanced rapidly . . . towards a great confusion of all racial elements and through numerous inter-racial marriages.

The result of such a progress will be a greater and greater similarity of human beings on the one hand, and on the other an increasing mediocrity of men's physical constitutions, of their beauty, and of their mind. Here we have the real triumph of mediocrity, since in this sorrowful inheritance (of race amalgamation) everybody must participate in equal proportion and there is no reason to expect that one would have a better fate than another. Like the Polynesians, all men shall be similar to one another,—in their stature, in their traits, and in their habits.

Human herds, no longer nations, weighed down by a mournful somnolence, will henceforth be benumbed in their nullity, like buffaloes ruminating in the stagnant meres of the Pontine marshes.

This means the death of society and the end of the whole human civilization.[22]

Such is the scheme and skeleton of the work of Gobineau. Written brilliantly, with the charm of an excellent stylist, the fascination of an original thinker, and marked by clearness and logicity of ideas, and finally, by unusual erudition, the book made, and makes up to this time, a strong impression. It gave a great impetus to many other racial theories, which will be mentioned later. Postponing my criticism of Gobineau's theory here, I shall mention only that which is an appreciation of the theory. The chapters of the book devoted to the criticism of different environmental theories are still valid in their essential objections to the environmentalism, and are quite fresh even at the present moment.

Houston Stewart Chamberlain (1855-1926).—Among the works which are similar to that of Gobineau in their method and character, a conspicuous place belongs to the work of H. S. Cham-

[22] *Ibid..* Vol. IV, pp. 318–359; Vol. I, Chaps. X, XI, XVI.

berlain: *The Foundations of the Nineteenth Century*.[23]   The son
of Admiral William Charles Chamberlain, born in 1855, the
author received an entirely foreign (principally German) education.   He travelled a great deal, and published several works such
as *Notes sur Lohengrin,* and *Das Drama Richard Wagners.*
However, his fame has been due to *The Foundations of the Nineteenth Century.*   In this historico-philosophical work, Chamberlain puts and answers the problem: What are the foundations or
the sources of the civilization of the nineteenth century?   The
essence of this answer is as follows: Contemporary civilization is
composed of four principal sources, namely, the contributions of
the Greek civilization, of the Roman, of the Jewish, and of the
Teuton.   From the Greeks we received poetry, art and philosophy;
from the Romans, law, statecraft, order, the idea of citizenship,
and the sanctity of the family and of property; while the Jews
gave us the elements of Judaism, and indirectly, of Christianity,
besides other good and bad legacies and influences which the
Jews have exerted since the moment of their entrance into Western history.   On the basis of these legacies the Teutons,—the
term by which Chamberlain understands the Germans, the Celts,
the Slavs, and all the races of northern Europe from which the
people of modern Europe and of the United States of America
have sprung,—have shaped and created the Western civilization
of the nineteenth century.[24]   Each of these fundamental elements
has been the work of the racial genius of the above groups.   Their
specific talents and contributions have been nothing but a manifestation of their racial qualities.   This leads Chamberlain to his
theory of the racial factor.

The human races are, in reality, as different from one another
in character, qualities, and above all, in the degree of their individual capacities, as greyhound, bulldog, poodle and Newfoundland dog.
Has not every genuine race its glorious, incomparable physiognomy?
How could Hellenic art have arisen without Hellenes? . . . Nothing

[23] It appeared in German under the title: *Grundlagen des Neunzehnten Jahrhundert,* in 1899.   I use its English translation by John Lees, London, John Lane
Co., 1911.   About Chamberlain see SELLIÈRE, E., *H. S. Chamberlain, de plus
récent philosophe du pangermanisme mystique,* Paris, 1917; HANKINS, *op. cit.,*
pp. 64 ff.
[24] CHAMBERLAIN, *op. cit.,* Vol. I, pp. 1–13, and *passim.*

is so convincing as the consciousness of the possession of Race. The man who belongs to a distinct, pure race, never loses the sense of it. The guardian angel of his lineage is ever at his side, supporting him where he loses his foothold, warning him where he is in danger of going astray, compelling obedience, and forcing him to undertakings which, deeming them impossible, he would never have dared to attempt. Race lifts a man above himself: it endows him with extraordinary—I might almost say supernatural—powers. It is a fact of direct experience that the quality of the race is of vital importance. [25]

The author proceeds further to show that the various races are different; that there are the superior and the inferior races; and that their difference is due not to environment, but is innate. The most superior race is the white, — particularly the Aryan race, to which in the past belonged the Greeks and the Romans, and at the present, the Teutons in the above indicated sense of the word. In these respects Chamberlain's theory is similar to that of Gobineau. Only in regard to the pure races does he differ from the French author. As we know, Gobineau regarded any mixture of the blood of a noble, pure race as its contamination. According to Chamberlain,

This supposition rests upon total ignorance of the physiological importance of what we have to understand by "race." A noble race does not fall from Heaven, it becomes noble gradually, and this gradual process can begin anew at any moment. [26]

Not only the Jewish, but the Aryan, and the Teutonic races, all emerged at the beginning from a fortunate mixture of different races. Such fortunate mixtures may take place in the future also. Therefore this future need not be necessarily as pessimistic as it was depicted by Gobineau.[27] The principal conditions necessary to create a noble race through mixture are as follows: First, "the presence of excellent racial material. Where there is nothing, the king has no right." Second, an inbreeding.

Such races as the Greeks, the Romans, the Franks, the Swabians, the Italians, the Spaniards in the period of their splendour, the

---

[25] *Ibid.*, Vol. I, pp. 261–262, 269–271 *et seq.* See also p. 317 *et seq.*
[26] *Ibid.*, Vol. I, p. 263.   [27] *Ibid.*, p. 263.

Moors, the English, and such abnormal phenomena as the Aryan Indians and the Jews,—only spring from continued inbreeding. They arise and they pass away before our eyes. Inbreeding means the producing of descendants in the circle of the related tribesmen, with the avoidance of all foreign mixture of blood.

Third, "artificial selection": that is, the elimination or hindering of the procreation of the inferior part of a race and the facilitation of that of the superior individuals. Fourth, the crossing of blood with other homogeneous racial groups. Fifth, "only quite definite, limited mixture of blood contributes towards the ennoblement of a race, or, it may be, the origin of a new one." [28] All known powerful and noble races sprang up under the operation of these five conditions.

Having given these principles, Chamberlain proceeds to his detailed analysis of the race and the contributions of the Greeks and the Romans. Beginning with the period of "The Chaos," at the beginning of the Middle Ages, he traces the origin and appearance of the Teutonic race; and the origin and entering of the Jews into Western history. On the one hand, the author admires the Jews for their preservation of racial purity, seeing in it the source of the increasing power of the Jews. On the other hand, like Gobineau and many others, he stresses their pernicious influence on our civilization. They remain always "the aliens among all peoples." With the help of the princes and the nobles who need their money, the Jews have always been the cruel exploiters and merciless destroyers of all nations.

The Indo-European, moved by ideal motives, opened the gates in friendship: the Jew rushed in like an enemy, stormed all positions and planted the flag of his, to us, alien nature — I will not say on the ruins, but on the breaches of our genuine individuality. Wherever the Jews are admitted to power, they abuse it.[29]

Owing to the humanitarianism, generosity, and disregard of the racial problem on the part of the Indo-Europeans for the last centuries, the influence of the Jews has been increasing and our time may be styled "The Jewish Age."

[28] *Ibid.*, pp. 276–289.
[29] *Ibid.*, pp. 330, 345, and the whole of Chap. V.

The Teutons, representing a fortunate mixture of different Aryan races, are the real creators of the civilization of the nineteenth century. Tall, fair, long-headed, they have been the bearers of courageous, energetic, inventive minds, and especially also of loyalty and freedom. "Freedom and loyalty are the two roots of the Germanic nature." [30] Having assimilated the heritage of the past civilizations, they have created the new, splendid, beautiful, and great civilization of ours.[31] Luther, Immanuel Kant, Newton, Charlemagne, Shakespeare, Dante, Nelson, Montesquieu, R. Wagner, and practically all the great leaders of the Middle Ages and of the new period have been Teutons. In the previous centuries the Teutons struggled and mastered all the other half-breeds and the Jews. At the present moment, the struggle between the Teutons and the Jews and other non-Teutons is being continued.

No arguing about "humanity" can alter the fact of the struggle. Where the struggle is not waged with cannon-balls, it goes on silently in the heart of society by marriages, by the annihilation of distances which further intercourse, by the varying powers of resistance in the different types of mankind, by the shifting of wealth, by the birth of new influences and the disappearance of others, and by many other motive powers. But this struggle, silent though it be, is above all others a struggle for life and death. [32]

Such is in essence this racial philosophy of history. His book touches many other important problems, and gives many interesting theories and interpretations, but we shall pass them by, because they do not have a direct relation to the racial theory in sociology.

3. THE RACIAL-ANTHROPOMETRICAL BRANCH OF THE SCHOOL

Before mentioning other works which have stressed the racial factor principally on the basis of historical evidences, let us turn to that branch of the school which has emphasized the importance of the race factor, principally on the basis of the data of anthropometry. The leading rôles in this field have been played by the works of a French anthropologist and biologist, G. Vasher de Lapouge, and by a German anthropologist, Otto Ammon, not to

[30] *Ibid.*, p. 574.   [31] *Ibid.*, pp. 321–328, and Chap. VI.   [32] *Ibid.*, p. 578.

mention other names. Their works have given a great impetus to the racial school, which tries to base its contentions on a new foundation, that is, on the data of anthropometry and biology. Through their works, the conception of the superior and the inferior races has become somewhat more definite. Let us briefly outline the essentials of their works.

G. V. de Lapouge.[33]—Of his numerous researches, the most important are summed up in his three books, the conclusions of which are now given: *Les sélections sociales* (Paris, 1896), *L'Aryen, son rôle social* (Paris, 1899) and *Race et milieu social* (Paris, 1909). In spite of the one-sidedness of these works, they belong to the type of books which are stamped by originality, independence of opinion, and erudition. From the sociological standpoint, the more interesting is the first book. It is opened with a discussion of Darwinism in social sciences. In regard to race, the author's starting point is that any population or any individual has in its veins the blood of numerous and various races. The number of the ancestors of every man, if they are traced back to the time of Jesus Christ, is no less than 18,014,-583,333,333,333. If we go further back, the number rapidly increases to an unthinkable figure. This means that there is no pure race in the absolute sense of the word.[34] This, however, does not mean that there do not exist different races in a relative sense of the word. Many crossings are purely incidental and cannot alter seriously either the purity of a race or its dominant characteristics. This is ascertained by the existence of races with different bodily, psychical, and physiological characteristics.[35] The population of Europe consists of three principal races, the word "race" being taken in its zoölogical sense. The first race is *Homo Europaeus,* or the Aryan race. Its characteristics are a tall stature (about 1m. 70), conspicuously dolichocephalic index, 76 and below, and blondness. Corresponding psychological traits are as follows:

A dolichocephal has great wishes and incessantly works to satisfy

---

[33] Concerning his works see KOVALEVSKY, M., *Contemporary Sociologists,* Chap. VIII; HANKINS, *op. cit.,* Chap. V., and works indicated further.

[34] *Les sélections sociales,* pp. 3–4.

[35] *Ibid.,* pp. 4–8.

them. He is capable rather of gaining than of preserving wealth. Being audacious in his temperament, he dares everything, and through this audacity achieves an incomparable success. He fights for the sake of fighting without a back-thought of profit. The whole earth is his own and the whole planet is his country. His intelligence may vary from dullness to genius. There is nothing that he does not dare to think or desire, and desire for him means to realize it at once. Progress is his most intense need. In religion he is a Protestant. In politics he demands from the State only the respect of his activity, and tends rather to rise himself, than to oppress others.[36]

The second principal race is the *Homo Alpinus*. His characteristics include a stature of from 1m. 60 to 1m. 65, and a cephalic index of 85 and above. Pigmentation is brown or even lighter. This is a typical man of the brachycephalic race:

He is frugal, laborious, remarkably prudent, and does not leave anything to chance. Not lacking in courage, yet he does not have a militant proclivity. He loves land and especially his native place. Being rarely a nullity, at the same time he rarely rises to a level of talent. His mental vistas are limited and he patiently works to realize his moderate purposes. He is a man of tradition and common sense. He does not like progress. He adores uniformity. In religion he prefers to be a Roman Catholic; in politics he craves for State protection and interference, and for equality and levelling. He sees excellently his personal interests, and partly those of his family, but the interests of the whole country are beyond his mental perspective. [37]

The third race is *Homo Contractus,* or *Mediterranean.* He has a low stature, dark color, and a cephalic index of about 78. He represents something midway between the two above races. According to his characteristics he must be ranked below even *Homo Alpinus.*[38]

Such are the principal racial types of the European population, the most important racial characteristics of which are the cephalic index and pigmentation. The combination of these bodily traits is connected with corresponding psychical and mental characteristics. This correlation is so close that the author says:

The strength of a character depends upon the length of cranium and brain. When the cranium is less than 0.19, the race lacks energy.

---

[36] *Ibid.,* pp. 13–14.   [37] *Ibid.,* pp. 17–18.   [38] *Ibid.,* pp. 23–28.

Such is the case with the brachycephalic race, which is characterized by insufficiency of individuality and initiative. Intellectual power, on the contrary, seems to be correlated with the breadth of the anterior part of the brain. Certain dolichocephals whose cephalic index is too low seem to be incapable of rising above barbarism. I do not know any superior people whose cephalic index would be below 74. An interval of a dozen units separates this limit of sufficient intelligence and maximal energy from that where the energy is insufficient. [39]

Having given these racial characteristics, Lapouge proceeds to show that practically all important achievements of culture have been made by the *Homo Europaeus,* the Nordic, or the Aryan race. They have been the leaders in every creative activity, and otherwise the dominant race. Within the same society the upper classes are composed predominantly of this race, while the lower classes are composed of the other two races or their mixture. There are racial differences, not only among various societies, but among various social classes of the same society, too. Correspondingly, the progress or regress of a society is determined principally by changes in the racial composition of its population. If the Nordic racial elements increase among it, society progresses, but if, on the contrary, its proportion decreases,—if, in other words, the cephalic index of the population becomes less and less dolichocephalic, this will result in a social regress and decay of the society.[40] These generalizations are corroborated by various and different anthropometrical data. They are intended to show that the cephalic index of the ancient aristocracy (and partly even of the contemporary one) has been lower (more dolichocephalic) than that of the lower social classes; that a more progressive city population has a more dolichocephalic index than that of a more backward country population; that in Greece and in Rome, parallel to the development of decay, the cephalic index of the population had been rising; that among contemporary societies, the most progressive have been those, in which, as in England and the United States of America, the population has been rich in the Nordic elements; that in France and in other countries during the last few centuries, a decrease of

[39] *Ibid.*, pp. 78–79.   [40] *Ibid.*, pp. 65 subsq.

the Nordic elements in the population has been accompanied by the process of decay; and so on. (See the *Social selections* and *L'Aryen, passim.*) On the basis of these data of anthropometry, Lapouge comes to conclusions similar to those of Gobineau about the rôle of the racial factor in the evolution of a country and a civilization.

Having formulated these conclusions, the author asked how these changes in the racial composition of a population could have happened. What factors are responsible for them? Why is it that a dolichocephalic race could not and cannot keep its own proportion within many societies? The answer to these questions leads us to the second, and from my point of view, to the more valuable part of the theory of Lapouge,—that is, his theory of social selection.

Changes in the population are possible either through the direct influence of environmental agencies which may modify, step by step, the bodily and mental traits of a population; or through selection,—that is, through a progressive decrease of certain racial elements and a progressive multiplication of other racial (hereditary) types in the population. The first way does not lead directly to a change of the racial (hereditary) type, but it may lead to it in a long period of time. The other way may change the racial (hereditary) composition of the population very efficiently, and in a relatively short period of time. In order to show this, the author analyzes the principal environmental agencies. He takes education and tries to show that its efficiency in this respect is very limited. It cannot change the race and the inherited traits of the population. It cannot make out of an innately stupid man, a talented one; out of an inborn idiot, an averagely intelligent man; or out of mediocrity, a genius. The best that education can do is to raise the mental level of mediocrity a little. But even in this respect its possibilities are limited. The importance of heredity is shown in the fact that education does not diminish the differences between individuals, but rather increases them. If a mediocre talent gains something by education, hereditary talent gains still more, so that after the education, the difference between the former and the latter increases, but does not decrease. Education, furthermore, is incapable of changing the temperament, the character, and the moral traits of people. This is witnessed by the fact that, in spite of a great increase of schools and educational institutions, the number of crimes has not diminished, but has rather increased. The cranial capacity also has not increased, but rather decreased during the last few decades. Finally, the results of education are not inherited; therefore, its fruits cannot be transmitted and fixed into posterity. These considerations must show that the educational factor is very limited in its efficiency to transform the race of a people.

More efficient is the influence of climate, as an environmental agency. Important also are the modifying agencies of food, alcohol, intermarriage, and some other environmental agencies in the alteration of the racial type of the population. Taken independently of selection, however, they would require hundreds of years to perform a noticeable change in the racial type of a people. For this reason their direct efficiency is limited. If it is somewhat greater, this is due to the indirect influence exerted through the channels of selection.[41] The most important, rapid, and efficient way of changing the racial composition of a population is not by the direct influence of environment, but by a selection which will lead to a survival and multiplication of one racial type, and to the extermination of another type. Through selection, the proportions of different racial types in a population may be changed greatly, and within relatively a few generations. If we imagine two different families, one producing four surviving children in each generation and the other only three offspring,— then in the course of about three hundred years, the total population will be 93 per cent the offspring of the first family, and 7 per cent that of the second.[42] This shows how rapidly the factor of selection works, and how efficient it is in changing the racial composition of a population. The degeneration or improvement of society has been due not so much to the direct influence of environment as to the factor of selection.

This leads to Lapouge's analysis of selection. He accepts Darwin's theory of natural selection and the evolution of organisms through the play of this factor, or through the elimination of the unfit and survival of the fittest. Among human beings,

[41] *Les sélections sociales*, Chaps. IV, V, VI.   [42] *Ibid.*, pp. 61 *et seq.*, 350.

however, he believes natural selection gives more and more place to social selection, natural environment being gradually superseded by social *milieu*. Therefore, natural selection is transformed into a social one, that is, the selection which goes on under the influence not so much of natural, as of social environment.[43] In the subsequent parts of his book, Lapouge analyzes the principal forms and effects of social selection within the past and especially in the present societies. As natural selection may be progressive and regressive, so may social selection lead to a degeneration or to a betterment of the racial (hereditary) composition of the population. Its dominant effects, however, are negative within present societies.

The first fundamental form of social selection is *military*, or the selection caused by war. Contrary to general opinion, Lapouge contends that wars do not decrease, but increase with the progress of civilization. Man is more warlike than any animal and contemporary man is more warlike than prehistoric man. With the exception of primitive times, war carries away the best racial elements of the population,—the healthiest, the strongest, the bravest, and the most audacious dolichocephals,—in much greater proportion than the inferior and the brachycephalic population. It facilitates the elimination of the belligerent Aryans and the survival of the Alpine or the Mediterranean races. In this military way the Aryans of ancient Greece and Rome, and the Nordic nobility of Gallia and of the Middle Ages perished to a great extent. As the Nordics are more belligerent and independent, they have been the greatest sufferers from war. Hence, if the fertility of these racial elements does not compensate for the losses of war, or should their propagation be retarded in comparison with that of other races, war leads to degeneration, that is, an extermination of the Aryan race in a society.[44]

The second form of social selection is *political*, performed under the influence of political factors and political struggles. Its results are also negative. Through revolution and civil strife, this selection facilitates an extermination of the best part of the population among both the aristocracy and the people. Again, the Nordics, who usually happen to be in both struggling factions,

[43] *Ibid.*, Chap. VI.   [44] *Ibid.*, pp. 207 *et seq.*

perish in a greater proportion than do the other racial groups. To this factor is greatly due the extermination of the Aryan aristocracy in ancient Greece and Rome, in the French Revolution, and in other similar cases. Further, in the past, but more especially in the present, political conditions have facilitated the social promotion of nullities, servile people, machinators, and politicians, while they have suppressed, especially in democracies, the social promotion of independent and creative minds. Through the political strife of parties, the chances of survival and procreation of such people are handicapped. Machinators, demagogues, politicians, who rarely belong to the best and creative type of men, greatly profit through this form of selection, while the best people, keeping themselves out of politics, rather suffer from such conditions.[45]

The third form of social selection is *religious,* which is due to the religious conditions. Religion leads directly to selection through the institution of celibacy required by several religions; and indirectly, through various religious institutions. In many religions the priests and the clergy must be celibate. This means that they cannot leave, at least legally, any posterity. As has been proved many times, church officials recruited from various social strata are usually superior physically, morally, and mentally to other people. Celibacy of this superior group prevents it from leaving superior posterity. In this way, celibacy impoverishes the fund of the superior racial elements of a population and facilitates its racial degeneration. From this standpoint, Mohammedanism with its polygamy is more eugenic than Christianity, especially, the Roman Catholic denomination. Religion leads to the same disgenic result through religious persecution, wars, and inquisition; and through the prohibition of sexual freedom, by favoring asceticism, its prohibition of marriages with those who have a different religion, and so on.[46]

The fourth form of social selection is *moral,* due to moral obligations and rules of conduct. It is closely connected with religious selection. It manifests itself in such phenomena as the repression and chastisement of sexual liberty, as the demands of decency, and as opposition to bodily nakedness, resulting in our

---

[45] *Ibid.,* pp. 243 *et seq.*   [46] *Ibid.,* pp. 263 *et seq.*

covering ourselves with unhygienic clothes which hinder free breathing, bar the beneficial influence of the sun and fresh air, and facilitate tuberculosis and other sicknesses. In addition, through philanthropy and its propaganda, moral rules facilitate the survival of the weak and the procreation of the inferior. In such ways morals contribute a great deal to negative social selection.[47]

The next form of social selection is *juridical,* being performed by law and law machinery. It operates through criminal law and the punishment of offenders by execution, imprisonment, banishment, ostracizing, and torture. Many of these offenders are political and this form of selection especially, often has negative effects, because its victims many times include people of superior character. Juridical selection operates further through civil law and its machinery, forbidding consanguineous marriages between relatives, and punishing bigamy and polygamy. Civil law prevents talented people from keeping purity of blood, and procreating more intensively, while it facilitates such disgenic institutions as prostitution.[48]

The sixth form of social selection is *economic,* due to the struggle for material necessities. For the best racial elements its results are disastrous also, because the superior people do not care much about money-making, and, as a result, the successful money-makers are rarely superior men. Enrichment is often the result of luck, or dishonesty, or cupidity, or machinations and manipulations. Within present societies the "machinators," especially the Jews, concentrate wealth. Through wealth they rise to the top of the social pyramid, and procreate themselves, while the mentally and morally superior individuals must limit their posterity to meet their own conditions. Many of them do not marry at all. In this way these precious racial elements are lost and the racial fund of a society is impoverished. Marriages dictated by economic reasons lead to the same result when a racially superior, but poor individual takes a rich, but racially inferior man or woman as his mate. In this and in similar ways the present "plutocratic" régime facilitates the procreation of the inferior and hinders that of the superior people. A régime based on wealth is the worst enemy of racial progress.[49]

[47] *Ibid.,* Chap. XI. [48] *Ibid.,* Chap. XII. [49] *Ibid.,* Chap. XIII.

The seventh form of social selection is *occupational,* called forth by occupational differentiation of the population. Its effects are again negative. Vital statistics show that the more qualified occupational groups have a lower fecundity than the semi-skilled and the unskilled groups. As the people engaged in the qualified occupations are more dolichocephalic than the people in unskilled occupations, this means that occupational selection facilitates the procreation of brachycephals and handicaps that of dolichocephals. It leads to the same racial degeneration to which lead other forms of social selection.[50]

The next form of social selection is performed by *urban and rural differentiation.* Growth of the cities and industrialization calls forth a permanent migration of the country population to the cities. The rural migrants are dominantly more dolichocephalic than those who remain in the country. The migrants, as a rule, are more energetic, enterprising, talented, and superior, than those who remain in the country. Cities permanently drain the best elements of the country population, and having drawn them from the country, they make them relatively sterile, either through city vice and sickness, or through their own voluntary restriction of fertility for the sake of social promotion. In this way urban selection diminishes the chances for the procreation of a relatively superior and more dolichocephalic people.

Such, according to Lapouge, are the principal forms of social selections and their factors. I have only outlined, schematically, what Lapouge brilliantly develops on many pages, full of statistical, historical, and psychological data. The result of all these selections is negative. They lead to an extermination of the Aryan elements within present societies, followed by their racial degeneration and ultimate decay. Excepting in Anglo-Saxon countries, where the Aryans are still in abundance, this race is already in the minority. Even among the upper classes they have been supplanted by a new brachycephalic aristocracy, representing the posterity of saloon-keepers, money-makers, and other racially inferior elements who promoted themselves owing to negative social selections. The triumph of mediocrity, demagogy, machinations, and the inability to create new, real values and to achieve

[50] *Ibid.,* Chap. XIII, pp. 355 *et seq.*

a real progress form the characteristics of our time and our culture. These are nothing but the symptoms of the beginning decay of Western civilization. Only in the Anglo-Saxon countries is the situation any better, and even there the condition is temporary, because, under present social conditions, the Aryans are doomed to extermination.

The above leads the author to his criticism of the Utopia of progress, and to the formulation of his law of the quicker destruction of the more perfect racial elements.[51] The concept of progress is a mere Utopia. Astronomy, paleontology, biology, and history testify against it. Astronomy tells us that the sun is becoming colder and that when it becomes cold, life on the earth, and consequently, the continuation of human history, will become impossible. Paleontology witnesses that in the course of the evolution of life many perfect species have perished, being unable to adapt themselves to the environment which much more primitive species have survived. Biology proves that selection may go on in regressive, as well as in progressive directions. History testifies that many a brilliant civilization has perished and many peoples, after a period of progress, have decayed.[52] All these undeniable facts show the chimerical character of the belief in progress, or of a perpetual betterment of mankind in the course of time. They also indicate that the more perfect organisms are liable to perish more easily than the less perfect or more primitive species. The social selection and elimination of the superior racial elements in a population, in favor of the inferior races, is only a particular form of this general phenomenon of the easier destruction of the more perfect forms in favor of the less perfect. The Aryan race has created almost all that is valuable in culture and civilization. Almost the whole of human progress is due to it; but these achievements and this progress have cost very much. They are now being paid for, and the price demanded is the destruction of this creative race itself. Now this process is approaching its end. The Aryan race has been rapidly disappearing and at the present moment it composes only a small fraction of the whole human population. Through some special eugenic measures, namely, the creation of a natural aristocracy according to

[51] *Ibid.*, Chap. XV.   [52] *Ibid.*, pp. 443 *et sea.*

the innate qualities of individuals, and through its inbreeding, its greater procreation and organization in a new dominant racial caste, it would be possible to slow the process of racial degeneration, but there is not much hope of realizing these measures, and, even at best, they would only serve to postpone, but not to avert, the elimination of the Aryans.

Such is the essence of the principal work of Lapouge. In his *L'Aryen* and *Le race et milieu social,* as well as in his numerous researches, he did not add anything substantially new to the principles given in *Les selections sociales.* In *L'Aryen,* Lapouge skillfully summed up the principal "laws" elaborated by himself and his collaborators. These laws will be given later on, after the characteristics of the theories of Otto Ammon and George Hansen have been disposed of.

Otto Ammon.—The second founder of the "Anthropo-sociology" is a prominent German anthropologist, Otto Ammon. His works began to appear almost at the same time as those of Lapouge. At the beginning they worked independent of each other, but somewhat later they came across the works of each other, and, after that, they began to coöperate in a popularization of their similar theories. Ammon began his scientific work with an anthropometric measurement of the recruits of the Grand Duchy of Baden in 1886.[53] These measurements have shown that the percentage of dolichocephals among the recruits of the cities (Heidelberg, Karlsruhe, Mannheim and so on) was much higher than among the recruits of the country, while the per cent of the brachycephals was in reverse proportion. This result was quite unexpected for Ammon himself, and he did not know at that moment whether it was due to the direct influence of the city environment or to a special selection of the city population. As a naturalist he thought he should test both possible theories, and he undertook such a test. He began by making further very careful anthropometric measurements of the students of the gymnasiums (high schools) and the recruits of Karlsruhe and Fri-

[53] Its results were published by Ammon in his *Anthropologische Untersuchungen der Wehrpflichtigen in Baden*, Hamburg, Richter, 1890. A short résumé of the evolution of the theories of Ammon in connection with the works of Lapouge is given by Ammon in his paper, "Histoire d'une idée. L'Anthroposociologie," in *Revue international de sociologie*, Vol. VI, 1898, pp. 145–181.

burg, with strong separation of the people measured according to their, and their parents', social position and according to their country or city origin. The results showed that the per cent of dolichocephals was again higher in the city population than in that of the country; that it was higher among those who migrated from the country than among those who remained sedentary; and that the upper social classes were more dolichocephalic than the lower ones.[54] These facts, being unaccountable through direct influence of the city environment, could be explained only through admission of selection. Ammon's explanation consists in the admission that the dolichocephals dominate among those who migrate from the country to the city. In other words, dolichocephals are more migratory than the brachycephals. This accounts for the predominance of the dolichocephalic type in city population composed of such dolichocephalic migrants, as compared with the country population. This form of selection is facilitated by an additional one which goes on in the cities, namely, by the fact that the brachycephals die out in the cities more rapidly than the dolichocephals, and that the dolichocephals climb up the social ladder in the cities more successfully than the brachycephals. The results obtained by these measurements may be accounted for by the hypothesis of selection. In this inductive way Ammon came to conclusions similar to those of Lapouge and George Hansen.[55]

In his *Die drei Bevölkerungsstufen* (first edition in 1889) George Hansen tried to show that the population of cities could not keep its biological balance if there were not a permanent influx of the country migrants to them. Their population would otherwise die out within two or three generations. Since this is not the case the cause must be the migration of the country people to the cities. The cities are incessantly draining the surplus and the best elements of the country population. The country migrants, having come to the city, usually enter the middle social strata; part of them climb up further. Having climbed, they become sterile, and die out, another part then dropping into the class of the proletariat. Thus, contrary to K. Marx's theory

[54] The detailed results of this study were published by Ammon in his book, *Die Natürliche Auslese beim Menshen*, Jena, 1893, G. Fischer.

[55] See AMMON, *Histoire d'une idée*, pp. 152–157.

there are not three, but only two principal social classes: the class of the agriculturists (farmers, landowners, peasants) and the class of the city proletariat; for the city middle and upper classes represent only a temporary transitional stage, of passage of the country migrants from the class of the agriculturists to that of the proletariat. Eventually the city drains all the valuable elements of the country population, and then a decay of the corresponding society becomes imminent.

Hansen's and Lapouge's theories helped Ammon to understand the general significance of the data disclosed by the above observations. Such was the way of Ammon's coming to conclusions similar to those of Lapouge and, later on, of his becoming one of the most prominent leaders of this school. Although agreeing substantially with the principles of Lapouge's theory, Ammon, nevertheless, stressed some points of difference. This was due in the first place to a greater accuracy and cautiousness of Ammon than of Lapouge. Contrary to Lapouge he indicated that even if dominance of the dolichocephals in the city population and in the upper classes is certain, the same cannot be said about pigmentation. Dolichocephals need not necessarily be blond in order to make a success in the city, and the same may be said of the dolichocephalic migrants from the country to the city. Further, contrary to Gobineau and partly to Lapouge, Ammon admits that a slight mixture of brachycephalic blood in the dolichocephals may be a rather favorable condition for scientific and similar activities. Contrary to Hansen, Ammon statistically showed that Hansen's time limit of two generations, within which the city population without an influx of the country migrants would disappear, is too short. Again, he indicated that the country migrants, having come to the city, enter not the middle classes, as Hansen thought, but from three-quarters to four-fifths of them enter the proletariat class at the beginning. Only during the next generations do their offspring gradually climb up, and climbing, become less and less prolific. He stressed also that within present cities, the brachycephalic population dies out more rapidly than the dolichocephalic type, though finally, the dolichocephals are to die out also.[56]

[56] AMMON, *Histoire d'une idée*, pp. 156–157.

Going gradually from a special type of research to more general problems Ammon published in 1895 his general sociological theory in the book: *Die Gesellschaftsordnung und ihre natürlichen Grundlagen* (Social Order and its Natural Foundations).[57] The essential points of this partly theoretical, partly propagandist book, are as follows: The principal defect of the existing sociological theories, Ammon says, has been their purely economic approach to social problems. The human being is, in the first place, an organism with certain qualities, and human society is a biological phenomenon in its essence; therefore, the biological approach to an interpretation of social phenomena seems to be necessary. This biological approach is provided by the principles of Darwin's theory. Heredity, variability, struggle for life, natural selection, and survival of the fittest, furnish the principles of Darwinism, which ought to be applied for an interpretation of social life also (§§ 1-9). They explain that social life appears only among such species as those for which social existence is useful from the standpoint of survival, among which are human beings. They show further that human beings are unequal from physical, mental, and moral viewpoints. This inequality is due mainly to the factor of heredity. Genius, talent, and any specific ability is primarily a result of heredity. Every society being in need of men of genius for its success in the struggle for existence, and men of genius being rare, it is in the interests of society to facilitate their production. To be successful in the struggle for existence, society must approach a type wherein all its members would be appointed to such positions as would be the most suitable for their abilities. Social order and social institutions, which make such a social distribution of its members, are not something incidental, but represent a wonderful machinery created in the course of generations to carry on successfully the struggle for existence (§§ 10-11). Reminding us of these principles, Ammon proceeds to interpret fundamental social phenomena from this standpoint. His interpretation leads him to an exclusively high appreciation of the existing social order and its wonderful character. Since human beings are naturally unequal, it is only natural that there should

[57] I give quotations according to its third edition, Jena, 1900, G. Fisher.

be no social equality. Since men of genius and leaders are necessary for the existence of any society, it is only reasonable that societies should have created many institutions whose purpose has been to facilitate their production. This purpose has been achieved on a large scale through the creation of a social stratification of the population into the upper and the lower classes, and in the prohibition or avoidance of interclass marriages. Thus, social stratification is completely justified from the biological standpoint. Since the best social order is that in which every member is put in such a position and to such work as corresponds to his innate ability, in every society there must exist special machinery which tests the individuals, sifts them, and appoints them to a suitable place and social stratum. Such a mechanism really exists. It functions in the form of schools which sift the incapable from the capable, hinder the incapable's social climbing, and facilitate the social promotion of the capable. Further, such a mechanism functions in the form of different religious, occupational, or institutional test examinations, and other handicaps which it is necessary to overcome before a relatively high social position may be occupied. Those who are talented successfully will pass such obstacles and climb up; those who are stupid will fail, and must remain in a relatively low social position. Police, criminal justice, and punishment are further forms of this machinery which is designed to exterminate the moral and social failures, and through this to perform a social selection. This social selection is only a particular form of natural selection, and it is inevitable, in view of the inequality of individuals (§§ 13-14). It is useful for a society because it permits the shifting of the capable from the incapable and because it places everybody socially according to his quality. Its natural result is the existence of social strata and social inequality. Such is their origin and their justification. Ammon indicates other reasons for the organization of social strata (§§ 23 *et seq.*). One of them is to facilitate the inbreeding of the natural aristocracy by the hindering of cross-marriages, and, in this way, to increase the chances for the production of men of genius. The second useful effect of the separation of the upper and the lower classes is that it permits talented children of the aristocracy to avoid the vices and evils of the lowest classes, while at the same time putting some obstacles in the way of easy climbing from the lower classes to the upper. Interclass barriers hinder the infiltration of incapable climbers into the upper strata while the capable can overcome these handicaps. The third benefit of such a stratification is that, thanks to the privileges of the upper classes, they have the material comfort absolutely necessary for a successful performance of the intellectual work of these classes. Better food, air, and other comforts are necessary for the right performance of the responsible social functions of the upper classes, while the same conditions are not so necessary for a successful performance of the unskilled work of the lower classes. The fourth benefit is that the privileges of the upper classes are efficient incentives for talented people among the lower classes to exert their talents to climb up to the upper strata. From such exertion, individuals and the whole society are greatly benefited. From the above it is clear that, in the opinion of Ammon, social stratification and unequal distribution of wealth are quite beneficial, useful, necessary, and therefore entirely justified. He indicates that the distribution of income and intelligence in a society are closely correlated, and that the one form of inequality is but a manifestation of the other. Summing up this part, Ammon stresses that all in all the existing social order is extraordinarily fine, and much better than any "rational" system invented by anybody.

This analysis leads Ammon to the second part of his book. Here he indicates that at the basis of social stratification lies the racial differences of individuals. Using some historical and anthropometrical data, he contends that the upper strata have been composed of the Aryans, while the lower social classes have been principally brachycephalic (§§ 27 et seq.). Here he gives the conclusions which I have already mentioned, which are the theories of migration from the country to the city; the dying-out process of the upper strata; the filling of their places by the climbers from the lower classes; the decrease of the fertility of the offspring of these climbers in the following generations; the process of their dying out; their replacement by the new climbers; and so on. In this way a permanent migration from the city to the country, and a permanent circulation from the bottom to the top of a society is constantly going on. The principal resource from which have been recruited the future climbers has been the class of peasantry. Thanks to the existence of barriers, only the talented upstarts may climb up successfully; and besides, as a general rule, they can climb only gradually, during the time of several generations. This is again beneficial to society. Up to this point, as we may see, the theory of Ammon is very optimistic,—he finds the existing social order almost perfect. Does this mean that his prospects concerning the future are also optimistic? Ammon indicates that, unfortunately, the proportion of Aryans has been decreasing. At the end of the nineteenth century in Baden they were already only 1.45 per cent of the total population (p. 132). At the most they can now only be found in the upper classes of society. In the opinion of Ammon such a fact is an additional reason to do everything possible to preserve this superior race from disappearance. According to Ammon the future is not very hopeful, and he agrees in essence with the law of decay given by Lapouge. On the other hand, he states that as long as the peasant class has a high fertility, there will be a possibility of filling the vacant places left by a dying-out aristocracy from the talented and severely selected country migrants and their offspring.

These are the essential points of Ammon's book. Its second part is devoted to rather political and propagandist purposes, in which Ammon strongly criticizes socialism, egalitarianism, and other similar theories and institutions. We need not enter into these details.

Laws of Lapouge-Ammon.—The best summary of these theories is a list of the laws which their authors claim as the scientific contribution and in which they try to sum up their principal generalizations. In Lapouge's formulation these laws run as follows : [58]

1. *Law of Wealth-Distribution.* In a country with a mixed Aryan-Alpine population, the wealth increases in reverse relation to the cephalic index. (This means that the more dolichocephalic is the population of a class or a region of the country, the greater is the wealth held by these groups, and *vice versa.*)

---

[58] See LAPOUGE, *L'Aryen,* pp. 412 *et seq.* See also CLOSSON, C. C., "La hiérarchie des races européennes," *Revue international de sociologie,* 1898, pp. 416–430.

2. *Law of Altitudes.* In the regions where the Nordic race coexists with the Alpine race, the Nordic race localizes in the lowest altitudes (in the plains but not in the mountainous regions).

3. *Law of Distribution of the Cities.* The most important cities are almost always situated in the region inhabited by the dolichocephals, and in the least brachycephalic parts of the brachy-cephalic regions.

4. *Law of Urban Index.* The cephalic index of an urban pop-ulation is lower than that of the country population around the city.

5. *Law of Emigration.* In a population which is going to dis-sociate it is the least brachycephalic elements which emigrate.

6. *Law of Cross-Marriages (Loi des formariages).* The cephalic index of the offspring of those parents who have different regions of origin is less high than the average index of the popu-lation of these regions. This means that the less brachycephalic elements of a population are more inclined to migrate and marry mates outside of their region.

7. *Law of the Concentration of the Dolichocephals.* In the regions where the brachycephalic type exists, it tends to concen-trate in the country, while the dolichocephals tend more to the city.

8. *Law of Urban Elimination.* Urban life tends to perform a selection in favor of the dolichocephals, and destroys or elim-inates the most brachycephalic elements.

9. *Law of Stratification.* The cephalic index decreases as we proceed from the lower to the upper social classes of the same locality. The average stature and the proportion of the high statures increase as we proceed from the lower to the higher strata.

10. *Law of the Intellectuals.* The cranium of the intellectuals is more developed in all its directions, and especially in its breadth, than is that of a common people.

11. *Law of the Increase of Index.* Since prehistoric times the cephalic index has tended to increase constantly and everywhere.

By this statement of the "laws" we will conclude our discussion of the characteristics of these theories.

4. BIOMETRIC BRANCH OF THE SCHOOL

The third principal branch of the anthropo-racial school is represented by the biometrical school, the ideas of which are set forth principally in the works of Sir Francis Galton and continued by Karl Pearson and his followers. Having started its studies with an investigation of individual differences among men, this branch has concentrated its attention on the study of heredity. These studies resulted in many generalizations of a purely sociological character, similar to the fundamental conclusions of other branches of the school.

Sir Francis Galton (1822-1911).—Among other scientists, a famous Belgian statistician, Adolph Quetelet [59] and Charles Darwin had especially great influence upon Galton and his works. To Quetelet he is indebted for an application, and the perfection of a quantitative study of individual differences and phenomena of heredity and talent. To Darwin he is indebted for many general principles applied by Galton in his theories of selection and variation. The principal works of Galton which are important from the sociological standpoint are: *Hereditary Genius* (first ed. in 1869. I use the edition of 1892, London); *English Men of Science* (1874); *Inquiries into Human Faculty and Its Development* (1883); *Natural Inheritance* (1889) and *Noteworthy Families* written in conjunction with E. Schuster (1906).

Various and different as were the problems studied by Galton, he stressed, none the less, in all his works, several fundamental ideas already set forth in his early work, *Hereditary Genius*. These ideas may possibly be summed up in the following way:

1. Human individuals are different in their bodily, as well as in their psychological characteristics. They vary in stature, weight, pigmentation, health, energy, sensitivity, power of hearing, mental imagery, gregariousness, intelligence, ability, and so on. Contrary to the popular idea of the equality of men, they are found to be unequal.

2. Physical, as well as mental, characteristics are distributed

---

[59] See QUETELET, A., *Sur l'homme et le développement de ses facultés, un essai de physique sociale,* 2 vols., Paris, 1835; *Anthropométrie ou measure des différentes facultés de l'homme,* Bruxelles, 1870.

according to a typical curve of frequency distribution among the individuals of the same society. From the standpoint of intelligence, for instance, one million individuals graded according to their intelligence from the highest genius to the most stupid, both below and above the average, into mental classes separated by equal intervals, will give approximately the following figures:

Grades of Natural Ability Separated by Equal Intervals		Number in Each Million of the Same Age
Below Average	Above Average	
a	A	256,791 or 1 in 4
b	B	162,279 or 1 in 6
c	C	63,563 or 1 in 16
d	D	15,696 or 1 in 64
e	E	2,423 or 1 in 413
f	F	233 or 1 in 4,300
g	G	14 or 1 in 79,000
x (all grades below g)	X (all grades above G)	1 or 1 in 1,000,000

On either side of average.......................... 500,000
Total, both sides.................................. 1,000,000

More than half of each million is contained in the two mediocre classes *a* and *A;* the four mediocre classes, a, b, A, B, contain more than four-fifths, and six mediocre classes more than nineteen-twentieths of the entire population. Thus the rarity of commanding ability, and the vast abundance of mediocrity is no accident; but follows of necessity, from the very nature of these things. [60]

3. Individual differences are due to two principal factors, — environment and heredity, but of these two factors, the factor of heredity is far more important. The standpoint of Galton may be seen from the following quotations:

I acknowledge freely the great power of education and social influences in developing the active power of mind, just as I acknowledge the effect of use in developing the muscles of a blacksmith's arm, and no further. Let the blacksmith labor as he will, he will find there are certain feats beyond his power.[61]

A man's natural abilities are derived by inheritance, under exactly the same limitations as are the form and physical features of the whole organic world.[62]

[60] GALTON, F., *Hereditary Genius*, pp. 30–31, London, 1892.
[61] *Ibid.*, pp. 12 *et seq.*
[62] *Ibid.*, pp. 1 *et seq.: Noteworthy Families*, pp. xx *et seq.*

4. The bulk of Galton's studies has been devoted to proving the decisive importance of the factor of heredity. In various ways he indefatigably tried to show this. The principal evidences given by him are as follows:

(a) The study of men of genius shows that talent and ability are inherited. Hence, "able fathers produce able children in a much larger proportion than the generality." Galton's study of English men of science, of men of genius, and of Fellows of the Royal Society has shown that the families which have two or more eminent men produce more famous men of genius than the families with only one eminent man; and that "the nearer kinsmen of the eminent are far more rich in ability than the more remote." In other words, we have "a rapid diminution in the frequency of noteworthiness as the distance of kinship increases." Correspondingly, "the expectation of noteworthiness in a kinsman of a noteworthy person is greater in the following proportion than in one who has no such kinsman: if he be a father, 24 times as great; if a brother, 31 times; if a grandfather, 12 times; if an uncle, 14 times; if a male first cousin, 7 times; if a great-great-grandfather on the paternal line, 3 and a half times." [63]

(b) Specific ability, like that of a mathematician, musician, eminent judge, or of a statesman is commonly inherited.

(c) Environment cannot create a genius out of a mediocre man; and, on the other hand, unfortunate environment is usually overcome by a man of talent or genius.

It is a fact, that a number of men rise before they are middle-aged, from the humbler ranks of life to worldly position in which it is of no importance to their future career just how their youth has been passed.

At that age they have usually overcome all hindrances, and have reached the position of those who were born into more fortunate conditions. As a result, such men of genius, though born in humble families, by the time of their maturity are in an equally fortunate position as those who were born amidst comforts. For instance, "the hindrances of English social life are not effectual in repressing high ability. The number of eminent men in Eng-

---

[63] *Hereditary Genius*, pp. 53 *et seq.*, 102 *et seq.*; *Noteworthy Families*, pp. xli *et seq.*

land is as great as in other countries, (*e.g.,* in the United States) where fewer hindrances exist." "Social hindrances cannot impede men of high ability from becoming eminent." "I feel convinced that no man can achieve a very high reputation without being gifted with very high ability." (*Hereditary Genius,* pp. 34 *et seq.*)

(d) A study of twins made by Galton has shown that similar nurture of the twins does not make them similar when the twins are biologically unlike, and that the dissimilarity of their training scarcely affects the similarity when they are biologically alike.

There is no escape from the conclusion that nature prevails enormously over nurture when the differences of nurture do not exceed what is commonly found among persons of the same rank of society and in the same country.[64]

(e) The secondary importance of environment is demonstrated also by the fact that the same objective environment is seen and perceived differently by people with different inheritance, stimulating them to quite different reactions, emotions, and interests. Furthermore, different environments often produce similar types of personality with great similarity in achievement, and *vice versa,* for from very similar environments often come quite different types of personalities with entirely different characteristics.

Such is the principal series of facts and statements which led Galton to the conclusion that the factor of heredity is more important than that of environment.

5. Having shown the differences among individuals, Galton applies the same principle to groups and races. In his works he indicated that the upper and the lower strata of a society are not equal in regard to ability; that the upper strata have produced more men of genius and talent than the lower strata; and that such a difference is due not so much to different environment as to heredity. Races are also unequal. If we judge their ability according to the number of the men of genius produced per a definite number of population, then it is clear that the ancient Greeks in Athens, especially in the period from 530 to 430 B.C., produced one genius of the first class per about 4,822 or even per

[64] *Inquiries into Human Faculty,* pp. 155–173.

3,214 population, while in England, this number of population per genius is much higher. As to the negroes, they have not been able to produce any man of genius in their whole history.[65]

6. From the above it follows that the historical destinies of a society are primarily determined by the changes in the hereditary qualities of its population, or in other words, through selection. Environmental changes taken separately have only secondary importance, and are rather the result than the cause of the changes in the hereditary qualities of the population. In this way Galton laid down the theory of selection and of racial factors which greatly influenced Ammon, Lapouge and other partizans of the anthropometrical school. Furthermore, Galton's works have given a great impulse to eugenics as a method of social reorganization based on the correct direction of the changes in the hereditary qualities of the population through selection and selectional agencies. It consists in the facilitation of the procreation and the fertility of the best — biologically, mentally, and morally, and in hindering the procreation of the socially inadequate and of the biologically and mentally inferior. Galton's work in this field has found a great many followers, and at the present moment eugenics is already becoming an important method of social reconstruction and social politics.

Such, in brief, are Galton's important contributions to the sociological viewpoint. Being the inferences from the factual material quantitatively studied, they have exerted a great influence on biologists, psychologists, and sociologists. Galton's work has been continued by many a prominent scientist and scholar, among whom an especially conspicuous place is occupied by Karl Pearson and his collaborators.

Karl Pearson (1857–   ).—The first great contribution of Karl Pearson consists in his perfecting the quantitative method for studying social, psychological, and biological phenomena. He was also one of the most prominent creators of the mathematical theory of correlation. This has been worked out in his series of biometric studies.[66] We do not need to enter here into their

---

[65] *Hereditary Genius*, pp. 325–337.

[66] See PEARSON, *Mathematical Contributions to the Theory of Evolution*, Series from I to XVIII, published in Biometric Laboratory Publications, and in the *Proceedings of the Royal Society*, and in *Biometrika*.

analysis. Their great value is recognized by all specialists and is beyond question.

The second category of Pearson's and his followers' contributions consists in a series of mathematical studies of the phenomena of variation and heredity in man. To Pearson's group, probably more than to any other, we are indebted for a quantitative study of these problems. The result of these researches has been to show "that man varies; that these variations, favorable or unfavorable, are inherited, and that they are selected." [67]

We not only know that man varies, but the extent of that variation in both man and woman has been measured by the Biometric School in nearly two hundred cases. The variability within any single local race of man amounts to from 4 or 5 to 15 or 20 per cent of the absolute value of the character.[68]

As to the inheritance of these variations, "there is not the slightest doubt. They are not mere somatic fluctuations, but correspond to real germinal differences."

These studies have shown that members of the same stock inherit not only the physical, but the psychological and pathological characteristics also. This is shown by the resemblance between the parent and his children, and by that among the siblings. The coefficient of correlation in man's inherited physique is almost the same as that in other species. The following tables give the essential results of the studies of inheritance in man, obtained by Pearson and his collaborators: David Heron, Ethel M. Elderton, Edgar Schuster, Amy Barrington, E. Nettleship, C. H. Usher, Julia Bell, Charles Goring, S. J. Perry, E. G. Pope, E. C. Snow, Lee and others.

Table II gives the coefficients of the correlation in the inheritance of pathological characteristics.

Table III gives the results of the studies of inheritance of psychical characteristics.

These tables show the principal results obtained by Pearson's school in its study of inheritance. The coefficients of correlation testify that physical, pathological, and psychical characters are in-

[67] PEARSON, K., *The Scope and Importance to the State of the Science of National Eugenics*, 2nd ed., p. 26, London, 1909.
[68] *Ibid.*, p. 26.

TABLE I. INHERITANCE OF PHYSIQUE IN MAN AND OTHER SPECIES [69]

Man—Paternal Inheritance, Males only		Fraternal Inheritance	
Character	Coefficient of Correlation or Intensity of Inheritance	Character	Coefficient of Correlation or Intensity of Inheritance
Stature..........	.51	Stature..........	.51
Span.............	.45	Span.............	.55
Forearm..........	.42	Forearm..........	.49
Eye colour........	.55	Eye colour........	.52; .54
		Head breadth.....	.59
		Head length......	.50
		Head height......	.55
		Cephalic index....	.49
		Health..........	.52
		Hair colour.......	.62
		Hair curliness.....	.52

PARENTAL INHERITANCE IN DIFFERENT SPECIES

Species	Character	Coefficient of Correlation
Horse....................	Coat Colour...................	.52
Basset hound.............	Coat Colour...................	.52
Greyhound...............	Coat Colour...................	.52
Aphis...................	Right Antenna (Frontal Breadth).	.44
Daphnia.................	Protopodite (Body Length).......	.47

TABLE II. PATHOLOGICAL INHERITANCE

Condition	Parental	Fraternal
Deaf-mutism....................................	.54	.73
Insanity.......................................	.58	.48
Pulmonary tuberculosis.........................	.50	.48
Mean value....................................	.54	.56

[69] *Ibid.*, pp. 27–29.

TABLE III. RESEMBLANCE OF SIBLINGS [70]

Character	Boys	Girls	Boy and Girl
Vivacity	.47	.43	.49
Assertiveness	.53	.44	.52
Introspection	.59	.47	.63
Popularity	.50	.57	.49
Conscientiousness	.59	.64	.63
Temper	.51	.49	.51
Ability	.46	.47	.44
Handwriting	.53	.56	.48
Mean	.52	.51	.52

INHERITANCE OF ABILITY, MALE AND MALE

Parental................... from .49 to .58 according to the groups studied
Fraternal.................. from .52 to .56 according to the groups studied

herited. In this way the school confirmed the principal statements of Galton.

Not mentioning other important contributions of Pearson and his school,— those which lie somewhat far from the field of sociology,—let us proceed to the sociological conclusions which have been inferred by Pearson from these and other biometrical studies. They have been laid down in his half-popular pamphlets and books, such as the quoted *The Scope and Importance to the State of the Science of National Eugenics, The Function of Science in the Modern State, National Life from the Standpoint of Science, Social Problems: Their Treatment, Past, Present, and Future, Eugenics and Public Health,* partly *The Grammar of Science* and some other works, not to mention Pearson's special researches.

In their essential points, the sociological teachings and practical advices of Pearson are identical to those of Gobineau and Chamberlain, Lapouge, Ammon and Galton. The primary sociological principles of Pearson's school are as follows: First, "the biological factors are dominant in the evolution of mankind; these, and these alone, can throw light on the rise and fall of nations,

[70] *Ibid.*, pp. 29–32.

on racial progress and national degeneracy." [71]   Man's evolution, like that of animals, is an evolution by natural selection.   It

is based upon four factors: (a) that characters are variable.   (b) that characters are inherited.   (c) that there is a selective death-rate, *i.e.,* that individuals possessing characters or combinations of characters in a higher or less degree than other individuals die, on the whole, sooner or later than the latter.   (d) That those individuals who die early leave fewer offspring than those who die late. [72]

From these principles it follows that changes in a racial stock of a population through selection furnish the most important factor in the rise or fall of a nation.   If selection proceeds in favor of survival and multiplication of the best stocks, the nation progresses; if its direction is opposite, it decays.   This is true in regard to the progress of a definite society, as well as to the whole of mankind.

If you have once realized the force of heredity, you will see in natural selection—the choice of the more physically and mentally fit to be the parents of the next generation—a most beneficent provision for the progress of all the forms of life.   Nurture and education may immensely aid the social machine, but they will not in themselves reduce the tendency toward the production of bad stock. Conscious or unconscious selection can alone bring that about.

What I have said about bad stock seems to me to hold for the lower races of man.   How many centuries, how many thousands of years, have the Kaffir or the negro held large districts in Africa undisturbed by the white man?   Yet their intertribal struggles have not yet produced a civilization in the least comparable with the Aryan. Educate and nurture them as you will, I do not believe that you will succeed in modifying the stock.   History shows me one way, and one way only, in which a high state of civilization has been produced, namely, in the struggle of race with race, and the survival of the physically and mentally fitter race.

This superiority of the Aryan race justifies, according to Pearson, that the white man "should go and completely drive out the inferior race."   From the same standpoint cross-marriage between different races is not desirable because through it, "if the bad

[71] *Scope and Importance of Science*, p. 38.
[72] *The Function of Science in the Modern State*, 2d. ed., p. 3, Cambridge, 1919.

stock be raised, the good is lowered." [73]   The struggle for existence goes on not only among individuals, but among groups and
races also.

The dependence of progress on the survival of the fitter race gives
the struggle for existence its redeeming features; it is the fiery
crucible out of which comes the finer metal.

You may hope for a time when the sword shall be turned into the
ploughshare, when the white man and the dark shall share the soil
between them, and each till it as he lists.   But, believe me, when
that day comes mankind will no longer progress; there will be nothing
to check the fertility of inferior stock; the relentless law of heredity
will not be controlled and guided by natural selection.   Man will
stagnate; and unless he ceases to multiply, catastrophe will come
again. [74]

For this reason, Pearson views pessimistically a decline in the
fertility of the civilized nations (p. 29); still more pessimistically
he regards the differential fertility of present society, where the
better social classes physically and mentally reproduce themselves
in a much less degree than the inferior stocks.   (See the statistical
summary of these studies of Pearson's school in his *Scope and
Importance of the Science,* pp. 36-37.)   He considers this fact
as the greatest danger confronting the progress of contemporary
society.

The above outlines Pearson's sociological position.   More specifically I will mention that he, like Ammon, views positively the
existence of different social strata.

Let there be a ladder from class to class, and occupation to occupation, but let it not be a very easy ladder to climb; great ability
(as Faraday) will get up, and that is all that is socially advantageous.
The gradation of the body social is not a mere historical anomaly;
it is largely the result of long continued selection, economically differentiating the community into classes roughly fitted to certain types
of work.

Accordingly, he suggests that education must be different for different individuals and groups, corresponding to their inner
ability.[75]

---

[73] PEARSON, K., *National Life from the Standpoint of Science,* 2d. ed., pp. 20-24.
[74] *Ibid.,* pp. 26-27.   [75] *The Function of Science* pp. 9-12.

I will not outline the other ideas of Pearson, for the above is sufficient to make his general sociological standpoint clear. We see that, in essence, they are very similar to the ideas given by the former representatives of this school, in spite of their different approach to the social problem.

5. OTHER ANTHROPO-RACIAL, HEREDITARIST, AND SELECTIONIST INTERPRETATIONS OF SOCIAL PHENOMENA

Besides the above theories, there are a great many other works which sustain the same or similar principles in an interpretation of various social phenomena. Among them the first group is composed of a series of works whose purpose is to show the inequality of races, the supremacy of the white race, and especially of certain of its varieties, such as the "Teutonic," or the "Nordic" or the "Anglo-Saxon" race. Representing in its bulk a mere modification and popularization of the principles laid down by the above authors, with a few exceptions, these works do not amount to much in their scientific value, and are mostly a kind of an intentional or unintentional propaganda literature. They have all the faults of the works of the preceding authors without their positive qualities. Their "superior" race is often made to correspond with a certain nationality or nation, and this superior "race-nation" is decided mainly by the nationality of the corresponding author. Accordingly, we have "the Teutonic," "the Anglo-Saxon," "the Celtic," "the Latin," and "the Jewish" theories of bio-social superiority of races or nations. The works of M. Grant, L. Stoddart, S. R. Humphrey, L. Woltmann, Wilser, Otto Hauser, J. L. Reimer, J. W. Burgess, A. Schultz, J. A. Cramb, W. S. Sadler, Ch. W. Gould, C. S. Burr, and partly even in some of the works of W. MacDougall, F. K. Günther, and F. Lenz are found samples of this kind of literature.[76]

[76] See GRANT, M., *The Passing of the Great Race*, 1916, (a fallacious vulgarization of the works of Gobineau, Lapouge, Ammon, Galton, and Pearson, without mentioning these names); STODDARD, L., *Racial Realities in Europe; The Rising Tide of Colour*, 1920; HUMPHREY, S. R., *Mankind, Racial Values and the Racial Prospect*, N. Y., 1917; WOLTMANN, L., *Politische Anthropologie*, Leipzig, 1903; *Die Germanen i.d. Renaissance*, 1905; WILSER, *Rassen und Völker*, 1912; HAUSER, O., *Der Blonde Mensch*, Weimar, 1921; REIMER, J. L., *Ein Pangermanisches Deutschland;* BURGESS, J. W., *Political Science and Comparative Constitutional Law*, Boston, 1890, (with the exception of the discussed trait, the work is very valuable in many other respects); SCHULTZ, A., *Race or Mongrel*, 1908; SADLER, W. S.,

The second category of such works deals principally with the various forms of social selection, with their results, and with the changes in the racial composition of a population as a factor of various social phenomena, such as the progress and decay of society and civilization. The works of this group are much more scientific, and, in the majority of the cases, are very valuable. Such are the works of P. Fahlbeck, S. J. Holmes, G. Sensini, C. Gini, Otto Seeck, W. Schallmayer, T. Frank, P. Jacoby, A. de Candolle, W. Bateson, E. Huntington, and partly of P. Sorokin, D. S. Jordan, V. Kellog, F. A. Woods, and many others.[77]

The third category of these works tries to establish a correlation between the various physical traits of a man and his moral, intellectual, temperamental, and socio-psychical traits. Side by side with this, many works of this group try to correlate the many bodily, vital and mental characteristics of social groups and classes, together with their social positions and historical rôles. In spite of several fallacies and hasty generalizations made in some of these works, they are, as a whole, very valuable, especially when they relate a series of special studies in this field. The writings of this group are too extensive to be enumerated here. A more or less complete bibliography of them may be found in my book, *Social Mobility* (Chaps. X-XII, and *passim*). Part of it will be indicated further in my criticism of the anthropo-racial

---

Long Heads and Round Heads, 1918; GOULD, CH. W., *America, a Family Matter*, 1922; BURR, C. S., *America's Race Heritage*, 1922; CRAMB, J. A., *The Origins and Destiny of Imperial Britain*, London, 1915; McDOUGALL, W., *Is America Safe for Democracy?* 1921, (there are several valuable and sound points, but the characteristic of the Nordic and other races is far from being scientific); GÜNTHER, F. K., *Rassenkunde des Deutschen Völkes*, 1924, a very valuable work, but in the discussed point is rather questionable. The same is to be said of F. Lenz's valuable theory in E. BAUR, E. FISHER, F. LENZ, *Grundriss der menschlichen Erblichkeitslehre und Rassenhygiene*, 2 vols., München, 1923; and of A. BASLER'S *Einführung in die Rassen u. Gesellschafts Physiologie*, Stuttgart, 1925.

[77] FAHLBECK, P., "La décadence et la chute des peuples," *Bulletin de l'Institut International de Statistique*, Vol. XV, pp. 367–389; *Der Adel Schwedens*, Jena, 1903; SENSINI, G., "Teoria dell' équilibrio di composizione delle classi sociali," *Rivista Italiana di Sociologia*, 1913; GINI, C., *I fattori demografici dell' evoluzione delle nazioni*, Torino, 1912; SEECK, O., *Geschichte des Untergang der antiken Welt*, 3rd ed., Berlin, 1910, all volumes; FRANK, T., "Race Mixture in the Roman Empire," *American Historical Review*, Vol. XXI, pp. 705 ff.; HOLMES, S. J., *The Trend of Races*, N. Y., 1921; SCHALLMAYER, W., *op. cit.;* JACOBY, P., *Études sur la sélection chèz l'homme*, 2nd ed., Paris, 1904; BATESON, W., *Biological Fact and the Structure of Society*, Lond., 1912; HUNTINGTON, E., *The Character of Races*, N. Y., 1924; SERGI, G., *La degenerazioni umane*, Milano, 1889; DE CANDOLLE, A.,

school. Here it is sufficient to mention merely a few names out of the great many who have made contributions in this field: C. Lombroso, and his followers, Ch. Goring, W. Healy, F. A. Woods, A. Niceforo, J. Bertillon, J. Beddoe, M. Muffang, E. M. Elderton, Pagliani, R. Livi, P. Ricardi, Pfitzner, Collignon, Topinard, Broca, Manouvrier, A. Hrdlička, Chalumeau, Oloriz, Anouchin, B. A. Gould, H. P. Bowdich, Talko-Hryncewitz, Ch. Roberts, J. F. Tocher, W. Porter, E. A. Doll, H. Goddard, Ch. Davenport, H. Ellis, F. Maas, E. B. Gowin, C. Röse, B. T. Baldwin, L. M. Terman, Samosch, E. Schlesinger, J. E. Young, J. G. Frazer, A. Vierkandt, P. Descamps, E. Mumford, Matiegka, Spitzka, F. G. Parsons, Shuster, A. MacDonald, Durand de Gross, A. Constantin, A. Binet, Deniker, Bushan, S. D. Porteus, J. Dräseke, W. Todd, E. Rietz, R. Pearl, McK. Cattell, E. L. Clarke, W. Z. Ripley, P. Tarnowsky, W. Clarke, A. E. Wiggam, A. Ploetz, P. Sorokin, W. R. Macdonel, A. Odin, J. Philiptschenko, W. Ogle, C. Novocelsky, C. Ballod, P. Mombert, L. Hersch, Fr. Prinzing, Körösi, E. Levasseur, A. Oettingen, G. v. Mayr, H. Westergaard, J. Wappäus, L. Dublin, L. March, F. Savorgnan, N. Humphreys, Dr. Farr, E. Wellman, W. Claassen, R. Thurnwald, Kozcinsky, W. MacDougall, and a great many other investigators have contributed to an elucidation of the problem,—as to whether there is a correlation between the bodily and the mental traits, between specific racial and intellectual qualities, between the social position of an individual, or of a group; and their physical, mental, and moral equipment. Also, whether a leading, or privileged group is composed of a selected people, or whether they represent a mere conglomeration of people, who "incidentally," and "thanks to a mere good luck," have succeeded in climbing up and enjoying their privileges.[78]

The fourth category of works deals principally with the rôle of heredity in man's nature and behavior, and in the various social processes. Stressing their rôle, the theories try to interpret, in

Histoire des sciences et des savants, Génève, 1885; SOROKIN, P., _Social Mobility,_ Parts III, IV; WOOD, F. A., _Mental and Moral Heredity in Royalty_, 1906; _The Influence of Monarchs_, 1913, and D. S. JORDAN's and V. KELLOG's works indicated further. Many of these works are discussed in the subsequent chapters of this book.

[78] See the works of these, and some further references of other authors, and their analysis, in my _Social Mobility_, Chaps. X–XII.

the light of the factor of heredity, a series of social processes. In this respect the group continues the studies of Galton, Pearson, and partly of Lapouge and Ammon. This type of literature is immense. The list of the works and their authors would be liable to occupy several dozens of pages. A legion of the biologists, psychologists, and sociologists compose it. Many of the above authors belong to this group also. Besides the names mentioned, I shall indicate here only a few names like E. Thorndike, A. Ploetz, R. M. Yerkes, Ch. Richet, P. Popenoe, R. H. Johnson, G. Poyer, and so on. The majority of the eugenists and of the investigators of human heredity have contributed to the achievements of this group.[79]

The fifth group is composed of historical works devoted to the problem of the Aryan race, and of the works in physical anthropology dealing with races and their history. As representative works of this group may be mentioned those of I. Taylor, S. Reinach, H. Peake, V. G. Childe, W. Ridgway, H. H. Bender, G. Kossina, and J. de Morgan on the one hand;[80] on the other, the anthropological works of P. Topinard, Morselli, G. Sergi, A. C. Haddon, R. A. Dixon, W. Z. Ripley, H. J. Fleure, A. Keith, Deniker, and of many other physical anthropologists.[81] Such are the principal groups of works which discuss the problems stressed by the leaders of the anthropo-social, the hereditarist, and the selectionist schools in sociology.

After this survey, let us now pass to an analysis of that which

[79] See the bibliography in HOLMES, S. J., *The Trend of the Race*, in P. POPENOE and R. JOHNSON, *Applied Eugenics*, N. Y., 1918, and in Holmes' special book of bibliography in eugenics.

[80] See TAYLOR, I., *The Origin of the Aryans*, London, 1890; REINACH, S., *L'origine des Aryens*, Paris, 1892; PEAKE, H., *The Bronze Age and the Celtic World*, London, 1922; CHILDE, V. G., *The Aryans*, N. Y., 1926; RIDGEWAY, W., *The Early Age of Greece*, Cambridge, 1901; ZABOROVSKI, M. S., *Les peuples Aryens*, 1908; BENDER, H. H., *The Home of the Indo-Europeans*, Princeton, 1922; KOSSINA, G., *Die Indogermanen*, Würzburg, 1921; DE MORGAN, J., *Prehistoric Man*, N. Y., 1925. See about other works in HANKINS, *op. cit.*, Chaps. II, III, IV.

[81] DIXON, R. A., *The Racial History of Man*, N. Y., 1923; RIPLEY, W. Z., *The Races of Europe;* TOPINARD, P., *Anthropology*, Eng. tr., 1878; MARTIN, R., *Lehrbuch des Anthropologie*, Jena, 1914; KEITH, A., *Man*, N. Y., 1913; *Anthropologie*, in HINNEBERG'S *Die Culture der Gegenwart*, Vol. V, Leipzig, 1923; FLEURE, H., *The Peoples of Europe*, Lond., 1922; HADDON, A. C., *The Races of Man*, N. Y., 1925; SERGI, G., *Le origine umane*, Torino, 1913; MORSELLI, *Antropologia generale*, Torino, 1910.

in the principles of the school is true, and also that which is a fallacy or guess.

6. CRITICISM OF THE SCHOOL

Let us take the principal statements of the school one by one and consider to what extent they are accurate.

1. *Hypothesis of the Polygenic Origin of Human Races.*— One of the bases for the theory of Gobineau, and of some other partizans of the school, is that different human races sprang from different sources and have different origins. This heterogeneity of origin is supposedly responsible for the relative superiority and inferiority of the races. Is the hypothesis true? We can answer only this: that the theory, as well as its opposite hypothesis of the monogenic origin of human races, is still nothing but a guess. We do not have any definite and decisive proof of the accuracy of either of these hypotheses.[82] For this reason, the argument of Gobineau, as well as the opposite arguments of his opponents, cannot have any conclusive value.

2. *Hypothesis of the Aryan Race.*—We have seen that almost all partizans of the school contend that the most superior race is the Aryan branch of the white race. Is this theory valid? Are the characteristics of this race definite? Are its origin and evolution, and the statement that all civilizations have been created by this race sufficiently proved? As we have seen, the Aryan race hypothesis has passed through two stages. In the writings of Gobineau the term is used rather indefinitely, without any attempt to outline its bodily or zoölogical characteristics. Only in the works of Lapouge and other anthropometrists do we find an attempt to indicate its zoölogical or bodily traits. Accordingly the discussion of the hypothesis must be divided into two parts. Let us first take the Aryan race as it appears in the writings of Gobineau and his predecessors. The origin of the Aryan race hypothesis is due to the works of the linguists who, since the formulation of William Jones's theory, have discovered that the Sanscrit language was the source of the European and a few

[82] See SERGI, G., *Le origine umane*, Torino, 1913; MORSELLI, *Antropologia generale*, Torino, 1910; SERGI, G., *Hominidae*, Torino, 1911; TOPINARD, *Anthropology*, London, 1878; HADDON, A. C., *The Races of Man,* N. Y., 1925; DIXON, R. B., *The Racial History of Man*, pp. 503 ff., N. Y., 1923.

other languages; and that the Greek, the Latin, and the European languages are related to one another. This fact led to the conclusion that all peoples who speak the "Aryan" languages compose different branches of the same race. Such an origin for the hypothesis of the Aryan race at once shows its weak point; for the fact that many individuals or social groups speak the same language does not necessitate that all of them must belong to the same racial group, in a zoölogical sense of the term, "race." At the present time peoples of very divergent racial stock speak English; while the peoples of one race may speak different languages. So it was in the past; and, therefore, it is impossible from the fact of a community or similarity of language to infer the community or identity of race. This is exactly what was done by the early "Aryanists." [83] In the second place, it is not known exactly where the Aryan race originated, nor what has been the area and the route of its migration. The Aryanists themselves differ in this respect greatly. All that is offered in this field is a mere hypothesis. As yet no unanimity is reached by their historians. In the third place, the theory that all, or at least the majority of the great civilizations, have been created by the Aryans is found to be still more hypothetical. Since the zoölogical traits of the Aryan race were not defined in early writings, their authors did not have any certain basis for saying that the ancient Egyptians, or the Assyrians, or the Greeks, or the Romans were Aryans in a zoölogical sense. Even in the linguistic sense, these peoples differed widely from one another; but granting that they had been alike in this respect, this would not have given any reason for concluding that they were near racially. These considerations are enough to show that the Aryan race hypothesis, in its early stage, was a mere guess which might, and might not, have been true; and on which it is impossible to build any valid scientific theory.

3. *The Nordic, or Homo-Europeus, Hypothesis of Lapouge*

[83] See the details in HOUZÉ, E., *L'Aryen et l'anthroposociologie*, pp. 1–33, Bruxelles, 1906; REINACH, SALOMON, *L'origine des Aryens: histoire d'une controverse*, Paris, Leroux, 1892; TAYLOR, I., *The Origin of the Aryans*, London, 1890; PEAKE, H., *The Bronze Age and the Celtic World*, London, 1922; quoted works of V. G Childe, M. S. Zaborovsky, H. H. Bender, G. Kossina, J. de Morgan. A good survey of the hypotheses is given in HANKINS, *op. cit.*, Chap. II.

and Ammon, and the Lapouge-Ammon Laws.—In the works of Lapouge and Ammon, the Aryan race hypothesis became more definite. As we have seen, Lapouge's race of *Homo Europeus* is tall, blond, and dolichocephalic. With these traits Lapouge correlated mental and moral superiority in connection with which he formulated the above "laws of Lapouge-Ammon." Now, to what extent is this theory warranted by the facts, and of what validity are the above "laws"? Since we have here more clearly-cut statements, it is easier to analyze them definitely than it was in the former case. Whatever may be the origin of this racial type,[84] the facts do not seem to corroborate the essentials of Lapouge's hypothesis, and the same is true of many of his "laws." In the first place, contrary to the conception of Lapouge and Ammon, dolichocephaly does not seem to be necessarily correlated with mental and intellectual superiority, extraordinary energy, or initiative and talent. The Australians, the Eskimos, the New Caledonians, the Hottentots, the Kaffirs, the Negroes of western Africa and some other primitive people have the most conspicuous dolichocephalic index (from 71 to 75)[85] and yet they are very primitive and have not shown any signs of mental superiority. Lapouge, confronted with this fact, tried to offset its significance by the statement that

I have never said or thought that the superiority of the homo-Europaeus is due to their mere dolichocephaly, but it is possible to claim that there is a general correlation between dolichocephaly and the greatest amount of impulsive activity. *Within any specific race,* its more dolichocephalic elements are dominant. In Mexico, in Java, and among the negroes, the dolichocephalic elements occupy the higher social strata, while the brachycephalic elements compose the bulk of the population of the lower social classes. All dominant races are dolichocephalic. [86]

This latter statement is somewhat self-contradictory, but, ignor-

[84] In the terminology and classification of Professor Dixon, this type is near the Dixon Caspian type. See Dixon's theory of the origin of different races, of their migration and distribution on the earth. DIXON, R., *The Racial History of Man*, N. Y., 1923, *passim*, and especially the chapter, "General conclusions."

[85] TOPINARD, *Anthropology*, pp. 240–242.

[86] LAPOUGE, *L'Aryen*, p. 395. Compare this with other statements of Lapouge in *Social Selections*, pp. 40, 78–79, 410 and *seq.*

ing this, is it true that within each race its dominant classes are composed principally of dolichocephals? Is it true among the leaders, the upper classes, or the prominent men of each race, that the proportion of the dolichocephals is much greater than among the lower classes and the common people? These questions must be answered rather negatively, since neither Lapouge nor any other Aryanist has given a satisfactory proof of this contention.

In spite of the common belief that the aristocracy of Europe has been composed of the dolichocephalic type, and that the higher social classes have been predominantly longheaded, this opinion may be seriously questioned.[87] First, the data concerning the past are very scarce and uncertain. Second, we certainly know that several prominent kings of the past, e.g., Tiberius, and some other Roman emperors were rather broadheaded. If it is more or less certain that the earliest prehistoric population of Europe, especially its lowest strata, was extremely longheaded,[88] we still do not have any reliable facts on which to base an opinion that the aristocracy and the leaders of that time were still more dolichocephalic. The data given by Lapouge [89] and by some others concerning the Greek, Roman, and mediæval aristocracy is extremely scarce and too uncertain to be a reliable basis for a more or less certain generalization. A few skulls, whose bearers and, consequently, whose social position, is unknown; and a few references to pictures and statues, with which it is possible to compare the opposite type of pictures and statues, furnish practically all the evidence upon which is based the hypothesis of the longheaded aristocracy of ancient times.[90] All that we have, as

[87] The recent attempt by B. S. Bramwell to prove it gives only a mass of incidental and self-contradictory data which cannot prove anything and which, as we shall see further, are disproved by the facts. See BRAMWELL, B. S., "Observations on Racial Characteristics in England," The Eugenic Review, October, 1923. The same must be said about H. ONSLOW's "Fair and Dark," The Eugenic Review, 1920–21, pp. 212–217, 480–491. Similar statements of McDougall and W. Ripley are also dogmatic. It is curious to note that K. Pearson in his earlier work set forth an opposite hypothesis of the superiority of brachycephals. See his The Chances of Death, pp. 290-292, London, 1897.

[88] See RIPLEY, W. Z., The Races of Europe, 1910, pp. 456–465.

[89] LAPOUGE, op. cit., pp. 40 ff., 410 ff.

[90] See the reasonable, critical remarks in HOUZÉ, E., L'Aryen et l'anthroposociologie, Travaux de l'Inst. de Sociologie; and in KOVALESKY, M., Contemporary Sociologists, (Russian) Chap. VIII; HANKINS, op. cit., passim; PEARSON, ibid.. p. 290.

proof of the hypothesis of the longheadedness of the higher classes, is the different group measurements of the contemporary populations of Europe.   It is true that much of the data obtained by Ammon and Lapouge and several other anthropologists seems to corroborate it; but other data, supplied partially by the same and other authors, contradict it.   We must conclude then that the hypothesis is, at best, still uncertain and not proved.   This may be seen from the following representative figures:

Niceforo [91] in his measurement of well-to-do and poor children found that in both groups there were both types, and that in this respect there was no significant difference.

In 594 of the most gifted children of California "various types of cephalic indices are found, but the majority of the children are of the mesocephalic type."   Cephalic indices are as follows:

Age	Boys	Girls
7	81	83
8	86	82
9	81	79
10	81	80
11	80	80
12	80	80
13	80	79
14	79	80
15	80	81

From this it is seen that the most gifted children of America (with I.Q. 151.33) are far from being dolichocephalic in their total.[92]

Data given by Dr. Parsons show that the cranial index of the higher social groups of the English population is by no means more dolichocephalic than that of the criminals or the general population.   This is seen from the following figures (See table on page 271).[93]   Besides, the index of the British population since the eighteenth century has become more and more brachycephalic, and yet we cannot say that during the eighteenth and nineteenth centuries the English people became stagnant and less progressive than they had been before.

[91] NICEFORO, A., *Les classes pauvres*, pp. 43–44, Paris, 1905.
[92] TERMAN, L., *Genetic Studies of Genius*, 1925, Vol. I, Table 35, pp. 148, 170.
[93] PARSONS, F. G., "The Cephalic Index of the British Isles," *Man*, February, 1922, pp. 19–23.

Social Groups	Cephalic Index
British criminals...	78.5
Population of the 19th century............................	74.9–77.5
Higher and educated groups (intellectuals, professors and students of Oxford, Cambridge, King's College, Royal Engineers, and so on)..	77.6–81.9

Measurements of American children by A. MacDonald show that "longheadedness increases in children as ability decreases. A high percentage of dolichocephaly seems to be concomitant with mental dullness." [94]

Furthermore, the data obtained by Dr. Röse, in spite of his own desire to corroborate the dolichocephalic myth, are quite contradictory and do not show any definite correlation. This is observable in the table on p. 272.[95]

These representative data, taken from many figures given by Röse, show that if there is any correlation between higher social position and dolichocephaly, it is so indefinite, and is contradicted by so many exceptions, that we are entitled to disregard it as being non-existent.

The measurements of the children of Liverpool by Muffang; of the skulls of the Polish nobility, educated groups, and common people by Talko-Hryncewitz; of Spanish students and people by Oloriz; of Belgian murderers by Heger and Dallemagne; of various classes in Italy by Livi; and other similar measurements do not show any evidence of this alleged dolichocephaly of the upper classes in Europe.[96]

These results, followed by Lapouge's own acknowledgment that "the necessary data about the cephalic index of the different

---

[94] MacDonald, A., *Man and Abnormal Man*, 1905, p. 19.

[95] Röse, C., "Beitrage zur Europaischen Rassenkunde," *Archiv für Rassen-und Gesellschafts Biologie*, 1905, pp. 760, 769–792. Recently J. R. Musselman and G. E. Harmon also did not find any correlation between the cephalic index and mental agility. See their papers in *Biometrika*, Vol. XVIII, 1926, pp. 195–206, and 207–220. The mean coefficient of the correlation between cephalic index and intelligence is .061. Pearson, K., "Relationship of Mind and Body," *Annals of Eugenics*, p. 383, Vol. I., 1926.

[96] See data and references in my *Social Mobility*, Chap. X.

Social Groups	Cephalic Index
Infantry Regiment in Bautzen	
Staff officers...	81.4
The chief lieutenants.......................................	86.3
Lieutenants...	84.4
Volunteers..	84.6
Under-officers...	84.9
Soldiers..	84.6
König-Ulanen Regiment in Hanover	
Officers..	80.2
Under-officers...	82.5
Soldiers..	82.4
Liebgarde Cavalry Regiment in Stokholm	
Officers..	81.9
Under-officers...	79.8
Soldiers..	78.9
Recruits in Copenhagen	
The sons of the farmer-owners..............................	81.6
The sons of agricultural laborers...........................	82.0
Recruits in Schwarzbourg	
The sons of the farmer-owners..............................	83.0
The sons of agricultural laborers...........................	81.6
The Pupils of the Real Schools in Dresden	
10 years old:	
All...	87.1
From the nobility......................................	83.1
11 years old:	
All...	86.8
From the nobility......................................	87.2
22 years old:	
All...	83.6
From the nobility......................................	85.4
Technische Hochschule in Dresden	
Full professors..	83.2
Associate and assistant professors...........................	83.2
Instructors...	83.8
Students...	84.0
Recruits generally...	85.2
The Pupils of Elementary Schools in Dresden	
Very superior...	85.8
Superior	86.4
Average..	86.4
Inferior..	86.4

social and occupational groups are lacking," are enough to warrant the statement that *the dolichocephalic hypothesis is still a mere belief, and nothing more.*

The theories in regard to pigmentation are no better supported. We have seen that, according to Lapouge, the second characteristic of the Aryan or Nordic race is its blondness. Like dolichocephaly, it is supposed to be correlated with energy, talent, and other superior mental qualities. Accordingly, the partizans of the Aryan or the Nordic race contend that the upper classes of the Western societies and their leaders are more blond than the lower classes and common people. In a recent paper H. Onslow and B. S. Bramwell repeat that "the ruling class has always been fair complexioned"; that the word "fair" means "bright and blond"; and that blondness is a characteristic of mental and social superiority.[97] To what extent is this contention true? So far as the collected data show, it is entirely baseless. Let us consider the pigmentation of the upper and lower social classes, putting aside the guesses about the color of past aristocracy, or the quite incidental references to the pigmentation of the few historical prominent men (which may be confronted by no less numerous opposite examples) and let us take to factual evidence. The study of Niceforo gives the results in this respect in the table on page 274.[98] The data contradict completely the criticized theory. The poor children have a higher per cent of fairness than have the wealthy.

Livi found that in Italy, among the poor, mountainous population and the peasants the per cent of light-colored persons was considerably higher than among the city population and the wealthier parts of Italy.[99] K. Pearson, having studied 1000 Cambridge graduates and 5000 school children, did not find any correlation between pigmentation and intelligence.[100] On the other

[97] ONSLOW, H., "Fair and Dark," *The Eugenic Review*, Vol. XII, pp. 212–217; BRAMWELL, B. S., "Observations on Racial Characteristics in England," *The Eugenic Review*, 1923, pp. 480–491. Even such an opponent of the exaggerated racial theory as Ripley, admits also the correctness of this theory. See his *The Races of Europe*, pp. 469, 548–550.

[98] NICEFORO, *op. cit.*, pp. 50–51.

[99] LIVI, R., report in *Bull. de l'Inst. Intern. de Statist.*, Vol. VIII, pp. 89–92.

[100] PEARSON, K., "On the Relationship of Intelligence," *Biometrika*. Vol. V, p. 139. Mean r=.08, *Annals of Eugenics*, Vol. I, p. 383.

Age Groups, Years	Per Cent of the Children Who Had Fair Eye-Color		Per Cent of the Children with Fair Hair-Color	
	Poor	Wealthy	Poor	Wealthy
7	19	18	26	21
8	18	18	26	20
9	17	17	25	20
10	16	17	24	20
11	16	15	22	18
12	16	15	23	18
13	16.4	14.8	22.1	17.2

hand, J. Jorger found that among the descendants and the members of such criminal and feeble-minded families as the Zero, there have been light-, as well as dark-colored people.[101]   J. F. Tocher, also, in a careful study of the criminals and feeble-minded in Scotland, did not find any difference in pigmentation between the inmates of prisons or asylums and the common population, with the exception that the insane exhibited a slight tendency to be lighter-eyed and darker-haired than the sane population.[102]   A study of the old Americans by Dr. Aleš Hrdlička showed further that the common opinion in regard to the supposed blondness of the old Americans is also fallacious.   About 50 per cent of them are midway between the blond and dark-haired.   One-fourth of the males have dark or dark-brown hair, and only one out of sixteen males and one out of 14.5 females are blond-haired.[103]   Omitting here other similar studies with the same results,[104] we find in the study of men of genius that, from the standpoint of pigmentation, neither do they support the criticized theory.   Of

[101] JORGER, J., "Die Familie Zero," *Archiv für Rassen und Gesellschafts Biologie*, 1905, pp. 494–554.

[102] TOCHER, "The Anthropometrical Characteristics of the Inmates of Asylums in Scotland," *Biometrika*, Vol. V, p. 347.

[103] HRDLIČKA, A., "Physical Anthropology of the Old Americans," *American Journal of Physical Anthropology*, 1922, No. 2, pp. 140–141.

[104] By H. G. Kenagy, N. D. Hirsh, Carret, Constantin and others. See LAIRD, D. A., *The Psychology of Selecting Men*, 1925, pp. 127–31; HIRSH, N. D. M., "A Study of Natio-Racial Mental Differences," *Genetic Psychology Monographs*, May and July, 1926, Chap. VIII; CONSTANTIN, A., *Le rôle sociol. de la guerre*, pp. 36–39, Paris, 1907.

such more or less systematic studies, I know only one,— that of
H. Ellis. The results obtained by this man in his study of
British men of genius are as follows:

Of 424 British men of genius,

> 71 were unpigmented (light).
> 99 were light medium.
> 54 were doubtful medium.
> 85 were dark medium.
> 115 were dark fully.[105]

These figures refute the alleged blondness of British geniuses.
More detailed data given by H. Ellis further confirm my criticism. Taking 100 as the index of the mean fairness, all indexes
above 100 as the indication of a greater blondness, and all figures
below 100 as the indication of an increasing darkness, we have
the following table: [106]

Categories of British Men of Genius	Number of Men	Index of Pigmentation
Political reformers and agitators.................	20	233
Sailors..	45	150
Men of science..................................	53	121
Soldiers..	142	113
Artists...	74	111
Poets...	56	107
Royal family....................................	66	107
Lawyers...	56	107
Created peers and their sons....................	89	102
Statesmen.......................................	53	89
Men and women of letters........................	87	85
Hereditary aristocracy..........................	149	82
Divines...	57	58
Men of genius of low birth......................	12	50
Explorers.......................................	8	33
Actors and actresses............................	16	3

This shows, first, that the royal family is very far from being

[105] ELLIS, H., *A Study of British Genius*, pp. 209–210.
[106] *Ibid.*, pp. 209–216; ELLIS, H., "The Comparative Ability of the Fair and
Dark," *Monthly Review*, August, 1901.

at the top of the list; second, that the pigmentation of the hereditary aristocracy is dark, and much darker, than that of the created peers who came out from the middle classes; third, that the statesmen and explorers—the men of energy—were dark. These facts refute completely the one-sided interpretation of this table which was given by H. Onslow. The figures do not give any confirmation of the "blond theory" and its variations. The above is enough to show that this theory, in spite of its popularity, has no scientific basis.[107]

Besides these anthropometric data, historical evidence seems to testify against the criticized theory, for the Nordic races of Europe were the latest to develop civilization.

Civilization was more precocious in the South of the European continent than in the North, and, of all the people of Europe, it was the population of North Europe and of the Baltic sea coast which remained the most retarded in regard to intellectual culture. Therefore it is absurd to pretend that the Nordics were responsible for the creation and promotion of culture in the remotest past. On the contrary, their invasions everywhere caused either stagnation or regress of development.

The cultivation of plants, the domestication of animals, and the use of bronze and metals were all developed long ago, since the neolithic epoch. The same is true in regard to many other fundamental inventions and discoveries in technique and religion, in *mores,* and in social institutions.[108] For these reasons, it is impossible to pretend that the blond, tall and dolichocephalic Aryans have alone been the conquerors, the aristocracy, and the bearers of mental superiority and progress.

On the other hand, Lapouge seems to underestimate the rôle and the achievements of the brachycephalic Alpine racial type. Nearer to the truth seems to be Dixon's statement that, "If in the history of the race as a whole, the Mediterranean and Caspian (Lapouge's Nordic race) peoples have played a great part, that of the Alpines seems hardly less impressive; and there is not a little reason to believe that only where these types have met and mingled have the highest achievements been attained." Accord-

---

[107] See other data in my *Social Mobility*, Chap. X, N. Y., 1927.
[108] Houzé, *op. cit.*, pp. 31–33: see first part of the book, *passim.*

ing to the author just such a blending took place when the Babylonian civilization rose to its climax; and when the Greek and the Roman, the Chinese and the Italian attained great achievements. Though these statements are rather guesses, nevertheless they appear to be nearer to the facts than Lapouge's one-sided theory. "To no one race or type (among the Nordic, Mediterranean and the Alpine races) can the palm be assigned, but rather to the product of the blending of those types which seem the most gifted,—the Mediterranean, Caspian and the Alpine." [109]

If this fundamental contention of the criticized theory fails, then many inferences from it, such as the theory of degeneration due to an increase of the cephalic index; such as the explanation of the decay of ancient Rome and Greece through the substitution of the brachycephals for the dolichocephals; such as the negative appreciation of the brachycephalic aristocracy of the democratic societies; and such as the alleged superiority of the blonds; all these popular inferences must fall down also, like a row of dominoes when the first one has been pushed over.

4. *Other Ammon-Lapouge Laws.*—Let us now briefly touch the validity of other laws indicated above. As for the *Law of Wealth-Distribution,* the above data have shown that it is not warranted by the facts, since there is no evidence that the wealthy classes are more dolichocephalic than the poor ones.[110]

The *Laws of Altitudes and of Distribution of the Cities* are, at their best, illustrative only of local phenomena, and in no way can pretend to be general formulas applied to all places and times.

The Law of Urban Index, according to which the population of the cities is more dolichocephalic than that of the surrounding country, is again quite a local phenomenon which cannot pretend to any degree of generality. If in some cities of Germany and France the population of the city happens to be more dolichocephalic, in other cities of the same and of many other countries (England, Italy, Belgium, Spain, Egypt, Grand Duchy of Lux-

[109] Dixon, *op. cit.,* pp. 514–516.

[110] This "law" by the way is in sharp contradiction with other statements of Lapouge where he slanders the present money-aristocracy as pseudo-aristocracy, as prosperous brachycephals, who, like a plague, devastate and impede the existence and procreation of the dolichocephals. See *Sélections sociales,* Chap. XIII, *passim.*

emburg, and so on) the situation is the reverse.[111]   In this respect
the formula of R. Livi is more correct.[112]   He states that the
cities attract their migrants from places far distant, rather than
near at hand; and that therefore, where the population surrounding a city is of the dolichocephalic type, the city population will
be more brachycephalic, and *vice versa*.   This shows the fallacy
of the discussed law and that of the supposition of "the Law of
Migration," according to which the dolichocephals are for some
mysterious reason more migratory than the brachycephals.   The
same is true concerning pigmentation.   The city population is
not more blonde, but rather, darker, than the country population.
The above refutes also "the Law of Concentration of the Dolichocephals and the Law of Stratification."   As to the "Law of
Urban Elimination," it is not proved either.   The data in its
favor are very scarce.   Besides, this law introduced by Ammon
contradicts other statements of Lapouge, given by him in the
chapter concerning Urban Selection.   Here he contends that the
present urban selection is very unfavorable to the procreation
of the dolichocephals.[113]

Finally, as to the *"law of a more rapid destruction of the more
perfect species,"* formulated by Lapouge as a universal law,[114] I
wonder, if this law were true, how any evolution of species from
the protozoa to *Homo Sapiens,* could have taken place.   It is
even incomprehensible how, under such a law, "the Aryan race"
could have appeared.   If this law is permanent and eternal, it
seems that such things could not have happened.   If *they happen,*
this means that the law is wrong, or rather, that it is not a law
at all.

[111] See CRAIG, F. J., "Anthropometry of Modern Egyptian," *Biometrika,* Vol.
VIII, pp. 72–77; RIPLEY, *op. cit.,* pp. 555–559; WISSLER, C., "Distribution of
Stature in the U. S.," *Scientific Monthly,* 1924, pp. 129–144; HOUZÉ, *op. cit.,* pp.
95 *et seq.*; BEDDOE, J., "Sur l'histoire de l'index céphalique dans les Iles Britan-
niques," *L'Anthropologie,* 1894, pp. 513–529, 658–673; PEARSON, K., *The Chances
of Death,* p. 290; LIVI, R., *Anthropometria militare,* Vol. I, pp. 86–91; RETZIUS, G.,
and FÜRST, *op. cit.,* Chap. IV.
[112] LIVI, R., "La distribuzione geografica dei charatteri anthropologici in
Italia," *Rivista Italiana di Sociologia,* II, 1898, fasc. IV; HOUZÉ, E., *Les indices
céphaliques des Flamands et des Wallons,* Bruxelles, Magden, 1882; VANDER-
KINDERE, L., *Nouvelles réchérches sur l'ethnologie de la Belgique,* (concerning
pigmentation), Bruxelles, Vander Auwera, 1879.
[113] *Sélections sociales,* pp. 407–409 and *passim.*
[114] *Sélections sociales,* pp. 456 *seq.*

This cursory analysis shows that little remains of these "laws." My criticism does not mean that the authors did not rightly observe the facts from which they inferred their "laws," but that they gave to their partial and local results a universal character, making their generalizations much broader than their material logically and scientifically permitted. Hence the fictitious character of their "laws." These remarks are enough to show the fallacies of the Aryan race hypothesis, and all the conclusions which have been made from it.

7. VALID PRINCIPLES OF THE SCHOOL

A. Does the above criticism mean that there is nothing valuable in the theories of the school? Does it mean that any theory of racial or individual differences is quite wrong? Shall we proclaim that all individuals and races are similar and equal? Shall we deny any importance to the factor of heredity and selection, and try to explain everything through environment? I do not think that such an attempt would be any better than the one-sidedness of the racial school. In other words, I think that side by side with the shortcomings of this school, there are valid statements in its theories.

In the first place, the school seems to be right in emphasizing the innate differences between races, social classes, and individuals.[115] Whatever characteristic we take for the classification of the races,—color, cranial capacity, cephalic indices, nasal index, hair, stature, or what not—we find different varieties among mankind.[116] The same is true in regard to individuals and social classes within the same race. Individuals of the same race are never identical. Social classes of the same society differ considerably in their physical, vital, and mental characteristics. As

[115] The terms, "superiority" and "inferiority" are subjective and their use by the school, as well as by many other scientists and scholars, is misleading.

[116] See any classification of races according to one or several of these traits, *e.g.*, the classification of Topinard, or of Haddon into Ulotrichi, Cymotrichi, Leiotrichi with the further subclasses, or that of Morcelli or Sergi, or the classifications of Dixon and Deniker. See HADDON, A. C., *The Races of Man*, pp. 1–36; MORSELLI, "Le razze umane e il sentimento di superiorita ethica," *Rivista Italiana di Sociologia*, 1911, pp. 325 *et seq.*; SERGI, *Hominidae*, 1911; DENIKER, J., *The Races of Man*, 1900, Chaps. I–III; DIXON, R. B., *The Racial History of Man*, 1923.

a general rule, the upper classes, compared with the lower ones, have a greater stature, a greater weight, greater size of head, or cranial capacity, or weight of brain. Vitally, they have a longer duration of life, lower mortality, and generally, better health.[117] This does not mean that each member of the upper class exhibits these characteristics when compared with any member of the lower class; it means only that such results are obtained when we compare the upper classes as a whole with the lower ones as a whole. Accordingly, differences amount to nothing but those of statistical averages, which does not prevent the existence of a great deal of overlapping, and cases where the member of an upper class may happen to have a lower stature, smaller cranial capacity, and poorer health than a member of the lower classes. The same is true in regard to the racial differences in the physical and the vital, as well as in the intellectual characteristics. If a part of these and other differences of various races and various social classes are due, no doubt, to differences in their environment, it seems to be certain that another part of them is due to the factor of innate heterogeneity or heredity, or to a selected group.[118]

B. In the second place, the school is right in its emphasis on mental and psychological traits, for individuals, the upper and the lower classes and various racial groups, as groups, exhibit considerable differences. In regard to individuals, the existence of differences in native intelligence, "will-power," sensitivity, temperament, emotionality and so on, can scarcely be questioned. It is manifested by common observation, by mental tests, by differences in achievements, by experiments, and by many other means. Individuals may range from idiocy to genius of the first degree; from the highly temperamental to the temperamentalless; from a man with great will power and resourcefulness to a man who is continually wavering. The same is true in regard to other psychical traits. The different social strata of the same society exhibit also in their averages considerable differences in intelligence, and in some other traits. Whether we take the

---

[117] See the data and the literature in my *Social Mobility*, Chaps. X, XI, XII.
[118] See an analysis of the problem in *Social Mobility*, Chap. XIII, *et seq.*, *passim.*

number (absolute and relative per thousand of population in each class) of men of genius yielded by the upper and the lower classes in England, Russia, Germany, the United States of America, and France, the proportion given by the upper classes is many times higher than that given by the lower classes, especially by common labor. If we take the data of mental testing and the corresponding I. Q., the results are similar. The I. Q. of both the children and the adults of the upper classes is generally higher than that of the children and the adults of the lower classes. There are overlappings, but they do not disprove the general rule. This means that the mental and social distribution of individuals is positively correlated. I shall give here only a few representative data which show this.

Among present European societies, the most "fertile" social group in the production of the men of genius seems to have been the royal families. The same families are at the apex of the social pyramid. Investigations of F. Adams Woods have shown that for about 800 individuals in this class, we have about 25 geniuses. "The royal bred, considered as a unit, is superior to any other one family, be it that of noble or commoner." [119] Granting that the data of Dr. Woods are greatly exaggerated, we still have a more abundant crop of men of genius from the royal families, than has been produced by any other social group. H. Ellis' study of the most prominent British men of genius has shown that the English upper and professional classes (composing only 4.46 per cent of the population) have produced 63 per cent of the men of genius, while the labor, artisan and industrial classes, composing about 84 per cent of the population, have produced only 11.7 per cent of the greatest leaders of Great Britain. Especially low is the percentage of British men of genius produced by common labor and artisans,—2.5 per cent from 74.28 of the total population. The figures include all British men of genius since the beginning of the history of England up to the twentieth century. During the nineteenth century, according to

[119] WOODS, FREDERICK A., *Mental and Moral Heredity in Royalty*, p. 301, N. Y., 1906. See also his *The Influence of Monarchs*, Chap. XVII, N. Y., 1913. See also SOROKIN, P., "Monarchs and Rulers," *Social Forces*, 1925-6.

A. H. H. MacLean's Study of 2500 Eminent British Men of the nineteenth century, the share of aristocracy during this period rather increased (26 per cent of all leaders, instead of 18.5 per cent); the share of the professions increased also (49 per cent instead of 44.5 per cent); while the share of the labor class and the artisans decreased, in spite of an increased literacy and greater educational facilities for the lower classes in the nineteenth century.[120]   According to the more detailed study of F. A. Woods, during the first quarter of the nineteenth century, the artisans and labor class produced only 7.2 per cent of the men of genius in England, instead of 11.7 per cent as during the preceding centuries; and during the second quarter of the nineteenth century, only 4.2 per cent.[121]   Thus, in spite of an increase of educational facilities, the great mass of the British population was, and still is, more than ever before, sterile in the production of geniuses. Similar results were yielded by Galton's study of 107 of the most prominent British scientists of the nineteenth century.[122]   Similar results have been obtained in France regarding all the prominent French men of letters.   The corresponding figures obtained by Odin in his careful study show the following number of prominent men in their ratio to the same number of the population of various classes.   The nobility (159) produced two and one-half times more literary geniuses in France than did the high magistrature (62); six and one-half times more than the liberal professions (24); twenty-three times more than the *bourgeoisie* (7) and two hundred times more than the labor classes (.8)![123] Classified according to different periods, the percentage of literary genius produced by different classes is shown in the following table.

The decrease of the share of nobility in 1775-1800 is a result of its extermination in the French Revolution.   Nevertheless, in the period of from 1800 to 1825 it shows again an increase of fertility in the production of genius.   Similar results were

---

[120] ELLIS, H., *op. cit.*, pp. 80 ff.

[121] WOODS, F. A., "The Conification of Social Groups," *Eugenics, Genetics and the Family*, Vol. I, pp. 312–328, Baltimore, 1923.

[122] GALTON, F., *English Men of Science*, p. 16, Appleton, N. Y., 1875.

[123] ODIN, A., *Genèse des grands hommes*, Vol. II, Table XXXII; Vol. I, p. 541, Paris, 1895.

Social Classes	Periods				
	1700–1725	1725–1750	1750–1775	1775–1800	1800–1825
Nobility...........	31.0	26.7	20.6	13.6	18.3
High magistrature..	50.0	52.6	50.0	54.9	53.1
Bourgeoisie........	7.1	10.35	18.5	18.6	15.2
Labor class........	11.9	10.35	10.9	12.9	13.4
Total...........	100.	100.	100.	100.	100.

obtained by de Candolle in his study of the illustrious men of science.[124]

Dr. Fritz Maas studied 4421 of the most prominent German men of genius in various fields of activity (writers, poets, painters, composers, scientists, scholars, artists, pedagogues, statesmen, captains of industry and finance, military men, and so on) who were born after 1700 and died before 1910. His study shows that the higher classes (nobility, professions, and the wealthy class of the big manufacturers and merchants), who have composed less than 20 per cent of the total population, produced 83.2 per cent of the men of genius; while the lower labor classes, which composed more than 80 per cent of the total population, have yielded only 16.8 per cent of the German leaders. Especially small has been the relative share of the proletariat, in spite of the rather large size of this class in the second half of the nineteenth, and at the beginning of the twentieth century. The percentage of the men of genius coming out of this class has been only 0.3 per cent. Again, in spite of the increase in educational facilities for the lower classes during the nineteenth century, these classes do not show any marked increase in their productivity of geniuses. This is seen from the following data:[125]

[124] DE CANDOLLE, A., *Histoire des sciences et des savants*, pp. 272–274, 279, Génève, Bale, 1885.
[125] MAAS, FRITZ, "Ueber die Herkunftsbedingungen der Geistigen Fürher," *Archiv für Sozialwissenschaft und Sozialpolitik*, 1916, pp. 144–186.

Social Classes from which the Men of Genius Came	Per Cent of Genius from Each Class in the Specified Historical Periods According to the Year of Birth		
	1700–1789	1789–1818	1818–1860
Nobility..........................	19.2	14.2	11.0
High magistrature and professions...	53.3	55.8	60.0
Bourgeoisie (commercial class)......	15.3	16.4	16.4
Labor classes.....................	11.9	13.6	12.4

According to the data of Professor J. McK. Cattell, the share of different classes from which the leading American men of science came, and the proportion of these classes in the total population of the U. S., were as follows:

Social Classes	Per Cent of Leading Men of Science from Each Class	Per Cent of the Class in the Total Population of United States
Professions....................	43.1	3.1
Manufacturing and trade.......	35.7	34.1
Agricultural class.............	21.2	44.1

The majority of the leading scientists came from the upper and middle classes and not a single one was produced by the group of domestic servants or by the class of day laborers.[126]

Dr. S. Visher studied the occupation of the fathers of 18,400 of the prominent Americans from *Who's Who* with the following results:[127]

---

[126] CATTELL, J. McKEEN, *American Men of Science*, 3d. ed., 1921, pp. 783–784.
[127] VISHER, STEPHEN S., "A Study of the Type of the Place of Birth and of the Occupation of Fathers of Subjects of Sketches in Who's Who in America," *The American Journal of Sociology*, p. 553, March, 1925.

Social Classes	Persons in Each Class per Notable	Notable Men per 10,000 Persons in Each Class
Laborers, unskilled............	75,000	0.013
Laborers, skilled and semi-skilled.	2,470	4.
Farmers.....................	1,100	9.
Businessmen.................	124	80.
Professions (except clergy)......	70	142.
Clergy......................	32	315.

Dr. E. L. Clarke, in his study of 1000 of the most prominent American men of letters, came to the following results: [128]

Social Class from Which Men of Letters Came	Number of Men of Letters from Each Class
Professional..	328
Commercial...	151
Agricultural..	139
Mechanical, clerical, unskilled......................	48
Unknown...	334
Total...	1000

Again the same picture: a numerically insignificant part of the total population—the professional and commercial classes—produced more than 60 per cent of all prominent men of letters in the United States.

My study of 476 American captains of industry and finance showed that 79.8 per cent of these leaders were produced by the commercial and professional classes; 15.6 per cent by farmers; and only 4.6 per cent by the skilled and unskilled labor class.[129] Here again, the share of the labor class in the production of the geniuses of industry and finance is not increasing but decreasing.

[128] CLARKE, EDWIN L., *American Men of Letters*, Columbia Univ. Studies, Vol. LXXII, 1916, pp. 74–76.
[129] SOROKIN, "American Millionaires," *Social Forces*, 1925, pp. 635–636.

Similar results were obtained by Ch. H. Cooley. Dr. Cooley's study of 71 of the most prominent poets, philosophers, and historians of all times and countries has shown that 45 of them came from the upper and upper middle classes, 24 from the lower middle class, and only 2 from the labor classes.[130] Dr. L. Terman quite recently came to a similar conclusion. The brightest children, (with an average I. Q. of 151.33) studied by Terman and his collaborators happened to come from the following social groups:

Occupation of Fathers of Gifted Children	Proportion among Fathers of Gifted Children	Proportion of Each Occupational Group in Population of Los Angeles and San Francisco
Professional...................	29.1	2.9
Public service.................	4.5	3.3
Commercial...................	46.2	36.1
Industrial....................	20.2	57.7
Total......................	100.0	100.0

PER CENT OF QUOTA OF EACH OCCUPATIONAL GROUP AMONG FATHERS OF GIFTED CHILDREN

Professional..	1,003
Public service..	137
Commercial..	128
Industrial..	35

In the industrial group only one man gives his occupation as "laborer" which is 0.2 per cent of our fathers as compared with 15.0 per cent of the total population classified as laborers in the census report. [131]

Jur. Philiptschenko's study of the contemporary Russian scien-

[130] COOLEY, CH. H., "Genius, Fame and the Comparison of Races," *Annals of American Academy*, Vol. IX, p. 15, May, 1897.
[131] TERMAN, L., *Genetic Study of Genius*, Vol. I, pp. 60 ff.

tists, scholars and representatives of the arts and literature gave the following results:[132]

Occupation of Fathers	Per Cent of Scientists and Scholars from Each Class	Per Cent of Representatives of Arts and Literature from Each Class	Per Cent of Great Contemporary Scientists and Scholars from Each Class	Per Cent of Greatest Scientists and Scholars,— Members of Academy of Science for Last Eighty Years
Professions...........	36.	44.6	46.	30.2
Officials..............	18.2	20.0	8.0	15.5
Military..............	9.4	7.7	14.0	16.2
Clergy...............	8.8	1.8	10.0	14.8
Commercial..........	13.0	6.7	12.0	5.6
Agricultural.........	7.9[a]	9.6[a]	6.0[a]	14.1[b]
Skilled and unskilled labor..............	2.7	9.6	4.	3.5[c]
Not known..........	4.0			0.1
Total..............	100.0	100.0	100.0	100.0

[a] Including the landlords and gentry.
[b] Only the landlords and gentry.
[c] Including peasants.

The labor classes (agricultural and labor) compose even in contemporary Russia more than 90 per cent of the population; and yet they yielded quite an insignificant percentage of the scientists and scholars, artists, literary men and so on. This percentage is still less among the great men of science.

I will not give other data obtained by different investigators in different countries.[133] They only confirm the above results. Passing from the bottom of a social pyramid to its apex we see a systematic increase of the number of men of genius—an absolute, as well as a relative increase.

Similar results have been obtained by the intelligence testing of various social groups. The general conclusion suggested by

[132] PHILIPTSCHENKO, *Bulletin of The Bureau of Eugenics* (Russ.), Bull. No. 1, pp. 11–12, 28; No. 2, pp. 11–12; No. 3, p. 35.
[133] See SOROKIN, P., *Social Mobility*, Chap. XII.

numerous intelligence tests is that the higher social classes are more intelligent than the lower ones. Of many data of this kind, I will mention here only a few which are representative. Other figures may be found in the sources indicated in footnotes and in my *Social Mobility.*

In the first place, we have the results of the intelligence tests given the U. S. Army. The I. Q. of various social groups obtained by this study is as follows: [134]

Occupation	I. Q.	Occupation	I. Q.
Civil engineers...............	274	Bakers and cooks...........	106
Lawyers and teachers.........	252	Printers....................	99
Chemists....................	205	Carpenters.................	91
Postal employees	200	Metal workers..............	88
Artists.....................	198	Leather workers............	88
Clerks......................	175	Horsemen..................	75
Salesmen....................	170	Teamsters..................	72
Merchants..................	138	Barbers....................	65
Policemen...................	119	Laborers...................	63
Machinists	107		

These data show a rather close correlation between social status and intelligence. Unskilled and semi-skilled laborers have a very inferior and low average intelligence; skilled labor groups are principally in the group of "high average" intelligence; superior and very superior intelligences are found only in the high professional and high business classes. On the other hand, it is necessary to mention that the testing disclosed a considerable overlapping in the intelligence of different social groups. This, however, does not disprove the indicated fact of the existence of superior intelligence in the higher social strata and inferior intelligence in the lower strata.[135]

[134] *Memoirs of the National Academy of Science,* Vol. XV, Wash., 1921, pp. 821 ff., Chap. XVII. See also YERKES, R. M., "Eugenic Bearing of Measurement of Intelligence," *The Eug. Review,* pp. 234 ff., January, 1923. See here the instructive figures and diagrams.

[135] See the details concerning the results of the U. S. Army mental test in the works indicated; see also GODDARD, H. H., *Human Efficiency and Levels of Intelligence,* 1920, pp. 1–30; PINTNER, R., *Intelligence Testing, passim* and chapter, "The Soldier and the Employees," and works indicated below.

Other proof of the superior intelligence of the higher social classes is given by the results of *intelligence testing of the children of different social classes*. At the present moment we have very numerous studies of this kind, and their results are almost unanimous in essence. The children of the professional and well-to-do classes, as a general rule, show a much superior intelligence than the children of the labor classes. The following figures may be taken as representative: According to the study of Dr. Terman, the median I. Q. for the children of the semi-skilled and unskilled labor classes has been 82.5 while the median I. Q. for the children of the professional and high business classes has been 112.5. The percentage of superior children with I. Q. 135–140 has been among the studied group, in the professional class, 53; in semi-professional, 37; in skilled labor, 10; and in the semi-skilled and unskilled, — 0.[136]

The I. Q.'s of 13,000 children, at the age of 11 and 12 years, studied by J. F. Duff and Godfrey H. Thomson in England, have been as follows (according to the occupation of their fathers):

Occupational Groups	I. Q.
Professional	112.2
Managers	110.0
Higher commercial class	109.3
Army, navy, police, postmen	105.5
Shopkeeping class	105.0
Engineers	102.9
Foremen	102.7
Building trades	102.0
Metal workers, shipbuilders	100.9
Miscellaneous industrial workers	100.6
Mines, quarrymen	97.6
Agricultural classes	97.6
Laborers	96.0

While of 597 children from the professions and higher com-

[136] TERMAN, L. M., *The Intelligence of School Children*, 1919, pp. 56 ff., 188 ff.; see also TERMAN, "New Approach to Study of Genius," *Psychological Review*, 1922, pp. 310–318.

mercial classes, 471 were above the average mental level and only 126 below the average; among 1214 children from the low grade occupations (laborers), 746 were below and only 468 were above the average mental level.[137]

Similar results have been obtained by C. Burt, H. B. English, Miss A. H. Arlitt, A. W. Kornhauser, Douglas Waples, G. Sylvester Counts, W. H. Gilby and K. Pearson, L. Isserlis, W. Stern, Holley, S. Z. Pressey and R. Ralston, J. M. Bridges and L. E. Coler, W. F. Book, M. E. Haggerty and H. B. Nash, and others.[138]   It is needless to multiply the examples.   We need merely to say that in the United States, Germany, England, and France almost all child mental tests have given similar results.[139]

The next proof of the correlation of social standing and intel-

---

[137] DUFF, J. F., and THOMSON, G. H., "The Social and Geographic Distribution of Intelligence in Northumberland," *British Journal of Psychology*, pp. 192–198, Oct., 1923.

[138] BRIDGES, J. M., and COLER, L. E., "The Relation of Intelligence to Social Status," *Psychological Review*, XXIV, pp. 1–31; BOOK, W. F., *The Intelligence of High School Seniors*, Chap. X, N. Y., 1922; PRESSEY, S. Z., and RALSTON, R., "The Relation of General Intelligence of the Children to the Occupation of their Fathers," *Journal of Applied Psychology*, Vol. III, No. 4.; HAGGERTY, M. E., and NASH, HARRY B., "Mental Capacity of Children and Paternal Occupation," *The Journal of Educat. Psychology*, December, 1924, pp. 563–572. See other facts in the indicated books of Terman and Pintner. See also MACDOUGALL, W., "The Correlation between Native Ability and Social Status," *Eugenics in Race and State*, Vol. II, pp. 373–376, Baltimore, 1921; ENGLISH, H. B., "Mental Capacity of School Children Correlated with Social Status," *Yale Psychological Studies*, 1917, *Psychological Review Monograph*, Vol. XXIII, No. 3; ARLITT, A. H., "Summary of Results of Testing 342 Children," *Psychological Bulletin*, Feb., 1921; KORNHAUSER, A. W., "The Economic Standing of Parents and the Intelligence of their Children," *Journal of Educat. Psychology*, Vol. IX; COUNTS, G. S., *The Selective Character of American Secondary School*, The U. of Chicago Educ. Monographs, No. 19, May, 1922, pp. 36–37 and *passim;* WAPLES, D., "Indexing the Qualifications of Different Social Groups for an Academic Curriculum," *The School Review*, 1924, pp. 537–546; GILBY, W. H., and PEARSON, K., "On the Significance of the Teacher's Appreciation of General Intelligence," *Biometrika*, Vol. VIII, pp. 94–108; HOLLEY, CH. E., *The Relationship between Persistence in School and Home Conditions*, U. of Chicago Press, 1916, *passim;* ISSERLIS, L., "The Relation between Home Conditions and the Intelligence of School Children," London, 1923, *Publications of the Medical Research Committee of the Privy Council;* YATES, "A Study of some H. S. Seniors of Super Intelligence," *Journal of Educ. Research*, Monos. No. 2; STERN, W., *Die Intellegenz der Kinder und Jügendlichen*, Barth, Leipzig; HART, H., "Occupational Differential Fecundity," *Scientific Monthly*, Vol. XIX, p. 531; DEXTER, E., "Relation between Occupation of Parents and Intelligence of Children," *School and Society*, Vol. XVII (1923), pp. 612–616; MURDOCH, K., "A Study of Differences Found Between Races in Intellect and Morality," *School and Society*, Vol. XXII, 1925, No. 568–569.

[139] See other data in my *Social Mobility*.

lectual level is given by mental tests of the intelligence of the adults of different social standing. They also yielded results similar to the above. (See *Social Mobility,* Chap. XII.)

As to an interpretation of these results, opinions differ; nevertheless, even those among the investigators who are inclined to account for these differences through the factor of environment, do not deny completely the rôle of heredity and selection. An attentive study of the data makes it reasonably certain that the differences are due to environment, as well as to heredity. At any rate, the series of facts could, in no way, be accounted for through the environmental agencies alone.[140] This means that the school's contention about the selected character of each of these classes has a great deal of truth. On the other hand, if it is fallacious to deny the rôle of heredity and selection in the creation of these differences, it is equally wrong to deny the rôle of environment in this field. The school seems to underestimate somewhat the importance of the environmental factor, and needs to be corrected in this point.

C. The school seems to be right also in its claim that racial groups are different physically and mentally. In regard to the existence of physical differences among various races, there is scarcely any doubt. The divergency of opinions concerns not the existence of these differences, but their significance as a basis for race classification and its history. Whatever the classification may be, the existence of different zoölogical racial types cannot be questioned. As an example of one of the best classifications of races, I give the following table of Professor Dixon.[141] That there are mental differences among races seems also to be definitely established; whether due to environment or to heredity, we find considerable mental differences between the principal racial (not national) groups. Their existence is witnessed in the first place by the quite different part which has been played by the various races in the history of mankind, and in their cultural achievements. Though almost all of these types have been given an opportunity to create the complex forms of civilization, and

---

[140] See *Social Mobility,* Chap. XIII.
[141] Dixon, *op. cit.,* p. 500; see here description of each of these types.

CHARACTER OF THE EIGHT PRIMARY RACIAL TYPES

Types	Head	Face	Nose	Prognatism	Cranial Capacity
Proto-Australoid.........	Long Low	Medium Broad	Broad	Moderate	Small
Proto-Negroid...........	Long High	Medium Broad	Broad	Moderate	Small
Mediterranean..........	Long Low	Narrow	Narrow	None	Large
Caspian...............	Long High	Narrow	Narrow	None	Large
Mongoloid.............	Round Low	Broad	Broad	Moderate	Medium
Palæ-Alpine............	Round High	Broad	Broad	Moderate	Medium
Ural.................	Round Low	Medium	Narrow	None	Largest
Alpine................	Round Low	Medium	Narrow	None	Largest

an almost unlimited span of time, nevertheless the rôle of the Proto-Australoid and Proto-Negroid races has been very modest in this respect, while the rôle of the Caspian, the Alpine and the Mediterranean races has been extraordinarily great. They have been the leaders in the creation of a complex form of culture. They have been the conquerors and subjugators of almost all the other races, driving them out, and spreading themselves throughout the world. The essence of Gobineau's deduction in this respect seems to be true. Professor Dixon says that "there is a difference between the fundamental human types in quality, in intellectual capacity, in moral fibre, and in all that makes or has made any people great. This I believe to be true, despite what advocates of the uniformity of man may say." [142]   No partizan of a belief in the uniformity of all races can disregard the discussed differences in the historical rôle and in the cultural achievements of different races.   They used to say that this was due to different racial environments, but we have already seen that it is impossible to give exclusive importance to geographical environment in this respect.   In the second place, the geographical environment of almost all of the races has been different, because each racial type has been spread over the vast areas of the earth with very different geographical conditions.   In the third place, nobody has shown as yet that the natural environment of the Caspian or the Alpine races has been more favorable than that of the Proto-Negroids or Proto-Australoids.   If the social environment of various races has happened to be different, this difference did not fall from heaven, but has been due to the fact that some of them have been able to create a complex social environment, while others have not been able to do so.

The difference in the cultural contributions and in the historical rôles played by different races is excellently corroborated by, and is in perfect agreement with, the experimental studies of race mentality and psychology.   The more perfect the technique of such a study becomes, the more clear and unquestionable become the mental differences among different races.   Fortunately science has already passed the speculative stage in this field, and has entered the stage of factual study, which has led to many interesting results.   I have just mentioned that the historical rôle of the Proto-Negroids and the Proto-Australoids has been very mediocre, — that their contributions to what we style complex culture and civilization have been very moderate.   Is this testimony of history corroborated by mental tests?   I should say that the verification has been complete.   So far as I know, all studies of the comparative intelligence of the contemporary negro and white races (the Caspian, the Mediterranean, the Alpine, and even in their blends with the yellow race) have unanimously shown that the I. Q. of the blacks, or even of the Indians is lower than

[142] Dixon, *op. cit.*, p. 518, see *passim*. The term "great" is evaluative. Whether the creation of complex forms of civilization is a good or a bad, a great or negative achievement, the fact of a different rôle for various races remains, regardless of any evaluation.

that of the white or the yellow. It is true that the difference is not so great as the school claims, and it is also true that there are individual exceptions, but they by no means disprove the rule. Below are a few representative figures of many available at the present time: [143]

MEDIAN OF MENTAL AGES BY OCCUPATION

Occupation	White	Negro
U. S. Army		
Farmers	9.5	8.2
Laborers	9.5	9.0
Miners	10.2	9.1

GENERAL INTELLIGENCE OF THE WHITE AND THE NEGRO DRAFT. PERCENTAGES MAKING THE GRADE

	D −	D	C −	C	C +	B	A
White	7.	17.1	23.8	25.	15.	8.	4.1
Negro	49.	29.7	12.9	5.7	2.0	0.6	0.1

[143] *Memoirs of the National Academy of Sciences*, Vol. XV., pp. 796, 707, Wash., 1921. Grades D − , D, C − , C, C + , B, A indicate a passing from the lowest I. Q. — border-line and dull — to the highest — bright and brilliant.

[144] FERGUSON, G. O., *The Intelligence of Negroes*, Virginia School and Society, 1919, Vol. IX, pp. 721–726; "The Mental Status of the American Negro," *Scientific Monthly*, Vol. XII, p. 533, June, 1921.

[145] TRABUE, M. R., "The Intelligence of Negro Recruits," *Natural History*, 1919, Vol. XIX, pp. 680–685.

[146] YERKES, R. M., "Psychological Examination in the U. S. Army," *Memoirs National Academy*, Wash., Vol. XV, 1921.

[147] PINTNER, R., and KELLER, R., "Intelligence Testing of Foreign Children," *Journal of Educational Psychology*, 1922, Vol. XII, pp. 214–222.

[148] THORNDIKE, E. L., "Intelligence Scores of Colored Pupils," *School and Society*, 1923, Vol. XVIII, pp. 563–570.

[149] MITCHELL, I., ROSANOFF, I. R., and A. J., "A Study of Association in Negro Children," *Psychological Review*, 1919, Vol. XXVI, pp. 354–359.

[150] HIRSH, N. D., "A Study of Nation-Racial Mental Differences," *Genetic Psychology Monographs*, 1926, May–July, p. 287.

[151] PETERSON, J., "Comparison of White and Negro Children in Multiple Choice in Learning," *Proceedings Amer. Psychol. Assn.*, 1921, pp. 97–98; "The Comparative Abilities of White and Negro Children," *Comparative Psychology Monographs*, 1923, No. 5.

Investigators	Race	Number of Cases	Year	Results
Ferguson [144]*.....	Mulattoes Negroes White draft	2288 155 —	1919	Negroes inferior mentally to the whites. Among mulattoes, the superior are those having the greatest percentage of white blood.
Trabue [145]*.......	Negroes	8244	1919	Whites are superior to the negroes.
Yerkes [146]*.......	Negroes (U. S. Army) Whites		1921	Negro mental age 10.4 years; that of the whites 13.1 years. The percentage of the very inferior among the negroes is higher, while the very superior are much scarcer.
Pintner [147]*....... Keller..........	Negroes Whites	71 249	1922	Negro I. Q., .88; white I. Q., .95.
Thorndike [148]*....	Negroes Whites	349 2653	1923	4 per cent of the negroes reach the median of the whites. Percentage of negroes with a superior I. Q. is very small, compared with the whites.
Mitchell [149]*...... Rosanoff.........	Negroes Whites	300 300	1919	The negro is far behind the white mental age.
Hirsh [150]*........	Negroes Whites	449 5055	1926	Negro I. Q., 84.6; all whites of different stocks, with the exception of the Portuguese, have higher I. Q., from 85.3 to 102.8.
Peterson [151]*......	Negroes Whites	315 311	1921	80–95 per cent of the whites surpass the intelligence of the negroes. The greater the proportion of white blood in a negro, the higher is his mental score.

*For footnotes see preceding page.

Investigators	Race	Number of Cases	Year	Results
McFadden....... Dashiell [152].......	Negroes Whites	77 77	1923	Whites have stronger personality. Only 15.4 per cent of the negroes exceed the median of the whites.
Brigham [153].......	Negroes Whites (U. S. Army)		1923	Results similar to those of Yerkes.
Sunne [154].........	Negroes Whites	1112 5834	1923	Mental age of negro 1-1½ years below whites.
Pressey-Teter [155]...	Negroes Whites	187 1022	1919	Negro's mental age two years behind that of the white's.
Arlitt [156]..........	Negroes Whites	71 191	1921	Negro's I. Q., 83; white's, 106. Besides, the I.Q. in negroes decreases with age and rapidly falls below that of the whites.
Derrick [157]........	Negro and white college students	52 (N.) 75 (W.)	1920	Negro's I. Q., 103; white's, 112.
Schwegler-Winn[158]	Negro	58	1920	Negro's I. Q., 89; white's, 103.
Murdock [159]......	Negro White	225 514	1920	White 85 per cent better than the negro.
Pyle [160]..........	Negro	758	1925	Negro scores in comparison with white scores taken as 100, are: in Manthan's meter test, 78; in substitution, 44; in rote memory, 68.5; and in logical memory, 80.3.

[152] McFADDEN and DASHIELL, J. F., "Racial Differences as Measured by the Dawney Will-Temp. Ind. Test," *Journal of Applied Psychology*, 1922, Vol. VII, pp. 30–53.

[153] BRIGHAM, C. C., *A Study of American Intelligence*, Princeton, 1923.

[154] SUNNE, D., "A Comparison of White and Negro Children," *School and Society*, 1924, Vol. XIX, pp. 469–472.

For the sake of brevity, instead of giving the detailed character-istic of the results of these studies, I have tabulated their principal results, with the methods employed in testing, referring to the indicated studies for the details.

There is no use to continue this list.[161] The above shows that practically without any exception, in spite of the different methods used in the studies, the results were unanimous. They all show that the I. Q. of the negro is comparatively lower than that of the white race. They are in perfect agreement with the historical data indicated above. If we take the number of men of genius yielded by a race as a criterion of its mentality, the results will also be unfavorable for the negro race, for it has been rather sterile in this respect. Finally, it is worthy of notice that the studies of Ferguson, E. B. Reuter, and of some others, have shown that the greater the infusion of white blood into the negro, the higher is his intelligence quotient. We have here, as well as in Hunter's study of the Indians, a partial corroboration of Go bineau's statement that the negro and other "inferior" races show intellectual ability only in proportion to their percentage of white blood.

This perfect agreement of all these tests: the historico-cultural, the mental; the absence of geniuses, especially of the highest rank;

---

[155] PRESSEY, S. Z., and TETER, G. P., "A Comparison of Colored and White Children, etc.," *Journal Applied Psychology*, 1919, Vol. III, pp. 277–282.

[156] ARLITT, A. H., "The Relation of Intelligence to Age in Negro Children," *Proc. 30th Ann. Meet. Am. Psy. Assn.*, 1921, 14; "The Need of Caution in Estab-lishing Race Norms," *Journal Applied Psychology*, 1921, Vol. V, pp. 179–183.

[157] DERRICK, S. M., "A Comparative Study of Seventy-Five White and Fifty-Two Colored College Students," *Journal Applied Psychology*, 1920, Vol. IV, pp. 316–329.

[158] SCHWEGLER, R. A., and WINN, E., "A Comparative Study of the Intelligence of White and Colored Children," *Journal Educational Research*, 1920, Vol. II, pp. 838–848.

[159] MURDOCK, M., "Study of Race Differences in N. Y. City," *School and Society*, 1920, Vol. XI, pp. 147–150; "A Study of Mental Differences that are Due to Race," *Proc. of 32d Ann. Meet. of Am. Psych. Assn.*, 1923, pp. 108–109.

[160] PYLE, W. H., *Nature and Development of Learning Capacity*, p. 93, Balti-more, 1925.

[161] See also ODUM, H. W., *Social and Mental Traits of the Negro*, (shows that the per cent of feeble-minded among negroes is higher than among whites); TERMAN, L., *Genetic Studies of Genius*, 1925, Vol. I, pp. 56–57; STRONG, A. C., "Three Hundred Forty White and Colored Children," *Ped. Sem.*, Vol. XX, pp. 485–515; REUTER, E. B., "The Superiority of the Mulatto," *American Journal Sociology*, 1917, Vol. XXIII, pp. 83–106.

and the "superiority" of the mulattoes, seems to indicate strongly (especially together with the further data concerning other races) that the cause of such a difference in the negro is due not only, and possibly not so much to environment, as to heredity.[162]   For a corroboration of their thesis, the partizans of one-sided environmentalism have been able to give nothing but speculation and reasoning.   This evidently is too little to make their position valid.

From the standpoints of cultural achievements, the results of mental tests, the number of geniuses produced, and the "superiority" of half-breed Indians over full-blood Indians, the red race makes a somewhat better showing than the negro, but one which is, nevertheless, "inferior" to that of the whites.   The results of these four tests are again in complete agreement with one another. It is enough to give merely the results of the mental tests, because of the lack of Indian cultural achievements, their backwardness, and their very low number of geniuses (if any).

From the same standpoint, it is interesting to take such racial varieties as the Chinese, Japanese, and the Hindus of the higher and the lower caste, and to ascertain to what extent the data of the historico-cultural achievements agree with the gradings of the mental tests.   We know that these peoples have, in the past, and

---

[162] References to environment are not convincing because if, in the present and past in America the environment of the negro has been less favorable, in Africa they had as many chances in the long course of history to create complex forms of culture as the white race had elsewhere and yet nothing has been created. Further, none of the environmentalists has shown that in this long course of race history the geographical environment of the negro has been less favorable than that of the white race.   Finally, in several of the mentioned experimental studies, the economic, occupational, and social status of the white and the negro has been taken into consideration; and attempts have been made to study the white and the negro in the same status and environment (studies of Arlitt, Hirsch and others), but the result has been the same.   The negro has been "inferior" when compared with the white in the majority of the studied mental functions.   Finally, the environment of either the Russian peasantry before the annihilation of serfdom, or of the mediæval serfs, or of the Roman and the Greek slaves was probably not any better, if indeed it was not worse than the environment of the American negro before 1861 or at the present moment.   Yet these slaves and serfs of the white race, in spite of their environment, yielded a considerable number of geniuses of the first degree, not to mention the eminent people of a smaller caliber.   Meanwhile, excepting, perhaps, a few heavyweight champions and eminent singers, the American negroes have not up to this time produced a single genius of great caliber.   These considerations and facts seem to point at the factor of heredity, without which all these phenomena cannot be accounted for.

Investigator	Race	Number of Cases	Year	Results
Garth [163]	Indians	190	1919	Negroes fatigue most, Indians least. Mixed-bloods excel in mental test, over full-bloods by 11 per cent. Full-bloods excel mixed-bloods in resisting mental fatigue. Nomads excel sedentary Indians in resisting mental fatigue. Indian mixed bloods have higher intelligence scores than full-bloods.
	Negroes	133	1920	
	Whites	711		
	Mixed-blooded Indians	215	1921	
	Full-blooded Indians	165	1922	
	Mixed-blooded Indians	82	1923	
	Full-blooded Indians	108	1923	
	Nomadic Indians	108	1922	
	Sedentary Indians	121	1922	
	Full-blooded Indians	559	1922	
Hunter and Sommermier[164]	Indian mixed and full-bloods	715	1921	The Indian I. Q. is inferior to that of the white. Mixed Indians made a better scoring in mental tests than full-bloods. The greater the proportion of white blood, the higher the grading. Correlation of .41 between degrees of white and Indian blood.
Pyle [165]	Indians	500	1925	Taking 100 as the scoring of the white Americans, in the substitution test, the score of the negroes was 44; of the Indians, 62; of the Chinese, 88.
	Negroes	758		
	Chinese	424		

[163] GARTH, T. R., "Racial Differences in Mental Fatigue," *Journal Applied Psychology*, 1919, pp. 235–244; "White, Indian, and Negro Work Curves," *Journal Applied Psychology*, 1920, pp. 14–25; "A Review of Racial Psychology," *Psychological Bulletin*, 1925, pp. 355–357.

[164] HUNTER, W. S., and SOMMERMIER, E., "The Relation of Degree of Indian Blood to Score on the Otis Int. Test," *Psychological Bulletin*, 1921, Vol. XVIII, pp. 91–92.

[165] PYLE, W. H., *op. cit.*, p. 96.

partly, even in the present, created a few of the most brilliant civilizations.   In their political and military history they have created world empires.   They have yielded a considerable number of the great geniuses in different fields of mental and social activity.   For this reason if this test and the mental tests are adequate, we must expect that their intelligence would be almost as high as that of the white race of which they are a blended variety. Results of the mental tests seem to corroborate this expectation.[166] The study of Pyle, and the investigations of K. Murdoch, Wolcott, K. T. Yeung, Symonds, and Porteus [167] have shown that their intelligence is either as high as the intelligence of the American and Anglo-Saxon whites, or is only a little lower, which may sometimes be explained by negatively selected groups of these peoples.   They have also been found very high in the tests of morality, and sometimes in school marks.   In this case also, we find then that the tests are in agreement.   Agreeing with the test of cultural and historical achievement are also the results of the mental tests of the Brahman (high) and the Panchama (lowest) castes in India, who belong to different racial types.   The scoring of the Brahman children is only a little lower than that of the American white children of the same age, while the scoring of the Panchama children is considerably lower than that of both these groups.   Besides, the Panchama children (as the negro children in some studies) "show no increase in the speed of their performance after the age of twelve. . . They have attained their

[166] Studies in the physical anthropology of these peoples have shown also that, from the standpoint of cranial capacity, these peoples rank as high as the white peoples.   For this reason, many prominent anthropologists and eugenists give them a very high qualification. See SCHALLMAYER, W., *Vererbung und Auslese*, 1910, Chap. XI; PORTEUS, S. D., and BABCOCK, M., *Temperament and Race*, Part IV, 1926.

[167] See MURDOCH, K., "A Study of the Differences Found between Races in Intellect and in Morality," *School and Soc.*, Vol. XXII, Nos. 568–569, 1925; SYMONDS, P. M., "The Intelligence of the Chinese in Hawaii," *School and Society*, Vol. LXXXIX, p. 442, 1924; WOLCOTT, C. D., "The Intelligence of Chinese Students," *School and Society*, 1920, Vol. XI, pp. 474–480; WAUGH, K. T., "A Comparison of Oriental and American Student Intelligence," *Psychological Bulletin*, 1921, Vol. XVIII; YEUNG, K. T., "The Intelligence of Chinese Children," *Journal of Applied Psychology*, 1922, Vol. V, pp. 267–274; YOUNG, KIMBALL, "Mental Differences in Certain Immigrant Groups," *Univ. of Oregon Public.*, 1922, Vol. I; see also TERMAN, *Genetic Studies of Genius*, Vol. I, pp. 56–57.

full mental growth at this age," while the American and Brahman children continue to show an intelligence growth after this.[168]

Finally, as to the so-called European nationalities or stocks, it is evident that they (as far as they are taken on the basis of their languages,—Anglo-Saxons, Germans, Swedes, Italians, and so on) do not represent racial groups in the zoölogical sense of the word. Within the same nationality we find different varieties of the white race; and *vice versa*. The same racial variety is spread among various national groups. Therefore, it is comprehensible that the results of the mental tests of these nationalities might be expected to be somewhat contradictory, showing differences that are not so great. These results could be easily accounted for, because all the principal varieties of the white race,— the Nordic, the Alpine, and the Mediterranean — in their cultural history have shown brilliancy and have never been so widely separated as the white and the black races. These expectations are considerably corroborated by the mental tests. The relative place of different European nationalities shifts from study to study, and the relative ranks of each nation are not identical with the ranks of other nationalities in different studies.[169]

The only conclusion which it seems possible to make from the above and similar studies is that the mentality of various races, and especially that of the white and the black races (as far as it may be judged by the tests given), is different. I do not say that one race is superior while another is inferior. Such an evaluation is subjective. But I do say that in the discussed respect, their "scores" are different. It is probable that in some other respects the blacks may score somewhat higher than the whites. But such a fact, if it is shown, would mean only that their difference is still greater and more many-sided. This means that the school is right as far as it maintains these differences in

[168] See HERRICK, D. S., "A Comparison of Brahman and Panchama Children in South India," etc., *Journal of Applied Psychology*, 1921, Vol. V, pp. 252–260. See also WAUGH, K. T., *op. cit.;* PORTEUS, and BABCOCK, *op. cit.*, Parts V, VI.

[169] See the above quoted works. Besides, see the studies of BROWN, G. L., "Intelligence as Related to Nationality," *Journal of Educational Research*, 1922, Vol. V, pp. 324–327; FEINGOLD, G. A., "Intelligence of the First Generation of Immigrant Groups," *Journal of Educational Psychology*, 1924, Vol. XV, pp. 65–83; PINTNER, R., *Intelligence Testing*, N. Y., 1923; YOUNG, K., "Intelligence Tests of Certain Immigrant Groups," *Scientific Monthly*, 1922.

various racial types, but that it is wrong in its exaggeration of them. As we have seen, they are considerably less conspicuous than the school contends. The difference between the upper and the lower classes of the same race is rather greater than that even of the white and the black races. The school is wrong also in so far as it finds in these differences the characteristics of "superiority" and "inferiority." In view of the subjectivity of these terms, it is possible to contend, with an equal right, that, for instance, an ability to abstain from the creation of a complex civilization is a trait of "superiority," while such a creation is a symptom of "perversion." From the standpoint of such criteria, the negro race would be "superior," while the white race would be "inferior." If we drop such evaluations, the above racial differences are as indicative of "superiority" as are the opposite ones.

The task of a science is not to evaluate, but to find the facts— in this case to find out whether or not the races are different, and, if they are, exactly what these differences are. The above survey answers the problem positively and shows the nature of the dissimilarities. This is all which is relevant from a scientific viewpoint.[170] Evaluations are to be left to the subjective taste of everyone. So much for this point.

D. Further, as I have already mentioned, the school is at least partly right in its contention that these differences are due, not

[170] In spite of a commendable cautiousness several careful authors, like E. B. Reuter, in his valuable study, go to the opposite extreme and beyond the facts known when they state that "all scholars accept as a provisional but fairly well-founded working hypothesis the position that the various races and peoples of the world are essentially equal in mental ability and capacity for civilization." REUTER, E. B., *The American Race Problem, A Study of the Negro*, pp. 95–96, 429. This statement is quite fallacious from the factual standpoint: the majority of the specialists do not recognize that "the various races and peoples of the world are essentially equal in mental ability and capacity for civilization." The statements contradict even the author's own statements that "there is a very considerable body of apparently unbiased scientific opinion on the side of Negro inferiority. And there are no competent students of racial matters who dogmatically assert an absolute racial mental equality." *Ibid.*, p. 92. This statement is much nearer to the truth than the preceding one of the same author. Putting aside "superiority" and "inferiority" as subjective evaluative terms, the problem of bodily and mental differences in various races, on the basis of the facts known, can be answered positively. Several recent studies, like that of Porteus and Babcock, as well as new devices to test chemically the reaction of the blood of various races to a certain reagent, make this statement still more certain.

only to direct environmental conditions, but also to the factor of heredity. That this factor plays a part in this respect may scarcely be questioned by any serious investigator of facts. There is no possibility of accounting for these differences through the influence of environmental agencies alone. From this standpoint, all the shortcomings of such theories as are indicated by Gobineau are valid. (See above. See also Chap. III.) The following categories of facts are especially unaccountable through environ-- mental agencies. First, in the same environment, some racial groups have created complex forms of culture, while others have not succeeded in doing it, and have remained in the simple forms of culture. Second, some racial groups have been able to create complex forms of civilization in the most different geographical environments, while others have remained stationary in various geographical conditions. Third, men of genius, and, partly, the idiots are unaccountable through environment alone. Fourth, men who came out of similar environments have achieved different things. Fifth, there are failures who have come out of the most favorable environment, and men of genius who have come out of the most unfavorable conditions. Sixth, there is a lack of increase in the number of men of genius from the proletarian class in the nineteenth and the twentieth centuries in spite of the increase of educational facilities. These, and other similar facts, may be accounted for only through the admission of the factor of heredity,[171] —through the fortunate and unfortunate combination of the *genes* of the parents. This does not mean that the direct influence of the environmental agencies, such as food, climate, occupation, education, and so on, do not play their part; but, in order that they may change directly the really racial or hereditary qualities of an individual or a group, it is necessary that a very long period of time should elapse.

The totality of physical and mental traits by which various races of man differ from each other is not unchangeable . . . but hundreds and thousands of years are always necessary for such a transformation

says Morselli.

---

[171] See an analysis of the problem in my *Social Mobility*, Chap. XIII.

I do not know of any case of racial transformation within one or two generations, unless it has been made through cross-marriage. The environment of a race cannot quickly change its physical and mental qualities. As for education, it is absurd to expect this to change the racial traits of a group within one or two generations. It is true that, at the present moment, it seems that the qualities of a people are changing often and easily; but scientific investigation shows that such changes belong to the history of a nation or people as psycho-social phenomena, rather than to the category of the racial changes.[172]

As far as the school insists on the important influence of heredity it is right, and, in this respect, it represents a good counter-balance against the one-sidedness of the exaggerated environmental school. But as far as some of the representatives of the school try to underestimate, or even to ignore, the influence of environment, they make the same mistake as the excessive environmentalists. There have been several attempts made to express quantitatively the relative importance of environment and heredity,[173] but they seem to remain somewhat subjective, and therefore inconclusive. Putting them aside, we may say with a reasonable degree of certainty that the factor of heredity plays an important part in determining the traits and behavior of individuals and groups. Thus far the contention of the school and its studies represent a contribution to the science, and deserve our appreciation.

E. The school is right also in ascribing a great importance to selection, and in giving significance to the racial changes of a population in explanation of the social phenomena and historical destinies of a cultured people. The school exaggerates somewhat the significance of these factors, but there seems to be no doubt

[172] MORSELLI, *Le razze humane*, pp. 331–332, 341 *et seq.* Dr. Franz Boas has tried to show that under the direct influence of environmental agencies, it is possible to change the racial traits of a group very quickly, but his interesting results are subject to very serious criticism, and cannot be taken as conclusive. See BOAS, F., "Changes in Bodily Form of the Descendants of Immigrants," *Senate Documents*, Vol. LXIV, Washington, 1911. See criticism in the works of G. Sergi, K. Pearson, C. Gini and others indicated in the chapter, "Geographical School."

[173] See, for instance, PROFESSOR STARCH, *Educational Psychology*.

that selection through differential fertility, mortality, and cross-marriages may efficiently, and in a relatively short time, change the racial stock of a population. Such a change may exert a tangible influence on social organization and social processes. If the changes consist in a survival of the "best," they may facilitate the progress of the society; if they are opposite, they may be one of the factors of a decay. We have a series of studies which rather convincingly show that the processes of a decay are usually accompanied by a change in the racial composition of the population. The best studied case of this type is the decay of Rome and Greece. All competent historians agree that Rome's population in the later period was different from that of the earlier period, and that the progeny of the earlier Roman aristocracy had already disappeared at the time of the first century, A.D. T. Frank has shown this convincingly. Otto Seeck made clear the "extermination of the best" in the war and revolution of Rome. Hence their conclusion that this racial change had to be one of the factors of Rome's decay.

What lay behind and constantly reacted upon Rome's disintegration was, after all, to a considerable extent, the fact that the people who built Rome had given way to a different race. The lack of energy and enterprise, the failure of foresight and common sense, the weakening of moral and political stamina,—all were concomitant with the gradual diminution of the stock, which, during the earlier days, had displayed these qualities.[174]

Even if it is questionable to explain Rome's decay only through this factor,[175] it is probable that it has played a part in Rome's disintegration. At least, such an admission is no less probable than its denial. It is probable also that the contemporary form of differential fertility and low birth rate in Western societies will exert some negative influences on their social life in the future. A lower procreation of the upper and the professional classes means a relative or absolute decrease of their progeny in

[174] FRANK, T., "Race mixture in the Roman Empire," *American Historical Review*, Vol. XXI, p. 705; see also SEECK, OTTO, *Geschichte d. Untergang d. Antik. Welte*, *passim*, and all volumes; PARETO, *op. cit.*, Vol. II, pp. 1694 ff.; FAHLBECK, P., *La decadance*, *passim*; SENSINI, G., *op. cit.*

[175] See ROSTOVTZEFF, *op. cit.*, pp. 485 ff., where the objections against such a theory are given.

the future population.   As far as their qualities are due to heredity also, this means an impoverishment of the racial fund of these societies.   A low birth rate, accompanied by a low mortality, means an elimination or weakening of the factor of natural selection; in other words, a survival of the weaklings who would be eliminated under the condition of high mortality which accompanies a high birth rate.   Under such conditions, the population of such a society is likely to be composed more and more of the progeny of the weaklings and less "superior" people.   The racial fund of the people being changed, their history is likely to be changed also.   These conclusions seem to be corroborated by a series of facts.   In the first place, Rome's and Greece's decay went on parallel to the extinction of their aristocratic stocks, and a fall in their birth rate.   In the second place, the long existing aristocracies, (the most durable among them being the Brahman aristocracy in India) have always been fertile, reproducing themselves in no less a degree than the lower classes.   In the third place, long existing societies, like the Chinese, Indian, or Jewish have always been fertile too.   In the fourth place, a series of studies in the mortality rate of age groups below 32 years and above; both in civilized countries like Germany, France, and England, which have low birth and child-mortality rates, and in less civilized countries with higher birth and child-mortality rates, like the Balkans, Hungary, and Russia; such studies have shown that in the last named countries, the mortality rates of the age groups above 32 years of age is not higher, but rather lower than that of the same age groups in more civilized countries.   Such a thing could be explained only by an admission that the weaklings in the less civilized countries are eliminated through high mortality,[176] and that those who survive to a greater age than 32 are relatively strong people.   For this reason, in spite of the less hygienic conditions, they show less mortality than the corresponding age groups within the more civilized and hygienic countries.

[176] See about the selective character of death rate SNOW, E. C., *The Intensity of Natural Selection in Man*, London, 1911; K. Pearson's paper in *Biometrika*, Vol. I, pp. 50–89; A. Ploetz's paper in *Archiv für Rassen und Gesellschafts Biologie*, Vol. VI, pp. 33–43, 1909; POPENOE, P., and JOHNSON, R., *Applied Eugenics*, Chap. VI, 1922.

Finally, medical investigations of the recruits of Germany, England, and France for the last few decades, have shown that the percentage of the biologically defective among them is not lower, but rather, higher than among the recruits of Russia, and that this percentage has been increasing in spite of an improvement in the standard of living in these countries at the end of the nineteenth, and in the beginning of the twentieth centuries. Such somewhat "unexpected" results testify rather in favor of the above negative "selection," due to low birth and child-mortality rates, and a still lower procreation of the "best" stocks. An improving environment does not seem even to compensate for that which the societies lose through the selection and impoverishment of their racial fund.[177]   These, and many other facts, make the school's conclusions in this field (minus their one-sidedness) probable, though they still remain in need of being tested.

F. As to Lapouge's theory of social selections, their forms and effects,—it must be considerably corrected in details.   He stressed too much the negative effects of the military, religious, legal, and other forms of social selection, overlooking entirely their positive effects.   For instance, in the next chapter we shall see that the effects of military selection are much more complex and many-sided than Lapouge thought.   The same is true in regard to other forms of social selection.   Lapouge's central idea being valid, his one-sided and simplicist characteristics remain to be seriously corrected.[178]

G. Ammon's and Pearson's conception of various social institutions as a kind of "sieve" which tests, sifts, selects, and distributes the members of a society according to their qualities, and their interpretation of class differentiation in essence seems to be valid.   The writer's study of the problem led to a similar con-

---

[177] See a more extensive discussion of this problem and its literature in my *Social Mobility*, Chaps. XX–XXII.

[178] Still more correction is needed by G. Hansen's theory of the migration from the country to the city.   We know now that not all rural migrants enter city positions higher than the native-born.   Further, the city population, since the end of the nineteenth century, has considerably improved its biological balance. It is also not quite certain that the best people always migrate from the country to the city, and that those remaining in the country are "inferior."   See the literature and details in my *Social Mobility*.

clusion. (See *Social Mobility, passim,* and Chapters VII-IX.) However, this sound kernel of theory is overgrown in the works of Ammon and Pearson by a series of "hasty" exaggerations of a "propaganda" character. They are to be discarded.

H. Gobineau's, Lapouge's, and many eugenists' theories of an inevitable harm in race blending seems to be one-sided also. The problem is by no means solved. The numerous data obtained are very contradictory. Hypothetically, the most probable solution of the problem seems to be as follows: The blending of blood between certain racial groups is likely to be beneficial, while that between other races seems to be harmful. On the other hand, inbreeding when the stock is good and not contaminated is likely to be beneficial, while, when the stock is poor or contaminated, it produces degeneration. Such is the answer which is possibly nearest to the truth. However, we still know very little of just exactly what are the conditions and races whose blending will be fortunate or unfortunate.[179]

8. GENERAL CONCLUSIONS

Space does not permit me to continue an analysis of the other statements of the school. On the basis of the above, we must conclude that it has been one of the most important and valuable schools in sociology. Rejecting its exaggerations and fallacies, we can be but grateful for its many contributions to our knowledge. Even the school's one-sidedness has been useful in counterbalancing the one-sidedness of the excessive environmentalists. Freed from their exaggerations, both schools complete each other excellently, and give "an aggregate key" to an understanding of a great deal of the mystery of human behavior and social processes.

[179] See DUNN, L. C., "A Biological View of Race Mixture," *Publications of American Sociological Society*, Vol. XIX, pp. 47–56; REUTER, E. B., "The Hybrid as a Social Type," *ibid.*, pp. 59–68; LINTON, R., "An Anthropological View of Race Mixture," *ibid.*, pp. 69–77; MJOEN, J. A., "Harmonic and Disharmonic Race-Crossings," *Eugenics in Race and State*, pp. 40–61, Baltimore, 1923; HOFFMAN, F. L., "Race Amalgamation in Hawaii," *ibid.*, pp. 90–108; SAVORGNAN, F., "Nuzialita e Fecundita delle Case Sovrane," *Metron*, Vol. III, No. 2, 1924; EAST, E. M., and JONES, D. J., *In-breeding and Out-breeding*, Philad., 1919; HANKINS, *op. cit.*, Chaps. VII, VIII. See there other references.

CHAPTER VI

SOCIOLOGICAL INTERPRETATION OF THE "STRUGGLE FOR EXISTENCE" AND THE SOCIOLOGY OF WAR

1. General Characterization of the Branch

I f t h e biological conceptions of organism, heredity, variation, and selection have inspired the series of sociological theories discussed above, the same must be said of what Darwin styled the "struggle for existence" and "adaptation." Though the theories of the "struggle for existence," "survival of the fittest" and of "adaptation" were set forth long before Darwin,[1] nevertheless his hypothesis has greatly influenced the sociological thought of the post-Darwinian period, and has been one of the principal factors in causing the appearance of numerous divergent theories interpreting the struggle for existence within human societies. These theories are either a mere application of the "biological law" of

---

[1] Conflict, opposition, and struggle were long ago declared a fundamental law of the universe, of life, and of man's existence; and the source of all change and progress. Even the theory of the "survival of the fittest" was outlined not later than the fifth century B.C. Heraclitus' "All is incessantly changing," and "War is the father of all things"; Empedocles' theory of the struggle for life and survival of the fittest; Seneca's *"vivere militare est"*; the Roman *"militia est vita hominis,"* show that. There is also the "Zend-Avesta's" fundamental principle that "the history of the world is the history of conflict" (of the opposite forces of good and evil); that "there is a war in nature, because it contains the powers that work for good and the powers that work for evil"; and that their struggle is permanent and omnipresent ("The Zend-Avesta," *the Sacred Book of the East.* Vol. IV, Oxford, 1880, pp. LVI–LVII, and *passim*). The dualism of the good and evil forces, with their attendant struggle is given in a great many ancient religions. Since that time, the philosophy of conflict and of struggle, whether in an application to the whole universe, or to the kingdom of life-phenomena, or to the history of man, has been running throughout the history of the social and philosophical thought of various peoples and societies. In the nineteenth century a great impetus to the idea was given by H. Spencer and especially by Charles Darwin. See a survey of the historical development of the theory of evolution in Osborn, H. F., *From the Greeks to Darwin*, N. Y., 1908. See also the very brief account of H. H. Newman in his *Readings in Evolution, Genetics, and Eugenics*, Chap. II; Judd, J. W., *The Coming of Evolution*, Cambridge, 1911; Spiller, G., "Charles Darwin and the Theory of Evolution," *Sociological Review*, April, 1926; de Quatrefages, A., *Darwin et ses précurseurs français*, Paris, Alcan; Perrier, E., *La philosophie zoologique avant Darwin*, Paris, Alcan; Nasmith, G., *Social Progress and the Darwinian Theory*, Chap. I, N. Y., 1916.

the struggle for existence to human society, or its variation. For this reason, the majority of them may be regarded as a branch of biological sociology. The purpose of this chapter is briefly to survey and analyze these theories, especially the various "sociologies of war."

Contemporary literature on "struggle sociology" is enormous. However, an incomparably greater part of it does not have any scientific value, being nothing but purely emotional and speculative "ideologies." Therefore this part may be dismissed without any analysis. What remains is well represented by a series of relatively few fundamental works, whose survey may be sufficiently representative to give an idea of the situation of sociological knowledge in this field. Before we analyze these theories, we shall "clear the ground" of a series of vague conceptions, which make a clear analysis impossible.

2. Uncertainty of the Meaning of "The Struggle for Existence" in Biological and Sociological Literature

As is generally known, Darwin took the idea of a struggle for existence from Malthus. Introducing it, he was aware of a vagueness in its meaning.

I should premise that I use this term in a large and metaphorical sense including dependence of one being on another, and including (which is more important) not only the life of the individual, but success in leaving progeny.

He further gives a series of examples of the struggle for existence, which give to the term a meaning almost identical with that of the "reaction of protection and preservation," a meaning far broader than a mere "extermination or elimination" of other organisms.

In these several senses, which pass into each other, I use for convenience sake the general term of "Struggle for Existence." [2]

This shows that Darwin practically left his conception of the struggle for existence undefined. In his work he uses the term in two different senses. The first is a broad one, which includes

[2] Darwin, Charles, *The Origin of Species*, p. 78, N. Y., 1917.

all the phenomena of the "dependence of one being upon another" (hospitable and inimical), and all the protective reactions such as mutual aid, sociality, coöperation, and so on. The second is a narrower sense, which principally means the inimical, antagonistic, and "struggling reactions." This divergency of the meanings and the somewhat interchangeable use of both of them has considerably vitiated even Darwin's theory.

In the works of the biologists and sociologists, the defect has grown enormously. In the first place, each of them interprets the meaning of the struggle for existence in his own way. There are authors who talk of the struggle for existence among atoms, planets, stars, and molecules, not to mention the struggle of organisms, human beings, and societies.[3] Some other authors use the term only in an application to living beings, but by the "struggle for existence" they understand not only inimical, antagonistic, or exterminating reactions; but mutual aid, solidarity, struggle for individuality and domination, coöperation, and so forth,—that is, practically all the reactions of an organism.[4] Finally there are the authors—though many of the above mentioned writers do the same too—who use the term in a narrow sense of the word, understanding by it only the antagonistic, and especially the injurious reactions occasioned by the extermination of one being by another. If to this anarchical use of the term in scientific works we add the incomparably worse anarchy in its journalistic and occasional usage, we cannot but agree with the ironical remarks of a prominent French biologist in regard to the factor of "struggle for existence."

Owing to a careless use of the term, "Struggle for Existence," a crowd of the superficial followers of Darwinism began to ascribe a magical power to the words. They are used now as the term "affinity" was once used,— in all cases when it was necessary to get out of a difficulty. Society men, especially journalists who talk of all

---

[3] See for instance NOVICOW, J., *Les luttes entre sociétés humaines et leur phases successives*, pp. 1–50, Paris, 1896; TARDE, G., *L'opposition universelle*, Paris, 1897.

[4] See for instance THOMPSON, J. A., *Darwinism and Human Life*, p. 91, N. Y., 1917; GIDDINGS, F., *Studies in the Theory of Human Society*, N. Y., 1922; BAGEHOT, W., *Physics and Politics*, N. Y., pp. 24, 50–52, 212–213, N. Y., 1884; NICOLAI, G. F., *Die Biologie des Krieges*, Vol. I, Chap. II, Zurich, 1919. (There is an English translation.)

this without serious training and knowledge, philosophers, metaphysicians, men who fetishize words, even some of the scientists, think that all problems are solved as soon as they have succeeded in indicating, especially in English, the factor of the "Struggle for Existence." Struggle for Existence! Nothing can resist that "Open sesame" which is supposed to unravel for us all the secrets of biology and sociology.[5]

If our discussion is going to be more or less fruitful, we shall have to omit all theories of a "struggle for existence" among atoms, planets, and so on. Let them be discussed by philosophers or by anyone else, but we are concerned only with human beings. We shall also have to omit all theories which give a very broad meaning to the struggle for existence, regarding as its varieties, mutual aid, coöperation, sociality, and what not. Such a broad interpretation of the struggle for existence makes the term practically meaningless; in this case it is possible, with equal right, to style all these phenomena as "A Life Protection" or "Help for Existence" or "Coöperation for Existence." It is an elementary scientific rule to style similar things with similar terms, and dissimilar things with different terms. The term, "struggle for existence," meaning the extermination of the other fellow, is so different from "struggle for existence" in the form of mutual aid with this fellow, that it is utterly impossible to cover them by, or identify them through, the same term. Moreover, if we should do that, it would be evidently impossible to find any clear and definite correlations between such a broad, indefinite, and self-contradictory factor, and some other phenomena. These reasons are sufficient for dismissing all such vague and "meaninglessly broad" biological and sociological theories. Let them be discussed by

[5] GIARD, *Facteurs primaires de l'évolution*, Paris, Librairie Croville-Morant, pp. xi–xii. Partly for similar reasons, such a prominent zoölogist as P. Charles Mitchell, a member of the Royal Society, and the secretary of the London Zoölogical Society, after his careful analysis of the problem as to whether the generalization of the struggle for existence could be regarded a scientific law answers: "It is rather ridiculous to claim that the natural selection and struggle for existence can demand a right to be considered as a scientific law. The pretension that 'the law of nature to which all other natural laws could be reduced is the law of struggle' is quite fallacious. It is not a law but only an intensively discussed hypothesis."—MITCHELL, *Le Darwinisme et la guerre;* French translation, p. 29, Paris, 1916. The book was published in English in 1915, but at the present moment it is not available to me.

those who like to wander in the wilderness of high-sounding, but vague and meaningless, phraseology.

This means that we are going to deal only with those theories of the struggle for existence which use it in the narrow sense of antagonism, conflict, and war among human beings. But even with such limitations, not all these theories are worthy of being surveyed or discussed. A great many of them represent nothing but superficial "ideologies" or an inadequate generalization, without any serious proof or any systematic analysis of the facts. These may be dismissed also. For this reason such "theories" and "statements" as: "The history of all hitherto existing society is the history of class struggle" (Marx-Engels); or "The law of struggle is an universal law" (Novicow); or "The struggle for existence is a law inherent in humanity as in all living beings" (E. Ferri); or "The law of struggle is a fundamental law of nature" (Bernhardi); and similar "figurative and meaningless generalizations," may be dismissed without any analysis.[6] The reason is that such statements, being incidental, do not give much; they mean something pretty indefinite, and they are obviously one-sided.

There is no doubt that, side by side with the phenomena of the struggle for existence, there exist the phenomena of mutual aid, coöperation, or solidarity. The studies of P. Kropotkin, W. Bagehot, and of many others, have made this clear.[7] These phenomena, although opposite to the struggle for existence, are as general in the human and the animal world as the relations of antagonism and war. For this reason, all theories which try to make the struggle for existence into a unique or primary factor of social evolution are obviously fallacious. Similarly, the same may be said of other "theories" of a like nature. After the above "clearing of the field" from pseudo-scientific "rubbish," let us turn to the sociological studies of war-phenomena, as the acutest form of the struggle for existence among human beings.

[6] MARX, KARL and ENGELS, F., *Communist Manifesto*, Kerr Edition, pp. 12–13, Chicago, 1913; NOVICOW, *op. cit.*, pp. 1–12; FERRI, E., *Socialism and Positive Science*, p. 25, London, 1909.

[7] See KROPOTKIN, P., *Mutual Aid*, London, 1902, *passim;* BAGEHOT, *op. cit.*, *passim;* MITCHELL, *op. cit.*, *passim.*

3. Forms of the Struggle for Existence, and Their Modification in the Course of Human History

J. Novicow's *Les luttes entre sociétés humaines et leurs phases successives*, M. Vaccaro's *La lutte pour l'éxistence et ses effets dans l'humanité*, and Vaccaro's *Les bases sociologiques du droit et de l'état* may possibly serve as representative theories in this field. At any rate, their statements, which are shared by a great many sociologists, furnish a convenient starting point for a discussion of the problem.

The essentials of Novicow's theory are as follows: Eternal struggle is a universal and everlasting law. Such a struggle goes on among atoms, organisms, human beings, societies, and among all kinds of units. Among animals the struggle for existence assumes two principal forms: elimination and absorption. However, even among them are found traces of the milder economic and mental competition. The result of the struggle is an elimination of the less fit, and a survival of those who are better adapted to the existing conditions. Experience and knowledge have played a great part in the successful struggle among animals. Those organisms which displayed this quality in the greater degree have had greater chances to survive. Through an elimination of the unfit the struggle leads to a better and better adaptation. Its progress means a greater happiness. In the course of time this progress of adaptation, especially among human beings, becomes more and more rapid. In fact, "progress itself is nothing but an acceleration of adaptation." [8] Turning to the forms and evolution of the struggle for existence among human beings, Novicow distinguishes at least four principal types. Their character and evolution may be seen from the following abbreviated scheme.[9] This scheme shows that there are many forms of the struggle for existence in human society. According to the author, in the course of time the ruder forms of struggle are superseded by milder ones. The physiological struggle has now almost disappeared, while the form tends to become more and more intellectual. War is more and more being superseded by mental and intellectual competition. Besides, as time goes on, the transforma-

[8] Novicow, *op. cit.*, pp. 1–12, 30, 50.   [9] *Ibid.*, p. 402 and *passim*.

The Principal Forms of the Struggle for Existence and Their Evolution

Forms of the Struggle for Existence	Purpose	Forms of Manifestation
1. Physiological	Elimination, extermination, obtaining food	Cannibalism, killing, murder, war for the sake of obtaining food and elimination of the enemy
2. Economic	Acquisition of the means of subsistence, and wealth; their accumulation, appropriation, etc.; economic wars	Brigandage, economic competition, and various forms of compulsion, with the direct purpose of robbing an enemy
3. Political	Obtaining various economic privileges through political means; political domination, with the purpose of profiting from it in various ways. The principal method is by the infliction of various punishments, by threatening execution, and so on. Political wars	Usurpation, enslaving, serfdom, spoliation, annexation, conquest
4. Intellectual	Struggle for an intellectual domination, for a victory of a religion, ideology, dogma, civilization, culture. Methods: propaganda, various methods of assimilation, training, criticism, intellectual persecution, and so on	Religious wars, revolutionary wars; intolerance, intellectual struggle, competition and so on

tion goes on at an accelerated rate. War, in a physiological sense, will disappear entirely in the future. Struggle will not disappear, but it will assume the forms of intellectual competition exclusively, without any bloodshed or extermination of fellow-men. The following quotation from another work of Novicow recapitulates his theory:

The apologists of war are quite right in this, that struggle is life.

Struggle is the action of the environment upon the organism and the reaction of the organism upon the environment, therefore a perpetual combat. . . . Without struggle and antagonisms societies would indeed fall into a state of somnolency, of most dangerous lethargy. That is perfectly true, but the great mistake consists in considering war the sole form in which humanity's struggle manifests itself. . . . Besides the physiological struggle, humanity has economic, political, and intellectual struggles, which do not exist among animals. It may even be stated that the physiological struggle, the dominant form in the animal kingdom, has ended among men, since they no longer eat one another.

Criticizing Ratzenhofer's and Gumplowicz's theories he continues :

No grim fatality obliges us to massacre one another eternally like wild beasts. . . . The Darwinian law in no wise prevents the whole of humanity from joining in a federation in which peace will reign. Within the federation of humanity the same will take place as takes place within each state. Here struggle has by no means disappeared but goes on under the form of economic competition, lawyers' briefs, judges' sentences, votes, party organizations, parliamentary discussions, meetings, lectures, sermons, schools, scientific associations, congresses, pamphlets, books, newspapers, magazines,—in short, by spoken and written propaganda. And we must not suppose that these methods have been preferred to bloodshed because men have become better. Idylls play no part in this question. These methods have been preferred because they were found to be the most effective, therefore the quickest and easiest. . . . All the methods of struggle just enumerated are constantly employed in normal times among 381,000,000 of English subjects inhabiting 25,000,000 of square kilometers. They could be equally well employed by 1,480,000,000 men inhabiting 135,000,000 square kilometers. Then the federation of the entire globe would be achieved.[10]

Such are the essentials of Novicow's theory.

[10] Novicow, *War and its Alleged Benefits*, translated by T. Seltzer, pp. 102–103, 113, 119, 125, N. Y., 1911. The French original edition was published in 1894, under the title, *La guerre et ses prétendue bienfaits*. In his later work, *La critique du Darwinism social*, Paris, 1910, Novicow makes some statements which are somewhat contradictory to the above theory, which will be indicated further. He published, further, a special monograph devoted to an analysis of the possibility and character of a federation of Europe, *La fédération de l'Europe*, Paris, 1901.

Vaccaro's (1854–   ) sociological theory of adaptation and the struggle for existence is drawn up along similar lines. Adaptation, in his opinion, is the final law to which all other biological and sociological laws could be reduced. Using Spencer's formula of life as an incessant adaptation of the inner relations to the outer, Vaccaro says that the essence of life is adaptation, and that adaptation consists of incessant efforts to establish an equilibrium between organism and environment. From this it follows that the more complex and dynamic the environment, the more complex and plastic the organisms will be; otherwise they would perish.[11] Combining Darwinian and Lamarckian principles, he discusses the evolution of organisms from this standpoint, the problems of heredity, and so on.[12]

Passing to man, he indicates that man's adaptation, compared with that of other animals, is more dynamic and complex, consisting not only, and not so much, in the modification of an organism, as in a modification and creation of the means of adaptation outside of his organism (tools, instruments, weapons, and other "artificial organs").[13] To adapt himself to his environment, man has had to struggle with cosmic forces injurious to him, with animal and plant organisms, and with fellowmen. The creation of various instruments to exterminate, annul, or modify the injurious effects of heat, gravitation, cold, and other cosmic forces, is nothing but an adaptation to a cosmic environment. The extermination of harmful organisms, cultivation of plants, and the domestication of animals, is again an adaptation to organic environment.[14] One of the most difficult tasks of adaptation has been that of man to man within a group, and of one society to another. This leads us to Vaccaro's theory of the struggle for existence among human beings, and of its evolution. Among other forms of adaptation among human beings, there has always been a form of the struggle for existence. In order to survive, human beings have had to adapt themselves to one another within a society, and to adapt one society to another. At the earliest stages this task was achieved with great difficulty and through the rudest methods: through a pitiless elimination of the

[11] VACCARO, M., *Les bases sociologiques*, pp. I–XX, Chap. I, Paris, 1898.
[12] *Ibid*, Chaps. I–II.   [13] *Ibid.*, Chap. III.   [14] *Ibid.*, Chap. IV.

weaker members of a group or of its "dissenters," and through a still more pitiless war and extermination of a weaker group by a stronger one. Vaccaro gives numerous facts to show that inner or exterior "war" at these stages was most bloody, inexorable, and permanent. Wars were incessant, and the conquered group was exterminated entirely. There was no pity for any member of a conquered group. The struggle was for absolute extermination.[15] Later on, however, this inexorability of the struggle gradually decreased. The factors of this quantitative and qualitative decrease of the inner and outer struggle for existence were: enlargement of the size of the groups and a decrease of their number, which made chances of inter-group conflicts less numerous; an increase in the size of the groups, which made it more difficult to start the social machinery for war at any moment, as was possible when the groups were small. Under such conditions wars have become less profitable; and an increase of social contacts, commerce, and similar factors has also contributed to this effect. For these, and similar reasons, the intra- and inter-group struggle for existence has been becoming less and less rude quantitatively and qualitatively.[16] In inter-group struggle this mitigation first manifested itself in the increased numbers of the members of a conquered group who were spared and permitted to live. At the beginning only some of the children were spared; later, women; then, all the non-dangerous members; and later still, the majority of the members of such a group. Instead of exterminating them, they were exchanged, turned into slaves, sold, and exploited in various ways. In this way the circle of pacified population has been expanding more and more. Furthermore, the treatment of the spared conquered people has been becoming more and more humane, until it has reached the present situation in which, as soon as the war is over, the conquered have almost as many rights as the conquerors.[17] Thus, quantitatively and qualitatively, the inter-group struggle—war—has

---

[15] *Ibid.*, Chap. V. See also VACCARO, M., *La lotta per l'esistenza e suoi effetti nell'humanita*, Rome, 1886, French translation, Paris, 1892. For an evolution of the intra-group struggle for existence (crimes and punishment) see his *Geneis e funzione delle leggi penali*, Rome, 1889.

[16] *Les bases*, Chap. VI. Other works *passim.*

[17] *Ibid.*, Chaps. VI–VIII.

been dying out, and inter-group adaptation has been gradually progressing.

Similar has been the trend in the evolution of intra-group struggle. At the earliest stages, the treatment of offenders against the members of a group was pitiless. Bloody revenge, expulsion, duels, and similar measures of elimination and extermination were the rule. Later on, these measures have also become more and more humane, until they have reached the present "penological" policy, in which the element of cruelty and torturing of an offender is reduced to a minimum, and tends to disappear completely.[18]

If now we glance at the struggle between the conquerors and the conquered forcibly subjected to the control of the conquerors, its evolution shows the same tendency. The conquerors used to become the privileged or governing stratum of the conquered society. Their interrelations at the beginning were those of a sharp antagonism in which the aristocracy, through a severe coercion and cruelty, forced the conquered or the lower classes to obey its despotic domination. The government was necessarily a military dictatorship of the conquerors over the conquered. As the mutual adaptation of both the classes grew, coercion and cruel despotism began giving way to milder forms of social control. The place of military despotism was taken by a theocratic government considerably milder than the former régime; then the place of theocracy was superseded by a still milder aristocratic régime; and its place, in time, by a democratic régime in which the differences between the conquerors and the conquered, between the governing and the governed classes, have been practically obliterated. Instead of an outside government, we have self-government; instead of a compulsory and tyrannical control, self-control, based on the will of the people and free from bloodshed and despotism. Thus in this field the tendency has been the same as that in other fields of the inter- and intra-group struggle for existence. All of them taken together show that the bloody forms of the struggle have been dying out in the course of time. Adaptation has been progressing, as a finer and more

[18] *Ibid.*, Chap. IX.

humane technique has been superseding the bloodier and ruder one. All this indicates that war, punishment, extermination, and elimination of human beings by their fellowmen will disappear in the future, and a mobile and harmonious adaptation will be established.[19]

Such is the skeleton of Vaccaro's theory. Each of his statements is supported by rich ethnographical, historical, and political materials. This, in addition to the harmonious and well-rounded character of the whole theory, greatly increases the convincing power of Vaccaro's conclusions.

It is scarcely necessary to say that the above conclusions of Novicow and Vaccaro are shared in their essentials by a great number of sociologists, economists, moralists, political thinkers, and historians; not to mention an immense number of journalists, publicists, preachers, politicians, pacifists, and others. They think that the outlined disappearance of war and the bloody forms of the struggle for existence within human societies is inevitable. G. Tarde, M. Kovalevsky, E. Ferri, G. de Molinari, G. Ferrero, N. M. Butler, G. Nicolai, W. H. Taft, R. S. Bourne, S. C. Mitchell, L. Petrajitzky, W. G. Sumner, A. G. Keller, the entire body of the Carnegie Endowment for International Peace, the enthusiasts of the League of Nations, various societies for the promotion of peace, and so on, may all be quoted as examples of the many people who believe this.[20]

---

[19] *Ibid.*, Chaps. X–XII.

[20] G. Tarde claims that the stage of opposition or conflict between the two subsequent,—old and the new—"adaptations" tends to become shorter and shorter, and less and less cruel as time goes on. See TARDE, *Social Laws*, pp. 105 and *passim*, 110–113, 132–133, N. Y., 1899. He was one of the earliest theorists who classified the phenomena of opposition into three principal forms: war, competition, and polemics,—the classification commonly accepted now, but sometimes wrongly attributed to Simmel. KOVALEVSKY, M., *Contemporary Sociologists*, pp. 164 ff.; FERRI, E., *Socialism and Positive Science*, pp. 24–25, and *passim;* DE MOLINARI, G., *Grandeur et décadence de la guerre*, Paris, Alcan, 1898; SUMNER, W. G., and KELLER, A. G., *The Science of Society*, Vol. I, 1927, pp. 16, 62 ff., 390 ff.; FERRERO, G., *Il militarismo*, 1898; NICOLAI, G., *op. cit.;* PETRAJITZKY, L., "Kvoprosou o sozialnom ideale," *Juridich. vestnik*, 1913, Vol. II, p. 34; see the statements of N. M. Butler, W. H. Taft, R. Bourne, S. C. Mitchell, in WOODS, F. A., *Is War Diminishing?* Boston, 1915, Introduction. A similar opinion was held by the writer in his book, *Crime and Punishment*, 1914, pp. 317–385, (Russian) and in his "The Trends in Evolution of Punishment," (Russian) in *Novyija idei v pravovedenii*, Vol. II.

CRITICISM

Can we say that the essentials of the above theories are scientifically proved and accurate? I am afraid not. They are very sympathetic, and therefore tempt belief; but a serious scientific scrutiny shows their fallacies.

In the first place, it is not true that among animals the struggle for existence assumes only the forms of elimination, extermination, and devouring of other organisms. We cannot say this of the majority of plants, or of many of the non-carnivorous animals. Besides, as a series of biologists have shown, the victory in the struggle for existence has not necessarily belonged to the most voracious beasts. Very often it has been obtained by those species which have been less cruel and voracious.[21] Furthermore, Kropotkin and many other investigators have shown that mutual aid is in no way restricted to human societies. It is quite common among animals. We cannot even say that the higher the place occupied by species on the "ladder of life" the less voracious they are. Such an assumption is quite false. Moreover, there is some truth in the ironical remark of Montaigne that "war is a specific characteristic of the human species"; and in a no less ironical epigram of Shaftesbury that Hobbes' famous *"homo homini lupus est"* is an insult to wolves, because they are less rapacious and cruel toward one another than is man toward man. These facts are sufficient to show the fallacy of Novicow's statement that, as we proceed from the lower to the higher animals, and from the animals to man, "the physiological struggle for existence" tends to disappear. The facts do not support such a pleasant "generalization" at all.[22] Now, considering man, can we say that the above scheme of the evolution of the inter- and intragroup struggle for existence is accurate? I am afraid it is not. In his later book, Novicow himself indicates that, at the beginning of his history, man was "a fruit-eater" and not "a flesh-

[21] See the corresponding facts in MITCHELL, *op. cit.*, Chap. II.

[22] It is curious to note that in his later book, in the heat of his criticism of sociological Darwinism, Novicow himself indicates that among animals, war, as a struggle of one group with another, is extremely rare, as is also an individual "physiological" struggle among the members of the same species. War is a conspicuous trait of human society. See NOVICOW, *La critique de Darwinisme social*, pp. 43, 47-48, 61, 153.

eater," and that man's strong herd-instinct made a peaceful fellow out of him. Only when the development of man's intellect broke the power of this instinct, did war appear in human history.[23] All this is but a speculation; but yet it shows Novicow's contradiction of his own statement that, in the course of human history, the struggle for existence has been perpetually decreasing, passing from the physiological to the intellectual form. Turning from this speculation to the facts, can we say that primitive man was more rapacious, bloodthirsty, and warlike than civilized man, as we are told by Novicow, Vaccaro, Sumner, Keller, and even by S. R. Steinmetz,[24] not to mention a crowd of incompetent asserters? If the facts, as far as they are known, do not permit us to answer the question negatively, still less do they permit us to answer it positively. Now we certainly know that a "savage" is in no way similar to a cruel, bloodthirsty, and voracious beast, as he has been often depicted.[25] The passage from the lowest hunters to the highest agricultural groups among the simple peoples is certainly great. If the criticized theory were right we would have to expect that war would be less known to, and the treatment of the vanquished more humane among, the high agricultural peoples than among the lowest hunters. Facts, however, do not support this expectation. The following table, in which the results of a study of 298 simple peoples are summarized, shows this. Only in nine cases has "no war" been found, and these instances have not been taken from among the high agricultural peoples, but from among the lower hunters and the lower agricultural peoples. This leads the authors of the study to the conclusion that "organized war rather develops with the advance of

[23] NOVICOW, *ibid.*, pp. 50, 53, 207. A similar speculation is repeated by Nicolai in his superficial *Die Biologie des Krieges*, Vol. I, pp. 29–32. Nicolai practically follows Novicow's work.

[24] As we shall see, Dr. Steinmetz very vigorously claims that war will not disappear in human history, and he is one of the most prominent scientific defenders of war. Nevertheless, he also states that "war is the usual business" of primitive tribes; that *"die Wilden, wahrscheinlich nach der alleersten Stufe, bludthurstig waren und ihre Kriege in der grausamsten Weise mit ungeheueren Verlusten an Menschen fuhren."*—STEINMETZ, *Die Philosophie des Krieges*, pp. 55–57, 190, Leipzig, 1907.

[25] See WESTERMARCK, E., *The Origin and Development of Moral Ideas*, Vol. I, pp. 334 ff., Chaps. XIV, XV, XVI, London, 1906.

industry and of social organization in general." [26]   The table is as
follows :

Number of Cases of Each Form of Treatment for the Vanquished Among Each
Class of People [27]

Classes of the Peoples	Vanquished Slain	Men Only Slain	Women and Children Enslaved
Lowest hunters..............	6	3	5.5
Higher hunters..............	23	17	10.
Lowest agricultural.........	15	6	1
Lowest pastoral.............	..	..	..
Higher agricultural..........	44	7	8
Higher pastoral.............	1	1	1
Still higher agricultural.......	16	7	6

Classes of the Peoples	Generally Enslaved	Adopted	Exchanged or Set Free
Lowest hunters..............	1	1	1
Higher hunters..............	11	9.5	7.5
Lowest agricultural.........	4.5	12.	..
Lowest pastoral.............	2	1	..
Higher agricultural.........	15	14	7.5
Higher pastoral.............	1	..	1
Still higher agricultural.......	35	2	1.5

The table probably contains a larger number of the simple peoples
studied from this standpoint than any other study.   Therefore it
is less fragmentary and incidental than many other studies of
primitive peoples based on one-sidedly few cases.   Being such,
contrary to Vaccaro's and Novicow's theory, it does not show any
noticeable quantitative or qualitative decrease of war as we pass
from the stage of the lowest hunters to that of the highest agricultural peoples.

If we turn to historical peoples, the discussed theories occupy

[26] HOBHOUSE, L., WHEELER, G. and GINSBERG, M., *The Material Culture and
Social Institutions of the Simpler Peoples*, p. 228, London, 1915.
[27] *Ibid.*, p. 232.

no better position. At the present moment we have at least two more or less systematic attempts to find out whether or not war has been decreasing among the European peoples during the last nine centuries. As a basis for deciding this problem the authors observed the number of years in each century spent by a country in war and in peace. One of them added to this the data which show what per cent of the fighting force (army) perished in all the principal wars of these centuries. The principal results of their study are as follows: [28]

Number of Years Spent in War in Each Specified Century in Each Specified Country

(The upper line of figures are those of F. A. Woods; the lower one, of Bodart.)

Country	1100–1200	1201–1300	1301–1400	1401–1500	1501–1600	1601–1700	1701–1800	1801–1900
England...............	54	36	65	57	54.5	43.5	55.5	53.5
France.................	36.5	49	43	52.5	60.5	46.5 / 64	50.5 / 52	35 / 74[a] 32[b]
Austria, and the Hapsburg					75.5	73.5	48.5	13.5
Austria-Hungary.........						77	59	25
Russia.................					78.5	57.5	49.5	53
Turkey.................					80.5	89	23	39.5
Spain..................					73	82	48.5	53.5
Poland.................					55	68	22.5	
Denmark...............					32.5	30.5	12	15
Holland................						62.5	29.5	14.5
Prussia of the Hohenzollerns						58.5	31	13
Sweden................					50.5	50	29.5	6.5

[a] with colonial wars
[b] without colonial wars

These figures show that only in regard to small countries whose total population composes an insignificant part of the European population, would it be possible to talk of the diminishing of war. The data concerning large countries does not give any valid

[28] WOODS, F. A., *Is War Diminishing?* pp. 34, 39, 43, 53, 64, 67, 73, 78, 85, 91; BODART, G., *Losses of Life in Modern Wars*, pp. 4, 75–78, Oxford, 1916. By the way, it is curious to note that the Hohenzollern Prussia, which in speeches used to be slandered as the very embodiment of militarism, was objectively the least militaristic of all large countries. This is a good illustration of a discrepancy between what is the objective truth, and what is subjective "public opinion."

basis for such a conclusion. If to this we add the appropriate consideration of F. A. Woods, concerning the long cycles in the movement of war; and finally the data of the twentieth century, we cannot but agree with Dr. Woods' conclusion that the "lines [in his valuable diagrams] for England, France, and Russia would never suggest that militarism is ceasing"; and that all the data can, at best, "do no more than throw a moderate amount of probability in favor of declining war years." [29]

If we take the per cent of losses for the belligerent armies in the wars of the seventeenth, the eighteenth, and the nineteenth centuries, we cannot see any tendency toward a decrease. Meanwhile, the size of the armies has been increasing not only in an absolute number, but probably even in proportion to the population. During the last war we saw that almost the entire population of nations was turned into an army. If, therefore, the per cent of the losses of the contemporary armies is no less than that of the armies of the past, this strongly suggests that, contrary to many authors, among them Steinmetz, there is no definite decrease in the number of war victims. Numerous and detailed tables given by Bodart of the losses in all the principal battles of the above three centuries, computed as a per cent of the total strength of the fighting armies, do not show even the slightest tendency toward a decrease of these losses.[30] These data seem sufficient to show that the

[29] *Ibid.*, pp. 29–30. J. de Maistre was the first who made such a tentative computation, and he came to the conclusion that *"la guerre est l'état habituel du genre humain dans un certain sens; c'est-à-dire, que le sang humain doit couler sans interruption sur le globe, ici où là; et que la paix, pour chaque nation, n'est qu'un répit."*—"Considérations sur la France," *Oeuvres*, Vol. I, pp. 28 ff. G. Valbert, on the basis of the computation of the *Moscow Gazette* says that "from the year 1496 B.C. to A.D. 1861, in 3,358 years, there were 227 years of peace and 3,130 years of war, or thirteen years of war to every year of peace. Within the last three centuries there have been 286 wars in Europe." He adds further that "From the year 1500 B.C. to A.D. 1860 more than 8,000 treaties of peace, which were meant to remain in force forever, were concluded. The average time they remained in force was two years."—VALBERT, G., in the *Revue des Deux Mondes*, April, 1894, p. 692. Having these facts in view, the Honorable George Peel in his *The Future of England*, p. 169, said that for fifteen centuries, since the full adoption of Christianity by the continent of Europe, peace has been preached, and for these fifteen centuries the history of Europe has been nothing but "a tale of blood and slaughter."

[30] Here again the popular writers have imposed upon the public quite a wrong picture of the militarism and enormous armies of past centuries, especially of the middle ages. The real situation was very different. The armies of the past, being mercenaries and professional fighters, were as a rule very small, sometimes

alleged disappearance of war is hard to prove by the actual data. Vaccaro's and Novicow's "tendencies" have been rather more a matter of imagination than an accurate description of the reality.[31]

As to the qualitative decrease of the cruelties of war, the criticized theories seem to be very doubtful also. Of course, some may believe the extermination of an enemy through machine guns, poisonous gas, crushing by tanks, big cannon shells, and other "scientific" methods more humane than that by arrow, or club, or spear; but this is a matter of personal taste. In the opinion of the author there is no substantial difference which would permit one to talk of a "progressive humanizing of war" in the course of time. The last war experience has shown also that in the twentieth century, women, children, and civil populations were often exterminated just as, according to Vaccaro, they were exterminated in the remotest past.[32]

These indications are possibly sufficient to show the illusionary character of the discussed theories. I am afraid the deeper we dig into the facts, the more conspicuous their fallacies are going to appear.[33] They are nothing but "derivations," in which the de-

---

amounting to a few dozen, or hundreds, or to a few thousand men. The figures for the Austrian, and other armies in the battles of the seventeenth, the eighteenth, and the nineteenth centuries are given in Bodart's study. Looking through these figures one sees how systematically the fighting armies have been increasing from the seventeenth to the nineteenth centuries. It is probable that the increase is greater than the increase of the population for the same period. See BODART, *op. cit., passim.*

[31] As I mentioned in my youthful work, I myself held the same belief; but a more careful study of the facts has made me change my opinion.

[32] If one takes the colonial wars of the European countries in the years of 1923–26, one will have a still more conspicuous example of the falseness of the alleged disappearance of war cruelties. Whole cities in Syria, Morocco, India, Afghanistan, etc., were shelled. Women, children, and the whole population were exterminated. A wonderful "humanizing of war," indeed!

[33] As a contrast to these theories we have the opposite ones whose authors try earnestly to show that, with a progress of civilization, the cruelties and the severity of the struggle have not been decreasing, but increasing. One of the most interesting treatises of this kind was published by A. N. Engelgardt in his book: *Progress as the Evolution of Cruelty* (Russian). The author collected an enormous amount of material from the histories of the past and the present wars, and of the colonization of the natives by the European nations, to prove his principal thesis. If this thesis cannot be accepted (it is also one-sided) the work at least shows the fallacy of the opposite opinion. As is known, B. Kidd, in studying the theories, ideologies, beliefs, and tendencies of the second half of the nineteenth century, also came to the conclusion that the West was becoming incomparably more brutal, warlike, and rapacious than it had been before. During this period there "was a recrudescence of the pagan doctrine of the

sirable trend is substituted for the real one. So much for this point.

Now, as to the *forms of the "struggle for existence," or the forms of antagonistic relationship among human beings, they are numerous.* Their classification depends upon the purpose of the study. The majority of the existing classifications represent a variety of Tarde's threefold classification:—war, competition, and polemics, which approximates Novicow's four forms of struggle.[34] Such are the classifications of G. Simmel, of L. v. Wiese, R. Park, and E. Burgess, E. A. Ross, and of some others.[35] There is no doubt that such a classification embraces only one aspect of the problem, and that it is only one out of many possible classifications. In the first place, it is possible to classify all antagonisms according to their specific characteristics. They may be, for example, *conscientious and unconscientious; one-sided,* as when they include only the antagonism between wolves and sheep; or they may be *mutual,* where both parties menace each other; *absolute,* where one party tends to exterminate another physically; or *relative,* where extermination is not necessarily an objective, but where subjugation, exploitation, domination, and competition of various kinds enters. In the second place, according to *"the diagnostic symptoms"* or *"manifestations of antagonistic attitudes"* (forms) there are antagonistic relations: *war, physical fight, competition, opposition, polemics, compulsion, coercion, and a series of inimical relationships.* According to the antagonizing units there are antagonisms between *individuals and between groups.* According to the nature of the antagonizing units there are antagonisms between *states, nationalities, races, religious groups, political parties, sex groups, social classes, occupational,*

---

omnipotence of force," a return to the religion of force, cruelty, slaughter, and so on. Kidd's conclusions are also one-sided, but again they stress the one-sidedness of the opposite opinions. See KIDD, B., *The Science of Power,* Chaps. I–III, N. Y., 1918.

[34] TARDE, *Social Laws,* pp. 110 ff.

[35] See further the chapter about the formal school. Competition, opposition, and conflict,—such are the principal forms in antagonistic relationship, according to L. v. Wiese, R. Park, and E. Burgess, who discriminate between competition (interaction without social contact) and conflict (interaction with social contact), which, in its turn, is divided into war and other forms of conflict. E. A. Ross enumerates a series of opposite forms; see ROSS, E. A., *Principles of Sociology,* 1923, Chaps. XI–XIX.

economic, ideological groups, and so on.[36] This brief enumeration shows the possibility of a divergent classification of human antagonisms. Which of these many possible classifications is to be used depends upon the purpose of the study.

4. SOCIAL FUNCTIONS AND THE EFFECTS OF WAR AND STRUGGLE

How little the phenomena of war and struggle have been studied, and how inadequate is our knowledge in this field, is conspicuously shown by the existence of two opposite types of sociological theory about social functions and the effects of war. According to one type of theory, war and struggle have been the principal factors of human progress and have exerted a series of most beneficial effects.[37] According to the other type of theory, war is "hell" and has exerted only the most disastrous influences on various sides of social life.[38] Both types of opinion are supported by prominent social thinkers, and the dispute between them continues to go on up to this day. Let us glance somewhat closer at the arguments of both parties. Their polemics and arguments are usually carried on in the form of "evaluating" judgments of

[36] Compare with J. Delevsky's classification of antagonisms given in his elaborate study: *Social Antagonisms and Class Struggle in History*, (Russian), St. Petersburg, 1910. See other classifications of antagonisms in SOROKIN, *System of Sociology*, Vol. I, pp. 207–211; PARK, R., and BURGESS, E., *Introduction*, Chaps. VIII–IX; SAVORGNAN, F., "Les antagonismes sociaux," *Scientia*, 1914, I–VII, pp. 138–146. See also *Annales de l'Institut International de Sociologie*, Vol. XI, devoted to the problem of social antagonism, and composed of the papers of prominent sociologists; CARVER, T. N., *Essays in Social Justice*, pp. 93–97, Cambridge, 1915.

[37] The representative theories of this type are given by J. de Maistre, who is regarded as the father of such theories in the nineteenth century. See his "Considerations sur la France," (1790), Chap. III; "Les Soirées de St. Petersbourg," septième entretien, in *Oeuvres*, Vols. I, V; STEINMETZ, S. P., *Die Philosophie des Krieges;* CONSTANTIN, A., *Le rôle sociologique de la guerre*, Paris, 1907; PROUDHON, *La guerre et la paix;* JAHNS, M., *Ueber Krieg, Frieden und Kultur*, Berlin, 1893; G. Valbert's paper published in the *Revue des deux mondes*, April, 1894; GUMPLOWICZ, RATZENHOFER, SOMBART, W., *Krieg und Kapitalismus*, München, 1913. Vaccaro's, and some others belong also to this group of works as far as they explain the origin of the state, social organization, and other social institutions through war and struggle. G. LeBon, L. Ward, and E. Renan, not mentioning such apologists of war as F. Nietzsche, Bernhardi and others, belong partly to this group, too.

[38] The representative works of this type are: the quoted works of Novicow, Nicolai, N. Mikhailovsky, Kropotkin, Molinari, Ferrero, Mitchell, B. Kidd, Lapouge, and the works of O. Seeck, V. Kellogg, D. S. Jordan, Nasmith, and of many others quoted further, not to mention a legion of pacifist pamphlets and publications.

"good" or "bad," "beneficial" or "harmful"; and the "desirable" or "undesirable" influences of war. Such a method inevitably introduces into the theories a series of non-scientific conceptions. They, in their turn, facilitate a misunderstanding between the parties, and very often shift the dispute from the field of a description of the facts as they are, into the field of moral evaluation and speculative reasoning. In order to avoid such an unscientific procedure, I shall split the problem into its important sub-problems, and, in this way, present a brief summary of what is known in this field, what is proved, and what is still uncertain.[39]

A. WAR'S SELECTION

Concerning the character of war selection there are two opposite theories. According to one the selection of war is negative; according to the other it is either neutral or positive. The first theory was brilliantly developed by H. Spencer, partly by Darwin, and by V. de Lapouge (see the chapter about the Racial School) and more recently by a series of authors such as J. Novicow, Nicolai, O. Seeck, D. S. Jordan, V. Kellogg, Charles Gide, and many others. The argument of this group runs as follows: Armies, as a general rule, are composed of the "best blood" of the population,—the healthiest, because the unhealthy and the physically defective are not taken into an army; the most efficient age groups, because the old and children are not recruited; the more honest, because criminals are not permitted to enlist in an army; and the brightest people mentally, because the mentally defective or feebleminded are excluded from an army. Through such a selection the army is somewhat superior physically, morally, and mentally to the common population of the country. During a war, it is the army which suffers losses; the civil population either does not suffer at all, or has incomparably fewer losses. This means that war exterminates the "best blood" of a nation in a far greater proportion than its "poorer blood." This means that war facilitates a survival of the unfit. Exterminating the best blood, at the age at which the reproductive capacity of the

[39] A very rich collection of war facts for future studies in this field is given in the works of VON BLOCH, *Der Krieg*, several volumes; and *Encyklopädie der Kriegswissenschaften*, several volumes; and BERNDT, O., *Die Zahl im Krieg*, 1900.

soldiers is far from being exhausted, war exterminates the best progenitors of the future generations,—the bearers of the best racial qualities. It favors a propagation of the poorer blood and in this way it is a factor of negative selection and of racial degeneration. Vaccaro stressed another form of this. In a long series of facts he has shown that, especially in the past, the conquerors aimed always to exterminate in the first place the strongest, the most courageous, the most intelligent, or the leaders of the opposite party. The Roman rule: *parcere subjectes et debellare superbos* (spare the submissive and demolish the proud men) has been a general rule of almost all wars. Such was the policy of the Spartans in regard to the strong Helots; of the Dorians in regard to conquered native peoples; of the Aryans in India; of the Romans in regard to many peoples conquered by them. The same is true in regard to civil strifes, where each victorious party pitilessly exterminates the leaders of the opposite group; and when success passes from party to party we have, as it was in Rome and Greece, a series of exterminations of the leading men of all parties by one another. "Since the submissive, to the exclusion of the brave and upright men, beget children, the traits of baseness and servility become fixed in the race." In this way military selection has exterminated millions of the best individuals, and through that has facilitated a procreation of the poorer elements of the population,—of the innate slaves and submissive peoples.[40]

Other negative influences of war and militarism on racial and biological composition of the population may be added. They make a great many wounded soldiers physically defective. They facilitate various epidemics and sicknesses, and undermine the health of the soldiers and population. What is more important, militarism, even in time of peace, is responsible for a very high per cent of venereal diseases, especially of syphilis, among the soldiers. Through this it directly contributes to the degeneration of the nation. Further, war exterminates the officers of an army in a greater proportion than the soldiers. Officers being superior to the soldiers, this means that war again works negatively. Such

[40] Vaccaro, *La lutte pour l'existence dans l'humanité*, p. 51, Paris, 1802.

are the principal considerations of those who maintain that selection through international, civil, or any kind of war, is negative.[41]

As the incidence of the death from the wounds and disease of war falls not at random on the general population, but on a specially selected part of it, namely, its sturdy young and middle-aged men, and men often not alone of especial physical fitness, but of unusual boldness and loyalty of spirit, and as these deaths may in times of severe and protracted wars be very considerable in number and take a heavy toll for several or many successive years from this particular part of the population, thus lessening materially the share which it would otherwise take in the reproduction of the population, it would seem to be inevitable, in the light of the knowledge of the reality of race-modification by selection, that serious wars should lead to a racial deterioration in the population concerned. [42]

Such is one of these formulas.

Some of the authors went so far in an evaluation of the negative selection of war that they made it responsible for the decay of nations. Such, for instance, is O. Seeck's theory. According to it the principal factor of the decay of Rome and Greece was an extermination of the best blood of the nations through bloody wars and civil strifes.[43] The theory is repeated eloquently by D. S. Jordan.[44] Later, he and H. E. Jordan illustrated it through a study of the effects of the Civil War on Virginia.[45]

The arguments of the opposite theory, which maintains that war selection is either neutral or even positive I shall use for aiding my criticism of the theory just outlined. Can we say

[41] See NOVICOW, *War and Its Alleged Benefits*, Chap. IV; NICOLAI, *op. cit.*, Vol. I, Chap. 3; NASMITH, G., *op. cit.*, p. 379; JORDAN, D. S., *The Human Harvest*, Boston, 1907; JORDAN, D. S., and H. E., *War's Aftermath*, Boston, 1914; GIDE, CHARLES, "La reconstitution de la population française," *Revue international de sociologie*, 1916; DARWIN, L., "On the Stat. Enquiries Needed after the War in Connection With Eugenics," *Journal of Royal Statistical Society*, March, 1916; OTLET, P., *Les problèmes intern. et la guerre*, 1916; KELLOGG, V., *Military Selection and Race Deterioration*, in Carnegie Endowment for International Peace Publications, Oxford, 1916; also "Eugenics and Militarism" in *Problems in Eugenics*, 1912, pp. 220–231; SOROKIN, P., "The Effects of War on Social Life," in *Ekonomist* (Russian) Petrograd, 1922, No. 2; *Sociology of Revolution*, Chap. XI.

[42] KELLOGG, *Military Selection and Race Deterioration*, pp. 197–198.

[43] See SEECK, O., *Geschichte des Unterganges der antiken Welt*, 3d. ed., Berlin, 1910, Vol. I, Chap. 3, and throughout six volumes.

[44] See JORDAN, *The Human Harvest*, pp. 28 ff.

[45] *War's Aftermath*, pp. 22 ff.

that the theory of negative selection is sufficiently proved? In the opinion of the writer, there seems to be a considerable portion of truth in the theory. Nevertheless, some of its propositions are questionable, and some others need to be tested further.

In the first place, even if negative selection takes place in present-day warfare, the same cannot be said certainly about warfare in the past. In the present warfare, which is carried on with poisonous gas, shells, bombs and so on, physical resourcefulness, courage, dexterity, intelligence, and cunning may not give any preference to the survival of the stronger men of an army. Shells, gas, and bullets exterminate them as easily as the weak soldiers. In wars of past history the situation was different. It is likely that the strong, skilled, dexterous, and clever fighter had then a greater chance than a weak soldier to go out of a battle alive. The reason is that in a fight with arrows, spears, lances, and so on, such a strong man could much better protect himself than a weak fighter.[46] Furthermore, because of starvation, lack of necessities, and other sufferings common in such wars, only those who could endure all this could survive, while the weak had to perish. Moreover, the stronger heroes seem to have had much greater chances for procreation (because of greater success among women, through polygamy, through the right of the stronger, through raping, and so on) than the coward, the weakling, and the physically and mentally defective. Even the facts indicated by Vaccaro are not quite general. The leading group very often obtained its life and freedom by means of concessions, ransom, and other values given to the conquerors at the cost of the masses ruled by such leaders. These considerations show how complex is the problem, and how difficult it is to find the real effects of war selection.

A number of authors indicate that, even at the present time, war's selection is far from being such as it is depicted above.

Also in modern warfare cunning and resourcefulness count for a great deal. It seems highly probable that more than ever before, superiority in intelligence is a great asset among fighting men.

[46] Compare Ross, E. A., *Principles of Sociology*, pp. 386–387; BUSHEÈ, F. A., *Principles of Sociology*, pp. 124–125.

Even in the present trenches,

the best shots are killing more peoples than the poor shots are . . . and the best shots will be themselves least often struck. . . So it is with other forms of killing. . . It is highly improbable that superiority in handling modern weapons is not correlated with general mental superiority. If it be admitted that intelligence is a factor at all, then the more intelligent must themselves tend to escape, from the mere fact that they tend to do more killing.

Furthermore, even in modern wars

the great mortality is really of advantage to the race, because, within the army itself, those who can survive hardship and disease must be by nature stronger than those who succumb. . . In whatever light we may view all these difficult questions. the great fact remains that somehow man has evolved, and he has fought, presumably, half of the time. If warfare is so deleterious it may be asked: How did he get where he is? We have thus seen how difficult and complicated is the philosophy of war. Yet most writers have been content to take one side or the other of the issue, so that we have scarcely begun to have a science of the subject.[47]

C. Gini and F. Savorgnan add to these considerations a new one. If, in regard to men, war's negative selection is true, its harm is compensated for through the positive selection of females due to war. Owing to the extermination of the males, the number of men decreases; and, because of this, the "supply" of females increases. Not all of them can now have a chance to be married and have children. Thanks to a "dearth" of males, only the relatively better females are now married. The poorest among them, who could have married had the war not taken place, now remain outside the "procreators" of the future generations. Thus, negative selection among males is compensated for by positive selection among females, because in determining the qualities of the offspring, the female parent counts as much as the male parent.[48]

[47] WOODS, F. A., *op. cit.*, pp. 23–27. Compare HOLMES, S. J., *Studies in Evolution and Eugenics*, N. Y., 1923; SUMNER, W. G., *War and Other Essays*, 1911; POPENOE, P., and JOHNSON, R. H., *op. cit.*, Chap. XVI.

[48] GINI, C., "The War from the Eugenic Point of View," in *Eugenics in Race and State*, pp. 430 ff., Baltimore, 1921; SAVORGNAN, F., "La gerra e l'eugenica," *Scientia*, June, 1926.

Dr. Steinmetz states generally that the losses and the negative selection of war are greatly exaggerated. On the basis of the losses of the Franco-Prussian War, he tries to show that they are less than the normal fluctuation of the mortality rate from year to year. Under such conditions it is impossible to talk about the deterioration of a race through war.[49] Besides, in modern wars about three-fourths of the losses are due to epidemics and only about one-fourth to warfare. This means that the stronger men survive while the weaker die. Other authors indicate that statistics and facts do not corroborate the statements of the opposite theory. If negative effects were noticed by Villermé and B. de Chateauneuf,[50] in contrast to their findings R. Livi did not find any trace of such deleterious effects on the Italian soldiers born in the years of war and after them.[51] To the same conclusion came Colignon in his study of the French recruits of 1892 from Dordogne who were born in the year of war and revolution.[52] A similar conclusion was reached by O. Ammon in his study of the Badenese recruits of the early nineties. F. Savorgnan found that the per cent of the still-born children and the death rate of the babies did not increase, and the weight of the new-born babies did not decrease in the years from 1914 to 1919 in comparison with the years from 1906 to 1914.[53] On the other hand, Claassen and some others have found that the per cent of defective recruits in Germany has been systematically increasing from 1902 to 1913, though the period from 1879 to 1892 and later was the period of peace in the history of Germany.[54] This means that a degeneracy in the vitality of a population may take place in the most peaceful times. These factual studies make

[49] *Philosophie des Krieges*, pp. 71 ff.

[50] VILLERMÉ, L., "Memoire sur la taille de l'homme en France," in *Annales d'hygiene publique*, Ier serie, t. I, pp. 351–399, 1829; DE CHATEAUNEUF, B., *Essai sur la mortalité, ibid.*, Ier serie, t. X, pp. 239–316, 1833.

[51] LIVI, R., *Antropometria militare*, Vol. II, pp. 89 ff., Rome, 1905.

[52] COLIGNON, R., "Anthropologie de la France," Dordogne, *Memoirs de Société de Anthropologie de Paris*, serie III, t. I, 1894.

[53] AMMON, O., *Zur Anthropologie der Badener*, 1899, Jena; SAVORGNAN, F., *op. cit.*, pp. 419–428.

[54] CLAASSEN, W., "Die Abnehmende Kriegstüchtigkeit in Deutschen Reich," *Arch. f. Rassen und Gesellschafts-Biologie*, Vol. VI, 1909, pp. 73–77; Vol. VIII, 1911, p. 786; Vol. X, 1913, p. 584. Similar results were found in France and in England before the War and during the War in regard to the recruits born and brought up in the period of peace.

the discussed theory still more questionable. Moreover, Steinmetz brings out two reasons in the endeavor to show that even if war selection is in some degree negative, this harm is far counterbalanced by war's positive effects. Following the opinion of Plutarch, Polybius, Aristotle, Machiavelli, Vico, and of many others, he claims that the peacetime selection is negative also. It leads to vice, loss of virility, and to a survival of the people who are far from being the best blood of the nation. "Peaceful competition leads to a regressive selection," too. This claim is not entirely denied even by those who, like Mallock, Jentsch, Ferri, Ploetz, Woltmann and others, insist upon the negative character of war selection.[55] Therefore it is questionable which of these two negative selections (of war and of peacetime) is more harmful and regressive.

> War that shatters her slain,
> And peace that grinds them as grain.

What, however, is especially important is that war is an instrument in the selection of the groups,—a selection whose importance is far greater than that of the selection of individuals. Like K. Pearson, Steinmetz contends that among men there is not only a struggle among individuals going on, but among groups also. Which of the two groups is better, more resourceful, more intelligent, and therefore more entitled to survive, could not be decided without war. War is the instrument of group-selection. It is the only test serving this purpose, and the test which is adequate because it tests at once all forces of the belligerent groups: their physical power, their intelligence, their sociality, and their morality. The victory is the result of a mobilization of all the forces of a nation. "The conqueror is always he who shall fatally conquer" on the basis of the superiority of all his forces. Without war such a group selection would be impossible. *"Sans guerre, tout le mond deviendrait rusé, dur et lâche comme les Juifs*

---

[55] STEINMETZ, "La guerre, moyen de sélection collective," in CONSTANTIN, A., *Le rôle sociologie de la guerre*, pp. 268 ff. See above about Lapouge's social selections theory. See MALLOCK, W. H., *Aristocracy and Evolution*, London, 1898; JENTSCH, *Socialauslese*, 1898; WOLTMANN, L., *Die Darwinische Theorie und Socialismus*, 1899; HAYCRAFT, *Darwinism and Race Progress*, 1896.

d'aujourd'hui." [56]   Compared with this positive group selection, the negative results of individual selection through war become quite insignificant.

The above shows that the character of war selection is much more complex than it is usually supposed to be. On the basis of what we now know about it, it is impossible to agree either with the "cursers" or the "praisers" of war selection. The truth seems to lie somewhere between these two one-sided theories.

B. WAR'S EFFECTS ON THE HEALTH OF THE POPULATION

Somewhat more certain seems to be war's influence on the health of a population, especially when the war is long and strenuous. The disorganization of economic conditions, and the increase of hardships make the satisfaction of primary necessities more difficult; and, in connection with this, tends to increase various epidemics, ailments, and sicknesses. In regard to venereal diseases the increase seems to be certain.[57]   In regard to epidemics of plague, influenza, cholera, typhus, etc., especially in the past, their increase could not be questioned. A great many mediæval wars were followed by various epidemics. The same seems to be true even in regard to modern wars, including the World War,[58] though the modern sanitary and hygienic measures have considerably decreased the chances for, and the severity of, epidemics. Less certain is the war influence on nervous or mental diseases. Several studies have found an increase and credited it to war,[59] but the data have always been fragmentary and incomplete. Where war hardships are great, a decrease in the weight of new-

[56] STEINMETZ, *La Guerre*, pp. 241, 251, Chap. III; also "Les sélections individuelles ou corollaires," in *Annales de l'Institut International de Sociologie*, Vol. IV, 1898.

[57] See KELLOGG, *op. cit.* Tuberculosis increased in the years of the World War, but after its end decreased again. *Handbuch d. sozialen Hygiene*, Vol. III, pp. 200–207, Berlin, 1926.

[58] It is enough to mention the post-war influenza which swept throughout all belligerent (and neighboring) countries.

[59] See, for instance, OETTINGEN, *Moralstatistik*, 1881, p. 68; GOROVOI-SHALTAN, "Mental Diseases Under the Existing Conditions," (Russian), the *Journal of Psychology, Neurology, and Experimental Psychology*, (Russian), 1922, pp. 34 ff.; OSIPOFF, "Mental Diseases in Petrograd," in *Izvestia of the Health-Commissariat*, 1919, Nos. 7–12 (Russian); SOECKNICK, ANNA, "Kriegseinfluss auf jugendliche Psychopathen," *Archiv für Psychiatrie*, Jahrgang 24, Bd. 70, pp. 172–186. See there other references.

born babies, an increase in the per cent of still-born children, and an increase of various deformities and ailments due to the abnormal conditions are probable. But again this is likely to be only one side of the complex picture. There may be several opposite influences which, however, scarcely counterbalance the above effects. From the standpoint of the future of the race, these negative influences, with the exception of venereal diseases, are scarcely important. Eliminating possibly the weakest elements of a population, they may be even beneficial from the standpoint of racial selection. But again, all these statements are still to be tested, and now represent only more or less probable hypotheses.

C. INFLUENCE OF WAR ON VITAL PROCESSES

In this field the effects of war, at least of modern wars, are more certain. They are as follows: With the beginning of war, the death rate of the whole population of a belligerent country begins to go up, and rises until the end of the war. After its termination it abruptly goes down, and sometimes falls below that of the pre-war level; but within one, two, or three years after the termination, it returns to pre-war level and assumes the pre-war trend of movement. The marriage rate falls at the beginning of a war, continuing this movement until the end, when it suddenly jumps up to the pre-war level, as a result of the many marriages which were postponed because of the war. Within one or two years, however, it returns to the pre-war level, and resumes its pre-war trend. In a somewhat similar way the divorce rate fluctuates. The birth rate begins to fall nine months after the beginning of war, and goes on decreasing up to nine months after its termination, when it jumps up above the pre-war level, as a result of the great increase of marriages in the post-war years; but within one or two years it returns to its pre-war level, assuming its pre-war trend. In details this scheme varies from country to country, and from war to war; but, in essentials, such was the fluctuation of the vital processes in the belligerent countries in the cases of the World War, the Prussian-Danish War, 1864; the Prussian-Austrian War, 1866; the Napoleonic Wars; the Crimean War; the Franco-Prussian War, 1870-71; the Russian-

Turkish War, 1877-78; the Serbian-Bulgarian War, 1885; the Balkan War, 1912-13; the Russian-Japanese War, 1904-5; the Civil War of the United States; and some others.[60]

D. INFLUENCE OF WAR ON ECONOMIC PHENOMENA

In this field the principal effects of war are: a waste of wealth (in the form of capital and human material) and an extraordinary shifting of it from society to society, and from group to group within the same society. As does any large enterprise, war requires a great mobilization of wealth. Furthermore, war destroys cities, factories, and other economic values. In this sense it may be regarded as a waste. If we agree to estimate an adult individual at 32,000 francs (as is done by some economists) then a loss of 20,000,000 individuals in war means a loss of 640,000,000,000 francs. In brief, the wasteful character of war may scarcely be questioned.[61] The next general effect of war is an extensive redistribution of wealth among societies, and among the groups and individuals of the same society. It is manifest in the shifting of the wealth of a conquered group to the conquerors; from the belligerent countries to neutral ones; in the economic ruin of some groups in favor of others of the same society; and in an impoverishment of the masses and an attendant enrichment of some individuals. In brief, war always is an important factor in the shifting or displacement of wealth

[60] See the figures in my "The Influence of War," in *Ekonomist*, No. 1, 1922, Petrograd, Russia; SOROKIN, "Influence of the World War upon Divorces," *Journal Applied Sociology*, 1925, No. 2; WOLFE, A. B., "Economic Conditions and the Birth Rate after the War," *Journal of Political Economy*, June, 1917; NOVOSELSKY, S. A., "War and Movement of Vital Processes," (Russian), *Obschestvenny Vrach*, Jan., 1915; NIXON, S. W., "War and National Vital Statistics," *Journal of the Royal Statistical Society*, June, 1916. See other data in the well-known works of G. v. Mayr, Levasseur, and Cauderlier. Less certain is the fact, accepted by some statisticians, (*e.g.*, by Oettingen) that in the post-war years there is an extraordinarily high proportion in the births of males, as a compensation for the males exterminated in war. In the last war such a phenomenon was not noticed.

[61] The purely economic literature in this field is enormous. About the general economic effects of war see NICOLAI, *op. cit.*, Vol. I, Chap. IV; NOVICOW, *War*, Chap. V; BOAG, H., "Human Capital and the Cost of the War," *Journal Royal Statistical Society*, Jan., 1916; OTLET, P., *op. cit.*, pp. 26 ff.; BOGART, E. L., *Cost of the War;* ROBINSON, E. VAN D., "War and Economics," in CARVER'S *Sociology and Social Progress*, Chap. IX.

from group to group, and from man to man.[62]   However, it must be noticed that the economic losses and destructions caused by war are often restored within an extraordinarily short time.   The explanations of this fact vary, but the truth is that it seems to have happened many times.

Furthermore, the unusual stimulation of the inventive power of a nation for the sake of military victory has often facilitated the invention of a new method or the improvement of the old methods of wealth production.   In this way it has indirectly contributed something toward economic progress and has, sometimes, at least partly compensated for its economic damages.[63]

E. WAR AS A MEANS OF EXPANSION FOR SOLIDARITY AND PEACE

That war stimulates animosity and the most inimical feelings among the enemies during the time of war is evident.   Less evident however, is the other side of the problem; the fact that war has been a powerful instrument in the process of expanding groups into larger and larger peace areas.   Yet even in the past it was said: *"si vis pacem para bellum"* (if you want peace, prepare for war).   Many ancient authors understood this function of war. More recently R. Jhering, in his brilliant essay [64] has shown that "the objective of Law is Peace, but the road to it is War."   At the present moment it seems to be certain that without war and compulsion this process of the unification of numerous and inimical groups into larger and larger pacified societies would have scarcely been possible.   War and other means of coercion have been instrumental in this respect.   Through them it has been possible to make the conquerors and the conquered into one group, to keep them together, to establish an intensive contact between them, to "level" their differences, and, after several generations of living together, to make out of them one social group in which previous differences and animosities are obliterated.   At the pres-

---

[62] See the data and literature in SOROKIN, *Social Mobility*, Chap. XVIII; LEWINSON (MORUS), R., *Die Umschichtung der Europäischen Vermögen*, Berlin, 1925; SCHIFF, W., "Die Agrargesetzgebung der Europäischen Staaten vor und nach dem Kriege," *Archiv für Sozialwissenschaft*, 1925, pp. 469–529; WHITE, E., "Income Fluctuation of a Selected Group of Personal Returns," *Journal of American Statistical Association*, Vol. XVII, pp. 61–81.

[63] See about that, SOMBART, W., *Krieg und Kapitalismus*, München, 1913.

[64] See JHERING, R., *The Struggle for Law*, translated by J. Lalor, Chicago, 1879.

ent moment this rôle of war seems to be certain, and is recognized by a great many investigators.[65]

F. THE MORAL EFFECTS OF WAR

Concerning this problem, opinions vary from the most positive apology for war to its most positive damnation. Let us briefly survey what in these opposite theories is more or less certain, and what is a speculation.

War, Brutalization and Corruption.—
Neither circumstances, nor human beings become better in the time of peace; it is from war, which may become more rare, that we must expect progress. . . From a biological standpoint, aggressiveness has been a condition necessary for progress.

Without it man could not emerge from his animal state, because he would be exterminated by other species. Without war an upward movement within humanity would not be possible, because any means of finding out which social group is superior and which is inferior would be absent. A long or eternal peace would make man an exclusively egotistical creature, without virility, courage, altruism, or bravery. Such a man would be entirely effeminated, and corrupted to the very heart of his nature. Degeneration, effeminacy, idleness, corruption,—such would be the results of an eternal peace. Such are the arguments of the defenders of the beneficial effects of war on man's conduct and behavior.[66]

War, an appeal to brute force, is always a degradation, a descent into the animalism that demoralizes the victors, as well as the vanquished. . . Bloodshed produces international hatred, and international hatred produces the most baleful evils. . . War is the most

---

[65] See STEINMETZ, *Philos. des Krieges*, pp. 27 ff.; SOROKIN, *Crime and Punishment*, pp. 216–247; GIDDINGS, F., *Democracy and Empire*, 1901, pp. 354 ff.; KELLER, A. G., *Through War to Peace*, N. Y., 1918; VINCENT, G. E., "The Rivalry of Social Groups," *American Journal of Sociology*, Vol. XVI, pp. 471–484; CASE, C., *Outlines of Introductory Sociology*, Chap. XXX, N. Y., 1924; SUMNER, W. G., *War and Other Essays*, New Haven, 1911; GUMPLOWICZ, L., *Der Rassenkampf*, Innsbruck, 1883, (see about Gumplowicz the chapter on the Sociologistic School); VACCARO, *Les bases, passim;* BUSHEE, *op. cit.*, pp. 130 ff. See, however, the opposite opinions of several writers in NASMITH, Chaps. III–VI; TODD, A. J., *Theories of Social Progress*, Chap. XIX.

[66] STEINMETZ, *La guerre*, p. 288, Chap. I.

active cause of our backwardness and mental stagnation. . . It brutalizes a man; strips him of all really human ethics, turns him into a beast, and entirely demoralizes him.

Such is the opposite opinion.[67]

I think that the mere contrasting of these opinions is sufficient to show their mutual fallacies. Steinmetz is right in maintaining that aggressiveness was necessary for man to survive and rise above an animal level; but it scarcely follows from this that courage and virility can be displayed only in the form of slaughtering other men, that war does not have any brutalizing effects, or that in peaceful coöperation no progress is possible. Novicow is right in maintaining that war demoralizes human beings greatly, but one fails to see how man really could survive by being quite pacifistic and non-aggressive. It is doubtful also that a safe and eternal peace is always beneficial. Still more questionable is it that war has not been instrumental in an increase of altruism and social devotion within at least a fighting group.

In brief, both sides are one-sided in their sweeping statements, and the truth again seems to lie somewhere between these extremes.

Criminality and War.—The influence of war on criminality represents one of the bases for a judgment concerning its moral effects. Does war favor or check criminality? The answer is that we do not know. There have been several statistical studies of the problem; they have shown that, for instance, in Germany in the years of 1866 (the Austria-Prussian War), of 1871 (Franco-Prussian War), in France in 1830 and 1871, the number of crimes decreased abnormally.[68] On the other hand, there are some data (principally concerning defeated countries) which show a sudden, though quickly passing, increase of criminality in the years of war.[69] This suggests that there is probably no general rule, and that the character of war effects depends greatly on

---

[67] NOVICOW, *War*, pp. 72, 74, Chap. VIII.

[68] See VON MAYR, G., *op. cit.*, Vol. III, pp. 947–949; STARKE, W., *Verbrechen und Verbrecher in Preussen, 1854–78*, Berlin, 1884, pp. 63 ff.; *Bijdragen tot de statistick van Nederland*, N. V. No. 231; LEVASSEUR, E., *La population française*, Vol. II, pp. 442–445; CORNE, A., "Essai sur la criminalité," *Journal des économistes*, 1868, (January).

[69] BOURNET, A., *La criminalité en France et en Italie*, 1884, pp. 42, 47, 114; SOCQUET, J., *Criminalité en France*, 1884, p. 25.

many conditions such as: whether the war is successful; whether it is carried on in the territory of the country, or in that of the enemy; whether it is accompanied by a great economic disorganization; whether it is popular among the people of the nation, and so on. This is confirmed by F. Zahn's study which did not find any uniform effect of the World War on the criminality of various countries.[70]   Furthermore, it is necessary to add that a decrease of criminality in time of war may also be due to the fact that many of the would-be criminals are enlisted in the army, and there find a full opportunity to satisfy their "criminal" proclivities in the form of heroic military exploits.   This consideration is supported by the fact that in France and in Germany, as soon as the war of 1870-71 was over, criminality began to go up again.[71]   The above seems to be true of civil and revolutionary strifes also, which are likely to be much worse in this respect than international wars.[72]

Granting that the hypothesis is true that sometimes war is followed by a decrease of criminality, Tarde seems to give an excellent interpretation of the fact, when he says:

The effect of militarism is to exhaust the criminal passions scattered through every nation, to purify them in concentrating them, and to justify them by making them serve to destroy one another, under the superior form which they thus assume. After all is said and done, war enlarges the sphere of peace, as crime formerly used to enlarge the sphere of honesty. This is the irony of history.[73]

As to the influence of military service and discipline on the criminality of the soldiers in time of peace, there seems to be no reason to think that it is noticeably positive or negative.   The attempts to show a greater criminality of the soldiers as compared with that of the common population are unreliable.[74]

War and Social and Anti-Social Forms of Conduct.—After all, criminal actions are only a small fraction of the socially and mor-

---

[70] See ZAHN, F. "Kriegskriminalität," *Schmollers Jahrbuch für Gesetzgebung,* pp. 243–271, 47. Jahrgang, 1924.

[71] TARDE, G., *Penal Philosophy,* p. 422, Boston, 1912; PARMELEE, M., *Criminology,* pp. 99–102, N. Y., 1923.

[72] SOROKIN, P., *The Sociology of Revolution,* pp. 146–147, Chap. IX.

[73] TARDE, *Penal Philosophy,* p. 422.

[74] See LOMBROSO, C., *Crime, Its Causes and Remedies,* pp. 201–202. Boston, 1911.

ally relevant actions. What is war's influence on the total group of such forms of conduct? Here again the truth probably lies somewhere between the apologies of the enthusiastic admirers of war and the curses of the war-haters. The admirers claim that war is an efficient school of altruism, solidarity for death and life, and of "a cure by iron which strengthens humanity." [75] The war-haters claim that war is the school of an exclusive egotism, bestiality, servility, brutality, harshness, slaughter, and of all imaginable mortal sins.[76] Both of these extreme views cannot stand even a quite superficial test. If the first opinion were true, the nations like the Swiss, the Dutch, and the Belgian, (before 1914) which did not have any war during two or three generations, would be the most egotistical and corrupted. The reality does not corroborate such an expectation. If the second opinion were true, the belligerent nations, especially in a period of a long-time war, would be the most anti-social and beast-like. The reality also does not support such an opinion. The Romans in the fifth, the fourth, and the third centuries B. C. were almost continually at war; while the Greeks in the time of the Greek-Persian wars also were in an incessant warfare, and yet we cannot say that the morals and sociality within their own nations were weakened. On the contrary, their inner-group sociality, morals, sacrifices for the sake of the country, the relative purity of the *mores,* lack of corruption, and so on, at that period were conspicuous. What is true of these groups is true of many other groups and individuals. There are "professional soldiers" who display all the harsh and ruffian qualities of an anti-social creature; and there are soldiers who are highly moral and social. There are cases in which war, especially an unsuccessful one, has demoralized a society; and there are cases of the opposite character. It is enough to confront the opposing arguments to see their mutual fallacies. A really scientific study must pass over emotional speculations, and get busy with the facts to be able to say what kind of war, under

---

[75] See, for instance, the quoted works of Steinmetz and Valbert.

[76] See, for instance, Novicow's *War,* Chap. VIII; NICOLAI, *op. cit.,* Chaps. III, IV, *passim;* NASMITH, *op. cit.,* Chap. IV; and almost all pacifist publications, and many of the publications of the Carnegie Endowment for International Peace, which represent nothing but propaganda wrapped into pseudo-scientific dresses. Much nearer to the truth are the views developed in SUMNER-KELLER, *The Science of Society,* Vol. I, pp. 397 ff.

what conditions, when, and in what respect, facilitates man's anti-socialization and society's demoralization; when, under what conditions, and what kind of war produces the opposite effects. Such studies are almost lacking up to this time.

G. INFLUENCE OF WAR ON POLITICAL ORGANIZATION

Possibly the most important generalization in this field was set forth by H. Spencer, in his theory of the militant and the industrial type of society. The essentials of Spencer's theory are: first, that war and militarism lead to an expansion of governmental control; second, to its centralization; third, to its despotism; fourth, to an increase of social stratification; and fifth, to a decrease of autonomy and self-government of the people. In this way, war and militarism tend to transform a nation into an army, and an army into a nation. Peace tends to call forth the opposite results: a decrease of governmental interference, an increase of the people's liberty and self-government, a weakening of social and political stratification, and decentralization. The reasons for such effects of war are as follows: Other conditions being equal, in a war the nation turned into an army and controlled by a powerful government has more chances to conquer than a nation in which everybody acts as he likes, and in which a strong control, centralization, and coördination of the activities of its members is lacking. Furthermore, military education, training, and discipline inculcate the habit of unquestioning obedience in the "rank and file," and that of control in the higher authorities. The very nature of the army, for the sake of victory, requires such a hierarchical and autocratic organization. Besides, the life in military barracks is one in which soldiers are controlled by the higher authorities. They do not have, and cannot have, a considerable amount of freedom and self-control. All this tends to ingraft into a nation which has many and long wars the habits of "military discipline," obedience on the part of the subordinated, and a despotical control on the part of the commanding authorities. This, in its turn, contributes to the expansion, centralization, and despotic character of governmental control. Such are the essential processes tending to be brought about by war and militarism. Being such, they, however, may assume various "dresses"—especially in the form of "ideologies" and "speech-reactions"—according to the circumstances. Sometimes they have the appearance of a despotism of military leaders, kings, and aristocratic dictators. But sometimes they assume the forms of "socialism" and "communism," "dictatorship of proletariat" or "nationalization." In spite of the difference in such "dresses," this difference is quite superficial. Both types of "dresses" wrap objective social processes of an identical nature. Both tend to realize an expansion of governmental control, (in the form of a "communist," "generals' " or kings' despotic government). Both tend to make it unlimited (in the form of an emperor's autocracy or of a despotic "dictatorship" of communist leaders) through the universal control of "nationalized" industry and wealth; through the limitation of private ownership, property, and initiative; through the control and regulation of the behavior and relationships of the people; both restrain the liberty of individuals up to the limit, and turn the nation into the status of an army entirely controlled by its authorities. The names are different in the two cases; the essence is the same. Thus, according to Spencer, militarism, "communism" and "socialism" are brothers. The increase of the former leads to the success of the latter, unless the tendency toward the expansion of governmental control assumes the "reactionary" form of an increase in the power of kings, lords, or military rulers.[77] Such is the essence of Spencer's correlation of militarism with the militant, and of peace with the industrial types of political organization.

In its essentials, Spencer's generalization appears to me to be valid.[78] The correlation between war and militarism, on the one hand, and a trend toward expansion, and a despotic form of cen-

[77] See SPENCER, *The Principles of Sociology*, Vol. I, §§ 258–263; Vol. II, §§ 547–582; Vol. III, §§ 840–853. Spencer even predicted a coming temporary rise of socialism as a contemporary "dress" for the expansion of governmental control due to militarism. Spencer's theory, with some modifications, has been further developed by W. G. Sumner in his *War and Other Essays*, New Haven, 1911. It was brilliantly corroborated by R. Pöhlmann, in his *Geschichte d. Antiken Kommunismus und Socialismus;* by V. Pareto in his excellent *Les systémes socialistes*, and by a great many other investigators of the problems of socialism, militarism, despotism, and étatism.

[78] Steinmetz's criticism of it does not appear to be valid. See STEINMETZ, "Classification des types sociaux et catalogue des peuples," *L'année sociologique*, Vol. III.

tralization of governmental control (whether in a "reactionary" or "communistic and socialistic" dress) on the other, seems to be tangible indeed. This does not mean that it may not sometimes be checked by the interference of a specific factor or that militarism is the only factor of these phenomena. There certainly are other factors, and among them an especially important rôle is played by the impoverishment of a society. This, however, does not annul the correlation so brilliantly outlined by Spencer.[79] Besides the past historical data, it has been conspicuously corroborated by the last war, and by the post-war years. We have had an extraordinary expansion of governmental control in all belligerent countries. There has been a rise in the success of socialist and communist parties which led in Russia, in Hungary, Bavaria, and so on, to the "Militant Communist Dictatorship" and to socialist governments in many other countries. We have seen, further, how, with the termination of the War and its post-War effects, and with the pacification of societies, the success of these groups in all these societies began to diminish. The despotic character of the groups' policies, and their unlimited communism (in Russia) began to become more and more moderate, until there remains very little of it even in Russia, and even there, the capitalist system, private property, and freedom of citizens and other characteristics of an "industrial" society, have been considerably re-established through the hands of the communists themselves.

In brief, Spencer's generalization seems to be valid in its essentials.

H. WAR, REVOLUTION, AND REFORM MOVEMENTS

Their interrelation has been studied little. Nevertheless, there seems to be a tangible correlation between these two phenomena,

[79] Such are the conclusions to which the writer has come in the process of his own study of the social effects of militarism, impoverishment, of the factors of an expansion of governmental control, socialism, and communism. See SOROKIN, *The Effects of War on Social Life*, (Russian) *passim;* "Impoverishment and Expansion of Governmental Control," *American Journal of Sociology*, Sept., 1926; "Famine and Ideology," *Ekonomist*, (Russian), No. 5, 1922, Petrograd; "War and Militarization or Communization of Society," (Russian), *Artelnoije Delo*, Nos. I–IV, 1922, Petrograd; *The Sociology of Revolution*, Chaps. XIII–XV. See also the indicated works of Sumner, Pöhlmann, and Pareto.

especially between an unsuccessful war and revolution.   Such
a war is in a great many cases followed by revolution (in 1917-
18 in Austria, Turkey, Hungary, Germany, Russia, Bulgaria,
Greece,and so on) ; in 1905 in Russia; in 1912 in Turkey; in 1870-
71 in France, and in a great many other cases in various countries
during the previous centuries.   On the other hand, many revolutions have led to wars.[80]   Generally they tend to breed each other.
The reasons for this are quite comprehensible.   An unsuccessful
war means that the society's organization could not meet the test
of war, and that it consequently needs a reconstruction.   Through
its calamities it breeds a dissatisfaction in the masses, and stirs
them to revolt against the existing conditions, especially against
the political régime.   Hence, revolution as a result of a military
defeat.   On the other hand, revolution itself tends to change so
radically the existing relationships within such a society and outside of it that it endangers the most important interests of many
social groups within, and outside of, that society.   Such an antagonism is likely to result in civil or international war as the final
method of solution for such antagonisms.[81]   Hence war as a result of revolution, and their functional relationships.   This correlation has been studied very little, but its existence seems to be
probable.

Even when there is no revolution after or during a war, it,
nevertheless, is followed by many a social reform and reconstruction.   War, especially a great or long war, inevitably causes so
many and so great changes, through the very fact of its existence, that no society can go on without alterations of its "social
machinery" or régime.   Whether these alterations are good or
bad is a matter of personal taste; but that they follow war, and
that war facilitates them can scarcely be doubted.

I. WAR AND SOCIAL MOBILITY

The above is corroborated in another form.   The mobility of
social objects, values, and individuals in time of war and immediately after, seems to become extraordinarily intensive.   War is
an "accelerator" of the horizontal, as well as the vertical shifting

[80] See SOROKIN, *The Sociology of Revolution*, pp. 336 ff.
[81] See an analysis of this problem in my *Sociology of Revolution*, Chap. XVII.

of social objects and individuals from one social status to another. Social climbing from the poor to the wealthy classes, from the lower to the higher strata, from disfranchised to the privileged groups; and the reverse process of a social sinking of individuals and groups, is more intensive in time of war than in time of peace. The same is true in regard to the shifting from occupation to occupation, from one territorial community, political party, or ideological group, to another. In this respect war plays the part of a fire which makes the particles of water in a kettle boil and move much faster. The same may be said of the vertical and horizontal mobility of social objects and values, (*mores*, fashions, beliefs, ideologies, opinions, tastes, and so on). They change and circulate within a society, and among societies, much faster in time of war than in time of peace. A quick and substantial modification of the "habits and *mores*" of a society, and various epidemics of "phobies" in time of war and immediately after have been many times observed, though they are only partial manifestations of this general phenomenon.[82]

J. WAR AND CHANGE OF OPINIONS, ATTITUDES, AND DISPOSITIONS

The above intensification of the mobility of social objects through war may be observed also in a sharp and quick change of opinions (ideologies and speech-reactions) and attitudes of the people with the beginning of war and after it. At the present moment we have several excellent studies in this field, such as A. L. Lowell's, W. Lippmann's, and some other works. President Lowell well described this process:

When civilians enlist in time of war their change of attitude takes place, not after long experience of army life and of battles, but almost at once; and it is due to a new orientation, a recognition of a different and paramount object, transcending in immediate importance the former ones. It is the result, in short, of a radical change in the focus of attention. . . . Moreover the change of sentiment is not confined to the army. The men and women who stay at home also assume a new attitude on the outbreak of a war that requires a great national effort. They are often no less ready than soldiers to restrict liberty. They do not shudder at reports of the loss of thou-

[82] See the data in SOROKIN, *Social Mobility*, Chaps. XVII–XIX and *passim*; and LOWELL, A. L., *op. cit.*, Chaps. V–VII.

sands of lives of their fellow citizens in a victorious battle, as they would at the loss of scores in an accident in time of peace. . . . They delight to work and deny themselves comforts in a way that they would otherwise think intolerable.[83]

The increase of patriotism, and hatred toward the enemy, readiness to underestimate his virtues and overestimate his defects, a willingness to believe anything favorable to their own country and unfavorable to the enemy,—all these, and many similar sudden changes of attitudes and disposition are usual in time of any war supported by the nation. There is no need to mention that the same fact may be observed in popular ideologies. Many ideologies, æsthetic values, political and moral opinions, literature, poetry, paintings, and so on,—popular in time of peace,—become unpopular in time of war, and *vice versa.*

This intensive circulation of social values continues to exist in the post-war years. They are marked by the changes in the way of readjustment to the new peace conditions. During the first few years after an armistice, society experiences an extraordinary change in this direction. One of its conspicuous characteristics is an increase in the unpopularity of many social values highly estimated in time of war, and an increase in the popularity of the values somewhat underestimated at that period.[84]

Such, in general, is the powerful influence of war in this field.

K. THE INFLUENCE OF WAR ON SCIENCE AND ARTS

Here again the existing opinions are quite opposite. According to the anti-militaristic writers, war's influence on intellectual progress of all kinds is entirely negative. *Inter arma silent musae,* was said long ago. "To actualize continually the entire capacity of the possible intellect" is possible only "amidst the calm tranquillity of peace" pleads Dante.[85]

War is a selection for the worse, which destroys the more cultivated and leaves the more barbarous. It has always held back mental progress, and at this very day it increases mental stagnation.

[83] LOWELL, A. L., *op. cit.*, pp. 223–234. See the whole of Chap. V.
[84] See in Lowell's work a concrete analysis of public opinion after the war. *Op. cit.*, Chaps. VI–VII.
[85] DANTE ALIGHIERI, *De Monarchia,* translated by Aurelia Henry, Boston, 1904, Chaps. II and III.

Such is a modern formula of the opinion.[86]   Another opinion was long ago formulated by J. de Maistre.   Following Euripides and Machiavelli, he says:

The best fruits of human nature, arts, sciences, great enterprises, great conceptions, and virile virtues, prosper especially in time of war. It is said that nations reach the peak of their grandeur only after long and bloody wars.   The climax of Greek civilization was reached in the terrible epoch of the Peloponnesian War; the most brilliant period of Augustus followed immediately after the Roman civil wars and proscriptions.   The French Genius was bred by the wars of the League, and was polished by that of the Fronde.   All great men of the time of Queen Anne (1665-1714) were born amidst a great political commotion.   In brief, they say that blood is a fertilizer of the plant which is called Genius.   I wonder whether they understood well when they say that *"arts are the friends of peace."*   Anyhow it would be necessary at least to explain and to clarify the statement because I do not see anything less pacifistic than the periods of Alexander the Great and Pericles; that of Augustus, Leo X, François I, Louis XIV and Queen Anne.[87]

These warring periods were marked by an extraordinary progress of science, arts, and philosophies, and of all kinds of intellectual achievement.   A more modern formulation of the same idea is as follows: "Unending peace would plunge all nations into a dangerous lethargy."   (Valbert, *op. cit.*, p. 692.)   "The certainty of peace would, before the expiration of half a century, engender a state of corruption, and decadence more destructive of men than the worst wars" (Melchior de Vogüé).

It is easy to see the fallacies of either of these opinions.   We know for instance that Japan, before its reformation, enjoyed a period of peace during almost three hundred years under the shogunate of Tokugawa.   And yet it did not corrupt it, nor did it render the country incapable of making wonderful progress when necessity came.   Nations like Switzerland, Holland, Norway, and Sweden have been enjoying peace during the last century; and yet their proportional contribution to the arts and

---

[86] Novicow, *War*, p. 59, Chap. VII; Nicolai, *op. cit.*, Chaps. II–IV; Nasmith, *op. cit.*, Chaps. V–VII; Todd, *op. cit.*, Chap. XIX.

[87] de Maistre, J., *Oeuvres*, Vol. I, pp. 36–37.   See the whole of Chapter III there.

sciences has not been less than that of many belligerent countries. We have also witnessed that the last war has considerably checked, at least temporarily, scientific and intellectual activities. There is no doubt also that war exterminates many scientists and literary men. It puts many obstacles in the way of creative intellectual activity. In brief, there is some truth in the statements of the war critics, but not in all of them. If the theory of de Maistre were quite wrong, the facts indicated by him could not have taken place. However, they happened; and, more than that, the correlation between the war periods and the extraordinary number of the great men of genius born in such a period, or immediately after it, seems to exist and is tangible in a much larger number of cases than those which are mentioned by de Maistre.[88]

Furthermore, we have seen that nations have been spending more time in war than in peace. If the influence of war were so deleterious as depicted by its critics, an intellectual progress could not possibly have taken place; but this happened. Furthermore, it is rather obvious that intellect counts a great deal in war. At such a time it is stimulated up to its limits in a specific direction. Its achievements for the purposes of war have almost always been used for quite peaceful purposes, and have contributed to intellectual progress in general. By its strong stimulation, excitement, and extraordinary conditions, the war situation has been responsible for the enlargement of human knowledge. In these and similar ways, war has exerted some beneficial effects on the development of sciences and arts. If there had been no war, we certainly would not have had either the *Odyssey, Iliad, Mahabharata, Makbet,* or a great many other poems, paintings, sculptures, architectural beauties, songs, symphonies, verses, and other works of art which have been inspired by war.[89] The same is true of a great many inventions beginning with various arms, and ending with aëroplanes, tanks, and poison gas.

This does not mean that we must close our eyes to the negative effects of war; it means only that the war influence is exceed-

---

[88] See some data in my *Social Mobility*, Chaps. XXI–XXII.
[89] See about this point, LEONTIEFF, K., *Visantism i Slavianstvo*, (Russian).

ingly complex and cannot be accurately described by a simple one-sided formula of its apologists or slanderers.

L. GENERAL CONCLUSION ABOUT THE EFFECTS OF WAR

The above survey shows that there is a series of correlations between the war phenomena, taken as an independent variable, and various aspects of social life taken as the dependent variable. Some of these correlations are seemingly certain and more or less studied. Some others, however, have been investigated little as yet, and represent guesses rather than scientific propositions. The authors have philosophized and moralized too much, and have studied objectively the facts in this field too little. If sociologists are going to promote our knowledge of war phenomena, they will have to quit moralizing (there are too many people who enjoy this business) and turn to a real study of the phenomena. Otherwise we are doomed to remain in the kingdom of half-truths.

5. WAR'S FACTORS

In the above, war has been taken as an independent variable and its "functions" have been traced. Now we may ask what are its factors or, in other words, what are the "variables" whose "function" is war. What phenomena facilitate the appearance of war and its increase, and what phenomena have the opposite results?

This part especially of the sociology of war, and of conflict, has been little investigated. We have dozens of varied theories which try to answer the question, yet the majority of them have scarcely any scientific value. In the first place, we have a series of theories whose answer consists in a mere reference to the "universal law of struggle" or to the "law of the struggle for existence." It is evident that such explanations do not contribute anything. We may grant that such a universal law exists, but the point is why, in a certain society at a certain period, there is no war; and why, in the same society at another period, war breaks out, expands, grows, and after some time, ends. The "universal law" does not help at all in answering the problem. A second variety of theories is represented by numerous "instinctive" theorists. Their general trait is that they look for the ultimate source of war in the field of instincts. Accordingly, we have "war instincts" and "patriotism instincts" as theories of war's causes. The "war instinct" is sometimes regarded as being similar to the "fighting instinct," as in the writings of Nicolai,[90] but in other cases the two are regarded as something quite different.[91] Other authors indicate a "fighting instinct" or an "instinct of pugnacity" as the source of war, (W. Mc-Dougall, H. R. Marshall, P. Bovet, and E. A. Ross).[92] Some sociologists indicate a "herd instinct" as indirectly responsible for the existence of war (W. Trotter).[93] Sociologists and psychologists, like Steinmetz, G. T. W. Patrick, W. H. R. Rivers, W. A. White, and some others indicate several varied instincts responsible for war, regarding it either as an outcome or as a drive for "rejuvenation," stimulated by a superabundance of the social bonds imposed by a social life and various social rules which finally repress the source of life itself; or as a form of relaxation from those conventional rules which, through their drudgery, monotony, and repression, tend to turn man into an automaton; or as an outlet for a satisfaction of the innate drives of anger, *wanderlust,* the military spirit, courage, the spirit of adventure, (*Mut, Wagelust, Grausamkeit*) and so on.[94] Some others have tried to connect war with hunger and the impossibility of satisfying the primary necessities of man, or with an increase in the number of obstacles before such a satisfaction.[95]

[90] See NICOLAI, *op. cit.,* Vol. I, pp. 20 ff.

[91] WOODS, F. A., *op. cit.,* pp. 17 ff.

[92] McDOUGALL, W., *Social Psychology,* pp. 280 ff.; MARSHALL, H. R., *War and the Ideal of Peace,* 1915, pp. 96 ff.; ROSS, E. A., *Principles,* pp. 44–45; BOVET, P., *The Fighting Instinct,* N. Y., 1923.

[93] TROTTER, W., *Instincts of the Herd in Peace and War,* London, 1916.

[94] STEINMETZ, *Phil. des Krieges,* pp. 233, 294; PATRICK, G. T. W., "The Psychology of War," *Popular Science Monthly,* 1915, pp. 166–168; WHITE, W. A., *Thoughts of a Psychiatrist on the War and After,* 1919, pp. 75–87; CRILE, G. M., *A Mechanistic View of Peace and War,* 1916; RUSSELL, B., *Why Men Fight,* 1917; CONWAY, M., *The Crowd in Peace and War,* 1916; ELTINGE, B., *Psychology of War,* 1915; THORNDIKE, E. L., *Original Nature of Man,* Chap. VI; WATSON, J. B., *Psychology,* Chap. VI; PARK and BURGESS, *Introduction,* Chap. IX; HALL, G. S., "Some Relations between the War and Psychology," *American Journal Psychology,* 1919; LE BON, G., *The Psychology of the Great War,* 1916; RIVERS, W. H. R., *Instinct and Unconscious,* Cambridge, 1921.

[95] SOROKIN, *The Influence of Famine and Food Factor,* Chap. VII; BAKELESS, J., *The Economic Causes of Modern War,* N. Y., 1921.

In brief, we have numerous and divergent "instinct" theories of war. Their kernel is probably true, but, unfortunately, the majority of them again do not solve the problem satisfactorily. We may grant that a fighting instinct, war instinct, or some other drive is the source of war; but does this explain why a society is in a state of war at a certain time, and in peace at another period, or why one society is very belligerent, while another one is relatively peaceful? If the source of war is a certain instinct or drive, it should exist permanently. Granting this, there is still no explanation that would make clear why at some periods it manifests itself, while at others it is ineffective. In order that these hypotheses might be satisfactory, they would have to explain from the "instinct" standpoint the real curve of war phenomena. They must show why, for instance, a "fighting instinct" called forth war in 1914 rather than in 1909; and why certain peoples participated in this war while other nations remained out of it. Why was the war terminated in 1918 rather than in 1915 or 1935? Why have there been relatively peaceful periods in the history of a nation, and other periods crowded with war? The majority of the discussed theories do not even attempt to answer such questions. For this reason their insufficiency is evident.

The same may be said of the majority of the other theories of war factors, which see these factors in "dynastic interests," in "religious heterogeneity," in "economic factors," in the "diplomatic and political machinations," in a lust for domination, self-expression, and what not. As far as such theories limit their "explanations" by merely mentioning these factors, and by a few considerations of their importance, they do not factually give any valid theory. To hold such a theory they must explain when, why, under what conditions, and in what way their factor is an efficient cause of war; and why, under what conditions, and so on, it has no such influence. In brief, such a theory must "interpret" the real fluctuation of the war curve. It must take the facts of war and correlate them with their factor, showing that it "fits" to the curve of war. Otherwise, such a theory is of no use. Only a very few of the existing theories make an attempt to perform such a factual verification. Unfortunately, a great many of such theories are defective too, sometimes even more defective than many instinctive theories.[96]

Here we may finish our analysis of what has been said above. So much for the Darwinian school of the struggle for existence and its interpretation.

The fourth important branch of biological sociology is represented by the "instinctivist interpretations" of social phenomena. However, in view of the mixing of "instinctive forces" with other psychological factors in such theories, it would be more convenient to analyze them in the chapters devoted to the psychological school in sociology.

6. GENERAL CONCLUSION ABOUT BIOLOGICAL SOCIOLOGY

In spite of its many defects, taken as a whole, the school has represented one of the most powerful currents of sociological thought; has thrown light on many social phenomena; has given a series of valuable correlations; and has shown many deep factors which lie under the picturesque surface of the social ocean. For these reasons it must be recognized as one of the most important sociological schools. Whether we like it or not, it will exist. The greater and more accurate are the findings of biology, the more accurate are going to be the biological interpretations of social phenomena, and the more powerful influence they are likely to exert on sociological thought in the future. It is useless and hopeless to try to shut the gates of sociology to an intrusion of biological interpretations, as is urged by some "formal sociologists" at the present time. Such an isolation will do no good to sociology, while its harmful results are rather evident. An in-

---

[96] As an example we may take E. Hovelaque's *Deeper Causes of the War*, London, 1917. Trying to elucidate the causes of the World War, he indicates purely "environmental" factors, such as Prussia's preceding history, its militant character, its militant leaders, "militant Prussian spirit," German philosophy, "belief in superiority," miraculous influence of F. Nietzsche, Treitschke, Bernhardi, and so on. It is needless to say how utterly fallacious the whole theory is. As a matter of fact, under the Hohenzollerns, Prussia had a fewer number of war years than any other big European country. (See the figures in this chapter.) It is fallacious to make only Prussia responsible for the war. It is certain also that among the English, the French, the Russian thinkers, historians, writers, and so on there has been a crowd of apologists for war, struggle, patriotism, nationalism, "militant spirit," and all this sort of thing. In brief, the whole theory represents a political pamphlet much less satisfactory than the above "instinctivist" theories of war.

crease of bad scholastics, useless word-polishing, and a sterile terminological discussion, on the one hand; and on the other, a backward "self-made" or "home-made" biology *ad hoc* fallacious in its essence, are likely to be the effects of such an isolation. This has happened in the past and it is probable in the future, if such a "formal" claim is carried on. To avoid it, we must follow the findings of biology, taking from them what is really scientific and throwing away that which is "pseudo-scientific." Such is the reasonable course which may be taken by the sociologists in regard to the "biological interpretation" of social phenomena.

CHAPTER VII

BIO-SOCIAL BRANCH: DEMOGRAPHIC SCHOOL

U N D E R this school I shall survey the theories which assume the demographic factor to be a primary or important "variable," and consequently attempt to interpret social phenomena as a function, or resultant of this factor. By the demographic factor is meant the increase or decrease of the size and density of a population. The qualitative aspect of population will be omitted here since it has been discussed in the chapter on the Racial School.

I. PREDECESSORS

The most ancient sources of social thought, and the oldest practices of ancient societies, show that human beings were aware, long ago, of the important rôle played by demographic factors in the field of social phenomena. Both the quantitative and the qualitative aspects of the population problem were appreciated to some degree. As a result, certain social practices arose. Their purpose was either to increase or to decrease the size of the population and to improve its quality. The Biblical admonition, "Be fruitful, and multiply, and replenish the earth" is a typical illustration of a great many ancient ideas and practices destined to increase the population—a condition believed necessary for the continued existence and prosperity of a given society. On the other hand, certain practices and *mores,* such as obligatory celibacy, the killing of old people and babies, prescribed abortion, etc., are found among many primitive societies.[1] These practices, whose objective was to check or to decrease the population, indicate that many societies were somehow aware of a danger of overpopulation. The statement in Genesis which says that Abraham's and Lot's herdsmen and cattle increased to such an extent

---

[1] See CARR-SAUNDERS, A. M., *The Population Problem,* Chaps. I, VII, VIII, IX, Oxford, 1922; REUTER, E. B., *Population Problems,* Chap. III, Philadelphia, 1923; STRANGELAND, C. E., *Pre-Malthusian Doctrines of Population,* N. Y., 1908.

that "the land was not able to bear them that they might dwell together; for their substance was great, so that they could not dwell together," and "The Zend-Avesta's" theory of the periodical over-population of the earth,[2] are typical illustrations of the same fact. With still greater reason it is possible to contend that ancient peoples also understood the qualitative side of the population problem. "Eugenics" is not an invention of the nineteenth century. Thousands of years before our era, eugenics was widely practiced in ancient Sparta and India, in China, and among the Jews, to mention only a few societies.[3]

There is no need to say that, since the appearance of individual social thinkers, a large number of them have paid attention to the factor of population. In their statements they have proposed practically all types of hypotheses which, in a more developed form, constitute the leading contemporary theories of population. Confucius, Mencius, Plato, Aristotle, Polybius, Seneca, Cicero, Lucretius, St. Thomas Aquinas, the Church Fathers, Ibn-Khaldun, Campanella, Machiavelli, J. Bodin, Luther, Botero, Colbert, W. Petty, Graunt, Justi, Sonnenfels, Zincke, the Cameralists, Ch. Davenant, W. Temple, Holinshed, the Mercantilists, the Physiocrats (Quesnay and others), Bruckner, C. Beccaria, A. Young, F. Briganti, J. J. Rousseau, J. Steuart, Hume, Wallace, Adam Smith, Price, Ortes,—these are only a few names from a long list of those who set forth various theories of population prior

---

[2] Genesis, xiii: 6; "The Zend-Avesta," *The Sacred Books of the East*, Vol. IV, Oxford, 1880, Farg. II: 9 ff. "The earth has become full of flocks and herds of men and dogs . . . and there is no more room for flocks, herds, and men." This led to the necessity of a periodical enlargement of the earth by Yima. "The Zend-Avesta" was composed probably about A.D. 325, though its contents are much older.

[3] See the chapter about the Racial School; ROPER, A. G., *Ancient Eugenics*, Oxford, 1913; SCHALLMAYER, W., *Vererbung und Auslese*, 2nd ed., pp. 142 ff.; SOROKIN, *Social Mobility*, Chap. IX. I cannot agree with Carr-Saunders that "the problem of quality did not arouse the same early interest" (as the problem of quantity), *op. cit.*, p. 18. Roper gives a quite sufficient proof that the qualitative side of the problem, at least in the way of trial and error, was understood as early as the quantitative side. A study of *The Sacred Books of the East*, especially of India and China, and the study of the practices of Sparta and other societies, does not leave any doubt that the "eugenic" side of the problem was understood in the past, perhaps even better than its quantitative aspect. In the *Laws of Manu, Brichaspat, Narâda, Gautama, Institutes of Vishnu*, and other books of ancient India, the "eugenic" side of the problem is the leading idea of all their contents.

to the time of Malthus (1766-1834).[4] After Malthus' epoch-making *Essay on the Principle of Population* (first edition in 1798), there have been few prominent economists, sociologists, political scientists, psychologists, practical reformers, demographers, statisticians, and eugenists who have not discussed the problem.[5] It is not my purpose to survey all these theories. In many of them the number and the density of population are viewed as an effect of other variables, rather than as their cause. My purpose is to take only such contemporary theories as interpret the social processes as a function of the demographic factor. Taking the principal theories of this type, we shall be able to cover the fundamental generalizations formulated in this field at least.

2. ADOLPHE COSTE

There is scarcely any other sociological theory which allots to size and density of population such importance as is done in the theory of Adolphe Coste, a former president of the Statistical and the Sociological Society of Paris. I shall begin my survey of the demographic theories with that of Coste, not because his works are especially valuable, or because he originated such a theory, but because of his attempt to make the demographic factor a kind of an all-sufficient key to account for important "social processes." The basic ideas of his theory were laid down before him by M. Kovalevsky, whom he mentions as his predecessor, and the originator of his theory,[6] by A. Loria, Yves Guyot, P. Mougeolle, and L. Winiarsky, whose works Coste did not know before the publication of his books.[7]

[4] See CARR-SAUNDERS, *op. cit.*, Chap. I; REUTER, *op. cit.*, Chaps. III, IV; STRANGELAND, *op. cit., passim;* SMALL, A., *The Cameralists;* HANEY, W. H., *History of Economic Thought;* REYNAUD, *La théorie de la population en Italie du XVI au XVIII siècle,* Paris, Lyon, 1904.

[5] The literature is enormous. See the principal theories in REUTER, Chap. V; THOMPSON, W., *Population; A Study in Malthusianism,* N. Y., 1915; the texts in economics by G. Schmoller, A. Marshall, F. Taussig, E. Seligman, R. Ely, or any other substantial text; LEROY-BEAULIEU, P., *La question de la population,* Paris, 1913; the treatises on demography by A. Oettingen, G. von Mayr, E. Levasseur, and others; WOLF, J., *Die Volkswirtschaft der Gegenwart und Zukunft,* 1912; *Der Geburtenrückgang,* 1912; BUDGE, *Das Malthus'sche Bevolkerungsgesetz und die theoretische Nationalökonomie der letzten Jahrzehnte,* 1912.

[6] See COSTE, A., *Les principes d'une sociologie objective,* p. 107, Paris, 1899.

[7] COSTE, A., *L'expérience des peuples et les prévisions qu'elle autorise,* pp. III-IV, Paris, 1900.

The essentials of Coste's sociological theory are as follows: 1. There are two fundamental categories of historical facts: the social and the ideological phenomena. By the "social facts" Coste means the phenomena of government, production, distribution of economic or useful things, beliefs, and solidarity. By "the ideological" fact he means the phenomena of non-practical arts, such as poetry, philosophy, various ideologies, including theoretical and non-applied sciences which do not have useful or utilitarian character. These two categories of phenomena must be discriminated between very decisively. While the social phenomena of government, production, belief, and solidarity are closely correlated with one another in their fluctuation and evolution, "the ideological" phenomena do not show any close correlation with "the social phenomena." In other words, "sociality" and "ideological mentality" are independent from one another. Four categories of facts corroborate this statement, according to Coste.

In the first place, the absence of a correlation between "the social and the ideological phenomena" is shown by the fact that the great "intellectuals" or creators of "the ideological values" have not regularly appeared within the most powerful societies, as would have been the case had there been a correlation between the "sociality" and "ideological mentality." The ideologies of Christianity, of Buddhism, and of Mohammedanism, appeared among the peoples who were far from being powerful or advanced. A small Greece produced the most wonderful poets, philosophers, intellectuals, and artists. But this abundance of ideological mentality did not much influence the sociality of Greece. Certainly, it did not make it a strong society. The Romans were much more ignorant and less cultured than the Greeks, the Egyptians, or many other peoples; but they succeeded in organizing a wonderful governmental, juridical, military, and social machinery; and in this way, in spite of being poor in the "ideological achievements," they rendered a greater service to the progress of sociality than did the Greeks. In the fifteenth and the sixteenth centuries Italy and France were incomparably superior, in regard to "ideologies," to Germany, Holland, and England; but these countries were far superior in their commercial, governmental, religious, and political organizations to France or Italy.

In the second place, the same absence of correlation is shown by the fact that the great intellectuals have appeared in the epochs of social progress, as well as in those of social decay. In the period of decay in sociality they appear even more often than in the period of political, economic, governmental, and religious well-being. This could not have happened if the two categories were correlated. In Greece and Rome the most brilliant "ideological" period (of philosophy, arts, poetry, architecture, literature and so on) was also the period of social disorganization and decay. We see the same in Italy in the period of the Renaissance.

In the third place, the absence of the correlation is manifest in the fact that the same race, the same epoch, and the same social conditions give rise to the most different ideological geniuses; and, *vice versa,* similar intellectuals appear under the most different social conditions. The "social" facts of each society are stamped by its racial or national traits, while the "ideological" facts are cosmopolitan, international, and free from any marks of the society in which they were originated. If the social and the ideological phenomena were correlated, this could not have happened.

In the fourth place, in the movement of the ideological phenomena there is no continuity, permanent progress, nor regularity. They appear and disappear whimsically, flourishing and decaying, while in social phenomena there is continuity, regularity, and mutual correlation.

Since the "ideological" facts are not influenced by the "social" phenomena, the latter are independent of the former, too. "Exterminate one or two dozen of the ideological Geniuses, and theoretical science and the non-useful arts would disappear." But this would not change the "social phenomena" at all. "The ideological achievements," whether they be the Pythagorean theory of numbers, Plato's theory of ideas, Epicurus' theory of atoms, the monadology of Leibnitz, the Newtonian law of gravitation, or the Lamarckian and Darwinian theory of evolution, are not known to the masses, and have no practical influence on them. If these theories should disappear, this would not noticeably influence the course of the "social phenomena." They are quite different from the social facts, which, besides being always useful, are the result of mass-activity, and of common needs, mutual suggestion, interstimulation, and division of labor.[8] The ideological phenomena are purely individual creations, and remain a possession of the few only. All this shows their difference and independence.

2. Since "the social and the ideological facts" are quite different, they must be studied by different sciences: the social facts by sociology, and the ideological facts by "the ideology." This would be a science somewhat similar to psychology but radically changed. The physiological part should go into biology, and the non-physiological part would be transformed, for the present, into "ideology."[9]

3. Correspondingly, in the classification of science, sociology must be put after biology, as was done by Comte, while ideology must follow sociology.[10]

4. Turning to the social facts,—government, production, beliefs, and solidarity,—Coste finds that they follow a definite sequence of five stages in their evolution, each stage being correlated with the others. The essentials of his theory of social evolution are given in the table on page 363.[11] Putting the amount and the concentration of the population at the basis of the classification, Coste gives the stages in the social evolution of the peoples who passed by purely animal stages in the same table. From this scheme it follows that in the development of the principal forms of social phenomena there is a definite sequence; that these forms are correlated with one another; and that there is a linear historical tendency toward a progressive division of social functions and an increase of free coöperation, at the cost of a progressive decrease in inequality.

5. If we ask now what factor is responsible for the above evo-

---

[8] *Principes*, Chaps. II, XXII; *L'expérience*, Chap. I.

[9] *Principes*, Chaps. III, IV; *L'expérience*, Chap. II.

[10] *Principes*, Chap. V. Coste's classification of sciences is a modified classification of August Comte; see p. 57.

[11] *Ibid.*, Chaps. IX, XII, XIV. See the Table on pages 150–151; *L'expérience*, Table on pp. 584–587. Practically the whole volume of Coste's *L'expérience des peuples* is devoted to the description of these five principal stages of social evolution.

Stages According to the Mass and the Concentration of the Population	Social Activities in Their Evolution of Differentiation and Their Character	Type of Solidarity and the Tendency Toward a Decrease of Inequality
I. Bourg	Lack of division of social activities	Absolutism of family, and supremacy based on birth
II. City superposed on bourgs	*Division of functions* Military government, socio-morphic and polytheistic religion; family-production	Military-religious supremacy Castes The only property: land
III. Metropolis superposed on cities	*Government* Two authorities: military and civil *Religion* Theistic and monistic, plus mathematical science *Production* Family-system, manufacture, commerce	Supremacy of state embodied in a prince and his officials; classes and privileges; *Property:* land and capital
IV. Capital superposed on the great cities	*Government* Three authorities: military, administrative, legislative *Religion* Half rational, mathematical science, physical science *Production* Family; manufacture; machinofacture; better transportation	Supremacy of wealth based on individualism and inequality of inheritance and instruction. *Property:* land, capital, mobile values
V. Center of Federation superposed on the capitals	*Government* Four authorities: military, administrative, legislative, judicial *Religion* Rational science: mathematical, physical, biological *Production* Previous forms plus "vivifacture" (utilization of vital forces)	Supremacy of free associations, tending to the supremacy of intelligence and the equality of protection for individuals *Property:* the preceding forms, plus patents on inventions and shares

lution of social phenomena, the answer is : *the growth of the population and its density.* Animal societies are stagnant because they are limited numerically. Human societies are progressive because they are ever increasing in their size and density. This leads to an increase of interaction, to its intensification, to an exchange of experience, and to its accumulation and transmission from generation to generation. The first great organized societies appeared where the concentration of the population (the valley of the Nile, in Chaldea, in India, in China) was great. The first brilliant civilizations emerged in Greece, Tyre, Athens, and Carthage, for the same reason. The first great military unification of societies by Babylon, Egypt, and Rome were made possible by the same factor of abundance of population, and its integration into compact social bodies. On the other hand, when the size and the density of a population decreases, the progress of a civilization stops, as happened after the depopulation of the Roman Empire, and during the first centuries of the Middle Ages. Omitting other arguments of Coste in favor of his hypothesis, we may say that the

numerical increase of the members of a society is the primary cause of its whole evolution. The increase of a unified population leads to an increase of social differentiation, and to a division of labor and of social aptitudes, facilitating the communication of various parts of the society, and making possible a better and more powerful coördination of the individual actions, and a more and more accurate representation of the unity of natural laws.

Soil, climate, and race may, to some extent, facilitate and check human aggregation, but they are not the primary factors of social evolution.[12]

6. Logically developing his idea, Coste finally tries to establish "the sociometrika" to measure the relative power of different societies. Since the mass and the density of a population are the primary factors of sociality, the social powers of various societies could be approximately measured through the number of its population and its density measured by the concentration of the population or the proportion of the population of the big and the small cities, to the whole population of the society. Combining

[12] *Principes*, pp. 95–103; *L'expérience, passim,* and pp. 588 ff.

these criteria, Coste gives the following final index of the social powerfulness of various nations: [13]

Table I			Table II
Power of the States (on the basis of the population at the end of the nineteenth century)			Sociality or Social Cohesion
States	Index of National Power [14] (France taken 100)		Index of Sociality [15]
A. *Great States*			
Great Britain..................	155		152
Russia........................	136		49
Germany......................	121		89
France........................	100		100
U. S. A.	70 or 74		44
Japan....................	73		66
Austria-Hungary...............	69 or 70		61
Italy.........................	49		60
Turkey.......................	45		70
Spain........................	36		77
Average for ten great states...	94		71
B. *Small States*			
Belgium......................	19		112
Holland......................	14		107
Sweden-Norway...............	11		60
Rumania.....................	9		64
Portugal...............	9		67
Switzerland..................	5		64
Average for six small states....	13		82

Since Social Power is equal to the size of the Population multiplied by Sociality (density)—Social Power $=$ Population $\times$ Sociality—it follows that a nation's sociality is equal to its so-

[13] The methods of computation are somewhat different in *Principes* and in *L'expérience*. Correspondingly different are his indices also. I give here the table from *L'expérience* because, according to Coste, it is more accurate. See *Principes*, Chap. XV; *L'expérience*, pp. 591 ff.

[14] *L'expérience*, pp. 602–603.

[15] *Ibid.*, p. 606.

cial power divided by the population— $\dfrac{\text{Social Power}}{\text{Population}} = \text{Sociality}$.
Table II gives the indices of the sociality of various nations computed according to this formula.

Such are the essentials of Coste's sociological theory.

Criticism.—Taken as a whole, Coste's theory represents a mixture of sociological objectivism and unbridled speculation; correct observations and fantastic generalizations.

1. His discrimination of "the social and the ideological phenomena" is vague and doubtful. One cannot understand why he puts some beliefs, arts, and theories within the category of "social facts," while some others are called "ideological facts," [16] or why the same "ideologies" like Buddhism and Christianity sometimes function as the "social", sometimes as the "ideological" phenomena. The criterion of "practical usefulness" does not help, because a great many purely abstract theories, like the majority of the theories of physics and chemistry, are, according to Coste, "ideological" phenomena. However, only a mentally blind man could deny the great practical utility which has come out of such abstract theories. On the other hand, a considerable number of beliefs which Coste regards as "the social, useful phenomena" seem to fail in showing their usefulness. It is also hard to see why religion is put among the "social" while arts and

[16] Coste's attitude in this respect is shown by the following quotation: "The Egyptians and the Babylonians *knew* how to build enormous constructions and how to solve practical, difficult problems long before algebra, geometry, and mechanics were established. Hannon encircled Africa; Himilcon discovered Great Britain; Columbus, Vasco de Gama, and Magellan crossed the Atlantic, the Indian, and the Pacific Oceans before Copernicus, Newton, and Kepler founded astronomy. The practical art of navigation preceded the science of astronomy as the social inventors preceded the 'ideological' ones. In the same way, agriculture, cattle breeding, medicine, and surgery did not wait until biology was founded by Bichat and Claude Bernard. Jenner made his discovery of vaccination in 1776,—a century before Pasteur's microbiology found its explanation. . . It goes without saying that science, after its establishment, reacts on useful applications through the generalization of empirical inventions, and the formulation of general laws. Ideology may be very useful for a society, but it does not precede it, and does not control it at all," *L'expérience*, p. 6. The table of multiplication and arithmetical rules seems also to be "ideologies," according to Coste. His fallacy is clear from the above. His so-called applied science is nothing but a preceding and a less generalized stage of knowledge confronting its later and more generalized stage. To differentiate one from the other, as something quite different qualitatively, is evidently fallacious.

sciences are placed among the "ideological" facts. From the standpoint of usefulness, science scarcely could be recognized as less useful than religion. Further, if we take from religion its cult, arts, ceremonies, architecture, paintings and music, I wonder how much there would remain of religion and its useful efficiency. More than that, if the ideological creations were really useless, they could not have survived, as useless things. In the process of elimination of values and activities, they would have been eliminated long ago. Yet they still exist and do not show any symptom of disappearance. There is scarcely any need to dwell longer on this point. Coste's classification is unsupportable. His estimation of science, and of a great many other "useless" things is fallacious. In brief, this part of his theory, and the discrimination of sociology and ideology resulting from it, are erroneous. The only sound point is Coste's insistence on the absence of a close connection between "sociality" and "mentality." As a counterbalance against the one-sidedness of the sociologistic theory, which explains the whole mentality as a product of social interaction or sociality, Coste's theory may be of service. But again, he, like L. Winiarsky,[17] falls into an opposite error. Both

[17] L. Winiarsky pretends that he was the first who indicated the antagonism of sociality and mentality. See L. WINIARSKY's "Réclamation au sujets des principes d'une sociologie objective de M. A. Coste," *La revue socialiste*, Vol. XXXI, 1900, pp. 419–421. In his interesting paper, "Essai d'une nouvelle interprétation de phénomènes sociologiques," *Revue socialiste*, Vol. XXIV, 1896, pp. 308–328, 430–454, Winiarsky tried to show first, that, as a biological type, those organisms are the most superior which are the most differentiated and the most integrated; second, that the social life, through division of labor, tends to decrease this differentiated integrity of an organism, and to substitute a one-sided "professional" type for it; third, that through this it favors the survival of narrow specialized types at the cost of the universal, many-sided type; fourth, that, through this, social life and social cohesion hinder the development of mentality, intelligence, or intellectual genius. The most important characteristic of a real genius is his universality, many-sidedness, and all-embracing mind. These become more and more impossible through social differentiation. Fifth, an ideal sociality means an ideal mental stagnation, and leads to it. These statements are supported by the fact that, among the animals, those who live in societies are inferior to the varieties of the same species which live an isolated life; that societies with a strong social cohesion are mentally dull, while the societies with a less strong social cohesion are superior in intelligence; and that, in the history of the same society, the periods of social disorganization are marked by an extraordinary intellectual achievement and an extraordinarily abundant number of geniuses, while the periods of strong social order are marked by a decrease in intellectual activity, organized "mob-psychology" and by mental stagnation. From this, Winiarsky concludes that the progress of social

authors are right as far as they contend that human intelligence
and mentality cannot be accounted for completely through social conditions.   They are right also in claiming that the correlation between "sociality" and "intelligence" is not close, and not
always positive.   Sometimes "progress of mind" and progress of
"social cohesion" are in conflict.   Within these limits, their
theory is generally valid.   It conspicuously shows the fallacies
of the sociologistic and the solidaristic schools, which insist upon
a complete parallelism in the development of mentality and sociality, making the former a mere result of the latter.   (See chapter about the sociologistic school.)   But both authors are wrong
as far as they regard mentality or "ideology" as something quite
independent from the "social" phenomena of Coste or the "sociality" of Winiarsky.   Even the fact of a greater intellectual
activity in the periods of social disorganization points to a correlation between sociality and mentality, mentioned by Winiarsky.
As I tried to show elsewhere, it is easily explained through social
conditions.   In addition, my study led to the conclusion that there
are also limits in this negative correlation.   Social disorganization which goes too far, leads to an intellectual decay instead of

cohesion and gregariousness leads to a lowering individual mentality, to a decrease
in the number of geniuses, and to a kind of mental sterility.   Such are the essentials of his study, and they are indeed similar to the theory of Coste.   Winiarsky's
claim that he originated this theory, however, is not valid.   Twenty years before
his paper came out, this same theory, only in a much better form, was published
by N. K. Mikhailovsky in his *What is Progress?*, *Darwinism and Social Sciences*,
Struggle for Individuality, and other works.   His name is not mentioned by
Winiarsky, but from the paper I conclude that Winiarsky is probably a Pole,
reads Polish, and may be even Russian.   It is probable that Winiarsky's theory
was elaborated not without the influence of Mikhailovsky, for even his terminology is practically identical with that of Mikhailovsky.   To this it is necessary
to add that the ineffectual rôle of ideologists and ideologies in Coste's sense was
indicated many centuries before by a great many authors.   It is enough for us
to remember Machiavelli's contemptuous estimation of ideologists and ideologies.
More recently the same opinion was held by Napoleon.   Furthermore, many
thinkers, like Fustel de Coulanges, many times stated the "striking inefficiency
of ideas and theories for the betterment of human existence."—DE COULANGES,
F., *Histoire des institutions politiques de l'ancienne France*, Vol. I, p. 200.   Finally,
in its own way, the same idea is maintained by the Marxian school of the economic
interpretation of history.   These remarks are sufficient to show that neither
Coste, nor Winiarsky, nor anybody else among the sociologists of the end of the
nineteenth century, can claim the privilege of originating the above, or practically
any other theory.   They have only been developing that which was known
many centuries, even thousand of years, ago.

an intellectual blossoming.[18]   This shows that the partial truth which is in Coste's statement is practically submerged in the greater fallacy of his sweeping generalization.   Furthermore, if the ideological phenomena are independent from the social phenomena (and also from race, geographic environment, climate, and soil), one wonders on what they are dependent.   Should we conclude that they represent a miracle?   It would be a waste of time if I were to array here the long series of other objections against the discussed proposition.

2. As to Coste's theory of the stages of social evolution, we may pass it without discussion.   It represents a variety of "the laws of evolution" or "historical tendencies" which, after Comte's "law of the three stages," became very fashionable.   At the present moment it may be enjoyed by freshmen only.   Neither the supposition of a similarity in the social evolution of various peoples; nor the linear conception of evolution, consisting in a definite sequence of certain "stages"; nor the optimistic, but quite speculative prophecy of the future millennium toward which "the evolution" is leading, have ever been proved, and they seem to have lost their fascination for contemporary social thinkers. All such theories have been nothing but a kind of metaphysics. (See the chapter about the linear and cyclical conception of the social process.)

3. It is curious to note that the fundamental point of Coste's theory—the primacy of the factor of population growth—remains almost uncorroborated by Coste.   He puts it flatly, gives a few of the mentioned illustrations, and that is all.   This naturally makes us conclude that he has not proved the thesis.   Such dogmatism naturally entitles us to leave it without discussion, as a thesis which has not been corroborated.

4. This may be done still more easily because Coste's "Sociometrika" shows conspicuously a fallacy in his theory.   É. Levasseur rightly remarks that, according to Coste's criterion, the

---

[18] See SOROKIN, *Social Mobility*, Chap. XXI. This, by the way, once more shows the necessity of finding the limits and optimum point of sociological correlations.   When an author fails to indicate the limits to which a correlation goes, and flatly states that it is positive or negative, and that with an increase of A its function B will increase (or decrease), he is bound to make a fallacy, because there are few cases, if any, where a correlation goes beyond all limits.

Shantung province in China, with an average density of population of 221 should be much more civilized and powerful than France, because France's average density is only 73. Such a conclusion will scarcely be accepted by many.[19]   I doubt also whether there are many sensible people who would agree with the indices of power and sociality of various nations given above. The years following the publication of Coste's works and the years of the World War seem to have disproved Coste's tabulation.   Such a "pragmatic" test is one of the most certain criteria of the validity or fallacy of "an ideology."   In this case it testifies against Coste's theory.

Nevertheless, the above does not mean a complete denial of the value of Coste's books.   In spite of the fallacies, they are suggestive and stimulating.   Coste's one-sidedness is a good anti-poison against the one-sidedness of other theories.   His statements are always clear, and are not wrapped in the thick cloak of abstract phraseology and conceptual definitions under which many "thinkers" hide a lack of thought.   Coste is a thinker, and a good one, but, unfortunately, one-sided.

Let us now pass to other more mature, though less sweeping theories which try to establish a correlation between the demographic factors and other social phenomena.

3.   SIZE AND DENSITY OF THE POPULATION AND VITAL PROCESSES

Can the size and the density of a population be a factor in the birth, death, and population-growth rates?   Is there any correlation between the first and the second series of phenomena?   The question has been answered positively by many a prominent investigator.   Let us notice in the first place the influence of the mentioned demographic factors on the death rate.

Demographic Factors and the Death Rate.—Already P. E. Verhulst, Dr. W. Farr, H. Westergaard, and several other demographers, have indicated the existence of a positive correlation between the density and the death rate of a given population.[20]

---

[19] LEVASSEUR, É., "La repartition de la race humaine," *Bulletin de l'Institut International de Statistique*, Vol. XVIII, 2-e. livr., p. 62.

[20] See VERHULST, P. E., "Recherches mathém. sur la loi d'accroissement de la population," *Nouveaux memoires de l'Académie R. des Sciences de Bruxelles*,

Later on, a series of investigators such as R. Pearl, T. H. C. Stevenson, Reed, S. L. Parker, J. Brownlee, A. Drzwina and G. Bohn, A. Bowley, and G. U. Yule have shown that there is at least a *tendency* toward an increase in the death rate with an increase in the density of the population, providing other conditions are more or less constant.[21]

The methods of obtaining these correlations, and of measuring the density of the population, have varied greatly, beginning with the experimental methods used in regard to *Drosophila* and some other organisms (by Pearl, Parker, F. Bilski, K. Semper, Drzwina, G. Bohn and others), and ending with various statistical methods applied to a human population. If, in the experimental works with *Drosophila,* the density could be measured accurately, and other conditions could be controlled, the same could not be said of a human population. To find an accurate criterion for the measurement of its density is very difficult. This explains the variety of methods used for this purpose. Some authors, like Dr. Farr, measured the density by the number of persons per unit of area, or (like Dr. Brownlee) by dividing the population of an administrative district by its area. Some others, like T. T. S. de Jastrzebsky, A. Bowley, and R. Pearl, measured it by the number of persons per room or by the indices of "crowding" and "overcrowding." Some other investigators have measured the density through the per capita wealth of the population. Whatever the methods employed, the authors properly recognize that at best they may give only an approximate index of the density of population. I mention this to show how

---

1845, t. XVIII, pp. 1–38; "Deuxième memoire sur la loi d'accroissement de la population," *ibid.,* t. XX, 1847, pp. 1–32; FARR, W., *Vital Statistics,* Stanford, 1885, pp. 172 ff.; "Causes of the high mortality in town districts," *Fifth Annual Report Registrar General, of Births, Deaths, and Marriages in England,* 2nd ed., pp. 406–435; "Effects of Density of Population on Health," *Supplement to the Thirty-fifth Annual Report of the Registrar General,* 1875, pp. XXIII–XXV; WESTERGAARD, H., *Die Lehre von der Mortalität und Morbidität,* pp. 455 ff., Jena, 1901.

[21] PEARL, R., *The Biology of Population Growth, passim* and Chap. VI, N. Y., 1925; BROWNLEE, J., "Density and Death-rate: Farr's law," *Journal of the Royal Statistical Society,* 1920, pp. 281–283; BOWLEY, A., "Death-rates, Density, Population and Housing," *Journal of the Royal Statistical Society,* 1923, pp. 516–539; YULE, G. U., "The Growth of Population and the Factors which Control It," *ibid.,* 1925, pp. 23 ff.; STEVENSON, T. H. E., "The Laws Governing Population," *ibid.,* 1925, pp. 67 ff.; see other references in these works.

great are the difficulties to be overcome in obtaining a valid association. To give an idea of the results obtained, I shall insert a
few figures. Here is the table obtained by the simplest statistical
method used by Dr. W. Farr: [22]

Number of Deaths Annually per 100,000 Population in England	Number of Inhabitants per One Square Mile
1,270	138
1,345	149
1,448	187
1,541	214
1,647	307
1,735	435
1,855	662
1,935	1,281
2,043	1,803
.....	.....
.....	.....
3,300	19,584

The density of the population increasing, the death rate increases
also.

Dr. Bowley's (1869–   ) coefficients of the correlation between the death rate and various indices of the density of the
population in England give an idea of the results obtained by
a finer method of statistical analysis. The coefficients of correlation of the standard death rate for specified parts of England
with a specified criterion of density are as follows: [23]

	London	South England	North England	Black Country	All Districts
With log. of density.	.635	.104	.429	.268	.246
Persons per room...	.842	.198	.477	.312	.581

[22] *Supplement to the Fifty-fifth Annual Report of Registrar General*, etc., 1895,
p. xlvii.

[23] BOWLEY, *op. cit.*, p. 522, Table I. In the table there are given more detailed
coefficients of correlation with "crowding" and "overcrowding," indices of
density, of the death rate and infant mortality, and corresponding regression
equations.

These, and the other studies mentioned, seem to suggest that a positive association between the population density and death rate exists. However, in spite of the considerable probability of such a correlation, the corresponding data suggest that either the association exists only within a definite range of density, beyond which it becomes intangible; or the effect of the density is so weak as to be overcome by the interference of other factors. There are also the possibilities that the correlation is due not so much to density, properly, as to poverty and similar factors, co-existing usually with "crowding" and "overcrowding"; or that the sum total of all these considerations is the cause. That the correlation may exist only within definite range of the density, beyond which it tends to disappear, is supported by Bowley's data concerning the rural district of England (*Ibid.*, p. 535). In the south of England and Wales, the correlation of the death rate with the number of persons per room is quite insignificant (0.05 and 0.16). That the possible influence of the density on the death rate of the population may easily be annulled by other factors, is shown by the fact of an all-European decrease in the death rate, especially since the second half of the nineteenth century, in spite of the great increase in the density of the population in these countries.[24] That these coefficients of correlation are a result not only of density, but are perhaps even more due to poverty or to sanitary and other conditions masked under the criterion of density, is shown by the fact that the coefficients vary greatly in different parts of England, though the conditions of density are approximately similar. While the coefficient for London is high, it is quite low for South England and the Black Country. This seems improbable if there were no "other variables" operating under "the density," as Professor Bowley himself and Dr. Greenwood indicate.[25] These considerations explain why the above correlation is often intangible. For instance,

[24] See the proper statement and the data in YULE, *op. cit.*, pp. 24–27. "The death-rate has persisted in falling, in spite of the increasing density of every country for which we have data. . . . Other influences have been much more important than the density of population." See also the remarks of Dr. Dudfield concerning this. *Ibid.*, pp. 540–541.

[25] See *op. cit.*, p. 535, Greenwood's remarks on p. 542, and A. Watson's remark on p. 544.

T. J. Le Blanc's study has shown that Farr's law does not hold in regard to the urban and the rural population of the United States.[26] From the above it seems reasonable to conclude that, while the existence of a positive correlation between the density and death rates is probable, we still do not know exactly how close it is, nor what part of the coefficients is due to density, and what to other factors acting under its cover. Dr. Greenwood says rightly:

We can decide between the various explanations (of these co-efficients) only after doing more and more work of this kind, and bringing other variables into the balance.[27]

Size and Density of the Population and Birth Rate.—What has been said of the association between the size and density of the population and the death rate is true of that between the size and the density of the population and the birth rate. A series of prominent investigators have claimed that these phenomena are negatively correlated. They maintain that an increasing density and size in a population as such, regardless of a lack of neces-sities, tend to decrease the fertility and birth rate. Recently this theory has been set forth by Dr. R. Pearl (1879–   ) in a series of his, and his collaborators', works.[28] This conclusion has been supported mainly by Dr. Pearl's experiments with *Drosophila* and fowls. The fowls in this experiment were handled in flocks of 50, 100, and 150 each. The pens in which they were kept were constructed in such a way that in the flocks of either 50 or 100 birds, there was an equal allotment of 4.8 square feet of floor space per bird, and other conditions were also equal. Therefore, if there happened to be a difference in the number of eggs laid in each flock per bird, this would be due to the factor of the flock size (50 and 100 birds) exclusively. In the flock of 150 birds there was an allotment of 3.2 square feet of floor space per bird. If there happened to be a difference in the number of eggs

[26] See LeBlanc, T. J., "Density of Population and Mortality in the United States," *American Journal of Hygiene*, Vol. IV, 1924, pp. 501–558.

[27] *Journal of Royal Statistical Society*, 1925, p. 542. See further Sir George H. Knibbs' sound statements in "The Laws of Growth of a Population," *Journal of Amer. Statistical Association*, Vols. XXI, XXII.

[28] See Pearl, R., *The Biology of Population Growth*, Chap. VI; see there other references.

per bird in this flock, it would be due to the factor of the density and size of the flock. The experiment was carried on during several years. The results are as follows: Mean annual egg production for the years of 1904-07 is: for the 50-bird pen, 129.69 per bird; for the 100-bird pen, 123.21; and for the 150-bird pen, 111.68. Thus the results show that the mere factor of the size of the flocks influenced the fertility of the fowls negatively. The same influence was shown as the density of the bird-population increased, as shown by the difference in the number of eggs produced in the 50, 100 and 150-bird pens.[29] Similar effects were yielded by the experiments with *Drosophila*. Here also the "rate of reproduction varies inversely with density." [30]

Similar results were obtained by some other investigators in their experiments with tadpoles (Bilski) [31] and other organisms.

Dr. R. Pearl thinks that the same must be true in regard to human population. However, the impossibility of obtaining an accurate measurement of its density makes it exceedingly difficult to prove the rule. Pearl made an attempt to verify the rule on the population of 132 American cities through the correlation of the birth rates, and the size and density of their populations. Measuring the density in various ways, he has obtained but a very slight correlation, the coefficient of the partial correlation between birth rate and density (as measured by the number of persons per acre) being $-.131 \pm .058$. On this basis Dr. Pearl concludes that in the studied urban population "the real net correlation between the birth rate and density is of the same character fundamentally as that we have found in experimental populations of flies and hens." The only difference is that among the human population, the influence of density upon the birth rate seems to be less marked than in the case of lower animals.[32] Dr. Pearl foresees a possible objection to his conclusion, in the well-known fact that the density, measured by the number of persons per room, is positively correlated with the birth rate. In many cities

[29] *Ibid.*, pp. 141 ff.
[30] *Ibid.*, pp. 133 ff. Notice how the experiments were conducted; and the tables and diagrams.
[31] BILSKI, F., "Über den Einfluss des Lebensraumes auf das Wachstum der Kaulquappen," *Pfluger's Archiv.*, Bd. 188, pp. 254–272.
[32] *Ibid.*, pp. 153–155.

the districts with a greater number of persons per dwelling show a higher number of children per family, or per 1000 population, or per married woman, than the districts with a less number of persons per dwelling or room.[33]   Correlating the number of persons per dwelling with the birth rate, Pearl himself finds the coefficient or correlation .456 ± .046, which is much higher than his above coefficient, and with a meaning opposite to it. He, however, declares this correlation false.   In his opinion, it is due to the physical and economic impossibility of obtaining a sufficient surplus of dwelling houses for new babies.   For this reason he discards it as fictitious, as "a mere mechanical consequence of putting more new babies into a lot of containers comparatively inflexible in respect of both number and size."[34]   In spite of this explanation, the very fact that among the human population Pearl's coefficient of negative correlation is low; that the method of his measuring the density by the number of persons per acre is very crude[35] and scarcely more adequate than that of measuring by the number of persons per room; that numerous studies (D. Heron's, Snow's, Pearson's, Johnson's, and others) have shown a greater fertility of the families living in crowded and overcrowded dwellings than that of the families living in less crowded houses,—in view of these and similar facts, the problem of the influence of density or size of the human population upon its birth rate, must still be regarded as open.   Even Pearl's study shows that the influence at the best is on a borderline between the tangible and the intangible.

Density of Population and Growth of Population.—A natural conclusion from the following studies of R. Pearl and others is that the size and density of the population greatly determine the rapidity of population growth.   In other words, the rate of

[33] Recently the same result was obtained by T. T. de Jastrzebsky, "Changes in the Birth-Rate . . . in London," *Journal of Royal Statistical Society,* 1923, Tables I–IV, pp. 40–43.   Grading the population of London into 21 groups according to the number of rooms per person (from .65 to 1.41 rooms per person) he shows that fertility per 1000 married women, or standardized fertility, or "effective" fertility, or crude birth rate goes down as we pass from the more "crowded" or dense to the less crowded and dense districts.

[34] PEARL, *op. cit.,* pp. 155–157.

[35] See Bowley's appropriate criticism of this method in his quoted paper, pp. 516–517.   See Knibbs' sound criticism of Pearl's theory, *ob. cit., passim.*

population growth is a function of the size and density of the population itself. This is the essence of the so-called "logistic law of growth of population." Since the birth rate decreases and the death rate increases with an increase in the size and the density of the population living in a limited area, the result is that, with an increase in the size and the density of the population, its rate of growth has to decrease. When, in a given limited area, the population reaches a point of saturation, it becomes stagnant. When a new invention or an expansion of the inhabited area occurs, and results in less density, the growth of the population may start again and follow the cycle passed through before. Such is the essence of "the logistic theory" in its primitive form. It was formulated at least seventy years ago by Verhulst (see his works). Later on, this cycle was outlined by several investigators, among them Dr. T. H. Stevenson (see his paper in *Journal of Hygiene,* April, 1904) ; and finally it was rediscovered and perfected by R. Pearl and his collaborators. In his own non-mathematical formulation, the logistic law of population growth runs as follows:

Growth occurs in cycles. Within one and the same cycle, and in a spacially limited area or universe, growth in the first half of the cycle starts slowly, but the absolute increment per unit of time *increases* steadily until the mid-point of the cycle is reached. After that point the increment per unit of time becomes steadily *smaller* until the end of the cycle. In a spacially limited universe the amount of increase which occurs in any particular unit of time, at any single cycle of growth, is proportional to two things, viz: (a) the absolute size already attained at the beginning of the unit interval under consideration, and (b) the amount still unused or unexpended in the given universe or area of actual and potential resources for the support of growth.

Under (b) should be included everything which may change the amount of necessities for a population, as for instance, inventions, potential development of transportation, power resources, etc. The law is valid only for a limited universe with a constant (b). When there is a new invention increasing potential and factual resources of the population, it breaks the limits of the universe and gives a check to the cycle of the growth which would have been followed had (b) remained constant.   In other words, the law, like many other scientific laws, is valid only under the indicated circumstances.[36]

R. Pearl, G. U. Yule (1871–   ) and several other statisticians have tried to compare the factual number and the factual rate of the growth in England's population, the United States of America's, France's, and of some other countries during the nineteenth and the twentieth centuries, with the number and the rate of the growth which had to be according to the mathematical formula of the "logistic law."   The results of the comparisons are very near to one another.[37]   On the basis of the same formula, they have made a computation of the future growth of the population in various countries, providing that (a) is well known and (b) remains constant.   Finally, guided by the same law, they try to explain the movement of the population, especially the trend of the falling birth rate, in the Western countries.   The essence of this explanation is as follows: During the nineteenth century the population of Western countries rapidly increased, growing in size and in density as it approached the limit of the population within its area ("the point of inflexion" of the curve).   Because of this reason, its further growth would naturally be slower.   This could be attained either by an increase in the mortality, or by a decrease in the birth rate, or by both ways.   Thanks to the progress of science and other factors, the mortality rate of Western countries has been decreasing rather than increasing.   As Dr. Yule remarks, "it has behaved as an independent variable."   Therefore, according to the law, there should be a decrease in the birth rate.   This is what really has happened.   Hence, the falling rate of births within these societies itself behaves according to the logistic law and once more corroborates its validity.[38]

Such are the essentials of the logistic law of the growth of population in which growth is regarded as a function of the size

[36] PEARL, *op. cit.*, p. 22.   See chapters I–III.   See also YULE, *op. cit.*, *passim.*
[37] See the tables in PEARL, *op. cit.*, Chaps. I–VI; *Studies in Human Biology, passim*, and pp. 567 ff.; BOWLEY, A., "Births and Population in Great Britain," *The Economic Journal*, 1924, pp. 188–192; WOOLSTON, H. B., "The Limits of American Population," *Social Forces*, Sept., 1925, pp. 5–16.
[38] See YULE, *op. cit.*, *passim;* PEARL, *Studies in Human Biology, passim;* and *The Biology of Population Growth, passim.*

and the density of the population itself. Being in its essence a better restatement of Malthus' laws, the logistic law is probably one of the valuable scientific formulas discovered in this field after Malthus. It has shown that among the factors controlling the movement of population, the population size and density are to be taken as one of the most important factors. The law helps us greatly in an understanding of the complex processes of the fluctuation of the death, birth, and growth rates of a population. In brief, its scientific value is beyond doubt. This, however, does not mean that the law is sufficient to account for all the fluctuations in the growth of a population, or that it gives a certain basis for predicting the future trend and size of a definite population, or that it even quite satisfactorily explains the changes in the movement of the vital processes. In the first place, the comparison of the actual and the computed growth rates of the population in various countries during the nineteenth century has shown, as Bowley rightly says, considerable discrepancy, in each decade the discrepancy being above one million. In the second place, as Bowley says further, "the justification for the logistic form is purely empirical; we are asked to accept it because it does give results which agree with the records of certain populations." But from this standpoint there are several other formulas which suit the actual population growth, as well as the logistic formula.[39] In the third place, Dr. Stevenson [40] seems to be right in indicating the fact of a simultaneous downward trend of the birth rates in many European countries whose populations are at very different phases of their development, and are dissimilarly situated on their various logistic tracks. Since, in spite of this difference, all these countries have shown a similar downward movement in the birth rate, this seems to be due to some other than "the logistic" factors. In the fourth place, since the law is valid only when at least (b) is constant, any change of (b), whether it is a new invention, or some extraordinary catastrophe, like a great war, revolution, or epidemic similar to the Black Death of

---

[39] See Bowley's remarks in *Journal Royal Statistical Society*, 1925, pp. 76-80.

[40] See Stevenson's criticism in his quoted paper, *ibid.*, 1925, pp. 69-75. See there also the critical remarks of Beveridge and Brownlee, who are inclined to explain the falling rate of birth through the popularization of contraceptive means since 1870 or 1880.

1348, or any other change in (b), calls forth a change of the limit for the population, and in this way upsets the prediction of the formula.[41] With these limitations, the scientific value of the law must be recognized. It has helped us to find a proper understanding of the correlation between the size and the density of the population and the rate of its growth. However, its help is much more moderate than its proponents assure us.

Such are the principal correlations of the demographic factors with the vital processes as set forth by various investigators.

4. SIZE AND DENSITY OF POPULATION AND MIGRATION

As the density of a population increases, in order to subsist it must either improve its methods for the production of necessities, make their distribution more equal, get an additional means of subsistence through the military plundering of other societies, migrate to some other less populated countries, or, if these outcomes fail to be realized, then the population must decrease its birth rate or increase its death rate, in order to reduce its density. We shall see further that an improvement of the technique of production sometimes happens, but not always. We have also seen that the eventual outcome is often found in the checked increase of the population through a decrease of the birth rate or an increase in the death rate (the logistic law). But, again, this outcome does not always take place in a sufficient degree. Sometimes a solution is found in the migration of a surplus of the population to, or a military plundering of, other countries. This explains the probable existence of a correlation between the fluctuation in the density of the population, and migration, or war phenomena. The existence of such a correlation has been indicated by a series of investigators. In regard to migration, the corresponding theories may be summed up as follows:

First Proposition.—In the history of the same society, the periods of rapid increase in the density of population are followed by an increase in emigration from the country, and by an inten-

---

[41] See this point in H. Woolston's quoted paper; see also L. Ayres' criticism of the law in the *New Republic*, Vol. XLV, pp. 223–224, Jan. 13, 1926. See other weak points of the theory in Knibbs' quoted paper; A. B. Wolfe's paper in the *Quarterly Journal of Economics*, Vol. XLI; and E. Krummeich's paper in the *Journal de société statist. de Paris*, 1927.

sive colonization of other territories by the emigrants; while the periods of stagnation, or of decrease in density, are followed by a decrease of emigration from the country, and sometimes, even by immigration to it from other places.

Second Proposition.—As a general rule, migratory currents move from the regions of a more rapidly increasing population (or population with a greater effective fertility) to those of a less rapidly increasing one.[42]   Many migratory movements have been going on following the lines of these propositions.   The history of the expansion of ancient Rome and Greece, and of their colonial activity, shows that they seem to have been the most intensive in the periods of a rapid increase in their population. A series of corresponding phenomena of later periods also show something similar.   Even now the countries or the regions of emigration have been the countries or the regions of a relatively intensive increase of population, while the countries or the regions of immigration have been either those of low effective fertility or low density of population.   Further, migration from the country to the city corroborates considerably the second proposition because, as a general rule, country population has been more "fertile" than city population.   In brief, it is probable that the two phenomena are somewhat correlated.

But again we must not exaggerate the correlation.   From the indicated reason that there are several outcomes (inventions, war, migration, reduction of birth rate, and increase of a death rate) of the conditions created by an increasing density of the population, it follows that, instead of migration, some other outcome may take place.   Under such conditions, the increase of a peaceful migration may not follow, and the correlation may not be realized.   On the other hand, migration may take place because of reasons different from the demographic causes: so-called religious, political, and other migrations.   As a result, the actual curve of migration coincides only in part with the one expected

[42] See, for instance, GINI, C., *I fattori demografici dell' evoluzione delle nazioni*, pp. 34 ff., Torino, 1912; HANSEN, G., *Die Drei Bevölkerungsstufen, passim*, München, 1889; also see HADDON, A. C., *The Wanderings of People*, 1912, pp. 2 ff., N. Y.; MYRES, J. L., "The Causes of the Rise and Fall in the Population of the Ancient World," *Eugenic Review*, Vol. VII, 1915.

on the basis of the demographic situation.   In other words, the correlation is tangible, but not close.[43]

5. DEMOGRAPHIC CONDITIONS AND WAR

Before Malthus, many authors indicated the demographic factor as one of the principal causes of war.   Malthus generalized the theories into a "law" where war functions as one of the effective checks of population.   Since that time, this idea has become quite common in various formulations.   "The World War was essentially an outgrowth of the pressing population problem which confronted the nations of Europe ten years ago." [44] Such is one of the varieties of the idea.   "The growth of population with the resulting desire for economic expansion is a necessary cause of War" is another formula of a correlation between the two phenomena.[45]   A. Dix, A. Wirth, von Bernhardi,

---

[43] Contrary to the authors who overestimate the correlation, some others, like Carr-Saunders, seem to me to underestimate it.   "Migration does not arise where a condition of overpopulation has come about," he states.   I regret to say that his whole discussion of the problem is rather speculative; and that his vague theory of ideas as the causes of migration is much more defective than even the one-sided demographic theory of migration.   From the fact that migration alone could not be so effective as to eliminate any possible surplus of the population due to a great potential human fecundity, it does not follow that migration cannot alleviate it to some extent.   We certainly know a series of cases when migration has done this task.   Due to the fact of the great potential fecundity of the human population, a migration of every hundred of possible progenitors has helped considerably to check a rapid increase in a given population.   Carr-Saunders' indication that migration is a rare phenomenon, which takes place only once in centuries, is also incorrect.   Any statistical census of migration from country to country, or from one region of a country to another, shows that the currents of migration are continual and quite considerable, even in normal times.   His indication that overpopulated societies usually do not exhibit initiative and energy, which are characteristics of the emigrants, and that overpopulated societies consequently could not originate migrants, is also fallacious.   Not every overpopulated society is marked in any or all of its periods by "the absence of hope, and the spirit of enterprise."   Gini's, and Carli's opposite thesis that the greatest spirit of enterprise and initiative usually coincides with the periods of a rapid increase in population seems to be nearer to the reality than Carr-Saunders' statement.   On the other hand, such a rapidly increasing society is likely to have a greater proportion of men with initiative and energy, and more stimuli to facilitate emigration.   See CARR-SAUNDERS, op. cit., pp. 291–304; GINI, op. cit., pp. 34–37, 48–53, and passim.   The data of the amount of permanent and normal migration may be found in SOROKIN, Social Mobility, Chap. XVI.

[44] DUBLIN, L., "The Statistician and the Population Problem," in Population Problems, p. 3.

[45] COX, HAROLD, The Problem of Population, London, J. Cape Co., p. 72 and Chap. III.

D. Frymann, W. G. Sumner and A. G. Keller, and scores of other authors have made similar statements. Many authors have elucidated the same correlation in a more detailed form. The argument runs in essence within the Malthus theory. One group explains the correlation through a lack of room under the sun, caused by an increase of population. This leads to the necessity for an expansion of room through war. Another group states that a discrepancy between the population and its means of subsistence tends to result in war.[46] A third group of authors offers a somewhat more complex explanation. According to them, the demographic factor of population growth is always a latent cause of war, but as an actual cause it varies: "the degree of latency of this factor is in reverse proportion to the degree of the political organization of a society." The more complex the latter is, the more serious is the rôle of the economic factors and the less actual is the rôle of the demographic factors.[47] Some others offer a still more complex interpretation of the correlation: The periods of rapid increase in a population are followed by an increase of the imperialistic attitudes and psychology. This leads to an increase in the tendency of expansion which in its turn facilitates an outbreak of war. Such is the essence of this theory.[48] The curves of the movement of the population and of the fluctuation of the imperialistic psychology are parallel. "That the substratum of military movement is to be looked for in demographic development, appears evident"; [49] but the correlation consists, especially in the World War, not so much in the form of a direct causation of the War by an increase of the population, as it does in a disruption of the equilibrium between the demographic, the economic, the psychical, and the political

[46] Examples of these types may be found in the quoted books of E. M. East, G. H. Knibbs, Novicow, Vaccaro; KEYNES, J. M., *The Economic Consequences of the Peace*, London, 1919, pp. 215 ff.; ROSE, H., *Origins of the War*, Cambridge, 1914; NICOLAI, *Die Biologie des Krieges*, 1919, pp. 34 ff.; SUMNER, W., and KELLER, A., *The Science of Society*, Vol. I, pp. 16, 42, 62 ff., 1927.

[47] GINI, C., "Fattori latenti delle guerre," *Rivista Italiana di Sociologia*, Jan.–Feb., 1915.

[48] See CARLI, F., *op. cit.*, pp. 289–303, 391–410, 600–603; MAROI, L., *I Fattori demografici del conflitto Europeo*, Roma, 1919, *passim*.

[49] CARLI, *op. cit.*, p. 392. "*Lo sviluppo numerico della popolazione fu la causa primaria delle grande variante economiche e sociali del secolo che precedette la guerra mondiale.*" *Ibid.*, p. 431.

variables within many European societies. The disruption was caused by a rapid increase of the European population in the nineteenth century resulting in a disruption of the equilibrium among many, especially in the Anglo-Latin and the German societies.[50]

Thus, whatever may be the explanation of the correlation, it seems to be thought of as existing, by a great many thinkers. However, some authors, for instance Carr-Saunders, are inclined to think that overpopulation is not a cause of war.[51] Nevertheless the existence of the correlation is probable. On the other hand, it is necessary to recognize that the partizans of its existence have not given any very satisfactory corroboration of their theories. Even the works of Gini, Carli, and Maroi, which seem to be the best in this field, are far from being convincing. They supply a series of historical facts which show that the periods of rapid population growth, and those of great demographic disturbances, have been usually followed by an increase of war;[52] but the greater part of these facts are taken from the earliest periods of Greece or Rome, whose population movement is practically unknown. Therefore their statements are rather guesses than factual corroborations. Other facts given from mediæval history are of the same kind, in that they give only a part of the truth. The remaining part of the facts may be accurate, but, unfortunately, they are contradicted by other no less ascertained facts. Can we say that every decrease in the density of a population leads to a decrease of war? Certainly not. The Black Death

[50] *Ibid.*, Libro IV, *passim*. See also MAROI, *passim*.

[51] CARR-SAUNDERS, *op. cit.*, pp. 305 ff. "The argument that war is due to over-population falls to the ground," says he. However, he practically does not give any arguments in favor of his theory. His own theory of the causes of war,— the instinct of pugnacity and traditions—is entirely deficient because of the uncertainty of the existence of such an instinct, and because of an absence of any explanation why, if such an instinct even exists, it is manifested in the form of war only from time to time. Why does the same instinct lead at one time to fighting and war, and at another time to peace? Carr-Saunders' theory does not answer the question at all. His account of the rôle of tradition and of highly organized government is so dark that the statements amount to nothing. Finally, he himself recognizes the rôle of war in eliminating a part of the population, and, in this way, he admits, contrary to his above statement, the existence of a correlation between the movement of the demographic processes and the war phenomena. See pp. 304–307.

[52] See GINI, *I fattori demogr. del' evoluz. delle nazioni*, pp. 35 ff., 48 ff.; CARLI, *op. cit.*, pp. 289–303, 391–410, 411–605.

of 1348 diminished the population of Europe enormously (by about one-third.) If the hypothesis were true, we ought to expect that in subsequent decades war would decrease in Europe. Such an expectation is far from being corroborated. According to F. A. Woods' and A. Baltzly's study, the number of years devoted to wars in France and England in the half century from 1350 to 1400, or in the century from 1350 to 1450, does not show any decrease. The corresponding figures are as follows:[53]

Countries	Number of Years Spent in War in Each Specified Period of Fifty Years							
	1100–1150	1151–1200	1201–1250	1251–1300	1301–1350	1351–1400	1401–1450	1451–1500
England..........	38	16	19	17	39.5	25.5	38	19
France............	26.5	10	31.5	17.5	18	25	35.5	17

This is one of the many cases where a sudden and enormous, or a low and gradual decrease in the density of the population was not followed by a decrease of war phenomena. With similar reason we are entitled to say that not every rapid increase of the population is followed by an increase of war. The population of Europe increased rapidly, especially during the nineteenth century. This would lead to an increase of war if the theory were quite general and valid. The reality is rather different. The figures in the table on page 386 may partly show this.[54] Though the number of years of warfare is not quite an adequate measure of the increase or decrease of war, nevertheless it is probably one of the best possible criteria. The figures show that the above century, in spite of its excessively rapid increase of the population, had a quota of war years not higher than other centuries. For other centuries also, the curves of the war years and of the population increase or decrease in these countries do not run parallel. These indications, which may be supported by

[53] WOODS, F. A., and BALTZLY, A., *Is War Diminishing?*, Boston and N. Y., 1915, pp. 43, 53.
[54] *Ibid.*, pp. 34, 39, 43, 53, 78. See there the figures for several other countries.

Countries	The Number of Years of War in Each Specified Period of 50 Years							
	1501–1550	1551–1600	1601–1650	1651–1700	1701–1751	1751–1800	1801–1850	1851–1900
Austria............	36	39.5	40.5	33	29	19.5	7.5	6
Denmark..........	22.5	10	21.5	9	11	1	10	5
England..........	16	38.5	17.5	26	29	26.5	26	27.5
France............	29.5	31	24	22.5	25	25.5	18	17
Russia............	42.5	36	18	39.5	29	20.5	35.5	17.5

other data, are sufficient to support the claim that, if the correlation exists, it is far from being close, and is much more complex than it is supposed to be by its many partizans. Here again the task of future study will be to promote an objective and quantitative investigation which would show under what conditions, and to what extent the correlation really exists (if it does) between the discussed phenomena. Though the trend of the studies has been drifting in this way, nevertheless it is still necessary to take many steps in order to clarify the relationship between demographic and war phenomena.

6. DEMOGRAPHIC FACTORS AND REVOLUTION

A correlation of these two phenomena has been alluded to by many thinkers of the past. At the present moment, a systematic theory of their relationship has been laid down by F. Carli. The essence of it is as follows: "The periods of intensive dynamics in demographic processes are also the periods of enormous psychical variations," revolutions, and inner crises.[55] Side by side with the rapid increase or decrease of the population, an important part is played in this respect by the differential increase of various classes of the same society. The greater this discrepancy is, and the greater the obstacles to an infiltration of talented peoples from the lower classes into the upper ones, the greater

[55] CARLI, op. cit., pp. 218–219, 369–389.

are the chances of revolution and inner crisis. Such is the essence of Carli's theory.

Is the theory accurate? I doubt it seriously. Not every increase in population leads to revolution. It is enough for us to look at Prussia, England, or Russia during the nineteenth century to see that. During this period the increase of their populations, especially that of Russia, was enormous, and yet these countries did not have any revolution. On the other hand, the population of France during the same period was almost stagnant. Its increase was less than in any other European country; and yet this did not hinder France from having at least three revolutions (1830, 1848, 1870-71) during that period. Again, the wave of revolutions and disorders in ancient Greece or Rome took place not so much in the periods of an increase of their population, as in the period of the depopulation of these countries. It is easy to multiply similar cases. They show that the increase or decrease of a population is not correlated, at least directly, with revolution. A more serious sign is noticeable in the differential increase of the upper and the lower classes, and in the intensiveness of the vertical circulation of the individuals from the lower to the upper classes, and *vice versa*. But even there the situation is much more complex than is depicted by Carli. It is not true that the more free the access of the individuals from the lower classes to the higher ones, the less are the chances of revolution. I have dealt with this problem in my *Social Mobility* [56] and my conclusions, based on careful study of the facts, are rather opposite. Mobile societies with an intensive vertical circulation are no more stable than immobile ones, though there is no general rule. The relatively closed aristocracies, when they are in proper conditions, have a longer span of existence than the open aristocracies. What is important is not so much the closeness or openness of the door to the upper classes, as the character of the aristocracy, and the conditions of its existence. Carli's corroborations of his hypothesis are rather few and not properly analyzed. It is only necessary to indicate that the European societies of the nineteenth century were more mobile, and their upper classes were more open, than many past societies, or many

[56] See SOROKIN, *Social Mobility*, Chap. XXII.

Eastern societies. This, however, did not prevent the European societies from having a series of revolutions. Meanwhile, in past societies with hereditary aristocracy, especially in Eastern societies, revolutions have been more rare than in the "open" societies of Europe or of ancient Greece and Rome since their aristocracy became relatively "open." Not repeating here other data given in my *Social Mobility*, I do not think Carli's theory is correct. In it there is only one correct point: the degeneration of the upper classes as a positive factor of revolution; but this is a quite different factor from the demographic forces. It may take place in an immobile, as well as in a mobile society, and with a closed, as well as open aristocracy.[57] For these reasons, Carli's theory of the correlation between the discussed phenomena must be judged as rather hasty.[58] The problem has not been studied seriously. It is up to future sociologists to elucidate it.

7. DEMOGRAPHIC FACTORS AND ECONOMIC PHENOMENA

Population Size and Density, and Technique of Production.— M. Kovalevsky (1851-1916), A. Coste, E. Durkheim, F. Ratzel, P. Mougeolle, E. Levasseur, E. Dupréel, C. Gini, F. Carli, W. Sumner and A. Keller, and others have tried to establish a correlation between these two series of phenomena. According to them, a growth of the population and its consequence, an increase in its density, have been responsible for an improvement in the technique of economic production and for a transition from less intensive forms of production to the more intensive ones. An increasing density makes the methods of production insufficient, which were quite satisfactory for a less dense population. Hence, the increasing pressure of this factor. It urges the invention of more efficient methods of production, which will be fit to satisfy the needs of an increased population. This leads to inventions and through them, to a betterment of the technique of production. On the other hand, an increased density of population means a more intensive exchange of experience, which is likely

[57] See SOROKIN, *The Sociology of Revolution*, pp. 397–413.

[58] With even greater reason, the same may be said of G. Ferrari's interesting theory developed in his *Teoria dei periodi politici*, Milano, 1874.

to result in a more rapid accumulation of knowledge and mental progress. In these ways, according to the theories,[59] societies have passed from the stage of hunters and fishers and collectors of natural products to that of agriculture and cattle-breeding; and from the primitive methods of agriculture and hand-industry, to the more perfect methods of machino-facture and agriculture. Thus, contrary to the economic interpretation of history, the demographic school is apt to regard the factor of production itself as a function of the demographic factor.

The attempt to establish the above correlation has been made in various ways. Libich, F. Ratzel, and E. Levasseur have indicated that there is a correlation between the density of the population and the technique of production, without, however, indicating which of the two is the cause, and which is the effect. According to Ratzel's computation, on 1000 square kilometers there exists the following density of population under the specified technique for procuring the means of subsistence:

Hunters and fishermen (in various regions and at various stages)	from 2 to 1770
Nomadic shepherds	1770
Agricultural peoples (in various regions and at various stages)	from 1770 to 35,000
The peoples with the most intensive agricultural technique.	177,000

As to the density of the population with a highly developed technique and commerce, as the contemporary industrial centers show, it exceeds the last figure many times.[60]

M. Kovalevsky, (1851-1916) in a series of his historical and sociological works [61] based on a concrete study of economic evolution, came to the conclusion that one of the "principal motors of economic evolution has been the growth of the population." According to his theory,

---

[59] See this argument in CARLI, *op. cit.*, pp. 145–183.

[60] See also LEVASSEUR, E., "La répartition de la race humaine sur le globe terrestre," *Bullétin Institut Intern. Statistique*, Vol. XVIII, 2ᵉ livr., pp. 48–64; CARLI, F., *L'equilibrio delle nazioni secondo la demografia applicata*, Bologna, N. Zanichelli Co., 1919, pp. 96 ff.

[61] See KOVALEVSKY, M., *Obschinnoje semlevladenie* (Communal Possession of Land), Moscow, 1879, pp. 6–7 and *passim; A Study of the Disintegration of Communal Land Possession in Waadt Canton*, Russ., 1876; "Évolution du régime economic," *Le devenir social*, June, 1896; *Die Ökonomishe Entwicklung Europas*, Berlin, 1908 and later, all volumes; in Russian the work began to be published in 1898; *Contemporary Sociologists*, pp. 260 ff., 200 ff.

this factor has been responsible for the transition from a stage of hunters and fishermen to agriculture, and from a primitive system of agriculture to a more intensive one with corresponding changes in the system of land ownership and land possession. . . To the same factor is due the substitution of a manufacturing system of production in industry for a domestic one; and that of the machino-facturing system for a manufacturing one, with a corresponding change in the division of labor, and in the interrelations of capital and labor. . . Thus, the simple fact of the growth of population called forth a division of labor, a social differentiation into castes, orders, and classes, and the evolution of the technique of production, as well as that of the economic régime.[62]

Such is the essence of Kovalevsky's theory, formulated and factually corroborated by him considerably earlier than was done by Coste, Durkheim, Mougeolle, or even by A. Loria.[63] Stressing the importance of this factor, Kovalevsky, however, strongly criticizes all those who would try to deny the existence and importance of other factors. He is a pluralist of a very definite type.[64] He makes a mockery of all those who "try to regard historical processes as a simple equation with one unknown." For him the very problem of the principal factor is a pseudo-problem, and wrongly set forth. In the future it must be put away.[65] As we shall see, Durkheim came to the somewhat similar conclusion that the process of the division of labor and economic evolution has been due to the growth of the population. (See chapter about Durkheim.)

Independently from Kovalevsky, A. Loria in his early work about land rent developed a theory very similar to that of Kovalevsky.[66]

Furthermore, P. Mougeolle and F. H. Giddings outlined a theory which also gave an important rôle to the factor of growth

[62] KOVALEVSKY, *Contemporary Sociologists*, pp. 200–201.

[63] See Loria's remark about priority in his *Il capitalismo e la scienza*, p. 251; Kovalevsky's answer, in *Contemporary Sociologists*, p. 261.

[64] See SOROKIN, P., "Kovalevsky's Theory of Factors," *In Memoriam of M. Kovalevsky*, Russ., Petrograd, 1917.

[65] KOVALEVSKY, *Contemporary Sociologists*, pp. vii ff.

[66] Kovalevsky elaborated his theory also independently from Loria three years earlier. For this reason, Loria's allusion that Kovalevsky only repeated his theory, is quite baseless.

and density of population.[67]   Quite recently, E. Dupréel, with Coste's one-sidedness and without Kovalevsky's reservations, without mentioning his predecessors, said that "Social progress and civilization is the fruit of the numerical increase of the population." [68]   F. Carli, on his part, states that "the denser population has more developed technique" and that "the non-densely populated societies have been poor in technical inventions." [69] There are other authors who have incidentally, or in a detailed way, insisted on the importance of the factor of population in the evolution of the technique of production.   We need not mention their names, because their statements add little to the above.

Criticism.—The above theories indicate two reasons why a growth in the number and the density of a population leads to an intensification of the technique of production: an intensification of social interaction which results in a more intensive exchange by experience, and an increase of need.   This means that both reasons are, so to speak, not inherent in the density and to the number of the population.   Only as far as an increase in the density and number of the population is followed by an intensification of interaction, and by an increase of the danger of starvation, need the demographic factor lead to an improvement of the technique of production.   Now, can we say that an increase of the population always and invariably gives an enrichment of human knowledge, and an increased lack of necessities?   Sometimes it does, but sometimes it does not give these results.   In order that the first result may take place, it is necessary that the corresponding *quality* of interacting people be sufficiently high.   Thousands of idiots may be in the most intensive contact; and yet probably only a Bedlam would result from it.   Again, if an increasing population has the complete possibility of satisfying its needs through emigration, war, plundering its neighbors, etc., without an intensification of the technique of production, as was the case in the past in regard to many tribes, a progress of the technique of production may not follow.   More than that, even the pressure of

[67] See MOUGEOLLE, P., *Statique des civilizations*, Paris, 1883; GIDDINGS, F. H., *Principles of Sociology*.

[68] DUPRÉEL, E., "Les variations démographiques et le progrès," *Revue de l'Institut de Sociologie*, pp. 359–385, May, 1922.

[69] CARLI, *op. cit.*, pp. 147–149, Chap. V.

needs being increased, a betterment of the technique of production may not follow, simply because new inventions do not always
come in proportion to the social need felt for them.   Poor health
urgently needs an efficient remedy; yet it often lacks this and
the man dies.   The same is true here.   During thousands of years,
thousands of societies have experienced poverty, famines, and
other miseries; and yet the necessary inventions have not been
created to alleviate these miseries.   In the majority of cases, the
outcome from overpopulation and misery has been found not so
much in a new invention, as in a death from starvation, in infanticide, in military robbery of neighboring peoples, in migration, in
strife, war, abortion, and so on.   Being unable to invent, the
people have "preferred" to die.[70]

These considerations are enough to show that if there is a correlation between an increase in the number and the density of the
population, and progress in the technique of the production of the
means of subsistence, it is not very close and perfect.   If the correlation were perfect, we should expect that the technique of economic production would be higher and the inventions more
numerous when the number and the density of the population is
greater.   The facts do not support the expectation.   While, at
the end of the nineteenth century, the average density per one
square kilometer in Australian Victoria was 5 inhabitants; in New
South Wales, 1.4; in the United States, 8; in Canada, 0.3; in
New Zealand, 2; in Finland, 7; in Sweden, 12; in Norway, 6;
in Denmark, 55; in France, 71; in Switzerland, 71;—at the same
time it was 182 in Bengal; in the northwestern provinces of
British India, 169; in India generally, 61; in China, from 60
to 94; in Italy, 96; and so on.[71]   Evidently we have no reason for
thinking that the first group of countries with a small density of

---

[70] My study of the correlation between famine and the invention of new
sources of means for subsistence has shown that if, under the influence of famine
(and overpopulation), there has sometimes been made a betterment of the methods for obtaining and producing necessities, there has more often been an increased mortality, while "preventive and repressive checks" have taken place.
If any increase of misery were followed by an improvement in the production of
economic necessities, the peoples with the most numerous famines should have
been the most inventive.   In reality, however, the facts do not support such an
expectation.   A detailed analysis of this has been given in chapter IV of my *The
Influence of Famine and the Food Factor*.

[71] VON MAYR, G., *op. cit.*, Vol. II, p. 48; LEVASSEUR, *La répartition*, p. 52.

population has a more primitive system of technique, industry or agriculture.[72]   Furthermore, if the discussed correlation were close, within the history of the same country the technique of economic production would make progress with every increase in the density of its population.   This expectation is corroborated to some extent, [73] but the exceptions are so numerous that the correlation must be considered rather imperfect.   Besides, the correlation seems to go only to a definite limit; after it the law of diminishing returns begins to operate, and tends to annul the potential benefits of an increased pressure in the population. Here are a few examples of the many possible.   Kovalevsky himself indicates that in England, in the period from the sixth to the sixteenth century, there was not any noticeable improvement in the technique of production, yet the population of England was increasing during this period.[74]   We cannot say that the population of the Roman Empire was less dense in the second century A.D. than in the third and in the second centuries B.C., yet the technique of production and invention in the second century A.D., especially at its end, was rather inferior to that of the preceding period.   Moreover, it began to deteriorate more and more, so that it eventually called forth a depopulation of at least some parts of Italy.[75]   Read the economic history of China.   In spite of the many waves of increase and decrease in its population, and in spite of its great density attained centuries ago, its industrial and agricultural technique has remained practically at the same stage which was attained centuries ago.[76]   In brief, the discussed cor-

---

[72] This shows that Carli's statement that industrial countries regularly have a greater density of population than agricultural countries is also extreme.   We cannot say that *"la coesistenza delle due serie di fenomeni ha una regolarita di legge."*   CARLI, *op. cit.*, pp. 9 ff.

[73] See facts in CARLI, *op. cit.*, Chap. V.

[74] KOVALEVSKY, *Contemporary Sociologists*, pp. 244–245.

[75] ROSTOVTZEFF, *The Social and Economic History of the Roman Empire*, pp. 166, 303–305; W. Simkhovitch goes even so far as to say that the evolution of the agricultural technique of production in Rome represents a passage from an intensive to an extensive system.   In ancient periods 7 jugera of land was enough to maintain a farmer's family.   In the time of the Gracchi, 30 jugera was necessary; in the time of Cæsar, 66; in the time of Augustus, 400.   Such a reverse movement, if Simkhovitch's conclusion is at least partly valid, was going on in the period of an increasing number and density of the Roman population.   SIMKHOVITCH, W., "Rome's Fall Reconsidered," *Political Science Quarterly*, 1916, p. 221.

[76] See LEE, M. P. H., *The Economic History of China, passim*, N. Y., 1921.

relation is tangible in many cases, but it has its limits [77] beyond
which no further increase of the population produces an improvement of technique among many peoples; and it has so many exceptions that the correlation cannot be regarded close or regular.
Finally, if the correlation were perfect, and there were no limits
beyond which it ceased to exist, there would be no danger of overpopulation; and no discrepancy between the means of subsistence
and an increased population could occur. Each increase in a population would secure new inventions and a corresponding improvement of the technique of production, and, in this way, the
need would be met. It is necessary to disregard all the facts of
human history to be able to support such a view. An innumerable
number of famines, miseries, economic impoverishments, migrations, and so on, show that in a great many cases an increased
population has not been followed by such inventions and improvements; and that the outcome of overpopulation has been found in
less pleasant ways of re-establishing the equilibrium between the
population and its means of subsistence.[78]   All Malthusian literature, and even the non-Malthusian theories of population, supply
abundant material which shows this.[79]

[77] This is recognized also by Carli; op. cit., pp. 172, 177 ff.
[78] See the facts in DESCAMPS, P., "Comment les conditions de vie de sauvages
influencent leur natalité," Revue de l'Institut de Sociologie, Sept., 1922; CARR-
SAUNDERS, op. cit., Chaps. VII–XI.
[79] The theory of the optimum number of population, and the possibility of de-
viating from this optimum by a too numerous population, is not denied even by
the opponents of Malthus.   Neither do they claim that each increase in the population will be followed by a corresponding improvement in the technique of
production.   They show conspicuously that in the past, as well as in the present,
the common method of re-establishment of "the optimum number" has been
not so much a betterment of the technique, as in methods of increased mortality,
decreased birth rate, infanticide, abortion, and so on.   About this, see the theory
of the optimum number of population, CANNAN, E., A History of the Theories of
Production and Distribution, Chap. V, London, 1903; NICHOLSON, J. SH., Principles of Political Economy, Vol. I, pp. 163 ff., London, 1893; CARLI, op. cit., pp.
98 ff.; CARR-SAUNDERS, op. cit., pp. 199 ff.; WOLFE, A. B., "The Optimum Size
of Population," in DUBLIN'S Population Problems, Boston, 1926; the quoted
works of Julius Wolf and Budge.   As to the pro-Malthusian theories, they show
the above facts of overpopulation, the limited possibility for an improvement in
the methods of production, and other facts where, in spite of an increased density
of the population, the needed improvement of technique has not followed.   See
THOMPSON, W. S., op. cit., passim, and Chaps. IX–XI; EAST, E. M., Mankind
at the Crossroads, 1923; KNIBBS, G. H., "The Problems of Population, Food Supply, and Migration," Scientia, Vol. I, No. XII, 1919; "The Mathematical Theory
of Population" in Census of the Commonwealth of Australia, 1917.

These considerations are sufficient to show that, even regardless of the fact that the number and the density of the population itself depend greatly on many factors, these demographic forces, taken as "variables," seem to show some correlation with the change in the technique of production; but the correlation is far from being close, general, or unlimited. This means that the evolution of the technique of production may be accounted for only in part through the demographic factor. We cannot say that this factor alone is always necessary or sufficient for producing inventions and improvements in the technique of production.

Population, Size, and Density Correlated with the Forms of Ownership and Possession.—Such Russian investigators of the forms of land property in Russia as M. Kovalevsky, A. Kaufmann, N. Organovsky, R. Kotcharovsky and others [80] have found that there is a correlation between the forms of landownership or land possession, and the density of the population in various parts of Russia. As we proceed from the less densely populated southeastern part (Siberia and central Asiatic provinces) to the more densely populated parts of central and northwestern Russia, the form of community landownership (*obschina*) is more and more superseded by private or individual landownership. The explanation of the correlation lies in the fact that a greater density in a population makes a more intensive agricultural production necessary, and this is more possible under a régime of private ownership and unhampered individual initiative, than under the régime of community ownership with its redistribution of land, with its inertia, and its limitation of private initiative and profit. This may serve as an example of the correlation between the density of a population and the forms of economic organization.

In Russia the correlation has been tangible, though it is far from being perfect.[81] It seems to be even less tangible in other countries, and at different times. I am a poor specialist in the economic history of the forms of landownership; but in studying

---

[80] See KOVALEVSKY, *Obschinnoie semlevladenie;* KOTCHAROVSKY, R., *Russian Obschina* (Russ.); KAUFMANN, A., *History of the Russian Common Land Ownership*, (Russ.).

[81] It is interesting to note that in the years 1917–1926 the number of persons in the territory of Soviet Russia decreased in comparison with that before 1917; and yet the forms of private land possession were growing at the cost of the *obschina* form, in spite of the communist régime.

the economic history of China and an alternation between the community landownership (so-called Tsing Tien System) and private landownership, I failed to find any definite correlation. Alternation has been going on continually, but without any correlation with fluctuation in the density of population.[82] The same seems to be true in regard to the forms of landownership in India, as far as they are known to us. During almost a thousand years (from the fifth century B.C. to the third and fourth centuries A.D.) the density of the Indian population probably underwent considerable changes. Nevertheless, the system of the common possession of land seems to have dominated in all this period.[83] Likewise, in the long history of ancient Egypt, the density of the population probably underwent considerable changes, but up to the Ptolemaic period, "there had been only two types of landed proprietors in Egypt,—the king and the gods." [84] I doubt also whether, in the evolution of the forms of landownership in Rome, there may be found any tangible correlation with the density of the population, except perhaps in the last period of the Western Roman Empire. Turning to our own times, we see in almost all Western countries the same system of private landownership dominating, in spite of the great difference in the density of their populations, ranging from 1 to 2 inhabitants to more than 200 per kilometer. If the correlation were close, such a thing could not have taken place. On the other hand, countries like India or China, in spite of a considerable density, have kept community landownership alive, while in Norway, Sweden, Finland, New Zealand and Australia, in spite of the small density of population, community landownership is practically absent.[85] These exceptions are sufficient to show that, even if the alleged correlation exists, it is very imperfect and far from being general.

[82] See LEE, M. P. H., *op. cit., passim;* CHANG, CHEN HUAN, *The Economic Principles of Confucius*, pp. 119 ff., 332 ff., 497 ff., N. Y., 1911.

[83] See *The Cambridge History of India*, Vol. I, N. Y., 1922.

[84] ROSTOVTZEFF, *op. cit.*, p. 262.

[85] To this it may be added that the table of the forms of property among the different hunting, pastoral, and agricultural peoples, given in the chapter about the Economic School (see further) also does not support the discussed correlation, in spite of the fact that, passing from the lowest hunters to the highest agricultural peoples, we pass from the societies with the lowest, to the societies with the higher density of population.

I do not here have space to scrutinize the series of other correlations between the density of the population and other economic
relationships claimed by the partizans of the demographic school.
To give an idea of their character I shall give the following quotation from Kovalevsky, which sums up the character of the cor
related economic phenomena.

In the field of economic relationship, changes in the density of the
population have manifested themselves in the substitution of a more
efficient bondage labor for a less efficient slave labor, and finally in
that of free labor for a bondage labor system. The liberation of
slaves *en masse,* and the emancipation of peasants, made at the beginning by individual feudal landlords, and later on by the governments of the city-republics and of the nations, have been possible
only through the inevitable increase of rent due to an increase of the
population. . . Parallel to these changes in the field of agriculture
and land possession, corresponding changes have been going on within
the field of industry and commerce, and in the field of organization
of the industrial and commercial classes. . . From the hands of the
slaves and the serfs . . . industry passes into the hands of the village artisans and the city-masters who, for the sake of mitigating
competition, have organized guilds and corporations. . . To this
evolution of industrial and commercial activity there corresponds a
process of differentiation between country-economy and city-econ-
omy, the appearance of markets and fairs, the organization of city-
economy and so on.[86]

Such is a brief résumé of the most important economic and social
effects of the growth of population, which have been shown by
Kovalevsky in eleven volumes of his *Die Ökonomische Entwicklung Europas.* From the quotation we see that the contended
correlations are highly important, and that the rôle ascribed to the
growth of the population is really great. I think that there is a
part truth in these contentions, but only a part, and that part defined rather vaguely. A severe statistical, historical, and logical
scrutiny of these correlations would probably make many of them
questionable, some of them fallacious, and part of them, so to
speak, local. As I said, I do not have space to test these contentions, but I am sure that such a testing would result in the above

[86] KOVALEVSKY, *Contemporary Sociologists,* pp. 245–246.

conclusions. With a corresponding modification, this may probably be said about other correlations in this field.

Demographic Factors Correlated with Economic Prosperity.— In this field the theories which have tried to formulate a series of definite correlations between the progress of industry, commerce, the standard of living, and economic well-being, on the one hand; and an increase or decrease in the density of the population, on the other, have been especially numerous. In the past, as well as in the present, the theories have been rather opposite. According to one group of theorists, represented by Malthus and the Malthusians, an increase in the density of a population tends to produce overpopulation, and influences the well-being of the society negatively. For this reason they view an increase of population negatively, and at the present moment especially, favor birth control, as a convenient means for checking population growth. Usually such theories come principally from the countries with a considerable density, and with a rapid increase in their population.[87] Another group of these theories, more typical of the past, and at the present moment supported principally in France, which is now suffering from depopulation, maintains a rather opposite view of the beneficial effect of an increase of the population on economic development and well-being of a country.[88] Finally, the third group of theories take a middle position, expressed in their somewhat vague conception of the *optimum number of a population* for any given conditions.[89] When the number and the density of a population is at this optimum point, the economic influences of such a situation are the best possible under the circumstances. When there is a deviation from the optimum point in the form of over or under population, the effects are negative.

Thus, all these theories explicitly or implicitly contend that

[87] The indicated books of East, Thompson, Sumner-Keller (Vol. I, pp. 42, 62 ff.), and J. Sweeney are examples of this type of theory. See also Cox, H., *The Problem of Population*, London, 1922. The author even offers an organization of a "League of Low Birth-Rate Nations," Chap. III.

[88] Typical samples of these theories are given in the mentioned book of P. Leroy-Beaulieu, and especially in BERTILLON, J., *La dépopulation de la France*, Paris, 1911. In America there recently appeared a current of thought pertaining also to this type of theories. It is represented by L. Dublin's last works. See his paper in *Population Problems*, 1926.

[89] The mentioned works of Carr-Saunders, A. B. Wolfe, Budge, Nicholson and Cannan are varieties of this type.

there is a definite correlation between the discussed demographic factors and the economic well-being of a society. Now, which of these theories is correct? In the first place, the very fact of the existence of such opposite theories makes one doubt the accuracy of each of them. In the second place, historical and statistical data do not entirely support any of the extreme types. Indeed, it is possible to contend that in many cases, a decrease in the number and the density of a population tends to raise its economic well-being. For instance, according to E. Meyer, in ancient Greece in the second century B.C., there was a considerable depopulation, and, at the same time, an increase of the material well-being of the decreased population.[90] F. Curschman, in his study of the famines in the Middle Ages, states also that often, after a great decrease of the population in famished areas (through great mortality, decreased birth rate, emigration from such districts, etc.), the well-being of those who survived became considerably greater.[91] D'Avenel, on the basis of his classical study of property, incomes, wages, and prices in France from 1200 to 1800, states also that the fluctuation of real wages of the labor classes during six centuries was independent of either the political régime, guilds, corporations and unions, or prices; the movement of their well-being was entirely determined by the law of supply and demand. Wages would rise in periods of a decrease in population, and a consequent dearth of labor, and they would go down in periods of a rapid increase in population, with an abundant supply of labor. Only the interference of science in the form of a new beneficial invention could sometimes counterbalance the downward trend of real wages caused by population growth.[92] M. Kovalevsky, on his part, has shown that one of the results of the Black Plague of 1348, which decreased the population of western Europe by about one-third, was a series of economic and social benefits for the laboring and unfree classes.[93]

[90] MEYER, E., "Die Bevölkerung des Altertums," *Handwörterbuch d. Staatswissenschaften,* 3d ed., Vol. II.

[91] CURSCHMAN, F., *Hungersnöte in Mittelalter,* pp. 41–47, Leipzig, 1900.

[92] D'AVENEL, VTE. G., *Découvertes d'histoire sociale,* pp. 8, 148–9, 155, 209, 230, and *passim,* Paris, 1910.

[93] See KOVALEVSKY, *Die Ökonomische Entwicklung Europas,* Vol. V, Chaps. V–XII, Berlin, 1911. "According to the law of demand and supply, labor wages had to increase in proportion to the decrease of the population, and this phenom-

In a similar way, many great devastations of the population in China have been followed by a comparative improvement of the material well-being of the surviving population.[94] These, and other similar facts seem to corroborate the accuracy of the pro-Malthusian theories; yet there are facts which show that decrease of the population may have the opposite result. The first example is given by the later period of Roman history. After the third century A.D., the process of depopulation took place in Italy, and in some other provinces of the Roman Empire. This, however, was not followed by betterment, but by great aggravation of the economic situation of Rome, and of the well-being of its population.

> Depopulation . . . became now the outstanding feature of the life of the Empire. . . . As a result, the general productivity of the Empire constantly decreased. Larger and larger tracts of land ran to waste. The exchange of goods became more and more irregular. . . . Hence the frequent occurrence of famines, and the decay of industry. No partial measures could counter this progressive decay.[95]

Another example is given by contemporary France. As we know, its population has been almost stagnant during the whole of the nineteenth and twentieth centuries. If the discussed theory were right, we should expect that its population would be much better economically than that of other European countries, whose population has been rapidly increasing during that period. Such a conclusion was indeed made by some authors.[96] Nevertheless, quite competent French investigators indicate that the real situation is quite different. Besides many non-economic disastrous effects in the field of purely economic life, an insignificant increase of the French population has caused the following results: A slower rate of increase in national wealth than in other countries with a more rapidly increasing population; and a slower increase of salaries and well-being of the population—in brief, brings

---

ena took place throughout all the countries of Western Europe because the number of the population decreased," p. 274.

[94] See LEE, M., *op. cit.*, *passim.*

[95] ROSTOVTZEFF, M. J., *op. cit.*, pp. 424–425.

[96] THOMPSON, W. A., *op. cit.*, pp. 156 ff.

results opposite to what should be expected.   The following table illustrates this.[97]

Countries	Population (Millions)		National Wealth (Billions)	
	1815	1914	1815	1914
Germany............	24	68	35–40	400
France..............	29	39	80	295
England.............	18	45	45.5	450

Furthermore, if the theory were right, we could expect that countries with a low density of population would have necessarily greater economic well-being than countries with a higher density of population.   But again, the facts do not support such an expectation.   Within countries with relatively low density we find a low standard (Russia) and a high standard of economic well-being (United States of America, New Zealand, Australia). The same is true in regard to other countries with a high density of population (Belgium, England, on the one hand; and by contrast many provinces of India and China on the other).

Without mentioning other similar cases, the above seems to entitle us to conclude that an absolute or relative decrease in the density of population is not always, nor everywhere, followed by a positive influence on the economic well-being of a society. This means, first, that the correlation between the two phenomena is much more complex and less close than the partizans of this type of theories assure us.   Second, the fluctuation of prosperity or impoverishment of a society cannot be accounted for through a quantitative fluctuation of the number and the density of the population alone.   Third, the correlation has been studied insufficiently.   In order to make it clear, the partizans of these theories must indicate under exactly what conditions, in what way, and to what degree, a decrease in the density of population may have

[97] GINI, C., *Ammontare e composizione della ricchezza delle nazioni*, p. 553, Torino, 1914.   See also BERTILLON, *La dépopulation de la France*, pp. 9–61.

positive effects; and when, under what conditions, and beyond what limits it begins to exert a negative influence.

With a still greater reason, the above may be said of the opposite type of theories, with their motto: "With every mouth God sends a pair of hands," and, the greater the population, the better the economic well-being of a society. I have already given some considerations which show the inadequacy of such a theory. Numerous computations of the demographers (R. Pearl, G. H. Knibbs, E. M. East, J. Sweeney, and others) show that, under the present rate of increase of population, if there are no miraculous inventions within a few generations the earth will be overpopulated and a consequent lowering of the standard of living may be expected.[98] History records too plainly the economic misery of many "overpopulated" countries to allow us to maintain the thesis of the discussed optimistic theory. In a few cases, an increase in the density of a population has been followed by a rising economic well-being; but in still more numerous cases it has had quite opposite effects. Therefore we must make the same conclusion in regard to these theories which I made in regard to the opposite hypotheses.

Thus we must conclude that the theories dealing with the optimum number of the population are nearer to the truth. The more a population deviates from the optimum number, either above or under it, the more negative will be the influence on the economic well-being. The nearer the number is to the optimum number, the better will be the economic influence. But unfortunately, just exactly what this "optimum number of the population" is, the theories do not declare. Their answer is rather a vicious logical circle: "The optimum number of the population is the optimum number which varies for various times and societies." [99] Some other writers, like Carr-Saunders, go even so far as to state that "There will, in fact, under any given circumstances, always be an optimum number." [100] But, according to the same author, it is

[98] See KNIBBS, G. H., *The Mathematical Theory of Population*, p. 453; EAST, E. M., *op. cit.*, Chaps. IV, VI; PEARL, R., "The Population Problem," *Geographical Review*, 1922, No. 4.

[99] This is all that is given by the "optimum number" theory of Cannan, Nicholson, Wolf, or some others.

[100] CARR-SAUNDERS, *op. cit.*, p. 200 ff. See the proper critical remarks against Saunders' "optimum number" in WOLFE, A. B., *op. cit.*, p. 68, note.

almost always broken by either over- or underpopulation. Thus, even this group of theories is far from being satisfactory.

Summing up this brief analysis, we conclude that a correlation seems to exist between the fluctuation of density in the population of a given society and its economic well-being, but exactly what this relationship is, we do not know as yet. It seems to be much more complex and less close than the theories claim. It is the task of the future to find out when, under what conditions, and to what extent, an increase or decrease in the density of a population facilitates an increase or decrease of its economic well-being; and what the optimum number for a given society should be. At the present moment, we still know very little in this field.

8. SIZE AND DENSITY OF POPULATION CORRELATED WITH THE FORMS OF SOCIAL ORGANIZATION

We have several theories which try to show that the demographic factors are responsible for the forms of social and political organization. *A priori,* it is possible to foresee that the family and marriage forms, and the political and social régimes will be different when a territory the size of the United States has a population of 10,000 and when the population amounts to 100,000,000 human beings. But exactly what the difference will be, and what it would be when the contrast in size and in density was not so enormous as in this case, remains an unsolved problem. Let us take a few of the theories which try to clarify some cases of this type.

Demographic Factors Correlated With Social Differentiation, Stratification and Segregation.—It is rather evident that the differentiation of a population into urban and rural groups, into various strata, classes, castes, and what not, depends considerably on an increase in population. As its size and density increase, the above forms of social differentiation progress also. The first phenomenon is shown by the history of cities; the second one, by a series of studies like Durkheim's study of the social division of labor. Admitting the existence of a correlation, at the same time it is necessary to indicate that it is not so close as to have no exceptions or deviations. The size of the cities, as well as the per cent of the urban and the rural population, only remotely depends upon the size of a country's population. This is shown by the fact that among countries with a small population, there are countries with both a low and a high per cent of urban population (for instance, Belgium, Finland, Korea). They are both with and without large cities. The same is true in regard to the countries with a large population. (Compare China, Russia, and the United States.) This means that the degree of a country's urbanization is a function not only of, and possibly not so much of, demographic factors, as of a series of other factors. The same is true in regard to the character and the degree of labor division and social differentiation. China is a more densely populated country, and has a larger population than the United States; and yet the technical division of labor in China is less developed than in America, or in other countries with a lower density and a smaller population. The same is true in regard to social differentiation. There are big and densely populated societies with and without the caste system (India, China, Russia, the United States of America). There are densely populated societies with and without nobility of birth (Belgium, many provinces of India, Germany). The same is true in regard to small countries, and the countries with a low density of population. These indications are sufficient for the claim that the correlation between the discussed phenomena is not perfect, knows many exceptions, and is less close than its partizans assure us.[101]

Thus, even these fundamental forms of social organization, stratification, and differentiation are only to some extent correlated with the demographic factors. There is a still smaller probability of finding a quite tangible correlation between the demographic factors and other less fundamental characteristics of social organization and institutions. Let us examine one or two examples to see if this be true.

Demographic Factors Correlated with Family Organization.— One of the best theories of a correlation between the forms of

[101] The above shows the one-sidedness of Coste's, Kovalevsky's, Carli's, and Durkheim's theories which regard urbanization, social division of labor, and social differentiation, as a function of the size and the density of the population alone, or almost alone. The table of the forms of government among the simplest peoples given in the chapter about the economic school, (see further) only supports what I have said above.

family and marriage, and demographic factors is set forth by J. Mazzarella in his explanation of exogamy, polygamy, and of "the ambilian" forms of marriage, characterised by the fact that the husband enters the family of his wife, and assumes there a servile and subordinated position. Mazzarella has shown that these forms of marriage are typical of the lowest primitive peoples, and that they are regularly followed by exogamy, polygamy, a matrilinear system of descent, and by a lack of social stratification in these primitive groups, (or by *"gentilisme,"* in his terminology). What factors are responsible for such a type of family, marriage, and social structure? Mazzarella's study leads to the conclusion that neither the geographic, racial, political, economic, nor religious factors can account for it directly, because the system is found among peoples who are different in all these respects. His analysis shows further that the discussed characteristics of family, marriage, and social organization are found among the peoples who (a) live in an area with unlimited potential economic resources; (b) which, however, for their utilization, and conservation require a great deal of human labor, especially the labor of adult males; though (c) they are, as a rule, groups of small size and not having a sufficient number of adult males (underpopulation, according to the theory of "the optimum number"). Hence, Mazzarella's conclusion: "Exogamy, polygamy, and the ambilian forms of marriage are an indication of the numerical weakness (underpopulation) of a social group, and a manifestation of its need for increasing its population (especially the adult males) through the adjunction of males of other social aggregates." According to Mazzarella, this hypothesis is in harmony with the facts, and explains many details of the ambilian and the exogamic forms of family and marriage.[102] Thus, these forms of family and social organization are in a close correlation with the size and the density of the population, according to the author. This means that they are in a considerable degree a function of demographic variables. I must confess that, unlike a great many works in ethnology, Mazzarella's works

---

[102] MAZZARELLA, J., *Les types sociaux et le Droit,* pp. 178 ff., 282–312, Paris. 1908; *Studi di etnologia guiridica, passim,* Catania, 1903.

are free from hasty generalizations, from the "method of illustration" and from the carelessness in scientific analysis which usually makes these works valueless scientifically. I am inclined to think also that in Mazzarella's generalization there is something scientifically valid. But, on the other hand, the generalization goes too far. Hobhouse's, Wheeler's and Ginsberg's studies have shown that polygamy, a high position for women, and matrilinear descent, are found among peoples with different sizes of population, with different forms of stratification, and with different natural environments.[103] Among the exogamic peoples, there are several who live in a poor natural environment, who have a patrilinear system of descent, and who practice various methods of checking the increase of their population.[104] These facts do not agree with the hypothesis. On the other hand, we cannot say that all peoples who have the wife enter the family of her husband and become *"filiae loco"* to the head of the husband's family (*pater familias*) or become entirely subordinated to her husband, (*manus mariti* and marriages *cum manu*) live in a poor geographical environment, or are not under the necessity of expending a great deal of labor in obtaining their means of subsistence, or are always overpopulated. Among the populations of Europe and America in the nineteenth century, we have had societies with the most diverse densities and sizes of population; but they have all been essentially identical in the system of family and marriage. In the history of the family and marriage relationships in Rome, Greece, Europe, or the United States, the later stages, when the density and the size of these societies was increasing, have not caused a further enslaving of wife to husband nor an increase of *manus mariti*, as would be expected according to the theory; but rather, an emancipation of women and a weakening of the authority of the husband. These contrasts are sufficient to show the shortcomings of the theory, and its generalization.

[103] See the table in the chapter about the Economic School.

[104] Study from this standpoint the peoples with exogamy in WESTERMARCK'S *History of Human Marriage*, the chapter about exogamy. Study in CARR-SAUNDERS, *op. cit.*, Chaps. VII-XI, the peoples among whom infanticide, abortion, drinking of various decoctions, tabooing of sexual intercourse, postponement of marriage, mutilations of genital organs, and other methods for decreasing the growth of population are practiced.

9. DEMOGRAPHIC FACTORS CORRELATED WITH FORMS OF POLITICAL AND SOCIAL INSTITUTIONS

In anthropological, historical, and sociological literature, there are several theories which attempt to view various political régimes (such as despotism, democracy, monarchism, or republicanism) and various social institutions (like slavery, serfdom, free classes, feudalism, "equal society" and so on) as a function mainly of size and density of population. Accordingly, the principal changes in these fields are accounted for through changes in demographic conditions. The above theories of Coste and Kovalevsky may serve as examples of these hypotheses. Since I do not have space here to analyze them, I can only say that if they are scrutinized in the manner of my above analysis of Mazzarella, and other theories, not much validity would remain to these hypotheses. The greater part of them are so vague in their meaning that if only because of this vagueness, they must be put out of science. Another part represented by Coste's theory of social evolution (see above) may be very "sympathetic" and "pleasant" for our wishes (it is not disagreeable to be drifting by a "law of social evolution" to an ideal paradise of perfect equality, liberty, and fraternity) ; and yet they are nothing but a kind of new "theology" in which the old-fashioned beneficial Providence is superseded by the "law of beneficial evolution or progress." This is the only difference between the old and this new theology. Happy are those who can believe! But for those who look for a seriously proved theory, Coste's "law" and hundreds of other "sympathetic" theories, are nothing but scientific "rubbish" contradicted at every step by stubborn facts. On what, for instance, does he base his statement that, at "the stage of Bourg," there was an absolutism of family and supremacy based exclusively on birth? On fiction, no more. Only a little study of the facts is necessary to see that the real situation is much more complex and quite different. On what is based his statement that with an approach to the stage of federation there is also an approach to the supremacy of intelligence and free associations? On nothing, also, except wishes. If I were a believer in any linear law of evolution, I would rather have reversed his theory, and have tried to show that, in the primitive stages, intelligence and free association played a greater rôle than they are playing in the last federative stage. But I am not a believer in either principle; therefore I simply state that both "laws" are "pseudo-laws." [105] In the history of a single country (especially of a long-existing society) study the alternation of monarchy and republic, the increase and decrease of despotism, the introduction and elimination of an elective system; and then confront these changes with the fluctuations in the size and density of the population, and the result will scarcely show any tangible correlation. Investigate the distribution of various political régimes, or of certain types of social institutions among various contemporary societies; then compare these with the size and the density of the population of these countries, and the result is again likely to be nil. In brief, if there is a correlation between demographic factors and the forms of social and political organization (which is probable), it is so remote, so complex, and so strongly masked by the interference of other factors, that we must regard it as a potential or intangible, rather than as a factual correlation. At any rate, only the future can establish it. The existing theories, with perhaps a very few exceptions, do not count much. As to these exceptions, I would mention only one type of correlation which appears to me more or less valid. This is the statement that, with an increase in size and density of the population, its social differentiation, whatever may be its form, and its technical division of labor, are likely to increase also. (See Durkheim's theory analyzed further.) But, as we have seen, even this broad correlation is far from being close, and the lines of both processes do not always go parallel. The curve of social differentiation often proceeds apart, sometimes even in the opposite direction from the curve of density and size of population, while their points of maximum and minimum, or points of inflection in their cycles quite often do not coincide. In brief, there is a tangible, but far from close correlation. With the exception of this, I wonder whether there is any valid correlation among the hun-

---

[105] See the facts in my *Social Mobility*, *passim*. See also FAHLBECK, P. E. *Die Klassen und die Gesellschaft*, Jena, G. Fischer, 1923.

dreds of "pseudo-correlations" abundantly supplied by various "sociological law-makers."

10. SIZE AND DENSITY OF POPULATION CORRELATED WITH INVENTIONS AND MEN OF GENIUS

Discussing the correlation between demographic factors and the progress of technical inventions, I indicated the principal reasons for expecting that an increase in the density and size of the population would favor an improvement in the technique of production. For similar reasons, a considerable number of the authors contend that increase in the density and the size of a population tends to increase the progress of mental activity, and the number of men of genius and talent. These theories have been laid down by A. de Candolle, A. Coste, McKeen Cattell, S. Fisher, P. Jacoby, A. Odin, G. R. Davies, F. Maas and others.[106] The principal inductive argument in favor of such a theory consists in the statistical finding that cities produce a greater quota of such men than the country; and the densely populated areas more than the less densely populated ones. Here are a few figures which may serve as examples of these findings. According to S. Fisher, per every 10,000 population of the specified categories in America, the following number of the notables mentioned in *Who's Who* (1922-23) were born in these different localities: farm population, 1; village (up to 8000), 8.5; small city (8000-50,000), 6.5; large city (50,000 and more), 6.0; suburb of large city, 11.6.[107] According to Davies, the coefficient of correlation between the density of the population and the fertility in prominent men of letters in America is: for 1850, +0.60; for 1860, +0.72; for 1870, +0.76.[108] The findings of several investigators

---

[106] See CATTELL, J. McK., *American Men of Science*, 2d ed., pp. 555 ff., 568 ff.; the same, 3d ed., pp. 784 ff.; DE CANDOLLE, A., *Histoire des sciences et des savants*, Génève-Bale, 1885; ODIN, A., *Genèse des grands hommes*, Paris, 1895; MAAS, F., "Ueber die Herkunftsbedingungen der Geistigen Führer, *Archiv für Sozialwissenschaft*, 1916, pp. 144–186; FISHER, S., "A Study of the Type of the Place of Birth," etc., *American Journal of Sociology*, March, 1925; DAVIES, G. R., "A Statistical Study of the Influence of Environment," *Quarterly Journal of the University of North Dakota*, Vol. IV, pp. 212–236; JACOBY, P., *Études sur la sélection chèz l'homme*, Paris, 1904; for other data and references see my *Social Mobility*, Chap. XII.

[107] FISHER, *op. cit.*, p. 552, Table I.

[108] DAVIES, *op. cit.*, pp. 221 ff.

are similar in their essentials. Shall we conclude from this that the greater the density, the greater will be the number of prominent men produced? Do these findings really prove that density, rather than any other factor, is responsible for the higher number of prominent men produced in the cities, and in the more densely populated areas? A mere glance at the given figures will make such a conclusion questionable. In the first place, we see that, though the number of prominent men produced in the cities is greater than in the open country, this number decreases as we pass from the villages to the cities, and from them to the big cities. The results obtained by Davies are similar. This contradicts the statement that the number increases parallel with the increase of the size and density. It also raises doubt as to whether density really is the responsible factor. Perhaps it is only a concomitant mask, under which quite a different factor operates. This hypothesis is supported by a series of facts. If density were the decisive factor, then the city proletariat would have to produce a greater number of prominent men than the peasantry of the open country. The facts collected by Maas and Fisher show that this expectation is not warranted. The city proletariat in the past, as well as in the nineteenth century, has been much less fertile in the production of prominent men than the peasantry. Furthermore, if the density of the population were the responsible factor, the number of the men of genius produced per a definite number of the population would have to increase along with an increase in the density of Europe's population during the nineteenth century. In spite of the great increase in density, and the great growth of cities, the quota of great men produced at the end of the nineteenth century seems not to have been greater. The same fact in regard to the eminent men of science in America has been indicated by McKeen Cattell. In the period from 1900 to 1910, the big American cities considerably decreased their quota of these men.[109] Furthermore, if density were the responsible factor, the districts of the cities with overcrowded dwellings would have to produce a high quota of the men of genius. As a matter of fact, they produce the smallest quota. The same conclusion is obtained by a comparison of dif-

[109] CATTELL, *op. cit.*, 2d ed., pp. 568 ff.

ferent countries according to their density, on the one hand, and according to the number of men of genius and talent, per 10,000 or 1,000,000 population, on the other. Not all densely populated countries top the list of those with the greatest number of geniuses and men of talent produced. Finally, even if the number of geniuses were increasing with an increase in the size of the cities, and not all the least densely inhabited countries were at the bottom of the list,[110] (which is not true), this would not prove that density is the responsible factor. This situation might have been due to the selective character of city population, to the attraction of all talented people to cities, and to the transmission of their talents to their posterity born in the city. It may be due also to the greater educational facilities of the big cities, and to other similar conditions. These considerations are enough to contend that, if density and talent are correlated, the correlation is loose.

What has been said of men of genius, may be said of inventions in their correlation with the size and the density of population. By making the interchange of ideas more intensive, a greater density and size of population may facilitate a lucky combination of ideas, resulting in new inventions. On the other hand, a greater density facilitates a too tight social cohesion, a mob-mind, and passive imitation of crowd-patterns; which rather hinders the development of the initiative necessary for new inventions and original achievements. For these reasons, it is quite understandable why the stream of inventions does not always increase with an increase in size and density of population; why many densely populated countries (like China or India) have been stagnant, tradition-bound, and poor in inventions during several centuries; why many of the greatest inventions ("domestication" of fire, domestication of animals, language, grammar, agriculture, use of metals, the first boat, first tools, machinery, utilization of wind, creation of pottery, building of dwellings, invention of first moral, juridical, and religious ideas, first mythology and poetry, and so on) were made under conditions where density of

---

[110] Compare for instance the list of densities of population of different countries with Huntington's table of their rank of civilization: *Civilization and Climate*, Chap. XI.

population was exclusively low and the size of the groups small; why a great many inventors and creators have lived a relatively isolated life; why men who spend their time in crowds, going from one group to another, are rarely the men of an original mind; and so on. In brief, density and size of population are, beyond some degree, neither sufficient nor necessary conditions for invention. In coöperation with other factors they may sometimes facilitate inventions, but no more. We must not overestimate their significance and their correlation.

11. DEMOGRAPHIC FACTORS CORRELATED WITH MORES AND CUSTOMS

J. Frazer, M. Kovalevsky, W. G. Sumner, H. Spencer, E. Westermarck, E. Waxweiler, A. G. Keller [111] and many others have shown that the folkways, *mores,* and customs of peoples are not something incidental, but represent the result of a great many trials and errors, or of the experiences of a great many individuals during several generations. In other words, they are, to a great extent, selected, and the most suitable under the existing circumstances. If not in all, at least in a great many cases, such a statement is likely to be true. For this reason it is probable that those *mores,* folkways, and customs which pertain to the practices connected with the phenomena of sexual intercourse, conceptions, birth, marriage, death, and generally with the phenomena of the regulation of the number of individuals, are to be directly or indirectly correlated with demographic factors. In groups which feel a pressure of population, or are overpopulated, there must appear "folkways" and *"mores"* whose purpose is to check an increase of their population. In groups which are underpopulated, there must appear "folkways" and *"mores"* whose purpose is to facilitate an increase of their population. Correspondingly, many practices, like infanticide, abortion, polyandry, postponement of marriage, or the utilization of contraceptive means, and

---

[111] See FRAZER, J. G., *Psyche's Task*, London, 1913; SUMNER, W. G., *Folkways,* 1906; WESTERMARCK, E., *The Origin and Development of the Moral Ideas*, Vol. I, London, 1906; KOVALEVSKY, M., *Coutume contemporaine et loi ancienne,* Paris, 1893; WAXWEILER, E., "Avantpropos" in *Bulletin mensuel of the Sociological Institute of Solvay*, 1910, No. 1; KELLER, A. G., *Societal Evolution*, N. Y., 1915.

so on, are likely to be permitted or approved in "overpopulated" societies, while the opposite practices and *mores,* whose purpose is to facilitate an increase of population, are likely to be approved in "underpopulated" societies. In this way, *the demographic factors may stamp, to some extent, the character of the moral, juridical, religious, and other forms of conduct pertaining to the above phenomena.* This expectation seems to be warranted to some extent. Carr-Saunders has shown this in regard to the simple peoples, as well as partly in regard to the more complex societies. The "population-politics" of France are rather opposite to the projected measures in Japan or China. Increasing pressure of the population of the European societies during the last few decades has been followed by an expansion of the methods of birth-control, and by factual and juridical legalization of their propaganda. In brief, the character and transformation of folkways in these fields seems to show some tangible correlation with the demographic factors. They must be taken into consideration in an elucidation of the problem of why the *mores* of a given society in this field are such and such, and why they are transforming in such and such direction. But, again, we must not overstress the rôle of the demographic factors even in this restricted field. Still less tangible is their rôle in the field of the *mores,* which are only remotely connected with the phenomena of population growth and vital processes.

12. DEMOGRAPHIC FACTORS CORRELATED WITH OTHER IDEOLOGICAL PHENOMENA

Several authors, among them F. Carli and C. Bouglé especially, have tried to interpret a series of ideological phenomena in the light of the demographic factors. Let us briefly glance at their theories.

Size and Density of the Population Correlated with the Evolution of Language.—Trying to prove a decisive rôle for the demographic factors in a causation of the ideological and psychical variations, Carli takes the evolution of language and the character of religious ideas to corroborate his fundamental proposition: "The denser a population, the bigger the size of the group, and the more heterogeneous its individuals; the richer will be the amount of experience of the society, and the more intensive its intellectual life." [112]   This general proposition is corroborated, in the first place, by the evolution of language. Carli's arguments are as follows: "The greater the density of a population, the greater the number of the substantives (and the verbs) in the language" because the experiences of the members of such a society are more numerous and manifold, requiring a greater number of words to express them than the experiences of a less dense society. To this he adds that the curve of the evolution of a language is parallel to that of an increase in the size and the density of population: the Roman language quantitatively and qualitatively reached its climax of development at about the first century A.D., and, after that time, began to go down parallel to the process of depopulation of Rome, so that it has almost disappeared since the fifth century A.D.[113]

I am not in a position to say to what extent Carli's proposition is true, but I can make the following statements: First, Carli's, and all "sociologistic" theories of language (see the chapter about the sociologistic school) are right as far as they contend that without social contact and some density of the group, language and grammatical rules could not appear and grow. I agree also that when the population of a society is decreasing, it is likely to be followed by a decrease in the area of diffusion of its language. However, I doubt seriously that the number of substantives and the verbs of a language is proportional to the density of a population. For instance, the density of the population of Russia is less than that of the majority of the European countries; nevertheless, the number of the substantives and the verbs of the Russian language is certainly not less than that of any other European language. I doubt also that the language of the denser city population is richer, better, and more colorful than that of the country population of the same society. I doubt again that the imagination and fantasy of the city population or those of densely populated industrial countries are richer than those of the country population; or those of the people of more densely populated industrial countries than those of the less densely populated agricultural countries. I think also that the grammar of a

<hr>

[112] CARLI, *op. cit.*, pp. 187 ff., 202 ff.   [113] *Ibid.*, pp. 202–205.

language was, in essence, created in the early stages of a group, when its size and density were insignificant. Furthermore, I do not see that the area of expansion of a language is in close proportion to the density of a country's population. The density of the population of Belgium, Holland, Bengal, or the northwestern provinces of India is higher than that of Great Britain; and yet, English is spoken in an area several times greater than the area where the Dutch, the French, or the Indian dialects are spoken. The density of Russia's population is lower than that of the majority of the European societies; but Russian is spoken by a number of people probably greater than the number speaking any European language, with the exception of English. The depopulation of ancient Greece began at about the end of the fourth century B.C., and yet the area of the Greek language in the third and second centuries B.C. was probably greater than it was before. I also doubt a close correlation between an increase and decrease of the population, and the qualitative progress and regress of a language. The rate of increase in the Roman population had already begun to go down at about 150 B.C. However, only at the end of the second century A.D. did there appear the first serious symptoms of decay in Roman literature and literary style. The density of the population of England, France, and Germany increased from 1820 to 1914. Yet one may doubt whether the English, the French, or the German languages and literature improved during this period, or are better now than they were in the eighteenth, or at the beginning of the nineteenth, centuries. The same is still more true in regard to music and many forms of arts.

These examples, which may be increased greatly, seem sufficient for raising a serious question as to the validity of Carli's proposition.

Size and Density of Population Correlated with Religion, Mysticism and Fetishism.—The psychology of a less densely populated society tends to be more religious, more mystical, more fetishistic, and less heterogeneous than the psychology of the more densely populated societies. Such is the next correlation which Carli tries to establish. The arguments given in favor of the proposition consist in the following indications: The thinner population of the country is more mystical and religious than the population of a city. In the less densely populated societies, words are given some mystical and sacred value, causing such societies to be predominantly "legend-making." With an increased density of population, irreligiousness, positivism, heresies, individualism of opinions, and heterogeneity, tend to increase.[114] I am afraid that in his proposition and arguments, Carli mixed quite a different series of facts. The few and one-sidedly interpreted facts given by Carli to corroborate his proposition may be confronted by a series of opposite facts. For instance, China, and many provinces of India are certainly more densely populated than America or many countries of Europe. However, we cannot say that in China or India there is less "legend-making" or a greater variety and heterogeneity of ideologies and various heresies, or less mysticism, than in the less densely populated European countries. It is doubtful also that the city population is less "mob-minded" than the country population. The opposite is likely to be more true. I doubt further that the city proletariat is less inclined to "legend-making" than the country population. The difference is rather in the kind of legend produced. The farmer makes a sort of hero out of some Christian individual, while the proletarian is doing the same out of some demagogue. The country people may make a legend out of one individual; the city people, out of some other one (out of Gloria Swansons, Valentinos, tennis stars, boxing and football stars, some "chiromancer," ballet-girls, Menckens, Bernard Shaws, Lenins, K. Marxs, J. J. Rousseaus, Voltaires, and so on). Pareto (see the chapter about Pareto) has shown that only the forms of superstitions and legends are changing while their essence remains practically the same. Instead of historical religion, the city population may have the religion of "socialism," "communism," "anarchism," "liberalism," "nationalism," the "religion of progress," of "pacifism," of "reason" or any other fashionable "ism." In spite of their pseudo-scientific forms they are as unscientific, mystical, and superstitious as the historical or traditional beliefs styled contemptuously by them as "superstitions." The same may be said of the tendency to ascribe to words some mystical and

[114] CARLI, *op. cit.*, pp. 206–211.

magic significance. Here also the more and the less densely populated societies, the city and the country, differ not in that one group does a thing while another does not, but only in the forms of doing it. In the country population there may be some words given a sacred or magic influence; in the city population the same is done in regard to some other words. "Fetishization" of words, as well as other phenomena, is an eternal fact. Its forms vary, but its essence remains.[115] That is all the difference.

For these reasons, I do not think Carli's correlations are valid. There is still less reason to admit any correlation between the character of religion (Buddhism, Christianity, Mohammedanism, etc.), and demographic conditions, because each of such religions has been spread among the large and the small, the densely, and the non-densely populated societies.

Demographic Factors Correlated with Equalitarian Ideology and Movements.—An attempt to establish a correlation between demographic and ideological phenomena is given by Professor C. Bouglé (1870–   ) in his book, *Les idées égalitaires.*[116] The purpose of the book is to answer the problem: What are the factors which are responsible for the growth and diffusion of the ideologies of equality, levelling, and democracy? The author's study leads to the conclusion that such factors are size, density, heterogeneity, and mobility of the population. An increase in these characteristics of the population tends to facilitate the diffusion, popularity, and power of ideologies of equality, and of democratic political institutions. The principal corroborations of this proposition are partly "speculative," partly factual. The speculative corroborations consist in some analogies with a complex biological organism, and in a series of statements typical of the sociologistic school. Some of these are, that with an increase in the size of the population and its density, social differentiation increases; that this frees an individual from a tight attachment to the group, making him more individualistic and "cosmopolitan" at the same time; that such a transformation naturally undermines the caste principle and facilitates an appreciation of the

---

[115] See Sorokin, *Sistema sociologii,* Vol. I, pp. 177–193.

[116] 2d ed., Paris, 1908; see also Bouglé, C., *La démocratie devant la science,* 3d ed., 1923.

human being generally, regardless of the group from which he comes and to which he belongs; that a greater density of population favors a greater intensiveness of mental interaction, in this way undermining many group prejudices and superstitions; and that an increase in the size and the density of the population makes more intensive the contact of the men of various races, classes, families, religions, and so on, helping to increase their mutual understanding. Such are the principal speculative reasons in favor of Bouglé's theory. His factual corroborations are essentially as follows: In the first place, he states that only twice in the history of mankind has an extraordinary diffusion of the ideologies of equality occurred,—once in the later period of the Roman Empire (in the period of Christianity and Stoic philosophy)—and again in the modern period of European history, opened by the great French Revolution. Analyzing the specific conditions responsible for the great diffusion of the equalitarian ideas at these periods, Bouglé concludes that they consisted in the above factors of large size, high density, heterogeneity, and mobility of the population. The same conditions are given within modern democratic societies. Further, Bouglé indicates that, in the Roman Empire, as the size, density, and heterogeneity of the population were growing, the privileges of birth and order were disappearing. The next proof is given in the indication that the ideologies of freedom, democracy, and equality were originated and developed in cities. To this is added the statement that the countries with a greater density of population, like Lancashire, where we have 707 inhabitants per square mile, are more democratic and equalized than the countries with a low density of population, like Russia. A series of other indications concerning the less intensive dogmatism of the followers of universal religions, compared with that of the followers of small religious sects; the increase in the popularity of equalitarian ideologies and institutions with an increase of social mobility and contact; and some other considerations of this kind, close the series of Bouglé's interesting and suggestive corroborations.

Shall we recognize Bouglé's theory as valid? I doubt it. Although we may find several interesting ideas in the book, the main contention of the author appears questionable to us. In the first place, I cannot agree at all with the statement that a diffusion of the equalitarian ideologies and institutions took place only twice in the history of mankind.   Omitting primitive societies for the moment, I still wonder why the democracies of Athens, the Italian mediæval City-Republics, the forest cantons of mediæval Switzerland, the Buddhist revolution in India and in several other countries of the East, the Republic of Geneva founded by Calvin, the Lollards' and Levellers' movement in England, and the Commonwealth of England, founded by the revolution of the seventeenth century, the great equalitarian and communistic movements in the history of Persia (Mazdack's revolution), in ancient Egypt (social revolution described by Ipuwer), a series of similar movements in the Arabian and the Mohammedan caliphates, the series of the mediæval equalitarians and communists; and the socialist movements and revolutions followed by a corresponding diffusion of the ideologies of equality, and democratic, communistic, and socialistic institutions (the Bohemian revolution of the fifteenth century, the foundation of the communist state of Taborites, the communes of Thomas Münzer, of John of Leiden, the sects and movements of the Katarrs, Patarens, the Lyon's Poor, the Arnold of the Breshia, the Ciompi, and so on); and a hundred similar phenomena are not mentioned by Bouglé?   Each of them, whether in their ideologies, practical demands, reforms, or institutions created, has been at least as radical in the recognition of the principle of equality as has Christianity, or the Stoic philosophy, or as the Declaration of the Rights of Man promulgated by the French Revolution. Even in their practical effects, many of these movements have been at least as efficient as Stoic philosophy and Christianity during the first three or four centuries of their existence.   In brief, Bouglé's very starting point is fallacious, and through its fallacy it naturally spoils the majority of his conclusions.   If the author had taken into consideration at least the above equalitarian movements, their ideologies, their reforms, and their diffusion, he evidently could not have come to the conclusion that the equalitarian movement is possible only in large, dense, mobile, and heterogeneous societies, because the above movements have happened in the large and the small, in densely and non-densely populated societies, and with both a homogeneous and heterogeneous population.

Now let us ask whether or not it is true that the greater the size, the density, and the heterogeneity of a society's population, the less it will be stratified; and the more equalitarian, democratic, and equal it will be. I am convinced that such a statement is fallacious. A great many primitive groups have been of small size, density, and heterogeneity of their population; yet they are less stratified, and rather more self-governed than almost all the large and densely populated societies with heterogeneous populations. In simple societies, economic contrasts were less than in any contemporary "equalitarian" society. Occupational stratification and differentiation were less also. Political privileges and disfranchisements of their members were less conspicuous than in any contemporary democratic society. These small groups did not often have any hereditary government or aristocracy, or any caste or class division. Their leaders were elected. They enjoyed self-government. To many of them it was possible to apply what Tacitus said of the ancient Teutons: *"Duces ex virtute legunt." "De minoribus principes consultant, de maioribus omnes."* Mazzarella, Hobhouse, Wheeler and Ginsberg, Lowie, and a series of other investigators have shown this clearly.[117] This means that, contrary to Bouglé, "the most equalitarian" organization is obtained where the size, and the density, and the heterogeneity of a population are the lowest. More than that, in my study I have come to the conclusion that each time the size or the heterogeneity of a society's population increases, social stratification, or inequality, increases rather than decreases.[118] Other conditions being equal, the groups with a smaller size and a less heterogeneous population are liable to be less stratified and more equalitarian than groups with a larger size and more heterogeneous population. This seems to be much nearer the truth than Bouglé's proposition.

[117] See Mazzarella, *Les types sociaux, passim;* Hobhouse, Wheeler and Ginsberg, *The Material Culture and Social Institutions of the Simpler Peoples,* pp. 50 ff. See the table given in this book in the chapter about the economic school. See the facts and other references in Sorokin, *Social Mobility,* Chaps. III–VI.
[118] See *Social Mobility,* Ch. V.

If further proof be needed it would be enough to compare existing societies according to the size and the density of their population, on the one hand, and the degree of democracy, self-government, political and economic equality, on the other. This would soon show that these two curves do not run parallel at all. China and many Indian states are populated more densely, and have a size much greater than Norway, or Sweden, or Denmark, or Finland, or Canada, or New Zealand; and yet, according to Bouglé's criterion of equality, the former societies are much less equalitarian than the latter. The density of the population of the United States of America is much less than that of France, or Italy, or Rumania, or Japan, not to mention many Asiatic countries; yet nobody would say that the United States is nearer to a caste régime, or is less democratic than any of these countries. In Rome, mentioned by the author, the process of equalizing its subjects in the form of an extension of the rights of citizenship went on not only in the period of an increase in the density of the Roman population, and during the enlargement of the boundaries of the Empire, but continued for a long time after the process of depopulation took place. (Caracalla's law was granted in A.D. 212, while the birth rate had begun to fall already at about 150 B.C.) I question also the validity of Bouglé's statement that cities with a more dense and heterogeneous population are more "equalitarian" or "democratic" than the country. If we ask where, in the city or in the country, are the greater inequalities of fortune, of privilege, of rank, and prestige, the answer is: in the city. Therefore it is hard to think that this case may testify in favor of the criticized theory. It is useless to continue these contradictions. The conclusion which follows from the above is clear: There is no definite correlation of the equalitarian movement with either the size or the density or the heterogeneity of a society's population. The illustrations given by Bouglé in favor of his theory may be confronted with facts which testify against it.

Bouglé's statements concerning the rôle of mobility are more valid in this respect. Yes, mobility in some cases facilitates the expansion of equalitarian ideology and institutions, but not always, and not so much in the sense that it makes social inequalities or social stratification less conspicuous, or less great, as in the sense that it substitutes some other basis for the social distribution of individuals within the social pyramid for the basis of birth or family status. The pyramid of social stratification or inequalities in mobile societies may be as high, and often is even higher, than in immobile societies (see my *Social Mobility,* Chaps. III-VI). The above reasons are enough to warrant questioning seriously the validity of Bouglé's interesting theory. I think it, like several other theories of the correlation of demographic factors with ideological ones, is far from being valid.

13. DEMOGRAPHIC FACTORS CORRELATED WITH THE PROGRESS AND DECAY OF SOCIETIES

As almost all sociological schools have, the demographic school also has its own theory of the evolution of societies, or the law of their origin, progress, and decay. The best theory of this type is formulated by Professor Corrado Gini [119] in his book *I fattori demografici dell' evoluzione delle nazioni.* F. Carli also added something of his own to the theory of Gini. Let us briefly outline the essence of Gini's theory of the progress and decay of societies.

The book opens with the statement that the decay of societies has taken place many times in human history. This leads to the problem of what the causes may be. After a criticism of several other theories, Gini comes to the conclusion that the principal cause of the evolution of a society is the demographic factor, which in various ways leads to many changes in the quality of the population, and in its economic, political, and cultural organization. The theory starts with a statement that, independent of immigration, emigration, war, and other catastrophic phenomena, the play of demographic factors, in a relatively short period, may change the biological characteristics of the population in quite a normal way. This is due to the fact that each later generation of a group represents the offspring of only a small fraction of the previous generation. From two-fifths to two-thirds of any

[119] Professor of Sociology at the University of Rome, president of the Italian Statistical Institute, editor of *Metron,* author of many a valuable work: *Il sesso dal punto di vista statistico,* 1908; *Problemi sociologici della guerra,* 1921, etc.

previous generation die before marriage. Of the remaining part who marry, not all leave any posterity. In this way, each subsequent generation comes practically only from one-third to one-eighth part of the previous generation. This shows that a normal play of the demographic factors may, in a short period of time, greatly change the racial or the biological composition of a society. This is still more inevitable, since, as a rule, the procreation of the upper classes is less than that of the lower classes. Therefore, owing to this differential fertility, plus the above play of the demographic factors, biologically a population changes very rapidly. At the same time, the lower procreation of the upper strata makes inevitable a permanent ascending current of climbers from the lower to the upper classes to fill the vacancies created by the lower fertility of the upper strata. They are doomed to die out, and their places are more and more occupied by newcomers from the lower strata. "The land of the conquered is the grave of the conquerors" is an expression of this general phenomenon.[120]

On the basis of these facts, Gini further formulates his "parabola of an evolution of the nations."

As the parabola of an organism's life has its reason in the different activities of its metabolism, so, I think, may the curve of the evolution of a people be correlated with the different stages of the demographic metabolism between various social classes.[121]

After this, Gini outlines his parabola of the evolution of societies. In essence, it is as follows:

Whether a society is founded by immigrants or by natives, at its earlier stages there is no conspicuous social differentiation. Such stages are marked by a high fertility of the population. (This is valid in regard to the past societies, such as Crete, Troy, Mycenae, Athens, Sparta, and others, and in regard to the population of colonial America, Australia, Canada, New Zealand, and so on.) As a result of it, the size and the density of the population begin to grow. This results in an increase of social differentiation within such a population and finally leads to the appearance of differential fertility in its upper and lower classes. At

[120] GINI, CORRADO, *I fattori*, pp. 1–33.   [121] *Ibid.*, p. 34.

the same time, the country becoming relatively overpopulated, a surplus of its population must emigrate, either peacefully or by means of war. Hence, intensive colonization and wars of expansion mark this period in the growth of a society. As a rule, those who are the most prolific, adventurous, and strong, are the principal ones to emigrate from the country, and go away on military enterprises. In the process of its expansion, society mainly loses these elements. Psychologically this stage is marked by great patriotic and nationalistic enthusiasm, by glorification of colonization and war for the country, by considerable solidarity, and a psychology of patriotic readiness to sacrifice individual happiness and life for the nation.

Then, sooner or later, comes the next stage. Through emigration and loss in wars of expansion, the society loses its most prolific, boldest and the most adventurous elements. As a result, the fertility of the society and the rate of increase of its population begin to diminish. This is augmented the more because the fertility of the already clearly separated upper classes has decreased enormously. The offspring of the lower classes, which also decrease their procreation, are more and more compelled to fill the vacancies left in the upper classes by its lower and lower procreation. The population increase stops. The ascending currents of social circulation from the lower to the upper classes become more intensive. Many of the previous obstacles for such a circulation are put away. Society becomes more "democratic." At the same time, thanks to the decline of population growth, and to the exploitation of colonies and subjugated countries, the economic well-being of the society rises. The standards of living of all classes go upward, their comforts increase, their tastes and desires become finer. The luxuries which could be found before only among the upper groups are now longed for by all classes. This leads to great progress in economic activity, and to the appearance of arts, music, and literature; while industries prepare on a large scale the objects of comforts and luxury. This is naturally followed by great industrialization of the society, by the growth of cities, by the development of commerce, and by increasing migration of country population to cities. Thus comes the period of commercial and industrial urban culture.

Politically, this is followed by a transformation of the society in the direction of democratization; psychologically, by a transformation of the previous prolific, adventurous, military, patriotic, and heroic people into a nation of the "small *bourgeois*"—into the business men who look for and long only for money, savings, and an income. Economic prosperity facilitates, so to speak, an "effemination" of the society. The elimination from it of its most prolific, adventurous, solidaristic, and patriotic elements in the previous period, and the exploitation of the colonies, accompanied by economic prosperity, make the society "pacifistic." Military glory is now no longer in vogue, and neither is nationalism. Vague pacifism and vague cosmopolitanism, side by side with a "small *bourgeois*" ideology, take its place. Arts, literature, poetry, and so on, begin to prosper. The society feels itself happy, and is sure in its future. Like Cicero, who lived approximately at such a stage of the Roman Empire, it thinks that "Rome will exist at least ten thousand years."

But, just as in the case of Rome, which existed only about five hundred years after Cicero, and which at his time was entering into the stage of its decline, the society does not see that it is also at the beginning of the stage of its decay. Sooner or later the preceding stage is superseded by a new one. The first symptom of this decaying stage is manifested in the process of depopulation in the rural parts of the nation. Owing to the great decrease in actual fertility of the population, and to a great migration of country people to the city, agriculture begins to decline, a lack of labor hands in rural districts begins to be felt more and more, many regions begin to be depopulated, and much land is forsaken. A series of economic conditions aggravates the situation of farmers and peasants still more, urging them still more to decrease their fertility. As a result, the country decreases more and more its inflow into the cities, whose fertility is still lower. The decrease of the country population, and its economic impoverishment, lead to a decrease in the demands for the objects of urban industry. The nation begins to produce more than it can digest. This reacts negatively on the development of industry, commerce, and the economic situation of city people. Industrial crises of "overproduction" become greater and more numerous. As a result, there comes an aggravation of the economic situation of the city laboring classes, and even in the city population as a whole. This is still further aggravated because the proportion of idle rentiers who live on the interest from their capital, and the professional classes who do not produce material values directly, is now much greater than it was before. Besides, in order to protect itself and its colonies and dominions, the government has to increase the taxes on a decreased population. All this results in an increase of social crises, disorders, and riots of the labor classes, who do not want to lower their standards of living. The class-struggle becomes bitter and more pitiless. This, in its turn, only contributes to the aggravation of the situation. The government, ideologists, and scientists try to cope with the difficulties. Governmental interference expands enormously. It begins to control more and more the economic life of the society. At that period a belief in the omnipotent rôle of science and the intellectuals is especially conspicuous. In vain! The process of the disorganization of the society continues to progress. Finally, either "peacefully," or in a military way, the society reaches its last stage,—decay. Its history is finished, and from the scene of history it is removed into its museum.[122]

Such is Gini's parabola of the social evolution of a society, interpreted in the light of demographic factors.

The next part of the book is devoted to a corroboration of the scheme by a factual analysis of the history of Greece, Rome, and several other societies, especially by an analysis of the present situation in France, which, according to the author, already is in its stage of decay (pp. 48-102). The majority of the European societies are supposedly about in the same stage. The final conclusion of Gini is that this parabola of social evolution is unavoidable. The only escape from it is through emigration and the founding of new colonies, by means of which it is possible to continue in a modified form the history of the metropolis, or the mother-country. *"Avviene nello sviluppo dei populi come in quello degli individui: raggiunta la maturità, cessa l'esuberanza delle manifestazioni vitali, si va a poco a poco chiudendo il ciclo del' esistenza; ad essi riapirne un altro. Ciò molte volte avviene."*

[122] *Ibid.*, pp. 34–47.

Such is the somewhat pessimistic conclusion of the author of the parabolic curve of the evolution of a society.

With a modification, but in essence similar to Gini's theory of the decay of nations, is the theory of Carli, which is as follows: With the decrease of the effective fertility of society, there comes a decrease in the number of inventions, and in the nations' "hope in possibilities" (*la fede nelle possibilita*). This reacts unfavorably upon the economic well-being of a society. All this is followed by a transformation of its dominant psychology; the solidarity of its members decreases, while individualism and economic egotism increase; the ideal of the glory and the magnificent grandeur of the nation is superseded by that of the savings account and the hunt for money; while the ideal of military heroism is replaced by that of pacifistic comfort. The upper classes degenerate more and more, ceasing to resemble their predecessors.

Of the more detailed statements, it should be mentioned that, according to Carli, the more closed the upper classes are, and the greater are the barriers for the ascent of the newcomers from the lower to the upper classes, the sooner the upper classes degenerate, and through that, the sooner comes the degeneration of the nation.[123]

Now what is to be said of the validity of these theories? At the beginning, let us put aside the details of Carli's theory which are far from being accurate. The longest aristocracy in the world, which I know of, is the Brahmanic caste in India which, without army, money, or even organization, has held its unquestionable superiority during at least two thousand years, and is holding it still. India continues to exist as a culture complex, while many other countries have disappeared. Yet, the Brahman caste is almost absolutely closed, at any rate more closed than any other aristocracy known to me. More than that, I am inclined to think that the closed aristocracies have been existing successfully for a period at any rate not shorter than the open upper classes. The Spartan aristocracy was more secluded than the Athenian one; and yet the Spartan aristocracy, and Sparta, which was con-

---

[123] CARLI, *op. cit.*, pp. 235–258, 362–368. Somewhat similar is G. Rageot's theory of the symptoms of decay, developed in his book, *La natalité, ses lois économiques et psychologiques*, Paris, 1918, especially pp. 12, 19, 152 and *passim*.

trolled by it, existed longer than the Athenian, with its more
open aristocracy. Rome's glorious period had a much more secluded aristocracy of patricians and senators than did her decaying period of the second and third centuries A.D., when her
upper classes were more open than before. Neither do we have
any serious reasons for thinking that the aristocracy of England
during the last thousand years, or during the last two centuries, has been more open than that of France.[124] For this reason, Carli's reference to the different fates of England and
France, as a proof of his contention, is unconvincing. Furthermore, the history of the secluded royal and old aristocratic families, when compared with that of the families of the new "aristocracy" which are less severe in their intermarriages, shows that
these old families have been degenerating rather more slowly
than the new ones. There is no need to increase these examples.
The statement of Carli is one-sided. The openness or seclusion
of an aristocracy seems to be not so important as its character.
If the aristocracy is biologically sound, and if it keeps its "blood"
from contamination through the exclusion of all contaminating
elements, (elimination of weaklings, deficient children, deficient
members, etc.), its seclusion and inbreeding seems to go on without degeneration.[125] If vigorous measures are not taken to
eliminate contaminating elements, then inbreeding may very
quickly lead to the aristocracy's decay. On the other hand, if, in
open upper classes, selection and recruiting of newcomers proceed
properly, then such an aristocracy may successfully exist and
rule for a long time. If the "refreshing blood" is picked up
wrongly, and the newcomers represent something far from superior, biologically and mentally,—which may easily happen if
access to the upper classes is too easy,—then such an aristocracy
is a pseudo-aristocracy; it is doomed to be incapable and through
its deficiency it may facilitate the ruin of the country.

Now let us turn to Gini's parabola of the evolution of nations.
In the first place, it cannot pretend to be universal. Like a great
many other theories of the progress and decay of societies, it is

---

[124] See my *Social Mobility*, Chaps. VII, XV, XXII.

[125] Compare SAVORGNAN, F., "Nuzialità e Fecondità delle Case Sovrane,"
Metron, No. 2, 1923, p. 224; PARETO, V., *Traité de sociologie générale*, Paris,
1919, pp. 1658 ff.

constructed principally on the basis of the history of Rome and
Greece. However, not all countries follow a similar "parabola"
in their history. Take, for instance, China or India. These two
countries have already existed several thousands of years, and yet
they are still alive, showing at the present moment some signs
of a new awakening. The whole scheme of Gini is practically inapplicable to their history. Perhaps this is due to the fact that
both countries seem to have always had a high procreation, and
their upper classes have probably not known differential fertility.
This, however, means that neither the fact of a decrease in the
fertility of a people in the course of its evolution, nor a lower
fertility of the upper classes is something universal and unavoidable. Since they are not unavoidable and not universal, the whole
scheme of Gini, which is based upon these two foundations, also
becomes not universal and not inevitable for all societies. The
theory, at the best, may be applied only to some peoples. Such
is the first limitation of the theory. Furthermore, it has several
assumptions which are questionable, and which could in no way
be regarded as universal rules. For instance, can we say that
the first stages of a society are always marked by an intensive
procreation and a rapid increase of its population? In some cases
it is so; in some others, it is not. The group or the society, on
account of many factors, (they are indicated by Carr-Saunders),
may be almost in a stationary state for an indefinite period of
time. Then the stage of expansion, colonization, and emigration,
with all the consequences of these phenomena, may not take place
for such a people, and their history may go on along quite different lines. Furthermore, granting that the first stages of a society
are marked by a rapid increase of its population, can we say that
emigration, colonization, and expansion are the only possible results of such an "overpopulation"? In the above we saw that
they sometimes take place, but sometimes not. The combination
of circumstances may be such as to make it impossible for the
society either to colonize, make a conquest, or conduct an emigration. Then there come other means for checking the population
surplus and growth; such as famine, increase of the death rate,
decrease of the birth rate, abortion, and all the other means described by Carr-Saunders. This means again that the subsequent

history of such a people will be different from Gini's parabola. Its generality thus becomes less and less universal. Let us go further. Is it true, for instance, that in the period of expansion of such a society, the most prolific, bold, and energetic elements of the population go away from the mother-country? Gini puts this statement quite dogmatically. His only argument in favor of his theory is that for the members of prolific families it is more difficult to find a place within the mother-country than for the members of the less prolific ones. But to this it may be objected that, since, according to Gini himself, the emigrating elements are more capable and energetic, they have more chances to find places within the mother-country than the less capable people. For this reason, we would expect that the emigrants are a rather less capable people than those who remain in the country. In brief, the discussed assumption of Gini is not proved, and we know little about its accuracy or inaccuracy. Therefore, all conclusions based on this assumption become uncertain, and the whole theory becomes something which may or may not be valid.

The next dogmatic assumption of the theory is an increase of economic well-being in society due to the emigration of its prolific members, and to the decrease of the effective fertility of the society. In the above we have seen that not every relative depopulation is necessarily followed by an increase of economic well-being. Sometimes it happens, sometimes not. If this is so, then, again, all later economic, political, and psychological changes depicted as the results of such an increase of well-being, might not happen, and the history of the society may follow quite a different curve of evolution than that depicted by Gini. A series of peoples have actually followed this curve, which differs much from Gini's parabolic line of development.

Without mentioning any of the further assumptions, the above is enough to show that Gini's scheme can in no way pretend to be a more or less general formula for the evolution of society. In the best case, it may be applied to some peoples. But, in view of the above assumptions of Gini, even there it remains uncertain as to what extent their decay is determined by demographic factors, as indicated by the prominent Italian statistician and sociologist.

His generalizations are still more questionable in view of the facts of the decay of many societies (Poland, Carthage, Bohemia, and so on) due to purely military causes; that is, to conquest by other peoples. In many other cases,—Babylon, Assyria, Egypt, the Arabian caliphates, Turkey, the empires of Genghis Khan, Tamerlane, and other old countries—we also do not find any serious reason for admitting that their decay was caused by Gini's demographic factors, or that it proceeded according to the line of his parabola.

Thus we come to the conclusion that Gini's theory must be limited greatly, and should be further tested even in those parts which seem to be valid. With these reservations and objections, it appears to contain a modicum of truth for the peoples to whose history it may be applied. One of its contributions is that it makes it impossible to disregard the rôle of the demographic factors in any scientific interpretation of the phenomena of the progress and decay of nations. Its practical value is in its warning to nations to be careful in their policy of birth-control and the reduction of their population, if they want to have a long and glorious history.

Gini's central idea that the depopulation or decrease of effective fertility is a factor of decay, seems to be near the truth, in spite of the popularity of the opposite opinion at the present moment. His arguments in favor of his statement may be backed by a series of others which point to the same fact. Among these arguments should be mentioned the following one: a low birth rate, and a low mortality through the elimination of natural selection are likely to lead to a survival of all the innate weaklings, and, through this, to a contamination of the innate quality of the people.[126] In this way they facilitate an aggravation of not only the quantitative side of the population problem, but its qualitative side also. This, in its turn, greatly contributes to the factors of a people's decay, and makes the attempt to stop this decay difficult.

14. GENERAL CONCLUSIONS

The preceding survey shows that the demographic school in sociology is one of the most developed. Numerous investigators

[126] See my *Social Mobility*, Ch. XX.

have succeeded in showing the importance and efficiency of demographic conditions in almost all fields of social phenomena. If we cannot say that all these attempts have been successful, or quite accurate, we have to admit that a considerable number of them are likely to be accurate, at least in part; and some of them are as near to reality as it is possible to arrive in the present stage of social science. The school has thrown light on a series of social phenomena. It has supplied us with a series of probable correlations. For these reasons the school has as much right to its existence as has any other sociological school. Putting away its mistakes and one-sidednesses, we may gratefully take its valuable contributions to the science of social phenomena.

CHAPTER VIII

SOCIOLOGISTIC SCHOOL

I. GENERAL CHARACTERISTICS OF THE SCHOOL

A s i s well known, in August Comte's classification of sciences into Astronomy, Physics, Chemistry, Physiology, and Social Physics, or Sociology,[1] sociology is put immediately after physiology or biology. Psychology, as a science preceding sociology, is omitted. This has called forth a serious criticism of Comte's classification by J. S. Mill, Herbert Spencer, and many others, who have insisted on the necessity of putting psychology after biology and before sociology, as its immediate basis. This has led to the appearance in sociology of the psychological school which tries to build sociology on psychology and to explain social phenomena by means of the psychological, rather than to explain psychological phenomena through the biological and sociological. Further characteristics of this school are that the majority of its partizans are inclined to interpret social phenomena as a derivative from the activity of individuals rather than trying to explain the individuals and their activity through social reality or society.

In spite of this, Comte's classification has found its followers. They think that in omitting psychology from his classification, he was quite right. They maintain that sociology has to be built immediately on biology, while psychology needs sociology as one of its bases. According to their opinion psychological phenomena need to be interpreted through sociological but not *vice versa*. Society, or sociality is the psycho-social reality of *sui generis* which exists apart, and is different from, that of the individuals who compose a society.[2] Sociological regularities are different from, and cannot be reduced to, the psychological. Such, in gen-

[1] COMTE, AUGUSTE, *Positive Philosophy*, tr. by Martineau, pp. 44-46, 394-395, N. Y., 1855.
[2] See the chapter about Bio-Organismic School, §1.

eral, are the lines of division between the so-called "psychological" and "bio-sociological," or, simply, "sociologistic" schools, which were quite conspicuous a few decades ago, and which, though much less definite now, are not yet entirely obliterated. The above, together with the fact that among the followers of "the sociologistic school" there are very prominent sociologists, and that they have contributed a great deal to the science of sociology through a clarification of problems only slightly touched by other schools, makes it appropriate to separate this group from other schools, and to survey briefly the works of its most prominent representatives. The very source and essence of sociality, these sociologists see in the phenomena of social interaction. Their investigations try to interpret social and psychical phenomena as a derivative of various forms of interaction. Their causal analysis consists essentially in a correlating of studied phenomena with various conditions of living together, or, in other words, with social conditions. Therefore all the theories which explain a certain social or psychical fact through its correlation with a certain social condition, are to be regarded as a variety of the sociologistic school.

For the sake of clearness, we shall take, in the first place, the most representative sociologistic theories which give *a general system* of sociologistic interpretation. This being done, we shall pass to *the special theories* which take a certain social condition as a variable (religion, *mores,* family, economic condition, etc.,) and try to show its effects, or its functions in various fields of social phenomena. In this way we shall be able to obtain a more or less adequate idea of the school. As a typical example of *the general* sociologistic theories we shall take: (a) the neo-positivistic school of E. De Roberty; and the theories of A. Espinas, J. Izoulet, Draghicesco, Ch. H. Cooley and others; (b) the school of E. Durkheim with his collaborators; (c) the theory of L. Gumplowicz and of his followers; (d) the "Formal School." [3]

---

[3] Among the earlier representatives of the contemporary sociologistic school we have Henri C. Carey. In his *Principles of Social Science*, Vol. I, 1858, he sets forth all the essentials of the school, and Durkheim's theory of the division of labor. Here, however, I do not give space to his theories because their characteristics are given in the chapter on the Mechanistic School. Similarly, the names of Lazarus and Steinthal are to be included among the "originators of

Having analyzed these general systems of sociology, we shall turn
to the principal types of the special sociologistic theories and
briefly survey them.   Such seems to me the best way to orientate
ourselves in the complex and vast field of contemporary sociologistic interpretations.   Now let us say a few words about the
predecessors of modern sociology.

2. PREDECESSORS

The ideas that man's mind, behavior and his other characteristics depend upon social interaction, and society; that social regularities are *sui generis;* that society is something different from
a mere sum of its individual members; and that there is a correlation between the fundamental categories of social phenomena
and those of personality-traits; these ideas were all known very
long ago.   The bulk of the old Indian philosophy and ethics,
(especially that of Buddhism,) is based upon the idea that our
"I" or "Self," with its empirical properties, sufferings, and joys
is a product of social contact and exists as long as the contact
exists.   "Self," the Hindu writers declared, can only be overcome
by: "destruction of contact," "separation," "isolation" or "giving
up."

Contact is the cause of all sensation, producing the three kinds
of pain or pleasure. . . Destroy contact and sensation will end . . .
names and things will cease . . . knowledge and ignorance will perish
. . . and the constituents of individual life will die.

This is the way to "escape from self, or from 'I.' " [4]   In modern
terminology this means that the very phenomenon of "I" or
an individual "Self" and its psychological qualities (desires,
emotions, ideas, etc.,) are the result of social contact and interaction.   Confucianism, as a system of applied sociology, is
essentially a socio-environmental theory.

---

the school."   Although giving an enormous mass of materials, they, however,
did not construct a clearly cut system of sociology.   See LAZARUS, M., and
STEINTHAL, H., *Zeitschrift für Völkerpsychologie und Sprachwissenschaft*, Vol. I,
1860, pp. 1–73, 437–477; Vol. II, pp. 54–62, 393–453; Vol. III, 1865, pp. 1–94,
385–486; Vol. XVII, 1887, pp. 233–264.

[4] "Life of Buddha by Asvaghosha Bodhisattva," in *the Sacred Books of the
East*, The Colonial Press, N. Y., pp. 369 ff.   See also "The Dhammapada,"
ibid., *passim* and Chaps. V–VI.   See also "The Upanishads," *The Sacred Books
of the East*, Vol. XV, *passim*, Oxford, 1884.

By nature, men are nearly alike; by practice, they get to be wide apart. . . There are only the wise of the highest class, and the stupid of the lowest class, who cannot be changed. . . When a child is trained completely, his education is just as strong as his nature; and when he practices anything perpetually, he will do it naturally as a permanent habit.

The habits are inculcated by family and other social groups with the help of ceremonies, music, poetry, imitation and other social agencies. Hence, an exclusive importance is given by Confucianism to "filial piety," the "five relationships," rules of propriety and to social environment generally. In this respect Confucianism contains all the essentials of the modern sociologistic theories, especially of the contemporary theory of *mores* developed by W. G. Sumner, and "the family-sociology" developed by Le Play's school and Ch. H. Cooley. Confucianism also stresses that "the heart of a man who observes no rules of propriety is the heart of a beast," which means that a man who is not modified by social environment is but an animal.[5]

Plato's *The Republic* is permeated with similar ideas. His system of a perfect state is based on selection, as well as on training, through a corresponding modification of social environment. In many places he draws a correlation between the character of the state and the character of the individuals, saying: "As the State is, so the individuals will be," and *vice versa*. Finally, he stresses the idea that man outside of social control is but an animal.

As the government is, such will be the man. . . . In the individuals there are the same principles and habits which there are in the State. . . . Governments vary as the character of men vary, and there must be as many of the one as there are of the other. Or perhaps, you suppose that States are made of "oak and rock" and not out of the human natures. . . . If the Constitutions of States are five, the dispositions of individual minds will also be five [and so on].[6]

When the reasoning and tamping and ruling power is asleep, the wild beast in our nature starts up and walks about, naked, and there

---

[5] See "Lî-Kî," *The Sacred Books of the East*, Vols. XXVII *passim*, and XXVIII, Book XVI, Hsio Ki.

[6] PLATO, *The Republic*, tr. by Jowett, pp. 435 ff., 456 ff., 544 ff., 557, N. Y., 1874.

is no conceivable folly or crime, however shameless or unnatural,[7] [which it may not commit].

Everybody knows Aristotle's saying that "man is a social animal" and his "without law and justice (and society) man would be the worst of all animals," [8] not to mention his developed theory of a socio-environmental determinism.

Later on there were few prominent social thinkers who did not stress the determining influence of various social conditions. On the other hand, we have already seen that an organic conception of a society, as a reality of *sui generis,* appeared long ago. (See chapter about bio-organismic theories.) This shows that the school, like almost all contemporary sociological systems, originated in the remote past. Since that time with variations the principles of the school may be traced throughout the history of social thought. Even the works of the eighteenth-century thinkers, "individualistic" though they may be, stress none the less a decisive determining power of social environment. The end of this century and the beginning of the nineteenth century were marked by a strong revival of the organic conceptions of society, by a sharp criticism of individualism and nominalism, by a reinstatement of the spontaneous evolution of social institutions independent from individual wishes, and by the idea of the theories of individual dependence upon society. The theories of J. de Maistre, de Bonald, E. Burke, and many others (see the chapter on the "Bio-Organismic School") furnish examples of the dominant sociological conceptions of that period. In their essentials they are conspicuously sociologistic.[9] These works influenced Auguste Comte in his principal theories in this field,[10] and in his turn Comte greatly determined the corresponding ideas of the contemporary representatives of this school. Let us now turn to their works.

---

[7] *Ibid.,* pp. 571 ff.

[8] ARISTOTLE, *Politics,* Book I, Chaps. I–III.

[9] See DE MAISTRE, J., "Considérations sur la France," "Les soirées de Saint-Petersbourg," *Le Pape,* "L'étude sur la souveraineté," "Examen de la philosophie de Bacon," in *L'Oeuvres completes de J. de Maistre,* Lyon, 1891–1892, Vols. I, IV, V; DE BONALD, L., "Theorie du pouvoire politique et religieux dans les société civile," *Du divorce,* "Essai analitique sur les lois naturelles," in his *Oeuvres,* Vols. I, II, III.

[10] See MOULINÉE, HENRI, *De Bonald,* pp. 145 ff., Paris, 1915

3. SOCIOLOGISTIC INTERPRETATIONS OF E. DE ROBERTY, A. ESPI-
NAS, J. IZOULET, D. DRAGHICESCO, CHARLES H. COOLEY
AND OTHERS

E. De Roberty (1843-1915), one of the earliest pioneers in sociology, was born and reared in Russia. He published his *Sociology* in Russian as early as 1876. Its French translation appeared two or three years later (second edition in 1886). Together with E. Littré and another prominent Russian thinker, Vyrouboff, he became one of the principal interpreters of A. Comte's positivism in a special journal founded by E. Littré for that purpose: *La philosophie positive*. A disagreement with some of Comte's theories, which he had already expressed in his "Sociologie," later led him to a formal rupture with positivism and to a designation of his own theory by the name of "Neopositivism." [11]   He spent many years outside of Russia and gave various sociological and philosophical courses at different foreign universities. After 1909 he was a professor of the Psycho-Neurological Institute in St. Petersbourg. In 1915 he was murdered in his home in Tverskaia Province, Russia. He was the author of many books in philosophy [12] and sociology.[13] Of his sociological works, the most important are *A New Program of Sociology* (Paris, 1904), and *Sociology of Action* (Paris, 1908), in which he sums up practically all the essentials of his theories. The philosophical and didactic character of his reasoning, together with a somewhat "heavy style," have probably been responsible for the fact that his name is much less known than that of Durkheim or Simmel, whose theories De Roberty set forth earlier, and, in some respects more consistently. Among his own predecessors, De Roberty mentions A. Comte, de Bonald, Herbart, Cattaneo, G. de Vitry, and George Lewes.[14]   De Roberty's sociological

[11] Besides in his books, the principal points of the disagreement are indicated in De Roberty's special pamphlet: *Pourquoi je ne suis pas positiviste.*

[12] *L'ancienne et la nouvelle philosophie; Inconnaissable; La philosophie du siècle; Agnosticisme; La recherche de l'unité; A. Comte et H. Spencer; F. Nietzsche; Les concepts de la raison et les lois de l'universe.*

[13] *La sociologie; L'éthique; Le psychisme social; Les fondements de l'éthique; Constitution de l'ethique; Nouveau programme de sociologie; Sociologie de l'action.*

[14] DE ROBERTY, *La Sociologie*, chapter, "Questions connexes."

system composes something inseparable from his whole philosophical system. Its essentials may be outlined as follows:

1. The world known to us — and it may be known adequately, contrary to the assertion of agnosticism — is composed of three fundamental forms of energy: the physico-chemical, or inorganic; the vital, or organic; and the social, or superorganic.

2. Physico-chemical phenomena are the result, or manifestation, of intra- and intermolecular interaction. Vital phenomena are the manifestation of an intra- and intercell interaction. Social or superorganic phenomena are the result of an intercerebral interaction. Each subsequent class of phenomena represents a specific complication of the preceding one.

3. The transition from one class to another is gradual and only relatively perceptible. This is true in regard to the boundary line between the inorganic and the vital, as well as between the vital and the superorganic phenomena. Besides the usual properties of living substance, life phenomena are often characterized by the presence of so-called elementary "psychical" processes, such as irritability, sensation, feelings, emotion and even by vague concrete images and representations.

4. Contrary to these elementary "psychical" phenomena, the very essence of superorganic phenomena is "thought" and abstract "knowledge" (connaissance). The highest forms of superorganic phenomena are the abstract and true concepts, categories and laws of science; generalizations of philosophy or religion; symbols and images of arts; and the rational prescriptions of applied thought, i.e., the rational theories of conduct (ethics). All these are various modes of social "thought" or "knowledge"; being found only among human beings, they are the very essence of civilization. "Thought," or "knowledge" or "concepts" are something entirely different from mere irritability, or sensation, or concrete images. In other words, in their pure form the superorganic phenomena are what are styled the highest forms of psychical phenomena.[15] They are embodied as we shall see, in the forms of scientific, philosophical, æsthetic, and applied

[15] See DE ROBERTY, *Nouveau programme de sociologie*, Chaps. I–IV, Paris, 1904; *Sociologie de l'action*, Chaps. I–VI, Paris, 1908; *La sociologie*, chapter, "Questions connexes."

thought or knowledge, based upon scientific premises. They compose a kingdom entirely different from vital phenomena. The gap between them is no less than between vital and inorganic phenomena. If this is so, then the problem arises, how have they originated? What is the source of their appearance? Why are they found among human beings only? These questions lead to the most important part of De Roberty's theory, which is his *"bio-social hypothesis."*

5. *Bio-Social Hypothesis.*—The factor responsible for the appearance and growth of superorganic "thought" or "knowledge" is the intercerebral, (intermental) interaction of biological organisms. The source of "thought" is two-fold. On the one hand, it is *purely biological,* in the form of vital factors which have created the highest organisms, with such a developed nervous system as is necessary for intercerebral interaction. On the other hand, it is *purely social — the factor of interaction itself —* without which "thought" in its scientific, philosophical, symbolical, and practical forms could not appear, however high might be the biological structure of an organism. The reasons for this last statement are as follows: (A) Contrary to mere irritability or sensation, "thought" cannot appear nor exist without language. Similarly, language could not have appeared without a long and permanent intercerebral interaction. *Ergo:* no thought could appear without interaction. This is corroborated by the fact that only among human beings do we find language and only among them do we find "thought." Human beings, also, have always been the most social animals. (B) Contrary to erroneous individual images and representations, "thought" and "knowledge" represent what is styled as "accurate" and "true" ideas. They are not an embodiment of incidental and fragmentary individual experience, but rather the incomparably richer *collective experience* of a multitude of generations which has corrected, verified, enriched, increased and completed the inadequate individual experiences. A scientific, philosophical, or any other kind of thought can be really accurate only after it is tested and found adequate by *collective experience.* Of individual experience, we cannot say anything until the experiences of other people have tested and either proved or disproved it. This means that logically and

factually "thoughts," or superorganic phenomena, could not have originated without interaction: it is their logical and factual condition *sine qua non*. (C) Without the permanent interaction of many generations of people, any accumulation of thought or, what is the same, any growth of superorganic phenomena, any development of civilization, any "mental progress" would not have been possible because, without interaction, any individual experience, however right it might be, is doomed to extinction; for it cannot be transmitted to any other man or to any later generation. Under such conditions an accumulation of culture or thought becomes impossible. Impossible also becomes the appearance, existence, and growth of superorganic, or the highest forms of "psychical phenomena." (D) One of the necessary conditions of a conscious psychical process is the existence of various and changing stimuli. When they are few and monotonous they lead to "a mental stupor" and to the transformation of even a conscious process into an automatic or unconscious one. If there had been only a natural environment, such an environment would have been a very poor incentive for the stimulation of mental processes in organisms because it is rather monotonous, it changes slowly, and its variation is limited. Once reached, an adaptation to such an environment would tend to become more and more automatic and instinctive, and no necessity for the development of thought would have been given. Human beings, like many animals, would have become "instinctive" creatures, without any "thought" or "mental life." Since this did not happen it must have been due to the social life of our human ancestors; to their intercerebral interaction; to their interstimulation; and to their "social environment," which is dynamic in its very nature. It is the permanent current of increasingly new stimulation, which, incessantly changing, gives no chance for the transformation of a habit into an instinct. On the contrary, it breaks instincts and forces human beings to make incessant efforts toward a new adaptation to their ever-changing social environments, which are stimulating and awakening conscious processes.

These reasons are sufficient to show that, besides the biological factors, social interaction is a condition absolutely necessary for the appearance and growth of "thought" or "mental processes."

This means that *"psychological phenomena" are the result, but not the cause of social interaction; therefore it is as wrong to try to explain social phenomena through the psychological as it is wrong to explain a cause through its effect.* This means that Auguste Comte was right in putting sociology immediately after biology and in omitting psychology. Sociology is a fundamental science of superorganic phenomena based on the data of biology, including that of "physiological psychology," which is biological but not psychological science. *Social phenomena are not to be explained through psychological causes, but psychological phenomena are to be explained through biological and social factors.* Such is the conclusion of De Roberty.

6. Psychology is not a generalizing, abstract science as is biology and sociology, *but is a descriptive and concrete science,*[16] which describes concrete psychological processes in an individual — psychological biography — or in a definite group — psychology of a definite race, nation or sect — explaining them through an application of the data of biology and sociology. Its position and character are similar to those of geology. Geology is also a descriptive and concrete science. It does nothing but describe the specific geological characteristics and processes of a unique concrete object — the earth — explaining them through an application of the general laws of physical mechanics, physics, chemistry, and biology. In this way, De Roberty draws a sharp boundary line between sociology and psychology. The above shows that De Roberty's insistence on an explanation of psychological phenomena through biological and social factors is not a trifling

---

[16] De Roberty classifies all sciences under two principal heads: (1) Abstract or generalizing sciences, which analyze the concrete world of the inorganic; the organic or the superorganic phenomena into their components, or elementary units, analyzing the relationship of the units, and formulating the laws of relationship. Such, for instance, are physics, chemistry, biology and sociology. (2) Concrete or descriptive sciences, which study a definite concrete object, for instance, the earth, a certain tree, a certain animal, man or group. They describe their object in its uniqueness and peculiarity, and, to explain its peculiar traits, they have to apply the laws of at least two different abstract sciences. Geology is one example of the concrete sciences. It has a specific and unique object: the earth. In order to explain its history and its geological characteristics, geology must apply the laws of chemistry, physics, and even of biology.

De Roberty's classification is, in many respects, near to the classification of sciences offered later on by H. Rikkert and W. Windelbandt. See DE ROBERTY, *La Sociologie,* and *A. Comte and H. Spencer.*

point, but something fundamental in his system.   Such is the essence of De Roberty's bio-social hypothesis and "sociologism."

7. Almost simultaneously with those, similar conclusions were set forth by A. Espinas in his valuable studies: *Les sociétés animals,* 1878; *Les origines de la technologie,* 1898; and *Être ou ne pas être,* 1901.   Omitting here the outstanding contributions of Espinas in the special fields of "animal sociology," and the origin and factors of the evolution of technology, it is enough to say that his special studies resulted in a series of conclusions very similar to those of De Roberty.   "The individual is rather a product than an author of a society," is one of Espinas' sociologistic formulas.   De Roberty, Espinas, and later on, E. Durkheim and his school,[17] have laid down many other reasons against a psychological interpretation of social facts, and a foundation of sociology on psychology.   They unanimously say that if the factor of social interaction is disregarded, then we have to come to the theory of "auto-genesis" of mind and thought, which is obviously unscientific and amounts to a mysticism.   In this case neither the appearance, nor growth of mind, nor continuity and accumulation of culture, becomes comprehensible.

8. Furthermore, under the influence of A. Espinas and E. De Roberty, and E. Durkheim, J. Izoulet in his *La cité moderne,*[18]

---

[17] Durkheim has formulated theories which are very similar in their essence to those of De Roberty and Espinas. I even think that Espinas' and De Roberty's formulas are clearer and better than the corresponding formulas of Durkheim developed in his "Représentations individuelles et représentations collectives," *Revue de methaphisique et de morale,* Vol. VI. S. Deploige in his *Le Conflict de la morale et de la sociologie,* and Ch. E. Gehlke in his *Emile Durkheim's Contributions to Sociological Theory* indicate a series of the authors from whom Durkheim could take several of his theories. Among these names I did not find either the name of De Roberty or Espinas. Meanwhile, their theories are probably nearer to those of Durkheim than the theories of Simmel, Wundt, and other German and French authors indicated by Deploige and Gehlke. *"La Sociology,"* of De Roberty and *"Les sociétés animales"* of Espinas were published earlier than the works of Durkheim. They could not have been unknown to him, as we see from his mention of Espinas and De Roberty's names in his works, and in his *L'année sociologique.* These references are not very complimentary for De Roberty, but such an attitude on the part of Durkheim is scarcely justified by comparison of De Roberty's and Durkheim's theories in the field of problems outlined above. By the way it is necessary to note that in Gehlke's work, the analogy between H. Bergson and Durkheim is erroneous. Their theories are quite opposite.

[18] See Izoulet, J., *La cité moderne,* 5th ed., Paris, 1901: 7th ed.. 1008, pp. 588–600.

and especially D. Draghicesco in his *Du rôle de l'individu*,[19] have each given a series of the more detailed corroborations of the bio-social hypothesis. In this respect, especially valuable is the book of Draghicesco. He, probably more clearly than anyone else, has shown the existence of a correlation between social and psychological processes, — the correlation in which psychological processes are interpreted as a result of the social processes of interaction. The essence of Draghicesco's argument runs as follows : One of the necessary conditions of intelligence is an existence *of changing and different stimuli*. Under monotonous and constant stimuli even the conscious psychical processes tend to turn into the unconscious and automatic. Geographic environment being relatively unchangeable cannot facilitate a progress of intelligence. Once achieved, adaptation to such an environment transforms even a conscious activity into an unconscious one. In the past this environment had to turn a human being into an instinctive creature and in no way could facilitate a development of his intelligence. If this happened, the responsible factor was social interstimulation. Incessantly changing and varying, it made necessary an incessant effort to a new and conscious adaptation. Through that, it incessantly stimulated development of human intelligence, weakened instinctive and automatic responses, undermined the importance of the factor of heredity, and made man plastic and mindful. Such is the first reason why the origin and progress of human intelligence has been due to social interstimulation. Man has lived in the largest and the most complex societies and on account of that he has become the most superior in intelligence in comparison with other animals. The second reason is this : An *ability of discrimination or analysis is a fundamental function of intelligence*. This function is the more developed the more complex is the world in which man lives. With an increase of an environment's complexity man's ability for analysis must increase also ; contrariwise, he cannot adapt himself to his *milieu*. Adaptation lacking, he is eliminated. The most complex environment is the social one ; and its complexity has been increasing in the course of history because an increase of social differentiation

[19] Draghicesco, D., *Du rôle de l'individu dans le déterminisme social*, pp. 121 ff., Paris, 1906.

has been a fundamental social process. *Ergo, a progress of an analytical or discriminative ability of mind has been due to social interstimulation and to progress of social differentiation.* The former has been but a reflection of the latter. The same is true of *the synthetic ability of mind as its second fundamental function.* It *again is but a reflection of a fundamental social process of an integration of small groups into larger and larger ones.* This social process has made necessary a parallel development of the synthetic ability of mind. Otherwise, man again could not adapt himself to the environment and had to perish. Thus we have a complete parallelism of the progress of social differentiation and that of the analytical function of mind; the progress of social integration, and that of the synthetic ability of mind. These two functions explained, the fundamental characteristics of a superior intelligence are accounted for. Further, intellectual and cultural progress has been made through inventions. Invention is a lucky marriage of two or more existing ideas. The more intensive is the exchange of ideas among the members of a society, the greater are the chances of an invention. For this reason, social interaction has been the source of intellectual progress. The same is true in regard to an accumulation of knowledge and storing of cultural values. Not being transmitted through biological heredity, cultural values could not have been accumulated had there not been social contact of individuals, groups, and successive generations. Likewise, an integration of human personality, the very idea of self, and the fundamental laws or logic could originate only in a social environment. On the other hand, the facts of disintegration of personality which are well known to psychiatrists are due mainly to the same factor of social interaction; to unexpected, sudden, and great shocks, or a too brusque passage from one social *milieu* to another.[20]

In a similar way, Draghicesco shows that neither memory, nor association of ideas, not even any concept and abstract generalization is explainable without the factor of social interaction, and its fundamental forms and characteristics. The psychical processes owe their existence to, and are but the psychological reflection of, the corresponding social processes.[21] Following De

---

[20] DRAGHICESCO, D., *op. cit.*, pp. 162–190.   [21] *Ibid.*, pp. 190–274.

Roberty, Durkheim and Simmel, he indicates that the individual soul is but a microscopic reflection of the social world. If an individual is a member of antagonistic groups, his psychology will be full of conflicts and contradictions; if he is affiliated only with solidary groups, his "soul" will be "solidary" also. An individual has as many different "selfs" as there are groups with which he is affiliated.[22] From this standpoint even men of genius are nothing but a product of social integration. They are the men who happened to be posted at the point of cross-section or the focus of the mental currents of society. Absorbing the dominant feelings and attitudes of the masses, they combine and systematize them and through them they exert their influence. An alleged irreducible originality of men of genius is due also to the same fact of their being at the points of the cross-section of ideas, feelings and attitudes of the masses.[23] Such is Draghicesco's interpretation of the bio-social theory.[24]

A few years before Draghicesco, and also partly under De Roberty's and Durkheim's influence, J. Izoulet, professor of the *Collége de France,* in his brilliantly written "The Modern Society," substantiated in detail the bio-social hypothesis, and like Draghicesco, showed that the factor of interaction and association has been responsible for the evolution of organisms from the lower to the higher ones, and for the origin and development of "the social, scientific, industrial, ideal, and moral senses" in man.[25] At the same time, G. Simmel and E. Durkheim in their works and in their own way, developed a series of theories which led to conclusions similar to the above; namely, that the social processes of differentiation and integration are correlated with psychological processes of discrimination and synthesis; that the human mind is but a reflection of a social world and its characteristics; that the logical categories of space, time, causation,

---

[22] Compare SOROKIN, *System of Sociology*, Vol. II, Chap. VI; PARK and BURGESS, *op. cit.*, Chaps. II–III; DURKHEIM, "Le dualisme de la nature humaine," *Scientia*, Vol. XV, pp. 206–221.

[23] *Ibid.*, pp. 295–335.

[24] In his later book *L'idéal créateur*, Paris, 1912, Draghicesco tried to show that the greatest contributions to culture have been made at these places and where and when interaction has been most intensive and manifold. It has led to a cross-fertilization of thought. In the same book he tries to show ideals as factors in human behavior.

[25] IZOULET, J., *La cité moderne, passim*, and especially Livre II.

quality, quantity and abstract concepts, religious ideas, and moral values originated and grew through the factor of social interaction; and that they are essentially the reflections or embodiments, or symbols of the society itself. (See also the chapters about Durkheim and Simmel.) [26] Somewhat later the above principles of sociology were brilliantly restated by many authors in various countries. Among their works a conspicuous place belongs to those of Professor Charles H. Cooley, born in 1864.[27] Starting from a somewhat different point, Cooley comes to conclusions similar to the outlined principles of sociology. Among his specific contributions should be mentioned his illuminating theory of primary and secondary social groups, and his analysis of the family, playground, and neighborhood as especially important among primary groups.[28]

Side by side with the treatises devoted to a general sociologistic theory, numerous special studies have been published in which certain "psychological" phenomena have been interpreted in the light of the sociologistic theory in detail. Of such studies, I shall mention in the first place a series of works devoted to the sociology of language;[29] another such study has been made by Professor E. Dupréel, who has tried to show that somewhat vague ideas like those concerning justice, righteousness, and so on, are but the reflections of certain social relationships, and are due to social environment.[30] Recently Professor M. Halbwachs, one of the most prominent followers of Durkheim, published a special monograph devoted to a sociologistic interpretation of

[26] Among Durkheim's works especially important in this respect are: *Le suicide, De la division du travail social, Représentations individuelles, The Elementary Forms of Religious Life.* In Simmel's works the above parallelism of the social and mental categories is especially conspicuous in his little book about religion, with its central idea that the concept of God is but "a translation of certain characteristics of society into a psychological language." See the chapter about the formal school.

[27] See COOLEY, CH. H., *Human Nature and the Social Order,* 1st ed., 1902; *Social Organization,* 1st ed., 1909; and *Social Process,* 1918.

[28] See especially *Social Organization,* Chap. III.

[29] Corresponding literature is enormous. See a good survey and analysis of the theories in POGODIN, A., *Language as a Creation* (Russ., *Iasyk kak Tvorchestvo,* Charkov, 1913); DE LA GRASSERIE, E., *Études de psychologie et de sociologie linguistique,* Paris, 1909; JORDAN, LEO, "Sprache und Gesellschaft," and VOSSLER, K., "Die Grenzen der Sprachsoziologie," both papers in the *Erringerungsgabe für Max Weber,* 1923, Vol. I, pp. 338–389; see in these works other references.

[30] DUPRÉEL, E., *La rapport sociale,* Part III, Paris, 1912.

memory.[31]   The author follows the method of Durkheim in his interpretation of religion, and tries to show that there exists a collective memory differing from the memory of an individual; that "a social frame-work of memory" is an indispensable condition for the existence of any individual memory; and that the character of a social organization stamps the character of its member's memory; the former being changed, the latter will change also.

The above shows that the principles of the sociologistic interpretation of various psychical phenomena have appeared almost simultaneously in various countries and have been progressing in their application to an explanation of the simple, as well as to the most complex psychical processes.   After this deviation, called forth by a desire to avoid a return to the characteristics of other sociologistic treatises, let us turn our attention back to the characteristics of other important points of De Roberty's sociology.

9. *Classification of Social Phenomena.*—The next important feature of De Roberty's system is its classification of the superorganic or social phenomena.   If, according to his definition, superorganic phenomena are social thoughts or conscious psychical phenomena, their classification should be that of the fundamental forms of social thought.[32]

---

[31] HALBWACHS, MAURICE, *Les cadres sociaux de la mémoire*, Paris, 1925.

[32] It is necessary to bear definitely in mind that, according to De Roberty, a concrete human behavior, or concrete historical and social processes, are not pure social phenomena.   In their concrete forms they are *cosmo-bio-social facts.* Man is not only an embodiment of the social, but also of the biological and physico-chemical forces because he is an organism, and any organism is a physico-chemical substance.   For an explanation of *concrete human behavior or historical events*, it is necessary to apply all the data and laws of physico-chemical sciences, which is done partly in the form of a study of cosmical or geographical factors; all the data and laws of biological sciences being in the form of a study of the biological factors of human behavior and history; and finally, all the data of sociology must be applied in the form of a study of the social factors of these phenomena.   This explains that human behavior and history are social phenomena only so far as they are a manifestation of social thought.   This explains also why, in his classification of purely social phenomena, De Roberty logically classifies only the forms of thought because other components of concrete human behavior or human history are not social phenomena.   This has not been properly understood by some critics of De Roberty's system who wrongly interpreted it as an attempt to explain through the factor of intellect alone the whole of human history.   Even P. Barth partly falls into this error.   As a matter of fact, De Roberty's system is free from such one-sidedness.   In his interpretation of the

In their causal sequence they are as follows:

1. Analytical, hypothetical, non-dogmatic thought — or Science

2. Synthetic or apodeictical thought — or Religion and philosophy

3. Symbolic or æsthetic thought — or Arts, and partly, love

4. Practical or applied thought which indicates on the basis of knowledge what ought to be done to achieve a definite purpose — All applied disciplines beginning with applied physical and chemical disciplines, and ending with ethics, or the theory of social conduct. Social Technology, in the broadest sense of the word

In causal sequence each preceding form of thought determines the later one. The scientific thought of society, determines the character of its philosophy or religion. This, in its turn, determines the character of the æsthetic thought or arts of a society; while all three forms of thought determine the character of the society's applied thought: its technology, industry, agriculture, economic and political organization, *mores,* customs, morals, ethics, and so on, as far as they are created or performed consciously.[33]

Since such is the causal sequence of the forms of thought, one of its results is *a law of lagging;* the philosophy or religion of a society lags behind its science; æsthetic thought lags behind its religion; and applied thought lags behind all previous forms of thought.[34]

Each of the forms of thought differs from each other qualitatively.[35]

concrete processes of history and of human behavior, he insists that they are the total result of all cosmical, biological and social factors. In this point De Roberty is very near to E. C. Hayes who also strongly separates "pure social phenomena" from the concrete facts of history and human behavior.

[33] DE ROBERTY, *Nouveau programme, passim; Sociologie de l'action,* pp. 163–304.

[34] *La sociologie de l'action,* pp. 182 ff.

[35] Compare De Roberty's conception of philosophy and science with that of G. Simmel; they are in many respects similar. See SIMMEL: *Hauptprobleme der Philosophie,* Leipzig, 1911; DE ROBERTY, "Le problème sociologique et le problème philosophique," *Revue Philosphique* No. 11, 1911. It is easy to see also that De Roberty's classification is the reverse of the Marxian classification of social factors. Here, the first factor is that which is last in the Marxian theory and the least important, and *vice versa.* Technology, or the forms of production

10. *Thought as Real Power, and Science as a Primary Social Factor.*—As I indicated above, De Roberty does not belong to the monistic sociologists who try to explain everything through one factor. On the contrary, he is a pluralist. He regards the human being, his behavior, and his historical processes as *cosmo-bio-social* phenomena determined by *cosmo-bio-social* factors. But as far as human behavior and historical processes are social, (*i.e.*, conscious and telic phenomena), they are determined by each of the fundamental forms of social thought. Like electricity "thought," as the highest form of energy, is a real force. It "moves" locomotives and machinery; it works in our factories and shops; it influences the behavior of human body-machinery, and manifests itself in the movements of individuals and masses. In brief, being the highest form of energy, thought is a great and real power,[36] whose function is to control and to dominate all other physico-chemical and biological forms of energy. There are few sociological systems, if any, which so strongly stress the general power of "thought," and probably there is none other which gives the first place to analytical or scientific thought. We know that Auguste Comte also attached great importance to ideas in determining human behavior and historical processes. But in Comte's system, as was rightly indicated by De Roberty,[37] the

---

as a variety of applied thought, is the primary factor in the Marxian theory. Here it occupies the last place. See De Roberty's interesting article about Marxism in *Annales de l'Institute International de Sociologie*, Vol. VIII.

[36] Here De Roberty's theory coincides with the conclusions reached from a different standpoint by A. Fouillée in his philosophy and psychology of idea-forces. According to Fouillée, an idea is not a powerless representation only, but a real dynamic force, which influences the behavior of individuals and masses. "Everywhere the 'idea' appears as a power which contains in itself the conditions for a change of consciousness and, thanks to a correlation of psychical processes with cerebral movements, the conditions for a change of cerebral processes themselves. . . . Every concept, like that of 'My Country,' 'Humanity,' and 'Universe,' excites an infinity of perceptions which contain the most powerful feelings and emotions. . . . 'My Country!' 'Humanity!' With these words they often carried and moved whole armies and peoples. . . ." Being social in their origin, "ideas compose the collective force stored (*emmagasinée*) in an individual; they have their own intellectual heredity which reacts on biological heredity and often, through education, may direct, and sometimes even dominate, it." Fouillée, A., *L'évolutionisme des idées-forces*, Paris, 1906, pp. XCI–XCIII. In his introduction Fouillée gives a concise summary of his theory of the idea-forces extensively developed in his books: *La psychologie des idées-forces; La morale des idées-forces; Eléments sociologiques de la morale*, not to mention his other books.

[37] See his *Pourquoi je ne suis pas positiviste*.

greatest importance is given not so much to analytical or scientific, as to synthetic or philosophical and religious thought. They are the basis of Comte's law of the three stages: his theological, metaphysical, and positive stages, which are based on the character of the synthetic and apodeictic conception of the world ascribed by Comte to each of its stages. This is one of the shortcomings of positivism, according to De Roberty. Contrary to Comte, De Roberty definitely gives first place to scientific or analytical thought. Its character and progress determine the character and progress of all the other forms of thought, and through these, the comparative power of thought as a factor of human history generally. If the analytical thought of a society is poor qualitatively and quantitatively, primitive and poor will be its religion, philosophy, arts, or applied technology. A "real revolutionary" is he who contributes to the progress of science. The man who, for the first time, discovered that "two and two are four," was one of the greatest revolutionists. Only the progress of science leads to an increase of the real freedom of man, and real freedom is nothing but knowledge. Knowing the phenomena and their relationship, we can command them to serve our needs. The real liberators of men have not been the ignorant revolutionaries or radicals, but only those who have really increased human knowledge. Either Pasteur, Newton, Faraday or Lavoisier increased the amount of human freedom incomparably more than all revolutions and revolutionaries taken together. In the fields where analytical thought achieves high perfection and accuracy, as is now the case in the field of natural phenomena, its power is manifested in a high efficiency of corresponding applied thought and in a successful subjugation of the natural forces of steam, electricity, and so on, to human purposes. Factories, locomotives, cars, aëroplanes, radios, and all industrial technique are nothing but a manifestation of the power of physico-chemical scientific thought. Considerable also are the achievements of biological sciences, with their consequent influence on human history and behavior. Modern agriculture, medicine, sanitation and hygiene are nothing but manifestations of the power of biological sciences. The poorest are the achievements of social sciences. We still know little about the nature of superorganic phenomena. Naturally, their applied technology is poor and insignificant, as is also their rational ethics, rational organization of social and political institutions, and rational theory of progress. Instead of a scientific technology in this field, there are only numerous Utopian schemes, pseudo-scientific plans of reconstruction, ignorant political propositions, and blind and elementary movements of suffering masses led by blind or dishonest demagogues. Until analytical thought in this field makes a real progress, no efficient and rational applied technology is to be expected there. All the high sounding phraseology of the reformers is doomed to be a mere phraseology and nothing more.[38] Such is the essence of this part of this theory.

11. *Criticism.*—Let us now take the principal statements of the sociologistic school and see to what extent they are valid.

A. The sociologistic theory is right in its contention that the factor of social interaction is to be taken into consideration in an explanation of the growth of the mind and the psychology of human beings. It is also right in its attempt to establish the correlation between social processes of interaction and psychological processes; and in insisting on the social origin of language, science,[39] concepts, logical categories, morals and religion and other social values. If such an approach were made as one among many possible approaches, I would not see any valid reason for opposing it.. But such is not the case. The theory pretends to be exclusive. It declares that any other approach is wrong. In so far it can scarcely be accepted. In the first place, let us ask, is the factor of interaction a sufficient explanation of the origin of thought or of superorganic phenomena? I do not think so. Among bees and ants and other animals we find permanent and

---

[38] See *Nouveau programme, passim; La sociologie de l'action, passim; Qu'est-ce que le progrès? Qu'est-ce que le crime?* Paris, P. Ollendorff Co.

[39] Recent experimental studies of E. V. Doran, E. A. Kirkpatrick, G. M. Whipple, E. H. Babbit, G. C. Brandenburg, F. M. Gerlach, L. Gerlach, L. Terman, V. R. McClarchy, H. L. Neher, E. L. Thorndike, G. C. Schweisinger and others have found a very high correlation—from $+ .39$ to $+ .85$—between vocabulary and intelligence of individuals. As far as language and vocabulary depend decisively on social contact the above correlation strongly testifies in favor of the contention of the sociologistic school. See a good summary of the mentioned studies and the literature in SCHWEISINGER, G. C., *The Social-Ethical Significance of Vocabulary*, N. Y. Teachers College, 1926, pp. 8-11 and *passim*.

complex interaction; yet it has not originated "thought" or any-thing like it. Furthermore, in accordance with the theory, we should expect that "the mentality" of species living in societies and continually interacting, would be higher than that of animals who are not living in societies. Facts do not corroborate this expectation. L. Morgan is right in declaring that we do not have any reason for saying that the non-social wasps are inferior psychologically to the social wasps, or that a non-social tiger is inferior to the social jackals, or that many non-social birds are more stupid than social birds.[40] If N. Mikhailovsky, G. Palante, and L. Winiarsky are not quite right in their contention that "living together," sociality and social cohesion always lead to the mental stagnation of a species, and that an individualistic and isolated manner of living always stimulates a development of mind, they give sufficient proof to show one-sidedness of the so-ciologistic theory. This means that the factor of interaction is not sufficient to explain the miracle of the origin and growth of mind. It is true that De Roberty and other prominent repre-sentatives of the sociologistic school mention that before inter-action can produce its effects, it is necessary to have a coöperation of biological factors in the form of a developed brain. This means, however, that through biological factors in some way it is possible (even without interaction) to produce as high a nerv-ous system as that of many animals who do not live in societies. If such a thing is possible, does not this admit the possibility of the origin of a relatively high nervous system and high mentality as the satellite, independent of the factor of interaction? If this is admitted, then social interaction is neither sufficient nor abso-lutely necessary for the origin of inferior thought forms at least. For the highest forms it is likely to be necessary, but will seldom be sufficient alone. Such is the first limitation of the theory of social interaction as a sufficient principle for an explanation of the

---

[40] See MORGAN, L., *Animal Behavior*, 1908, pp. 229 ff. See also PARMELEE, M., *The Science of Human Behavior*, N. Y., pp. 391 ff.; AMMON, O., *Die Gesellschaft-sordnung*, Part I. These facts also contradict another assumption that "sociality" is always useful for all species, and that the more social they are the higher they are in their structure, and the greater chances they have to survive. This idea is especially strongly expressed by P. Kropotkin in his *Mutual Aid* but it is not warranted by the facts.

origin and development of "thought" or superorganic phenomena.[41]

This conclusion is reinforced by the following considerations.
According to the theory, the more intensive, complex, and the
longer the interaction among human beings has been, the greater
will have been the progress of thought. Just exactly what is
meant by intensity and complexity of human interaction, the
school has not defined. If they consist in a direct, excited, and
manifold interstimulation, such conditions are given in mob and
crowd-interaction which are intensive, complex, and full of excitement. And yet it is a mere platitude to say that a mob or
crowd's thought rarely produces anything really fine and superior
in the field of thought. Its psychology is stamped by what is
termed the "mob-mind," which gives something quite opposite to
real thought. If the intensity and complexity of interaction are
measured by the density of the population, as some of the representatives of the school say, then again, in the past and in the
present, the distribution of societies according to their cultural
standard and according to their density, does not show any close
correlation. Many regions of India and China are in the most
densely populated areas, and yet they are far from being at
the top of the cultural ladder. The density of population in
the United States is far from being the highest; yet the country
occupies one of the highest positions on the cultural ladder.
The same is true in historical perspective. If we try to correlate
the cultural progress or regress of a country with an increase
or decrease of the density of its population, we shall scarcely
obtain any noticeable correlation. (See the chapter about the
Demographic School.) Further, a continuation and prolongation
of interaction does not necessarily guarantee either progress of
thought and culture or even the maintenance of its previously
achieved standard. In Rome after the second century A.D.; in
ancient India after the fourteenth century A.D. (the end of the
Cholas Empire—the climax of Hindu culture); in China after

---

[41] C. Bouglé, in his later work, rightly indicates that a "social *milieu*" is not a
unique creator of mind. See BOUGLÉ, *Leçons de sociologie sur l'évolution des
valeurs*, 1922, p. 193; see also DUPRAT, I., "La psychosociologie en France,"
Archiv für Geschichte d. Philosophie und Soziologie, B. XXX, heft 1–2; PAULHAN,
FR., *Les transformations sociales des sentiments*, Paris, 1920.

the Ming dynasty; in ancient Egypt, after the eighteenth and the nineteenth centuries; and in Greece, after the third century B.C., social interaction certainly continued to exist and sometimes became more complex; yet historians assure us that since these times the thought and the civilization of these countries has gone down, and never has been able to reach the level which was before achieved. Consequently, permanency and continuation of social interaction is not a sufficient guarantee even for maintaining an achieved level of thought. Further, there seem to be various intensities and complexities of interaction. If some of their forms are favorable for mental progress, some others seem to be disastrous. An increasing number of mental diseases within our complex and strenuous civilization shows this. With a reasonable degree of certainty we can say that their increase is due, in a considerable degree, to the intensity, complexity, and manifoldness of the social interstimulation of Western society.[42] Finally the results of experimental studies of the effects of social stimulation on mental work also do not testify in favor of the criticized hypothesis. From the qualitative standpoint performance of more complex mental functions in a group of persons working together is not better than the performance of the same functions by the same persons when alone. If from the quantitative side, in working together the output of work increases, the quality of the work does not improve. It rather suffers when the more delicate are the tested mental operations.[43] Even quantitative improvement takes place not always and is still questionable.[44]

[42] See my *Social Mobility*, Chap. XXI.

[43] See the data and the description of the experiments in the following works: GATES, G. S., "The Effects of an Audience Upon Performance," *Journal Abnormal Psychology*, Vol. XVIII, pp. 334–344, 1923–24; GATES and RISSLAND, "The Effect of Encouragement and of Discouragement Upon Performance," *Journal Educational Psychology*, Vol. XIV, No. 1; LAIRD, D. A. "Changes in Motor Control and Individual Variations Under the Influence of Razzing," *Journal Experimental Psychology*, Vol. VI, No. 3; TRAVIS, L. E., "The Effects of a Small Audience Upon Eye-Hand Coördination," *Journal of Abnormal and Social Psychology*, Vol. XX, pp. 142–146, 1925–26; ALLPORT, F., *Social Psychology*, 1924, Chaps. XI, XII; MAYER, A., "Einzel und Gesamtleistung des Schulkindes," *Archiv für Gesamte Psychologie*, 1903; MEUMANN, E., *Haus-und Schularbeit*, Leipzig, 1914; MOEDE, W., "Einzel-und Gruppenarbeit," *Praktische Psychologie*, 1920–21.

[44] See WILLIAMSON, E. G., "Allport's Experiments in Social Facilitation," *Psychological Monographs*, Vol. XXXV, No. 2, 1926, pp. 138–143. M. Skalet's and my experiments with the pre-school children have shown that their work

Further, superior individuals, when alone, work rather better than in a group under a social stimulation.[45] Such are the effects of social stimulation on performance of very simple mental functions. It is to be expected that the results found in the study of social stimulation in a co-working group will be still more negative in the performance of such a remarkable mental function as the composition of Beethoven's Symphony, Newton's *Principia*, Kant's *Kritik der reinen Vernunft*, Lobachevsky's *Geometry* or any other work of genius. These experimental results suggest again that the problem is very complex. There probably are forms of social stimulation highly beneficial for mental progress, and other forms harmful for it.

These considerations are sufficient to prove the contentions that, *first, the factor of interaction is not sufficient to explain the origin and development of thought; second, it is not sufficient for an understanding of mental progress or regress; third, the discussed theory has not made an analysis of what is to be understood by intensity, complexity, and duration of interaction, nor how they are to be measured. For this reason, its propositions remain somewhat vague and uncertain. Fourth, even though they are clarified, the facts do not corroborate the expectations of the theory.* Such are its first shortcomings. The above does not deny an importance to the factor of interaction; but it denies the exaggeration of the rôle ascribed to it by the sociologistic school. It suggests also a need for more detailed studies in the field of interaction to clarify when, where, and under what conditions certain forms of interaction are the "generators" of thought; and when, where and what forms of interaction are rather the obstacles for its progress. Vague and general formulas are not sufficient now.

B. *The second objection to the sociologistic theory is that its claim of interpreting psychological phenomena as a mere function of social processes and an individual as a mere "reflection" of a group is not justifiable as far as it pretends to be exclusive,*

---

in groups is worse qualitatively and quantitatively, than when each of them worked alone. The study will be published together with my other experimental studies and that of my collaborators.

[45] See Allport's summary in *Journal of Abnormal Psychology*, Vol. XVIII, pp. 341–344.

and as far as it pretends to explain all the phenomena of human psychology, human thought, and human genius in terms of social processes alone. But as one of the many possible interpretations, the theory is certainly valuable. However, it claims more than this by declaring fallacious any attempt to interpret psychical phenomena from any other standpoint. This claim is to be rejected. Methodologically, an attempt to correlate social phenomena with the psychological characteristics of individuals in such a way that social phenomena are viewed as "functions," while certain psychological properties of individuals are taken as "variables," is as logical as the opposite attempt of the sociologistic school. The same may be said of an interpretation of group-phenomena through the properties of the members of the group, taken as variables. I do not see any methodological sin in the attempts of G. Palante, J. M. Baldwin, G. Tarde, Ch. A. Ellwood, W. McDougall, F. Allport, G. Le Bon, E. A. Ross, E. C. Hayes, or any of the Freudian School,[46] who, in their ap-

[46] The position of these and many other sociologists in the dispute between sociology and psychology, or "the group" and "the individualistic" interpretations, varies, beginning with clearly-cut psychologists and individualists of the type of G. Palante and F. Allport, partly of G. Tarde and McDougall, and passing through intermediary types like Ellwood, Baldwin, Ross, Hayes, Giddings, and ending with the sociologists of the type of Cooley, whose position practically coincides with that of the sociologistic school. The first psychological branch starts with the instinctive or acquired psychological characteristics of man, and views social life and processes as the result and manifestation of these psychological "variables." Many of the representatives of this branch do not admit any "social entity" in the form of a "social mind" or "social reality" apart and independent from individuals. See PALANTE, G., *Précis de sociologie*, 2d ed., Paris, 1903; *Combat pour l'individu*, 1904; *Antinomies entre l'individu et société*, 1912; ALLPORT, F., *Social Psychology*, Chap. I; TARDE, G., *Études de psychologie sociale*, pp. 169–175, Paris, 1898; *La logique sociale*, 3d ed., pp. 1 ff.; *Les lois de l'imitation*, *passim*. W. McDougall's *An Introduction to Social Psychology* is also an example of the interpretation of social processes as derivatives of inherited and acquired properties of man. Ch. A. Ellwood's and J. M. Baldwin's position is somewhat intermediary and synthetic. In his paper, "The Origin of Society," *American Journal Sociology*, Vol. XV, pp. 394–404, Ellwood views social life and institutions as an outcome of instincts; and interprets the "social" through the "psychological." In chapter II of his *The Psychology of Human Society*, N. Y., 1925, he puts "mental evolution" before "social evolution" as its basis. On the other hand, he stresses the importance of inter-mental interaction as a necessary condition for the development of mind and culture. Somewhat similar is the position of J. M. Baldwin. He stresses the interdependence of the social and the psychological, but at the same time claims that "the sociologist is at every turn dependent upon the psychologist to inform him of the movements of the individual mind which incorporate themselves in social institutions." His interpretation of social life is a deduction of the latter

proach, have taken certain psychological characteristics of man as variables and have tried to correlate certain social phenomena as their functions.   If some of the attempts of this kind are defective the fault is not in the method of starting with properties of an individual and passing from them to social phenomena; but in some other mistakes which are outlined in the chapter on the psychological school.   These defects once overcome, the psycho-individualistic interpretation is as legitimate as the sociologistic, and it has already given valuable results.[47]   The

from the psychological characteristics of man.   "Personal individualism shows itself in social competition; personal sympathy and morality in social solidarity; personal loyalty in civic institutions," and so on.   See BALDWIN, J. M., *The Individual and Society*, pp. 14–17 and *passim*, Boston, 1911.   See also *Social and Ethical Interpretations*, 1907, *passim*.   Near to the conceptions of these authors are the positions of E. C. Hayes, E. A. Ross, F. S. Chapin, and E. S. Bogardus.   In Hayes' *Introduction*, an analysis of the inherited and acquired characteristics of man precedes an analysis of the social activities and social life; while psychology is declared standing in the same relation to sociology as chemistry does to biology.   On the other hand, the author does not take an individual as a social unit but regards him as a complex phenomenon.   See HAYES, E. C., *Introduction to the Study of Sociology*, 1920, pp. 354–361; "Classification of Social Phenomena," *American Journal Sociology*, Vol. XVII, pp. 109–110.   See ROSS, E. A., *Principles of Sociology*, 1923, Chaps. IV, VIII, IX, X; BOGARDUS, E., *Fundamentals of Social Psychology*, 1924, Part I; CHAPIN, F. S., *An Introduction to the Study of Social Evolution*, 1920, pp. 102 ff.   F. H. Giddings' position in this respect seems to be a little nearer to that of "sociologism."   He says that "considerable mental development is possible only to creatures physically but not mentally separated" and that "acquaintance, talk, and the consciousness of kind are the specific determiners of (human) association."   On the other hand, he is free from an extremism of "sociologism."   See GIDDINGS, *The Scientific Study of Human Society*, 1924, pp. 32–34; *Studies in the Theory of Human Society*, 1922, Chap. XV and his definition of society, p. 202.   Still nearer to the sociologistic position is that of W. Wundt, Sumner and Keller, Ch. H. Cooley, and O. Spann.   Cooley's statements like "self and society are twin-born," "social consciousness is inseparable from self-consciousness," "a separate individual is an abstraction unknown to experience, and so likewise is society when regarded as something apart from the individual"; and his conceptions of the "social mind" and the whole character of his books separate him from the psychologists; but at the same time it seems to me that he does not go as far as the sociologistic school.   See COOLEY, CHARLES H., *Social Organization*, pp. 5–7, Chaps. I–II, VI, N. Y., 1924; *Human Nature and the Social Order*, pp. 35 ff., and *passim;* WUNDT, WILHELM, *Völkerpsychologie*, Vol. I, pp. 1–6, 1900.   Also sociologistic is Spann's *"universalismus."*   See SPANN, O., *Gesellschaftslehre*, 1914, pp. 244–284; SUMNER, W., and KELLER, A., *op. cit.*, Vol. I, pp. 40 ff.   See an able survey of other theories in DAVIS, MICHAEL M., *Psychological Interpretations of Society*, pp. 15–83, N. Y., 1909.

[47] The dispute between "sociologism" and "psychologism," or between "the group" and "individualistic" interpretation of social facts, appears to me both fruitless and baseless.   Both of the methods are admissible; when properly used both have shown themselves workable; and either one may be used according to the nature of the problem studied, the purpose of the study, and the tech-

above does not deny the method and the valuable contributions of the sociologistic school, but it denies its pretension for a monopoly on interpretation.

C. The third objection to the school is that, contrary to its assertion, *it has failed to reduce successfully either logical categories, concepts of science, genius, or inventions, to purely social sources.* Something in this way the school has achieved, but far less than it claims. When we are told that the conception of God, or the Sacred, or the Mana, or the Totem, is nothing but hypostatized society itself, and that God's characteristics like omnipotence, eternity, omnipresence, omniscience, omni-justice, etc., are nothing but the corresponding characteristics of a society as it appears to an individual, (Simmel, Durkheim), we may learn something from the statements; but do they explain completely the mystery of the conceptions of God or of "the Sacred"? Do they exhaust the limits of our ideas about such phenomena or superphenomena? I am afraid not. When we are told that the categories of force, space, time, efficacy, kind, and so on, are nothing but a reflection of the characteristics of society, we again learn something from such explanations. But how pale they seem when put face to face with the immensely complex reality of the human logical and psychological kingdom! More than that, in spite of widely diverging forms of society, we see that these fundamental logical categories are essentially the same in the minds of Confucius, Aristotle, St. Thomas Aquinas, Immanuel Kant, Newton, Pascal, Durkheim and Mendeleeff. This could not be if they were a mere reflection of the characteristics of a particular society, because the societies in which these men lived are quite different. We may agree that a genius might be interpreted as the focus of currents of social thought and the spokesman of what in society already exists in a diffused form. This may be true, but does it exhaust the mystery of genius?

nical conveniences of the investigator. The dispute reminds me of that one as to whether egg produced hen or hen produced egg. The sooner it is dropped, the better. In a similar way, I find rather useless the dispute about the boundary line between sociology and social psychology. There is no such line. Attempts to draw it are either vague or purely conditional, stimulated mainly by "departmental considerations." Comparisons of "social psychology" and "sociology" by the same author show that under different names there is given practically the same bulk of theories and problems.

Does this explain why we have not a Mr. Smith, but a Sir Isaac Newton; not a somebody else, but Napoleon, or Buddha, or Mahomet, at the center of "the foci"? The theory, in its somewhat vague statement, does not answer our question at all. Neither does it attempt to offer its partizans any prediction regarding who, in the next five years, will become such "foci," and what will be their characteristics; for, to be sure, they could not predict it. If A. Coste, in his flat denial of any correlation between the social *milieu* and the appearance of a genius in philosophy, morals, arts, music, goes too far, he is right, nevertheless, when he claims that the correlation is often loose and almost intangible. (See above, the chapter on the demographic school.) As an argument in favor of the criticized thesis, W. Ogburn sets forth a list of 148 inventions made independently by two or more persons.[48] But the very fact that out of millions of inventions made only 148 have been listed, and the fact that these 148 inventions were made by the persons who lived in quite different societies and under different conditions, testifies rather against than in favor of the hypothesis. Further, it is probable that complexity and fluidity of social environment somewhat weakens the factor of heredity; but is it sound to say that heredity does not play any more an important part? Is it possible to contend that education makes all human beings similar? Under conditions of similar environment and training, are all individuals to be equally capable or incapable, equally stupid or clever? Is it true that their equality is realized more and more; and, in the future, will it be realized completely? Alas! Such an assumption is pure metaphysics, contradicted at every turn by facts, by experiments, and by less speculative biological, psychological, and educational researches. These short statements allude to what I style as the failure of the school to reduce psychological and logical phenomena, and the peculiarities of individuals to their essential social sources. Some part may be reduced to them, but there still remains a great bulk which is irreducible.[49] The school boasts more than it can accomplish.

[48] OGBURN, W., *Social Change*, pp. 90–102.
[49] One of the best and sharpest criticisms of the sociologistic school has been given by G. Palante in his *Les antinomies entre l'individu et société, passim*. See also a sound criticism of Durkheim's theories in GEHLKE, CH. E., *op. cit., passim*

D. As to De Roberty's classification of social phenomena, it is sound in many respects. It is logical; it embraces the principal forms of social thought; it properly grasps their characteristics; and it is good as a counterbalance to the opposite classification of the economic interpreters of history. (See the chapter on the economic school.) Through its emphasis on scientific thought as a primary social factor, it indicates a factor whose importance may scarcely be overestimated. The pages and the chapters devoted in De Roberty's works to an analysis of this factor are really brilliant. At the present moment we have numerous factual studies of the rôle of science in social and historical processes, and there is no need to say that these studies only confirm the theory of De Roberty. Any attempt to disregard, or to give an insignificant rôle to this factor, would scarcely be recognized at the present moment. It is enough to remember a simple computation like that of Professor Umoff, according to which the approximate amount of energy now used in our factories is no less than 20 billion horse-power. Translated into human labor, this means the work of 200 billion men doing purely physical work for ten hours a day.

By turning the whole of mankind into slaves who would do only manual work and by stopping all other kinds of human activities, we could not obtain even one hundredth part of that mechanical work which is given to us by modern technique created by chemical and physical science. . . . During millions of years, nature has increased human population to one and a half billion, while boisterous thought of physical science, during one and a half centuries had created one hundred times greater number of unanimated and unpaid workers who, (in the form of harnessed energy) serve our needs.[50]

Further, De Roberty's idea that any change in the field of science calls forth a corresponding change in other fields of social thought — in religion, philosophy, arts, applied thought, human behavior and historical processes, — could scarcely be denied either. A series of facts and corresponding researches shows that such a

[50] UMOFF, N. A., "Physical Sciences in Mankind's Service," Russ., *Priroda*, February 1913.

correlation exists and is quite tangible.[51] We must admit also that the law of lagging indicated by De Roberty is, to some extent, likely to be true also. The principal shortcomings of this part of De Roberty's theory, as well as that of other intellectualists, are two: first, its pretension of exclusiveness; and second, its assumption that the correlation between each preceding and each subsequent form of thought is quite perfect. As I have mentioned in the field of social phenomena, we rarely have one-sided dependence and one-sided causal relationship, but have, factually, almost always the relations of the interdependence of different factors. It is reasonable to take science as a "variable" and to try to correlate it with other phenomena such as religion, arts and economics, which are regarded methodologically as its "functions." But it is also reasonable to take an "economic or any other factor" as a "variable," and to regard all others, including science, as its "functions." Since we deal with the phenomena of interdependence and with the "functional relations" of various components of social life, there is no objection to such a procedure. For this reason, we must recognize the value of De Roberty's classification while rejecting its pretension of monopoly.[52] As to the second shortcoming, the facts do not show that De Roberty's perfect correlation is true. Here he becomes a victim of his "intellectualism" and forgets that man is not only a "logical and rational animal" but, being a biological organism,

[51] See LITTLE, A. D., *The Fifth Estate*, published by The Chemical Foundation; DANNEMANN, FR., *Die Naturwissenschaften in ihren Entwicklung und in ihrem Zusammenhange*, Leipzig, 1923; NEUDECK, G., *Geschichte der Technik*, Stuttgart, 1923; KNOWLES, L. C. A., *The Industrial and Commercial Revolution in Great Britain*, London, 1922; CUNNINGHAM, W., *The Growth of English Industry and Commerce*, Cambridge, 1907; ESPINAS, A., *Les origines de la technologie;* VEBLEN, T., *The Place of Science in Modern Civilization*, N. Y., 1919; FISKE, B. A., *Invention: The Master-Key to Progress;* MARVIN, F. S., (ed.), *Science and Civilization;* CALDWELL, O., and SLOSSON, E. E., *Science Remaking the World*, N. Y., 1924; CRESSY, E., *Discoveries and Inventions of the Twentieth Century;* TILDEN, W. A., *Chemical Discovery and Invention in the Twentieth Century*, Dutton & Co.; SODDY, F., *Science and Life*, 1920; FLEXNER, S., *Twenty-five Years of Bacteriology*, Science, 1920; DUCLAUX, *Pasteur, The History of a Mind*, Philadelphia, 1920; ANDREWS, B. R., *Economics of the Household*, N. Y., 1923; EDDY, W. H., *The Vitamine Manual*, Williams & Wilkins Co.; BUCKLE, T., *op. cit., passim;* ESPINAS, A., *La philosophie sociale du XVIIIe siècle et la révolution*, Paris, 1898. These works show clearly how every scientific progress has influenced various aspects of human thought, behavior, industry, social, economic, moral, religious, and historical processes.

[52] This pretension vitiates almost all sociological theories.

he is also illogical and irrational. Owing to this illogicality, especially stressed by Pareto (see the chapter about Pareto), man often thinks very irrationally. His reasoning is almost always disfigured by "various biases," emotions, affections, and so on. Often, when new scientific ideas contradict his interests or mental attitudes, they are simply rejected without any influence on his religion, æsthetics, and practice. Often a new idea is reconciled with the existing ideologies in the most illogical way without changing these ideologies. Sometimes it is disfigured in such a way that there remains very little of it. Such facts are quite common in human behavior and in the mental history of mankind. This explains why it is that not every change in scientific thought leads to a corresponding change in synthetic thought, or why it is that not every change in the field of religion influences æsthetic or practical thought. Often such a change in a preceding form of thought passes without exerting any influence on the subsequent one. Sometimes such changes are suppressed and disappear, to be discovered again centuries later. De Roberty's law of lagging is a partial corroboration of this. Therefore, though De Roberty's correlation is tangible, it is far from being close and perfect.

Such are the principal limitations and objections to this branch of the sociologistic school. Outside of these defects, the remaining part of its theories are to be recognized as valuable. Let us now pass to Durkheim's variety of the school.

4. E. DURKHEIM AND HIS SCHOOL [53]

The second fundamental variety of the sociologistic school is represented by E. Durkheim and his collaborators. Among con-

---

[53] Born in 1858 in France, died in 1917, professor of Social Science at the University of Bordeaux; later professor of Sociology and Education at the University of Paris. Founder and editor-in-chief of *L'année sociologique*. Author of numerous articles and books, among which the most important are: *De la division du travail social*, 1893; *Les règles de la méthod sociologique; Le suicide*, 1897; *Les formes élémentaires de la vie religieuse*, 1912. About Durkheim there is considerable literature. Besides the mentioned works of Gehlke and Deploige, see BARTH, P., *op. cit.*, pp. 628–642; BRANFORD, V., "Durkheim," *Sociological Review*, 1918; HALBWACHS, M., "La doctrine de E. Durkheim," *Revue Philosophique*, 1918; BARNES, H. E., "Durkheim's Contribution to the Reconstruction of Political Theory," *Political Science Quarterly*, 1920; BOUGLÉ, C., "Die Philos. Tendenzen der Soziologie E. Durkheim," *Jahrbuch für Soziologie*, Vol. II. 1926;

temporary sociologists, Durkheim has occupied one of the most important places. In France only G. Tarde has possibly been as influential as Durkheim. Besides several heterogeneous causes, this has been due to the character of the sociological works of Durkheim. He fortunately combined the ability of broad, logical, and philosophical thought with the scrupulous and careful method of a scientist. Every hypothesis formed by him is formulated on the basis of patient study of the corresponding facts. After the formulation, he carefully tries to verify it again through an inductive study of the factual data. This has made his works quite superior to the purely speculative philosophizing in social sciences, as well as to the narrow, matter-of-fact descriptions of a definite phenomenon. Hence the eminence of Durkheim.

General Characteristics of Durkheim's Sociology.—The above mentioned characteristics of the principles of the sociologistic school are practically the same as those of Durkheim's sociology. For this reason, there is no need to repeat them.[54]

It is enough to indicate only briefly a few specific traits added by Durkheim to the theories developed before him. In accordance with the position of sociology he stresses that "collective consciousness specifically differs from individual consciousness"; that "they are composed of different elements"; that "sociology is not a corollary of psychology," and that "not in psychology, but in the very nature of society, it is necessary to look for an explanation of social life."[55] In order to discriminate collective consciousness from individual consciousness, and social fact from purely psychological fact, Durkheim introduces two objective criteria: *exteriority* and *constraint*. The psychical nature of social phenomena separates them from purely biological phenomena. The fact that collective representations exist outside of the individual and come to his mind as something exterior in the

---

Duprat, G. L., "La psycho-sociologie en France," *Archiv für Geschichte der Philosophie und Soziologie*, Vol. XXX, heft 1-2; Sorokin, P., "E. Durkheim's Theory of Religion," Russ., in *New Ideas in Sociology*, Vol. II; Kovalevsky, M., *op. cit.*, pp. 134-164; Sorel, G., "Les théories de M. Durkheim," *Le devenir social*, Vol. I, 1895; Bouglé, C., "Revue générale des théories récentes sur la division du travail," *L'année sociologique*, Vol. VI; Fauconnet, *op. cit.*

[54] This side of Durkheim's theory is quite satisfactorily analyzed in Gehlke's work on Durkheim.

[55] Durkheim, E., *Règles de la méthode sociologique*, 1895, pp. 125-128.

form of various moral, religious, juridical and logical rules; and the fact that they are endowed with a power of coercion, which allows them to impose themselves upon an individual regardless of his individual desires, — these two characteristics indicate a boundary line between social and purely psychological phenomena.[56] This logically leads Durkheim to an admission of the reality of the social mind; collective representations; and a society independent and different from the reality of individual minds, representations, and psychology.

Society is not at all the illogical or a-logical, incoherent and fantastic being which it has too often been considered. Quite on the contrary, the collective consciousness is the highest form of the psychic life, since it is the consciousness of consciousness. Being placed *outside of* and *above* individual and local contingencies, it sees things only in their permanent and essential aspects, which it crystallizes into communicable ideas. . . Society sees farther and better, than individuals. [57]

In this way, the criteria of the social facts of exteriority and constraint lead Durkheim to a recognition of the existence of a social mind independent from, and exterior to, individuals,—a peculiarity not so much stressed by De Roberty, but typical of a great many of the representatives of sociologistic realism or psycho-organicism.[58] Before going further, let us discuss briefly to what extent this part of Durkheim's sociology is true. As far as it means that the psychical phenomena undergo a change in the process of social interaction and would become different if there were no interaction of individuals; and as far as he states that the regularity of social processes does not coincide with the regularity which may be expected from the activities of iso-

[56] *Les règles*, Chap. I; *Representations individuelles, passim;* in this point Durkheim's position is identical with Stammler's theory. See STAMMLER, R., *Wirtschaft und Recht nach der materialist Geschichtsauffassung*, 1896.

[57] DURKHEIM, *The Elementary Forms of Religious Life*, tr. by Swain, p. 444 and *passim.*

[58] Besides Gumplowicz, Espinas, De Roberty and Durkheim, similar in this respect is the attitude of the organic school, (see the chapter about it); GIERKE, *Deutsche Privatrecht*, Vol. I, p. 468, 1895; POSADA, A., "Les sociétés animales" in *Annales de l'Institut. Int. de Sociologie*, Vol. III, p. 271; BOODIN, J. E., "The Existence of Social Mind," *Amer. Journal Sociology*, July, 1913; FERRIÈRE, *La loi du progrès en biologie et sociologie*, 1915, part III; COSTE, A., *Les principes d'une sociologie objective*, pp. 1 ff., 26 ff., and of a great many others.

lated individuals; the statement may scarcely be questioned. But as far as it means an existence of mind or psychical phenomena *outside* of the mind of individuals, and an existence of a society *independent* from its individual members, the proposition could scarcely be accepted. It creates a kind of fictitious entity. In this case Tarde's criticism of Durkheim's realism seems to be valid. "I confess," he says, "that it is difficult for me to understand how, after excluding the individuals, we can have a society as a remnant. If the students and the professors are excluded from a university, I do not think there remains in it anything but the name. Durkheim apparently tries to return us to the realism of the Middle Ages." [59] This is the more true because the difference between social and individual regularities can be explained much more simply, through the fact of neutralization of individual phenomena in a mass of individual actions and reactions. In brief this side of Durkheim's realism is scientifically wrong and ought to be rejected, as it is nothing but unjustified mysticism. This also concerns similar conceptions of the sociological realism of other mentioned sociologists.

The criteria of exteriority and constraint as the characteristics of social phenomena, may be useful in a study of some particular problems, as, for instance, in a study of juridical and moral phenomena. Nevertheless, when Durkheim says that only the phenomena which are compulsive are social phenomena, he unreasonably limits their field. Here, Tarde's criticism is again valid. In this case, says Tarde, it seems that only the relationship of the conqueror to the conquered, the facts of enslaving, and the phenomena of compulsion would be social phenomena. Meanwhile, all instances where there is free coöperation, like a free conversion of a people into a new religion, free contractual relations, free mutual aid, free solidarity, free imitation, free learning and thousands of similar facts; all these are to be excluded from the field of social facts. Such a conception of social phenom-

[59] TARDE, G., *La logique sociale*, pp. 1 ff.; *Études de psychologie sociale*, pp. 69–75, Paris, 1918. Recently F. Allport, in his *Social Psychology*, gave a similar criticism of the sociological realism generally. See also my *System of Sociology*, Vol. I, Chap. VI; DUPRAT, G., *Science sociale et démocratie*, 1900, pp. 59, 68–69; LITT, T., *Individuum und Gemeinschaft*, 1924, pp. 151 ff.; HAFF, K., "Kritik der Genossenschaftstheorie," *Jahrbuch für Soziologie*, B. II, pp. 288 ff.

ena is evidently fallacious.[60] I think that Tarde's remarks are quite valid.

Now let us pass to the special works of Durkheim. His real contributions consist not so much in his general statements, like the above, as in his factual studies and in the series of correlations which he tried to establish, to support his fundamental principles.

Durkheim's Analysis of Social Solidarity, its Causes, Forms and Effects.—This study was given in Durkheim's *De la division de travail social.*[61] Under this somewhat misleading title, Durkheim made a careful study of social solidarity, in which field he had many predecessors. Plato, Aristotle, Comenius, W. Petty, A. Ferguson, Adam Smith, Saint-Simon, and more recently, A. Comte, H. Spencer, J. S. Mill, H. C. Carey and many other economists outlined the essentials of Durkheim's theory. Six years before Durkheim, Ferdinand Tönnies,[62] and three years before, Georg Simmel,[63] set forth theories of social differentiation almost identical with those of Durkheim. This, however, does not mean that Durkheim did not show any originality, or that he did not add anything new to what had been written by his predecessors. The work contains many propositions based on a careful analysis of factual material which we cannot find in the earlier works. In the first part of the book Durkheim takes division of labor as a "variable" and tries to correlate its forms and variations with other social phenomena viewed as "effects" or "functions." The principal conclusions and correlations obtained may be summed up in the following table, which shows what socio-psychical phenomena are influenced by changes among the variable. Such are the principal effects of the variation of labor division, as a social factor, on different sides of social life and psychology. From the above it follows that a series of psychological changes are a mere "function" of the corresponding

[60] TARDE, G., *Études*, pp. 69-75. The same may be said against Stammler's conception.

[61] See BOUGLÉ, C., "Théories sur la division du travail," *L'année sociologique*, Vol. VI.

[62] TÖNNIES, F., *Gemeinschaft und Gesellschaft*, Leipzig, 1887.

[63] SIMMEL, G., *Ueber soziale Differenzierung*, Leipzig, 1890.

WITH WHAT PHENOMENA THE VARIABLE IS CORRELATED, AND HOW

Variable: Division of Labor

1. Lack of or a slight division of labor in a society is followed by the specified effects in each of the specified fields of phenomena:

Human Behavior and Psychology	Mental, moral and social homogeneity of individuals. Their beliefs, convictions, opinions, manners, conduct and so on are alike. Differences are due only to heredity. Domination of tradition, lack of individuality and individualism.
Law, Morals, and Social Control	Thanks to the homogeneity of the social conscience and of social consciousness, they are strong, unanimous, and non-atomized. Crime is the action which offends the strong and intensive social conscience and calls forth a strong repression. Domination of criminal law,—repression and punishment—over civil law in the law code of a group. The purpose of justice is not a restitution of the harm done by the offender to his victim but "repression" and, through that, reinforcement of the moral conscience of the group.
Solidarity and Social Ties	"Mechanistic solidarity" based on homogeneity of individuals. The tie which binds them in one solid unity is this strong unanimity of public opinion, based on mental and moral homogeneity of individuals.
Political Régime	All important social affairs and acts of justice are enacted by the whole body of the group, in the public meetings of its members.
Economic Organization	Communal property.
Religion and Ideology	Belief in impersonal totemic force, free from an individuality or personality. Lack of individuality in the members of a group is reflected in the lack of individuality in sacred power. Local and tribal patriotism.

2. In the process of time, division of labor grows. This is an historical trend. When division of labor becomes great, it determines the following changes in the same fields of social phenomena:

Human Behavior and Psychology	Disappearance of mental and moral similarity of individuals. Increase of their individuality and peculiarity. Their tastes, beliefs, opinions, morals become less and less alike. Specialization of labor causes that of individuals. Specialization causes a decrease in tradition. The determining rôle of heredity becomes less and less important. This facilitates weakening of walls of caste, and of the transmission of occupation and social position from the father to the children.
Law, Morals, and Social Control	General and common social conscience and consciousness decrease. Crimes begin to offend less intensively thus decreasing common social conscience. Offensive acts begin to be regarded as only something harmful to a part of the members. They lose their sacrilegious character. As a result, law loses more and more in "repressive" character. Punishment also decreases, because now there is no need of punishment to reinforce the moral conscience of the whole group. The offender has only to restore the harm done to his victim. Social control becomes less rigid and more loose. Only few general spheres of conduct are prescribed. In other fields everybody may act as he pleases. Increase of individual freedom and increase of a contractual law and relationships based on free agreement of parties.
Solidarity and Social Ties	Since homogeneity of individuals does not exist any more, it cannot now play the rôle of a social bond. If there were no new ties, the unity of a group would be ruined. Division of labor becomes such a new tie: solid unity of a group now is based on non-self-sufficiency of heterogeneous individuals caused by division of labor. They now "need" one another and cannot exist without coöperation because everybody does only a special part of the work. Thus is "mechanistic" solidarity transformed into the "organic."

Political Régime	Specialization of political functions. Tendency to a decrease of inherited political status. Contractual relationship of government and citizens.
Economic Organization	Private property; economic individualism; contractual coöperation; "open door" system which permits everybody to enter any occupation. Decay of inherited social position facilitated by a decreasing inheritance of specific abilities which in its turn is caused by division of labor.
Religion and Ideology	Transition to polytheism and monotheism. "Individualization" and "personalization" of God accompanied by a universalization of religion. Waning local and tribal patriotism and an increase of cosmopolitanism or internationalism.

variation of labor division, as an objective social process. In this way, Durkheim remains faithful to his sociologistic position.

In the second part of the book, the author, so to speak, reverses his equation, and asks: What are the causes responsible for an increase in the division of labor itself; or, in other words, what are the variables of this phenomenon now viewed as a mere "function"? The answer to this question is less elaborate, but, nevertheless, it is clear that Durkheim remains faithful to the position of "sociologism." The usual answer that an increase in the labor division is due to a psychological tendency to happiness does not account for the fact at all. There is no reason for thinking that, with an increase in the division of labor, happiness increases. On the contrary, an increasing number of cases of suicide, nervousness, and dissatisfaction within highly differentiated societies, on the one hand; and on the other hand, the well-proved fact of the happiness and satisfaction of primitive peoples testifies that happiness tends to decrease with the progress of labor division. Therefore, this, and similar psychological hypotheses, cannot explain any progressive increase of social differentiation. Its causes are to be looked for in the objective social conditions themselves. One of the principal factors has been the increase in population, with its increasing density, or "the dynamic and moral density" of the morphological structure of a society. Such an increase leads to an intensification of the struggle for life. If all members of an increasing society would perform the same functions, as for instance, if all would become tailors, they would have less opportunity to procure the means of subsistence. Competition is the sharpest among members of the same occupation when there is a superabundance of membership. When they follow different occupations, they may exist side by side without an intensive struggle, and with greater opportunity to obtain their means of subsistence. Hence, an increase in the density of a population leads to an increase in the division of labor; which result leads to the above effects in the social processes, organization, and psychology of the individuals. Such, in brief, is the skeleton of Durkheim's well rounded and harmonious theory of forms, causes, and effects of social solidarity. His "sociologistic" position must be clear from the above.

The same sociologistic principles permeate other monographic studies of Durkheim. In his excellent investigation of suicide,[64] he shows, in the first place, that the suicide movement cannot be accounted for either through psychopathic factors, through race and heredity, through geographical factors, or through imitation and other purely psychological factors, or by poverty, or unhappy love, or other personal motives. A careful analysis of the statistical data contradicts all such hypotheses. After this, in a brilliant manner, Durkheim shows that all the principal types of suicide— the egotistical, the altruistic and the anomique—are due entirely to social causes.

Egotistical suicide is due to an increase in the social isolation of an individual or, what is the same, to a decrease in the intensity of the social cohesion of a group. For this reason, the single and the divorced give a higher per cent of suicide than the married people because family bonds make the isolation of the married less intensive. Roman Catholics, whose religion is more dogmatic and integrates its members strongly, show a smaller percentage of suicides than do Protestants or free-thinkers, who are removed from such ties. For the same reason, the periods of social move-

---

[64] *Le suicide*, Paris, 1887. I quote the edition of 1912.

ment or war, when individuals go out of "their individual shells," decreasing their isolation and increasing their social cohesion, are marked by a sudden decrease of suicide; while the ends of such movements, when the individuals again confine themselves within their "shells," are marked by a sudden increase in suicides.

Anomique suicide is due to a sudden shattering of the social equilibrium and moral constitution of a society. Suicides after economic crises and bankruptcies are examples of this type. The usual explanation, that they are due to an increase of poverty, is not valid, because there are plenty of poor people and classes among whom suicide is almost unknown; and because suicide increases not only when the disturbance of equilibrium leads to impoverishment, but also when it leads to prosperity. The cause is the mentioned increase of *l'anomie sociale*.

Altruistic suicide is due to an increased engulfment of an individual in a group when an individual is regarded only as a member of a group, without much regard for his own personality or individuality and when he is controlled completely by the group. This engulfment is psychologically expressed by the feeling of duty in an individual to sacrifice himself for the group at any moment when it is necessary; or when he may, through his actions, disgrace the group. Among the members of primitive groups, this psychology of engulfment and duty is expressed with mechanistic solidarity; in an army, by a soldier; and in a definite group with a strong *ésprit de corps*, by its members (Livre II). Thus, "the curve of suicide" "may be accounted for only sociologically. It is the moral constitution of a society which at any given moment fixes the number of suicides. For every society there exists a collective force of a certain energy, which pushes individuals to kill themselves. The movements which are performed by such a person, and which, on the first approach, may appear as a manifestation of their individual temperament, in reality are nothing but the result and exterior manifestation of a corresponding social constitution. Each society according to its morphological structure and collective constitution has its own collective proclivity to the act of suicide, and it is this collective proclivity which determines individual proclivities to suicide, but not contrariwise." Such is the final result of the study, which again stresses "the sociologistic" position of Durkheim.[65]

Finally, in his book upon religion, Durkheim has given a very penetrating analysis of the nature, sources, forms, effects and variations of religion from the same "sociologistic" standpoint. After a destructive criticism of the common definition of religion, such as a belief in God or in supernatural forces, he defines religion as "a unified system of belief and practices relative to sacred things; that is to say, things set apart and forbidden—beliefs and practices which unite into one single moral community called a Church, all those who adhere to them." [66]

Its essence is the division of all things and phenomena into two kingdoms: the profane and the sacred. Its teachings urge the members of a religion not to mix these two kingdoms because mixing is a sin or religious sacrilege; and it teaches them to approach the kingdom of the sacred or, when mixing does happen, in order that they may annul its sinful results, it urges them to perform religious purification, whatever its concrete form may be. These functions and characteristics of religious phenomena are manifested in thousands of forms: in a special separation of the places for religious services from the places of usual profane activities; in a prohibition to use such places for everyday affairs; and in a separation of the time devoted to the sacred from that devoted to the profane; hence arise holidays when it is forbidden to do profane things, as is specified in the fourth Commandment. The same essence of religion is exhibited by religious ceremonies whose purpose is either to purify man from sin, as is the case in confession; or, like the Eucharist and baptism, to make a profane man a participant of the sacred; or, like a consecration, to give him an additional portion of the sacred. In the next part Durkheim criticizes the animistic and the naturistic theory of the origin of religion. The first theory, which is set forth by E. Tylor and H. Spencer, tries to explain the appearance of religious belief through such bio-social factors as dreams, visions of shadows, death, psychoses, and other bio-psychological phenomena. The second theory, represented by M. Müller and others ascribes the

[65] *Ibid.*, p. 336.
[66] *The Elementary Forms of the Religious Life*, tr. by Swain, London, p. 47.

origin of religion to impressive cosmical phenomena, like thunder, storms, lightning, earthquakes, the sun, the moon, rivers, and so on, which primitive man cannot control, and which impress him enormously. Durkheim convincingly shows the fallacies and inadequacy of these theories.[67]   Finally, after a careful and painstaking analysis of the elementary forms of religious phenomena, he sets forth his own theory,—that the source of religion is the society itself; that religious conceptions are nothing but symbols of the characteristics of the society; that the sacred, or God, is but a personified society; and that the substantial social function of religion has consisted in the creation, reinforcement, and maintenance of social solidarity.   For this reason, religion has played a great and beneficial rôle in history.   In spite of the temporary crisis of a certain religion, it will exist in some form as long as social solidarity exists.   Concrete forms of religion change but its essence is eternal.   In brief, Durkheim has given us a harmonious sociologistic theory of religion.[68]   Together with this, he gives the sociologistic theory of knowledge generally.   In the words of Durkheim himself, the essence of his general conclusions are as follows:

Religious representations are collective representations which express collective realities; the rites are a manner of acting which take rise in the midst of the assembled groups and which are destined to excite, maintain, or recreate certain mental states in these groups. . . The religious life is the concentrated expression of the whole collective life. . . The idea of society is the soul of religion.   Religious forces are therefore human forces, moral forces. . . Religion, far from ignoring the real society and making abstraction of it, is in its image; it reflects all its aspects, even the most vulgar and the most repulsive.

Similar to religious ideas and concepts, there are other general concepts of the human mind, such as the concepts of *time, space, class, force, personality, efficiency,* and so on; all of which are due to the same social factors.

[67] *Ibid.*, Chaps. II–III.

[68] As I shall show further, Durkheim had many predecessors who expressed similar ideas. Among relatively recent writers, it is enough to mention the names of J. de Maistre, De Bonald, Saint-Simon, A. Comte, B. Kidd, and especially, F. de Coulanges (see his *La cité antique*), J. Frazer, and G. Simmel, who, in his small pamphlet, *Religion*, gave the skeleton of Durkheim's theory.

Try to represent what the notion of *time* would be without the processes by which we divide and measure it. . . This is something nearly unthinkable! Now what is the origin of this differentiation [of time into days, weeks, years]. It is not so much our personal experience because it is not *my time* that is thus arranged; it is time in general. . . That alone is enough to give us a hint that such an arrangement ought to be collective. The divisions into days, weeks, months, years, etc., corresponds to the periodical recurrence of rites, feasts, and public ceremonies. A calendar expresses the rhythm of the collective activities, while at the same time its function is to assure their regularity.

It is the same thing with *space*. [Without its differentiation, space, like time, is almost unthinkable, too.] But whence come these divisions [of space] which are so essential? By themselves, they are neither right nor left, up nor down, north nor south, etc. All these distinctions evidently come from the fact that different sympathetic values have been attributed to various regions. [Besides, representations of space show their social origin. In some groups in Australia] space is conceived in the form of an immense circle because the camp of the tribe has a circular form; and this special circle is divided exactly like the tribal circle.

Analogous proofs will be found presently in regard to the ideas of *class, force, personality* and *efficacy*. It is even possible to ask if the idea of *contradiction* does not also depend upon social conditions. [Evidently] if men did not agree upon the essential ideas, if they did not have the same conception of time, space, cause, number, etc., all contact between their minds would be impossible, and with that, all life together. Society could not abandon its categories to the free choice of the individual without abandoning itself.[69]

Such, in brief, are the contributions of Durkheim and his sociologistic interpretation of social and psychical phenomena. As we see, in essence his sociology coincides with that of De Roberty's school. Leaving without discussion [70] Durkheim's

[69] *The Elementary Forms of Religious Life*, pp. 10–17, 419–21; see the whole introduction and conclusion. See also LEVI-BRÜHL, *Les functions méntales dans les sociétés inferieur*, 1910; HUBERT ET MAUSS, *Mélanges d'histoire des religions;* LEVY-BRÜHL, *La moral et la science des moeurs*, Paris, 1903. In these works of Durkheim's collaborators are expressed the theories similar with that of Durkheim.

[70] A relatively good account of this side of Durkheim's ideology is given in the mentioned works of Deploige, Bouglé, Gehlke, and in the mentioned paper of H. E. Barnes.

political and ethical ideas, which pertain to the field of practical
judgments, let us now turn to a brief criticism of the above theories of Durkheim.

Criticism.—The above criticism of the general principles of
the sociologistic school concerns Durkheim's sociology also.
Therefore there is no need to repeat it. We may say only that
Durkheim's monographic studies have shown clearly that purely
social factors in the form of social interaction, (morphology of
society, its organization, and its social processes) cannot be ignored in an explanation of social and psychical phenomena.
Durkheim's works made this especially clear. But recognizing
this value of the sociologistic interpretation, shall we follow
Durkheim as far as to exclude all other interpretations? I think
we shall not, and Durkheim himself gives a sufficient reason for
such a conclusion. Take his explanation of the origin of the idea
of the sacred, of the concepts of time, of space, of efficiency, and
so on. He states that religious belief in the kingdom of the
sacred was caused by the alternation of periods of dispersion and
of gathering of primitive groups. In the period of dispersion
they lead a dull, monotonous, and tedious life; while in the period
of gathering, like the *corroborri* of the Australians, they experience a complete change of psychology in the form of great excitement, joyful madness, feverish impulsiveness resulting from
interstimulation, drink, food, dances, and so on. Being unable
to account rationally for such a transformation of their feelings,
primitive men explained it through some impersonal sacred force
which entered their body and made them "sacred" also. Is such
a theory sufficient? It is not. In the first place, the very fact
of the alternation of periods of dispersion and of gathering of a
primitive tribe is considerably controlled by climatic seasons: a
tribe disperses into parts during a season poor in natural products, and gathers together in a season of natural abundance.
This means that, at least indirectly, these social processes are controlled by geographical factors; if they were different, the social
processes would likewise be different, and through that, the
psychical states of the people. Other evidence we have in the
facts that the totems of tribes are local plants or animals; that the
ideas of heaven and hell, of good and evil gods, and so on, are

marked by the local color of geographic environment; that the deification of the moon, the sun, the thunderstorm, and of other cosmic phenomena is quite common; all these and a thousand similar properties of religious representations indicate the rôle played by cosmic environment in the origin and development of such representations.   It is improbable that the cosmic phenomena could have failed to impress the minds of primitive peoples who greatly depend upon cosmic forces, when they impress even the mind of a cultured man.   Furthermore, Durkheim and other representatives of sociology, exaggerate the static character of *cosmic milieu*.   Still clearer is the rôle of this *milieu* in the origin and development of the ideas of *time, space, efficiency* and so on.   If division of time into days, weeks, months and years, expresses the rhythm of the collective activity, it even more clearly expresses the rhythm of natural phenomena: the division of time into days, months, years and seasons coincides with the daily alternation of light and darkness; with the rhythm of the moon's cycles; and with the sequence of the seasons and the sun's yearly cycles. [71] This is so evident that only a strong preconception may hinder our seeing it.   The same is true in regard to *space*.   The natural *milieu* is not something so formless as to lack coördination with spacial location of events and things.   "Farther than this tree," "to the right of that hill," "below this mountain," "up or down the river," — these spacial coördinations are quite natural and practically known to all primitive peoples.   No less known to them is spacial orientation according to the position of the sun, the stars, the moon, and thousands of other cosmic phenomena. Their rôle in this respect is likely to be more conspicuous than that of the forms of a tribal camp.   This is also corroborated by the fact of relatively uniform representations of space and time in a great many social groups with the most different political and social organization.   If the hypothesis of Durkheim were accurate, this could not have happened.   These indications are enough to see the one-sidedness of Durkheim's sociology and the undeniable rôle of *cosmic milieu* in the origin and shaping of religious representations, and of the ideas of time, space, and other conceptual categories.

[71] See the facts in NILSSON, MARTIN, P., *Primitive Time Reckoning*, Lund, 1920.

With still greater reason this may be said of the rôle of *biological factors* in this respect. Take the character and purpose of the fundamental religious rites among primitive, and even cultured peoples. Is it not true that one of the principal rites among primitive peoples is the rite for the *multiplication of food and means of subsistence?* Is it not true that the same motive fills a great many religious prayers beginning with the Christian: "Give us this day our daily bread"? Is it not true that a similar rôle is played by the *biological phenomenon of procreation and sex interrelations?* If these and similar biological phenomena had not existed, fully half of the religious ideas, rites, prayers and so on would not have appeared. Furthermore, did Durkheim succeed in showing that such biological phenomena as dreams, psychoses, mental diseases, and so on, did not play any part in the origin and shaping of the religious-animistic-representations? He did not. What he has shown is only that they alone cannot account for them. More than that, it is evident that if human beings had possessed quite a different nervous system and biological constitution, their ideas would have been quite different, or there would have been no ideas. In order that social contact may play its rôle, it is necessary that man have a biological constitution, and, especially, a nervous system. Rats or sparrows may interact as much as you please, and yet their interaction cannot yield anything like religious representations or concepts. For this reason it is utterly fallacious to ignore the rôle of biological forces, as is done by Durkheim in his "sociologistic enthusiasm." C. Bouglé, one of the most eminent collaborators of Durkheim, had to acknowledge that

there are two elements which cannot be accounted for through, or created by, any collective enthusiasm: the nature of the things and the nature of human mind. [It is true that social *milieu* plays an important part in the mental development.] But he who says development says germ. The most various experiences and interactions could not have produced ideas and concepts known to us if man, before such experiences, had not reacted in a certain way predetermined by his nature. Is this nature itself also an entirely social creation? Is such a precious intellectual instrument as an arm a social gift also? . . . The forces born from collective living always have

worked on a certain number of the forms given before their interference. . . . You may prove that these forces have played a modifying, facilitating, or hindering rôle; nevertheless, you cannot prove
they have been the only creative forces.[72]

These brief allusions are sufficient to show the fallacious one-
sidedness of Durkheim's sociology. So much for this point. The
above criticism is corroborated by Durkheim himself in his study
of the division of labor. Granting that his correlations of the
division of labor with other phenomena are correct,[73] what factors

[72] BOUGLÉ, *Leçons de sociologie sur l'évolution des valeurs*, p. 193, Paris, 1922.

[73] However, this admission is not quite justified. Some of the correlations are
very questionable. Some of the premises and statements of Durkheim are
fallacious. I cannot enter here into a detailed criticism of all his mistakes. Instead of this, I shall simply refer the reader to the quoted work of M. Kovalevsky,
Contemporary Sociologists, and to N. K. Michailovsky's article about Durkheim's
book on the division of labor, where is given, as far as I know, the best factual
criticism of Durkheim's theory of the division of labor. Unfortunately these
works are in Russian, and are, therefore, not available to non-Russians, ("*Rossica
sunt, non leguntur*"). Here I can only enumerate some of his mistakes without
any corroboration of my statements. Durkheim's assumption that law is rarely
in conflict with ethics or morals is questionable. His assumption that the less
there is of the division of labor, and the more homogeneous is the moral consciousness of a group; the more repressive will be the law, and the more abundant and
cruel the punishments; is in no way a general phenomenon. A variation of this
idea is given by Durkheim in his article: "Deux lois de l'évolution pénale,"
L'année sociologique, Vol. IV, which is fallacious. See SOROKIN, *Crime and
Punishment*, Russ., pp. 433 ff. His theory that the most ancient institution of
justice is the public meeting of the whole tribe, is also erroneous, as is his theory
that the primitive tribes knew only a communal form of property. His claim
that a great division of labor results in an increase of freedom, independence,
solidarity, hearty coöperation, unvariable mental progress, and so on, is more
than questionable. A moderate but valid criticism of this, besides Kovalevsky's
and Michailovsky's works, is given in Bouglé's mentioned *Revue général des
théories sur la division du travail*, pp. 90 ff. Durkheim's faith in the beneficial
results of governmental regulation and control of contractual relations between
capital and labor in forms which remind one of "the Russian Communist System,"
or the mediæval reglementation of labor, is a mere faith which, having been disproved many times, is disproved still more by the opposite result of the Russian
experiment. Durkheim's assumption that the struggle for life is always stronger
between the members of the same occupation than between the members of
different occupations, is again a wrong generalization of a partial fact into a
general law. He forgets the other side of the phenomena, namely, the solidarity
of the members of the same occupation, which is so conspicuously manifested
in labor and occupational unions, in "class-struggles," where not the members
of the same class, but those of different classes fight each other, and so on. See
SOROKIN, *System of Sociology*, Vol. I, pp. 351 ff. Durkheim's theory does not
give any account as to how the solidarity of tribes not having division of labor
appeared. His claim that, with an increase of labor division, the inheritance of
social position and the caste-principle invariably decrease, is not warranted by
the facts. See SOROKIN. *Social Mobility*, Parts I and II. His similar assumption

have been responsible for the very fact of the modification of labor's division itself? As soon as Durkheim puts this problem, he has to recognize at once its dependence on the factor of procreation and multiplication of the people,—a factor essentially biological. Increase of labor division is principally the result of an increase of population. Such is his answer. Is this not an evident proof that division of labor, or any other social factor is not self-sufficient, and can be taken as variable only methodologically? As soon as we try to turn this conventional "primacy" of a factor into a substantial or dogmatic one, or to regard it as independent of other factors, the insufficiency of such a method at once becomes evident.[74] Without continuing this chain of thought, the above is enough to conclude that, although recognizing the claim of "sociologism" for its interpretation of social phenomena, and its valuable contributions to the science of sociology, we should unhesitatingly reject its claim of scientific monopoly of investigation. Let us now turn to the third branch of the sociologistic school, represented by the works of L. Gumplowicz and his followers.

5. L. GUMPLOWICZ,[75] F. OPPENHEIMER, AND OTHERS

The purely philosophical part of the theories of Gumplowicz which are embodied in his series of "the laws" of Causation,

---

that the rôle of heredity decreases with an increase of labor division is questionable also. These are a few of the many questionable assumptions and even plain blunders given in Durkheim's book.

[74] This concerns also Durkheim's study of the factors of suicide. If his study has made evident the rôle of the social factors in the movement of suicide, it did not succeed in showing that all other factors do not have any influence. Many fluctuations of the suicide-curve are unaccountable through Durkheim's theory. On the other hand, a series of investigators have shown quite a tangible correlation of the suicide movement with other biological, psychological, geographical, and social influences. See VON MAYR, G., *op. cit.*, Vol. III, pp. 258-405.

[75] Ludwig Gumplowicz, of Polish-Jewish stock, was born in 1838 and committed suicide in 1909. He was professor at the University of Gratz in Austria. The principal works of Gumplowicz are: *Rasse und Staat*, 1875; *Allgemeines Staatsrecht*, 1877; *Der Rassenkampf*, 1883; *Grundriss der Soziologie*, 1885; *Soziologie und Politik*, 1892; *Die soziologische Staatsidee*, 1892; *Geschichte der Staatstheorien*, 1905. About Gumplowicz see ZEBROWSKI, B., *L. Gumplowicz*, Berlin, 1926; SALOMON, G., *Preface* to the new edition of *Geschichte des Staatstheorien*, 1926; KOCHANOWSKI, L., "Ludwig Gumplowicz," *American Journal Sociology*, Vol. XV; WARD, L., *L. Gumplowicz, ibid.*, Vol. XV; corresponding chapters in SMALL, A., *General Sociology;* JACOBS, P. P., *German·Sociology*, N. Y., 1909; BARNES, H. E., "The Struggle of Races and Social Groups," *Journal of Race De-*

Development, Periodicity, Complexity, Parallelism and so on,[76] I shall leave entirely out of the discussion. As a logical analysis of these fundamental principles of science, it is too elementary; and as a sociological interpretation of these scientific categories, it is somewhat out of date.

Gumplowicz's "Sociologism."—Of the sociological characteristics of Gumplowicz's theory, the most obvious is his "sociologism," in the most conspicuous form. He declares that the chief concern of sociology is not the individuals, but exclusively the groups; and that individuals in themselves are nothing but the mere product of a group. Two brief quotations are sufficient to show his position.

We contend that the real elements of a social process are not separate individuals but social groups; in history we shall study not the regularities of the behavior of individuals, but that of the movements of groups.[77]

The great error of individualistic psychology is the supposition that man thinks. It leads to a continual search for the source of thought in an individual, and for the reason why the individual thinks so and not otherwise. . . . A chain of errors: for it is not man himself who thinks but his social community; the source of his thought is in the social medium in which he lives. . . . Man's mind and thought are the product of his social medium, of the social element whence he arose, in which he lives.[78]

Criticism.—There is no need to continue these quotations: we are already well acquainted with this kind of thought. What is to be noted is that Gumplowicz's "sociologism" is much ruder and rougher than that of the previous two branches. For this reason it is still more objectionable. I wonder how one can understand a group completely ignoring individuals. His declaration is identical to that of a biologist who would declare that, in order to

---

velopment, Vol. IX; BARTH, P., *op. cit.*, pp. 266 ff.; KOVALEVSKY, M., *op. cit.*, pp. 89–134; Ross, E., *Foundations of Sociology*, p. 4; TODD, A. J., *Theories of Social Progress*, 1919, pp. 133 ff., 276 ff. Furthermore, considerable attention is given to his works in a great many of the sociological works of F. Oppenheimer, F. Savorgnan, M. Vaccaro, Ratzenhofer, and others; LICHTENBERGER, J., *Development of Social Theory*, pp. 436 ff.

[76] See GUMPLOWICZ, *Outlines of Sociology*, tr. by Moore, pp. 76–82, N. Y., 1899.
[77] GUMPLOWICZ, *Der Rassenkampf*, pp. 39–40, Innsbruck, 1883.
[78] *Outlines of Sociology*, pp. 156 ff.

study the structure and the function of a complex organism, a biologist needs to study only tissues and not the cells; and that the cells should be entirely eliminated from the study.[79]   The biologists will scarcely give credit to such a contention.   The sociologists unfortunately, have given it.[80]   I wish I could see also how "not a man, but a community thinks."   Unfortunately I have failed in this desire.   All that I have seen is this: The decisions and opinions enacted by a group of individuals are often different from those of *some* of the individuals; and sometimes the opinion of certain individuals prevails, while at other times, the ascendancy is obtained by the opinion of other members.   However, I never have seen a "community's thought."   Moreover, I do not think anybody has observed one.   Gumplowicz's claim is either an inaccurate *façon de parler,* or a simple "blunder." [81]   So much for this point.

Principles of Gumplowicz's Theory.—Further principles of Gumplowicz's theory are as follows: First, *the theory of polygenesis,* or the multiple origin of mankind developed by Gobineau thirty years before Gumplowicz.   Second, *the assumption of an inherent and deadly hatred in the relationship of one group to another,* resulting in an inevitable and deadly struggle between the groups (*Rassenkampf*).   Third, the assumption that *only through such a struggle has any enlargement of the social group, or any consolidation of two or more groups into one social body, been possible.*   Fourth, the victorious group, having conquered its victim, pitilessly exploits it, turning it into slaves or subjects.

---

[79] SOROKIN, *System of Sociology*, Vol. II, p. 14.

[80] I regret to say that L. Ward, A. Small, Kochanowsky, A. J. Todd and others greatly overestimated the value of Gumplowicz's theories.   In this, as well as in several other cases, Small's and Ward's thinking is rather loose and misleading.   See correct remark of P. BARTH, *op. cit.,* p. 270, note 4.

[81] The fallacy of Gumplowicz's "sociologism" is shown by his own theories.   Having excluded the individuals, he had to explain how "the groups," or his "syngenetic hordes" have originated.   His explanation asserts that these groups are the union of *individuals* bound together by the community of language, religion, occupation, locality, consanguinity, and common interests.   *Der Rassenkampf,* chapter about Syngenism; *Outlines of Sociology,* pp. 92 ff., 100.   Such an explanation means, first, mixing the race as a zoölogical type with social or ethnic groups; second, an admission of individuals who were excluded before; and third, the *petitio principii.*   Gumplowicz says that there are inimical groups because their language, religion, etc., are different.   When we ask how these differences in religion, language, etc., have arisen, he answers: because there have been different groups.   Unfortunately sociology is rich in this kind of theory.

For the sake of successfully controlling them, it enacts laws, and in this way we have: (1) *the origin of the states* as a union of the victorious and the subjugated groups, in which the conquerors become the privileged and governing body, while the conquered become the exploited and disfranchized body; (2) *the origin of law* as a totality of compulsory rules enacted by the governing group for the sake of controlling and exploiting the subjugated group; (3) *the origin of social stratification* and *inequality* causing the conquerors to become the aristocracy, while the conquered become the lower strata. The fifth principle is that in the course of time differences between the conquerors and the conquered decrease. The conquerors take over the language and the religion of the conquered, and the gap between them is more and more obliterated. In this way the group becomes more and more solidified until it subjugates, or is subjugated, by another group, when the above process is repeated again. In the repetition of such *"ricorsi"* we find an essential process of history. Such is a concise summary of Gumplowicz's sociological theory. The above set of hypotheses, or a part of them, have found several supporters. Besides A. W. Small, L. F. Ward and Kochanowsky,[82] it is possible to name here Professor Franz Oppenheimer of the University of Frankfurt, a.M., who in his valuable works [83] has followed the line of Gumplowicz's and Marx's sociology; F. Savorgnan,[84] though his later works have little in common with Gumplowicz's speculation; G. Ratzenhofer,[85] partially, and some others.[86]

Criticism.—In regard to the above theory, our critical remarks may be summed up as follows:

[82] For me it is rather impossible to see how Small and Ward could have reconciled Gumplowicz's theories with their own, because, logically, they contradict each other.

[83] See OPPENHEIMER, F., *Der Staat*, Frankfurt, a.M., 1908; *System der Soziologie*, Vol. I, Jena, 1923; Vol. II, 1926.

[84] See SAVORGNAN, F., *Soziologische Fragmente*, Innsbruck, 1909; and partly *Studi critici di sociologia*, Modena, 1925.

[85] RATZENHOFER, G., *Wesen und Zweck der Politik*, Leipzig, 1893; *Die Soziologische Erkenntnis*, Leipzig, 1898; *Soziologie*, Leipzig, 1908.

[86] Dr. G. Salomon mentions also Vaccaro among the partial followers of Gumplowicz, but Vaccaro's theories are considerably different from those of Gumplowicz and Vaccaro stressed his disagreement explicitly in the introduction to his *Les bases sociologiques du droit et de l'état*.

1. The principles of the theory are not new. As we have seen, (see the chapter on struggle for existence), the principle that struggle is the source of all changes, including that of human history, was proclaimed by Heraclitus, the *Zend-Avesta*, by the oldest religions, by the Church Fathers, by Machiavelli, J. Bodin, Thomas Hobbes, mentioning only a few examples from the past. Among the many writers who much earlier and less one-sidedly than Gumplowicz, indicated war as a source of social stratification, we will name John Millars, and Simon Linguet.[87] After Darwin and Spencer, the social theories of the struggle for existence (ideas similar to those of Gumplowicz) became so numerous that it is rather useless to enumerate all the authors and works.[88]

2. As I have already indicated, the polygenesis theory of the origin of mankind, which was reinstated by Gumplowicz, represents an hypothesis which cannot be proved or disproved.

3. Gumplowicz's assumption that the relationship of different ethnic groups is always absolutely inimical, and that they are always in the state of permanent warfare, greatly exaggerates the situation. If it were so, the groups would have exterminated each other, and the history of mankind would have been finished long ago. Factual studies show that among primitive peoples, there are groups which do not know war at all; that among those who have war, it is by no means a permanent state; and that there is a considerable number of tribes which set free, exchange, or adopt the war prisoners.[89] On the other hand, there are well ascertained facts of a quite peaceful relationship of primitive peoples toward one another. As it was in the past, so it is in the present. War certainly continues to exist among contemporary nations, but he who would conclude from this that it is permanent among them

---

[87] MILLARS, J., *Observations Concerning the Distinction of Ranks in Society*, London, 1771; LINGUET, S. N., *Théorie des lois civiles ou principes fondamenteaux de la société*, London, 1767.

[88] See some of them in the mentioned *Preface* of G. Salomon to the new edition of Gumplowicz's *Geschichte der Staatstheorien*, Innsbruck, 1926; see above for the theories of the struggle for existence.

[89] Out of 298 primitive peoples studied by Hobhouse, Wheeler and Ginsberg, there were nine peoples who did not know war at all. Among others, war was by no means a permanent state. Out of 298 peoples, about 57 used to adopt, set free, or exchange their prisoners. See HOBHOUSE, WHEELER, and GINSBERG, *The Material Culture and Social Institutions of the Simpler Peoples*, pp. 231 ff. See also STEINMETZ, *Philosophie des Krieges*, 1907, Chaps. I–III; KOVALEVSKY, *op. cit.*, pp. 109 ff.

or that their mutual attitude is always deadly inimical, would be obviously wrong.[90]

4. The contention is also incorrect that all consolidations of two or more groups into a bigger one have been achieved only through war. Many such consolidations have been really made through war and compulsion, but many others have been achieved without it. It is enough to mention the relatively peaceful foundations of the Russian, the Roman, the Athenian, the Swiss, the Iroquois, the American, and the Australian states. There are many cases in ancient, mediæval, and modern history where some autonomous countries have freely adjoined some other country, and in this way produced a consolidated body. There are also several leagues and unions which have been composed in a contractual way. Rightly also, M. Kovalevsky indicates that among primitive groups, and at the early stages of present nations, many such consolidations have taken place through the activity of special mediators, namely, wise and esteemed men. This series of facts is sufficient to show the one-sidedness of Gumplowicz's conception.

5. It is also fallacious to claim that social stratification is due exclusively to war, that all governments and aristocracies have arisen exclusively in a military way, and that they invariably have been composed of foreign conquerors, while the lower classes have been composed of the conquered. In some cases the situation has been such, but in other and more numerous cases, it has been quite different and has had nothing to do with war. In my *Social Mobility* (Chap. XIV), I have shown that social stratification arises regardless of any war in any group of men living together, be it a gang of children, a pioneer settlement, a society of ascetics, a group of levellers, or what not. It is a close correlate of any human association. We do not know any single

[90] Here Gumplowicz makes the same mistakes as Marx in his statement, "The history of all hitherto existing society is the history of class struggle." A partial fact is reared into the universal; one aspect of the whole historical process of group or class-interrelations is substituted for the whole process; some moments of the time-process marked by struggle are taken for all moments and, among them, the moments of peace and solidarity. Such is "the logic" of this construction. It is as sound as the statement: "The history of individual life is the history of eating." "*Pars pro toto*," such is the fault in the terminology of the old logicians.

example where, in a group of men more or less permanently living together, and having no war, social stratification did not exist.[91] Inherited differences between men and differences in environment, regardless of any war, are responsible for the fact of stratification. War only facilitates it. In cases where war has established a new aristocracy of the conquerors, we have not had the creation of an aristocracy where it did not exist before. Rather, we have the mere substitution of a new aristocracy for the previous one. This means that Gumplowicz's factor is neither necessary nor even sufficient to account for the origin and existence of stratification.

6. One-sided also is his assumption that the government and the upper class have always been composed of the victorious conquerors. In some cases it is so, but in numerous cases it is not. Studies of primitive leadership, the origin of early kingship, the history of social stratification, and the composition of upper classes in different societies of the past and the present, all contradict Gumplowicz's hypothesis. The first great leaders and rulers of many old societies, (like Oknirabata of the Central Australia tribes, Manco Ccapac and Mama Occllo among the Incas, Moses among the Jews, Fu Hi among the Chinese and so on), are depicted not as foreign conquerors, but as great native inventors, teachers, judges, sages, and lawgivers. The same is true of many a king in the early stages of civilization, and of the "ruling class" of many a primitive tribe, or the ancient Teutons (*duces ex virtute sunt*, says Tacitus).[92] Whether we take the

---

[91] Dr. F. Oppenheimer is wrong in supposing that pre-state groups are not stratified, while state groups are stratified. Since this premise is not valid, not valid becomes also his interesting attempt to build on this difference the definition of the state. See OPPENHEIMER, F., "Soziologie des Staates," *Jahrbuch für Soziologie*, B. II, pp. 85–87. The same mistake is made by J. Mazzarella in his valuable *Les types sociaux et le droit*, p. 64 and *passim*. He himself shows that in his "unstratified" (*le gentilice*) group there are chiefs and the ruled, the servile and the dominating classes.

[92] See the facts in SOROKIN, *Social Mobility*, Parts I, II, III and *passim;* FRAZER, J. G., *Lectures on the Early History of the Kingship*, London, 1905; VIERKANDT, A., "Führende Individuen bei den Naturvölkern," *Archiv für Sozwissenschaft*, XI, 1908, pp. 542–553, 623–639; KOVALEVSKY, M., *Sociology*, (Russ.) 1910, Vol. II; *Contemporary Sociologists*, pp. 112 ff.; MUMFORD, E., "The Origins of Leadership," *American Journal of Sociology*, Vol. XII; MAUNIER, R., "Vie réligieuse et vie economique," *Revue Internat. de sociologie*, Dec., 1907, Jan., Febr., 1908; LOWIE, R. H., *Primitive Society*, 1920, Chap. IX; DESCAMPS, P., "Le pouvoir publique chez les sauvages," *Revue internat. de sociologie*, 1924;

class of priests, or rulers, or even military leaders in a great many societies, we find that they have been composed of natives. Later stages of the history of various peoples show the same picture. It is needless to insist any longer on these facts. Here again we see the same mistake: a partial fact is made universal; a particular case is transformed into a general rule.

7. Finally, I wonder whether there is any competent investigator of the history of law, judicial institutions, morals, *mores,* and customs, who would agree with Gumplowicz that all these "compulsory" rules of conduct have originated through and are due to, war; and are consequently nothing but the rules of the conquerors enacted for the sake of exploiting and controlling the conquered subjects. Neither the comparative histories of law like those of Brunner, Post, Mayer, Dargun, Kohler, Efimenko, Thurnwald, B. Spencer and Gillen, M. Kovalevsky, Henry Sumner Maine, Mazzarella, Steinmetz, Makarewicz, and so on; nor the histories of moral ideas like those of Westermarck, Letourneau, Frazer, Durkheim, Huvelin, Hubert, Mauss, H. Spencer, Hobhouse, W. G. Sumner, etc.; nor contemporary ethnography, ethnology, or cultural anthropology, give a serious basis for such a theory of the origin of law and compulsory forms of conduct. No doubt in some cases Gumplowicz's factor has played some facilitating rôle, but it is fallacious to contend that without it human societies would never have had any law, or that all compulsory rules of conduct have originated in the way traced by Gumplowicz.

These indications are sufficient to show the fallacies of Gumplowicz's theories. However, Gumplowicz's works have not been useless. Through his one-sidedness and exaggeration of the above points, he has facilitated concentration of the attention of investigators upon these phenomena. This has led to a series of more careful studies, which have permitted us to judge more accurately of the discussed facts. In this sense, Gumplowicz's sociological works [93] have served the science of sociology.

GOLDENWEISER, A., *Early Civilization.* THURNWALD, R., "Soziale Organization" in *Zeitschrift f. vergleichende Rechtswissenschaft,* Vol. XXXVI, and a series of his valuable articles in *Reallexikon der Vorgeschichte.*

[93] I estimate Gumplowicz's studies in the history of social theories much higher. Here his works were really valuable.

CHAPTER IX

SOCIOLOGISTIC SCHOOL (*Continued*): THE FORMAL SCHOOL AND A SYSTEMATICS OF SOCIAL RELATIONSHIP

I. THE CHARACTERISTICS OF THE SCHOOL AND ITS LEADING REPRESENTATIVES

T H E fourth principal variety of the sociologistic school is the formal. It maintains the fundamentals of the sociologistic school, which are interaction and interrelations as the essence of social phenomena, the superindividual conception of social reality, the interpretation of an individual as a group product, group interpretation of social phenomena, etc.; but in addition it stresses that the proper object of sociology, as a specific science, is the study of the *forms* of social interaction, or of social *relationship,* as contrasted with its *contents,* as studied by other social sciences. Its partizans, contrary to "encyclopedic" sociology, which treats everything and represents a "hodgepodge" of various problems, try to build sociology as a specific and systematic science, with a limited but quite definite field of study. In this field are the forms of human relationships, or of socialization, regardless of any concrete, historical society. Such a sociology is, in the first place, an analytical science. In the second place, since it studies the forms of social relationships, it can be more accurate than any encyclopedic sociology. In the third place, compared to other social sciences, it occupies approximately the same position which physical mechanics, or especially mathematics, has in regard to physical or technical sciences,—the latter cannot exist without the former. The better the mathematics or theory of social relations, the greater will be their service to technical or other social sciences.[1]

The school claims that it is new and much younger than the

[1] See an able summary of the formal school in VIERKANDT, A., *Gesellschaftslehrs,* pp. 1–19, Stuttgart, 1923.

"encyclopedic" sociology. F. Tönnies and G. Simmel [2] are regarded as the founders of the school. Its history is computed only by some thirty years. Leaving this claim without discussion for a moment, let us briefly outline the principles of the school as they are given in the works of its most prominent representatives. These representatives are: F. Tönnies, R. Stammler, G. Simmel, G. Richard, L. von Wiese, A. Vierkandt, T. Litt, C. Bouglé, partly E. A. Ross in his last works, R. Park and E. Burgess, to mention only a few names.

Possibly George Simmel's (1858-1918) conception of sociology is the most characteristic of the school. It is as follows: In order to be a really separate science, sociology, like other special sciences, should have its own field of study which is not investigated by other social sciences, or, what is the same thing, its own point of view. The lack of such a special field for sociological study would necessitate the barring of sociology as a special science. Now what field or viewpoint is sociological? From the standpoint of *content* all fields of social phenomena such as the economic, religious, linguistic, moral, historical, and other phenomena are already studied by corresponding social sciences. In regard to content, there is no room for sociology. The only field or viewpoint which is not taken by other sciences is the field of the *forms of socialization,* or the *forms of human relationship.* This field, or viewpoint, is exactly what belongs to sociology, making of it an independent and special science. In regard to other social sciences, sociology has the same attitude as geometry has to other natural sciences. Geometry studies the spatial forms of physical objects but not their content. Sociology does the same in regard to social phenomena. The same geometrical form, as a ball, may be filled with different contents, and different geometrical forms may also have the same physical content. The content and form are quite separate phenomena, or viewpoints toward phenomena. In a similar way, the same forms of human relationship may have different social content; the same social content may have different forms of social relationship. In other words, in the field of human interrelations, form and content are

---

[2] *Ibid.*, p. 1; SPYKMAN, N. J., *The Social Theory of Georg Simmel*, pp. XIV, XV, 263 ff., Chicago, 1925.

something quite different, and consequently each of them may be the object of a special study. Each of the forms of human inter-relations (domination, subordination, competition, imitation, division of labor, formation of parties, and many other forms of relationship) are found in a civic group, in a religious community, in a band of brigands, in a business organization, in a family, in a school, and, in brief, in the most different social groups from the standpoint of their content; and *vice versa*. Hence, the possibility and even the necessity for the existence of sociology as a special science whose aim is a description, classification, analysis, and explanation of the *forms* of human relationship, the forms of socialization, or even the forms of social organization rather than their contents, which are now studied by other sciences.

Such, in brief, is Simmel's conception of sociology as a specific social science.[3]

In his *Soziologie,* which incorporates his previous sociological studies: *Über soziale Differenzierung, Das Problem der Soziologie, Comment les formes sociales se maintiennent,* and some others,[4] Simmel attempts to give an analysis, classification, and interpretation of several forms of social relations, such as isolation, contact, superordination, subordination, opposition, persis-

---

[3] SIMMEL, G., *Soziologie,* 1908, pp. 1–14, and *passim.* See also SPYKMAN, N. J., *The Social Theory of Georg Simmel,* 1925, Book I, *passim.* The book is good from the standpoint of a summary of Simmel's theories. From the standpoint of a criticism and estimation of Simmel's contribution it is rather elementary. About Simmel's sociological works see SOROKIN, P., *Systema Soziologii,* Vol. I, pp. 25–35, 322 ff.; BARTH, P., *Die Philosophie der Geschichte als Soziologie,* 1922, pp. 149 ff.; BERNHARD, E., "Simmel als Soziologe und Sozialphilosoph," *Die Tat,* 1913–14, No. 10, pp. 1080–1086; FRISCHEISEN-KOHLER, M., "Simmel," *Kantstudien,* Vol. XXIV; KRACAUER, S., "Georg Simmel," *Logos* IX, 1920, pp. 307–338; SCHMALENBACH, H., "Simmel," *Sozialistische Monatshefte,* 1919, pp. 283–288; a series of authors in *La philosophie allemande au XIXe siècle,* Paris, 1912.

[4] Some of these works have been published in English. See "The Problem of Sociology," *Annals of the American Academy, of Political and Social Science,* Vol. VI, pp. 412–423; "Superiority and Subordination as Subject Matter for Sociology," *American Journal of Sociology,* Vol. II, pp. 167–189, 392–415; "The Persistence of the Social Group," *ibid.,* Vol. III, pp. 662–698, 829–836; Vol. IV, pp. 35–50; "The Number of Members as Determining the Sociological Form of the Group," *ibid.,* Vol. VIII, pp. 1–46, 158–196; "The Sociology of Conflict," *American Journal of Psychology,* Vol. IX, pp. 490–525, 672–689, 798–811; "Fashion," *International Quarterly,* Vol. X, pp. 130–155; "A Contribution to the Sociology of Religion," *American Journal of Sociology,* Vol. XI, pp. 359–376; "The Sociology of Secrecy and the Secret Society," *ibid.,* Vol. XI, pp. 441–498; "How Society Is Possible," *ibid.,* Vol. XVI, pp. 372–391. For a complete list of the works of Simmel see Spykman's book, pp. 277 ff.

tence or continuity of social group, social differentiation, integration, and some other forms.

F. Tönnies, (1855–   ), professor of the University of Kiel, had already published in 1887 his *Gemeinschaft und Gesellschaft,* in which he laid down a conception of sociology which was in essence similar to that which was later formulated by Simmel.[5] In this valuable work, Tönnies gave not only a mere outline of "pure" or "formal sociology," but, by way of making a factual analysis of the fundamental forms of social relationship, he demonstrated the essential character of such a sociology. According to Tönnies there are two fundamental forms of society or social relationship: "Community" (*Gemeinschaft*) and "Society" (*Gesellschaft*). The *Gemeinschaft* is a union of individuals with an "organic will," whose solidarity springs from the natural forces of consanguinity. It is a product of nature, or a kind of natural organism. There is no personal will. Individuals are only members of a general body with a natural solidarity, harmonious interrelations, and an identity of will because the individual will is suppressed by the community will. As the result of such an "organic" solidarity, we have a community of property, and a law which is nothing but a family law. It is easy to see that Tönnies' *Gemeinschaft* is identical to what Durkheim later styled a "group with mechanical solidarity." The *Gesellschaft* is a totality of individuals who enter interaction according to their own individual will, (*Kürwille*) for an achievement of their own purposes. It is not a product of nature, and is in no way a natural organism. It is rather an artificial mechanism.[6] This form is styled by Durkheim as a group based on "organic solidarity." One cannot help thinking that Durkheim intentionally gave to his social types names which were opposite to those given by Tönnies. Further differences of both these forms of society are as follows:[7]

[5] Spykman's sketch of the precursors of Simmel and ot the state of the pre-Simmelian sociology is unsatisfactory. Being generally wrong in his claim that the formal school is new (see further) and making some mistakes in his characterization of the pre-Simmelian sociology, he is wrong also in his contention that Simmel was the first who set forth the theory of the formal school.

[6] TÖNNIES, F., *Gemeinschaft und Gesellschaft,* 3d. ed., pp. 1–102 and *passim,* Berlin, 1920.

[7] *Ibid.,* pp. 22, 42, 126, 148, 152, 157 and *passim,* 191.

Gemeinschaft	Gesellschaft
Common will	Individual will
No individuality of members	Individuality of members
Domination of the community interests	Domination of the individual interests
Belief	Doctrine
Religion	Public opinion
Mores and customs	Fashion, fads, mode
Natural solidarity	Contractual solidarity, commerce and exchange
Common property	Private property

Historically, the *Gemeinschaft* appeared earlier than the *Gesellschaft,* because primitive groups, family, and tribes are concrete examples of this form of society. In the course of time, however, the *Gemeinschaft* began to disintegrate and *Gesellschaft* appeared. It has been progressing at the cost of the *Gemeinschaft* type. Man has been becoming less and less attached to any community. Instead of it, in temporary and contractual ways, he has been tending to become a member of more and more numerous and larger groups. In this way history goes from the community to the society, from "the culture of the people to the civilization of State." This process is irreversible. Such, in brief, is Tönnies' theory, in many respects similar to what later on was developed by Simmel in his *Ueber soziale Differenzierung,* and by a Russian professor, B. Kistiakowski, in his *Gesellschaft und Einzelwesen,* 1899.

The next considerable contribution to the principles of the formal school was made by R. Stammler in his *Wirtschaft und Recht nach der materialistischen Geschichtsauffassung* (Leipzig, 1896), where Stammler very conspicuously developed the difference between the concepts of social *form* and social *content* and gave a systematic theory of law as the form, and of "economic phenomena" (*Wirtschaft*) as the content of social relations. Furthermore, G. Richard (1860–   ), professor at the University of Bordeaux, editor of the *Revue internationale de sociologie* and previously a collaborator of Durkheim, but later a critic of several points in Durkheim's theory, in his *La so-*

ciologie générale et les lois sociologiques (Paris, 1912) also assumed a position especially near to Tönnies' sociological conception. Richard states that the field of sociology is neither all social phenomena, nor various phenomena of human behavior, nor analogies between society and organism, nor any philosophy of history, nor any "encyclopedism." Its field is more limited and more definite; namely, the "relationship between Community and Society, between the phenomena of coöperation and mental interaction (*society*), and the phenomena '*communautaires*' (*Community*)." [8] Accordingly, the greater part of Richard's work is devoted to an analysis of the relationship between these two forms in the course of history, and to the formulation of several laws of their development similar to those given by Tönnies, Simmel, and Durkheim. They indicate an historical tendency toward a decrease of community-form and an increase of society-form in the course of time.[9]

Of the other prominent representatives of the school and their works, it is necessary to mention Professor A. Vierkandt's (1867–) *Gesellschaftslehre* (1923) and Professor L. von Wiese's *Allgemeine Soziologie* (1924).[10] Vierkandt's course is built along the line of the school, but is less "formal" than the work of L. von Wiese. "*Allgemeine Soziologie als Lehre von den Beziehungen und Beziehungsgebilden der Menschen*" by Professor Leopold von Wiese (1876–), may be regarded as the

[8] RICHARD, G., *La sociologie générale et les lois sociologiques*, pp. 180, 227, 345–372, Paris, 1912.

[9] The first law is that, in the course of history, the society-type relations (economic, intellectual and so on) tend to expand progressively and to extend finally over the whole of mankind in the form of a world market, world religion, world intelligence, and other intercourse. The second law is that the community-type of social group tends to be more and more differentiated into a series of "society-type" interrelations. The third law is that the community-type of a group has more chances of being preserved as it becomes more isolated from intercourse with other groups. This means that the development of a relationship between the community and society-types is negatively correlated. See *ibid.*, pp. 227–277 and *passim*.

[10] There is a considerable number of other sociologists who belong to the same school; for instance, the majority of the collaborators of the "*Kölner Vierteljahrshefte für Soziologie.*" On the formal position also stands C. Bouglé, in his *Qu'est-ce que la sociologie?*, and *Les sciences sociales en Allemagne;* and T. Litt, in his *Individuum und Gesellschaft*. See other names in VIERKANDT, A., "Die Uberwindung des Positivismus in der deutschen Soziologie der Gegenwart," *Jahrbuch für Soziologie*, B. II, and VON WIESE, L., *Allgemeine Soziologie*.

most systematic development of Simmel's conception of sociology. The author acknowledges his indebtedness to Simmel, E. Waxweiler, E. A. Ross, and Max Weber; but it is evident that Simmel's and Ross' influence on the book is far greater than that of the other mentioned sociologists. Like Simmel, Dr. von Wiese is trying to establish sociology as an independent science.

My aim was to shape sociology into a distinct science, definitely separated from other sciences, firmly jointed, and consistently systematized.[11]

Like Simmel he thinks that the only way to attain this aim is by conceiving sociology as the science of the forms of human relations or, what is the same, the forms of social processes. The book, in its essence, represents an attempt to give a systematic classification of the forms of human relationship. At the back of the book the reader finds a chart classifying human relations or social processes. The essential features of the classification are as follows. The author discriminates the relationship *between individuals* from that *between groups,* which represent a kind of crystallized formation of interindividual relations (*Gebilden*). Each of these orders of relationships is divided into classes: I. *Interindividual* relations are classed into three principal forms— 1. *toward* each other (contact, approach, adaptation, combination, and union); 2. *away* from each other (competition, opposition, and conflict); 3. *mixed* form, which is partly a relation toward, and partly away from each other. II. *Intergroup* relations, or social processes in a narrower sense of the word are classified into four principal divisions: 1. *differentiating processes,* like social promotion and degradation, domination and subordination, stratification, selection, and individualization; 2. *integrating processes* such as uniformization, stabilization, crystallization, and socialization; 3. *destructive processes* like exploitation, partial favoring, corruption, formalization, commercialization, radicalization, spoliation; 4. *modifying-constructive processes,* which embrace institutionalization, professionalization, and liberation. Such are the substantial forms of social relationships or social processes.

[11] VON WIESE, L., *Allgemeine Soziologie,* Teil I, Beziehungslehre, München und Leipzig, 1924, p. VIII.

Each of the mentioned subdivisions in its turn is subdivided into many sub-subclasses which, in their totality, give about 650 forms of human relationship.[12] The book as a whole is a foundation, motivation, and interpretation of this classification and of each class, sub-class, and sub-subclass of human relations given in the table. This is followed by some logical discussion and a psychological interpretation of some of the classes, but they compose the secondary matter of the book. From the above one can see that Dr. L. von Wiese, more systematically than anybody else, pushed the formal conception of sociology to its logical end. In order to prevent a contamination of "pure sociology" by the "content" of social relations he cut all ties between social "form" and "content." He tries to compress an immensely complex world of human relations into a classification based on formal logic. This explains why von Wiese's book must be regarded as "a leading expression of the present animus of post-Simmelism." [13] For this reason it may serve well to show the pluses and the minuses of the formal school.

2. CRITICISM

Before discussing what is valid in the claims of the formal school, let us indicate at once what is questionable. In the first place, the school's claim that it is a new one is baseless. It is a very old school, perhaps even older than any other school of social science. In the second place, the fundamental discrimination between form and content of social relationship is either fallacious, or represents something on which it is impossible to build sociology as a special science. In the third place, the claim that forms of social relationship are not studied by other than sociological disciplines, is not warranted by the facts. Thus far, Simmel's attempt to build sociology as an autonomous science of the forms of social relationship is not valid. In the fourth place, Simmel and other "formalists" do not keep to their principles, but transgress their own definition, contradict it, and often interpret the same terms in quite different senses. In the fifth

---

[12] See at the end of the book *"Tafel der Menschlichen Beziehungen"*; see Chapters I and II.

[13] A. Small's review of the book by L. von Wiese, in *American Journal of Sociology*, Vol. XXXI, p. 87.

place, even if the Simmelian concept of the forms of social relations were true, this would not mean that sociology, as a science of general characteristics of, and the correlation between, social phenomena, could not, or should not, exist. The following considerations will show the validity of these critical propositions : [14]

A. The claim that the forms of social relationship are not studied by other sciences is not warranted by the facts. It is sufficient to take the science of law in order to see that all Simmel's, or Tönnies', or Vierkandt's, or Richard's, or von Wiese's forms of social relationship have been studied in an excellent and more precise way by the science of law. Is it not evident that such "forms" as "domination" and "subordination" have been always a fundamental object of so-called public, constitutional, or administrative law? The very essence of the phenomena of sovereignty, authority, prestige, power, government, ruling, conflict, domination, subjection, subordination, obedience, together with their forms, origin, and functions have always been one of the fundamental objects of the science of law. And more than that, the science of law, through the Roman jurisconsults, has already given excellent, clear, and brilliant definitions of these phenomena : *Potestas, Majestas, Imperium, Dominus, Princeps, Dignitates, Subjecti,* etc. Any serious book on constitutional law will show that these "forms" of social relationship are its principal objects.[15] The same is true of the other forms of formal sociology. If we take international law, we find that such forms of intergroup relationships as contact, isolation, agreement, opposition, conflict, war, and so on, are studied very attentively, and again more clearly and more formally than is done by the partizans of the formal school. Furthermore, such fundamental forms of social relationship as obligation or duty, dependence,

[14] They were formulated already in my *System of Sociology.* See SOROKIN, *Systema Soziologii,* Vol. I, pp. 24–35, Petrograd, 1920.

[15] See PETRAJITZKY, L., *Introduction to the Science of Law,* and *Theory of Law and State,* Vols. I, II, St. Petersburg, 1907 and 1909 (Russian); DUGUIT, L., *Droit constitutionel;* STAMMLER, R., *Theorie der Rechtswissenschaft,* Halle, 1911; SOHM, *Systemaische Rechtswissenschaft,* 1906; IHERING, R., *Geist des romischen Rechts,* Vols. I, II, III; MOMMSEN, T., *Romische Staatsrecht, passim;* LASKI, H. J., *Studies in the Problem of Sovereignty,* 1917; SOROKIN, *Theory of Law and State,* 1919 (Russian); KISTIAKOWSKI, B., *Social Sciences and Law,* (Russian), Moscow, 1915; POKROVSKY, T., *Fundamental Problems of Civil Law,* (Russian), 1913.

contractual relations, stratification, exploitation, transgression, spoliation, persistence, and continuity, show that all these forms of social relationship have been studied, analyzed, described, classified and compared by the civil, criminal, processual and other branches of the science of law since immemorial times. All this is so evident that there is no need to insist longer upon it.

What has been said about the science of law may be said of a great many other sciences. They have also studied the forms of social relationship. Take economics. Does it not study division of labor and social differentiation?—coöperation and association? —the forms which Simmel styles *"Die Treue"* and *"Dankbarkeit"?*—or that of exploitation and spoliation?—and a great many other forms of social relations?[16] Dr. O. Spann is quite right in saying that almost all the laws of economics are quite formal and describe what Simmel styles the forms of relationships.[17] The same is true in regard to political science, and practically in regard to almost all social sciences. In brief, it is not easy to find a social science which does not study the forms of social relationship in the sense of the formal school, and from a standpoint which is identical with, or similar to, the school's standpoint.

The above means that this claim of the school is not valid. If it is not valid, then the attempt to build sociology on such a claim fails. Since the "forms" are studied by other sciences, there is no room for sociology as a science of the forms of human relationship.

B. The above explains why, in my opinion, the formal school is very old. Its founders were neither Tönnies nor Simmel, as Dr. Vierkandt claims;[18] nor Kant, Hegel, Herbart, Ferguson, Fichte, L. von Stein, Gneist, Jellinek, nor Spencer, as G. Richard

[16] To see this it is enough to take any serious course in economics.

[17] O. SPANN, rightly indicates that the theory of value describes nothing but a specific form of Simmelian relationship. *"Auch andere national ökonomische Gesetze erweisen sich als rein formale. In Thünens Gesetz der relativen Rationalität der Landbausysteme und ihrer abnehmenden Intansität bei wachsender Entfernung vom Marktorte sind rein 'formale' Beziehungen geschildert. . . . Es muss daher abgelehnt werden, dass die formale Natur des Gegenstandes der von Simmel angestrebten 'Soziologie' alleineigen wäre. Diese fehlt nirgends, und der ganze Gesichtspunkt erweist sich daher als unrichtig."* SPANN, O., *Kurzgefasstes System der Gesellschaftslehre*, pp. 17–19, Leipzig, 1914.

[18] VIERKANDT, *op. cit.*, p. 1.

indicates more rightly.[19]   Its founders were all lawgivers who formulated the first rules of social relations, and especially all jurisconsults and theorizers of law.   Beginning at least with Confucius [20] and the Roman jurisconsults, who so brilliantly formulated the principal forms of social relations, and ending with the theorizers of law, all have been "formal sociologists." If they are not regarded as the predecessors and the representatives of the formal school, this is probably due only to the fact that their works have been styled juridical but not sociological. In their character, however, their works, even the very codes of law, beginning with *Corpus Juris Civilis* of Justinian, and ending with new codes of the civil, the constitutional, the criminal, and the processual law (not to mention corresponding theories) are the most brilliant samples of the formal analysis of human relationship or of the forms of social interaction.   Their formulas of *Potestas, Imperium, Majestas,* and *Manus* are incomparably better and more formal than the forms of domination in the characteristics of the contemporary formal school.   Their formulas of *commercium, consensus, cessio, beneficium,* various *obligationes,* contractual relations, *dominium, proprietas,* and *possessio;* their definitions of the *status libertatis, status civitatis,* and *capitis diminutio;* of marriage, family, consanguinity, inheritance, and so on, represent an "ideal formal sociology" which the formal sociologists may only envy and try to approach as near as possible.

The classification of the social forms of either Tönnies, Simmel, Vierkandt, or von Wiese, is but an incomplete and less formal enumeration of the forms classified, defined, and analyzed in the codes and in the theories of the law.   Further, it will be shown that in the classification of the forms of social relations the formal school follows the path trodden by many "non-formal" sociologists.   Hence the conclusions : First, that the formal school is a very old one.   Second, all great jurisconsults and theorizers of

---

[19] RICHARD, G., *op. cit.,* Chaps. I, IV.

[20] It is enough to remember Confucius' theory of "the five relationships" and their analysis in the Confucianist teaching to see that a "formal sociology" — and a good one — existed six centuries B.C. See *Lî-Kî,* Book I, pp. 62–63; Book VII, p. 3; Book VIII, pp. 1, 15; and *Doctrine of the Mean,* translated in J. LEGGE'S *The Life and Teachings of Confucius,* pp. 313 ff., London, 1895. See also *Policraticus* by John of Salisbury, Books V and VI, where the relationship of domination and subordination is treated in a perfectly formal way.

law have been its founders and representatives. Third, the contemporary formal sociologists, contrary to their claim, are less formal in their constructions than the mentioned jurists. Fourth, a further purification of the principles and aspirations of the formal school must lead it to a greater and greater approach to the works of the theorizers of law, and to the codes of law which are nothing but an "ideal formal sociology." If the theories of the present formal school do not coincide completely with the latter, this is due, as we shall see, to the fact that the formal sociologists are not consistent. They often transgress their own contention of being "formal," and pour into their books a great deal of the "content" of social phenomena.

The above leaves the school in a dilemma : either to be perfect and consistent in its formality, thus becoming nothing but a variety of the theories and codes of law ; or to lose its "formality" and become the kind of "encyclopedic" sociology which is criticized so severely by the formalists. In its present stage, the school represents a mixture of "formality" and "encyclopedism," and, like any imperfect mixture of this kind, it has the shortcomings of both, often without the superiorities of either of these types of sociology.

C. The school's concepts of form and content are somewhat unsatisfactory also. Since at least the time of Aristotle, philosophical concepts of form and content, or substance, have been very common, and have been given different meanings. Neither Simmel nor his followers, however, have taken care to clarify these somewhat indefinite conceptions. Speaking of the objects which have spatial characteristics these concepts may be applied easily and properly ; but how can they be applied to such phenomena as power, authority, domination, subordination, competition and other forms which do not have geometrically-spatial dimensions? Since they have not, it is then clear that to make an analogy between a geometrical form, as a ball, which may be filled by different content, and a social form which may be filled by different content, is rather fallacious. Still more fallacious is it to isolate the "social form" from its content (which in the field of geometrically spatial objects is possible) and then to state that "social forms can remain identical while their members change." [21]   We may fill a glass with wine, water, or sugar without changing its form; but I cannot conceive of a social institution whose "form" would not change when its members, for instance, Americans, were superseded by quite a new and heterogeneous people, *e.g.,* by Chinese or Bushmen.   Even if the written constitution of the institution remained untouched on paper, nevertheless its form and organization would change, in direct proportion to how dissimilar the new members were as compared with the previous ones.   Quite questionable also is the statement that social "form" may exist independent of "content."   Simmel himself has shown that even such a "content-condition" as the number of the members of a group decidedly influences the "form of the group."   These examples show how vague are the terminology and analogies of the Simmelian school.   In some cases its followers use the concepts of form and content just in this inadmissible "geometrico-spatial" sense.   In some other cases, however, they somewhat change their meaning, and use them in the sense of Aristotelian logic, where form designates a broader class of phenomena or concept, while content means a subclass, or a concept which designates this subclass.   In this sense the class, and consequently the concept, "human beings," is a form of the subclasses and corresponding concepts, "man" and "woman," which may function as "content" in regard to the "human being" as a form.   The same may be said of an "organism," "plant," or "animal," where "organism" is a form for "plant" and "animal" "content." [22]   If such is the logical interrelation of these concepts, then it is clear that they cannot be associated with one another as something logically heterogeneous.   With this interpretation, Simmel's claim that sociology studies the forms of social phe-

[21] SIMMEL, "Comment les formes sociales se maintiennent," *L'année sociologique*, Vol. I.   This theory of the persistence of the social group is in its essence nothing but a somewhat shortened and modified theory of the juridical existence of so-called juridical personalities, which was many centuries ago brilliantly elaborated by jurists and lawyers.

[22] Dr. R. Stammler, like Simmel, always uses these terms in his scientific works.   On the discrimination of form and content is based his discrimination of law as a form, and economic processes as a content of social life.   When, however, Stammler has to define the concepts of form and content, he says that the form means a broader, and the content, a narrower concept for a classification of the same series of phenomena.   In other words, form is a *genus;* content is a subclass of the same *genus.* See STAMMLER, R., *Theorie der Rechtswissenschaft,* pp. 7 ff., Halle, 1911; also, *Wirtschaft und Recht, passim.*

nomena may mean only that, contrary to other social sciences, sociology studies the most general characteristics of social phenomena which belong to all specific forms of human relationship, while other sciences study these specific characteristics (content). This means that sociology is not a science which studies the specific characteristics of social phenomena, as Simmel claims, but a generalizing science, which Simmel denies. Thus, we come to the conclusion that Simmel's conceptions of form and content are either meaningless and inapplicable to social phenomena; or that they lead to the conception of sociology as a generalizing science, which conception contradicts Simmel's pretensions of building sociology as a specific science.[23]

Furthermore, one who reads attentively the works of Simmel or of the other "formalists" can easily detect a permanent, sometimes quite a strong alteration, in the meanings which they give to many terms, and especially to those of form and content. On one page we are told that the object-matter of sociology is the forms of human relationship; a few lines or pages further on, we are suddenly told that this object is the forms of socialization! [24] Nevertheless, these two concepts of the forms of human relations, and the forms of socialization mean something quite different. The forms of human relationship may mean not only the forms of socialization, but those of desocialization also; not only association, but dissociation; not only coöperation, but warfare, also.[25] If we define sociology as the science of the

---

[23] Compare SPANN, O., *Kurzgefasstes System der Gesellschaftslehre*, pp. 9–19.

[24] See SIMMEL, *Soziology*, pp. 4 ff.; *Grundfragen der Soziologie*, pp. 22 ff. It is curious to note that one of the recent propagandists of Simmelianism in this country, being quite accurate in his characterization of Simmel's theory, makes such a shifting of meaning in the following way: "This concept of society as form, or rather of the form of the socialization," etc. The author, like Simmel, seems not to see that "forms of human relationship" and the "forms of socialization" mean something quite different and by "simple" or "rather" it is impossible to jump from one to another and identify their meaning. See the whole of Book I, in Spykman's quoted work where he, like Simmel, uses interchangeably these two definitions.

[25] E. A. Ross and E. Dupréel, who, independent of Simmel, have very ably tried to outline the concept of sociology as a science of human relations, and who give one of the best analyses of human relations, are free from this *quaternio terminorum* of Simmel and the Simmelian school. See Ross, E. A., *Principles of Sociology*, Part III; DUPRÉEL, E., *Le rapport social, Essai sur l'objet et la méthode de la sociologie*, Paris, 1912, Chap. IV and *passim*. See also his "Sociologie et psychologie," *Institut Solvay, Bullétin mensuel*, pp. 180–186, Jan., 1911. Ross and Dupréel being relationists in sociology, do not belong to the formal school.

forms of human relationship, then the processes of dissociation, opposition, conflict, and warfare must be included in the field of its study. If we define it as a science of the forms of socialization, then these processes, as opposed to those of socialization, must be excluded from the field of sociology. For Simmel and some of the Simmelists, this heterogeneity of the two definitions does not exist. They use them interchangeably, and without any attempt to reconcile them. This naturally results in a series of logical inconsistencies, and in a vagueness of theoretical constructions.

What has been said of the fundamental conceptions of Simmelian sociology, may be said of its many other propositions. Although valuable in some respects, they are stamped by the same vagueness, indefiniteness, changeable meanings, and often by a purely speculative character. In this respect they are still in the stage of a purely philosophical or speculative sociology.[26]

Finally, the insufficiency of formal sociology is shown also by the transgression of its principles by the "Formalists" themselves. In spite of their severe criticism of the "encyclopedic" sociology, their own works have the same "encyclopedic char-

[26] From a purely methodological standpoint, Simmel's sociological method lacks scientific method. I must express my complete disagreement with Dr. R. Park's or Dr. Spykman's high estimation of the sociological method of Simmel. Besides the above logical deficiency, Simmel's method entirely lacks either experimental approach, quantitative investigation, or any systematic factual study of the discussed phenomena. In vain one would look in his work for a systematic method like that of the Le Play school, or of the methodological principles of social sciences developed by A. Cournot in his *Considérations sur la marche des idées*, etc.; *Essai sur le fondements de nos connaissances; Traité de l'enchainement des idées fondamentales dans les sciences et dans l'histoire;* or some principles like those of H. Rikkert and W. Windelbandt concerning the classification of sciences and of their methods of generalizing (nomographic or nomothetic) and individualizing (ideographic) sciences; or something like Max Weber's method of the "ideal typology"; or Galton's, Pearson's, and A. Tchuproff's quantitative methods of investigation; or even a simple, careful and attentive study of the facts he is talking about. All this is lacking. What there is represents only the speculative generalization of a talented man, backed by the "method of illustration" in the form of two or three facts incidentally taken and often one-sidedly interpreted. Without Simmel's talent the same stuff would appear poor. Simmel's talent saves the situation, but only as far as talent compensates for lack of scientific methodology. Under such conditions, to call the sociologists "back to Simmel," as Drs. Park and Spykman do, means to call them back to a pure speculation, metaphysics, and a lack of scientific method. Speculation and metaphysics are excellent things in their proper places, but to mix these with the science of sociology means to spoil each of those sciences.

acter." They are "contaminated" by a great deal of the "social content" poured into their "forms." Dr. Vierkandt's book may serve as an example. In spite of Vierkandt's declaration that he is going to deal only with the forms of social phenomena, he fails to carry on his program. Beginning with the second chapter of the book (pp. 58-179) it is filled with the "content"; with a long discussion of human instincts (of self-feeling, subordination, of mutual help, pugnacity, sympathy, and so on), together with their modification in the process of interaction; with sketches of the history of family, professional groups, classes, orders, nations, and states; with a philosophy of social unity and reality; and with imitation, suggestion, mob-mind, and so on;—in brief, with the usual "stuff" found in all non-formal sociological books. With a modification, the same may be said of all the works of the formal school. I do not know any one which would not have an "encyclopedic character," and in which the data of biology, ethnology, anthropology, history, psychology, political science, economics, and literature, are not mixed and used. In brief, "the sin of encyclopedism" is as common within the formal sociology as within the "non-formal" sociology it criticizes.[27]

The above should be sufficient to show that the formal school has failed to build sociology as an "autonomous and independent science" on the discrimination of the categories of form and content. To this it is possible to add that even the attempt itself to build such an independent science of sociology or of any other science, as far as it pretends to be something more than a mere conditional and approximate limitation of its field for the sake of a mere practical conveniency, is rather fallacious. Many sociologists [28] seem to be very anxious to construct such "an independent sociology." For this purpose they are ready to prohibit all sociologists from using the data and the materials used by other sciences. They dream of a "pure sociology," absolutely inde-

[27] This makes baseless the pretension of formal sociology to play the same rôle for other social sciences which is played by mathematics or physical mechanics in regard to other physical and technical sciences. Neither the pretension nor the analogy are justified in any way.

[28] See for instance ZNANIECKI, F., "The Object Matter of Sociology," *American Journal of Sociology*, January, 1927. See also SPANN, O., *op. cit.*, pp. IV, VII, Chapter I and *passim*.

pendent from, and not contaminated with, the data of other sciences. To achieve this fantastic goal they write and publish hundreds of volumes filled with a discussion of what sociology, as an independent science, ought to be, how it ought to be built, and how it ought to be separated from all other sciences. I confess that I find almost all such reasoning fruitless. If an author knows a wonderful secret about building such a sociology, let him show the validity of his secret by its factual building, but not by a mere reasoning of "how scientific sociology ought to be built." The success of his factual building is a much more convincing argument in favor of his secret than mere reasoning.[29] As a matter of fact, these reasonings are only a proof of the helplessness of such an author. Likewise, the attempt itself to build "an independent sociology" is rather fallacious. There is practically no science (except perhaps mathematics and formal logic) which is independent and "uncontaminated" by data taken from other sciences. I do not know any chemistry which would not use the data of physics, or even of biology. I do not know any biology which would not use the data of chemistry, physics, or some other sciences. There is no anatomy which does not contain the data of physiology, ecology, systematics, histology, or what not. Various branches of physical, chemical, and biological sciences are so closely interwoven and mixed and some of them, like organic or colloidal chemistry, are such a *"mixtum compositum"* of "different sciences" that only by completely ignoring their real character is it possible to dream of "an absolutely independent science." The same "mixture" of data and premises is still more conspicuous in the field of social sciences, or those which deal with human beings. I cannot imagine psychology without the data of biology, anatomy, and physiology. I have not seen any important treatise in economic or political sciences which did not use the data of psychology, biology, history, demography, ethics, or even philosophy.[30] More than that, practically all the most

---

[29] Pareto, who devotes only five lines to his definition of sociology in his fifteen-hundred page treatise on the subject, and Ross, who, in his *Principles of Sociology* does not give any definition of sociology, but starts at once to build it, proceed much better than all those who extensively discuss what sociology is, and by this discussion complete their "books."

[30] A sociologist cannot be troubled much by the divergency of the existing definitions of sociology. This situation is not worse than that of the economists.

important books in cultural, psychological, and social sciences, even in biology, have been those which have been rich in such a mixture of the data of various sciences. Whether I take *Philosophy of Zoölogy* by Lamarck; or *The Origin of the Species* by Darwin, I find it difficult to decide exactly to what branch of science these works belong. The data of various, even of social sciences, are so mixed in such works that it is not easy to decide the question. At any rate they do not belong to the kind of "formal and independent works" of which "sociological autonomists" dream. The same is still more true in regard to the epoch-making works in the field of cultural and social sciences. Whether we take *The Republic* of Plato, or *The Politics* of Aristotle, *La Scienza Nuova* by Vico, *Discourse on Livy* by Machiavelli, Montesquieu's *The Spirit of Law,* Malthus' *Essay on Population,* or the works of Adam Smith, Saint-Simon, I. Kant, Auguste Comte, H. Spencer, and so on,—all these great works are composed from, and on the basis of, the data of various sciences, to such an extent that we cannot say exactly to what "department" of science—economics, or sociology, or philosophy, or psychology, or political science—they really belong. On the other hand, I do not know any "formal" work which has produced anything above an average scholastic value. For these reasons I do not see why sociologists need to have "an absolutely independent sociology" not contaminated by the data of other

historians, theorizers of law, and psychologists, or the students of any other of the cultural sciences. All these sciences still wait for their definition, and are understood in very different ways. An illustration of this is given by the papers of the most prominent economists, published in *The Trend of Economics,* N. Y., 1924. The volume conspicuously shows that there are as many different definitions of economics as there are economists. The most modern definition of it is that "economics is a science of behavior." (MITCHELL, WESLEY C., *ibid.*, pp. 22 ff.) Psychology is defined now also as a science of human behavior, as is sociology. Thus, if we must be guided by definitions of "pure sciences," psychology, economics and sociology cannot exist, because they are all "sciences of behavior." Is it necessary to add that such independent sciences do not exist indeed; but on the other hand, the identity of the definitions does not hinder the study of the phenomena of human behavior from somewhat various standpoints; and in somewhat different combinations, which give a basis for a relative and conditional separation of these disciplines. In all these respects, the situation of sociology is not worse than that of these cultural sciences. It is worse only in the sense that while economics and psychology have been busy with the study of facts, sociologists have greatly wasted their time in a discussion of the "object-matter of pure sociology." But, luckily for us, now they also are dropping this fruitless business, and are getting busy with factual study.

sciences, and not overlapping their fields. Neither do I see how such a fantastic goal could be achieved, whether in the field of sociology or of any other science. I do not believe that such a formalism can produce anything valuable. The attempt sacrifices the real unity of human knowledge to purely **accidental** and practical subdivisions required by "departmental subdivisions," and by other similar needs external to science itself. This means that the very attempt of formal sociology to build "an independent sociology" is rather fallacious.[31]

The above, however, does not mean that the formal school has been quite fruitless in sociology. Through its analysis of human relations and their types it has contributed something valuable to a definite part of sociology in *systematizing human relations and social processes.* The multitude of concrete human relationships and the complexity of social processes make it necessary to classify them into a few large classes, with further subdivisions, in this way preventing us from becoming lost in a wild forest of interrelations. Like zoölogical or botanical systematics, sociology must have, among its parts, at least an approximate classification of social relationships in order to make orientation possible in the vast field of social phenomena. For this part of sociology, the formal school, with its consideration of "the forms of human relations" and with its efforts to classify them, has contributed something valuable. However, in this respect also, the school must share its contributions with other sociological schools which have contributed to this field, at any rate no less than the formal school. It is enough to remember H. Spencer's

[31] The same is true of the recent attempt of Professor F. Znaniecki to define the "object-matter of sociology." After his severe criticism of all "hodgepodge" sociologies instead of a "pure sociology" he gave an additional "hodgepodge" conception of sociology as a science of human interinfluence and relationship, which embraces criminology, ethics, educational theory, political science, and so on. It is evident that the conception has all the sins of other "hodgepodge" definitions so severely criticized by the author. Nevertheless, such a sin is better than the "purity" of the "pure sociologists," which has never been attained by anybody. For my part, as far as some guiding and approximate definition of sociology is necessary, I find the most suitable definition of it as a science of the most general characteristics common to all classes of social phenomena and the correlations which exist between these classes. (See the *Conclusion* of this book.) However, several other definitions are as good as this, and I do not think it is necessary to argue much about them. It is much better to "build" than to argue about "how to build." See ZNANIECKI, *op. cit.*, pp. 558–584.

discrimination of the processes of social growth, differentiation and integration, and dissolution and disintegration; or G. Tarde's fundamental classification of social processes into three groups: *repetition, opposition,* and *adaptation* or *invention;* in order to see that neither Tönnies, Simmel, nor any other partizans of the formal school could be regarded as the initiator in the classification of social relations and processes. Even the detailed table of Dr. von Wiese, in its three principal divisions of human relations,—*toward* each other, *away* from each other, and *mixed*— follows pretty closely Tarde's classification, but not that of Simmel. Similarly, von Wiese's classification of social processes: *differentiation, integration,* and *destruction,* is but a slightly changed classification of H. Spencer. These indications are enough to show that even in this field the contribution of the formal school does not represent a monopoly.

3. THE FORMAL SYSTEMATICS OF SOCIAL PROCESSES AND HUMAN RELATIONSHIP IN CONTEMPORARY SOCIOLOGY

Here it is appropriate to cast a glance at the present situation as regards the problem of a formal systematics of social processes and human relations in contemporary sociology. The results of such a survey show: first, that there is a considerable diversity of opinion; second, that some sociologists are inclined to identify the terms social process and human relations, while some others give them a different meaning; third, that some sociologists mention and analyze processes and relations somewhat incidentally, not trying to give their systematic classification, while others seemingly try to do the reverse; fourth, that the basis of the classification (*fundamentum divisionis*) used by sociologists is different; and fifth, that the majority of the systematic classifications go on along the lines of the classifications offered by Herbert Spencer, and especially by Gabriel Tarde.

All this means that the discussed problem is far from being definitely settled, and makes it necessary for greater attention to be paid to it by sociologists. Here are some typical examples which may corroborate the above statements. As a group of sociologists who do not try to give a formal systematic classification of social relations and processes, I will mention the names of Charles A. Ellwood, E. C. Hayes, E. Waxweiler, Charles H. Cooley, and Franklin H. Giddings. They give very valuable classifications of social processes, but not from the "formal" standpoint. In the group of sociologists who try to do it, there are besides L. von Wiese, Edward A. Ross, Robert E. Park, Ernest W. Burgess, Emory Bogardus, and the writer.

In the works of Charles H. Cooley, there is a brilliant analysis of such social processes and human relationships as : social organi⁺ zation and disorganization, ascendancy, domination, leadership, formalization, individualization, socialization, conflict, hostility, and suggestion; but all these are given without any attempt to classify them from the standpoint of a formal systematics of social processes, or of human relations.[32] In a similar way, Charles A. Ellwood gives an illuminating analysis of such social processes as association, social coördination, socialization, co-adaptation, coöperation, social assimilation, social organization, social continuity, and social disintegration; [33] but all this is ana-lyzed not for the sake of classifying social processes, but for other, no less important, purposes. The same may be said of the works of Franklin H. Giddings. He gives one of the most interesting and valuable classifications of societal facts,[34] but his "categorical scheme of societal genesis" is constructed for other purposes and from another standpoint than that of a formal systematics of social relations. Again, his analysis of such social processes as adjustment, concourse, achievement, amelioration, variation, so-cialization, concerted volition, organization of action, and plural-istic behavior, is generally made from another standpoint than that of their formal classification.[35]

A somewhat more detailed and careful classification of human relations—but not that of social processes—is given by Edward C. Hayes. He discriminates thirteen classes of human relations : social suggestion of ideas, sympathetic radiation of feelings, imita-

---

[32] See COOLEY, CHARLES H., *Social Process; Social Organization; Human Nature and the Social Order.*

[33] See especially ELLWOOD, CHARLES A., *The Psychology of Human Society*, 1925, *passim.*

[34] See GIDDINGS, FRANKLIN H., *Scientific Study of Human Society*, 1924, Chap. IV and pp. 70–79.

[35] See *ibid., passim.* See also GIDDINGS, *Studies in the Theory of Human Society*, N. Y., 1922, Part III.

tion of overt practices, inducement, deterrence, accommodation, corroboration, emulation, domination-subordination, competition, conflict, coöperation, and organization.[36] It is easy, however, to see that these classes are not given from the "formal" standpoint, and that they represent partly the "forms" of human relations, like association, conflict, competition, accommodation; and partly the methods of influencing one individual by another through suggestion, inducement, deterrence, emulation, etc. The same may be said of Waxweiler's classification of "social activities" in the following groups: conjunction, protection, competition, divulgation, gregariousness, repetition, initiation, acquisition, and selection.[37]

More "formal" are the classifications of the other mentioned group of sociologists, especially that of E. A. Ross. His *Principles of Sociology* is a systematic treatise on the forms of human relations or social processes. He discriminates between and very ably analyzes the following forms of social processes; preliminary socialization, genesis of society, association, domination, exploitation, opposition, stimulation, antagonism:—competition, conflict, class struggle, war,—adaptation, coöperation, organization of social effort, will and thought, deterioration, stratification, gradation, segregation and subordination, equalization, selection, socialization, estrangement, social control, individuation, liberation, commercialization, professionalization, institutionalization, expansion, ossification, decadence, transformation, and re-shaping.[38] This book, being free from the above sins of the formal school, together with Leopold von Wiese's book, furnishes probably the most conspicuous examples of a formal classification of social processes. Along the same lines R. Park's and E. Burgess' *Introduction to the Science of Sociology,* and Emory S. Bogardus' *Fundamentals of Social Psychology* are built. R. Park and E. Burgess try to give an analysis of all essential social phenomena

[36] See HAYES, E. C., "Some Social Relations Restated," *American Journal of Sociology*, pp. 333–346, 1925; *Sociological Construction Lines*, 1902; *Introduction to the Study of Sociology*, Chaps. XIX–XXIV; see also a very good summary of Hayes' sociological theories in *Vox Populorum*, No. 21, September, 1925.

[37] See WAXWEILER, E., *Esquisse d'une sociologie*, 1906, Chap. VII.

[38] See ROSS, E. A., *Principles of Sociology*, part III, N. Y., 1923. Somewhat similar also is the character of the book of a Russian professor, TAKHTAREFF, K. M., *Science of Social Life*, Nauka ob obschestvennoi jizni, Petrograd, 1920.

in the form of a study of a few fundamental social processes such as: isolation, social contact, social interaction, competition, conflict, accommodation, assimilation, amalgamation, social control, and progress.[39] Similarly, E. Bogardus discriminates between the following forms of interstimulation: isolation, stimulation, communication, suggestion, imitation, diffusion, discrimination, discussion, accommodation, assimilation, and socialization.[40] E. H. Sutherland's classification is fourfold: conflict, avoidance, submission, supplementation.[41]

In a sense systematic, but yet considerably different, is the classification of the forms of human relationship given by the writer. In this classification are indicated the following classes of interrelations: 1. Relationship (or interstimulation) achieved through the actions of doing and not doing, since individuals may influence one another not only through doing something, but also through not doing it. 2. Relationship of a two-sided and one-sided character, as when one party influences another which is not influenced by it, as takes place in the cases when the living generation is influenced by those who have already died. 3. Long-time and permanent relationship, and relationship which is incidental or temporary. 4. Antagonistic and solidaristic. 5. Direct (face to face) or indirect. 6. Conscious or intentional; and unconscious, or unintentional. 7. Formal, or institutionalized, and informal, where there is no generally accepted pattern. Each of these seven classes of relationship is discriminated from the "exterior" or "objectively tangible" standpoint. Being divided into subclasses, they are enabled to embrace all the fundamental forms of human relations.[42]

These examples are sufficient to give a pretty accurate idea of the present status of the classification problem of social relations and processes in sociology. We see that the statements given at the beginning of this paragraph are seemingly accurate. The principal conclusions which follow from the above may be summed up as follows:

[39] PARK, R. and BURGESS, E., *Introduction to the Science of Sociology*, Chaps. IV–XIV.

[40] BOGARDUS, E. S., *Fundamentals of Social Psychology*, Part II, N. Y., 1924.

[41] SUTHERLAND, E., "The Biological and Sociological Processes," *American Journal of Sociology, Proceedings*, Vol. XX, p. 62.

[42] See SOROKIN, *Systema Soziologii*, Vol. I, Chap. V.

The need of a systematics of social processes and human relations in sociology is evident. Paying great attention to this
problem, the formal school and other "relationists" have contributed something to the science of sociology, but the problem is
far from being solved. The very fact of the above heterogeneity
of the classifications means that as yet no unanimity has been
achieved. The existing classifications, and among them even the
most elaborate ones are somewhat imperfect. An example is
given in Professor Ross' or Professors Park and Burgess' classifications. There we find several forms of social processes which
have been somewhat doubled. In Ross' nomenclature, it is hard
to see the reasons for a discrimination between such processes as
association, socialization, coöperation, adaptation, and organization of social effort, will, and thought; or between such processes
as deterioration, decadence, ossification, and exploitation. In a
similar way, it is incomprehensible to me why Professors Park
and Burgess treat separately such processes as social contact and
interaction; accommodation, assimilation, socialization, and
adaptation. The boundary lines between such processes and some
others are drawn indistinctly, and their separate treatment looks
somewhat incidental. As a result, the relations of these social
processes become somewhat confused, especially when they are
very numerous. For this reason, the task of a sociologist in this
field consists in giving a better classification, free from the indicated shortcoming. E. A. Ross' revised classification and that
of L. von Wiese are possibly a step toward a solution of the task.
F. H. Giddings' "scheme of societal genesis" is already an excellent tool for a systematization of types of social groups and
dynamic and genetic relationships typical for each of them.

The second defect of the above classifications is the lack of a
clear definition for many social processes. In our common talk,
and in sociological literature, there are a great many terms which
are supposed to be quite clear and which, in fact, are entirely
indefinite. Examples are exploitation, equalization, individuation, organization, disintegration, decadence and some others.
What social relations are to be styled as exploitation is a problem
remaining to be solved. Permeated by the Marxian conceptions,
we are prone to see exploitation in almost all the actions of a

capitalist, slave-master, or an aristocrat; yet a slight analysis is sufficient to show the fallacy of such a conception. Often the interrelations of a wage-earner and a capitalist, or a slave and his master, are free from antagonism, reminding one rather of the protection of a weaker party by a stronger one, than an exploitation. It is not a rare fact for a class of unskilled laborers to appear rather as exploiters than as those who are exploited.[43]   Many interrelations would appear to be exploitation if we assumed the standpoint of "arithmetical equality"; and the same interrelations would appear in quite a different light if we assumed the standpoint of "proportional equality."   These brief allusions are sufficient to suggest why such terms, without a preliminary analysis, could not be used for the designation of social processes, and why their use without analysis leads to a confusion instead of a clarification.   The same may be said of the processes of organization, disorganization, adaptation, and decadence, not to mention such absolutely subjective evaluations as progress, regress, aggravation, betterment, and so on.   This means that one of the urgent tasks of sociology in this field is to begin a careful, monographic, and objective study of these processes, which will lead to a clarification of their nature, and through that, will give a better basis for their scientific classification.

The third defect of the above classifications is that they do not discriminate between which of these processes are permanent and universal, found within any social group; and which are particular, and temporary, found only among specific groups at a definite period.   As far as the fundamental task of sociology consists in an analysis of the permanent and universal social processes, it is extremely important to separate them from those of a local and temporary character.   This separation is not made in a majority of the existing classifications.

Finally, in view of the tendency of the formal school and of

[43] "We are told that unskilled labor creates the wealth of the world.   It would be nearer the truth to say that large classes of unskilled labor hardly create their own subsistence.   The laborers that have no adaptiveness, that bring no ideas to their work, that have no suspicion of the next best thing to turn to in an emergency, might much better be identified with the dependent classes than with the wealth creators," rightly says Professor Giddings in his *Democracy and Empire*, p. 83, N. Y., 1900.

some of the relationists to limit the content and the task of sociology by a study of the forms of social relations and processes, it is necessary to stress that such pretensions are fallacious. Like botanical or zoölogical systematics of plants and animals, the classification and analysis of social relations and processes composes only a part of sociology. To limit its contents to this part means to cut from sociology its other more vital parts. Any classification is descriptive and gives very little opportunity for a causal analysis of the phenomena. If we had followed literally the pretensions of the formal school, the result would have been a transformation of sociology into a purely scholastic and dead science, a kind of almost useless catalogue of human relations.[44] Accordingly, this pretension must be rejected, and the study of the "forms" of human relations must be made only one of the parts of sociology.

With the formal school we shall finish our survey of the principal types of the *general* sociologistic theories. Now we shall pass to a survey of the *special* sociologistic theories, which take a definite social condition or factor and try to interpret many social phenomena as its function. We shall begin an analysis of the special sociologistic theories with the economic school, as one of the most popular at the present moment. Its analysis done, we shall survey other special sociologistic studies. In this way we can obtain an adequate idea of the present situation of the sociologistic school.

[44] If von Wiese's, Tönnies', Simmel's, Park and Burgess', Ross', Vierkandt's and Bogardus' works have not become such a scholastic catalogue, it is because of the fact that they themselves have not followed the "formal pretension." The best parts of their works are exactly those in which they forget this pretension, and plunge into an investigation of the "content" phenomena.

CHAPTER X

SOCIOLOGISTIC SCHOOL (*Continued*): ECONOMIC SCHOOL

U N D E R this school I include those theories which have taken one of the so-called "economic factors" as the independent variable and have tried to find out its effects on or its correlations with other social phenomena.

I. PREDECESSORS

At the present moment only persons quite innocent in knowledge of the history of social thought could claim that this school originated with Karl Marx' and Friedrich Engels' works. The fact is that since immemorial times thinkers were aware of the important rôle played by "economic factors" in human behavior, social organization, social processes, and in the historical destiny of a society. Already in the teachings of Eastern sages like Confucius and Mencius and Hindu thinkers we find many statements which, implicitly and explicitly, stress the importance of economic conditions. Confucius and Mencius indicated that poverty calls forth dissatisfaction of the people and social disorders and that a satisfactory economic situation of the people is a necessary condition of social order. They also pointed out that "economic factors" condition religious and political phenomena. This explains why the securing of food and other economic necessities is regarded by them as a primary task of a good government;[1] and why in Confucius' Law of the Three Stages the most important characteristic of each stage is given in the form of its economic features, correlated with corresponding political and moral phenomena; and, finally, why in the long history of China we meet so many economic reforms and such a vivid dis-

---

[1] See LEGGE, J., *The Life and Works of Mencius*, Philadelphia, 1875, the works of Mencius, pp. 20–24; 48–49; "The Lî-Kî," pp. 12 ff., in *The Sacred Books of the East*, Vol. XXVIII; CHANG, CHEN HUAN, *The Economic Principles of Confucius and his School*, pp. 52 ff. and *passim*, N. Y., 1911.

cussion of various economic systems.[2] The same may be said of the Hindu sacred books, and Hindu sages. To Buddha is ascribed the statement that "around hunger and love is centered the whole history of mankind." The very fact of the great attention which *The Sacred Books of India* give to a regulation of economic relationship, to economic organization, and to economic problems testifies that in ancient India thinkers were well aware of the importance of economic conditions for human behavior and social life.[3] The same is true of such a relatively ancient source as *"The Zend-Avesta"* [4] or the Bible.[5]

As to ancient Greece, its historians and philosophers, like Thucydides, Plato, and Aristotle, to mention only a few names, methodically used economic factors for an explanation of many social processes. Aristotle's theory of the forms of government consists of a correlation of political and moral phenomena with economic conditions. His theory of social changes and revolutions explicitly states that "the causes for which men will be seditious are profit and honour; and their contrary: for, to avoid dishonour or loss of fortune by mulcts, either on their own account or their friends, they will raise a commotion in the state. . . . What influence ill-treatment and profit have for this purpose, and how they may be the causes of sedition, is almost self-evident." Further, Aristotle gives his explanation and factual

[2] See *The Sacred Books of the East,* Vol. III, Texts of Confucianism, *passim;* Vol. XXVII and Vol. XXVIII, "The Lî-Kî," *passim;* CHANG CHEN HUAN, *op. cit., passim;* LEE, MABEL PING-HUA, *The Economic History of China,* N. Y., 1921, *passim.*

[3] See in the same series of *The Sacred Books of the East, The Institutes of Vishnu, The Laws of Manu, Narâda, The Vedanta Sutras, Brichaspati, Gautama, Apastamba;* throughout them are scattered many statements which express the above idea; a painstaking regulation of economic relationship shows also that the authors of these books well understood the significance of economic conditions for the well-being of a society.

[4] "He who sows corn, grass and fruit, sows holiness; he makes the law of Mazda grow higher and higher," this is one of many statements showing an influence of economic factors upon morals and religion. "The Zend-Avesta," *The Sacred Books of the East,* Vol. IV, Farg. III, 31.

[5] The very statement: "man doth not live by bread only but by everything that proceedeth out of the mouth of Jehovah doth man live" (Deuteronomy, viii: 3) indicates an understanding of an importance of bread-factors. The statements that in conditions of economic welfare the people are prone to forget God and morals (Deuteronomy, viii: 11-17), while in poverty people are prone to riots; and the very fact of a detailed regulation of economic relations given in Deuteronomy and other books of the Bible are sufficient corroborations of my statements.

corroboration of this generalization.[6] Thucydides' *The History of the Peloponnesian War* opens with a short sketch of the early history of Greece. Tracing Greece's evolution Thucydides conspicuously stresses the fundamental rôle of changes in production, wealth, commerce, and other economic conditions which determined, and were correlated with, changes in political and social organization, in behavior and psychology.

The coast populations now began to apply themselves more closely to the acquisition of wealth, and their life became more settled; some even began to build themselves walls on the strength of their newly-acquired riches. For the love of gain would reconcile the weaker to the dominion of the stronger, and the possession of capital enabled the more powerful to reduce the smaller towns to subjection. And it was at somewhat later stages of this development that they went on the expedition against Troy. . . . As the power of Hellas grew, and the acquisition of wealth became more an object, the revenues of the states increasing, tyrannies were by their means established almost everywhere, and Hellas began to fit out fleets and apply more closely to the sea.[7]

These are the samples which show Thucydides' attentive consideration of economic factors in the social evolution of Greece, in social changes, and in originating the Peloponnesian War.

In Plato's *The Republic and Laws,* a series of generalizations concerning the influence of economic conditions on human behavior and social phenomena are given. First, in his classification of human needs Plato indicates eating, drinking, and sexual intercourse as fundamental needs.[8] Second, with a great insight

[6] ARISTOTLE, *Politics*, Book V, Chaps. II and III. I quote Everyman's Library Edition, Dutton Co., pp. 144–147. In this and other works of Aristotle there are scattered numerous statements concerning the effects of economic conditions on social life, their rôle in social antagonisms and class-struggle, and so on.

[7] THUCYDIDES, *The History of the Peloponnesian War*, tr. by R. Crawley, Dutton Co., Chap. I. The majority of the Greek writers, beginning with Hesiod and Theognis and ending with the "proletarian" ideologists of ancient Greece, its demagogues and propagandists, did not fail to mention, to stress, and to analyze the rôle of "economic factors" in social and historical processes. See KOVALEVSKY, M., *Sovremennya Soziologi*, 1905, Chap. V, pp. 225 ff.; PÖHLMANN, R., *Geschichte des Antiken Sozialismus und Communismus*, 2d ed.; HANE1, L. H., *History of Economic Thought*, Chaps. I–V; MONROE, A. E., *Early Economic Thought*, Chaps. I–II; ZIMMERN, A. E., *The Greek Commonwealth;* see especially *The Comedies of Aristophanes.*

[8] PLATO, "Laws," *Dialogues of Plato*, tr. by B. Jowett, Oxford, MDCCCXCII, Vol. V, pp. 782–783.

he characterizes the effects of poverty and wealth on human psychology and behavior. Here is a sample. Poverty and wealth are the causes of deterioration. "One is the parent of luxury and indolence and the other of meanness and viciousness and both of discontent." They are the causes of social and class-struggle. "Any ordinary city, however small, is divided into two cities, one of the city of the poor, the other of the rich, at war with one another." [9] In his classification of the forms of government he correlates economic organization with a corresponding political organization and with the dominant psychological and ethical characteristics of the people. In this way he shows a full understanding of the conditioning rôle of economic factors and their correlation with other social phenomena.[10]

A complex system of economic organization of Roman society, in its later period,[11] naturally called forth, as in Greece, an intensive turning of social thought upon economic problems. It would have been strange indeed if the Roman social and economic thinkers had failed to understand such a simple idea as the conditioning rôle of economic factors. Whether we take the works of Cicero, Sallust, T. Livy, Seneca, Ammianus Marcellinus, Varro, Lucretius, Cato, Columella, Tacitus, Pliny, or Polybius, we easily find a series of statements which describe, indicate, and analyze many effects of various economic conditions upon social life, historical processes, human behavior, and psychology. Such for instance, are Pliny's formula of the fall of Rome: *"Latifundia perdirere Italiam, jam vero et provincias"* (the large

[9] PLATO, *The Republic, The Dialogues of Plato*, tr. by Jowett, Vol. II, pp. 422 ff., 547, N. Y., 1874.

[10] A clear understanding of the important rôle played by economic conditions in human behavior is the reason why Plato planned communism of property and women and children for the Guardians in his ideal Republic. The Guardians' "means of subsistence should be such as will neither impair their virtue, nor tempt them to prey upon the other citizens." Plato hoped that communism of property would lead to such effects. Whether his hope is reasonable or not, this shows that he well understood the effective influence of economic conditions on human conduct: changing the former, through this he hoped to change the latter. Generally, throughout *The Republic*, especially in its eighth and ninth books, there are given many valuable generalizations concerning the discussed problem.

[11] See ROSTOVTZEFF, M., *The Social and Economic History of the Roman Empire*, Oxford, 1926; SALVIOLI, J., *Der Kapitalismus in Altertum*, Stuttgart, 1912; FRANK, T., *Economic History of Rome*.

estates, the latifundia, were ruining Rome) ; [12] a similar statement of Seneca; [13] Sallust's statements like the following one:

When the people were gradually deprived of their land, idleness and poverty left them without a place to live on; they began to wish greedily for other men's property and to regard their liberty and the interests of their country an object for sale. Thus the people . . . became degenerate; and instead of supporting their commonwealth brought upon themselves individual servitude.[14]

Polybius' theory of the cycles of the forms of government correlated with corresponding changes in economic conditions; these and hundreds of similar statements [15] show clearly that the Roman writers were well aware of the importance of economic factors, of their influence on many social processes, including even such a fundamental process as the decay of Rome. There is no need to say that they were aware of class-struggle and of its economic causes, and that there was an abundance of many radical and "proletarian" ideologies with the slogans and shibboleths identical with those of contemporary socialism, communism and Marxianism. [16]

Similar was the situation in the later periods of the Middle Ages, especially in the period of the Renaissance and the Reformation. M. Kovalevsky rightly says:

It is hard to find a writer of this period who, discussing the problem of a change of political forms, would not correlate it with the changes in economic conditions and with the origin of a new economic class in whose interests the political régime had to be altered.[17]

In this respect among these writers especially prominent are

---

[12] PLINY, H. N., xviii. 7.   [13] SENECA, Ep. 89.   [14] SALLUST, I. 5.

[15] Even such a relatively detailed correlation as that between occupation and economic status on the one hand, and ideological, moral and biological characteristics of a man on the other, was many times stressed by various writers. Here are the samples: "It is from the tillers of the soil that spring the best citizens, the staunchest soldiers," CATO, De Agricultura, pp. 19 ff., N. Y., 1913. See in VARRO, Rerum Rusticarum Libri Tres his characterization of the city and the country people from a biological and psychological point of view, a characterization which shows his full understanding of the occupational and economic influences on human body and mind.

[16] Even the famous phrase of Marx-Engels' Communist Manifesto, that in the class-struggle the proletariat can lose nothing but its chains, is but a repetition of the statements of M. Agrippa and Sallust. See PÖHLMANN, R., op. cit., passim.

[17] KOVALEVSKY, Sovremennya Soziologi, p. 227.

N. Machiavelli and Guicciardini, to mention only a few names. Both of them, and Gianotti also, pay great attention to economic factors in their interpretations of historical processes; both of them viewed a change of government in the light of a class-struggle, and the class-struggle itself was explained through a conflict of economic interests of different classes. [18]

Of writers of the seventeenth century the name of James Harrington, a contemporary of the English revolution, occupies an especially conspicuous place in this respect. In his *The Commonwealth of Oceana* (1656) he laid down a systematic theory of economic interpretation of history. His motto is: "Such as is the proportion or balance of dominion or property in land, such is the nature of the Empire." Political power is based on property. When one man owns the greater part of the property in a country, in such a country there would exist an absolute monarchy. When the property (or wealth) is concentrated in the hands of a few men, this leads to a "gothic or mediæval monarchy," to a mixed form where the political control is in the hands of the king and a small group of the privileged classes. When the property is distributed throughout the whole population and no group has an exclusively great wealth, which would outbalance the wealth of the whole people, in such a country there would be a republic or a democracy. When in the distribution of national wealth there happen to be changes, they naturally call forth corresponding changes in the political régime, and in other fields of social life and organization. Such is the essence of the theory of Harrington. These and a great many other propositions given in his work are inferred from a study of historical facts, as far as they were accessible at that time. This still increases the value of Harrington's theory.[19]

Of the writers of the eighteenth century it is possible to mention the names of Garnier,[20] Dalrymple,[21] Möser, Reinhard,

[18] See MACHIAVELLI, *The Discourses on Livy, passim,* and Book III, Chap. XVI; Book I, Chaps. V, XI, XII; Book II, Chap. II; *History of Florence, passim.* See GUICCIARDINI, *Opere inedite,* Ricordo, Vol. I, *passim;* see KOVALEVSKY, *op. cit.,* pp. 227–229.

[19] See *The Oceana and Other Works of James Harrington,* London, 1747, *passim,* and pp. 4 ff., 39 ff., 291 ff.

[20] GARNIER, *De la propriété dans ses rapports avec le droit politique,* 1792.

[21] DALRYMPLE, *An Essay Toward a General History of Feudal Property in Great Britain,* 1757.

Mably, John Millar,[22] Barnave, Schlözer, Adam Smith, Adelung, Turgot, and especially Raynal.[23] In the writings of these authors almost all the theories, which later on were developed by the writers of the nineteenth century and K. Marx and F. Engels, were laid down.

Finally, if we turn to the writers of the first half of the nineteenth century, whose works were published either before or simultaneously with that of Karl Marx, their number is so great that I can here only enumerate their names without any attempt to give an idea of the character of their theories. Since the end of the eighteenth and in the first half of the nineteenth centuries, the "intellectual atmosphere" has been satiated with the idea of the "economic or materialistic interpretation of history." Some of the more ardent followers of Marx, and even some of the prominent academic writers, used to depict K. Marx's theory as *deus ex machina,* as though it did not have any predecessors, or only a very few like Hegel, Feuerbach, Saint-Simon, or L. Blanc; and they correspondingly proclaimed Marx the "Galileo" or the "Darwin" of the social sciences.[24]

---

[22] Möser, *Vorrede zur Osnabrukschen Geschichte,* 1768; Millar, John, *Observations Concerning the Distinction of Ranks in Society,* 1771.

[23] See an appropriate analysis of their works from this standpoint in Sulzbach, W., *Die Anfänge der materialistischen Geschichtsauffassung,* Karlsruhe, 1911; von Below, G., *Die Deutsche Geschichteschreibung,* 2d ed., München und Berlin, 1924, pp. 161–194; Roger, P., "La théorie de la lutte de classes à la veille de la révolution," *Revue d'économie politique,* 1911, No. 5. See also Salomon, G., "Historische Materialismus und Ideologienlehre," *Jahrbuch für Soziologie,* Band II, 1926, pp. 386–423.

[24] For instance P. Barth mentions only the names of Saint-Simon, Hegel, Feuerbach, Bruno Bauer, Louis Blanc, and Lorenz von Stein, as the predecessors of Marx. A. W. Small goes so far in his eulogy of Marx, that he "confidently predicts that in the ultimate judgment of history Marx will have a place in social science analogous with that of Galileo in physical science." Small, A. W., "Socialism in the Light of Social Science," *American Journal of Sociology,* Vol. XVII, May, 1912, p. 812. Even such a careful author as Professor E. R. A. Seligman indicates some of the predecessors of Marx's theory, in criticizing it; nevertheless he states finally that "Marx must be recognized as in the truest sense the originator of the economic interpretation of history." Seligman, E. R. A., *The Economic Interpretation of History,* pp. 52–53, N. Y., 1907. As far as the originality and the content of the theory of Marx's materialistic conception of history is concerned (but not that of Marx's practical influence) at the present moment, especially after the studies of von Below, Sulzbach, Roger and some others, there seems to be no possibility to claim that Marx added any single new idea in this field or gave a new and scientifically better synthesis of the ideas which existed before him. From this standpoint earlier opinions of such scholars as A. Menger, W. J. Ashley, S. H. Patten and of some others who

The facts are that practically all the sociological ideas of Marx in an identical or even a more accurate form were published by other authors either before or simultaneously with the publication of his *Communist Manifesto, Die Heilige Familie, Misery of Philosophy,* and *Zur Kritik der Politischen Oeconomie,* where there is found for the first time a more or less systematic formulation of Marx's materialistic interpretation of history. Many historical, economic and philosophical works of the first half of the nineteenth century were characterized by concentration of attention on economic conditions, by a study of the influence of these conditions on various phases of social life, and by an explanation of many political, social, religious, æsthetic, and moral phenomena in terms of economic influences.

To show this it is enough to mention the names of Niebuhr, Böckh, K. W. Nitzsch, Savigny, V. A. Huber, Heinrich v. Sybel, K. D. Hüllman, H. Leos, G. A. H. Stenzel, Adam Müller, G. L. v. Maurer, W. Arnold, M. Töppen, L. Giesebrecht, F. v. Bilow, Neumann, K. F. v. Klöden, Stüve, Höfler, Hassler, Franz Kurz, J. v. Koch-Sternfeld, Chmel, K. F. v. Rumohrs, A. v. Haxthausen, Roscher, B. Hildebrand, Lorenz v. Stein, Drumann, S. Hirsch, G. v. Raumer, Thierry, Rüge, Rodbertus, Lassal, Le Play, partly Proudhon, not to mention many others. In their works, in the way of a factual analysis of historical data, these authors formulated practically all that is sound in a speculative and a more defective form of Marx's and Engels' formulas of the economic or materialistic interpretation of history.[25] Finally, it is necessary to mention the name of Georg Wilhelm von Raumer, who in 1837, and in 1851, earlier rather than Marx, formulated a theory of the economic conception of history, which is

---

much more moderately estimated Marx's scientific contributions seem to be completely warranted by the facts. See especially S. H. Patten's criticism of Small's "scientific blunder," PATTEN, S. H., *Essays in Economic Theory,* pp. 287–288, N. Y., 1924. See further the text of this book.

[25] See a very good analysis of the works of the mentioned authors from this viewpoint in VON BELOW, G., *Die Deutsche Geschichteschreibung,* pp. 161–194. See also SULZBACH, W., *op. cit.;* partly, HAMMACHER, E., *Das philosophisch-ökonomische System des Marxismus,* 1909; WOLTMANN, L., *Der historische materialismus,* 1906; partly PLECHANOW, G., *Beitrage zur Geschichte des Materialismus,* 1896; partly CUNOW, H., "Zur Geschichte der Klasskampftheorie," *Jahrbuch für Soziologie,* Bd. II. Two last works are defective.

almost identical with that of Marx.[26]   This theory was formulated as a result of a painstaking historical study of Raumer. Here are a few quotations from his theory which may show its mottoes :

All political changes are nothing but a result of the changes in the condition of production, manner of living, and in a new situation of different classes called forth by the changes in commerce and trade (*Verkehrsverhaltnisse*). . . . The political changes in their final analysis are but the results, and even the necessary results, of the changed social and economic conditions of the people which by and by change not only the morals, and *mores,* and manners of living and thinking but also the relations of various social classes toward one another. . . Of course, this does not mean a denial of an importance and power of the spiritual (*geistigen*) movements within a people; but it is also true that such movements in the majority of the cases are either induced through economic changes, or are followed and carried on by them.

Summing up the theory of Raumer one can say : first, the character and the conditions of production are the most important and primary factors; they condition all other social phenomena : a change in the conditions of production calls forth a corresponding change in distribution of wealth and property : this, a change in the class-differentiation, class-composition and class-interrelations of society and in its family organization; these changes condition a corresponding modification of social relations and juridical institutions; and these are followed by a corresponding modification of the *mores,* habits, customs, manners, ideologies, beliefs, and psychology of society.   In brief, we have a theory practically identical with that of Marx.   This, however, does not mean that both theories were something extraordinary among other theories of that time.   On the contrary, "in the German (and the same is true in regard to the French and the English) historical and economic literature of the middle of the nineteenth century there was such a vivid interest in economic problems, that an author,

---

[26] See VON RAUMER, G. W., *Neumärkischen Landbuchs von,* 1337; and especially *Die Insel Wollin und das Seebad Misdroy,* 1851; about Raumer's work see VOIGT, A., "Georg W. von Raumer und die materialistische Geschichtsauffassung," *Preussischen Jahrbüchern,* Bd. 103, 1901, pp. 430 ff.; VON BELOW, G., *op. cit.,* pp. 161 ff.

simply being within the current of this literature, could easily come to a stronger appreciation of the economic causes." Raumer, as well as Marx and Engels, "were simply within this current, and depended on it in a degree much greater than it was supposed up to this time. Their originality, as far as their general formulas are concerned, consists only in an exaggeration and generalization of what other authors said before." [27] Such is the real situation.

The above brief survey of the predecessors of the economic school in sociology shows that it is as old as human thought itself; that it is not a monopoly of the nineteenth century; that, sometimes in a vague, sometimes in a clearly-cut form, the influence of economic conditions on human behavior, body and mind, and on social processes was understood, and that long ago a series of correlations of economic conditions with various social processes were formulated.

Now let us turn to a survey and analysis of the principal contributions made in this field during the last few decades.

2. K. MARX's (1818-1883) AND F. ENGELS' (1820-1895) THEORIES

The socialistic dogmas of the founders of the Marxian socialism,[28] and their economic theories in the narrow sense of the

---

[27] VON BELOW, G., *op. cit.*, pp. 179 and 191.

[28] In regard to these parts of their "ideology" it is enough to say that at the present moment it is scarcely possible to support them as scientifically accurate. Marx's theory of the progressive impoverishment of the laboring classes, of the concentration of wealth, of the disappearance of the middle classes, and of the catastrophic advent of socialism proved to be fallacious. Still more fallacious happened to be his beliefs in the beneficial results of the annihilation of private property, and a disappearance of exploitation and misery, as the results of the socialization of the means and the instruments of production, and all this from the wonderful effects of "the dictatorship of the proletariat." The most important part of his economic theory, the labor theory of value, and the theory of the surplus-value, in their Marxian forms, are (practically) not sustained by contemporary economists. See SIMKHOVITCH, V., *Marxism vs. Socialism*, N. Y., 1913; SOROKIN, P., *Social Mobility*, 1927, Chaps. III and IV; MICHELS, R., *La teoria di C. Marx sulla miseria crescente*, Torino, 1922; NOVGORODZEFF, P., *Ob Obtschestvennom ideale*, 1924. About the contribution of Marx-Engels to economics see BÖHM-BAWERK, E., *Karl Marx and the Close of His System*, N. Y., 1898, and the courses in economics of G. Schmoller, F. Taussig, A. Marshall, J. B. Clarke, R. Ely, M. Tougan-Baranovsky and practically any solid course in economics. See also SOMBART, W., *Der Proletarische Sozialismus*, new and greatly changed edition of his *Sozialismus und soziale Bewegung*, Vols. I, II,

word do not concern us in this book.   Only their sociological generalizations are discussed here.   In view of a somewhat ambiguous terminology of Marx, the best way to characterize his conception is to do it in his own words.   The essence of his theory is given in his *Critique of Political Economy,* published in 1859.   Here we read:

The general conclusion at which I arrived and which, once reached, continued to serve as the leading thread in my studies, may be briefly summed up as follows: In the social production which men carry on they enter into definite relations that are indispensable and independent of their will; these relations of production correspond to a definite stage of development of their material power of production. The sum total of these relations of production constitutes the economic structure of society — the real foundation, on which rise legal and political superstructures and to which correspond definite forms of social consciousness.   The mode of production in material life determines the general character of the social, political and spiritual processes of life.   It is not the consciousness of men that determines their existence, but, on the contrary, their social existence determines their consciousness.   At a certain stage of their development, the material forces of production in society come in conflict with the existing relations of production, or what is but a legal expression for the same thing — with the property relations within which they had been at work before.   From forms of development of the forces of production these relations turn into their fetters.   Then comes the period of social revolution.   With the change of the economic foundation the entire immense superstructure is more or less rapidly transformed.   In considering such transformations the distinction should always be made between the material transformation of the economic conditions of production which can be determined with the precision of natural science and the legal, political, religious, æsthetic or philosophic — in short, ideological forms in which men become conscious of this conflict and fight it out.   Just as our opinion of an individual is not based on what he thinks of himself, so can we not judge of such a period of transformation by its own consciousness; on the contrary, this consciousness must rather be explained from the contradictions of material life, from the existing conflict between

Jena, 1924.   In brief, the Marxian variety of socialism has no more right to claim to be "scientific" than any other variety of socialism.

the social forces of production and the relations of production. No social order ever disappears before all the productive forces, for which there is room in it, have been developed; and new higher relations of production never appear before the material conditions of their existence have matured in the womb of the old society. Therefore, mankind always takes up only such problems as it can solve; since, looking at the matter more closely, we will always find that the problem itself arises only when the material conditions necessary for its solution already exist or are at least in the process of formation. In broad outlines we can designate the Asiatic, the ancient, the feudal, and the modern bourgeois methods of production as so many epochs in the progress of economic formation of society. The bourgeois relations of production are the last antagonistic form of the social process of production — antagonistic not in the sense of individual antagonism, but of one arising from conditions surrounding the life of individuals in society; at the same time the productive forces developing in the womb of bourgeois society create the material conditions for the solution of that antagonism. This social formation constitutes, therefore, the closing chapter of the prehistoric stage of human society.[29]

If we add to this Marx's theory of class-struggle, all essential features of his economic interpretation of history are at hand.

The history of all hitherto existing society is the history of class struggle. Freeman and slave, patrician and plebeian, lord and serf, guild-master and journeyman, oppressor and oppressed, stood in constant opposition to one another, carried on an uninterrupted, now hidden, now open fight, a fight that each time ended either in a revolutionary reconstitution of society at large, or in the common ruin of the contending classes. . . . The modern bourgeois society that has sprouted from the ruins of feudal society, has not done away with class antagonisms. It has but established new classes, new conditions of oppression, new forms of struggle in place of the old ones. . . Our epoch, the epoch of the bourgeoisie, possesses, however, this distinctive feature; it has simplified the class antagonisms. Society as a whole is more and more splitting up into two great

[29] MARX, K., *Zur Kritik der Politischen Oekonomie*, 1859, pp. IV–V; *A Contribution to the Critique of Political Economy*, tr. by Stone, pp. 11–13, N. Y., 1904.

hostile camps, into two great classes directly facing each other: Bourgeoisie and Proletariat.[30]

Such is the essence of Marx's-Engels' sociological theory.[31]

[30] *Communist Manifesto*, pp. 12–13, Kerr, Chicago, 1913.

[31] These other works of Marx are important sociologically: *Die Heilige Familie; Das Elend der Philosophie; Die Klassenkampf in Frankreich; Lohnarbeit und Kapital*, and a few places in the first, in the second, and especially in the third volumes of his *Das Kapital*. Of the works of Engels the most important are: *Ludwig Feuerbach und der Ausgang der klassischen Philosophie in Deutschland; Die Entwicklung des Sozialismus von der Utopie zur Wissenschaft; Die Lage Englands; Der Ursprung der Familie, des Privateigentums und des Staate; Hern Eugen Duhrings Umwälzung der Wissenschaft*. Besides, several important works of both authors are published in the volumes, *Aus dem literarischen Nachlass von K. Marx, F. Engels und F. Lassalles, herausgegeben von F. Mehring*. Of an immense literature devoted to Marxianism besides the already quoted works the most important are: *Annales de l'Institut Internationale de Sociologie*, Vol. VIII, Paris, 1902, devoted to an analysis of Marxianism by various prominent sociologists; BERNSTEIN, E., *Die Voraussetzungen des Sozialismus und die Aufgaben der Sozialdemokratie*, 1899; STRUVE, P., "Die Marxsche Theorie der sozialen Entwicklung," *Braun's Archiv*, Bd. XIV, pp. 677 ff.; MASARYK, TH. G., *Die philosophischen und soziologischen Grundlagen des Marxismus*, 1899; KAUTSKY, K., *Ethik und material. Geschichtsauffassung; Das Erfurter Programm;* BARTH, P., *op. cit.*, pp. 657 ff.; ELLWOOD, CH., "Marx's Economic Determinism," *American Journal of Sociology*, Vol. XVII, July, 1911; LABRIOLA, A., *Essays on the Materialistic Conception of History*, tr. by Kerr; LORIA, A., *The Economic Foundations of Society*, London, 1899; LORIA, A., *The Economic Synthesis*, tr. by E. Paul, N. Y., 1914; SPARGO, J., *K. Marx, His Life and Works*, N. Y., 1910; CROCE, B., *Historical Materialism*, tr. by C. Meredith; NOVGORODZEFF, P., *Ob obschestvennom ideale*, Social Ideal, 3d ed.; TUGAN-BARANOVSKY, M., *Theoretical Foundations of Marxism*, Russ.; KAREEV, N., *Old and New Essays on Economic Materialism*, Russ.; BELTOV-PLEKHANOV, G., *The Monistic Conception of History*, Russ., tr. into German; BUKHARIN, N., *Theory of Historical Materialism* (Marxian Sociology), tr. into German and English; CUNOW, H., *Grundzüge der Marxschen Soziologie*, Vols. I, II, 1920, 1921; TSCHERNOFF, V., *Essays in Economic Materialism*, Russ.; HANSEN, A., "The Technological Interpretation of History," *Quarterly Journal of Economics*, Vol. XXXVI, 1921; COMMONS, J., "K. Marx," *Atlantic Monthly*, 1926; ADLER, M., *Marx als Denker; Marxistische Probleme; Kant und der Marxismus;* TÖNNIES, F., *Marx Leben und Lehre;* SOREL, G., *Reflections on Violence*, N. Y., 1912; MICHELS, R., "Die Ital. Literatur über den Marxismus," *Archiv für Sozialwissenschaft*, Bd. XXIV and XXV; *Matériaux d'une théorie du proletariat*, 1919; SCHMIDT, K., "Marxistische Orthodoxie," *Sozialistische Monatshefte*, 1913, Bd. I, 8 Heft.; GEHRLICH, *Der Kommunismus als Lehre von Tausendjährigen Reich*, 1920; STAMMLER, R., *Wirtschaft und Recht nach der materialistischen Geschichtsauffassung*, 1896; GENTILE, G., *La filosofia di Marx*, 1899; ILIJN, W. (Lenin), *State and Revolution*, Russ.; KELSEN, H., *Sozialismus und Staat*, 1920; TROTSKY, L., *Terrorisme et communisme* (tr. into English also); KAMPFFMEYER, P., "Zur Kritik d. philos. Grundlagen des Marxismus," *Sozial. Monatshefte*, IX; KORSCH, K., *Marxismus und Philosophie*, 1923; UNTERMANN, E., *Marxismus und Logik;* PENZIAS, A., *Die Metaphysik der materialist. Geschichtsauffassung*, 1905; OPPENHEIMER, F., *Das Grundgesetz der Marxschen Gesellschaftslehre*, Berlin, 1903; PARETO, V., *Les systèmes socialistes*, 2 Vols.; LICHTENBERGER, P., *op. cit.*, pp. 291–302; TODD, A. J., *Theories of Social Progress*, Chaps. XIV–XV, N. Y., 1926.

INTERPRETATION AND CRITICISM

The ambiguity of Marx's wording is responsible for the different interpretations of his theories and those of Engels' theory by various writers, Marxian as well as non-Marxian. One who is well acquainted with the pertinent parts of the writings of Marx cannot help thinking as he reads the commentaries of the Marxians, that he is reading a kind of purely dogmatic interpretation of a "sacred revelation" by its enthusiastic followers. Omitting such interpretations, let us briefly indicate the principal shortcomings of the main points of the theory under consideration.

A. *Its first shortcoming is its conception of causal relation and determinism.*—It is easy to see that an expression like "the mode of production determines the general character of the social, political and spiritual processes of life," presupposes an anthropomorphic and one-sided conception of causal relation: the cause as something active, which one-sidedly determines, "acts," "creates," "produces" its result, (*causa efficiens* of the Middle Ages) and the result, which is something inert and completely depending on its cause. At the present moment, it is rather hard to sustain such a conception. Being metaphysical in its essence it cannot be applied to a great many relationships of various phenomena which, especially in the social field, are not one-sidedly but mutually dependent. This explains why in the methodology of contemporary natural science the conception of functional relation ("variable" and its "function," which may be one- and two-sided), is being substituted for that of one-sided causal relation, and correlation for that of one-sided and metaphysical determinism. That is, the scientist asserts only that associated phenomena are in functional relations or are correlated to a degree indicated by the coefficient of correlation of a certain probability.[32] Such substitution frees us from all an-

---

In these works are represented all principal varieties of interpretation and criticism of the Marx-Engels' theory.

[32] See COURNOT, A., *Essai sur le fondements de nos connaissances*, Paris, 1851; *Considérations sur la marche des idées*, Paris, 1872; *Traité de l'enchainement des idées fondamentales dans les sciences et dans l'historie*, Paris, 1861; MACH, E., *Erkenntnis und Irrtum*, 1906; *Beiträge zur Analyse der Empfindungen*, 1903;

thropomorphic elements in the connection of cause and determinism, and gives the possibility of studying one-sided and two-sided relations. Such a conception presents the possibility of treating any "factor" as a variable and trying to find to what extent and with what phenomena it is correlated. In a great many cases it permits also inverting such a functional "equation": *i.e.,* taking a function as a variable and trying to find its functions. For instance, we may take, in one case, an "economic factor" as a variable and study to what extent it is correlated with religious phenomena. In another case, we may take religious phenomena as a variable and try to investigate their "functions," among them, the functions in the field of economic phenomena.[33] In the field of social phenomena we almost always deal with relations of interdependence but not with that of one-sided dependence. The application to such phenomena of the conception of one-sided causal relations leads to a series of logical and factual fallacies, (see above paragraphs about Pareto). And this is just what happened with the Marxian theory. Its conception of a one-sided causal relation, when applied to socially interdependent phenomena, is responsible for some logical and factual fallacies of the theory, contradictory interpretations, and for endless dispute among Marxian followers and among the critics of the Marxian theory. It is the source of many shortcomings of the theory. Let us look at the problem closer. The first idea of Marx's theory is that the economic factor is the primary or the most important factor which determines all others. The primacy may mean either: (a) that in a causal chain this factor is the first which determines all

---

BOREL, E., *Le hasard*, Paris, 1914; REY, ABEL, *Die Theorie der Physik bei den modernen Physikern*, Germ. ed. by Alfred Kröner; POINCARÉ, H., *La science et l'hypothèse*, Paris, 1908; PEARSON, K., *The Grammar of Science*, Chap. III; PARETO, V., *Trattato di sociologia generale*, Chaps. I and II; TSCHUPROFF, A., *Essays in the Theory of Statistics*, Russ., tr. into English; TSCHUPROFF, A., *Das Gesetz der grossen Zahlen und der Stochastisch-Statistische Standpunkt in der modernen Wissenschaft*, Nord. Stat. Tidskrift, Bd. I, heft 1; SOROKIN, P., "M. Kovalevsky's Theory of Social Factors," in *In Memorium of M. Kovalevsky*, Russ., 1917; DUHEM, P., *La théorie physique, son objet et sa structure*, Paris, Chevalier et Riviere Cie.; WEBER, M., *Gesammelte Aufsätze zur Wissenschaftslehre*, pp. 87 ff., 112 ff., 420–445 ff.

[33] Precisely this was done by M. Weber in his *Gesammelte Aufsätze zur Religionssoziologie*, 3 vols., *passim*. In his study religion is taken as a variable and its "effects" on economic phenomena are carefully studied. M. Weber stressed the fact that such a study is but one of many possible studies.

other social phenomena or (b) that its efficiency in determining social phenomena is far greater (say its influence is 90 per cent) than that of all other factors (whose total efficiency is, say, 10 per cent only). The first interpretation is nothing but the foregoing conception of one-sided and irreversible causal relations. The second may be reconciled with the functional conception, but, unfortunately, neither Marx and Engels nor any one of their followers has tried to indicate either the means of measuring the comparative effectiveness of various factors in conditioning social phenomena, nor have they given the indices of the comparative effectiveness of various factors in this respect. According to the literal and logical meaning of the theory under discussion the primacy of the economic factor is to be interpreted in the first sense; *i.e.,* the economic factor is primary and is the most important one because, as has been said, it determines all other social phenomena in the causal chain, or because it is "the starter" while all other ones are the "started."

It is evident that such a conception cannot be accepted: factually, such factors as geographical conditions and biological drives inherent in man appeared and operated earlier than economic factors. Other social factors, such as intelligence, experience, religious ideas or superstitions, rules of taboo or *mores,* primitive art, activity devoted to what could be called ideal aims, play and so on, are found in the most primitive human societies known to us and operated as early as economic conditions. The idea of a primitive man as a mere stomach can scarcely be supported at the present moment. A series of careful studies have shown its fallacy.[34] Furthermore, we cannot say that among man's inherent drives or instincts there is only an instinct of food, or even that it is the strongest. Such an assumption is likely to be a fallacious

[34] See WODON, L., *Sur quelques erreurs de méthode dans l'étude de l'homme primitive*, Inst. Solvay; THURNWALD, R., "Die Gestaltung der Wirtschaftsentwicklung aus ihren Aufangen heraus," Münich, 1923; "Psychologie des primitiven Menschen," *Handbuch für Verglichende Psychologie*, München, 1922; MALINOWSKI, B., *Argonauts in the Western Pacific*, London, 1922; SCHWIEDLAND, E., *Anfänge und Wesen der Wirtschaft*, Stuttgart, 1923; SOMLÒ, F., *Der Güterverkehr in der Urgesellschaft*, Inst. Solvay, 1909; MAUNIÈR, R., "Vie religieuse et vie économique," *Revue Inter. Sociologie*, Dec., 1907, Jan., Febr., 1908; LOWIE, R. H., *Primitive Society*, 1920; WALLIS, W. D., *An Introduction to Anthropology*, N. Y., 1926.

530   CONTEMPORARY SOCIOLOGICAL THEORIES

speculation not warranted by the facts.[35]   We cannot even claim
that man is an economic creature and always acts "economically,"
as it was supposed by the classical economists.   Facts strongly
contradict such a contention.[36]

Furthermore, a series of investigators such as Espinas, Durkheim, P. Huvelin, Thurmvald, Malinowski, Hubert and Mauss
have shown that, even in primitive stages, the technique of production and the whole of economic life are absolutely inseparable
from, and incomprehensible without, a consideration of contemporary religion, magic, science, and other intellectual phenomena.[37]

[35] THORNDIKE, E. L., *Educational Psychology*, Vol. I, The Original Nature of
Man, N. Y., 1913; SOROKIN, *Sociology of Revolution*, Chaps. I–III, especially
the note on p. 33; WALLAS, G., *Human Nature in Politics*, 1919; the courses in
psychology by W. McDougall, R. S. Woodworth and others; PAVLOV, I., *Twenty
Years of Objective Study of the Higher Nervous Activity of Animals*, Russ., 1923.

[36] See especially WEBER, M., *Gesammelte Aufsätze zur Religionssoziologie*, 3
vols., *passim*, and Vol. I, pp. 12, 21–22, 37, 38, 82, 183, 233–237; WEBER, M.,
Wirtschaftsgeschichte, 1924, pp. 238, 308–315; MITCHELL, W. C., "Human Behavior and Economics," *Quarterly Journal of Economics*, Vol. XXIX, pp. 1–47;
"The Prospects of Economics," in *The Trend of Economics*, N. Y., 1924, pp.
3–34; DOUGLAS, P. H., "The Reality of Non-Commercial Incentives in Economic Life," *ibid.*, pp. 153–193; TAUSSIG, F., *Inventors and Money-Makers*, N. Y.,
1915; SOMBART, W., *Der Bourgeois;* SLATER, G., "The Psychological Basis of
Economical Theory," *The Sociological Review*, July, October, 1923; TUGWELL,
R. G., "Human Nature in Economic Theory," *Journal of Political Economy*,
Vol. XXX, pp. 317–395; CLARK, J. M., "Economics and Modern Psychology,"
Journal of Political Economy, Vol. XXVI, pp. 1–30; PARKER, C. H., "Motives
in Economic Life," *American Economic Review, Suppl.*, Vol. VIII, pp. 212–213;
VEBLEN, T., *The Instinct of Workmanship*, N. Y., 1918.

"*Wir haben uns angewöhnt, als Wirtschaft ein Handeln zu betrachten, das von
einem künstlich konstruierten 'homo normalis rationalis' ausgeht.   Ein Mensch ohne
Seele, eine Art puppenhafter Rechenmaschine.   Dieser homunculus versagt aber
sofort seinen Dienst, wenn wir die grosseren Zusammenhänge ins Auge fassen.
Denn allen intelligenten Berechnungen liegen affecterfullte Strebungen zur Er-
haltung, Sicherung und Functionsbetätigung zugrunde.*" . . . Even a seeking for
luxuries is universal and exists among the most primitive groups.   "*Alle Zeiten
kennen ihren Luxus.*"   "*Ehrgeiz und Prunk, Liebe und Hass sind in alle wirt-
schaftlichen Zweckbetätigungen eingewoben-keineswegs Hunger und Durst allein.*"
Thurnwald clearly shows a mutual dependence of economic and non-economic
phenomena and concludes his interesting analysis by saying about "the economic"
and opposing one-sided interpretations of history: "*Die einseitige 'wirtschaftliche
Geschichtsauffassung' ist ein rationalistisches Truggebilde, sowie die nur 'idealis-
tische' ein romantisches Phantasma.*"   Thurnwald, *op. cit.*, pp. 274–278, 328.

[37] The conclusions at which Espinas arrives in his study of the origin of technology are as follows:

"General law dominates the development of technology.   Speculation precedes
action (or technique) to some extent, and in certain cases; but a more systematic
theory of the corresponding facts of technique becomes possible only when these
facts have already existed for some time."

For the later stages, a conditioning of economics by religion, magic, rationalism, or traditionalism, and even a religious origin of modern capitalism itself (from Protestantism), has been elucidated by Max Weber.[38]

"It is impossible to deny the existence of a correlation between mental and practical functions." This is shown schematically in the following table:

Mental Stages	Corresponding Stages of Technique or Practice
1. Elementary *sensations*	1. Elementary *reflexes*
2. *Perceptions:* individual and concrete representations of forms and events	2. *Individual habitudes:* actions controlled by inner, socially unconscientious impulses
3. *Connaissances* (types and laws): A totality of representations already collective and, in a degree, abstract, composed of aggregate individual perceptions	3. *Customs:* practical or collective institutions, a totality of individual habitudes controlled by opinion
4. *Sciences*, a totality of systematic, rational conceptions	4. *Arts or techniques*, a totality of customs organized with deliberation and knowledge

(ESPINAS, A., *Les origines de la technologie*, pp. 10–11, and *passim*, Paris, 1897.)

"Development of economic organization goes hand in hand with the psychical evolution of man. It is influenced in the first place by technique and the form of political organization." But the technique itself is nothing but *"die Anhäufung von Kenntnissen und Fertigkeiten,"* determined by the psychically constant factors, by the spacially varying geographical factors, and by the factors varying in time, like inventions, discoveries, and so on. (THURNWALD, *op. cit.*, pp. 274 ff.)

See DURKHEIM, *Elementary Forms of Religious Life*, *passim.*; HUVELIN, P., "Magic et droit individuel" *L'année sociologique*, Vol. X; HUBERT *et* MAUSS, *Esquisse d'une théorie générale de la magie*, *ibid.*, Vol. VII; see also KAPP, *Grundlinien einer Philosophie der Technik*, 1877. See in this book the chapter about the sociologistic school.

[38] M. Weber has shown especially clearly how strongly the character of the economic organization of China, India, the ancient world, the Middle Ages, and of the present time has been conditioned through the character of the corresponding religions, magic, traditions, or rationalisms. He has also clarified the rôle of the Protestant religion in the origin and development of modern capitalism. In his study he quite rightly outlines the methodological principles of the mutual dependence of religious and economic phenomena upon each other, as well as upon all other social factors. He rightly says that there may be studies in which the economic factor can be taken as a variable, with religion or magic as its function; and there may be studies in which economic phenomena are viewed as a function of religion. His own study belongs to this type. His attitude may be seen from the following quotations: *"Eine Wirtschaftsethik ist keine einfache 'Funktion' wirtschaftliche Organizationsformen, ebensowenig wie umgekehrt diese eindeutig aus sich heraus prägt. Keine Wirtschaftsethik ist jemals nur religiös determiniert gewesen."* Taking the religious factor methodologically as a variable, he has shown that *"die Wurzel des modernen ökonomischen Menschentums ist religiöse"*; that without the Reformation it would have been impossible, and that an economic specification of China, or India, or of Judaism is unaccountable

Therefore, the economic factor is not older than the other factors. This means that social phenomena are, and always were, mutually, but not one-sidedly, dependent. For these reasons, there is no basis for claiming that the economic factor is the first in the causal series, and therefore, the primary one. So much for the factual side of the problem.[39]

But beside the factual, there is a logical side to it. L. Petrajitzky and R. Stammler indicated that law and social order are the logical and the factual preconditions of economic relationship, because, without a code of obligatory rules of conduct, the very facts of social relationship and mutual living are impossible.[40] Furthermore, if the economic factor is always "a starter," and all changes in the field of social life are due to changes in economic conditions, how can we explain the dynamics of the economic factor itself? Are they, due to its mystical property, a *perpetuum mobile* or a self-starter; or are they due to some other factor? Since the primacy of the economic factor is based on its being always "the starter," this has to be accounted for. The hypothesis of "the self-starter" amounts to the worst kind of mysticism, where the economic factor becomes a kind of God. For this reason it must be rejected. If the Marxians, like Engels, Labriola, and Plechanow, would refer to a "reverse influence of the secondary factors on the primary one," [41] then the starting point of the theory, and the basis of the primacy of the economic factor would be invalidated. Then we would no longer have a one-sided dependence of other factors on the economic one, but a mutual interdependence in which there would be neither the "starter" nor the "started" factors; but all would be "the starters"

without a knowledge of the corresponding religions of those peoples. See the chapter about M. Weber in this book. See his *Gesammelte Aufsätze zur Religions soziologie*, Tubingen, 1922–23, Vol. I, pp. 12, 21–22, 37–38, 82, 183, 233 ff. and *passim;* Vol. II, pp. 363–378; Vol. III, *passim.* A short summary of the principal conclusions reached in these volumes is given in his *Wirtschafts-Geschichte*, pp. 30, 239, 240, 300–315, München, 1924.

[39] Comp. HANSEN, A., "The Technological Interpretation of History," *Quarterly Journal of Economics*, Vol. XXXVI, pp. 80–82.

[40] See STAMMLER, R., *Wirtschaft und Recht, passim;* PETRAJITZKY, L., *Die Lehre v. Einkommen.*

[41] See Engels' statements in his letter of 1894, *Der Sozialistische Akademiker,* 1895; Marx himself was forced also to admit such a reverse influence of the non-economic factors on the economic ones. See also LABRIOLA, *op. cit.,* pp. 110, 201 ff.; PLECHANOW, *Kvoprosou o rasvitii monisticheskago vsgliada na istoriu.*

and "the started" at the same time.   Through this, the primacy of
the economic factor is taken away, and consequently, the theory
loses its characteristics.   Every Marxian who admits such a reverse influence of other factors on the economic one, logically
abandons his theory and comes to the conception of a functional
interdependence, reducing his claims simply to the statement that
the economic factor is correlated with some others.[42]   This shows
one side of the wrong causal conception on which the theory was
based, and some of the fallacies which result from such a conception.   They finally destroyed the theory as far as it represented
something specific.

B. *The second fundamental shortcoming of the theory is an
ambiguity and indefiniteness in the expression: the economic
factor is the last, the final, and the most important factor of
social phenomena.*—As is known, this claim has been interpreted
in two senses.   Some of the Marxian and the non-Marxian writers
(*e.g.,* Plechanow and Ellwood) have interpreted it in the sense
that the economic factor is exclusively sufficient to explain all
historical and social processes, as was believed by Marx.   Meanwhile, some other writers, including Engels, interpreted it in the
sense that it is only the principal factor, side by side with which
there are some other less important factors, (*e.g.,* Seligman,
Labriola, Marx, and Engels, in the later period of their writings).[43]   If we take the first of these interpretations, it leads to a
series of absurd statements.   If we take the second one, it amounts
to an abandonment of the theory.   The first interpretation is a

[42] Marx himself, in his later writings, and also Engels, having made this inevitable concession, practically abandoned their earlier claims, and almost
reduced "the economic interpretation of history" to a very general, common,
and sound recognition of the economic factor as one among many others.

[43] In my opinion, both of these interpretations are correct, but the first is true
in regard to the earlier writings of Marx and Engels, while the second one is true
in regard to their later writings, after they had abandoned many earlier exaggerations.   At this period, Engels wrote that "Marx never meant to claim an absolute
validity for economic considerations, to the exclusion of all other factors.   It is
not that the economic situation is the cause, in the sense of being the only active
agent, while all phenomena are only a passive result.   It is, on the contrary, a case
of mutual action on the basis of economic necessity (quite a dark expression,
amounting to the statement: 'white blackness' or 'wooden iron') which, in the
last instance, always works itself out." Letter of 1894, *Der Sozial. Akademiker.*
See similar statements of LABRIOLA, *op. cit.,* pp. 110 ff., which are as dark and
contradictory as this.

kind of monistic conception where an attempt is made to account for the whole of social life, and the whole process of history, through the economic factor alone.   Its hopelessness is shown by the following considerations.[44]   First, if the whole of social life, war and peace, impoverishment and prosperity, enslaving and liberation, revolution and reaction, are the results of the same factor, this gives the equation:

A and non-A $= f(E)$, that is, the most opposite phenomena are the result of the same cause.

Such an equation is logical nonsense; it contradicts the fundamental principle of science,—the uniform connection of cause and effect.   It admits that the same cause may have the most different and opposite results.   Under such a premise, the very conception of regularity and causal or functional relation is destroyed.   Indeed, if A and non-A are the results of the same cause, E, it is hopeless to try to find out any regularity or causal relation.   The premise is a denial of causality or regularity. Such a monistic factor becomes a very *coincidentia oppositorum* (reconciliation and identification of opposite phenomena)—the same kind of definition through which the mediæval scholastics characterized God.   In other words, such a monistic conception amounts to the equation:

$$E\text{(economic factor) is the cause of}\begin{cases} A \text{ and non-A} \\ B \text{ and non-B} \\ C \text{ and non-C} \\ D \text{ and non-D} \\ F \text{ and non-F} \\ \dots \dots \dots \\ N \text{ and non-N} \end{cases}\begin{array}{l} \text{that is,—the cause of all} \\ \text{forms of behavior, so-} \\ \text{cial processes, and his-} \\ \text{torical events.} \end{array}$$

No mathematician, logician, or scientist could formulate any law, any causal relation or any formula of regularity with such a premise.   Furthermore, if, in the equation, the factor E means a universally broad conception equal to that of "All," or "God," or "the universe," or "the whole social life," the equation becomes

[44] This criticism of economic monism may be applied to any kind of monistic theory of factors

tautological. "All" or "God" is the cause of "All," or "God." "The whole social life is the cause of the whole social life." Being tautological, it is sterile. If, by such a monistic factor, E is understood to be something narrower (as is the case), then, instead of tautology we have something still worse,—*pars pro toto,* a part of something as the cause of the whole something; an economic factor (a part of the whole social life) as the cause of the whole social life. This amounts to the statement: "Out of the part may be the whole; out of nothing, something." Such are the logical fruits of the monistic interpretation of Marx's contention.[45]

The factual hopelessness of such an attempt is clear from the following consideration. Even the simplest dynamic phenomenon of our universe,—the movement of physical objects—could be accounted for by contemporary physical mechanics through at least two factors, inertia and gravitation. To hope for an explanation of the most complex dynamics of social life and history through only one factor amounts to nothing but idiocy. At the most, such an attempt will give only tautology, nothing more.

The above is enough to show the scientific hopelessness of such a conception of economic materialism. This hopelessness was possibly the reason for the shifting of Marx and Engels, in their later writings, to the second interpretation of their claim.

But this second interpretation, which admits other factors side by side with the economic one, is practically an abandonment of the theory. It means a pluralistic theory of the factors, signifying that the economic factor is only one among many others. It is not necessary to be a Marxian to accept this, and, as we have seen, in such a pluralistic interpretation, the economic factor was recognized, stressed, and studied by hundreds of thinkers many hundreds of years before Marx and Engels. It is true that, having shifted to such a pluralistic conception, Marx, Engels, and the Marxians still add: "but among these many factors the economic one is the most important and primary." But even this contention was expressed by many non-Marxian writers before and after Marx and Engels. Therefore, this addition does not give them any right to claim originality. Furthermore, their

[45] Compare CROCE, B., *Historical Materialism,* pp. 28 ff.

addition has not been corroborated by any clear logical or factual proofs. Marx and Engels did not even attempt to give any method for measuring the importance or efficiency of various factors, neither did they give any indices of the "primacy" of the economic factor, nor any logical motivation of their claim. This is enough to contend that the pluralistic interpretation of the Marx-Engels theory strips it of any originality, and amounts to its abandonment.[46]

C. *The third shortcoming of the theory is that the definitions of the terms "the economic factor," "forces and relations of production" and "economic basis" are not sufficiently exclusive and specific.*—To the ambiguity of Marx's wording is due the fact that some of his interpreters, like K. Kautsky, W. Sombart, A. Hansen,[47] and others, understand this factor to be only a kind of technique, while other interpreters like Engels, Masaryk, Seligman, Cunow and others understand it to mean the general conditions of production, including geographical environment, natural resources, extraction, fashioning, transportation, trade, mechanism of distribution and so on.[48]

If we accept the first interpretation, we have the proposition: Technique is the primary factor, and through technique it is possible to explain all the miracles of history. Taking into consideration the fact that technique is only a part of social reality, the above is logically absurd (*pars pro toto*). Further, in view of

---

[46] Trying to save the originality of Marx's theory, Professor Seligman contends that such a pluralistic interpretation does not mean its abandonment. Unfortunately, he does not give any proofs of this statement, except the purely dogmatic assertions that "the chief considerations in human progress are the social considerations (this is not at all characteristic of Marxian economic determinism); that the important factor in social change is the economic factor (Confucius, Mencius, Plato, Aristotle, Thucydides, Plinius, Machiavelli, Guicciardini and hundreds of other writers stressed that); and that they exert not an exclusive, but a preponderant (why and on what reasons?) influence in shaping the progress of society." (SELIGMAN, *op. cit.* p. 67.) Furthermore, mention of the name of Demolins does not strengthen, but only aggravates the position of the author, because Demolins' "economism" is quite different from that of Marx, and it originated not from Marx, but from a better theory of Le Play, who, rather earlier and better than Marx, described the influence of economic factors. See the second chapter of this book.

[47] SOMBART, W., "Technik und Kultur," *Archiv. für Sozialwiss.*, Bd. 33, 1911, p. 315; HANSEN, A., "The Technological Interpretation of History," *Quarterly Journal of Economics*, Vol. XXXVI, 1921, p. 73.

[48] SELIGMAN, *op. cit.*, Chap. V; CUNOW, *Die Marxsche Geschichts-Gesellschaft und Staats-Theorie*, Vol. II, 1921, pp. 158 ff.

the fact that the technique itself requires a certain amount of experience and knowledge of society,[49] Marx's differentiation between technique and science becomes a separation of what is identical (science, as a component of technique, as opposed to science generally), and the establishing of identity between that which is different, (between technique as something existing separately from science, and technique composed only of science). Old logicians used to style such illogical procedures by the name, *quaternio terminorum*.

If we accept the second and broader interpretation, we have an increase of vagueness in the theory and the concept of the economic factor itself. It becomes a kind of bag filled with geographic conditions; technique, and followingly, science; and by the whole complex machinery of trade, commerce, and distribution; which involves juridical and political institutions, and what not. To take such an indefinite complexity as a cause or variable, and try to explain something by means of it is a hopeless enterprise. We would be dealing with that which we do not know, and we would be trying to find its effects on the phenomena which directly or indirectly make up the composition of the factor itself. Under such conditions, it is not likely we could reach any clear and definite correlation, and it is probable that we would find the most absurd correlations, as actually happened with many followers of Marx, and with Marx himself.[50] In this case we

[49] This is recognized by Marx himself: "Although technique is mainly dependent on the conditions of science [which he attempts to account for completely through technique] it is still more true that science depends on the condition and needs of technique." (True, but how can it follow from this that technique is an omnipotent factor, while science is something secondary?)

[50] It is enough to remember Marx's correlation between the hand-mill and feudal society; between the steam-mill and capitalist society; the explanation of the Reformation *exclusively* through the economic revolt of the German nation against the exploitation of the Papal Court; the accounting of the whole character of Babylonian culture and organization exclusively through the canalization of Mesopotamia; and that of ancient Egypt, through the channeling of the Nile; the development of science, arts, and inventions exclusively through the needs of technique, and so on. Some time ago such childish "explanations" and correlations were produced by the Marxians in so great an abundance that the sober Marxians themselves had finally to protest against it. "In this way (by childish explanations) the simpletons might reduce the whole of history to commercial arithmetic; and, finally, a new and authentic interpretation of Dante might give us the Divine Comedy illustrated with the process of manufacturing pieces of cloth, which the wily Florentine merchants sold for their greater profit." indignantly exclaims Labriola; *op. cit.*, pp. 204–205.

are confined to statements and formulas whose indefinite contents and meanings do not permit us either to prove or to disprove them. A sterile verbalism is an inevitable result of such a method.

D. *As a result of this indicated indefiniteness, the exact meaning of the Marx-Engels' causal sequence of factors, or the sequence of their dependency also becomes somewhat indefinite.*— In the technological interpretation, this sequence is as follows: (1)—Changes in the technique of production determine (2)—the changes in the economic structure of society—in "the relations of production" and the "property relations,"—which, in their turn, determine (3)—changes in the political, social and intellectual life of a society. In the second, and broader, interpretation of the economic factor, the sequence assumes a somewhat different form: —1—, changes in the general conditions of production and exchange determine, —2—, modifications in class-composition of a society, which, in their turn, call forth, —3—, a modification of class-antagonisms resulting in —4— a modification of the social, political, and intellectual "superstructure" of a society. Whatever interpretations we take, both sequences may have only a relative value at best,—the value of one of many possible sequences and alignments of social phenomena. In the above I indicated that there is no reason for thinking that, among the forces which mold social and historical processes or human behavior, only the economic factor is "active" or is "the starter." I indicated also that the "functional conception" of "causation" and the fact of the interdependence of social phenomena, permit us to take any factor as "variable" (not only "technique," but "science," "religion," "law," and what not) and attempt to find its "functions" or "effects" in any field, as in the fields of technique and economic phenomena. We have seen, and shall further see, that such attempts have been made and have not been fruitless. As far as Marx and Engels pretend to make their sequence the only one possible, their claim is unacceptable. It may be met by an opposite claim, in which law, religion, or the "intellectual factor" is set forth as the "starter," with the economic factor as a function.[51] As far as we take this in a relative sense, with

[51] Professor John Commons' *Legal Foundations of Capitalism;* R. Stammler's *Wirtschaft und Recht* and L. Petrajitzky's *Die Lehre v. Einkommen* are examples

"the economic factor" as "a variable," but without any claim for its exclusiveness, the sequence may be accepted, and its value decided by the results of a study of its correlation with other phenomena. If the study shows that its correlation with other phenomena exists and is universal and constant, and that its coefficient is high, this will be proof of the sequence's scientific value. If the results of the study are opposite, this would mean that it is of small value for scientific sociology.[52] Later on, I shall show to what extent a correlation exists between the economic factor and other social phenomena, and how high it is. Here I only mention that the Marx-Engels' expectation that the correlation would be very high and universal, and that it would follow the sequence exactly was greatly exaggerated.[53] So much about this point.

---

in which law is taken as a "starter" (variable), and economic system as a function. M. Weber's *Religionssoziologie* is an example of where religion is taken as a variable, and economic organization as a function. Geographic and racial schools take as variables the geographic and the racial factors. An intellectual factor as a starter is taken in the theories of De Roberty and Tarde. "What!" exclaims Tarde in his criticism of the Marxian theory, "Science and religion . . . are made dependent on economic conditions! But is it not true that the social and economic environment itself has been created through diffusion and vulgarization of scientific and religious ideas? Is it not true also that the density and numbers of the population (and economic conditions) are dependent upon the character of the decisions in a series of political problems?" "The very progress of industry and technique has been due to a series of thinkers with their love for the truth. Gun-powder, as well as the steam-engine, were discovered by dreamers." See Tarde's paper in *Annales of the Institut International de Sociologie*, Vol. VIII; also De Roberty's paper where Marx's sequence is inverted. This is an example of Marx's reversed sequence, in which science is made a variable, while economic phenomena are viewed as its "function." Scientifically, such a sequence is as appropriate as Marx's sequence. If the authors had understood "the functional conception of causality" there would not have been any such conflict of opposite theories. But since the authors held conceptions of "one-sided causality," their sequences naturally could not be reconciled and they argued endlessly with one another. A similar reason is at the basis of the endless disputes between the partisans of various "primary" factors. Compare SOMBART, W., "Technik und Kultur," *Archiv für Sozialwissenschaft*, 1911, pp. 312 ff.

[52] However, in such an interpretation of the sequence, Marx's theory, while losing its "sins," at the same time loses its specific "originality" and becomes something that has been said many times before.

[53] For instance, a change of technique or economic basis is not an absolutely necessary condition for many changes in the field of economic, social, political and intellectual phenomena. M. Kovalevsky properly indicates that in England in the period from the sixth to the sixteenth century, the technique of agriculture, and the means and the instruments of production remained practically the same.

E. Of the other characteristics of the Marxian theory, its
*fallacious and contradictory conception of historical determinism
should be mentioned. It represents an incongruous reconciliation
of fatalism with free will.*—Let the reader read attentively the
above long quotations from Marx. Here we read that the relationships of production entered into by men "are indispensable
and independent of their will." The forces of production are
depicted as developing *sua sponte,* independently of human beings
and other social factors. The whole process of human history
is depicted in the way "men are agitatedly acting, while, in fact,
they are led by the economic factor," or, in the paraphrase of
Bossuet: "Men are agitatedly acting while, in fact, they are
led by God." The very expectation of the victory of socialism is
based on the same idea of the omnipotent, fatalistic, and inevitable
play of the economic factor, which will lead to the destruction of
capitalism and to the victory of socialism.

This fatalistic interpretation of determinism would be quite
objectionable from the scientific standpoint alone, because scientific determinism has nothing in common with fatalism; scientific
determinism states only that, on the basis of the theory of probability, the appearance, connection, or disappearance of such and
such phenomena is probable or improbable with such and such a
degree of probability, and that is all. All terms, like "inevitable,"
"necessary," and so on, are not a part of science, or of the
scientific conception of determinism.[54]

To this sin, however, Marx and Engels add two others: first,
an eschatological, "historical" tendency toward socialism and a
future earthly paradise guaranteed by the "inevitable" play of
human factors; and second, the belief that as soon as the socialistic

---

In spite of this, in the field of economic relations, social and political institutions,
and in the mental and moral life, a series of the most important changes occurred.
On the other hand, we have many instances where a modification of technique,
or of economic basis is not followed by any noticeable change in the ideologies,
ethics, or art of a people. See KOVALEVSKY, *op. cit.,* pp. 244 ff. See also SOM-
BART, *op. cit.,* pp. 315 ff.

[54] See PARETO, *op. cit.,* Chaps. I, II. See also the quoted works of A. Tschuproff,
Pearson, Cournot, Mach, A. Rey, and so on. The contemporary theory of cause
and effect, variable and function, determinism and indeterminism is based on,
and expressed in, the concepts of probability and its coefficient.

paradise is reached, fatalism ceases to exist, and mankind "jumps from the kingdom of necessity into that of freedom." [55]

The incongruous mixture of these components (fatality, freedom, and eschatology) makes any criticism of the Marxian conception of determinism unnecessary. Its weakness is evident.[56]

F. Finally, the Marx-Engels' theory of class-struggle, being very old, has a series of defects. It is evidently fallacious to say that "the history of all hitherto existing society is the history of class struggle," as far as this means that there has not been a coöperation of social classes. It is a fallacy because class coöperation has been an even more universal phenomenon than class-antagonism. As far as this means that class-struggle alone has been the dynamic factor to which the progress of mankind has been due, it is again wrong. After a series of investigations, like Kropotkin's "Mutual Aid," it is certain that the progress of mankind has been due rather to coöperation and solidarity than to

[55] This eschatological belief,— a variety of many forms of belief in a millennium, —Marx expressed many times. For this reason he views all the history of mankind up to this day as "the prehistory of the human race." "The productive forces developing in the womb of bourgeois society create the material conditions for the solution of that antagonism." *Crit. of Polit. Econ.*, pp. 12–13. "To the old bourgeois society with its classes and class antagonisms will succeed an association in which the free development of each is the condition of free development of all." *Communist Manifesto.* "It is only when the order of things will be such that there will no longer be classes and class antagonisms, that social revolutions will cease to be political revolutions." *Misère de la philosophie*, Paris, 1847, p. 178. Engels, as is well known, speaks plainly about "jumping from the kingdom of necessity into that of freedom" where "human beings will be the masters of nature and the masters of themselves." See ENGELS, *Die Entwicklung des Sozialismus von der Utopie zur Wissenschaft*, pp. 51–53, Berlin, 1907; *Herrn E. Duhring Umwaltzung der Wissenschaft*, p. 305, Stuttgart, 1894. See also LABRIOLA, *op. cit.*, pp. 154 ff., 234, 244. This part of the Marxian theory, according to P. Struve's appropriate opinion, "is not a scientific theory of evolution, but an evident theory of progress which supposes that the evolution of mankind is an inevitable betterment and a growth of positive values." Gehrlich, Novgorodzev and some other investigators style with reason the evolutionary theory of Marxianism as "a variety of the belief in a millennium,"— a kind of religious orthodoxy, as an incongruous mixture of science and ethics, necessity and freedom, the theory of evolution and progress, primitive materialism, and fantastic or Utopian idealism. See the quoted works of Novgorodzev, Gehrlich and Struve.

[56] This incongruity is still further aggravated by the self-contradiction of Marx's theory. It claims that up to this time any social change or progress has been due to class-antagonism and class-struggle. Now, if it is going to disappear in the future millennium, does this mean that with this millennium the history of mankind will stop and stagnation take place? If it does not mean this, what will be the dynamic force instead of class-antagonism? And if it will be solidarity, why did it not work in the past and how may it appear suddenly, as *deus ex machina?*

class-struggle, antagonism, and hatred. In this respect Tarde's sharp remarks seem to be accurate: "Since the beginning of the history, classes and armies could have struggled with one another endlessly; and yet, this could not have created either geometry, mechanics, or chemistry, without which it would be impossible for man to subdue nature and make progress in industry or military art. All this became possible only through the fact that in the noise of this destructive struggle, a few thinkers and seekers for the truth silently worked in their laboratory and study." As far as Marx's class-theory means that only an antagonism of economic classes exists or that it is the most important, it is again wrong. There have been many other forms of antagonism other than that of class, — as the struggle of racial, national, religious and state groups. These antagonisms, being quite different from the antagonism of the economic classes, have been sometimes more important than the former.[57]

Finally, apart from the above defects, the Marx-Engels' conception of social or economic class is indefinite and self-contradictory. In the *Communist Manifesto,* they use this term in the broadest sense, embracing under it caste, occupational group, estate or order, guild, and political ranks. In their other works, (in *Misery of Philosophy* and *Capital*) they used it in a narrower sense, and discriminated the social class from the occupational group, order, and so on.

The manuscript of the third volume of Marx's *Capital* ends with the beginning of an analysis of social classes, but the analysis is not finished. Therefore, we do not gain any clear conception of social or economic classes from the works of Marx and Engels. Owing to this, their whole theory of class-struggle becomes indefinite also. Some of the Marxians have tried to elaborate a concept and classification of social classes (K. Kautsky, Overberger, S. Solntzev, E. Bernstein, H. Cunow and others).[58] This resulted in a production of contradictory and unsatisfactory definitions of social class. Interpretations of Marx's concept given

[57] See SOROKIN, *Systema Soziologii*, Vol. II, *passim;* DELEVSKY, J., *Social Antagonisms*, Russ., *passim.*

[58] See my *Systema Soziologii*, Vol. II, pp. 283–306; DELEVSKY, *op. cit., passim;* SOLNTZEV, S., *Social Classes*, Russ., Tomsk, 1917; CUNOW, *op. cit.*, Vol. II, pp. 50 ff.

by various Marxians have happened also to be quite different. Therefore, the Marxian theory of social class, as well as the common terms of "proletariat," *"bourgeoisie,"* and so on, are still undefined. They are the "shibboleths" whose exact meaning is not known.[59] For the above reasons it is possible to say that this part of the Marxian theory is quite unsatisfactory.[60]

G. Perhaps the most valuable part of the theory of Marx is his analysis of the dependency of our ideologies upon our environment, and especially upon socio-economic environment; and his contention that the "objective social situation" is very often reflected, or thought of, in individual minds in an inadequate and

[59] The problem of who a proletarian is became practically important in the Communist régime of Soviet Russia. Studying the theoretical discussions of the Communist leaders and their practical attempts to separate the proletarians from the non-proletarians, one comes to the conclusion that the theoretical conceptions of the Communists are vaguely different and contradictory. In their practice, however, a proletarian has been regarded as anyone who has supported the Communists although he occupied the position of a capitalist or was a privileged and a wealthy man. The non-proletarians have been regarded as all who have not supported the Communist government, though they were the common laboring men in factories. See *e.g.*, *Petrogr. Pravda*, 1919, No. 162, where some peasants, sympathizing with the Communist government, are styled "proletarians" while the working people of the Obouchov and Poutilov factories, who displeased the Soviet government, are styled as *"bourgeois."* This additionally shows that Marxianism does not have any clear conception of social class, and consequently, slogans like: "proletariat" and "dictatorship of proletariat" are far from having a clear and definite meaning.

[60] It is rather surprising that A. W. Small found this part of Marx's theory especially valuable. I cannot style his statements in this respect as otherwise than a "blunder." As we have seen, class-struggle was discovered thousands of years ago. Even the terminology of the *Communist Manifesto* could be found in the writings of the Roman and the Greek writers, not to mention the thinkers of the later periods. Therefore in no way is it possible to ascribe to Marx the merit of discovering the class-struggle factor. As to the specific traits of the Marxian theory of class-struggle, the above shows that they are nothing but fallacies. Another thing to be mentioned here is the lack of a generally accepted definite conception of social class in contemporary sociology. The majority of sociologists continue to use this term carelessly. Those who have tried to define it have given different definitions. In my *System of Sociology* I give thirty-two of the principal forms of these definitions. Evidently such an anarchy cannot be continued. It is high time to end it. See an analysis and survey of the definitions and classifications of social classes in my *System of Sociology*, Vol. II, pp. 283–306. See also Michels, R., "Beitrag zur Lehre von den Klassenbildung," *Arch. f. Sozialw.*, Vol. XLIX, 1922, pp. 561–593; Mombert, P., "Zum Wesen der sozialen Klasse," *Erinnerungsgabe für Max Weber*, 1923, Vol. II, pp. 239–278; Bauer, A., *Les classes sociales*, Paris, 1902; Schmoller, G., *Grundriss der Volkswirtschaftslehre*, 1901, Vol. I; Solntzev, S., *op. cit.;* Loria, A., "Beiträge zur ökonomish Theorie der sozialen Klassen," *Arch. f. Sozialw.*, 1923; Mombert, P., "The Tatsachen der Klassenbildung," *Schmoller's Jahrbuch für Gesetzgebung*, etc., 1920, pp. 93–122; Fahlbeck, P., *Die Klassen und die Gesellschaft*, Jena, 1923.

disfigured form. This is the idea which he expresses in the words : "Just as our opinion of an individual is not based on what he thinks of himself, so can we not judge of such a period of transformation (of productive forces and the relations of production) by its (society's) own consciousness." In this, and similar statements, Marx and Engels indicate the fact that our "speech-reactions" and our subjective interpretations of social phenomena (ideologies) are often misleading; that they reflect reality inadequately; and that it is impossible to grasp the objective social reality, the nature of social processes, or the nature of the social group or individual exclusively on the basis of the "speech-reactions" (ideologies) of a man, group, or society.[61] Even the real function of many "ideological phenomena," like religion and belief, is often different from that which the ideologists themselves say of it. The essence of this statement is sound, but again, this was expressed by Marx with his usual exaggeration and ambiguousness in statements like this : "It is not the consciousness of mankind that determines its existence, but, on the contrary, its social existence that determines its consciousness." Furthermore, the theory is far from being new. It was expressed, and more clearly, many centuries before Marx.[62] Therefore, even this part of his theory cannot pretend to be an original discovery.

GENERAL CONCLUSION

Summing up what has been said of the Marx-Engels' sociological theory, it is possible to say : first, from a purely scientific

[61] See SOROKIN, *The Sociology of Revolution*, Chaps. III and IV; SOROKIN, *Social Mobility*, Chap. II; SOROKIN, "Die Russische Soziologie," *Jahrbuch für Soziologie*, B. II, pp. 473–477; PARETO, *op. cit.*, Vol. I, Chap. III and *passim* (his analysis of the "derivations").

[62] A sufficient example is furnished in *Defensor Pacis* by Marsilio of Padua, where we find quite a "materialistic" interpretation of the rôle of religion, and of the discrepancy between the objective reality and its disfigured reflection in beliefs and ideologies. Similar ideas of Machiavelli were expressed in his *Discourses on Livy*, Book I, Chaps. XI–XVI; Book II, Chap. II. Quite an adequate expression of the theory may be found in the works of P. Bayle, with his theory that "opinions and ideologies are not the rules for actions, and men do not follow them in their conduct. The Turks believe in Fatalism and Predestination; and yet, they flee from a danger just as the French who do not have such a belief." See BAYLE, *Pensées divers. . . a l'occasion de la comète*, etc., pp. 266, 272 ff., Paris, 1704. Among the writers of the eighteenth, and of the beginning of the nineteenth centuries, there were a great many who laid down such a theory. See the immediate predecessors of Marx in this respect, Salomon, G., *op. cit.. passim.*

point of view, as far as its sound elements are concerned, there is nothing in their theory that was not said by earlier authors; second, what is really original is far from being scientific; third, the only merit of the theory is that it in a somewhat stronger and exaggerated form generalized the ideas given before the time of Marx. However, as we have seen, the general formulas are expressed in an obscure and ambiguous form, and they are not so much the results of any inductive or factual study as of a speculative and dogmatic deduction. Therefore, from a purely scientific standpoint, there is no reason for regarding Marx and Engels as the "Darwins" or "Galileos" of the social sciences. There is no reason even for regarding their scientific contributions as something above the average. The great influence which their works and names have acquired are due, not to the scientific merits of their writings, but to quite dissimilar circumstances.[63] If they gave an impetus for some few fruitful scientific studies,[64] at the same time they have originated an enormous number of wrong hypotheses and ideologies, and an enormous bulk of literature whose essence consists only in a "theological" interpretation of the "scripture" of Marx and Engels, similar to the theological interpretations of the Koran by theologians.

[63] Such a phenomenon is rather common in the history of social thought. From a purely scientific viewpoint, the works of Rousseau, Voltaire, or of many Church fathers, or popular authors, are far from being perfect. Their leading ideas are, rather, fallacious from the scientific standpoint, and yet, this did not prevent their obtaining great popularity and great influence in certain societies at certain periods. We see something similar to that at the present moment in the great popularity in Germany in 1919–1923 of the work of O. Spengler. This phenomenon is interesting and worthy of study. The popularity and influential rôle of the works of Marx and Engels is a case of this general phenomenon.

[64] Many authors, and among them even such as Professor Seligman, have given credit to Marxianism for works which in no way have been due to direct or indirect influence from him. For instance, Seligman mentions the works of M. Kovalevsky, L. H. Morgan, Francotte, R. Pöhlman, Nietzche, Mommsen, Lamprecht, and E. Demolins, under a misleading title, "Recent Applications of the Theory" (of Marx). This title, and some of Seligman's statements may give an impression that these works have been written under the influence of the theory of Marx, or for the sake of an application and corroboration of his theory. See SELIGMAN, op. cit., Chap. VI. The truth is that all these works (some of which appeared even before Marx's works) have appeared without any influence of Marx's theory, and Marxianism could not be given any credit for their appearance. This remark may be applied to many similar statements which give to Marxianism credit for that which does not belong to it.

This literature is practically out of the field of science.[65]   All in all, Marx and Engels have rather hindered the progress of social sciences than facilitated it.   At the present moment, as we shall see, their theory is in the past.   It is outdistanced and repudiated in its specific traits by numerous careful and factual studies. Only a metaphysician could now be busy with the Marx-Engels conceptions.   A scientist will pass them over and will turn to the inductive and factual studies of the correlations between economic and other sides of social life.

3. Contemporary Studies of the Correlation Between Various Economic Conditions and Other Social Phenomena

Their General Characteristics.—While the Marxian theorizers have been busy with a theological exegesis of the "revelation" of their teachers; while many distinguished thinkers have been wasting their time and energy in criticism and repudiation of Marx's statements; and while many speculative minds appeased themselves in a scientifically fruitless meditation on what the meaning of such and such a Marxian conception is, such as the relationship between Kant and Marx, or whether his categories are logical or historical and so on; while all this was going on, a great many investigators, before and after Marx, and regardless of his theory, have been busy with really scientific studies of the correlations between various economic factors and other social phenomena.   If, at the present moment, we know something in this field, our knowledge is primarily due to such studies.   Almost all such researches have taken this or that economic condition not as "a primary factor" or "principal cause," but simply as a "variable."   Regardless of the "materialistic conception of history" or of any ranking of the importance of various factors, without any preconceptions, they have proceeded to find out what the correlations are, how close they are, and with what phenomena they are related.   *The first result is that the relationship between various economic and non-economic phenomena has been found to be much more complex than it was supposed to be by*

---

[65] The stamp of this scientific sterility lies even on such recent works as N. Bucharin's *Marxian Sociology*, conspicuous only by its ignorance and arrogant pretentions.   Even Professor Cunow's good book is marked by the same stamp of "theological" spirit.

Marx or by any other writer who advanced the deductive theory of the economic interpretation of history. Their second general result is that various social phenomena are correlated in the most different degrees of closeness with various economic conditions, although, between some of the economic and non-economic phenomena the correlation is pretty high, between some other non-economic and economic conditions the correlation is almost nil. Their third result is in ascertaining that there is almost no case when the correlation is quite perfect. This means that, practically, there is no social phenomenon of the non-economic character whose "nature," variation, movement, or change could be explained exclusively through the "economic factor." Their fourth result is in finding out that the economic phenomena themselves are not to be regarded as something which only condition other phenomena, but as something which is conditioned by these other phenomena also. Their relationship is not one-sided dependence, but mutual interdependence. Therefore, we cannot regard the economic factors as "the cause," and all other phenomena as "the effects." Only methodologically, or conditionally, can an "economic factor" be taken as "an independent variable," while all other phenomena are taken as "functions." With the same right, these other phenomena may be taken as "independent variables," while the economic factors may be viewed as their "function."

Such, in brief, are the results of these studies. At the present moment we have a rather enormous number of such investigations. In this book it is impossible to give an exhaustive account of them. Therefore, in the following pages I will mention only the principal and representative types of such studies. They will give a sufficient idea of the present situation of social sciences in this respect.

4. The Economic Conditions, and Bodily and Mental Characteristics of Population

Numerous statistical, anthropometrical, and experimental studies have shown that there is a series of correlations of various degrees between economic position (degree of poverty or wealth) and the bodily, biological, and mental characteristics of the population of the same age and sex in the same society.

Among these correlations possibly the most important are as follows:

The poor classes when compared with the well-to-do of the same society (a) are smaller in stature; (b) have less weight; (c) probably a lower weight of brain or cranial capacity; (d) more physical ailments; (e) a shorter duration of life; (f) a somewhat inferior intelligence. The studies of investigators like V. de Lapouge, O. Ammon, A. Niceforo, K. Pearson, E. Elderton, Pagliani, N. Viazemsky, Wateff, Beddoe, Ch. Roberts, M. Muffang, H. Schwiening, R. Livi, A. Binet, A. Constantin, F. G. Parsons, A. MacDonald, G. Bushan, S. D. Porteus, W. Pfitzner, Matiegka, P. Ricardi, J. Bertillon, Villermé, P. Topinard, Carlier, Longuet, B. Rowntree, C. Röse, F. A. Woods, A. Odin, J. Mc-Keen Cattell, F. Maas, S. Fisher, J. Philiptschenko, L. Terman, R. Yerkes, A. Geissler, Weisenberg, Talko-Hryncewitz, Manouvrier, A. Hrdlička, Oloriz, Anoutchin, H. H. Goddard, J. Duff and G. Thomson, M. Haggerty, J. Bridges and L. E. Coler, W. Mc-Dougall, B. A. Gould, Wachter, W. Porter, E. A. Doll, H. Ellis, E. B. Gowin, B. T. Baldwin, P. Sorokin and of many others have made these correlations rather certain.[66]   However, the correlation is not perfect, and there is a great deal of overlapping.   This means that the rôle of economic conditions is limited.   The limitation becomes still greater if we take into consideration that even these, though tangible, are still the imperfect correlations of economic conditions with the above differences, and they are due not only to differences in economic position, but to many other factors.   The mere fact of correlation does not necessarily mean that these differences of various economic classes are the direct result of the "economic differences."   The correlations indicate only that such is the factual relationship between the economic positions of these classes of the population and their characteristics.   Whether the poorer classes have a lower intelligence because they are poor and do not have much opportunity for intellectual training, or whether they are poor because they have an inferior intelligence, the correlation cannot decide.   In a short

[66] For the sake of brevity I do not give here the corresponding data and references.   They are given in my *Social Mobility*, Chaps. X, XI, XII; see also Chap. V of this book.

formula, it simply describes the factual situation, and that is all. To make a decision in the indicated dilemma we have to take further special studies. They seem to indicate that the above differences are due to the social and economic conditions of the poor and the well-to-do classes, as well as to the innate differences between the upper and the lower classes. Both factors are necessary for an "explanation" of these differences.[67]

5. Economic Conditions and Vital Processes

Differences in Vital Processes among the Poor and the Rich Classes.—Of a great many correlations found between various economic conditions (measured by amount of income, the number of rooms occupied, the standard of living, and so on) and birth, death, marriage, and divorce rates, and their fluctuations, the most important ones are possibly as follows:

First: *As a general rule, within contemporary Western societies and some societies of the past, the poor classes have a greater mortality and a greater birth rate than the well-to-do classes of the same society, and of the same sex and age.* Many censuses, and the studies of the mentioned investigators, besides those of Körösi, Ollendorf, Oettingen, E. Levasseur, G. U. Yule, A. L. Bowley, N. A. Humphreys, W. Farr, F. Prinzing, L. Hersch, H. Westergaard, W. Ogle, J. Wappäus, J. C. Dunlop, T. H. Stevenson, L. March, G. von Mayr, L. Dublin, C. Gini, F. Savorgnan, D. Heron, R. May, R. Pearl, W. Willcox, A. Powys, and a great many others, have made this proposition rather certain.[68] However, here again these correlations, being quite noticeable, are not perfect. There are many exceptions to the rule and a great deal of overlapping. This means that the rates of these vital processes depend on many other than economic factors. Again, even the imperfect correlations could not be regarded as controlled exclusively by economic conditions. There is scarcely any doubt that a series of other factors participates in the conditioning of the mentioned differences of various classes. Furthermore, there have been societies in which such correlations, es-

---

[67] See Sorokin, *Social Mobility*, Chap. XIII.

[68] See the data and references in my *Social Mobility*, Chaps. XI and XV. See also a good summary in Mosse, M., and Tugendreich, G., *Krankheit und Soziale Lage*, München, 1913.

pecially in regard to the birth rate, have not existed. A lower procreation of the well-to-do classes, compared with that of the poorer classes, seems not to have taken place in many past societies, and in Eastern societies (India, China) of relatively recent time. This is especially true in regard to the societies practicing polygamy, which shows some preferences for the procreation of the well-to-do classes. This means again that the correlation is not universal, and that the movement of these vital processes is controlled by economic conditions still less than is shown by the above imperfect correlations found within modern Western societies. Again, as we shall see further, a study of the fluctuation of the death and the birth rate in connection with business conditions, gives results rather opposite to the above. Instead of a decrease in the period of business prosperity, the death rate in many cases has risen in such periods, and has decreased in the periods of business depression. In spite of the improvement of economic conditions in Western societies during the second half of the nineteenth century, their birth rate did not go up, as might be expected, but went down. Such an unexpected result seems to suggest that there are limits in a correlation of the vital processes with economic conditions. These limits being passed, the correlation becomes either intangible, or assumes the opposite character. A great impoverishment, amounting to starvation, leads, no doubt, to an increase in the death rate, and to a decrease in the birth rate. A relatively slight change of economic conditions, however, may not influence the fluctuation of the vital processes, or its effects may be overweighed by those of other non-economic factors, resulting in a movement of the vital processes which is different from that determined by a great change of economic conditions, or from the one which may be expected on the basis of the discussed statistical findings. This again shows the limited influence of the economic factor in this field. Finally, even the above greater mortality and greater birth rate of the poor classes when compared with those of the well-to-do strata, in their limited sense, could not be regarded as a "function" of exclusively economic conditions. It is probable that they are the result of many other agencies besides that of the economic factor. With a reasonable degree of probability we can say that the poorer classes have a greater mortality, not only because they live in less healthy economic conditions, but also, that they are poor because they have poor health and a weak inherited constitution, leading to a higher mortality. This means that the vital, and the economic and other social phenomena, are interdependent. Consequently, economic conditions cannot be ignored in an explanation of vital processes, but, at the same time, they alone are not sufficient to account for them, and their rôle must not be overestimated.[69]

In regard to such criteria as the marriage and divorce rates, the differences between the poor and the rich classes are still less definite, and are somewhat contradictory. Correlations found in some societies,—for instance, a greater divorce rate in some of the well-to-do classes than in the poor classes,—have not been found in other societies. In general, the correlation between the rates of these phenomena and economic conditions seems to be so complex that they may be regarded only as local and temporary. This means that these phenomena depend upon purely economic conditions in a still less degree than death and birth rates, and that they seem to be controlled in a greater degree than birth and death processes by the non-economic conditions which may mask, change, or disfigure the "influence" of the economic factors.

Fluctuation of Vital Processes Correlated with Business Conditions.—Correlations between economic conditions and the birth, death, marriage and divorce rates, have been found also through

[69] There have been many other attempts to account for a higher birth rate in the poorer classes. Some authors like Thomas Doubleday tried to explain a lower procreation of the upper classes through an overabundance of their food, and the constitutional change due to it. See DOUBLEDAY, THOMAS, *The True Law of Population*, London, 1843, *passim* and pp. 67 ff., 128 ff. Darwin, as is known, sharply criticized the hypothesis and laid down a series of facts which contradict Doubleday's hypothesis. Recently F. Carli, on the basis of the studies of Pignini and others set forth a hypothesis similar to that of Doubleday. "Beyond certain limits, an increase of wealth goes against the interests of the species and checks fertility." CARLI, *op. cit.*, pp. 177 ff.; PIGNINI, *La biochimia del cervello*, pp. 100 ff., Torino, 1915. R. Pearl, on his part, explains the difference through a greater sexuality of the poor classes compared with that of the well-to-do and upper classes. His study of the frequency of the sexual activity of the poorer, and the wealthier and professional groups, has shown that the unskilled and poorer groups have a higher frequency than the well-to-do and more intellectual groups. PEARL, R., *The Biology of Population Growth*, Chap. VIII, pp. 198 ff. Without mentioning several other hypotheses, the above shows how complex is the situation, and how necessary it is to abstain from an assertion of any "unlimited correlations" in this field. Besides, it means again that these phenomena cannot be accounted for through economic factors alone.

the study of the variation of both phenomena *in time* within the same, or approximately the same, social unit, as distinguished from the above studies of their correlation in *"social space"* among different economic classes at the same time. Many investigators, among them, H. Denis, Pokrovsky, Oettingen, Levasseur, J. Lescure, G. von Mayr, W. Beveridge, Tugan-Baranovsky, Aftalion, Farr, A. L. Bowley, Bodio, Longstaff, Ogle, Hooker, Juglar, and more recently W. Ogburn, G. P. Davies, G. U. Yule, L. March, D. Thomas, and M. Hexter, have studied the effects of business cycles (the rhythm of prosperity and depression) on the variation in marriages, births, deaths, and divorces.[70]

A. In regard to the marriage rate, the statisticians of more than half a century ago had already noticed that, in agricultural countries, in years of a good harvest, which mean prosperity, the marriage rate went up; while, in years of poor crops, the movement was opposite. With the industrialization of these countries, the harvest ceased to play an exclusively important part in the economic well-being of the country, industrial prosperity or depression having taken its place. Accordingly, many authors have tried to show that years of industrial prosperity or revival tend to increase the marriage rate, while years of industrial de-

---

[70] See OETTINGEN, A., *Die Moralstatistik*, 1881; VON MAYR, G., *Statistik und Gesellschaftslehre*, Vols. II and III; LEVASSEUR, E., *La population française*, Vols. I and II; TSCHUPROFF, A., and POSTNIKOW, *The Influence of the Harvests on Various Sides of Social Life*, Vols. I and II, Russ.; DENIS, H., *La dépression économique et sociale et l'histoire des prix*, Bruxelles, 1895; "Les index numbers des phénomènes moraux," *Memoirs de l'Academie Royale de Belgique*, Vol. IV, 1911; LESCURE, J., *Les crises générales et périodiques de surproduction*, 1910; TUGAN-BARANOVSKY, M., *Les crises industrielles en Angleterre*, 1913, (orig. Russ.); AFTALION, A., *Les crises périodiques de surproduction*, 1913; FARR, W., *Vital Statistics*, 1885; OGLE, W., "On Marriage Rates and Marriage Ages," *Journal of Royal Statistical Society*, June, 1890; BEVERIDGE, W., *Unemployment*, 1912; HOOKER, "Correlation of the Marriage-rate with Trade," *Journal of Royal Statistical Society*, 1901, pp. 485–492; JUGLAR, C., "Y-a-t-il des periodes pour les mariages," etc., *Bulletin de l'Institut Intern. de Statistique*, Vol. XIII, 1903; YULE, G. U., "On Changes in the Marriage-Birth-rates in England and Wales during the Past Half-Century," *Journal of Royal Statistical Society*, Vol. LXIX; DAVIES, G. P., "Social Aspects of the Business Cycle," *Quarterly Journal of the University of North Dakota*, Jan., 1922; BOWLEY, A. L., *Elements of Statistics*, 1907; OGBURN, W. F., and THOMAS, D. S., "The Influence of the Business Cycle on Certain Social Conditions," *Journal American Statistical Society*, Sept., 1922; THOMAS, D. S., *Social Aspects of the Business Cycle*, London, 1925; HEXTER, M. B., *Social Consequences of Business Cycles*, Boston and N. Y., 1925. In the last two books there is given a good summary of the principal studies in this field.

pression are marked by its decrease. The greater the contrast between the period of depression and revival, the more noticeable is the fluctuation of the marriage rate. The correlations obtained by different authors between various economic conditions, and the fluctuations of the marriage rate, are as follows:

Kind of Correlation	Author	Years and Country	Coefficient of the Correlation
Between marriage rates and: Exports per head.......	Hooker	England, 1861–1895	+ .80 (method of moving averages)
Imports per head.......	Hooker	England, 1861–1895	+ .79
Total trade per head....	Hooker	England, 1861–1895	+ .86
Price of wheat..........	Hooker	England, 1861–1895	+ .38
Sauerbeck index numbers	Yule	England, 1865–1896	+ .795
Unemployment index...	Yule	England, 1870–1895	− .873
Unemployment index...	March	England, 1870–1895	− .73
Trade of the same year..	March	England, 1870–1895	+ .78
Wholesale index numbers	Davies	U. S. A., 1887–1906	+ .67
Complex business barometer.................	W. Ogburn and D. Thomas	U. S. A., 1866–1906	+ .66 and + .87
Complex business barometer.................	D. Thomas	England, 1854–1913 England, 1854–1874 England, 1875–1895 England, 1895–1913	+ .67 + .64 + .84 + .57
Wholesale prices........	Hexter	Boston, U. S. A., 1900–1920	+ .469 (marriage lags 1 month)

These data show that there is a pretty high correlation between economic conditions and the marriage rate. However, we see from the data that it is not perfect. It fluctuates considerably from country to country, and from period to period. This, together with the above mentioned fact, indicates that the movement of marriages is considerably determined by economic conditions, but not entirely by them. The differences between the perfect coefficient, 1, and the obtained coefficients indicate roughly the amount of influence of other non-economic factors on the movement and the fluctuation of the marriage rate. If we also take into consideration the "trend" of the marriage rate, the rôle of the non-economic factors will possibly be still more important, because all attempts to correlate the trends with economic conditions have not yielded any unquestionable results.

B. The above mentioned studies, and some others have also shown that there is a noticeable correlation between the *fluctuation of economic conditions and the birth rate.* With a lag of about one or two years the birth rate tends to increase in the periods of economic prosperity, and to decrease in those of depression. The coefficients of correlation on page 555 show the situation.

These data show that the birth rate seems to be less closely correlated with business cycles than the marriage rate. The coefficient of correlation is lower here than in the marriage rate. Hexter's relatively high coefficients are related to periods which are somewhat questionable, since we do not know whether or not, "psychologically," there is a possibility for individuals to foresee or to feel the approaching improvement or aggravation of the economic conditions. However it may be, a lesser dependence of the birth rate upon economic conditions is suggested by these data. With the exception of periods of great economic misery, amounting to famine, when the birth rate falls considerably (look at the data of India for the years of famine, and the famine of 1917-1922 in Russia for this purpose) the usual normal fluctuations of business conditions seem to influence only slightly, though noticeably, the fluctuation in the birth rate. Taking also into consideration the fact that trends in the movement of the birth rate have not been satisfactorily explained by economic factors, we are forced to think that, in this field, the rôle of economic factors is still less marked than in the field of marriage fluctuation.

C. As to *the death rate,* among the investigators previous to the great work of Malthus, there was a somewhat greater unanimity in admitting a close correlation between the fluctuation of the death rate and that of economic conditions. There is no doubt that a great economic impoverishment, amounting to misery and famine, greatly increases the death rate; but it was also

Correlation between Birth Rate and the Indicated Economic Conditions	Author	Country and Period	Coefficient of Correlation
Trade of two years earlier.	Yule	England, 1850–1896	+ .479
Business barometer of one year earlier...........	Ogburn and Thomas	U. S. A., 1870–1920	+ .33
Business barometer of one year earlier...........	Ogburn and Thomas	England and Wales, 1874–1910	+ .15
Business barometer of one, two, three years earlier..	D. Thomas	England and Wales, 1854–1913	+ .29, + .30
	D. Thomas	England and Wales, 1854–1874	"no significant coefficient"
	D. Thomas	England and Wales, 1875–1894	+ .35, + .34
	D. Thomas	England and Wales, 1895–1913	+ .64, + .42
Wholesale prices of one month earlier..........	Hexter	Boston, 1900–1920	+ .705; synchronous, + .516
Or when conceptions lead by eleven months.......	Hexter	Boston, 1900–1920	
Employment with a lag of seventeen months.......	Hexter	Boston, 1900–1920	− .696; synchronous, − .090

Seasonal synchronous fluctuations of birth rate and unemployment leading 10 months... − .474
Seasonal synchronous fluctuations of birth rate and unemployment leading 2 months... + .440

thought that any economic depression had to increase it proportionately, while any economic improvement decreased it. More recent and careful studies have yielded results which either do not show any noticeable correlation between business fluctuation and that of the death rate, or else give somewhat contradictory results. Dr. Yule found that since 1850 (in England and Wales) "there is no evidence that the death-rate has tended to rise in time of depression. For a very striking instance of this we have only to turn to the records of the past few years. 1921, 1922 and 1923 have been years of record low death-rates, in spite of the greatest and most widespread depression of industry to which we have ever been subject." [71] For several states of the United States, in the period from 1870 to 1920, W. Ogburn and D. Thomas found the correlation a pretty high one: +.57; and with cycles from nine-year moving averages, +.63; but, contrary to expectation, the correlation happened to be positive. Instead of a decrease, the death rate in the period of prosperity increased, and *vice versa*. Dr. Thomas' study of the data for England and Wales in 1854 to 1913 yielded a correlation which with the death rate lagging a year behind the business cycle, is positive also: +.30. For the subperiod from 1854 to 1874, the coefficient is +.24; for the period 1875-1894, +.32; [72] for the period 1895-1913, +.35. [73] M. B. Hexter's results are considerably different. The correlation between the death rate and wholesale prices obtained by him is +.613 (death lead by 17 months); that between the death rate and unemployment is —.361 (death lead by 10 months). [74] These data are nearer to the usual expectation, and to the results of the earlier investigators.

The above entitles us to think that, at the present moment, the relation between business fluctuation and the death rate is much more complex and not so close as we used to think. Economic conditions probably exert some influence on the death rate, but it is rather remote, often intangible, and sometimes it is modified

[71] YULE, G. U., "The Growth of Population and the Factors which Control It," *Journal of Royal Statistical Society*, 1925, p. 30; also his quoted paper: *On the Changes in the Marriage*, etc., *passim*.

[72] THOMAS, D., *op. cit.*, p. 69.

[73] *Ibid.*, p. 109. Among recent studies which show the insignificant rôle of economic and occupational conditions on the infant mortality rate and on children's health, and the more important rôle of an inherited constitution, are to be mentioned the studies of E. Elderton (*Annals of Eugenics*, Vol. I) with the coefficient of correlation 0.03 between infant mortality and all environmental conditions; of D. N. Paton and L. Finlay (*Medical Research Council*, *Special Report Series*, No. 101, London, 1926); of M. Greenwood and J. Brown (*Journal of Hygiene*, Vol. XII). On the other hand, see COLLINS, S., *Economic Status and Health*, 1927; WOODBURY, R. M., *Infant Mortality*, 1926.

[74] HEXTER, *op. cit.*, pp. 144–150, 161.

by the non-economic factors. In brief, it is far from being the principal factor in this field, unless economic impoverishment amounts to starvation and a lack of the minimum necessities. In this case, Malthus' laws begin to work.

D. Somewhat indefinite, and contradictory also, are the correlations between the fluctuation of *business conditions and that of the divorce rate.* The data of W. Wilcox, W. Ogburn, and D. Thomas for the U. S. yielded a noticeable positive correlation, $+.70$ for 1867 to 1906; and $+.33$ for the thirteen states in the period 1867-1920. The data of England, studied by Thomas, did not give any noticeable or uniform correlation.[75] The coefficients obtained by Hexter also happened to be very low, the highest being $-.308$ (with divorce lagging by 24 months). These results would seem to entitle us to think that the divorce movement is still less dependent on economic conditions than the birth, death, and marriage rates.

The above shows approximately the character of the correlations between economic factors and vital processes, its degree of closeness, and the methods of contemporary study of these correlations. If, on the whole, the vital processes are sensitive to economic conditions, they could, in no way, be accounted for only through the economic factor taken as an independent variable.[76]

6. ECONOMIC CONDITIONS, SUICIDE, PAUPERISM, AND CRIME

Suicide.—Long ago, many investigators noticed some correlation between economic conditions and suicides. A considerable number of them have thought that impoverishment or poverty favors suicide, while economic betterment and wealth favors its decrease. Later investigations, and among them especially Durkheim's study, have showed that the relation between the discussed phenomena is more complex and less close. Statistics show that the poorer classes do not give, as a general rule, a higher per cent

[75] THOMAS, D., *ibid.,* pp. 67-68, 90-93.

[76] By the way, the above and the following pages show how far the scientific study has left behind the metaphysical, speculative, and verbal Marxian discussions about "the basis" and "superstructure," "primary" and "secondary" factors, and so on. The difference between these and the "Marxian" studies of the rôle of the economic factor is scarcely less than between the alchemy of the Middle Ages, and contemporary chemistry.

of suicide than the well-to-do classes. They show also that, in spite of a general rise in the standard of living in the nineteenth century, the suicide rate increased rather than decreased. Furthermore, the wealthier geographical regions of the same country often give a higher per cent of suicide than the poorer ones. These, and some other considerations, indicate that, if there is a correlation between economic conditions and suicide, it is rather indirect and somewhat complex.[77]   On the other hand, it has been observed many times that periods of acute economic panic are almost invariably followed by an increase of suicide.[78]   Recent studies of the correlation of the suicide rate with business conditions made by Ogburn and Thomas, have given the coefficient of the correlation —.74 for the U. S. and — .50 for England and Wales.[79]   Durkheim's theory that poverty or wealth are only indirect facilitating factors of suicide—as far as they increase social isolation (*l'anomie sociale,* liberation of an individual from social rules) seems to be more in harmony with these contradictory data than any other.[80]   This means again that, in this field, the rôle of economic conditions is far from being decisive.   Even if we do not accept Durkheim's theory, the results obtained show a tangible, but not exclusive, influence of economic conditions on suicide.

Pauperism.—A close correlation in the fluctuation of pauperism with that of other economic conditions results simply from the fact that pauperism itself is an economic phenomenon.   What is more interesting is that, in spite of this, the correlation is not perfect.   Miss Howland's study of poor relief in Massachusetts and F. S. Chapin's study of the dependency index for Minneapolis yielded the following coefficients of correlation :

---

[77] See DURKHEIM, E., *Le suicide,* Chap. V;   see VON MAYR, G., *Statistik und Gesellschaftslehre,* Vol. III, pp. 258–406, especially pp. 353–359.   See in these works the literature and the data.

[78] See DURKHEIM, *op. cit.,* pp. 264 ff.

[79] THOMAS, *op. cit.,* pp. 73 and 114–116.

[80] "*Si donc les crises industrielles ou financières augmentent les suicides, ce n'est pas parce qu'elles appauvrissent; c'est parce qu'elles sont des crises, c'est-à-dire des perturbations de l'ordre collective.   Toute rupture d'équilibre, alors même qu'il en résulte une plus grande aisance et un rehaussement de la vitalité générale, pousse à la morte volontaire.   Toutes les fois que de graves réarrangements se produisent dans les corps social, qu'ils soient dus à un soudain mouvement de croissance ou à un cataclysme inattendue, l'homme se tue plus facilement.*"   DURKHEIM, *ibid.,* p. 271; see the whole of Chapter V.

Between the number receiving poor relief and wage
index .... —.62
Between the number receiving poor relief and business
failures .... +.44 [81]
Between the dependency index in Minneapolis and C.
Snyder's Clearing Index of Business for a six-
months lag .... —.556 [82]

Dr. D. Thomas' study in England gave the coefficient of correlation —.52, between indoor relief and the business barometer, with a one-year lag for relief. For the outdoor relief (relief of paupers in their homes) the coefficient is —.32.[83] This means that even this phenomenon, which might be expected to be in the closest dependence on economic conditions, is, in fact, influenced by many other factors. As far as the phenomenon of poverty and pauperism generally is concerned, an attempt to account for their existence, amount, character, and social distribution through economic conditions alone is a rather hopeless business. These complex phenomena are the resultant of many and various factors, economic, as well as non-economic. A series of studies has made this more or less clear.[84]

Crimes.—The correlation between economic conditions and crime, especially crime against property, was known long ago. Investigations have shown that often the poor classes give a higher quota of crime against property than the well-to-do classes; and that the geographical districts of a country, or city, which are inhabited by the poor, give a higher rate of criminality than the districts of the well-to-do classes. Further, many authors have indicated a parallelism in the movement of crime against property

[81] HOWLAND, K. E., "A Statistical Study of Poor Relief in Mass.," *Journal of American Statistical Society*, Dec., 1922.

[82] CHAPIN, F. S., "A Dependency Index for Minneapolis," *Publications of the American Sociological Society*, Vol. XIX, pp. 200–202; also "Dependency Indexes for Minneapolis," *Social Forces*, May, 1926.

[83] THOMAS, *op. cit.*, Chap. VI.

[84] See the literature, the data, and the factors in GILLIN, J., *Poverty and Dependency*, N. Y., 1922; ROWNTREE, B. S., *Poverty*, London, 1906; PARMELEE, M., *Poverty and Social Progress*, 1921; LIDBETTER, E. J., "Pauperism and Heredity," *The Eugen. Review;* BOOTH, CHARLES, *Life and Labor of the People of London*, all volumes; DEXTER, R. C., *Social Adjustment*, N. Y., 1927.

For a correlation between business cycles and unemployment see *Business Cycles and Unemployment*, the papers of W. A. Berridge, W. C. Mitchell, F. R. Macaulay, W. J. King, P. F. Brissenden, S. A. Rice, N. Y., 1923.

and that of the price of wheat or bread in agricultural countries; many other investigators have shown that, in industrial countries, the periods of depression have been marked by an increase in crime against property, while the periods of prosperity have been marked by its opposite course.   So-called "seasonal fluctuation" of crimes against property, when the cold winter months show an increase, and the warm months show a decrease, seem to point at the same economic factor.   In brief, a series of such studies seems to have made certain the existence of a correlation between economic conditions and crime, especially crimes against prop erty.[85]   Admitting the correlation, it is necessary, however, not to exaggerate it.   Many of the investigators have shown that not only the movement of crime generally, but even that of crime against property, could not be accounted for through economic factors alone.   Several studies, and among them that of G. Richard and my own, have shown that an extraordinary increase of crime in the periods of social upheaval is due to other than purely economic conditions.[86]   Secondly, not everywhere nor always do the poor show a greater proportion of crime.   Third, many poorer countries have had less crime than the richer countries. Fourth, the improvement in the economic conditions of the population of the Western countries in the second half of the nineteenth century, and at the beginning of the twentieth, has not been followed by a decrease of crime.   Fifth, among those who commit crime against property there is always a considerable number of well-to-do people, and, on the other hand, many of the poorest

[85] A. Quetelet, A. Oettingen, E. Levasseur, G. von Mayr, Tarnovsky, Bosco, H. Denis, L. Moreau-Christophe, A. Corne, M. Gernet, Foinitzky, Charykhow, A. Meyer, W. Starcke, Tugan-Baranovsky, J. Bertillon, Villermé, B. Weisz, H. Müller, E. Fornasari di Verce, A. Lacassagne, A. Corre, P. Lafargue, P. Hirsch, M. Yvernès, G. Tarde, E. Ferri, R. Mayo-Smith, Van Kahn, Bonger.—These are a few of the great many who have studied crime from the discussed standpoint. See the data and the literature in VON MAYR, G., op. cit., Vol. III; BONGER, W. A., Criminality and Economic Conditions, Boston, 1916; VAN KAHN, J., Les causes économiques de la criminalité, Paris, 1903; GILLIN, J., Criminology and Penology, 1926; PARMELEE, M., Criminology, 1923; the quoted works of Levasseur and Oettingen; GERNET, M., Crime and Its Prevention, Russ.; CHARYKHOW, Factors of Criminality, Russ.; JIJILENKO, A., Factors of Crime, Russ.; ASCHAFFENBURG, G., Crime and its Repression, Boston, 1913.

[86] See RICHARD, G., "Les crises sociales et les conditions de la criminalité," L'année sociologique, 1899; SOROKIN, P., Crime and Punishment, Russ., Chap. X; Sociology of Revolution, 1925, Chap. IX.

people do not commit such crimes. Sixth, it is an ascertained fact that, in the causation of crime and criminals a great many non-economic factors play an important rôle.[87] Seventh, practically all correlations between economic conditions and crime are far from being perfect, or even notably high. Eighth, there is only a relatively low coefficient of correlation found between crime and business conditions, through a relatively fine mathematical analysis.[88] These, and many similar facts, do not at all permit us to think that the phenomena of crime are controlled by economic conditions only. They do not permit us even to think that these conditions are the most important factor. All that they entitle us to conclude is that economic conditions play a serious rôle in this respect.

7. ECONOMIC CONDITIONS AND MIGRATION

With a reasonable degree of certainty, it is possible to contend that the phenomena of migration in a population (its direction, character, and amount) are considerably correlated with the economic phenomena. An aggravation of the economic situation in a country of emigration, and an improvement of it in the country of immigration, facilitates the increase of emigration from the first to the second country, and *vice versa*. A series of studies relative to the migration of primitive tribes and many ancient peoples, of the statistics of emigration and immigration for the last few decades, and of the data of migration in various countries at the periods of famine, corroborate this expectation.[89] In

[87] See the works of von Mayr, Oettingen, Gillin, Levasseur, Parmelee and others. See also SUTHERLAND, E., *Criminology*, 1924.

[88] According to G. Davies, the annual admissions to N. Y. state prisons, 1896–1915, correlated with the price index, gives a coefficient of − .41; W. Ogburn's and D. Thomas' coefficient of the correlation between the business cycle and movement of crime is − .35. For crimes against the person it is only − .12. Thomas' coefficients of the correlation for England and Wales, 1857–1913, are: for crime generally, − .25; for crimes against property only, without violence, − .25; for crimes against property with violence, − .44; for crimes of violence against the person, .06; for crimes against morals, .05. DAVIES, *op. cit.;* OGBURN, W., and THOMAS, D., *op. cit.;* Thomas, D., *op. cit.*, pp. 143–144. These coefficients show how naïve is the expectation that with an improvement of economic conditions the phenomena of crime will disappear.

[89] A detailed study of this was given in my book destroyed by the Soviet government: *The Influence of Famine and the Food Factor on Human Behavior, Social Organization, and Social Processes*, Chap. VI; see the data in PHILIPPOVICZ, "Auswanderung," in *Handwörterbuch d. Staatswissenschaften*, ed. by Conrad, 3d.

a recent study, D. Thomas corroborates this expectation by correlating the number of emigrants from the United Kingdom to the United States, (1870-1913) with the business conditions in the United States, and she found the coefficient +.77. Correlating emigration with the business cycle in both countries she found the coefficient +.65.[90] Both coefficients are sufficiently high to warrant the above established contention. A similar conclusion is reached in a recent study of the problem by H. Jerome.[91] Other similar facts seem to show that human migrations, being considerably controlled by economic conditions, are, at the same time, controlled by many other factors.[92] This is recently shown by the facts of Soviet Russia, where, owing to the internal prohibition against leaving, and the opposition from other countries, there has been little emigration in spite of the famine conditions prevailing. The United States' law which limits immigration is another case in point.

8. ECONOMIC CONDITIONS, SOCIAL ORGANIZATION, AND INSTITUTIONS

We have seen that Marxianism and the economic interpretation of history claim that the character of the means, and the instruments of production, determine the social, political and ideological superstructure of society. Guided by this simplicist theory, many "investigators" have tried to "corroborate" it through some "factual" studies. Studies in the field of the "economic interpretation" of social organization and institutions of primitive people are especially numerous. Some authors like F. Engels, E. Grosse, H. Cunow, and partly G. De Greef have tried to show that the forms of production and economic relationship determine the

---

ed., Vol. II; DENIS, H., "Le mouvement de la population" in *Memoirs of the Belgian Academy of Science*, Vol. LIX, 1900; TUGAN-BARANOVSKY, M., *op. cit.;* VON WALTERSHAUSEN, SART., "Einwanderung," in *Handwörterbuch d. Staatswissenschaften*, ed. by Conrad, 3d ed., Vol. III; VON MAYR, S., *op. cit.*, Vol. II; MAYO-SMITH, *Statistics and Sociology;* COLETTI, FR., *Dell' emigrazione italiana*, Milano, 1912; several articles in the volumes of the *Bulletin de l'Inst. Intern. Stat.;* RAVENSTEIN, E. G., "The Laws of Migration," *Journal Royal Statistical Society*, Vol. XLVIII, pp. 167-227.

[90] THOMAS, *op. cit.*, p. 151.

[91] JEROME, HARRY, *Migration and Business Cycles*, Chaps. IV–VIII, National Bureau of Economic Research, N. Y., 1926.

[92] JEROME, H., *op. cit.*, Chap. VI.

types of family, property, and political institutions.[93] Some others, like A. Loria, K. Kautsky, and A. Groppali went still further and pretended to establish a close correlation between economic factors and the forms and variation of political and juridical institutions, religious beliefs, morals, *mores,* ideologies, literature and arts. All these phenomena are depicted by such authors as a "mere bizarre reflection" of, or a "superstructure" on, an economic "basis." [94] All the mysteries of human history are made "simple," and even too "simple" in these works. Any social process they solve as a simple equation with one unknown.[95]

---

[93] ENGELS, F., *Der Ursprung der Familie, des Privateigentum und des Staates;* GROSSE, E., *Die Formen der Familie und die Formen der Wirtschaft,* Freiburg, 1896; DE GREEF, G., *Introduction à la sociologie,* Vol. II., pp. 142 ff., Paris, 1889; CUNOW, H., *Die Verwandschafts organisationen der Australneger,* Stuttgart, 1894; *Zur Urgeschichte der Ehe und Familie,* Stuttgart, 1912.

[94] See LORIA, A., *The Economic Foundations of Society,* London, 1899; *Le leggi organiche della costituzione economica i le forme storiche della constituzione economica,* Torino, 1889; *Sociology,* 1901; *The Economic Synthesis,* N. Y., 1914; GROPPALI, A., *Lezioni di Sociologia,* Torino, 1902; *Elementi di Sociologie,* Genova, 1905; KAUTSKY, K., *Foundations of Christianity,* N. Y., 1925; CUNOW, H., *Ursprung der Religion und des Gottesglaubens,* Berlin, 1913; *Die Marxsche Geschichts—, Gessel—, und Staatstheorie,* Bd. II; KELLES-KRAUZ, C., "Influences du facteur économique sur la musique," *Annales de L'Institut Intern. de Sociologie,* 1903, pp. 305–321; EULENTHROPOULOS, ABR., *Wirtschaft und Philosophie,* Vols. I, II, 1900–1901. Less one-sided is KINDERMAN, C., *Volkswirtschaft und Kunst.* A cheaper and more primitive type of the same kind of "interpretation" is given in an enormous number of essays by the Marxian journalists and by socialistic and communistic propaganda literature. An example of such a cheap "interpretation" of literature from the Marxian standpoint is given in LEO TROTSKY'S, *Literature and Revolution,* N. Y., 1925. This old European kind of interpretation is now being introduced into the United States as something quite modern by a group of journalistic writers in "Modern Review," and in other socialistic and communistic periodicals of America.

[95] Here are the most conspicuous examples of such "interpretations": "Pantheism and migration of the soul of Kabbala is nothing but a metaphysical expression of the value of merchandise and its exchange."—LAFARGUE, P., *Die Geschichte des Sozialismus im Einzeldarstellungen,* Stuttgart, 1895, Vol. II, p. 489; "the philosophy of Hartmann is an expression of the disintegration of the German bourgeoisie" (A. Eulenthropoulos); "the Reformation is nothing but a revolt of the German countries against Papal exploitation." (Loria, Kautsky); "the disappearance of Palestrina's quiet sweetness in music, of the eighteenth century, is caused by the development of capitalism and its satellite, class-struggle." The introduction of the fugue into music by the second Venetian school is interpreted as a "musical reflexion of the passionate social fights" (Kelles-Krauz). The origin of picture-painting is explained through the appearance of the *bourgeoisie.* The whole of religion, law, morals, and "public opinion" is interpreted as a mere system of control by the upper classes for the sake of an exploitation of the lower classes and a prevention of their revolt. (LORIA, *Economic Foundations of Society,* 1899, pp. 9 ff.) See other examples in KOVALEVSKY, M., *Contemp. Sociologists,* Chap. V; BARTH, P., *op. cit.,* pp. 677 ff.

All they contend is that there is the closest correlation between the economic factor and other social phenomena, including science, philosophy, religion, literature, arts, and what not. This contention they "prove" very simply by the method of speculation and illustration. Having a definite preconception in mind, they, consciously or unconsciously, take one or two suitable examples, especially from narratives about the primitive peoples, and the desired correlation is proved and the economic factor corroborated.

The data (of ethnology, anthropology, and history of civilization) are so vast and so various that it must be an unskilled selector who is unable, by giving prominence to the instances which agree and by ignoring those which conflict with his views, to make out a plausible case in support of some general notion (of human evolution).[96]

These words explain the essence of the method of "illustration" used by such writers, and generally by the early ethnologists, anthropologists, and historians of culture. It is evident that the scientific value of such a method is nil.[97]   Nil also is the value of the results obtained through such a method.[98]   In the last few decades, luckily for social science, this was understood by many

[96] HOBHOUSE, L., WHEELER, G. C., and GINSBERG, M., *The Material Culture and Social Institutions of the Simpler Peoples*, p. 1, London, 1915.

[97] See its criticism in SOMLÔ, F., *Zur Grundung einer beschreibenden Soziologie*, Berlin, 1909; also STEINMETZ, S. R., "Classification des types sociaux," *L'année sociologique*, Vol. III.

[98] Take Loria's works as an example. They are, comparatively, the best in this kind of literature. To Loria everything is simple. If there is a free land it determines a lack of class division, of exploitation, religion, law, and of morals. In this case we have a society of free producers,—happy, equal and wisely controlled by their "enlightened egoism." If, owing to some miraculous machinations of the capitalists (miraculous because Loria does not explain how these "capitalists" could enslave and subjugate the laborers, nor how they have succeeded in instilling into their minds, with moral, religious, juridical and public opinion, rules of conduct whose only purpose is to help to exploit the labor ng man), they succeed in barring a free access to the land, then class differentiation, exploitation, and so on appears, and with them, law, morals, religion, and public opinion. However, a reader of Loria is consoled, for he (Loria) guarantees that "the final economic form of society," which will be free from "all manner of usurpation and every species of conflict" is coming, and everything will be harmonious and perfect. It would take hundreds of pages to indicate the shortcomings of Loria's *Economic Foundations of Society*. It is enough to say that the whole theory is speculative, and has only a very remote relationship to either scientific methods, or to a scientific scrutiny of facts. See, for instance, the whole of Parts I and II. Factual criticism of the book may be found in KOVAL-EVSKY, *op. cit.*, pp. 249–286.

investigators, and, as a result there appeared a series of works which permitted the establishment of more accurate relationships between economic factors, and other social phenomena. On the other hand, they gave a solid basis for deciding to what extent the pretentious generalizations of the "economic interpreters of history" were valid.

Let us survey the principal results of these more scientific works, and, through them, find out what the correlations between economic conditions and various complex social phenomena are.

9. ECONOMIC CONDITIONS, INCLUDING THE TECHNOLOGY OF PRODUCTION, AND FORMS OF SOCIAL ORGANIZATION AND POLITICAL INSTITUTIONS

One of the most important works in this field is *The Material Culture and Social Institutions of the Simpler Peoples* by L. T. Hobhouse (1864–   ), G. C. Wheeler and M. Ginsberg, together with the studies of J. Mazzarella, summed up in his *Les types sociaux et le droit*.[99] The principal purpose of the first study is to determine whether or not there is a correlation between economic conditions and social institutions, and, if it exists, just what it is. As a starting point the authors take "material culture" as "the control of man over nature as reflected in the arts of life." This corresponds to the Marxian economic factor; they, however, take it not as the Marxian "primary cause," but as a methodological "independent variable." The authors differ from Marx in saying that "material culture is a fair index of the general level of knowledge, and, if we may use a more general term, of mentality" (pp. 6, 16). In order to avoid a use of "the method of illustration" the authors carefully classified all more or less studied peoples (more than four hundred) according to their material culture or means and instruments of production, or their methods for procuring a living. This gives the following classification of the peoples:

[99] See the excellent volumes of his *Studi di etnologia guiridica*, Catania, 1903, and subsequent years. Mazzarella was the first author who took pains to avoid "the method of illustration" in ethnology. He elaborated the principles of a much better and sounder stratigraphic method for analyzing social organizations and causal relations.

lower hunters
higher hunters

agricultural (lowest)	pastoral (lower)
agricultural (higher)	pastoral (higher)

agricultural (still higher)

After this they proceeded to find out the correlations between these forms of material culture and various social institutions. They did this by making a careful statistical study of all these peoples one by one, and by giving the results in the form of quantitative tables and diagrams, which permit one roughly to measure the closeness of the correlations. The tables on page 567, a few out of the many given by the authors, may give an idea of the results obtained. (*Ibid.*, p. 50.)

The table shows, first, that the same form of material culture (economic basis) is connected with the most various forms of government (read horizontal lines), and *vice versa;* and that the same form of government is found among various economic cultures (read vertical lines). This means that there is no basis for claiming that "the character of the forces of production and relationships of production" are closely correlated with definite forms of political "superstructure," or that the political institutions are but the function of the economic factor. On the other hand, the table shows also that some forms of government are more conspicuous among the peoples of a definite stage of material culture than among other peoples. For instance, the per cent of cases with slight or no government is 47 per cent for "lower hunters" and nothing for the "agricultural peoples III." This suggests that some correlation exists between "economics" and "government," but it is far from being high or close. The same conclusion is corroborated by the data which show that "trends" in the evolution of the forms of government, as we pass from the lower hunters to the agricultural peoples III, are rather fanciful and capricious.

Practically the same conclusions are suggested by all other tables given by the authors. Here are some of them in an abbreviated form:

CORRELATION BETWEEN THE FORMS OF MATERIAL CULTURE AND THE FORMS OF GOVERNMENT

Classes of Peoples	Total Number Studied	Government Hereditary	Government Personal	Powerful	Influential	Powerful in War	Powers in War and Peace Distinct	Council Powerful	Government Slight or Nil
Lower hunters........	36	8	6	3	10	0	0	5.5	17
Higher hunters	75	20.5	17	13.5	32.5	1	2	9	19
Dependent hunters.....	8	1	1	4.5	0	0	0	3	1
Agricultural I	37	7	10	7	13.5	4	5	8	10
Pastoral I...........	16	1	4	2	8	0	1	4	2
Agricultural II........	119	34	22	20	34.5	9	4	24	12
Pastoral II..........	16	2	5	1	6	0	1	3.5	0
Agricultural III.......	96	16.5	14.5	7	23	2	0	19	0
Total.............	403	90	79.5	58	127.5	16	13	76	61

MATERIAL CULTURE AND FORMS OF JUSTICE

The per cent each of the four forms of justice composes to the total number of cases of each class of people

Classes of Peoples	Total Per Cent	Self-Redress and No Law	Self-Redress with Public Intervention	Public Intervention with Elements of Self-Redress	Public Justice as a Regular System
Lower hunters.......	100	40	58	2	0
Higher hunters......	100	62	30	3	5
Dependent hunters...	100	17	11	61	11
Agricultural I.......	100	48	21	10	21
Pastoral I..........	100	28	32	24	16
Agricultural II......	100	35	18	23	24
Pastoral II..........	100	19	19	13	48
Agricultural III.....	100	11	17	30	41

Somewhat similar are the data in regard to the methods of punishment (retaliation, composition, atonement, etc.), and in regard to the forms of procedure (trial, ordeal, oath).—(See the tables on pages 569 to 573.)

Similar are the pictures given in regard to chastity, public control of marriage, and so on. The tables show even more clearly than the table concerning government and justice, that there is no more or less high and convincing correlation between the economic factor and the forms of marriage and family. Some correlation seems to exist, but it is very low and almost intangible in regard to many traits of family and marriage institutions.

Material Culture and War.—Of the 298 peoples studied, only in nine cases has "no war" been found. There were four cases among the lower hunters, two cases among the higher, and two among the lower agricultural peoples. Thus, contrary to popular opinion, "organized war rather develops with the advance of industry and of social organization in general" (p. 228). The tables show that even in relatively primitive societies, where the power of purely economic needs is supposed to be especially

MATERIAL CULTURE AND FORMS OF FAMILY, KINSHIP AND MARRIAGE

The Traits Studied	The Number of Cases Where Each Specified Characteristic of Family and Marriage Is Found in Each Class of the People							
	Lower Hunters	Higher Hunters	Dependent Hunters	Agri-cultural I	Pastoral I	Agri-cultural II	Pastoral II	Agri-cultural III
Descent								
Matrilineal..........	23	14	—	5.5	3	21	1	20
Patrilineal..........	14	12	—	6	6	15.5	6	24.5

	Per Cent of the Peoples of Each Class, Among Whom Each Specified Form Is Found, to the Total Number of the Peoples in This Class							
	Lower Hunters	Higher Hunters	Dependent Hunters	Agri-cultural I	Pastoral I	Agri-cultural II	Pastoral II	Agri-cultural III
Forms of Marriage								
Consideration given for the bride...	47 of all cases studied	66	5	61	72	76	88	81
Purchase.........	10 of all cases studied	42	38	31	61	53	83	69
Capture.........	24 of all cases studied	6	0	6	11	2	2.5	7.5

MATERIAL CULTURE AND FORMS OF FAMILY, KINSHIP AND MARRIAGE (Continued)

	Per Cent of the Peoples of Each Class, Among Whom Each Specified Form Is Found, to the Total Number of the Peoples in This Class							
	Lower Hunters	Higher Hunters	Dependent Hunters	Agricultural I	Pastoral I	Agricultural II	Pastoral II	Agricultural III
Consent of the bride is required	29	56	100	78	35	62	14	70
Not required	71	44	0	22	65	38	86	30
Total	100	100	100	100	100	100	100	100
Polygamy general	29	32	33	18	53	43	74	64
Polygamy occasional	57	61	55.5	59	40	39	26	25
Monogamy regular	14	6	11	23	7	17	0	11
Total	100	100	100	100	100	100	100	100
Divorce								
At will	40	59	4	53	5	49	29	44
At will of husband	25	26	—	25	19	14	43	31
Divorce conditioned	25	14	6	17	23	32	29	23
At will of wife	—	2	—	—	—	1	—	—
Marriage indissoluble	10	0	—	5	8	5	—	2
Total	100	about 100	100	100	100	about 100	about 100	100

Marriage	Lower Hunters	Higher Hunters	Dependent Hunters	Agricultural I	Pastoral I	Agricultural II	Pastoral II	Agricultural III
Is stable	35	14	18	22	31	36	29	25
Unstable	65	86	82	78	69	67 (?)	71	75
Total	100	100	100	100	100		100	100

Position of Women	Hunters	Pastoral	Agricultural
Good	14	10	19
Bad	82	87.5	73
Indifferent	4	2.5	8
Total	100	100.0	100

great, there is no close correlation between the methods of production (economic basis) and the forms of various social and political
institutions.   This is in spite of the fact that the studied societies
belong to quite different economic ages.   There seems to be some
correlation, but it is imperfect and loose.

Essentially similar are the results obtained by Mazzarella in his
painstaking studies of the forms of family, marriage, and priest-
hood; and of the forms of political, judicial, property, inheritance,
punishment, and other institutions.   After a most careful study

NUMBER OF CASES IN EACH FORM OF THE TREATMENT OF THE VANQUISHED [100]

Classes of Peoples	Van-quished Slain	Men Only Slain	Women and Children Slaves	Gener-ally Slaves	Adopted	Ex-changed or Set Free
Lower hunters.......	6	3	5.5	1	1	1
Higher hunters.......	23	17	10	11	9.5	7.5
Agricultural I........	15	6	1	4.5	12	0
Pastoral I..........	0	0	0	2	1	0
Agricultural II.......	44	7	8	15	14	7.5
Pastoral II..........	1	1	1	1	0	1
Agricultural III.....	16	7	6	35	2	1.5

MATERIAL CULTURE AND NOBILITY AND SLAVERY [101]

Classes of Peoples	Per Cent of Peoples in Each Class Who Have Slavery to the Total Number of the Peoples in This Class	Per Cent of the Peoples of Each Class Who Have Social Ranks of Nobility to the Total Number of the Peoples in This Class
Lower hunters........	2	0
Higher hunters........	32	11
Agricultural I..........	33	3
Pastoral I.............	37	20
Agricultural II.........	46	15
Pastoral II............	71	24
Agricultural III........	78	23

---

[100] *Ibid.*, p. 232.   [101] *Ibid.*, p. 236.

MATERIAL CULTURE AND FORMS OF PROPERTY [102]

Classes of Peoples	Per Cent of the Peoples Who Have a Specified Form of Property, to the Total Number of the Peoples in the Same Class					
	Com-munal	Inter-mixed	Private	Chief's Property	Nobles' Property	Total
Lower hunters......	69	15	15	0	0	about 100
Higher hunters......	80	6	5	3	5	about 100
Agricultural I.......	64	18	18	0	0	100
Pastoral I..........	57	0	35	0	9	about 100
Agricultural II......	54	21	13	8	4	100
Pastoral II.........	62	0	5	33	0	100
Agricultural III.....	29	24	10	27	10	100

of the area of diffusion of matriarchy, its variations, its fluctuations, and so on; and after a still more painstaking study of the "ambilian" form of family (where the bridegroom enters the family of the bride) he concludes: "These institutions do not depend directly on economic causes . . . because they are found among a great many peoples quite different in regard to economic conditions." [103]   If there is a correlation, it is remote and exceedingly indefinite. It consists in:

a lack of the labor forces necessary for the utilization and conservation. of the natural economic resources of the autonomic social groups (among whom these forms of family and marriage are found),—a lack which is determined by an insufficient number of the adult males of the groups, [and] in an existence of natural economic resources potentially or really unlimited, which require a great amount of labor to be used and preserved.[104]

The dependence of the forms of family (and of a series of other

[102] *Ibid.*, p. 251.
[103] MAZZARELLA, J., *Les types sociaux et le droit*, pp. 179–180.
[104] *Ibid.*, p. 311 and *passim*. See also CARR-SAUNDERS, A. M., *The Population Problem*. Having surveyed a series of customs (infanticide, sexual regulations, abortion, war, etc.), the author came to the conclusion that "there is no apparent connection between the practice of any of these customs, and the different economic stages," p. 237.

social institutions) rests then only very indirectly on the economic conditions of a society.

If such is the real situation, it is quite reasonable to suppose that in a more complex society, where social forces are more numerous, and their interrelations are more complex, the correlation could not be closer than in the above simple societies. The facts seem to corroborate this expectation. For the sake of brevity I shall quote Sombart's statements, which depict the situation quite accurately. Sombart convincingly shows that, contrary to Marx, technique (or the means and the instruments of production) does not tangibly determine the forms of social and economic organization.

As far as history shows, a close and necessary correlation evidently does not exist between the technique of production and the definite economic system of a society. . . . Often an already existing better technique is not applied. On the other hand, the cultural situation of a society may be such, and it has often been such, that an already existing technique becomes forgotten and ceases to be applied, either because the people become too indolent, or because they do not want to do it. If possession of a definite technique must exert a necessary influence upon the culture-complex of a society, how can we explain the decay of a whole culture without any change in the technique of production, which does not become obsolete until later? Some of the inventions which we now use were made by the Chinese thousands of years ago; and yet these did not force them to abandon their system of tiresome cultivation. In what way then does technique determine all kinds of culture?

In a similar way, we find that there is no close correlation between the character of the technique of production which is used, and the definite economic system of social organization.

There are plenty of cases where the same economic system is in use on the basis of quite different techniques of production; and there are cases where the same technique is applied in quite different economic systems. We have had, and do have, a Capitalistic system of economic organization on the basis of a technique of handwork and machine-work. The principal forms of the Capitalistic economic organization . . . remain in their substantial traits unchanged after the introduction of quite a new modern technique of production, and *vice versa.* The three-field system of farming has been applied in the economic systems of the free farmers, as well as in that of the dependent serfs. For centuries the Capitalistic system, with the same technique of production, was served here by the slaves, and there by the free working men. All this would have been impossible had the economic organization of a society been a mere function of production technique.

The dependence of non-economic cultural phenomena on the technique of production and economic organization of a society is still less pronounced, because

quite heterogeneous culture-complexes have existed under the same economic organization; and similar culture complexes have existed under heterogeneous economic systems. We have the same Capitalism in the small and in the great states; in republics and in absolute monarchies; and in the Protestant and Catholic countries. Within the same Capitalist system, we have most different forms of arts, and "sciences" such as the Catholic and the "Unprejudiced" science; and the religious-ethical and the materialistic ideological currents. The opposite is also true. Scarcely anyone may really prove that Plato, Spinoza, and Hegel belong to the three economic systems; that they are necessarily bound with the three various systems; or that they are only a function of these systems.[105]

These words sum up well that which was shown by the preceding tables. This does not mean, and Sombart does not believe, that there is no correlation between the technique of production and the economic system, or between them and the non-economic social phenomena. It means only that the correlation is remote, less definite, and more varying than has been thought by "the economic interpreters of history." Being always imperfect, the correlation in regard to some phenomena is sometimes sufficiently tangible. Sometimes, in regard to other phenomena, it is almost unnoticeable, or nil.[106] This conclusion is practically corrobo-

---

[105] SOMBART, *Technik und Kultur*, pp. 317 ff.

[106] Without regarding the technique of production as a "primary factor" it is fruitful to study its influence on various social phenomena, not in a general and speculative way, but taking in each case a definite technical object and a definite social phenomenon to be correlated. Such a study is exemplified by K. KRIES' *Die Eisenbahnen und ihre Wirkungen* (1853) and by *Sociological Aspects of Automobile Accidents in Omaha*, published by the University of Omaha, and by R. H. LOWIE's *Primitive Society*, pp. 198–201, where he indicates the changes among

rated, as far as I know, by all careful and really scientific studies of the correlation between the economic and the complex social phenomena. The following may serve as additional representative examples.

10. Economic Conditions, Strikes, Disorders, and Revolutions

One of the best studies of the correlation between the economic factors and the movement of strikes is A. H. Hansen's analysis of the number of strikes and strikers in the United States (and Canada) for the period from 1881 to 1919. Correlating it with the business cycles, he found for the period of the falling prices, 1881-1897, the coefficient of correlation between the wholesale prices and the number of the strikers,—.338; and for the second period of the rising prices, 1898-1919, the coefficient, + .494. "Strikes correlate inversely with the business cycles in periods of long-run falling prices, while they correlate directly with business cycles in periods of long-run rising prices." The coefficients are "not entirely convincing"; nevertheless, they are quite tangible.[107] This shows that even such phenomena as industrial strikes and their fluctuation are far from being accounted for completely through economic conditions.

Somewhat similar conclusions have been reached in a study of the correlation between the fluctuation of economic conditions (prosperity and poverty taken as an independent variable) and the movement of revolts, disorders, and revolutions, methodologically taken as "functions." For a relatively recent period, including the years preceding the Russian Revolution and the years of the Revolution, it has been possible to obtain comparatively

---

the Chukchee due to a shifting from fishing to reindeer-breeding; or by C. Wissler's "The Influence of the Horse in the Development of Plains Culture," *American Anthropologist*, N. S., Vol. XVI, No. 1; they are scientifically fruitful indeed. With the above limitation, the theory of a cultural lag which was developed by W. Ogburn and F. S. Chapin along the lines of the economic interpretation of history, may be accepted also, as far as it does not pretend to be exclusive, and does not insist on a close correlation between material culture and "adoptive culture." See Ogburn, W. F., *Social Change*, N. Y., 1923, Part IV, pp. 265 ff.; Chapin, F. S., "A Theory of Synchronous Culture Cycles," *Journal of Social Forces*, May, 1924, for further study of the theory.

[107] Hansen, A., "Cycles of Strikes," *American Economic Review*, Vol. XI, Dec., 1921, pp. 616–621.

detailed data. For the past history of various countries I used the method of a rough historical correlation. It consists in an opposing to the periods of improvement or aggravation of the economic situation of the masses of ancient Rome and Greece, or mediæval and modern England, France, Germany, Bohemia, and Russia, on the basis of the testimonies of contemporaries; the periods immediately preceding great revolutions and social upheavals, or those periods having a relatively stable social order. This study led to the following principal conclusions: In great social disorders, riots, revolutions, strifes,—whatever their concrete form,—the participation of economic factors seems to be certain. The periods immediately preceding such upheavals coincide usually with the periods of an aggravation of the economic situation in the corresponding society; while the periods of social order coincide with those of an improvement in economic status. The degree of aggravation and its tempo or velocity have an important significance. On the other hand, this factor alone seems to be insufficient for producing a revolution or upheaval. There have been periods of great economic aggravation (famines) which were not followed by revolution. Again, some of the upheavals happened to be in relatively prosperous periods. In order that an upheaval or revolution may take place, the combination of many other factors is necessary. Combining with the economic factors, they may produce revolution, but, when opposed to them, they may annul their effects and thwart revolution. Among such factors are the degree and the character of social differentiation; the character of political organization, of social control, of the nature of the government, of the *mores,* habits, and traditions, of religion and education, of racial qualities, of the intensity of social mobility, and of many other non-economic conditions. This means that the discussed correlation exists, but that it is far from being close.[108]

The results obtained by Professor N. Kondratieff in his study of long-time business fluctuations with a period of from 48 to 60 years gave similar results. These long-time business cycles are

[108] This study composed chapters VII and IX of my above mentioned book, *The Influence of Famine and Food-Factor,* destroyed by the Soviet government. I gave a brief summary of it in my *The Sociology of Revolution,* Chap. XVII. See also SOROKIN, *Social Mobility,* Chap. XXII.

correlated also somewhat with social upheavals, though the correlation is far from being close.[109]

11. Economic Conditions, and Various Political Phenomena and Attitudes

Among the valuable studies in this field, I may mention the works of Charles A. Beard, R. Michels, and of some others, who have elucidated the problem of an interrelation of economic and various political phenomena. Professor Beard's work, based on a careful study of a large amount of factual data, shows the rôle which economic factors had in shaping the Constitution of the United States. His principal thesis is that "the Constitution was essentially an economic document." It was created and carried through by those groups of the American population who had an economic interest in it, and it was opposed by those groups whose economic interests were opposite.

In the ratification [of the Constitution] it became manifest that the line of cleavage for and against the Constitution was between substantial personalty interests on the one hand, and the small farming and debtor interests on the other.

The movement for the Constitution of the United States was originated and carried through principally by four groups of personalty interests which had been adversely affected under the Articles of Confederation: money, public securities, manufactures, trade, and shipping.

The first firm steps toward the formation of the Constitution were taken by a small and active group of men immediately interested through their personal possession in the outcome of their labor. The members of the Philadelphia Convention which drafted the Constitution were, with few exceptions, immediately and directly and personally interested in, and derived economic advantages from, the establishment of the new system.[110]

---

[109] See KONDRATIEFF, N., *Large Cycles of Conjuncture*, Russ., in *Voprosy konjunctury*, Vol. I, pp. 45 ff. There seems to me to be one unfortunate statement in his work, when he says that the periods of upheavals are more common in the upward period of the large cycles. A study of even his own data shows that the upheavals begin at the end of the downward periods,—(of long-time cycles or at the end of a period of depression),—as he himself states in another place.

[110] BEARD, CHARLES A., *An Economic Interpretation of the Constitution of the United States*, pp. 324 ff., N. Y., 1913. See also his *Economic Basis of Politics*.

The author has succeeded in showing the existence of the correlation, but at the same time his general conclusion seems to exaggerate it somewhat.   To give a more adequate picture of the real correlation, I will take two or three of the tables given by him.[111]

PENNSYLVANIA.   NUMBER OF VOTES FOR AND AGAINST THE CONSTITUTION, ACCORDING TO ECONOMIC GROUPS

Economic Classes	For	Against
Merchants...	4	1
Doctors...	2	
Clergymen..	2	
Farmers...	10	13
Capitalists..	12	3
Lawyers...	8	1

Of the 128 men who, in the Connecticut Convention voted in favor of the Constitution, only about 65 men held public paper in such an amount as, according to the author, to make it an economic motive for favoring the Constitution.   These data are representative for all states.   Granting that the author's theory is right, his concrete figures nowhere show that the correlation between the economic interests and the favoring or disfavoring of the Constitution is perfect.   Not all the capitalists voted for the constitution, as they should have, had the correlation been perfect, but only 12 out of 15.   Not all the farmers voted against the Constitution, but only 13 out of 25.   Only 65 voters in Connecticut holding public papers (economic interests) voted for the Constitution, although a total of 128 voted.   For the remaining 63 the author does not indicate any economic motive.   These deviations apparently cannot be accounted for through economic interests.   This means that if "the line of cleavage for and against the Constitution" was correlated with economic interests, this correlation was far from being perfect; and, in many places, the line seems to have passed in quite a different direction from that of cleavage between personalty and the small farmer-debtor interests.   On the other hand, situations in which there has been a

[111] *Ibid.*, p. 280.   See the whole of Chap. X.

conflict between the interests of farmer-debtors and personalty interests have taken place several times in history; and yet they have never produced a constitution remotely similar to that of the United States.[112]   These reasons are sufficient to show that in this, as well as in all studied cases, the correlation studied is tangible but far from being perfect.

This conclusion is sustained by many similar studies of the correlations between political attitudes of various social groups and their economic interests.   Professor Robert Michels' valuable studies in the sociology of political parties,[113] especially of the socialist parties, have shown that although the socialist parties are composed principally of proletarians whose interests may be in accordance with the aspirations of the socialist parties, nevertheless, especially among their leaders there always has been a considerable number of capitalists, rich men, members of nobility, and intellectuals   On the other hand, a very considerable number of working men have always been affiliated with other than the socialist and "labor" parties.   This fact has been shown by many other studies and censuses.[114]   They show that each political party is composed of members of various economic classes.   On the other hand, members of the same economic class are affiliated with different parties.   Furthermore, the number of votes for different political parties in a country fluctuates greatly and in very short periods of time,—in France in the years from 1870 to 1911,

[112] As an additional reason, the author indicates that "a majority of the members [of the Convention] were lawyers by profession," who had the same personalty interests.   There have been few conventions in history where lawyers have not composed a considerable part; and yet, in spite of this, the laws and the constitutions framed by them have been most heterogeneous, and there have been none similar to that of the United States.

[113] See MICHELS, R., Political Parties, passim, and pp. 79 ff., 264 ff., N. Y., 1915;   Le prolétariat et la bourgeoisie dans le mouvement socialiste italien, Paris, 1921.

[114] See OSTROGORSKI, M., La démocratie et les partis politiques, Paris, 1912. R. Blank's study has shown that in Germany in 1903 about one-third of the proletariat was affiliated with other than the socialist parties, while about half a million voters for the socialist parties belonged to the "bourgeois class."   BLANK, R., "Die soziale Zusammensetzung der socialdemocratischen Wählerschaft Deutschland," Archiv für Sozialwissenschaft, 1905, Heft III.   The census of 1913 in Germany has shown that out of 5,391,000 proletarians organized in labor unions, only 2,573,000 were affiliated with the socialist parties, while the remaining part was affiliated with other than socialist parties.   See LURJE, The Composition of the Proletariat, Russ., 1918, p. 10; see other data and the literature in my System of Sociology, Vol. II, pp. 198–220, and passim.

within nine months on the average; in England, 1846 to 1924, within two years and nine months on the average. The victory used to pass from one party to another.[115] This means that within this short period the political attitude of a great part of the population changed, and changed greatly. It is evident that the composition of economic classes of the population cannot change noticeably within such a short period. We must conclude therefore that this fluctuation of the political attitudes of the population does not coincide with, is not parallel to, is considerably independent from, and could not be accounted for through fluctuation in the economic classes of the population.[116] Such discrepancies between the supposed line of cleavage of economic interests and that of political party affiliation and attitudes is again an indication of the looseness of the supposed correlation. Economic interests alone cannot account for the distribution and variation of political attitudes among the population.[117]

The same phenomena are shown still more conspicuously by W. Ogburn's and D. Peterson's study of the political thought of various social classes. They have studied the nature of the votes cast by five different social economic classes in Oregon: the rural population, the urban population, the upper class, the middle class, and the laboring class, on 103 different political matters. The votes of each class were divided into groups "for" and "against" each of these matters; and the corresponding per cent of "pros" and "cons" in each class on each measure was also computed. The results are given in Table I. In regard to all 103 political matters, there is no single case in which the whole class voted for or against a measure. In each instance a part of the same class voted against, and another part for, the measure. As a result, the votes of the members of the same class are different, and the votes of a part of the members of different classes are similar. The following few figures from the long table may illustrate this:

[115] See facts and data in SOROKIN, P., *Social Mobility*, Chap. XVI. See also TAYLOR, C. C., *Rural Sociology*, 1926, p. 447.

[116] See my *System of Sociology*, Vol. II, pp. 205–211.

[117] Statements like Kautsky's contention that "to the three big classes of present society correspond the three big political parties,—liberals (to the capitalist class), conservatives (to the landlord class) and the socialists (to the labor class)" are nothing but an inaccurate simplification of the real situation. The real correlation is much less definite and much more "loose."

Titles of Measures	Per Cent of Votes in Favor of a Measure in Each Specified Class				
	Rural	City	Upper Class	Middle Class	Laboring Class
Woman suffrage...............	46	32	21	45	29
State construction of railroad...	39	44	33	38	52
Eight-hour on public work......	53	67	49	61	80
Proportional representation....	21	25	15	16	25
Prohibition..................	61	50	46	65	31
Abolition of death-penalty.....	47	51	41	47	53

This shows that there is some correlation between the social-economic position of a people and their political attitudes, but it is far from being close.[118]

The results of S. A. Rice's study of the political votes of farmers, laboring men and of their representatives in several states of America are similar. These also show that there is a "cohesion" among the votes of the same class somewhat above a chance expectation, but it is far from being perfect and stable.[119]

Similar conclusions follow from a series of other studies. As an example I may mention W. G. Sumner's and my own study of *the factors of expansion and shrinking of governmental interference in the regulation of economic and other social relations of the population.* The amount of governmental interference is not constant; it fluctuates from society to society, and from period to period within the same society. What are the factors of this fluctuation? My study led me to the conclusion that they are numerous. Among them an especially prominent part is played by the factors of militarism, indicated by H. Spencer and W. G. Sumner, and by the economic factor in the form of improvement or aggravation of the economic situation of a considerable part of the population. Under definite conditions, impoverishment facilitates an expansion of governmental interference, while prosperity

[118] OGBURN, W., and PETERSON, D., "Political Thought of Social Classes," *Political Science Quarterly*, 1916, pp. 307 ff.
[119] See RICE, S. A., *Farmers and Workers in American Politics*, Chaps. V–VI, N. Y., 1924. The results of C. Taylor's and C. Zimmerman's study are similar.

acts in the opposite direction. Thus there is a correlation, but again it is far from being perfect.[120]

These facts and considerations lead to the conclusion that economic conditions cannot be discounted in an explanation of the various political phenomena and political attitudes of the population. Their influence is tangible in the majority of cases; but, on the other hand, they are far from being sufficient to account entirely for such phenomena. If it is unscientific to deny the existence of a correlation between the discussed phenomena, it is no less unscientific to exaggerate it, as is done by the one-sided Marxian economic interpretation of history. Factual and inductive studies do not warrant such speculations.

12. Economic Conditions and Ideologies, Religion, and Arts

In spite of the voluminous literature devoted by various investigators, especially by the Marxians, to the establishment of a correlation between economic factors and the character and fluctuation of ideologies, beliefs, and phenomena of arts and literature, it does not amount to much in a scientific respect. The speculative character of the works, the preconceptions of the authors, the permeation of the studies by a cheap propaganda spirit, the lack of scientific methods of study, the complex and delicate nature of the phenomena and many similar reasons make the value of the works questionable.[121]

[120] This study *in extenso* was given in Chapter XII of my *Influence of Famine and Food-Factor*. In a greatly abbreviated form, parts of it were published in my "The Influence of Famine on Social-Economic Organization of a Society," in the *Russian Ekonomist*, 1922, No. 2; and in my "Impoverishment and the Expansion of Governmental Control," *American Journal of Sociology*, Sept., 1926. Compare SUMNER, W. G., "State Interference" in his *War and Other Essays*.

[121] The scientific technique of experimental and quantitative study of "speech reactions" and ideological phenomena and their correlations with various factors has only recently begun to be developed. As examples of such studies, I may mention the following works: The quoted works of Ogburn and Peterson, and Rice; ALLPORT, F., and HARTMAN, D., "A Technique for the Measurement and Analysis of Public Opinion," *Proceedings Amer. Sociological Society*, Vol. XXXII, 1926; ALLPORT, F., "The Influence of the Group upon Association and Thought," *Journal Experim. Psychol.*, Vol. III, pp. 159–182, 1920; GATES, G. S., "The Effect of an Audience upon Performance," *Journal of Abnormal Psychology*, Vol. XVIII, pp. 334–345, 1924; ROOT, W. T., "The Psychology of Radicalism," Vol. XIX, pp. 341–356, 1925; MOORE, H. T., "Innate Factors in Radicalism

Of the more serious attempts, I will now mention a series of hypotheses which *try to correlate the number, the movement, and the character of inventions with various phases of business fluctuation.* Such, for instance, is the theory of Kondratieff, which contends that at the end of the downward period of a long-time business cycle, the number of inventions increases in a somewhat greater proportion than in the period of the upward movement of such a cycle.[122]   Somewhat similar is the theory briefly outlined by V. Pareto, partly by W. Ogburn, and by some others.[123]   They claim that between these phenomena there is some (not high) correlation.   The hypothesis may be probable, but the corresponding studies being somewhat rough, the hypothesis still needs to be tested.   There have been some attempts to correlate economic condition with not only a *general trend* of inventions, or of ideologies, (scientific, philosophical, religious, literary, æsthetic, moral and so on), but even in *their details.*   These hypotheses declare that "such and such an economic situation sufficiently explains how that Christianity, Kant's philosophy, or Macbeth had to *appear* at such and such a period in such and such a society; and that, if the economic conditions were known, their appearance could be predicted exactly."   These, and similar audacious attempts, are to be regarded as baseless and wrong.   I do not know any theory of this kind which is in a remote way successful in proving such a contention.[124]

---

and Conservatism," *ibid.*, Vol. XX, pp. 234–244, 1925; LUNDBERG, G., "The Newspaper and Public Opinion," *Social Forces*, June, 1926, pp. 709–715; PATERSON, D. G., and LANGLIE, T. A., "The Influence of Sex on Scholarship Ratings," *Educational Administration and Supervision*, Sept., 1926; SOROKIN, P. "Experimental Studies of the Effects of Equal and Inequal Remuneration and Pure Competition on the Efficiency of Work, etc.," *Kölner Vierteljahrshefte für Soziologie*, Vol. V.

[122] See KONDRATIEFF, *op. cit.*, pp. 47 ff.

[123] OGBURN, W., *Social Change*, 1924; PARETO, *Traité de sociologie générale*, pp. 1655 ff.

[124] The invention or creation of a definite ideological value is the function of such a multitude of different "variables," and of such complex combination, that no mathematician can disentangle them, or solve such an "equation" and establish the formulas of correlation.   For this reason, the appearance of each certain value we must regard as something which amounts to a "mere chance." It is impossible either to foresee or to predict where and when each value will be invented or created.   The authors who bravely state "that such and such an invention, religion, ideology, or theory had to be expected at a definite time, and could be predicted" practically say no more than that "Christianity appeared in Rome in the first century A. D.   Therefore it had to be expected there and

More serious and successful are the hypotheses which try to correlate the *fluctuation of popularity (contagiousness or diffusion) of a certain ideological value among certain social groups with certain economic conditions.* The above theories of Charles A. Beard, R. Michels, and so on, are samples of such theories. Further examples are Kautsky's interpretation of the origin of Christianity,[125] G. Isambert's theory concerning the factors of fluctuation in the popularity of socialist ideologies, and my own study of the same problem. In such a setting, the correlation becomes tangible in regard to certain ideologies, though not all. The following propositions may serve as examples. They concern the correlation of the character of economic groups among which communist-socialist ideologies have or have not had success; with the fluctuation of their popularity and contagious quality during certain economic conditions. Understanding communist-socialist ideology to be any ideology which requires and stimulates the actions of encroachment, expropriation, redistribution, levelling and "socialization" of the property of the well-to-do classes, regardless as to whether this is required in the name of Christ or Marx, justice or progress; it is possible to make the following propositions:

---

then." Try to make them predict three years in advance some of the ideological values which will be created, and, on the basis of some experiments made by me in the University of St. Petersburg, I do not hesitate to predict that their prophecy will fail. Not only such capricious phenomena as the appearance of a definite ideological value in a certain society at a certain period cannot be foreseen, but, unfortunately, we cannot predict with an accuracy of 100 per cent even incomparably more regular and simple social events. We cannot predict even our own to-morrow's behavior, as my study of several hundred time-budgets of the students of St. Petersburg University, kept during several months, has shown. Still less can we predict our to-morrow's "mood," or "kind of thoughts," or *"the points of mental interests"* or *"fancies";* and even still less can we predict their character and fluctuation in some other fellowman, especially in a man whom we do not know. This is enough to show the fictitiousness of the statements of the mentioned omniscient prophets.

[125] See KAUTSKY, K., *Foundations of Christianity, passim;* ISAMBERT, G., *Les idées socialistes en France de* 1815 à 1848, Paris, 1905; SOROKIN, P., "Famine and Ideology of a Society," *Ekonomist,* Russ., 1922, No. 5. Kautsky's study, however, suffers from a one-sided exaggeration of correlation, and a great simplification of reality. Isambert's theory is defective because it tries to correlate with economic conditions not only diffusion and fluctuation in the popularity of an ideology, but the moment of its creation also. The fact of creation is a function of a great many variables, and for this reason could scarcely be accounted for through economic conditions.

1. *Other conditions being equal,* a communist-socialist ideology has a greater success, and infects the poor more readily than the well-to-do classes. The well-to-do groups are more immune toward it than the poor classes.

2. *Other conditions being equal,* an increase in the economic differentiation of a society, or an impoverishment of its population, or, especially, a simultaneous increase of economic differentiation followed by an impoverishment of the masses, facilitates and increases the success of such an ideology within a society. The stronger the differentiation, the more intensive these processes will be.

3. A decrease in differentiation, or the improvement of the economic situation of the masses, or both these phenomena, lead to a decrease in the popularity or contagiousness of such an ideology.

4. When economic differentiation grows, but the economic situation of the masses improves, or when it becomes worse, but differentiation decreases, each of these variables may then neutralize each other and the popularity of such an ideology may remain constant.[126]

A series of historical and statistical data show that these propositions are likely to be accurate. They, however, stress the reservation: *"other conditions being equal,"* indicating by this that, when they are unequal, other factors may mask, annul, and disfigure the correlation, giving a fluctuation of the popularity of such an ideology, or its contagiousness among the poor and the rich which is different from the above. This means that the correlation is imperfect, and that the fluctuation and contagiousness of such an ideology depends not only upon the economic, but on many other factors.

Such an imperfect correlation is likely to exist in regard to many ideological phenomena, but scarcely in regard to all, and where it is tangible, it is never perfect. Acceptance or non-acceptance of a series of ideological values, such as the truths of mathematics and natural sciences, physics, chemistry and so on, seem not to show any tangible correlation with the economic conditions of the poor and the rich. The rules of arithmetic are accepted by both groups equally, and they are valid in the period of impoverishment, as well as of prosperity. The same may be said of many other scientific propositions. If, sometimes, some of

[126] SOROKIN, "Famine and Ideology," *Ekonomist,* Russ., 1922, No. 5, p. 6. See there the corroborations of these propositions.

them are opposed by some groups, and favored by other groups, the factors responsible for such phenomena are usually considerably different from economic ones. It is probable that, besides such scientific values, there are other ideological values (phenomena of music, art, literature, fashions, etc.), which, in their contagiousness or fluctuation of success, are also "neutral" in regard to economic factors. But even those ideological values which may not be "neutral" do not often show any noticeable correlation with the economic conditions; and if it exists, it is very loose, as in the case of all great religions. Among the Christians, the Buddhists, and the Confucianists, we find the poor and the rich. These religions have existed in periods of impoverishment, as well as of prosperity; under the system of primitive production as well as of manufacturing and the machino-manufacturing technique of production; and under slavery and serfdom, as well as in the free capitalist-economic systems. The same is true in regard to a great many other ideological (moral, literary, musical, æsthetic, and what not) systems and values. On the other hand, members of the same economic class living under the same economic system, even in the same community, usually have various and different ideologies. They often belong to different religions, have different philosophies of life, æsthetic tastes or moral convictions. They like different literature, different pictures, and different music, and belong to different parties and organizations. These obvious facts mean that even if there is a correlation of these phenomena with economic conditions, it is often intangible or very low.[127]

The task which sociologists now face in this field is to drop the discussion of the general influence of economic factors on ideologies, and to begin to study carefully the fields of ideology in which an influence of a certain economic factor exists, how close it is, and in what fields it is intangible. When such studies have

[127] Compare SOMBART, *op. cit.*, pp. 323 ff. M. Weber also says: "*Ausserlich anliche ökonomische Organisationsformen mit verschieden Wirtschaftsethik vereinbar sind und je nach deren Eigenart dann sehr verschiedene historische Wirkungen zeitigen. Ein Wirtschaftsethik ist keine einfache 'Function' wirtschaftlicher organizations formen.*" *Gesammelte Aufsätze zur Religionssoziologie*, Vol. I., p. 238. "Cultural phenomena are neither the result (*Ausfluss*) nor a mere function of economic phenomena, as is claimed by the materialistic interpretation of history." —WEBER, M., *Wirtschaftsgeschichte*, p. 16.

become numerous, we should have a series of more accurate correlations, which would give a better insight into the problem. Otherwise, we are doomed to go on teaching these indefinite and doubtful generalities which may be, and may not be, true.

13. Economic Conditions, and Decay or Progress of a Society

There are several theories which try to correlate the rise or decay of a nation with various economic factors exclusively, or with their pre-eminent influence. As the very conception of the decay or ascendancy of a nation in these theories is vague, it is hard either to prove or to disprove them. They slip between the fingers as the ancient Proteus. Until their authors take care to define more clearly what they mean by the terms "decay" or "ascendance," such theories may be discussed very briefly as something which has not yet reached the maturity of scientific hypothesis. This explains why my survey of the economic theories of decay will be brief.

Since ancient times we have had a theory which teaches that economic prosperity leads to corruption, demoralization, effeminacy, and finally, to decay (Diodorus, Q. Metellus, Polybius, Seneca, Machiavelli and others). Since ancient times, also, we have had the statements that impoverishment and poverty breed crimes, sickness, dissatisfaction, revolt, anarchy and decay. With variations, these theories have been repeated many times and are repeated now. It is evident that as a universal explanation both of the theories are fallacious. We know some "decays" which happened in the period of impoverishment,—the Western Roman Empire, for instance. The same Roman Empire, however, in its earlier history passed several periods of impoverishment, and did not decay. The majority of existing nations and empires, especially China, have known several periods of the greatest impoverishment, and have not decayed. This simple induction is sufficient to show the fallacy of the theory of decay through impoverishment. With some variation, the same may be said of the theory of decay through prosperity and economic luxury.

Let us now pass to some more complicated theories, which try to account for the phenomena of decay through the influence of economic factors. As examples I may take Brook Adams', V. Simkhovitch's, and partly, R. A. Freeman's theories. Brook Adams' theories were given in his *The Law of Civilization and Decay,* and in his *The New Empire.* Generally speaking, B. Adams gave not one, but a series of different and somewhat contradictory theories. In one place he says that the "preponderating" factor is a geographical one; [128] in another place, the racial; in still another, the economic, or the "redistribution of cosmic energy." [129] Nevertheless, the most elaborated part of his theory of decay may be styled as an "economic interpretation of decay." Its essence is as follows:

In an unavoidable struggle for life, men have striven to equip themselves well for the combat, and, since the end of the Stone Age, no nation has been able to do so without a supply of relatively cheap metal. Thus the position of mines has influenced the direction of travel.

This determined the places of market. Markets, with their tributary territory, led to the organization of states and empires. Thus the prosperity of a nation is dependent upon the markets, and the ways to and from them. "When trade-routes shift, markets move; and the seat of empire is displaced." This, being followed by wars, revolutions, and other upheavals, leads to a decay of the nation from which the dominating markets have been shifted, and to the ascendancy of a new nation, which now becomes the seat of commercial centers, and wealth.[130] Such is the essence of the theory. It is complicated by a further "sub-theory." The well-endowed races, according to Adams, do not spend their whole energy in a daily struggle for life and store of their surplus in the shape of wealth. By conquest and economic competition, it is transferred from community to community. As a result, in some communities the surplus energy (wealth) becomes "accumulated in such bulk as to preponderate over productive energy." Then wealth becomes the controlling social force. This is manifested through a shifting of the social domination from priests

---

[128] See ADAMS, B., *The New Empire,* p. III, N. Y., 1902.

[129] See ADAMS, B., *The Law of Civilization and Decay,* Preface, N. Y., 1897.

[130] See *The New Empire,* pp. 193–211, where Adams sums up his theory better than in his *The Law of Civilization.*

and military men to commercial men; military and intellectuals cease to reproduce themselves, and the dominant figures become "the usurer" and the "peasant." Such a point reached, sooner or later a decay of the society becomes inevitable.[131]

It would be necessary to devote many pages to enumerating the historical inaccuracies of the author.[132] Still more pages would be needed to show that, even granting the validity of his theory, it does not explain hundreds of the most important facts pertaining to the phenomena of decay, and to the shifting of social domination from country to country. This, however, it is not necessary to do. In order to show the inadequacy of the theory, it is enough to ask what the causes responsible for the shifting of the trade-routes are, and, through that, the markets and the seat of empire. B. Adams' theory does not answer the question. Next, we may ask what the causes are which are responsible for the assumed fact that some races are able to store their surplus energy in the form of wealth, while some others cannot do it. What factors are responsible for the fact that some nations, through military conquest and competition, can encroach upon the wealth of other nations and can change the trade-routes and market-places and, through that, the seat of powerful empires? B. Adams assumes this as something given. He does not even try to analyze the problem. However, if it is possible, as he states, to transfer the wealth and the trade-routes, through the superiority, sagacity or military valor of a race, this practically means that race and its hereditary and acquired traits determine the trade-routes and markets, and the direction of wealth transference. In other words, it is the racial factor which is predominant rather than that of trade-routes and markets. This means, further, that for the decay of a nation neither trade-routes nor the directions of shifting wealth are decisive, (they, according to the author, may be altered by a capable race); but race-factor, its training, its equipment, and its natural sources, and so on, exercise this influence. In brief, the theory turns against itself. Furthermore, there is no need to say that, during the thousands

---

[131] See *The Law of Civilization and Decay*, Preface and *passim*.

[132] Part of them are indicated in ROOSEVELT, T., *Administration, Civil Service*, N. Y., 1900, Essay VIII; see also KOVALEVSKY, M., *op. cit.*, pp. 299–302.

of years of existence of the trade-routes to China and India, routes have changed many times; and yet these countries still exist, and have not decayed. These indications are sufficient to indicate the fallacy of the theory. A portion of truth there is in the theory, but only a part.[133]

Let us now turn to an interesting theory of decay set forth by several German authors and recapitulated again by Professor V. Simkhovitch in his theory of Rome's fall.[134]

Properly speaking, this is not exactly the theory of the economic interpretation of decay. It is rather a "geographico-economic" theory, because Simkhovitch's factor of decay, *exhaustion of soil,* is a result of physico-chemical-cosmic forces on the one hand, and on the other, of the economic exploitation of the soil. The essence of the theory is simple and clear. It contends that neither corruption, nor latifundia, nor wars, nor racial depletion, nor any other factors were the primary factor in Rome's decay. Rather, they all were secondary results of a deeper cause, the exhaustion of Rome's soil. Its increasing sterility, carefully traced by the author, determined the transition from a more intensive form of agriculture in Rome to a less intensive one; from farms of small size to larger ones; and to latifundia. The exhaustion of the soil was the cause of the decay of agriculture, of the desertion of land by farmers, of the transition of farmers into landless proletarians, of the concentration of wealth, of the increasing economic disorganization, of depopulation, of corruption, and, finally, of decay. Summing up his theory, the author says:

All that this study shows is that the progressive exhaustion of the soil was quite sufficient to doom Rome, as the lack of oxygen in the air would doom the strongest living being. . . . His moral or immoral character, his strength or his weakness, his genius or his

---

[133] Some of the details of Adams' theory are valuable; his analysis of the negative side of the dictatorship of commercial men (money-lenders and money-makers) is true; his theory of rhythm of the domination of priests, military men, and of the money-makers (a theory which reminds us of Pareto's similar one) grasps something important; even his analysis of the social effects of the shifting of trade-routes, free from its exclusive pretension, is likely to be accurate in many respects.

[134] SIMKHOVITCH, V. G., "Rome's Fall Reconsidered," *Political Science Quarterly,* June, 1916; see also his "Hay and History," *ibid.,* Sept., 1913.

mental defects, would not affect the circumstances of his death. He would have lived had he had oxygen; he died because he had none. But it must be remembered that while the presence of oxygen *does not explain his life,* the absence of it is sufficient to explain his death.[135]

This shows that the author's claim consists not in the simple contention that, among the various factors of Rome's decay, the progressive exhaustion of the soil has to be taken into consideration; but that this exhaustion was the deepest and quite sufficient factor for causing the decay,—the factor whose effects could not be averted either by "Rome's moral or immoral character," or by "its genius or mental defects," or by anything else. This interpretation makes Simkhovitch's theory "monistic," or a type of the above "one-sided theories of causation." Though the very fact of the exhaustion of Rome's soil is denied by the most prominent historians of Rome,[136] we may grant that Simkhovitch's factor played its part in the disintegration of Rome. In spite of this admission, however, we must reject his claim for "primacy" or "exclusiveness" for his cause. In the first place, a series of historical facts show that exhaustion of the soil does not necessarily lead to decay. M. Ping-Hua Lee has shown that in China, with its long history and overpopulation, exhaustion of the soil has taken place many times, and yet China still exists. After the periods of exhaustion, through the activity of her people, the soil has been made fertile again, and the disastrous results of permanent soil sterility were prevented.[137] This shows that the results of soil exhaustion are avoidable, and do not lead necessarily to decay. In the second place, we know that the process of a progressive sterility of soil can be stopped, if the corresponding measures, particularly soil fertilization, are taken. This means that in no way could it be regarded as something unavoidable, and that "the genius, morals, strength, and other qualities of the population" can affect it, and can prevent decay as a result. This means that the exhaustion of the soil itself is not a

[135] *Ibid.,* p. 241.

[136] See ROSTOVTZEFF, M., *The Social and Economic History of the Roman Empire,* p. 495, Chap. VIII.

[137] See LEE, M. PING-HUA, *The Economic History of China,* Columbia Univ. Studies, Introduction and *passim,* N. Y., 1921.

cause independent of everything, but a resultant of many other cosmic, as well as social, biological and mental forces. Its rapidity and intensiveness are determined by the amount and the density of the population, by climatic and cosmic influences, by the agricultural technique of the population, by its genius or stupidity, by peace or war, and so on. These obvious reasons do not permit us to interpret it as an independent, primary, or sufficient cause of decay. Furthermore, if the theory of the author were true, one should wonder why existing nations have been able to live, and why the territory of Rome continues to support vast aggregates of population. Since the exhaustion of Roman soil has been progressive and unavoidable, it should have continued, consequently making the existence of social bodies there less and less possible. If the exhaustion was stopped in some way, at some period, this means that it was not imminent and unavoidable. Many European countries have been overpopulated many times, and many times have known famine and starvation.[138] One may wonder why exhaustion of the soil did not take place in those countries; or, if it has taken place, why it did not lead to their final decay. Finally, the parallel of the author with the lack of oxygen, as an imminent cause of death, is still more fallacious. It is true that the lack of oxygen may be a sufficient cause of death, but death may be caused also by lack of water, food, or shelter; and by poison, by infection, by bullet, and by hundreds of other factors. Any of them may be a sufficient cause of death. In a similar way, the cause of the decay of a social body may be military extermination, death from starvation, degeneration of the population, great and prolonged anarchy, great demoralization, depopulation, inundation, geological catastrophe, and so on. The mere theoretical possibility of death from one of these causes does not entitle us to take one of them and to say: "This is the cause." We must ascertain which of the hundred possible causes factually was present, and why it could not have been averted or counterbalanced. Granting that in Rome, Simkhovitch's cause existed, it is still more certain that other possible causes, such as war and the invasion of barbarians, anarchy, racial transformation of the population, demoralization, depopu-

[138] See CURSCHMAN, F., *Hungersnöte in Mittelalter*, 1900. *passim.*

lation, economic disorganization, and so on, were also present. For this reason, any one following the logic of the author could pretend, with the same right, that his factor was the cause. If we ask why the sterility of the soil was not averted in Rome, we do not find any answer by the author. If we add to this that Rome's fall was the result of a concurrence of many factors,[139] the inadequacy of Simkhovitch's theory becomes clear.

Besides the uncertainty of the very fact of the exhaustion of soil in Rome, the theory, as far as it claims exclusiveness and primacy for its factor, is scarcely better than seventy-seven other exclusive theories of Rome's fall. Generally speaking, it is improbable that such a complex phenomenon as the decay of an empire could be accounted for through any single factor, whatever it might be.[140] Any such theory is doomed to be fallacious, or, if the factor chosen is too broad, it would also be too indefinite, and would mean no more than the statement: "All is the cause of all."

The study of the negative effects of "mechanism" or "machino-technique of production" and especially of contemporary machino-facturing on human beings and social life, offered by R. Austin Freeman, is quite different. It does not take the studied factor as a primary cause, but, contrariwise, it shows that machino-facturing itself is something which has been created and determined through other factors. The theory does not claim to give a universal explanation of the phenomena of decay; neither does it claim that the traced effects of "mechanism" are unavoidable. It simply takes the factor of mechanism or "machine-industry" as a given variable, and tries to trace its principal effects on first, mechanism or machine-industry itself; second, on the human environment; third, on man collectively; and fourth, on man individually. This shows that Freeman's claims are moderate, and his setting of the problem is appropriate. As his conclusions sum up a great many negative effects of contemporary machino-technique, and do it, it seems to me, rather accurately, they deserve to be quoted as valuable sociological propositions. In

[139] See ROSTOVTZEFF, M., op. cit., passim, and Chaps. VIII–XII.
[140] Compare ROSS, E., Principles of Sociology, 1923, Chap. XLIII.

an abbreviated form, in the words of the author they are as follows:

I. The reactions *of mechanism on itself* are manifested in three directions: (a) In a tendency of mechanism to beget further mechanisms; (b) in a tendency of the power-generating machine to beget power-consuming machines, machine tools, and producing machines; (c) in a tendency of both types of machines to evolve in the direction of increased automatism, with a correlative elimination of the human factor.

II. A.—*On the natural environment of man,* mechanism has reacted (1) by producing a general deterioration of those regions which have come under its influence; a destruction of natural beauty and the creation of areas of devastation; (2) by the creation of great industrial towns, adjusted to the needs of the machine but unadjusted to those of the multitudes of human beings who are compelled to live in them; (3) by inducing a gigantic and wasteful consumption of the natural resources, both capital and replaceable, whereby the available wealth of the world is appreciably reduced and there is set up a condition relatively unfavorable to posterity. The general tendency of these reactions is to reduce the suitability of the world as a habitat for man, *i. e.,* to transform a favorable environment into one less favorable.

B.—*On the secondary environment,* reactions are manifested [through the locomotive-mechanism]—(1) in an apparent contraction of space and a reduction of the effects of distance. This tends to result in an increasing uniformity in the appearance of places and in the suppression of local characteristics; and this uniformity extends to natural products, which become available in regions far distant from their place of origin. Facility of transport tends to be accompanied by ever-increasing centralization of the means of locomotion, by the loss of their control by individuals, by insecurity of their possession, and by compulsion as to their use. (2) Machine tends to supersede manual skill . . . and man, as the agent of production; [leads to the centralization of manufacture, with resulting extinction of small local industries; and to a substitution of complex and costly means of production for simple and inexpensive ones. In regard to the products of industry, the effects of machine-mechanisms is an increase in the quantity of produced commodities, with a decrease in their cost; a tendency to deterioration of commodities in

quality of material, workmanship, durability, and beauty; reduction
of the adaptation of products to individual, or even to human, needs;
repetition, uniformity, and lack of interest and character in commodities. Thus, in these respects, the reactions] in the main, are unfavorable.

III. *Reactions on man collectively,* (a) the transformation of the
working class from a discrete body of skilled men of a relatively
high type, living under fairly good conditions and fairly satisfied
therewith, into a concrete body largely composed of comparatively
unskilled men of a relatively low type, living under conditions which
are incurably unfavorable, with which they are dissatisfied;[141] (b)
as a consequence, the creation of a great organization—the federated
trades unions—whose members conceive their interests to be antagonistic to those of the rest of the community, and whose political
activities are of an anti-social character; (c) the appearance of an
international movement,—syndicalism—of which the declared purpose is the destruction of the existing order by revolutionary methods;
(d) transfer of the initiative of production from individual craftsmen
or small bodies of skilled workers to a financial operator—the manu-
facturer—controlling automatic machines and a large body of relatively unskilled workmen; (e) the chronic disturbance of social
order and economic stability; (f) the formation of anti-social organizations (combines, cartels, trusts, etc.), the purpose of which is to
control the supply and prices of commodities; (g) the accumulation
by a relatively small number of men of enormous wealth, and through
it, a great controlling power over men; (h) the transfer of large
portions of the population from the producing to the non-producing
class.

IV. *Reactions on man individually,* (a) the extinction of the
craftsman and his replacement by the machine and the factory hand
(by unskilled men). (b) The change of the character of the individual; a lack of "handiness" and self-helpfulness begets a lack of self-
reliance. He becomes willing and even anxious that his personal
activities and duties as a citizen shall be taken over by the state. (c)
A general decrease in pleasurable mental states, consequent on the
exchange of the pleasant, varied, and interesting work of the craftsman for the disagreeable, monotonous, and dull occupations of the
factory hand; (d) exchange of the relatively good and human condi-

[141] Compare PATRICK, G. T. W., *The Psychology of Social Reconstruction,*
Boston, 1920.

tions of life of a craftsman for the bad conditions of a factory hand, with his dwelling in an industrial district, his time spent in a factory, his loss of liberty, and his subjection to rigid discipline; (e) lowering of the social status of the worker and loss of equality of opportunity; (f) lowering of the æsthetic taste and standards and substitution of æsthetic obtuseness and vulgarity of taste for fine taste and perfect æsthetic arts; (g) loss of culture, resulting from an individual's transference from the position of an executant to that of a passive spectator or listener. (h) As a result of a growing locomotive mechanism,—social mobility,—we have "a loss of the complete social adjustments which are possible in areas inhabited by a stationary population." (i) Reduction of sustained, concentrated effort; (j) reduction of leisure and increase in the amount of time wasted in traveling; (k) evolution of the locomotive man, or "hustler", and increase of restlessness and unpurposed strenuousness; (l) diminution of the interest of travel, and lack of curiosity respecting remote regions and their inhabitants.

Thus, taken as a whole, the reactions of mechanism have not been favorable to man.[142]

I have made this long quotation from Freeman's book because, in this dry summary, he, probably more fully than anybody else, indicates the various effects of the machino-technique of production contributing to a decay of society. Though the list of the effects is somewhat one-sided because it does not mention many beneficial influences of the studied factor, nevertheless its enumeration of "the evils" of machino-industry seems to be accurate, and therefore valuable. As machino-industry is regarded as an economic factor, this is the reason why I have mentioned Freeman's work in this section. This part of his book is an example of the tentative correlation of the means and instruments of production with the complex phenomena of social decay.

14. General Conclusions of the Economic School in Sociology

(1) The above shows that the school is old. (2) The school is one of the most important in social sciences. (3) Marx and

Engels can in no way be regarded as the founders of the school, and as the thinkers who contributed more than hundreds of other investigators. (4) Studies of a great many investigators have shown that so-called economic conditions are correlated with various and numerous social phenomena. For this reason, in an interpretation or an analysis of social phenomena, they cannot be disregarded. (5) In many fields social science can now tell not only whether the correlation of a certain social phenomenon with a certain economic condition exists, but even the degree, or coefficient of the correlation. (6) These coefficients show that there is scarcely any social phenomenon which can be correlated perfectly with the economic factor. Some of them are correlated quite tangibly; others, only slightly, and some others do not show any noticeable correlation. This means that in no way is it possible to take the economic factor as the omnipotent, primary, or the final cause, or even as the only "starter," while all others are "only dependent" on it. (7) This conclusion becomes still more valid if we take into consideration that social phenomena are interdependent, but not one-sidedly dependent. For this reason the non-self-sufficiency of the economic factor shown by the character of the correlations becomes still greater if we take it by itself as a "function," and show its dependency on other factors taken in the above studies as "mere functions." This is done by other sociological schools which are logically and factually entitled to proceed in this way as much as the economic interpreters in their way. (8) The above reasons require that the sterile and fruitless debate as to which factors are primary and secondary, which the "starters" and the "started," which the cause and the effects, which the more and the less important, and so on, be ended. (9) The above shows also that, at the present moment, the task of sociologists in this field consists, not in a production of vague and ambiguous and speculative generalizations, and not in a "metaphysical brooding" on a somewhat indefinite economic factor generally, and not in the creation of sensational though one-sided all-explaining hypotheses; but in a factual, inductive, careful, and quantitative study of the existence or non-existence of a tangible correlation between a certain well-defined economic condition, and a certain and well-defined social phenomenon; and, if the correlation exists, in the study of its degree, universality, character, and variations. Every study of this kind is likely to contribute more to the science of sociology than any sweeping and speculative generalization. When such studies accumulate in a sufficient amount, this, and only this, will permit us to climb from narrower conclusions to broader generalizations. (10) The above shows that contemporary sociology is already drifting that way.

CHAPTER XI

THE PSYCHOLOGICAL SCHOOL

IT has been mentioned before that the boundary line between the Psychological and the Sociologistic schools is pretty indefinite. It reminds one of the difference between the Republican and the Democratic parties in America. Each of them is republican and democratic, but at the same time there are some indefinite differences which lead to the independent existence of these parties. In a similar way the Sociologistic school is essentially psychological, and the Psychological school is essentially sociologistic. Nevertheless, there are some differences which have caused the independent existence of both streams of sociological thought during the last few decades. Of these differences the most tangible has been a methodological one. The Sociologistic school tries to explain psychical phenomena through social conditions. It makes them a derivative of the transindividual processes of interaction and societal circumstances. The Psychological school, on the contrary, starts with the psychical characteristics of an individual, takes them as variables, and tries to interpret social phenomena as their derivative or manifestation. The difference is put here in a somewhat schematical form, and many sociologists occupy a position intermediary between these poles; nevertheless, the difference has existed, and the subsequent paragraphs will show this clearly.

I. PREDECESSORS AND PRINCIPAL BRANCHES OF THE SCHOOL

The majority of the predecessors of the various branches of the sociologistic school may be practically regarded as sharers of the psychological interpretation of social phenomena. That the human mind, soul, spirit, desires, wishes, instincts, or other psychical characteristics of man "count" in conditioning social events; and that they are the most important agencies of human behavior and social processes, was stressed in the most ancient

thought. Primitive "animism," which views the bodily movement of man and all the changes in nature as a mere manifestation of various spiritual or psycho-magical agencies, is perhaps
the most conspicuous form of the primitive psychological interpretation of the dynamics of the universe and human history.

Action springs from the mind.

Mind is the instigator . . . even to that action which is connected
with the body.

The universe rests on the Self; for the Self produces the connection of these embodied spirits with actions.[1]

Beyond the senses there are the objects, beyond the objects there
is the mind, beyond the mind there is the intellect, the great Self
is beyond the intellect. . . . He who has perceived that [Self] which
is without sound, without touch, without form, without decay, with-
out taste, eternal, without smell, without beginning, without end,
beyond the Great, and unchangeable, is freed from the jaws of death.
[Such a man, being the] "Lord of the past and the future, hence-
forward fears no more. This is that." [2]

All that we are is the result of what we have thought; it is founded
on our thought, it is made up of our thought.

A well directed mind will do us great service.

Thoughtlessness is the path of death.[3]

These brief quotations from the ancient Hindu, Buddhist,
and Chinese sources well illustrate my statement. The Confucianist and the Taoist philosophy, Plato, Aristotle, Zeno, Epicte-
tus, Polybius, and other Stoics,[4] the Church Fathers, and the
majority of the mediæval thinkers stressed the same idea in various ways, partly in the form of ethical and religious teaching,
and partly in the form of various philosophical and psychological
theories, but principally in the form of the applied arts of the
re-education of human beings successfully practiced in the monas-

---

[1] *Laws of Manu*, XII, pp. 3–4, 119.

[2] "The Upanishads," Part II, third Vallî, 10–15; fourth Vallî, *passim; Sacred
Books of the East*, Vol. XV.

[3] *The Dhammapada*, Chap. I, p. 1, Chap. III and *passim*, The Colonial Press.
Compare *The Texts of Taoism*, The Classic of Purity, Chap. I; *The Thâi-Shang,
passim; Tao-Teh-King, passim; Sacred Books of the East*, Vol. XL.

[4] Stoicism, with its motto: "Dig within," and "The aids to noble life are all
within," in "our own will and the formation of our judgments and opinions"
occupies a position similar to that of Brahmanism, Buddhism, and Taoism.

teries and similar institutions.[5]   This branch of psychology is now represented by various "introspective," "purposive," or "structural" psychologies.

Side by side with this "introspective" psychological interpretation of human behavior, the past also knew the mechanistic, or behavioristic, psychological interpretation of human conduct and psycho-social phenomena.   Democritus and Titus Lucretius Carus, with their purely materialistic and mechanistic theory of psychical phenomena, show this.   This stream of interpretation has been going on throughout the subsequent history of social thought.[6]   As we have seen, in the seventeenth century it manifested itself as the mechanistic psychology of the thinkers of that period.   (See the chapter about the mechanistic school.)   In the eighteenth century it was recapitulated by such "materialist philosophers" as Condillack or La Mettrie; and in the nineteenth century by Huxley, H. Spencer, and many others.   Now it assumes the forms of various factions of the behaviorist school in psychology.   In brief, the patterns of all the contemporary schools in psychology were given long ago, as also were set forth the corresponding interpretations of human actions and social phenomena from the standpoint of each specific variety of psychological theory.[7]   At the present moment we still have no generally accepted psychology, but various psychologies almost as numerous as are the psychologists themselves.[8]

[5] A more attentive study of these measures and the corresponding ascetic technique of the re-education of individuals practiced therein is quite necessary from the standpoint of the theory of social control, and the practical art of education.   We must recognize that in practical ways these educatiors knew rather more than we know about these problems.   According to my suggestion, one of my students, Mr. Timofeevsky, has found forty-four different methods of modifications of human conduct practiced in mediæval monastic and ascetic orders. All these methods were very efficient and must be recognized as quite appropriate from the standpoint of modern science.   The reading of such books as Ignatius Loyola's *Spiritual Exercises* clearly shows the deep insight of their authors into the mechanism of human conduct and an ingenuity in the invention of efficient methods for its modification in a desirable direction.   It is unnecessary to add that this technique was "psychological" in its essence, and was based on the change of human psychology and mind.

[6] See LANGE, FR. A., *Geschichte des Materialismus*, 2 vols., 3d ed., 1877.

[7] See some fragmentary data in BARNES, H. E., *New History and Social Studies*, Chap. III; DAVIS, M. M., *Psychological Interpretations of Society, passim.*

[8] An idea of this is given by the volume: *Psychologies of 1925*, Clark University, 1926, where there are represented at least six various psychologies which are as

Leaving their mutual dispute to the psychologists themselves, of these numerous psychologies we shall take only those which have really attempted to interpret social phenomena from the standpoint of their leading principles. This leaves us the following principal branches of psychological sociology: First, the *instinctivist;* second, the *behaviorist* interpretations; and third, the *introspectivist interpretations in terms of desires, ideas, beliefs, conations, interests, wishes, sentiments, and other psychical experiences.* If to our analysis of these fundamental branches of the psychological school we add a survey of the theories of the social rôle of religion, *mores,* public opinion, law, and other psycho-social or cultural factors, our knowledge of the present situation of the school may be sufficient. Adding to this a survey of the quantitative and experimental studies of various psycho-social phenomena—the studies which occupy a position intermediary between the sociologistic and the psychological schools—we shall obtain a still more adequate idea of today's stand of sociology in this field.

We will now turn to a concise analysis of the instinctivist branch of the psychological (and, partly, the biological) school.

2. INSTINCTIVIST INTERPRETATIONS

It is not my intention to enter here into a controversy over the conception of instinct, or instinct classifications, or other phases of the problem so vividly and somewhat fruitlessly discussed now.[9] One thing is clear, that even the most extreme

different from one another as the most different sociological schools of the present moment.

[9] See PAVLOV, I., *Twenty Years of Experimental Study of the Highest Nervous Activity of Animals* (in Russian), Petrograd, 1923; THORNDIKE, E. L., *The Original Nature of Man*, N. Y., 1913; McDOUGALL, WILLIAM, *An Introduction to Social Psychology*, Boston, 1923; "Can Sociology and Social Psychology Dispense with Instincts?" *American Journal of Sociology*, Vol. XXIX, pp. 657–670; PETRA-JITZKY, LEO, *Introduction of the Theory of Law and Morals* (in Russian), 1907; WAGNER, W., *Biological Foundation of Comparative Psychology*, (in Russian), Vol. II; FARIS, E., "Are Instincts Data or Hypotheses?" *American Journal of Sociology*, Vol. XXVII, pp. 184–196; DUNLAP, K., "Are There any Instincts?" *Journal of American Psychology*, Vol. XIV, pp. 307–311; ALLPORT, F. L., *Social Psychology*, Chap. III; FROLOFF, J. P., "The Problem of Instincts from the Standpoint of the Physiology of the Conditioned Responses," (in Russian), *Isvestia Voenno-Medizin. Akademii*, 1913, Vol. XXVI; TOLMAN, E. CHASE, "The Nature of the Fundamental Drives," *Journal of Abnormal and Social*

opponents of instincts cannot give them up entirely either in psychology or sociology. On the other hand, the discussion has shown that the term has been considerably misused and now requires a great deal of care in utilizing it.[10] Putting aside this general discussion, which lies practically outside of sociology, and leaving the general sketches of "instinctive" sociology, which because of their generality cannot show to what extent they are plausible, let us take the monographic "instinctive interpretations" of social phenomena, and find to what extent they are scientifically fruitful. Instead of the mere plan of interpretation offered by general theories, monographic works try to interpret social phenomena in fact; therefore, they are much more symptomatic of the pluses and minuses of this branch. The monographic works of this type are already numerous. As representative samples I shall take, first, a series of monographs devoted to a study of the social functions of the gregarious, herd, or

---

Psychology, 1925–26, pp. 349–358; BALDWIN, J. MARK, *The Individual and Society*, Boston, 1911; LARGUIER DES BANCELS, J., *Introduction à la psychologie; l'instinct et l'émotion*, Paris, 1921; FREUD, SIGMUND, *Group Psychology and the Analysis of the Ego*, translated by J. Strachey; KOFFKA, KURT, *The Growth of the Mind*, pp. 84–114, N. Y., 1924; BERNARD, L. L., *Instinct*, N. Y., 1924; ELLWOOD, C. A., *The Psychology of Human Society*, Chap. IX, N. Y., 1925; ROSS, E. A., *Principles of Sociology*, Chap. IV; ELDRIDGE, S., "Instinct, Habit and Intelligence in Social Life," *Journal of Abnormal Psychology and Social Psychology*, Vol. XIX, pp. 142–154; JOSEY, C. C., *The Social Philosophy of Instinct*, N. Y., 1922; WOODWORTH, R. S., *Dynamic Psychology*, Chaps. III–V; WELLS, W. R., "The Anti-Instinct Fallacy," *Psychological Review*, Vol. XXX, pp. 228–234; WATSON, J. B., "What the Nursery Has to Say about Instincts," *Pedagogical Seminary*, Vol. XXXII, pp. 293–326. See other literature in these works and see the works quoted further.

[10] The majority of the functional, structural, and the *Gestalt* psychologists recognize their existence. The same is true of the dynamic psychology of the type of R. S. Woodworth, and of the biological psychologies of the type of W. Wagner. Of the behaviorist psychologies, the Russian school of Pavlov recognizes a great many instincts, identifying them with the unconditioned reflexes. The behaviorists of the type of F. Allport operate with the prepotent reflexes and drives whose difference from the instincts is practically intangible. The same is true of other moderate behaviorists. The behaviorists of the type of R. B. Perry and E. C. Tolman are explicit instinctivists. Finally, the behaviorists of the type of John Watson emphatically deny the instincts, but through their admission that a difference in structure leads to a difference in forms of behavior, and through their recognition of a series of the unconditioned reflexes, among which we find "love behavior," "fear reflexes," "rage behavior," "defensive movements," "vocal responses" and so on, they practically reintroduce them also. Some other "anti-instinctivists" do the same under the name of the "physiological needs" or "drives" or "impulses." In brief, there are very few, if any, psychologists or biologists who really do not use (explicitly or implicitly) something like instincts.

social instincts; second, a series of monographs dealing with the social functions of the sex instinct; and, third, the studies devoted to the sociology of the pugnacious or fighting instinct, the parental instinct, and of other instincts such as "workmanship," "freedom," "collectioneering," and so on. A concise analysis of two or three groups of these works is enough to show the strong and the weak points of all "instinctive sociologies."

A. *Social Functions of the Sex Instinct and Sex Difference.*—Take, in the first place, the sex instinct and sex difference as factors of human behavior and social processes. At the present moment we have several monographic studies which take these biological factors as variables and try to indicate their "functions" in the field of social phenomena. Let us see how they work, and what results they yield.

Take first S. Freud's school, which gives such an exclusive importance to the libido and sex. The principal sociological correlations of this factor with other social phenomena, as claimed by the school, are as follows: First, the very fact of social life and the appearance of human society are due to libido or eros in the sense given to these terms by the Freudian school. Second, the tie which binds human individuals into a social group is the libidinal tie. Third, large human societies are due to the specific variety of the sex impulse of man to man (but not to woman). Fourth, in any attachment of followers to the leader, of the members of a society to one another, the same libido operates. Fifth, the phenomena of crowd, suggestion, imitation, and so on, are but libido manifestations. Sixth, a series of other phenomena like totemism, religion, taboo, and so on, are again but various manifestations of the same factor. A few quotations will illustrate the above. "Love relationships constitute the essence of the group mind. . . . Libidinal ties are what characterize a group." [11] Suggestion is only a screen for libido. Herd instinct is another name for libido.[12] These ideas of Freud were developed more extensively by Hans Blüher. In his work he tries to show that the force which attracts man to man and leads to his living together, and to the creation of large social bodies,

[11] FREUD, S., *Group Psychology and the Analysis of the Ego*, pp. 37, 40, 54, 80, 88, 92.

[12] *Ibid.*, pp. 85, 89, and *passim*. See also FREUD, *Totem and Taboo*, N. Y., 1918

is neither economic necessity, nor self-protection, nor any other factor, but sexuality or libido in its particular form of the gravitation of male to male. Blüher especially strongly stresses the idea that if small family groups have appeared through the operation of male-female libido relationship, large societies are due, by their existence, only to male to male libido relationship, and are possible only where male-female libido relationship is either weakened or destroyed; [13] because the male and female "coming together for the purpose of sexual satisfaction, in so far as they seek for solitude, are making a demonstration against the herd instinct, and the group feeling. The more they are in love, the more completely they suffice for each other." In this way group solidarity and sex love between male and female are in antagonism, and where one is strong the latter cannot develop the former. Therefore "it seems certain that homosexual love is far more compatible with group ties." [14]

It is scarcely necessary to go into other details of Freud's constructions. The above shows that this popular theory is utterly inadequate. One may only wonder at such unscientific constructions finding the relatively numerous supporters that they did. Indeed, take in the first place the Freudian conception of libido, or eros, or sexuality itself. Here it is:

We call by libido the energy of those instincts which have to do with all that may be comprised under the word "love." The nucleus of what we mean by love consists in sexual love with sexual union as its aim. But we do not separate from this, on the one hand, self-love, and on the other, love for parents and children, friendship, and love for humanity in general, and also devotion to concrete objects and to abstract ideas.[15]

---

[13] BLÜHER, HANS, *Die Rolle der Erotik in der männlichen Gesellschaft*, Vol. I, pp. 4, 6, 37, 190, Jena, 1921; Vol. II, pp. 2–8 and *passim*, Jena, 1920. Here is Blüher's own summary of the hypothesis: All social relations being a modification of sexuality, "*So ist auch klargelegt, dass das, was letztes Endes und zwingend den Mann zum Manne drängt, genau dasselbe ist, wie das, was ihn zum Weibe treibt: seine Sexualität. Liegt die mannweibliche offen und unverleugnet da, so ist diese durch ein vielgestaltiges System psychischer Mechanismen verschüttert und zersprengt. Aber sie ist, und wäre sie nicht, so fiele noch am morgigen Tage der Menschenstaat auseinander.*" *Ibid.*, Vol. I, p. 190.

[14] FREUD, S., *Group Psychology*, pp. 121–123.

[15] FREUD, S., *Ibid.*, pp. 37, 65, 77, 85, 93, and *passim*; "Zur Sexuellen Aufklärung der Kinder," *Soziale Medizin und Hygiene* Bd. II, 1907.

Further, we read that the herd instinct is also the sexual instinct; that suggestion, self-preservation, like-mindedness, the hypnotic state, and many other phenomena are also libido or love.[16]

The definition shows that the Freudian libido, love, or sexuality is a bag filled with everything, beginning with sexuality in a narrow sense and ending with hypnotism, sociality, idealism, parental love, friendship, self-protection, and what not. It is as broad as the conception of life itself. Shall we wonder therefore that the school regards the whole activity of man as a sex activity; man himself, beginning with a baby, as a mere sex-machinery; and social phenomena, beginning with a society itself and ending with religion, magic, law, arts, and sciences, as a manifold manifestation of the sex-factor? This procedure is identical to that of the ancient philosophers who, like Thales, viewed the whole universe as a manifestation of water. From a metaphysical standpoint such a philosophy may be all right, but from a scientific standpoint it is fruitless because it is tautological. The above libido conception and theory give us no more than the statement: "The life-activities of man and society are the function and manifestation of the life factor," because the Freudian libido is identical to the conception of life. Such a statement may be true, but unfortunately it is meaningless. Furthermore, the theory transgresses the fundamental logical law of identity. "To explain all behavior by one formula is to explain nothing," properly say R. Park and E. Burgess.[17] To the term of "libido" it gives quite different meanings,—sometimes quite narrow, sometimes unlimitedly broad. As a result, neither the authors nor the readers know what they are dealing with, and talking about. Under such circumstances it is impossible to establish any clear correlation, any causal relation, or any definite relationship between the phenomena. We do not know what we are trying to correlate with what, and we wander in the forest of undefined phenomena and shadows of phenomena. If we are lost, as factually the Freudian theorizers are, this is only natural. In brief, the theory is utterly inadequate and unsatisfactory. It

---

[16] Still more indefinite is Blüher's definition of *Sexualität*. See BLÜHER, *op. cit.*, Vol. 1, pp. 15–16, 37.

[17] PARK and BURGESS, *op. cit.*, p. 497.

is hard to admit that it has contributed anything to our understanding of social phenomena, or the relationship between the sex
factor, and other categories of social facts.[18]   So much for this
group.

The next group of works in this field is represented by Havelock Ellis' *Studies in the Psychology of Sex* (six volumes), W.
I. Thomas' *Sex and Society,* E. Westermarck's *History of Human Marriage,* and by chapter X of W. McDougall's *Introduction
to Social Psychology.*   The first three works are sociological
only in part.   Their bulk consists either in treating the physiology
and psychology of sex, or in a purely descriptive analysis of the
historical development of sex, marriage, and family phenomena.
If we squeeze the principal sociological statements from these
works, we shall receive the following propositions:

1. The reproductive instinct is "one of the strongest of the
instincts." [19]

2. Its psychological accompaniment is "sexual jealousy and
female coyness." [20]

3. It is responsible for the reproduction of human beings and
for the gravitation and love behavior of the sexes.

4. The organic differences between the sexes are responsible
for a series of social phenomena.   For instance, "the earliest
groupings of population were about the females rather than the

---

[18] This naturally does not concern the contributions of the Freudian school in
the field of psychology.   But even there, it seems to me, the importance of the
school has been greatly exaggerated.   See *Psychological Review,* Vol. XXXI,
May, devoted to *Contributions of Freudism to Psychology,* especially the paper
of LASHLEY, K. S., "Physiological Analysis of the Libido."   See also W.
McDougall's paper in *Problems of Personality,* N. Y., 1925.   The most valuable
part of the Freudian contribution is its method in the treatment of psychoses,
and its hypotheses of repression, displacement, projection, sublimation, compensation, and rationalization of desires.   But again all this in no way is a discovery of the Freudian school.   For instance, the Freudian method of treatment
of psychoses was practiced thousands of years before Freud on the largest scale,
in the form of confession practiced in many religions.   Both methods are essentially identical.   This, by the way, shows that many religious practices, which
often are styled superstitions, in fact have a very serious reason for their existence
and perform the most important functions.   An even superficial study of the
technique of social control practiced in the old and the mediæval religious orders
shows that other mentioned principles of the Freudian school were well known
to them, and successfully practiced.
[19] McDOUGALL, W., *op. cit.,* pp. 272 ff.
[20] *Ibid.,* Chap. III.

males." [21]   "The movement towards exogamy doubtless [!]
originates in the restlessness of the male," [22] while the organic
differences of the sexes have called forth the occupational differences of the sexes, and division of groups into male and female
social classes.[23] "Marriage by capture is an immediate expression
of male forces." [24] The sex impulse is one of the principal forces
"in the development of the ideal, moral, and æsthetic sides of
life." [25] Sex attraction is one of the principal sources of family
and marriage.[26] Sex finds its expression in poetry, religion, law,
and so on.[27]

These statements are a few among the many given in the quoted
and similar works. The majority of such statements appear to
be valid, yet one who was seeking for somewhat more accurate
and more important correlations in this field would remain unsatisfied with the above and similar statements. We may agree
that marriage and family are a result of the sex instinct, but
does such an admission explain the infinitely numerous variations in the forms of these institutions in space and time? If
the instinct is something constant, the variations cannot be accounted for through it. If, in its intensity and forms, the instinct
varies from man to man, and from period to period, then these
studies must show this and must show a correlation of the variation of this instinct with that of other phenomena. Unfortunately, as yet such a study has not been made in a really
systematic way. We may grant that "the movement toward
exogamy doubtless [!] originates in the restlessness of the
male." If it be so, and if the restlessness of the male is an innate
trait, then how can we explain the phenomena of endogamy or
the disappearance of exogamy? If the restlessness varies in
time, may it not be an acquired trait erroneously taken for an

[21] THOMAS, WILLIAM I., *Sex and Society*, 7th ed., p. 55; ELLIS, HAVELOCK, *Man
and Woman*, Chap. I, N. Y., 1904.
[22] THOMAS, *ibid.*, pp. 57, 196 ff.
[23] *Ibid.*, pp. 51, 61, 67.
[24] *Ibid.*, p. 80.
[25] THOMAS, *ibid.*, pp. 119–120; McDOUGALL, *ibid.*, Chap. X.
[26] McDOUGALL, *ibid.*, Chap. X; ELLWOOD, CHARLES A., *The Psychology of
Human Society*, pp. 288–290.
[27] See HOWARD, CLIFFORD, *Sex Worship*, Chicago, 1917; papers of Albert Moll,
G. Bushan, and S. Ribbing, in *Handbuch der Sexualwissenschaften*, herausgegeben
von A. Moll, Leipzig, 1921.

innate one? Evidently endogamy, monogamy, and marriage by mutual agreement cannot be accounted for through the premise of restlessness of the male, and we are forced to conclude that either the premise itself is inaccurate, or that the theory is insufficient to explain the basic phenomena in the field. The same is true about "marriage by capture as an immediate expression of male forces," and other similar statements. If these "male forces" are responsible for it, then why has such marriage disappeared? We may grant again that the phallus cult in religion is a manifestation of the same instinct, but again, why is it not found in all religions, and why does it vary in its forms? If the sex instinct is one of the most powerful, then how explain the facts of absolute sexual asceticism, or sexual modesty?

These allusions show the weak points of the discussed theories. They cannot account for the infinitely rich variation of the phenomena. They claim many correlations which have not been proved. They do not show exactly what actions are a specific manifestation of the sex impulse, and which are acquired or originated from other instincts. They do not discriminate clearly between the permanent and direct manifestations of the instinct, and its indirect and varying effects. The theories cannot account for the greater part of the variations either in the methods of copulation, or in the forms of love-conduct, courtship, marriage, or family, not to mention other fields. For instance, the instinct theory does not explain why among some people monogamy is the form of marriage, while among other peoples it is polygamy. Why is homosexual love permitted in some societies, while in others it is punished? Why is asceticism or divorce high in some periods and low in others? Why does the sexual tie increase sympathy between male and female in some cases, while in others it leads to an increase of hatred? Why are jealousy and female coyness found in some cases, while they do not exist in others? Why does the birth rate fluctuate in time and space? In brief, the existing instinct theories do not account for the most important phenomena in the field. If they want to justify their pretensions, they must explain all these phenomena in a thorough way. Otherwise they have formed a mere hypothesis, which may have a part of the truth, but how large this part really is neither the authors of the discussed theories nor their critics know as yet.[28] The field is extremely interesting and important; and yet, from a purely sociological standpoint, it has been cultivated but little.

B. *Social Effects of the Parental Instinct.*—All that is included in this term represents in fact a bunch of various reflexes or instincts mixed with a great many acquired reactions. Granting, however, that the parental instinct exists as a bunch of the simpler reflexes, let us ask what are its effects in human behavior and social life. The answer is as follows: "The parental instinct is the foundation of family." "It impels to actions of self-sacrifice"; to exertions in favor of children, to marriage ceremonies, and formal laws concerning the family. It is "the source of all tender emotions and truly benevolent impulses"; it is the great spring of moral indignation and "enters in some degree into every sentiment that can properly be called love." To it is due the charity of such religions as Buddhism or Christianity. "No teaching and no system of social or religious sanctions could induce benevolence in any people if their minds were wholly lacking in this instinct."[29] I will not continue the list of the effects of the instinct in human behavior and social life.

If the above effects are really the manifestations of the parental instinct, then how can we explain the facts of the killing, tortur-

[28] It is possible to hope that the recent studies of the nervous mechanism of sex-reactions will help to promote our knowledge of the sociological effects of the sex-reflexes. I mean in the first place an application of the theory of the conditioned and the unconditioned reflexes in this field, the study of "the sex-center of the nervous system," the conditioned and unconditioned stimulation, including the stimulation through the hormones, and so on. On the other hand, the study of sex-differences is entering into a more careful stage of experimental investigation. Besides the studies in purely physiological differences in metabolism and anatomy of the sexes, we already have several experimental studies in their mental differences. A continuation of these researches promises to be very helpful for the sociology of the sex instinct which, as yet, remains unwritten. See some data about the mental differences in the works: PATERSON, D. G., and LANGLIE, T. A., "The Influence of Sex on Scholarship Ratings," *Educational Administration and Supervision*, September, 1926, (see there other references); STARCH, D., *Educational Psychology*, pp. 68 ff., N. Y., 1919; JASTROW, J., *The Psychology of Conviction;* THOMPSON, H. B., *Psychological Norms in Men and Women;* THORNDIKE, E. L., *Educational Psychology.*

[29] McDOUGALL, W., *op. cit.*, Chap. X. Compare SUTHERLAND, A., *The Origin and Growth of the Moral Instinct*, 2 Vols., London. 1898; WAGNER, W., *op. cit.*, Vol. II; WESTERMARCK, E., *The Origin and Development of the Moral Ideas.* Vol. I, Chaps. XVII and XXV.

ing, and persecuting of children by parents, facts which are pretty common among many preliterate groups,[30] and in a milder form in modern society? If such an instinct exists, why do thousands of parents avoid having children in present society? Why are there so many careless parents? If the parental instinct is an instinct, such facts could not have taken place, because the instinct would have made them impossible. If they happen, it is certain then that either such an instinct does not exist, or that it is destroyed or repressed through some other agencies. The last explanation is usually given. But in this case, in order that the theory may be clear, it is necessary to indicate when, under what conditions, and with what means the instinct is repressed. Are the facts of its repression in some cases and its existence in others due to a different intensity of the instinct among various individuals and groups or is it constant, and are the above facts due to the difference in the pressure of various agencies of repression? Unfortunately, the authors do not give anything but purely dogmatic statements in this field. As a result, a great many contentions become highly hypothetical, while manipulations with the instinct become highly questionable. Here is an illustration of this: [31]

The Effects of the Parental Instinct

1. It is "the source of all benevolent impulses" not only within but outside the family.

1. Savage, "a tender father may behave in an utterly brutal manner to all human beings other than the members of his tribe."

2. Sacrifice for the family.

2. Infanticide.

3. "No teaching and no system of social or religious sanctions could induce benevolence in any people if their minds were wholly lacking in this instinct."

3. "The great extension of benevolent action in the civilization of ours is not necessarily due to an increase in the innate strength of this instinct." (This means that a

[30] See CARR-SAUNDERS, *op. cit.*, *passim.*
[31] *Ibid.*, pp. 274–275, 277, 281–283, Chap. X.

great increase of benevolence is possible without an increase of the instinct—the judgment contradicting that on the left.) Without the support of religious and social sanctions the instinct fails and leads to infanticide.

The table shows that to the same instinct are ascribed the opposite effects. This means that A and non-A are regarded as the effects of the same factor—a logical operation of highly questionable validity. With such operations the theories of this, as well as other instincts, are full. In one place is ascribed to the instinct one effect, in another place, without any sufficient explanation, the opposite one. These indications show how unsatisfactorily the problem is studied, and how great are the shortcomings of the discussed theory of the sex and the parental instincts. What we now have does not go any further than to give general, half-true and half-wrong sketches, which in no way could be regarded as something accurate and exhaustive in a scientific respect.

C. *Social Effects of the Gregarious or Herd Instinct.*—With still greater reason the above may be said of the gregarious or the herd instinct. Without entering into a discussion as to whether such an instinct exists or not, we need only to look attentively at the functions ascribed to the instinct by various, and even by the same, authors to see how little has been the study made in this field. Here is a brief list of these functions taken from only two books. To it are due by its existence the social phenomena of coöperation, recreation, growth of cities, attraction of the migrants to the cities, parades, crowds on the streets, and consciousness of kind.[32] Social life of man, suggestion-imitation, altruism, intolerance, fear of solitude, sensitiveness to the voice of the herd, standardization of *mores,* the passion of the pack in mob violence, the passion of the herd in panics, suscep-

[32] McDougall, W., *op. cit.,* Chap. XII.

tibility to leadership, and striving for popularity, are also similarly explained.[33]

If all these phenomena are really a manifestation of the same instinct, then this is excellent evidence that there is no such instinct, because an instinct with such divergent manifestations is not an instinct at all. If such an instinct exists, then many of these "manifestations" are wrongly ascribed to it. Whichever of these inferences we take, both indicate a great deficiency in the theories. It is easy to see that some phenomena are quite wrongly correlated with the instinct. For instance it is rather fallacious to explain through it the phenomena of the growth of cities. If such a theory were right, we must conclude that those who do not go to the city are devoid of the instinct, and that in the past when there were no big cities the population seems not to have had such an instinct. This inference leads further to the conclusion that the instinct appeared recently, and that it has been acquired, which means that it is not an instinct at all, because an acquired instinct is a self-contradictory conception. If the phenomenon of leadership were a manifestation of the instinct of the herd, then numerous phenomena of anarchy, and a lack of obedience to any leader, must be interpreted as a manifestation of the instinct of "independence" denied by Dr. Trotter. If the fear of solitude is a manifestation of the herd instinct, then evidently the ascetics, the hermits, and all those who run away from the crowd either do not have Trotter's instinct or do have "an instinct of solitude," denied by him. If suggestibility and imitation are a manifestation of the herd instinct, then evidently there exists "an instinct of originality and stubbornness," because almost every man is susceptible to suggestion in some respects and quite insusceptible in some other respects. I will not continue my criticism. The above is rather enough to show how highly speculative are these theories, and how fragile they become after a slight criticism.

D. *Other Instincts.*—Similar shortcomings of the theories of the fighting or pugnacious instinct were indicated above in the chapter devoted to the theories of the struggle for existence.

[33] TROTTER, W., *Instincts of the Herd in Peace and War*, pp. 17, 112–120, and *passim*.

With still greater reason all the above objections may be applied to a great many other instinctive interpretations of social phenomena, such as the "instinct of fear," "curiosity," "religion," "freedom," "acquisition," "construction," "affection," "property," "workmanship," and so on.[34] For the sake of brevity I shall omit their analysis and criticism. It is enough to say that the corresponding theories are much more defective than the above ones.

E. *General Conclusion about the Instinctivist Interpretations.* —To the above shortcomings of the discussed theories it is necessary to add one more, namely, their "animistic" character. The primitive animistic interpretation of any given phenomena consists in viewing them as the results of the activity of mysterious spirits hidden within. A thunderstorm is a "manifestation" of the activity of Zeus; death, the result of a spirit's departing from the body; birth, of a spirit's entering into a female, and so forth. The instinctivist theories are but a refined form of the same animistic interpretation. Behind a man and his activities they place a certain number of spirits styled instincts, and interpret all the phenomena as a manifestation of the instinct-spirits. Sexual activity is regarded as a manifestation of the sex impulse; the relationship between parents and children is accounted for through the mysterious activity of the parental instincts; war, through the fighting instinct; peace, through the peace instinct, and so on. The essence of the interpretation consists in the following operation: man is taken and, according to the whims of an instinctivist, is filled with a certain number of instinct-spirits. Some investigators put into man only three or four instinctive agents; others pack him with some one hundred and fifty instinctive agencies. Having done this "filling," they take a certain activity of man, for instance fighting, and explain that all "fighting activity is a manifestation of the fighting instinct." You want to explain crowd behavior? Take the herd instinct, and the ex-

[34] See, for instance, VEBLEN, THORSTEIN, *The Instinct of Workmanship and the State of the Industrial Arts*, N. Y., 1914. With a reasonable degree of certainty, it is possible to state that there is no such an instinct as workmanship, and the very starting point of the work is consequently wrong. See further WALLAS, GRAHAM, *Human Nature in Politics*, London, 1919, pp. 1–56; ELDRIDGE, S., *Political Action*, 1924; PATRICK, G. T. W., *The Psychology of Social Reconstruction*, Boston and N. Y., 1920.

planation is ready. Why do parents care about their children? Nothing to be wondered at, because the "parental instinct" is the cause. Men are hunting? Quite comprehensible, because they have the "hunting instinct." Men go to church? Very simple indeed; they have a religious instinct. And so on and so forth. The method of the explanation is ingenuously simple indeed. It is clear, however, that in its essence it is identical with the animistic explanation. The surface difference is that the old-fashioned words, "spirit," "soul," "God," or "devil," are replaced by a more fashionable term, "instincts."

Shall we wonder that in such an explanation everybody is free to pack a man with as many and as various instincts as he pleases? It is evident, however, that such a procedure is nothing but an explanation of *obscurum per obscurius*—of what is dark through what is still darker. Such an explanation naturally is not an explanation at all. Furthermore, since an "instinct" itself is something intangible, it is exceedingly difficult to establish any certain correlation between this immaterial "variable" and some "material" phenomena viewed as its "manifestation." Imagine that A is the parental instinct. The instinctivist claims that a series of phenomena: a, b, c, d, are the functions of this "variable,"—a, b, c, d $= f(A)$. To verify this equation we need to know A. But since it is immaterial we cannot grasp it, measure it, and test the validity of the equation. The very fact that a, b, c, d are material or trans-subjective phenomena (actions), and that A is a subjective "force" of an immaterial nature does not permit us to throw any bridge between them which may be objectively measured and tested. Therefore, all equations of this type, where one half consists of trans-subjective phenomena (a, b, c, d) while the other half consists of purely subjective (psychical) experience (instinct, idea, feeling, wish, desire, conation, etc.), are doomed to remain unverifiable, and as such, will remain an assumption whose validity nobody knows. Evidently such a situation is not very hopeful.

Let the reader notice that in all the above criticism I have not denied the existence of instincts. In the terminology of the German philosophers, my criticism has been "immanent." I have taken the existence of the instincts for granted; and under this assumption I have tried to show the deficiencies of the existing theories. For the above reasons the theories should be recognized as insufficient and defective, in spite of some truth which they seem to have. What it is we shall now see.

3. BEHAVIORIST INTERPRETATIONS

A. *General Characteristic.*—At present we have not one but many and various psychologies styled "behavioristic." Let it be understood that under behaviorism here is meant a branch of the experimental study of animal and human behavior which has been developed by C. S. Sherrington, Magnus, and especially by Ivan Pavlov and his school. This school has contributed to the science of human behavior possibly more than any other behavioristic school, and is relatively more free from many a speculation so common in other behavioristic and pseudo-behavioristic "psychologies." One of its principal achievements is the theory of the conditioned and the unconditioned (or innate) reflexes. The existence of the latter has been proved beyond doubt. It has been shown that all the conditioned or acquired reactions are inculcated on the basis of the unconditioned ones. It has also been proved that the conditioned reactions, repeated many times without the support of the unconditioned ones, tend to become "extinguished," and finally disappear. The mechanism of the relationship between the conditioned and the unconditioned reflexes and between various conditioned responses, their inculcation, their modification, extinction, weakening, reinforcement, and inhibition, has been studied also. As a result we now know something in this mystery. Among other things, the study of the unconditioned reflexes has corroborated the existence of numerous innate or instinctive drives with their importance in the behavior of either animal or man.[35]

[35] See PAVLOV, I., *Twenty Years of an Experimental Study of the Higher Nervous Activity of Animals,* (in Russian), 1924; *Lectures in Functioning of the Hemispheres of the Brain,* (in Russian), 1927; BEKHTEREFF, W., *General Foundations of Reflexology,* (in Russian), 1918; see also the experimental studies of G. V. Anrep, V. M. Arkhangelsky, B. P. Babkin, M. Besbokaia, M. F. Belitz, V. V. Beliakoff, V. N. Boldyreff, V. A. Bourmakin, A. S. Bylina, P. Vasilieff, E. Voskoboinikova, L. N. Voskresensky, E. L. Gorn, F. Grossman, M. Gubergritz, V. A. Demidoff, V. A. Degtiareva, V. S. Deriabin, V. M. Dobrovolsky, I. E. Egoroff, M. N. Erofeeva, I. V. Savadsky, G. P. Seleny, B. A. Kogan, P. S. Kupalov, S. P. Kuraieff, N. I. Leporsky, I. S. Makovsky, G. Mishtovt, E. A. Neitz, N. Kasher-

Does this mean that the behaviorist interpretation of human activity and social processes is identical with the instinctivist one? Not at all. There is a great difference. It is that the behaviorists do not assume the existence of any "mysterious agents" behind the objective data of the behavior itself. The very conception of the unconditioned reflex means that between such and such stimuli and such and such responses of an organism, the connection is innate, rather than learned. Whether it is innate or not is decided again on the basis of several sorts of purely objective data. The same is true in regard to conditioned responses, that is, the responses where the connection between the stimulus and response is acquired. In other words, all equations of the behaviorist school are the equation between trans-subjective phenomena, but not between the subjective and trans-subjective realms as is the case in the instinctivist theories. In the lectures of Pavlov one cannot find any "subjective" term and any operation with "idea," "emotion," "desire," and so on. Being such, the behaviorist equations do not have the impassable gap between the trans-subjective and subjective realms, and they can be tested, verified, and proved. For this reason they can establish certain definite correlations not according to the whims of an author, but according to the evidence of the trans-subjective phenomena. This is enough to show the difference between the instinctivist and the behaviorist analysis of human actions and social phenomena. Although in agreement in regard to the ex-

ininova, N. I. Krasnogorsky, A. N. Krestovnikoff, L. A. Orbelli, A. Palladin, M. K. Petrova, O. S. Rosental, A. A. Savitch, I. P. Frolov, D. C. Foursikoff, I. S. Tzitovitch, and others indicated in PAVLOV, *Twenty Years of an Experimental Study,* and in his epoch-making *Lectures,* all in Russian. Claiming that there is no substantial difference between the innate reflex and instinct, the school recognizes a great many innate reflexes, and among them, such ones as the "reflex of investigation," "the reflex of freedom," "the reflex of purpose" (similar to "purposive actions" of W. McDougall), and many others. In this respect there is a conspicuous difference between Pavlov's school and such behaviorists as John B. Watson and others, who flatly, though perhaps without consistency, deny the existence of instincts in man. See especially Pavlov's "Reflex of Purpose" and "Reflex of Freedom" in his *Twenty Years,* and pp. 13–21 in *Lectures.* See also FROLOV, I. P., "The Problem of Instinct from the Standpoint of the Physiology of the Conditioned Reflexes," *Isvestia Voenno-Medizinskoi Akademii,* Vol. XXVI, 1913. The writer must acknowledge here his indebtedness to Ivan Pavlov for kindly sending to the writer his new book, *Lectures* in which is given a summary of all the important results of the researches of Pavlov and his pupils.

istence of a certain number of innate responses, they are quite different in the method of their study.

Accordingly, their approaches to the interpretations of social phenomena are also different. Any really behavioristic interpretation must start with a trans-subjective variable, go to the trans-subjective phenomena, and establish the correlation between trans-subjective phenomena. The chain of the phenomena must not be disconnected anywhere by the insertion of a "psychical agent." Only when such a task is done, is it permissible to try to establish correlations between trans-subjective and subjective phenomena, but even this can be done only as far as these subjective phenomena are expressed in the trans-subjective forms of speech-reactions, gesticulations, exclamations, and other phenomena observable outwardly.

B. *Relationship of the Behaviorist and the Non-Behaviorist Methods of Study of Human Activity and Social Processes.*—In a broad sense every sociological study which correlates one trans-subjective phenomenon with another trans-subjective may be regarded as behavioristic. For instance, the above correlations of a certain geographical condition with an economic one, or a certain economic condition with a certain form of religious cult expressed in overt actions, is a behavioristic theory. All such studies do not involve in a causal or functional chain any purely psychic or subjective link. They start with trans-subjective data, go to the trans-subjective phenomena, and finish with the trans-subjective facts, also. In this broad sense we have a great many behavioristic studies in sociology.

In a narrow sense of behaviorism, as a specific interpretation of human behavior and psychology from the standpoint of the formula:—trans-subjective stimuli-responses with an elimination of any introspection and introspective methods—the behavioristic interpretations of social phenomena are relatively few. Even those which exist are devoted not so much to the factual interpretation of a certain category of social facts as to a mere discussion of the plan and program of such an interpretation.[36]

[36] Such, in fact are BENTHLEY, A., *Process of Government*, 1908; SELIONY, G. P., "Ueber die zukünftige Soziophysiologie," *Archiv für Rassen-und Gesellschafts-Biologie*, pp. 405–430, 1912; a series of articles of the same author in Russian See a criticism of his theory by ELLWOOD, CHARLES A., "Objectivism in Soci-

Furthermore, a considerable number of them, being strong in their critical part, often fail as soon as they pass to their constructive part, where they become either pseudo-behavioristic,[37] or speculative and metaphysical.[38] In view of the heated dispute

---

ology," *American Journal of Sociology*, Vol. XXII, pp. 289–305; partly WAX-WEILER, E., *Esquisse d'une sociologie*, 1906, pp. 169 ff.; KENAGY, H. G., "The Theory of the Social Forces," *The Psychological Review*, Vol. XXIV, pp. 376–390; BERNARD, L. L., *The Transition to an Objective Standard of Social Control;* ALLPORT, F., *Social Psychology.* Examples of a factual interpretation of various social phenomena are given in PAVLOV, I., "Reflex of Purpose" and "Reflex of Freedom," in his *Twenty Years*, pp. 204–212, (in Russian); SAVITCH, V. V., "An Attempt at an Interpretation of a Creative Activity from the Standpoint of Reflex-Theory," (in Russian), *Krasnaia Nov.*, 1922, No. 4, pp. 207–223; VASI-LIEFF, *Essays in Physiology of Mind*, (in Russian), 1923; ROSENTAL, O. C., "Influence of Inanition on the Conditioned Reflexes," (in Russian), *Archive of Biological Sciences*, Vol. XXI, Nos. 3–5; and a considerable number of other works of the laboratory of Pavlov enumerated in his *Twenty Years*, pp. 238–244; SOROKIN, P., *System of Sociology*, Vols. I, II.

[37] Such, for instance, are the works of Durkheim, Coste, Waxweiler; and such, in their constructive part, are the works of A. Bentley, who operates with the term, "interest," which is as subjective as the terms "ideas," "feelings," "desires" and so on, criticized by him in the first part of his *Process of Government*. Pseudo-behavioristic also are the works of L. L. Bernard, with his "psycho-social," "symbolical" and "neuro-psychic" categories, with his "attitudes of sympathy," "emotional, intellectual, and psychic attitudes"; practically with the whole set of the methods and concepts of the subjective or introspective psychology altered only in name in a behavioristic fashion. Non-behavioristic also is his discrimination between "instincts" and "physiological needs." See BERNARD, L. L., *An Introduction to Social Psychology*, *passim*, N. Y., 1926. The same is to be said of R. PARK's, *Principles of Human Behavior*, 1915. In some cases the term "behavioristic" is utterly misused. For instance, one will wonder why J. Davis' and H. E. Barnes' *Introduction to Sociology* (1927) has a subtitle: "behavioristic" sociology, while in the whole book there is absolutely nothing from "behaviorism." All who really care for and know "behaviorism" can but protest against such a misuse of the term.

[38] Speculative, for instance, is A. P. Weiss' reduction of psychic phenomena to the electron-proton aggregations. Besides, like the above mechanistic theories (see the chapter on the mechanistic school) it is useless. Granted that, like a stone, dog, or plant, human consciousness is an electron-proton aggregation, does it follow from this that the stone, the dog, the plant, and human consciousness are identical things or phenomena? If not, which seems to be certain, then what is the difference between each of the electron-proton aggregations which compose the dog, the stone, the plant, and consciousness? The answer is not given and, of course, cannot be given. Like any "monistic formula" which tries to explain everything, Weiss' formula is meaningless, and at the same time illogical. See WEISS, A. P., *A Theoretical Basis of Human Behavior*, Columbus, Ohio, 1925. Many sweeping statements of John B. Watson go far beyond the factual and experimental data, and in this sense are also quite speculative. Such, for instance, is his contention that all men of all races are exactly alike as regards their innate mental endowment. This conclusion is based practically on nothing, and contradicts somewhat his own statement that the difference in the structure of a body leads to a difference in behavior and functioning. Speculative also is his flat denial of instincts, which again contradicts his theory of innate reflexes and of the

which is going on now in psychology as regards the possibilities and the limits of the behaviorist interpretation of human behavior; and in view of the fact that this problem will confront us throughout the discussion of psychological theories, and that it practically confronts every sociologist in any investigation, let us dwell a little on the problem as to whether the behaviorist approach is the only possible approach to the study of human behavior and social phenomena; whether it has its own limitations; whether the method of introspection is necessary; and if both approaches are possible, where and in what form they are appropriate.

The extreme behaviorists of the type of Watson claim that the behaviorist method is quite sufficient for the analysis and description of all human behavior and psychology, and that introspective methods are quite unnecessary, giving nothing valuable from a cognitive standpoint. They go so far that they believe in the possibility of describing in a strictly behavioristic or trans-subjective terminology even the inner or psychic experiences of man, beginning with consciousness and ending with ideas, emotions, desires, and so on. Accordingly, their "philosophy" tends to assume the forms of a kind of a materialism, for which all psychic phenomena either do not exist or are something fictitious, at any rate devoid of any cognitive value.

On the other hand we have a series of psychological and sociological theories which claim that the methods of introspection are the primary methods of the cognition of human behavior and psychology. In their opinion, psychical phenomena like desires, ideas, wishes, volitions, sentiments, and so forth, are real forces which determine human behavior in its overt or trans-subjective forms. These overt actions are but a manifestation of these psychic forces—the trans-subjective social processes are conditioned by, and could not be understood without, them. Consequently, their causal explanation consists in the insertion of these

---

connection of structural peculiarities with the forms of reactions. Speculative too are many references to the nature of processes going on within the nervous system. In brief, we must carefully discriminate what in behaviorism is really proved by experimental and other data, and what is a mere guess based on nothing. See Watson's papers and the criticism of his behaviorism in the papers of K. Koffka, W. Kohler, M. Prince, and especially W. McDougall, in *Psychologies of 1925.*

subjective forces into a chain of trans-subjective phenomena (see further).

Which of these opposite standpoints is accurate? In the opinion of the writer, from a purely methodological standpoint both are wrong. The extreme behaviorism is wrong because inner experiences cannot be adequately described in the terminology of a strictly overt action. When it is done, the description becomes either extremely poor and inadequate, like the speech of a stutterer, or it turns into a disguised introspectivist description and becomes pseudo-behavioristic. Here are examples:

Consciousness is an electron-proton aggregation (A. P. Weiss).

Consciousness is "a complex integration and succession of bodily activities which are closely related to or involve the verbal and gestural mechanisms, and hence most frequently come to social expression" (K. S. Lashley).[39]

Emotion is "a particular stimulus-response relationship" (W. S. Hunter).[40]

If I had not put at the beginning of these definitions the words "consciousness" and "emotions," nobody would have guessed that these formulas were the definitions of consciousness or emotions. To such an extent they are poor, inadequate and "deaf-mute." Furthermore, my table is also an electro-proton aggregation. Does this mean that it is "consciousness"? A frog exhibits "a complex integration and succession of bodily activities which involve the vocal and gestural mechanisms." Does this mean that the frog is a "consciousness," or that its consciousness is identical to that of man? A snake certainly shows "a particular stimulus-response relationship." Shall we conclude that the snake is "emotion," or that its "emotions" are identical to those of man? These remarks are sufficient to show why such a description is poor and utterly inadequate. They show also that these "scientific" formulas are in fact the worst kind of metaphysics. Here are a little better samples. Let the reader guess what phenomena or kind of behavior is described by the following definitions:

[39] LASHLEY, K. S., "The Behavioristic Interpretation of Consciousness," *Psychological Review*, 1923, Vol. XXX, pp. 237 and 329.
[40] HUNTER, W. S., "The Problem of Consciousness," *Psychological Review*, 1924, pp. 1–31; "Psychology and Anthroponomy," *Psychologies of 1925*, p. 91.

No. 1—"Checking of breathing, jump or start of whole body, crying, often defæcation and urination."

No. 2—"Cessation of crying; gurgling, cooing and many other not determined (reactions). Predomination of visceral factors shown by changes in circulation and respiration, erection of penis."

No. 3—"Stiffening of the whole body, screaming, temporary cessation of breathing, reddening of face, changing to blueness of face." [41]

If one would say that these descriptions represent a kind of an incomprehensible hieroglyphic without a key to read them, one would not be far from the truth. Furthermore, the formulas are so vague that by them it is possible to understand a dozen of various forms of behavior. Finally, one scarcely would guess that formula No. 1 describes "fear" behavior; No. 2, "love" behavior; and No. 3, "rage" behavior. Only with the introduction of these introspective keys: "fear," "love," and "rage" do these formulas acquire a real cognitive value and some scientific meaning. This fact testifies that our experience obtained in an introspective way is neither valueless, nor nil. This shows also that a purely behavioristic description of human conduct, with a complete disregard of the knowledge and the terminology of introspective psychology, is doomed to be extremely poor and inadequate.[42]

But that is not all. Further inadequacy of the strictly behaviorist description of human actions and psychology is shown

[41] WATSON, J. B., "Experimental Studies of the Growth of the Emotions," *Psychologies of 1925*, pp. 49–50.

[42] Dr. W. Kohler is quite right in saying that even the behavior of a monkey could not be described adequately if we had to follow the advices of the extreme behaviorists. In this case "one consequence would be unavoidable: Our description of behavior would become extremely poor, and our concepts would very soon be exactly as poor as our material."—KOHLER, W., "Intelligence of Apes," *Psychologies of 1925*, p. 153. It is comprehensible therefore that a great many of the prominent behaviorists, like W. Bekhtereff, I. Pavlov, W. Wagner, E. C. Tolman, even F. A. Allport, either explicitly recognize the cognitive value of the introspective method and the necessity of combining both the inner and the behavioristic methods of studying human psychology and behavior, or else they implicitly use such terms as in their essence are "introspective." See BEKHTEREFF, W., *General Foundations of Reflexology*, p. 128, (in Russian); WAGNER, W., *Bio-Psikhologia*, Vol. I, pp. 157–249; see other references in my *Systema Soziologii*, Vol. I, pp. 50–76; see also ELLWOOD, CHARLES A., "Objectivism in Sociology," KOFFKA, K., *The Growth of the Mind*, Chaps. I, II, N. Y., 1924.

in that it cannot grasp at all what is styled the "meaning" of either overt actions or subjective psychical processes, or that of symbolic social phenomena like science, religion, ideology, church, school, and so on. "Meaning" is generally indescribable in the terminology of strict behaviorism, because "meaning" is not a trans-subjective or overt phenomenon which may be observed in a change of muscles, or glands, or nervous system. The meaning of Kant's philosophy, or of Newton's "Principia" or Confucianism, or of "two and two is four," is neither a physical phenomenon, nor a description in terms of muscular and glandular contractions; nor may it be seen in a microscope, or studied through a chemical analysis. A "behaviorist net" cannot catch "meaning" at all, as a unit of weight cannot be used to measure space. The expression: "The distance from New York City to Los Angeles is five thousand pounds" is absurd. No less absurd is the expression: "The consciousness is vocal or subvocal reflex," or "Kant's ethics is a totality of the electron-proton aggregations," or "the phenomena of property are a combination of the grasping and collecting reactions of an organism followed by such and such a secretion of a certain kind of glands." Not only the meaning of these complex experiences, but even ˉthe meaning of such things as "love and hatred, reverence and devotion, rage and fear, happiness and suffering," could neither be grasped, nor described by strictly behavioristic methods, providing "the introspective experience" is really excluded. Watson writes: "Negroes show fear," or "awe" or "reverence." [43] This is not a behaviorist description because all that negroes may show to an observer who excludes introspection and psychical experience is this or that change of muscles, reactions, and other trans-subjective movements among which there is nothing of "fear," or "love," or "awe," or other psychic experiences. The mere introduction of these and similar terms is a contamination of pure behaviorism by "introspection." The same must be said of such popular behaviorist terms as "symbolic stimuli," or "attitude," or "psycho-social pattern of behavior." A symbol is inseparable from a meaning and its meaning is different from

---

[43] WATSON, JOHN B., "Experimental Studies of the Growth of the Emotions," *Psychologies of 1925*, p. 37.

the physical character of the symbol stimuli. The national flag is physically only a bit of cloth attached to a stick. As a symbol, however, it means something quite different and incomparably more complex. Physically, Plato's *Republic* is only a paper with some black figures on the white field. As Plato's *Republic* it means something absolutely different from paper and figures. As far as a behaviorist refuses to use the inner experience, and limits his task by a description of overt and physical phenomena, the very conception of a symbol does not, and cannot, exist for him. And the real and great behaviorists, like Pavlov or Sherrington, do not deal with any phenomenon of behavior which is unobservable from "outside," and do not use any of the terms of an overt or masked introspective psychology, and do not try at all to "measure distance by the unit of weight" or to study "behavioristically" inner and subjective phenomena. If a behaviorist uses "inner experience" he ceases to be a pure behaviorist, and in a disguised form introduces "an introspectivism" previously expelled by him. The same may be said of the "attitude," [44] "adjustment," "behavior pattern," and other popular terms of the behaviorists. These terms, in a disguised form, contain a great deal from "inner psychic experience," and through it they are given a more or less clear meaning. In fact all the extreme pseudo-behaviorists do this, and, in a disguised form, reintroduce what they banished before. This means that they are inconsistent, and themselves show the inadequacy of their method. This leads also to another inconvenience from a methodological standpoint. Owing to this disguised use of introspective terminology, their descriptions of human behavior become vague, dull, and unclear, like the above behavioristic formulas.

These indications are sufficient to show some of the fallacies of an extreme pseudo-behaviorism.[45] Does this mean that the

---

[44] See, for instance, ALLPORT, F., *Social Psychology*, pp. 244 ff.; BERNARD, L. L., *Introduction to Social Psychology*, pp. 246 ff.

[45] Many other shortcomings of extreme behaviorism in psychology and sociology are indicated in the papers of K. Koffka, W. Kohler, W. McDougall, M. Benthley, M. Prince, and R. Woodworth, in *Psychologies of 1925*. See also ROBACK, A. A., *Behaviorism and Psychology*, Cambridge, 1923; ELLWOOD, CHARLES A., "Objectivism in Sociology"; FARIS, ELLSWORTH, "The Subjective Aspect of Culture," *Publications of the American Sociological Society*, Vol. XIX, pp. 37–46; OGDEN, C. K., *The Meaning of Psychology*, N. Y., 1926. See also the quoted works of W. Wagner, Bekhtereff, P. Sorokin, and Petrajitzsky.

extreme introspectivists are right? Not at all. Behaviorism in its proper limits is certainly a most valuable method for making a scientific study of human behavior, and through that, of social phenomena. Without the study of the mechanics and the forms of overt or trans-subjective human actions, we never can obtain anything objective and accurate in this field. Within the world of trans-subjective phenomena, behaviorism is the only method which may be used scientifically. As I tried to show, its shortcomings begin when it intrudes into the field of subjective experience, and begins to measure distance by the units of weight, and when, being unable to do so, it begins to deny the value of all other methods, and even of the existence of the realm of inner psychic experiences themselves. Without such missteps, from which the real behaviorists (Pavlov, Sherrington, Magnus) are free, behaviorism is entirely right in its claim that it studies human behavior as a trans-subjective phenomenon, without any insertion of the psychical agencies in a causal chain of trans-subjective events or reactions. This, however, does not entitle it to, and the real behaviorists do not, deny the cognitive value of introspection, nor exclude the possibility of a description of human experiences from the inner side through the method of introspection. The terms, "fear," "love," or "rage," when put side by side with the above formulas of Watson, do not spoil either their objective character, or rob their significance; but rather, they increase their scientific value, and our own knowledge of human behavior. The behaviorist formula shows the outer or trans-subjective side of the phenomena, and the introspective describes the inner experience correlated with them;—both together, their mutual correlation and the phenomena in their entirety. From such a combination our knowledge increases; each set of descriptions becomes more accurate and valuable; and their meaning is mutually supplemented. From a purely cognitive standpoint, one cannot see any defect arising from such a mutual supplement, when it is properly done.

But in order that the above advantages may accrue, both methods must be used in their proper fields. Neither of them is entitled to intrude upon the field of the other with its quite heterogeneous methods absolutely unsuitable for the other field's study. Each description must stand side by side, but not be mingled with another. The introspective experiences in no way may be introduced into the causal chain of the trans-subjective behavior, and the trans-subjective concepts and approaches cannot be used for a description of inner experiences. The type of their relationship must be as follows:

Fear—(introspective description from the inner side)	checking of breathing, jump, start of whole body, etc. (behaviorist description from the outer side)

Each of the descriptions, like different languages, designates in different terms two sides of the phenomena and their correlation. Let behaviorism study its trans-subjective phenomena with its objective methods, and let the introspectivists do the same in regard to the inner experience of man. As soon as they intrude into the field of the other they begin to measure distance by the units of weight.[46] In regard to extreme behaviorism this has been shown above. In regard to introspectivism and introspective sociology this will be shown further *in extenso*. Meanwhile, these remarks are sufficient to outline the position which we must assume in the discussed problem, and to make comprehensible the criticism of the introspectivist psychological interpretations of social phenomena given further. Now let us return to the concrete studies of the behaviorist type of sociology.

C. *Influence of Food Stimuli on Human Behavior, Social Processes, and Organization.*—As yet, we have very few factual interpretations of social phenomena from a behaviorist standpoint. Some of them were mentioned above. There are others, but they also represent either a mere plan of behaviorist study, or are too general to be a real factual interpretation. As an example of the few factual studies of social phenomena from the standpoint of the outlined moderate behaviorism, I will take the liberty to give here a skeleton of my study of the correlation of

[46] The reader should notice that the solution is not a psychophysical parallelism in its philosophical meaning, but a mere methodological parallelism quite different from it. This methodological parallelism of two methods of the study does not pretend to solve the problem of the mind and the body in any way, and does not attach itself to any one of the existing solutions of the problem.

the food stimuli with human behavior, psychology, social processes, and social organization. Its defects may serve as a warning, its virtues as an incentive to other behaviorist interpretations
of social facts.[47]

The guiding principles of this study were those which were
outlined above. First, to start with a trans-subjective stimulus
which may be measured, to proceed to trans-subjective phenomena, and to finish with the trans-subjective facts. Second, the
causal chain of the trans-subjective phenomena must not be
broken by the insertion of the inner psychical experiences or
agencies. Third, a description of the inner psychical experiences
which are concomitant with the changes in the quantity and
quality of the food consumed is to be added to, but not to be
mingled with, the description of the changes in the field of the
trans-subjective phenomena. Fourth, as a starting point in the
study is taken Pavlov's theory of the nutrition process; the theory
of the nervous center which controls it; and the mechanism of its
operation—the unconditioned and the conditioned ways of the
stimulation and inhibition of "the nutrition center of the nervous
system" through the blood and nervous system itself—in brief, all
the essentials of Pavlov's theory.[48] Omitting here the details,
the methodology, and many points and reservations, the essential
results obtained may be summed up as follows:

Taking the quantity and the quality of food consumed as an
independent variable, and concentrating attention on the cases
when this variable is below the physiological minimum, or when
we have physiological inanition, we obtain in the first place a
series of *correlations between this variable and the bodily characteristics of man and animals,* established by many investigators.
The quantity and the quality of food determine many characteristics of the alimentary tract and its organs, the stature, the

[47] SOROKIN, P., *Influence of Inanition on Human Behavior, Social Organization,
and Social Life,* Petrograd, 1922, Kolos Co. The book was destroyed by the
Soviet government in the process of printing. From a volume of about 600 pages
I have about 300 pages in galley proofs.

[48] See PAVLOV, IVAN, *Lectures in the Activity of the Principal Alimentary Glands,*
(in Russian), 1897, *The Work of the Digestive Glands,* London, 1902; BABKIN, B.,
Exterior Secretion of the Alimentary Glands, (in Russian), 1915; LONDON, E.,
Physiology and Pathology of Digestion, (in Russian), 1916; PAVLOV, I., "The
Nutrition Center" and "The Real Physiology of the Brain," in his *Twenty Years,*
pp. 92–99. See other readings in these works.

weight, the chemical composition of the body, the size of the chest, the form of the cranium, and other bodily traits. In all these respects inanition calls forth considerable changes. For this reason, a series of bodily differences of various social groups who consume food in different quantity and quality may be accounted for through this factor. Such, for instance, are the greater weight and stature of the well-to-do classes as compared with those of the poor classes.[49]

In the second place, *inanition calls forth a fundamental change in all physiological processes,* which has been pretty well studied by physiologists.

In the third place, *the changes in a body and its physiology, caused by inanition, are paralleled by a series of changes in subjective psychical experience.* (A) At the beginning of physiological and comparative inanition, *in the field of feeling and emotions* we have the appearance of "appetite." Inanition continued, "appetite" turns into a quite different feeling of "hunger"; and later into different and complex feelings of weakness, dull pain, "emptiness," and apathy, interrupted by moments of irritation, angriness, low feeling, and general psychical depression. (B) *In the field of sensation, perception, and attention,* the first stages of inanition are followed by a decrease of sensitiveness and attention toward all phenomena which do not have a relation to food and nutrition, and by a sharp increase of sensitiveness and attention toward all phenomena which directly or indirectly are related to food and nutrition. Man becomes dull and deaf toward everything but food and nutrition phenomena. Continuation of starvation finally leads to a general dullness and apathy. The whole receptive system becomes disorganized and loses its ability of analyzing the exterior world and its components. (C) *In the field of the reproductive imagination and association of ideas,* inanition is paralleled by a driving out of the field of consciousness of all images, representations, and ideas heterogeneous to food and nutrition phenomena, and by filling the field with images, representations, and ideas of "food character." At the same time, a free course of idea association is interrupted more and more by the involuntary intrusion of "the alimentary represen-

[49] See also ARMITAGE, F. P., *Diet and Race,* London, 1922.

tations, images and ideas," which often leads to "food" hallucination and delirium of inanition. Men become more and more unable to think about anything but food and phenomena related to food. (D) In the field of *the speech-reaction* this is expressed by the fact that "food-topics" begin to occupy more and more place and drive out all other topics from the conversation of starving people. (E) In the field of *memory,* in the first stage inanition is paralleled by a weakening of the memory of things and events unrelated to food, and by an intensification of it in regard to food phenomena. In the later stages of inanition memory generally weakens and leads to the forgetting of even a man's own name and address. (F) In the field of *desires and wishes,* we have a weakening of all wishes unrelated to food, and a reinforcement of the wishes for food. (G) In the field of *volitions,* as an intentional effort, we have their weakening, which, under a continued inanition, makes an individual apathetic, indifferent, and incapable of any deliberate effort. (H) In the field of the *whole psychical life,* inanition is paralleled by a revolution of its whole course. Inanition being strong and long enough, it is paralleled by a disintegration of "self"; a disorganization of personality, its harmony, and oneness, by a weakening of the ability of cohesive thinking, and concentration of thought; and by an increase of psychoses and mental disease.[50] Thus, with inanition, man's body, physiology, and psychology greatly change.

In the fourth place, *inanition changes all of human behavior.* Since man changes physically, physiologically, and psychologically under the influence of deficient food, his behavior changes, too. The central phenomenon in this change may be styled as *an increase in the attraction of a hungry man toward food objects or their substitutes whose possession helps to obtain food.* In other words, all behavior tends to assume the character of the food

---

[50] SOROKIN, P., *op. cit.,* pp. 1–112; see also PETRAJITZSKY, LEO, *Introduction to the Theory of Law and Ethics,* Part II; LUCIANI, *Das Hungern,* 1890; PASHUTIN, *General and Experimental Pathology,* (in Russian), 1902, Vol. II; BORING, E. G., "Processes Referred to the Alimentary and Urinary Tracts," *The Psychological Review,* No. 4, 1915; MARSH, "Individual and Sex Differences," *The Psychological Review,* 1916, pp. 434–445; CANNON, W. B., *Bodily Changes in Pain, Hunger, Fear, and Rage,* D. Appleton Co.; ARMITAGE, F. P., *Diet and Race,* London, 1922. Other literature was given in my book.

obtaining reactions, or that of approaching to food and its substitutes. The very fact of such an attraction is not learned but innate. The technique or the concrete manifestation of it in certain patterns of behavior is learned and varies according to circumstances. From this standpoint, the totality of the food-approaching actions may be subdivided into the *pure,* stimulated exclusively by lack of food, and the *mixed,* stimulated by lack of food and other factors. Both varieties may be subdivided further into the *simple* food-approaching reactions (taking the food, chewing, and swallowing it) and the *complex* food-approaching reactions, consisting of a long chain of various actions whose objective is to obtain the food, (the reactions of taking a job, doing it, going to shop, buying the food, cooking it, and finally swallowing).

Analyzing the part of such actions in the total budget of human actions, it is possible to make the following generalization: *The greater are the obstacles to be overcome in order to obtain food, the greater is the proportion of the food-approaching actions in the whole of human behavior.* When, as in the case of a great famine, these obstacles become extremely great, the whole of human behavior tends to become a mere food-searching behavior composed of the pure and the mixed; of the simple and the complex food-tropic activities. Study of the budget of time in man's behavior, and the budget of income and expenses corroborates this. However, the intensity of the food-tropic tendency is not constant, but varies according to the length and the degree of inanition. In absolute starvation it usually reaches its climax on the third, fourth, and fifth day. After that its intensity begins to go down, as a result of the general weakening of man's vitality and energy.

The above means that hunger tends to drive out all other activities unrelated to nutrition from our behavior, and to turn the body-machinery into an exclusive mechanism of nutrition. Consequently, under the stimuli of a lack of food, men risk doing many dangerous actions which they would not have done had they not been hungry (repression of self-protective reactions by hunger). The same is true in regard to the group of actions whose purpose is to protect the interests of the group to which man belongs.   Such actions as are harmful to the group or other fellow men, but which may help under the circumstances to satiate the hunger, tend to increase.   Therefore people who have a horror of cannibalism when they are well fed often become cannibals and kill their neighbors, children, and fellow men to eat them when they are starving.   For the same reason we have an increase in the killing of useless members of a group to alleviate starvation.   Under such conditions, an honest man may become a traitor to his friends and relatives in order to obtain bread.   In a similar way, the group of sex reactions undergoes a direct and indirect change also.   The sex appetite falls down and weakens. The actions of copulation decrease in number.   Sex love and romance tend to disappear.   On the other hand, sex chastity may be thrown away if an act of prostitution may help to obtain food.   Hence the increase of such actions on the part of women in time of famine, if there are buyers.   In a similar way all other purely acquired actions,—religious, moral, social, æsthetic, and conventional—tend to cease to be performed if their performance hinders a satiation of hunger under the circumstances.   The non-thief becomes a thief; the proud man, meek; and the independent like Esau, is ready to sell his birthright, dignity, and freedom for bread and a pottage of lentils.   Finally, convictions, opinions, and beliefs also undergo a change if they hinder satisfaction of hunger.   Thus the whole human behavior changes.

In the fifth place, the *above change of human behavior makes comprehensible the noticeable changes in the field of social phenomena when a considerable part of the population begins to starve or experiences an aggravation due to lack of nutrition.*   As the actions of nutrition are performed several times every day this explains the existence of several social institutions which are, so to speak, *constant functions* of the factor of nutrition in any existing society.   All activities and institutions in a society whose purpose is to obtain food for its members, to prepare it, and to distribute it are to be regarded as such constant social functions of the factor of nutrition.   A considerable part of the so-called economic institutions of production, distribution, exchange, and consumption are of this nature, whatever may be their concrete forms.   Side by side with these constant functions there are sporadic social functions of the factor when it assumes the forms of mass starvation. In this case, the behavior of all the starving population assumes the above food-tropic character. Under such conditions plus the existing concrete circumstances of a starving society, one or several of the following social effects may be expected: *First, the invention of new, or the improvement of old methods of obtaining food; second, an increase in imports of food from other societies; third, an increase of peaceful or violent emigration from the starving country to other non-starving ones; fourth, invasion of non-starving societies by the starving people, or prevention of such an invasion of the non-starving societies by force, which results in the phenomena of war and conflict; fifth, an increase of crimes against property and in a less degree against persons; sixth, an increase of disorders and revolution as a form of violent appropriation of the wealth and food of the well-to-do classes by the poor and the starving; seventh, an increase of governmental interference in economic affairs and governmental control of food-supply and distribution (starving state-socialism); eighth, an enslaving or increasing dependence of the poor upon the rich in exchange for bread; ninth, if all these manifestations of the food-tropic activities fail to satisfy the need, either the mortality rate increases, or the birth rate decreases, or both of these phenomena take place; tenth, the speech-reactions of the society change also in the direction of an increase of "food-speech reactions" measured by the space in the paper given to food-topics, by the number of meetings of parliament and other bodies politic for a discussion of the food problem, by the topics of private conversations, and so on; eleventh, among the ideologies of society, those which under the circumstances stimulate to actions which promise a satisfaction of starvation (for instance, confiscation of the wealth of the rich or invasion of a rich country) tend to become more contagious, while the ideologies of the opposite hindering character lose their popularity.*

One, or in the majority of cases, several of these effects invariably take place in a society where the nutrition of a considerable part of its population becomes deficient or worse qualitatively and quantitatively. An inductive verification of these statements through historical data, statistical data, experimental materials, and observation, justifies the expectation and makes tangible the correlation between the fluctuation of the quality and the quantity of food consumed by a society and the phenomena of migration, war, crime, revolution, expansion of government control, increase in the death and decrease in the birth rate, and the increase and decrease of the popularity and contagiousness of various ideologies.

Although the social effects of the same factor are manifold, they must not embarrass us because the circumstances a, b, c, d, e, f, under which the factor operates are different in various societies. Naturally, the concrete effects of the discussed factor must be different. Thus, the above must show that the social effects of such a prosaic factor as the quantity and the quality of food consumed are enormous. They go so far as to influence phenomena so remote as social ideologies and beliefs. Nevertheless, the correlation is tangible, and, being such, should be stated.

This study has convinced the writer of the important rôle of the unconditioned reflexes.[51] Though the concrete forms of the "food-approaching" reactions may vary and a great number of them have been learned, yet the "food-approaching" direction of behavior, many "nutrition-reflexes" beginning with the kind of materials suitable and unsuitable for food, and the fundamental mechanism which controls the essentials of the process of nutrition, and so on, are certainly innate. They "give a tone" to the whole "complex symphony" of the actual behavior of a starving man and to his learned reactions. These innate reflexes, being eliminated, the whole behavior of a starving man becomes incomprehensible. The same is true in regard to many other unconditioned reflexes. This means that extreme "environmentalism" is unsupportable from the behaviorist standpoint.[52]

[51] I can say the same on the basis of my study of the phenomena of revolution. Without an admission of the repression of a series of unconditioned responses, it is impossible to understand the most important features of these phenomena. See my *Sociology of Revolution*.

[52] In a general discussion about instincts or learned actions it is easy to construct any kind of a one-sided theory. Not being put into operation, they may look all right. As soon, however, as an investigator takes a factual problem and begins to analyze it, a great many one-sided and "well-combed" general theories do not work. This is the reason why here, as well as in other chapters of the

I have already indicated the main weaknesses of the instinctivist theories. In a proper behaviorist interpretation there are all the strong points of the instinctivist theories, without their weaknesses. Furthermore, when the number of really behavioristic studies is sufficiently great; when the existing unconditioned responses and their typical combinations into the more complex bunches are sufficiently studied; when their mechanism of stimulation, inhibition, modification, and interrelations is properly investigated; when their periodicity is properly analyzed and the interrelationship of the conditioned responses is investigated further; and finally, when the relative powerfulness of various conditioned and unconditioned responses is measured and a rough index of this comparative powerfulness is outlined,[53]—then we will have every reason for expecting that the behaviorist interpretation of social phenomena will throw a great light on the mystery of human behavior and history. The prospect is rather bright, but in order that it may be realized, it is necessary to forsake the existing "flapping" around "instincts"; or the metaphysical intrusion into the field of inner experiences; or extreme speculation. It is necessary that we get busy with a careful objective study of the unconditioned and the conditioned responses along the lines outlined above.

---

book, I usually take the principal factual studies rather than the general "Outlines," "Fundamentals," and "Introductions," which are full of these non-tested reasonings. By the way it is curious to note that while many a pseudo-behavioristic sociological treatise denies the existence or important rôle of the unconditioned responses or "instincts," real behaviorism views them as the very basis of all the conditioned responses. "The totality of reflexes (or "instincts") composes a basic fund of man's or animal's nervous activity," says Pavlov: *Lectures*, Chap. I and *passim*.

[53] As far as I know only very few attempts have been made to measure the comparative power of various "drives" and to find methods for such measurements. See MOORE, HENRY T., "A Method of Testing the Strength of Instincts," *American Journal of Psychology*, Vol. XXVII, pp. 227–233. The method appears to me unsuccessful. Much better seem to be the experimental methods applied in Pavlov's school in their attempts to study the problem. See ARKHANGELSKY, B. M., "A Comparative Power of Various Forms of Inhibition" (in Russian), *Works of Pavlov's Laboratory*, Vol. I, Book I, 1924; TIKHOMIROFF, N. P., "Power of a Stimulus," *Publications of the Society of the Russian Physicians*, 1910 (in Russian); CHAPIN, F. S., "Measuring the Volume of Social Stimuli," *Social Forces*, Vol. IV, pp. 479–495. Using "the method of conflict," and observing which of the conflicting reactions stimulated by different stimuli is driven out and which remains in body-machinery, I have tried in a rough way to give tentative indices of the comparative power of the principal "drives" in my study of hunger.

4. INTERPRETATIONS IN TERMS OF DESIRES, CONATIONS, PAIN
AND PLEASURE, INTERESTS, WISHES, WANTS, VOLI-
TIONS, AND ATTITUDES

A. *General Characteristic of the Branch.*—The third dominant
variety of the psychological school is represented by numerous
theories which take the psychological experiences of man as the
key to an understanding of human behavior and social processes,,
classify them into a number of groups, view them as the dynamic
agencies of human behavior and social processes, and interpret
these processes as a manifestation of the dynamics of these agencies. It is needless to say that the essentials of such an interpretation are very old. Beginning with the ancient sources of
Indian, Chinese, Grecian, and Roman thought, and passing
throughout the mediæval works, everywhere we find statements
which ascribe to human desires, affections, wishes, lusts, conations, and similar subjective psychical agencies a good or bad,
but great, influence. In the same sources we find several classifications of these agencies. At the present moment there are
rather numerous theories of this type. Their terminology is
somewhat different, but their essence is similar, in that they all
take psychical experience as a "variable" for the interpretation of
human behavior and social processes, and regard the latter as a
function of the play of these variables. The principal varieties
of these theories will next be described.

B. *Interpretations in the Terms of Beliefs, Desires, and Conations. Gabriel Tarde.*—Possibly the most prominent modern
representatives of this type of interpretation are Gabriel Tarde
(1843-1904) and Lester F. Ward (1841-1913). Among the
sociologists of the end of the nineteenth and the beginning of
the twentieth century, Tarde occupied one of the few very prominent positions. Born in a small town in France, he held the positions of judge, criminal statistician, editor of a scientific journal,
and finally, the position of a professor of modern philosophy in
the Collége de France. Among his numerous works the most
important are: *Les lois de l'imitation,* (1890, English translation by E. C. Parsons, 1903), *La philosophic pénale,* (1890), *Les
transformations du droit,* (1893), *La logigue sociale,* (1895),

Essais et mélanges sociologiques, (1895), *L'opposition univer-selle,* (1897), *Les lois sociales,* (1898, English translation by H. C. Warren, 1899), *Études de psychologie sociale,* (1898), *L'opinion et la foule,* (1901). A short summary of the essentials of his sociological doctrine is given in Tarde's *Social Laws.*[54]

A brilliant writer and inspirational thinker, Tarde left a great many original plans, ideas, and theories in sociology, social psychology, criminology, economics, and philosophy. Although marked by originality, inspiration, and intuitive insight, his theories show also that Tarde was rather a social philosopher than an accurate scientific scholar. Many of his theories lack the necessary accuracy and clearness; and some others are rather speculative. None the less, Tarde has exerted an enormous influence on contemporary sociological thought. Leaving here without discussion his metaphysics, monadology, criminology, and other theories which do not directly belong to sociology, the essentials of the Tarde sociological system may be summed up as follows:

1. Social phenomena are psychical in their nature. They consist in an interaction of individual minds. They are made up of beliefs and desires of the interacting individuals. Where such a psychical interaction is found there also is found society and social phenomena in their pure form. Where such psychical relations are lacking there is no society.[55] This shows that Tarde, although a psychological sociologist, at the same time refuses to join either psycho-social or biological organicism. He emphatically rejects all theories of a "social mind" or "collective soul," and so on. He remains a representative of "nominalism" in sociology.

[54] About Tarde see DAVIS, M. M., *op. cit.,* pp. 83–260. Notice the good bibliography of the writings of Tarde, pp. 254–260; the articles of R. Worms, É. Levasseur, M. Kovalevsky, P. Grimanelli, Charles Limousin and others in *Revue international de sociologie,* Vol. XII, 1904; BOUGLÉ, C., "Gabriel Tarde," *Revue de Paris,* Vol. III, 1905; BELOT, "La logique sociale d'aprés M. Tarde," *Revue philosophique,* Vol. IV, 1896; VIERKANDT, A., "G. Tarde und die Bestrebungen der Soziologie," *Zeitschrift für Sozial-Wissenschaft,* Jahrgang II, 1899; TOSTI, G., "The Sociological Theories of G. Tarde," *Political Science Quarterly,* Vol. XII, 1897; WARD, LESTER F., "Tarde's Social Laws," *Science,* Vol. XI, 1900; KOVALEVSKY, M., *Contemporary Sociologists,* Chap. I; LICHTENBERGER, J. P., *op. cit.,* Chap. XIV; SQUILLACE, F., *op. cit.,* pp. 321 ff.

[55] See TARDE, G., "La psychologie intermentale," *Revue intern. de sociologie* Vol. IX, 1901, pp. 1–13; *L'opposition universelle,* pp. 165, 336, Paris, 1897; *La logique sociale,* p. 87, Paris, 1895; *The Laws of Imitation,* preface.

2. The mental or inter-cerebral interaction of individuals,— that is, the exchange and circulation of the desires and beliefs which compose the essence of social processes,—has three principal forms: repetition or imitation, opposition, and adaptation or invention. Any new idea or belief which appears in the mind of an individual tends to be repeated or imitated by other individuals. It originates a wave of imitation and tends to spread throughout society. In the process of its diffusion it meets, sooner or later, another wave of imitation coming from another center of invention. The meeting of the two or more different waves of imitation results in the phenomena of their opposition. Thus imitation produces opposition, as the second fundamental form of social processes. Opposition of two or more waves of imitation may result either in a mutual destruction of both waves, when they are equally strong and irreconcilable; or in a destruction of the weaker imitational wave by the stronger one; or in a mutual adaptation of the two imitational patterns, which means a new invention. Thus, opposition calls forth adaptation or invention as the third fundamental form of social process. Any invention adaptation is a "lucky marriage" of two or more imitational patterns (ideas, beliefs) in the mind of an individual. A new invention being made, a new wave of imitation takes place; and spreading, it meets another wave of imitation. This results in their opposition; opposition leads to a new invention, and so on.

Such is Tarde's conception of the social process, its dynamics, and its fundamental forms.[56]

3. From the above it follows that, according to Tarde, invention is the source of social change. Any new idea, belief, or form of behavior which is invented is similar to a stone thrown into the water of a social sea. It produces a wave of imitation, and this spreads until it meets another wave. They clash and either annul each other, or one of them annuls the other, or they originate a new invention. Such incessant inventions, imitations, oppositions constitute the dynamics of social life.

4. Of these three forms of social process, imitation and invention have been studied by Tarde especially attentively. He tried

[56] Tarde, G., *Social Laws, passim; L'opposition universelle*, pp. 88–98, 331–332, 428. *La logique sociale*, pp. 166 ff.

to indicate the factors which facilitate or hinder inventions. Innate mental ability, social need, and social conditions are among these factors. Among Tarde's laws of imitation should be noted the following: The imitation-wave tends to spread from its initial center in geometrical progression. "Imitations are refracted by their social media": a physical or racial heterogeneity of population is a condition which checks the successful diffusion of an imitation-wave. Imitations themselves may be either logical or extra-logical. Both forms usually proceed from the socially superior to the socially inferior. Inner imitation in mind precedes an overt imitation in practice. In the life history of a society there is a rhythm of the period of custom and of fashion. In the period of custom it is the ancient patterns which are predominantly imitated, while, in the period of fashion, it is the most modern patterns of beliefs or conduct which have prestige and are imitated.

Such is the skeleton of Tarde's sociological theory. It shows that his conception of social life, its dynamics, its forms, and factors are entirely psychological. The purpose of sociology is not to explain the trans-subjective events of history or of the behavior of men in their concrete psycho-physical form, but in the dynamics of ideas, beliefs, desires, and other inner experiences. Men's behavior, relationship, historical and social events, as trans-subjective phenomena, are interesting to Tarde's sociology only so far as they are a manifestation of mental phenomena, and as far as they may influence the psychic processes of invention, opposition, and imitation. Outside of this they lose any interest for his sociology.[57] This signifies that the very objective

[57] In the above we saw that the attitude of De Roberty is similar. For him the subject matter of sociology is also "social thought," but not a "cosmo-bio-social" phenomenon of history or human behavior. Of present-day sociologists a similar conception is logically developed in E. C. Hayes' (b. 1868) *Introduction to the Study of Sociology*. Interrelated psychical activities ("experience-activity") are the essentials of social life or social process. They compose the object matter of sociology; and the study of their relationship (suggestion of ideas, radiation of sentiments, and imitation of overt practices), their intercausation, their forms, and so forth, is considered to be the proper task of sociology. Physical phenomena, such as the geographic environment, the artificial physical environment—technique—or the psycho-physical traits of the population, are only "conditioning factors" of social life, and are taken into consideration only so far as they are "manifestations" of social "activity-experiences." Ideas, sentiments, and other psychic phenomena are regarded as agencies which

of Tarde's sociology is quite different from that of many other sociologists who try not so much to study the psychic interaction of individuals, but human behavior, human interrelations, social and historical events, as such, regardless of whether they are "manifestations" of mental processes or not. Tarde, and other psychological sociologists, try to decipher the dynamics of ideas, desires, beliefs, in their social circulation, while other sociologists. on the contrary, try to decipher the dynamics of a trans-subjective human behavior and social events, as such. This is the great difference in the understanding of the very nature and objective of sociology. It is responsible for many other differences between these two classes of sociologists.

Lester F. Ward.—Another of the most prominent representatives of an interpretation of social phenomena in terms of desires and conations is Lester F. Ward (1841-1913).[58] Together, Henry Cary, W. G. Sumner, and L. Ward represent probably the most conspicuous figures of the earlier generation of Ameri can sociologists who ranked at that time among the most prominent sociologists of the world. In Ward's numerous works, and especially in *Dynamic Sociology* (1883), *Psychic Factors of Civilization* (1893), *Outlines of Sociology* (1898), *Pure Sociology* (1903) and *Applied Sociology* (1906), he laid down a broad system, not so much like a sociology as social philosophy. Putting aside the philosophical part of his system, which does not concern us here, we find that its purely sociological part consists in his theory of social forces, and in his comparison of the teleological or conative character of social process to the blind character of natural process.

---

determine human behavior and social processes. "The human organism is a mechanism adapted to function under the stimulation of ideas." See HAYES, EDWARD C., *op. cit.*, Chaps. XVII–XXI and *passim*, and especially pp. 302-306, 311-316, 340-347.

[58] About L. F. Ward see LICHTENBERGER, J. P., *Development of Social Theory*, Chap. XIII; DEALEY, JAMES Q., *Sociology, Its Development and Application*, N. Y., 1920; "L. F. Ward," *Social Forces*, Vol. IV, pp. 257–272. See further the articles of E. A. Ross, F. H. Giddings, U. G. Weatherly, C. A. Ellwood, A. W. Small, published in *American Journal of Sociology*, Vol. XIX, July; BARTH, P., *op. cit.*, pp. 446 ff.; SOROKIN, P., "Principal Theories of Progress" (in Russian), *Vestnik Snania*, September, 1911; HOUSE, FLOYD N., "The Concept 'Social Forces' in American Sociology," *American Journal of Sociology*, Vol. XXXI, September, pp. 156 ff.

Ward's theory of social forces is marked in the first place by a discrimination of the dynamic and the guiding agencies among these forces. Dynamic agencies are desires or feelings; the guiding agency is the human intellect. The first supplies the dynamic energy; the second perceives the ways and means of attaining ends. "It is no force, but only a condition. It does not propel, it only directs" (the blind force of desires).[59] Desires as real social forces are classified as follows:[60]

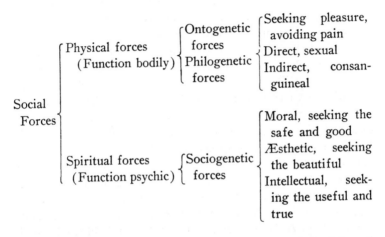

These desires are the "motor-power" of human behavior and social processes. Intellect's function, since the time of its slow evolving, has been the guidance of the blind forces of desires. This function of intellect is gradually increasing. Accordingly, under its influence the social adaptation of man assumes a more and more teleological and circuitous or indirect character, instead of a blind and direct character of the natural process not guided by intellect. This means that the social adaptation of man becomes more and more artificial, calculated, self-directed, and self-controlled by intellect. Ward depicts a rather optimistic prospect of the future of mankind, and his theory stimulates human

[59] See the details in WARD, *Dynamic Sociology*, Vol. I, pp. 69, 468 ff.; Vol. II, 89 ff., 93 ff.; *Pure Sociology*, pp. 256 ff.; *Psychic Factors of Civilization, passim* and Chap. XXXIII.
[60] *Pure Sociology*, p. 261. Compare *Dynamic Sociology*, Vol. I, p. 472.

efforts, guided by knowledge, to an organization of universal happiness as the ultimate end of conation.[61]

Partly under the influence of Ward, partly independent from him, many a prominent sociologist has set forth theories similar to those of Ward's. Such is, for instance, E. A. Ross's theory of desires as social forces. The desires are classified into two large classes: the natural and the cultural. The natural desires are: (a) appetitive (hunger, thirst, sex-appetite); (b) hedonic (fear, aversion to pain, love of ease, warmth, sensuous pleasure); (c) egotic (shame, envy, love of liberty, of glory, of power); (d) affective (sympathy, sociability, love, hate, jealousy, anger, revenge); (e) recreative (play impulses, love of self-expression). The cultural desires are: (a) religious; (b) ethical; (c) æsthetic; (d) intellectual.[62]

Professor Charles A. Ellwood, in his later works, side by side with the geographic and biological forces, gives great importance to psychic factors, to impulses, to feelings, and to intelligence.[63] In his opinion, "all our social life and social behavior are not only embedded in feeling, but largely guided and controlled by feeling." Again, "intelligence is the active agent in social progress" and it plays an exclusively important part. Several other authors, like W. G. Sumner and A. Keller (hunger, love, vanity and fear), F. A. Bushee, and partly O. Spann, hold similar positions.[64] Such is this hedonistic plus intellectualistic variety of the school.

C. *Interpretations in Terms of Interests.*—The second variety

[61] See *Dynamic Sociology*, Vol. I, pp. 15, 18, 29, 487 ff.; Vol. II, pp. 2, 13, 93, and *passim; Pure Sociology*, pp. 15–29, 545, and *passim.*

[62] Ross, EDWARD A., "Moot Points in Sociology," *American Journal of Sociology*, Vols. VIII, IX, X, especially Chap. V. Professor Ross's position in this respect has undergone slight changes in his writings. His present attitude in this point in essence is still essentially the same. "The immediate causes of social phenomena are to be sought in the human mind." The original social forces are human instincts. The combination of these instincts or cravings, or wants, gives "the derivative social forces" in the form of the "interests" like wealth, government, religion, and knowledge. To these forces is attached the race factor and geographic environment. Such is the latest theory of Ross as outlined in his *Principles of Sociology*, Chaps. IV to VII.

[63] ELLWOOD, CHARLES A., *Introduction to Social Psychology*, pp. 75–77, 1917; *The Psychology of Human Society*, pp. 316 ff., 365 ff., and Chaps. III, X, XII.

[64] SUMNER-KELLER, *op. cit.*, pp. 21 ff. and *passim;* BUSHEE, F. A., *Principles of Sociology*, pp. 57 ff.; SPANN, O., *op. cit.*, p. 20. Spann regards *"Emphindungen"* and "actions" as the final "elements" of society.

of the discussed group of introspectivist psychological interpretations is represented by theories which take the "interests" as a variable of human behavior and social processes. The term, "interest," is different from that of "desire" or "feeling," and the classification of the interests also varies from author to author. But, in essence, the character of the interest theories is essentially the same as that of the desire theories. Gustav Ratzenhofer's [65] and Albion Small's theories of the interests as the permanent and fundamental factors of social dynamics, are representative. According to Ratzenhofer, "in the beginning were interests." Viewing them as "the inner necessities" or drives he claims that "it is the key of interests that unlocks the door of every treasure house of sociological lore." Social life is a huge bundle of interests; social groupings are but the groupings of individuals around the interests; and social dynamics itself is but an incessant conflict, adaptation, and inter-play of the interests of the members of a society. The principal interests, according to Ratzenhofer, are: (1) the racial or sexual; (2) food and self-preservation or physiological interest; (3) the individual interest; (4) the social interests, (in family, class, nation); (5) the transcendental interests, (in an unseen and ultimate absolute or in religion and philosophy).[66]

Albion Small's [67] theory of interests represents a modification of Ratzenhofer's theory. For Small also "interests are the stuff that men are made of."

The whole life-process, whether viewed in its individual or in its social phase, is at last the process of developing, adjusting, and satisfying interests [understood as] the unsatisfied capacity, corresponding to an unrealized condition, and predisposition to such rearrangement as would tend to realize the indicated condition.

[65] Born in 1842, died in 1904. About Ratzenhofer see LICHTENBERGER, J. P., op. cit., Chap. XV; BARTH, P., op. cit., pp. 472 ff.; JACOBS, P. P., German Sociology, N. Y., 1909; SMALL, A., General Sociology, 1905, Chap. XIII.

[66] RATZENHOFER, G., Die soziologische Erkenntnis, pp. 55–66, Leipzig, 1898; some other works of Ratzenhofer are: Wesen und Zweck der Politik, 3 volumes Leipzig, 1893; Soziologie, Leipzig, 1907.

[67] Born 1854, died 1926. Principal works are: An Introduction to the Study of Society (in collaboration with George E. Vincent), 1894; General Sociology, 1905; Adam Smith and Modern Sociology, 1907; The Cameralists, 1910; The Meaning of Social Science, 1910; Origins of Sociology, 1924. About Small see the articles of several authors in American Journal of Sociology, Vol. XXXII, No. 1; HAYES. E. C., "A. W. Small," Social Forces, Vol. IV. No. 4.

In this sense the theory of interests is "the latest word in sociology." [68] The interests are classified by Small into six classes: health, wealth, sociability or prestige, knowledge, beauty, and rightness.[69]

There is no need to enumerate the many other theories which use the concept of interests for an explanation of social phenomena and as a principal or partial social force. It is used by Ross, Spann and even by A. Bentley.[70] It is extensively used by economists, but their use of this term is considerably different. Their "interests" have a stick for measurement, and they represent almost always some trans-subjective phenomena. For this reason they must not be mixed with the above sociological concepts of interests, especially in Ratzenhofer's and Small's interpretation.

D. *Interpretations in Terms of Wishes, Volitions, Attitudes, and so on.*—If, instead of the interests and desires in the preceding theories we put the word "wishes," and slightly modify the above classifications, we shall find the interpretation of social phenomena in terms of wishes. The theories of W. I. Thomas (1863–), R. Park (1864–), and E. Burgess may be regarded as the modern forms of this old type of the interpretation of human behavior and social dynamics. Similarly to Ward, Small, Ratzenhofer and others, who, like the social physicists of the seventeenth century, regard the "desires" or the "interests" as the final atoms into which the social life is dissolvable, Professors Thomas, Park, and Burgess regard wishes as the most elementary component of social phenomena. In a sociological analysis the wishes play a rôle similar to that of the electrons in chemical analysis. Wishes are numerous. But they may be classed into a few fundamental classes. Such classes are four: the wish for security, the wish for new experience, the wish for response, and the wish for recognition.

---

[68] SMALL, A., *General Sociology*, pp. 197–198, 282–284, 425–426, 433.

[69] *Ibid.*, pp. 197–198. See the details in HOUSE, F., *op. cit., American Journal of Sociology*, Vol. XXXI, pp. 507–512.

[70] Through the identification of the concepts of social group activity and interests, and through the further replacement of group activity by interests, A. Bentley skipped from a behaviorist position into that of the psychological interpretation of social phenomena in terms of interests. See BENTLEY, A., *Process of Government*, pp. 258 ff.; see also his "Simmel, Durkheim and Ratzenhofer," *American Journal of Sociology*, Vol. XXXII, pp. 250–256.

The combination of wishes and sentiments composes attitudes or behavior patterns which stand toward the wishes in the same relationship as the electrons in chemistry toward the elementary substances.[71] Further examples of the operations with the wishes as a cognitive principle are given in the works of the Freudian school, many psychologists, social philosophers, and ordinary philosophers.[72]

E. *Interpretations in the Terms of Ideas, Sentiments and Emotions.*—The most conspicuous samples of the interpretation of social phenomena in the terms of ideas, and especially of scientific ideas, were given above in characterizing the theories of De Roberty and A. Fouillée. (See the sociologistic school.) Therefore, we need not recapitulate these and similar theories here.

Furthermore, it is needless also to give a detailed analysis of other interpretations of social phenomena in terms of the sentiments, affections, emotions, or other "components" of psychical experience. It is enough to say that such interpretations are not lacking,[73] but on the other hand, they represent rather a terminological than a substantial difference from the above psychological theories. Like them they, under the name of the sentiments, affections, and emotions, take an intra-individual psychical datum,

[71] See PARK, R., and BURGESS, E., *Introduction to the Science of Sociology*, pp. 435–443 and Chap. VII; THOMAS, WILLIAM I., *The Unadjusted Girl*, pp. 4 ff., Boston, 1923; THOMAS, W. I., and ZNANIECKY, F., *The Polish Peasant in Europe and America*, Vol. I, pp. 21–23, 72–73. In this earlier work Thomas' conceptions of attitude, value, causation, and wishes is somewhat different from that given in *The Unadjusted Girl*.

[72] See, for instance, HOLT, E. B., *The Freudian Wish and Its Place in Ethics*, N. Y., 1915; WATSON, JOHN B., "The Psychology of Wish Fulfillment," *Scientific Monthly*, pp. 479–486, 1916. The most important parts of these works are given in PARK and BURGESS, *op. cit.;* SUTHERLAND, E., *Criminology*, pp. 118 ff., 1924; VAN DER HOOP, J. H., *Character and Unconscious*, Chap. III. The enormous literature of the voluntaristic psychology and philosophy represents a modified variety of the discussed group of the theories, with the difference which is given between the meaning of the "wish" and the "will." The philosophies of Schopenhauer, Nietzsche, and to some extent of Hegel, are samples of such a philosophical interpretation of the universe in terms of volition.

[73] See, for instance, RIBOT, T. A., *Psychology of Sentiments*, Russian translation, pp. 15 ff. and *passim*, 1898; LANGE, *The Dynamics of Emotions*, Russian translation, pp. 14 ff., 1896; PETRAJITZKY, L., *Introduction to the Theory of Law and Ethics, passim;* PATTEN, SIMON S., *The Theory of Social Forces*, Philadelphia, 1896; see also Pareto's classification of the residui; and Sumner's four "motive-interests": hunger, sex passion, vanity, and fear.—SUMNER, W. G., *Folkways.* §§22 and *passim.*

and, taking it as a variable, try to show its "operations" in human behavior and socio-historical phenomena.[74]

F. *Criticism.*—The above gives all the essential theories of the interpretations of social phenomena in the terms of introspective psychology. Let us now turn to a criticism of the theories. In spite of their difference in terminology and other details, their essential "introspective" character is similar. Therefore their weak and strong points are practically the same. The principal shortcomings of the theories seem to be as follows:

1. *In so far as the theories make of psychic experiences the causes which determine the dynamics of trans-subjective phenomena, they are a variety of an animistic interpretation.* In the above criticism of the behavioristic interpretations I indicated that their fundamental shortcomings consist in their intrusion into the field of the inner experience which is indescribable at all in the terms of, and could not be studied with the methods of, behaviorism. The same error is made by the discussed theories with the difference that with their introspective terminology and methods they unlawfully invade the field of the trans-subjective phenomena of behavior and social events, for which their methods and terminology are also unsuited. They claim that these trans-subjective phenomena are determined by the ideas, the wishes, the desires, and so on. These psychical experiences are made the agencies which govern the dynamics of the trans-subjective processes, cause, determine, and control them. In so far the theories must be regarded as a variety of animistic interpretation. In this sense, they are pseudo-scientific. Indeed, in what consists their explanation? It is very simple. Each author fills a man with a certain number of desires, interests, wishes, sentiments, and emotions. Furthermore, he takes a man's behavior and explains it in a very simple manner. Man performs a series of sexual activities because he has the "sex-desire," "sex-wish," or "reproductive interest." Man goes to a court and sues another man because he has the "desire, or the wish, or the interest" of "rightness." And so on. The wishes, the desires,

---

[74] See, for instance, FAIRBANKS, A., *Introduction to Sociology*, 3rd edit., pp. 108–141; DE GREEF, G., *Introduction à la sociologie*, Vol. I, pp. 214 ff., 1896; TAKHTAREFF, K. M., *Soziologia*, pp. 25–26, 47–48, 1918 (in Russian); STUCK-ENBERG, J. H. W., *Sociology*, Vol. I, pp. 203 ff., 1903.

the interests and the sentiments here play the same rôle which in primitive animistic theories is played by various "spirits" or supernatural agencies. The explanations are a replica of Moliére's famous sarcasm: "Opium makes man sleepy because it has a sleeping power." Like a prestidigitator, the authors betimes put into a man-bag a series of wishes and desires, and after that, with a serious expression, they take out of the bag one or several of the desires and wishes, according to the circumstances, and convincingly add: "This agency is responsible for the actions or events studied." The procedure is certainly easy, but one may seriously doubt as to whether or not it has any cognitive value.[75]

2. *The very nature of the theories makes exceedingly difficult or even impossible any causal or functional analysis of the trans-subjective phenomena.* As we have seen, the theories pretend that the psychical experiences, like desires, wishes, interests, and so on, are the forces which causally determine the movements of the body and the dynamics of the trans-subjective social and historical events. The theories try to bridge the psychic and the trans-subjective sets of phenomena. The first consequence of such a claim is that the theories should meet all the objections which are directed against similar theories in psychology and philosophy. How an "idea," or "desire," or "wish," as a pure psychic experience, can influence the receptors, conductors, and effectors of the nervous system and bodily movements, together with such trans-subjective phenomena as fighting, or the decreasing birth rate, and so on, is the problem to be met by these theories. It is needless to say that, being pretty crude in their philosophical part, the theories are likely to find difficulty in meeting this and many other objections.[76] Meanwhile, without

---

[75] In this sense A. Bentley's criticism of all such theories appears quite valid. See his *Process of Government*, Part I. I have already mentioned that in his constructive part this author fell into the same error of "animism" with his theory of "interests-groups."

[76] See WEISS, A. P., "Relation between Structural and Behavior Psychology," *Psychological Review*, pp. 301–317, 1917; "Relation between Functional and Behavior Psychology," *ibid.*, No. 5, 1917; PERRY, R. B., "Docility and Purposiveness," *ibid.*, No. 1, 1918; ORJENTZKY, R. M., "The Nature of Economic Phenomena and the Methods of Their Study," (in Russian), *Iuridichesky Vestnik*, No. 5, 1914. Take further any substantial text in psychology and study the arguments of the partizans of various theories against their opponents.

a satisfactory answer to the above and many other objections, their fundamental contention remains unproved and questionable. Questionable also become all their other claims. Owing to this, they are vitiated from their starting point.

Granting, however, that in some way they will cope with this difficulty, the theories are very unsatisfactory from the standpoint of a scientific methodology. Instead of alleviating the difficulty of the study, they greatly increase it. This may be seen from the following considerations.

Their causal analysis of human behavior or social events may be schematically depicted as follows:

A	B	A'	B'	A''	B''
desire or wish A causes	overt action B	desire or wish A' causes	overt action B'	desire A'' causes	overt action B''

If a psychical agency is regarded as the cause of an overt action, then, besides the mystery of such a causation, we have a causal chain in which the trans-subjective phenomena: B, B', B'' are disconnected from one another by the insertion of the psychic links: A, A', A'' into the causal chain. The whole chain represents thus an incessant mental *salto mortale* from the realm of psychic experience to that of the trans-subjective phenomena, and *vice versa*. It is possible of course to talk of such a causal chain, but science knows nothing similar to it. The very character of such a chain is a denial of the causation known to other sciences, because all causal formulas start with trans-subjective phenomena, use them, and finish with them too. They nowhere admit a discontinuing of their causal sequence by the insertion of the non-trans-subjective links. From this standpoint the above "causation" is sheer mysticism. It precludes any causal analysis of the phenomena. Such is the first methodological inconvenience of the theories.

Their second inconvenience may be seen from their analysis of the stages through which human action passes. Here are two examples: According to Novicow, any conscientious action is started with some trans-subjective stimuli; being started it enters "the inner or psychic stage" and passes there through the substages of sensation, representation, idea, desire, and volition; only after this does it assume again the form of an overt action which becomes "an incarnation" of all these sensations, representations, ideas, desires, and volitions. According to M. E. Mayer, the genesis of an overt action is still more complex. Both theories may be represented schematically in the following way.

Novicow's stages of the genesis of a response:[77]

B→sensation→representation→idea→desire→volition→C

| trans-
subjec-
tive
stimulus | psychical link of the causal chain of an action
and its successive psychical stages | trans-
subjec-
tive
reaction |

M. E. Mayer's genesis of human action:[78]

| B | idea of reaction | motivating power of image | stage of a struggle of motives | influence of char-acter | purpose | consideration of the means | volition | C |

| trans-
subjec-
tive
stimulus | psychical link of the causal chain of an action
and its successive psychical stages | trans-
subjec-
tive
reaction |

With some variation, all the discussed theories explicitly or implicitly presuppose something similar. According to the theories we must take the psychical link as an agency or variable which produces the overt action C. This means that we must keep an account of all components of the variables: sensation, representations, desires, motives, ideas, purposes, and volitions.

[77] NOVICOW, I., *Conscience et volonté sociale*, pp. 89 ff.
[78] MAYER, M. E., *Die Schuldhafte Handlung und ihre Arten im Strafrecht*, 1901, Chap. II. Possibly the most detailed psychological analysis of a human action from the psychological standpoint has been given in numerous works of the criminologists of which Mayer's work is a sample.

Each of them represents a sub-variable of the whole psychical variable. Take further into consideration that all these psychical sub-variables are extremely unstable, since they incessantly fluctuate and change. Consider also the lack of method in their measurement. When only these circumstances are taken into consideration, it becomes quite clear that even the greatest mathematician cannot keep account of all these sub-variables and their fluctuations; therefore, a computation of their "function," that is, a single overt action, becomes impossible. Only God can solve an equation in which are analyzed a series of actions of several individuals from the standpoint of the criticized theories. An investigator is as though in the midst of a great multitude of psychical shadows, which incessantly dance, change, and transform. These shadows he must take as "variables" to explain through them a single, or a set of trans-subjective phenomena! The method is really that of an explanation of *clarum per obscurium*. The overt actions are much simpler than these psychic variables offered to explain them. Instead of an alleviation of the difficulties of the study, the theories pile them up to an extent which makes scientific analysis of behavior impossible.

No better becomes the situation if the above scheme is replaced by the following one:

Let AB represent the chain of the overt action or trans-subjective phenomena and CD the stream of the desires, wishes, ideas, or volitions. Each of the series develops without interruption. The series CD is the variable, the series AB its "function," result, or manifestation. The analysis remains impossible still, because the series CD is more complex than the series AB. The multiplicity and incessant turmoil of the wishes, desires, etc., make the variable so complex and poorly defined that the correlation of both series and their links is practically excluded.

This is not all. According to the scheme, the proposition: "The trans-subjective phenomena A are a result of the wish, or desire, or idea *a*" presupposes that the wish *a* manifests itself in the form of an overt action A; the wishes $b, c, d, e,$ in the forms of the corresponding actions $B, C, D, E;$ otherwise, the whole contention becomes empty. Meanwhile, the establishment of such propositions is impossible because the same desire a may be accompanied by various forms of overt activity, and the same overt activity may be paralleled by the most different wishes or desires. My desire to eat may be followed by the actions of entering a restaurant, or of digging potatoes from a kitchen garden, or of working in a factory to get money to buy the food, or of singing in a theater for a dinner. The overt action of a typist may be paralleled by her dreaming of a trip to Florida, or by thinking of a dress to be bought for the money obtained by typing, or by the thoughts of spending the money in a dance hall.[79] If such is the case, an explanation along the line of the criticized theory becomes impossible. No certain correlation between a certain part of the series CD and a certain part of the series AB can be established. The whole theory goes to the wall.[80]

[79] Compare HAYES, E. C., "Classification of Social Phenomena," *American Journal of Sociology*, Vol. XVII. The same is true of the attempts to deduce certain social institutions from certain desires or wishes or interests. For instance, Sumner and Keller regard the industrial organization, property, war for plunder, and the regulative organization as the phenomena "summoned by hunger into being"; marriage and family as an outcome of "love-interest"; ostentation in dress, ornament, social etiquette, war for glory, games, gambling, narcotics, etc., as a function of "vanity"; religion as an outcome of "fear-interests." SUMNER and KELLER, *op. cit.*, pp. 89–90. It is easy to see that the attempt is a mere variety of the above "instinctive drives" theories, though the authors deny the instincts; furthermore the authors themselves recognize an unsatisfactory character of the theory, saying that these correlations are rather hopeless because "the categories run into one another across zones of transition, and no such zones are clean-cut but all are blurred." "Property goes back in no small degree to vanity; marriage is not by any means to be connected solely with sex and love," and so on. And factually the above correlations are of no use in the analysis of these authors except in the rôle of a purely exterior frame in their presentation of the materials.

[80] No better is that variety of these theories which is represented by Professors Park and Burgess in their theory of the wishes and the attitudes. Their very conception of an "attitude" introduced to help the conception of wish, is a logical monster. We read, "An attitude is the tendency of the person to react positively or negatively to the total situation." They "are the mobilization of the will of the person. . . . The wishes enter into attitude as components. . . . The clearest way to think of attitudes is as behavior patterns or units of behavior. The two most elementary behavior patterns are the tendency to approach and the tendency to withdraw." Thus we have a concept which on the one hand is something purely psychological (a wish), and, on the other hand, something trans-subjective and physical ("behavior unit" or "pattern"). In fact, it is a kind of a bag (tendency) into which are put several wishes, sentiments, emotions.

3. *As a matter of fact, the theories explain little, and are not used even by their authors.* The above criticism is excellently warranted by the discussed theories. First, their classification of the number of desires, wishes, interests, sentiments, or emotions varies from author to author. Some discriminate four or six classes, while some others have more than one hundred. Who is right? No one, because the classifications are not based on any factual reality, but are purely speculative, and based on the whims of the authors. Second, if we ask, for instance, why Small discriminates six, but not thirty-six classes of interests, or why Thomas indicates only four, but not one hundred forty-four "wishes," we would not find any satisfactory answer. The situation is similar to that in the classifications of instincts, with this difference, however, that many of the instinct-classifications are better, being based on observed uniformities, while in these psychological theories it is hard to find even such an approximation to reality. Consider the classes of the desires, interests, or wishes, as, for example, "the interests in rightness," or "sociability," or "vanity," or the "wish for response" and "new experience." Is it not clear that these very classes represent a kind of a dark cellar which you may fill with whatever you please and as you please? Something more indefinite it is hard to imagine. We are told that the wish for new experience may "incarnate" itself in the forms of hunting, athletics, gambling, crime, scientific research, exploration, and even a craving for a variety of sex affairs. Likewise, the wish for security manifests itself in the actions of securing food and the means of subsistence, in that of avarice, systematic labor, conservatism, flying from danger, attacking and fighting activities, and so on. Or vanity-interest "materializes" itself in practices of ostentation in dress, ornament, social eti-

---

even instincts, and some other psychical phenomena. Side by side with them there is also a "reaction," "behavior pattern," and "behavior units," "withdrawing" and "approaching" as something trans-subjective. I am sorry to say that such a monstrous hodgepodge of the psychical and the trans-subjective elements is unthinkable, and still less may it be one of the fundamental concepts of sociology. In this as well as in many "modern psychologies" we have some new terms which in spite of their popularity, are in fact quite defective and unsuitable for any scientific analysis. The fault, however, is not with the authors. It lies partly in the nature of the problem itself, and partly in the magic of words which still reigns in social and psychological sciences. See PARK and BURGESS, *op. cit.*, pp. 438–439; read attentively the whole of Chapter VII.

quette, war for glory, games, gambling, the use of stimulants, narcotics, dancing, play-acting, the fine arts, etc. This variety and heterogeneity of the forms of the "incarnation" of each of the wishes or interests testifies clearly that each of them represents a bag filled by chance with the most heterogeneous activities, unrelated either neurologically, psychologically, or logically to one another. Any classification of wishes may be as good as this. The same is true of the classification of desires, interests, and so on.

Furthermore, in order that the wishes, desires, or interests may serve as variables, we must know whether or not they are constant, or whether they are varying in their intensity and stimulating power. Are they given an identical proportion among all human beings, or is their distribution among them varied from man to man, from sex to sex, and within the same man from moment to moment? We must know further which of the wishes, desires, interests, and so forth are stronger or weaker, what their relationship is, whether antagonistic or solidary, and when, where, and why. We must also know how to measure their intensity and variation. Only when these and many other problems are solved may these "variables" be used as real variables and we may attempt to correlate them with overt actions and to interpret them as functions of the "wish-desire-interest-variables." It is needless to say that nothing like this has been done, or even attempted. Therefore it is a rather hopeless enterprise to make such "foggy blots" the fundamental "variables" of human behavior and to try to explain something through such variables. Even the studies of the authors show this clearly. Have Small, Ward, Sumner and Keller, or Thomas, or any others succeeded in building something with their help? Nothing. In their works they play the rôle of an incidental appendix which is mechanically attached to their other valuable theories. The categories are not used at all upon their factual analysis. If, sometimes, they are incidentally mentioned, they do not add any cognitive value to what has been obtained by the authors in other ways and without these instrumental concepts.[81] It is natural,

---

[81] This is especially true in regard to the works of Thomas. The psychology of the Polish peasant or the unadjusted girl is given by concrete cases. The

therefore, that operating with such "forces" can aid little in a causal or functional analysis of the trans-subjective phenomena.[82]

4. *Several Specific Points of the Theories are Questionable.*— Besides the above shortcomings common to all the theories, their specific features are also questionable.

Take, for instance, Tarde's *conception of imitation,* and the rôle ascribed to it. The very concept is extremely vague. It is so broad that practically every phenomenon of similarity in the behavior of men or in the social characteristics of a group is a manifestation or result of imitation, according to Tarde. It is needless to say that such an all-embracing concept, like the Freudian libido, ceases to have any definite contents, and becomes scientifically useless. Taken in a narrower sense, it does not justify at all that enormous rôle which has been ascribed to it by Tarde and many others.[83]

---

four wishes do not add anything to what is depicted in the concrete cases given in the letters.

[82] From this methodological standpoint one cannot but agree with the following statement of Ivan Pavlov: "During thirteen years of my study of behavior, in no single case have 'psychological interpretations' happened to be useful for an analysis of the phenomena. A reflection of the nervous processes in an inner experience is very peculiar and disfigured, and, all in all, is exceedingly inaccurate and conditional."—PAVLOV, IVAN, "A Genuine Physiology of the Brain," *Twenty Years,* p. 182; *Lectures,* Chaps. I and II.

[83] Tarde, V. Sigele, P. Rossi, B. Sidis, W. Bekhtereff, G. Le Bon, Marpillero, A. Vigouroux, P. Juquelier, G. Dumas, P. Aubry, J. M. Baldwin, S. Freud, N. K. Mikhailovsky, and the majority of the writers about imitation, suggestion, mob-mind, and psychology of a crowd have greatly exaggerated the importance of imitation-suggestion and uncritically ascribed to these factors a great many effects which do not belong to them. Likewise, there is a considerable exaggeration of the "mobbish" traits in a description of the mob-mind and crowd-psychology. Even such relatively good works as *The Behavior of Crowds* by E. D. Martin are not entirely free from the same mistake. The more the corresponding phenomena are studied, the less important becomes the rôle of imitation-suggestion, and the less "mob-minded" becomes a mob at the virtue of these factors. See a sound criticism of the imitation-suggestion theories in DURKHEIM, E., *Le suicide,* chapter about imitation; in KOVALEVSKY, M., *Contemporary Sociologists,* Chap. I; ALLPORT, F., *Social Psychology,* pp. 239 ff.; especially FARIS, ELLSWORTH, "The Concept of Imitation," *American Journal of Sociology,* Vol. XXXII, pp. 367–379; MOEDE, WALTER, "Die Massen- und Sozialpsychologie im kritischen Überblick," *Zeitschrift für pädagogische Psychologie und experimentelle Pädagogik,* 1915; a history of the corresponding theories is given in DAVIS, M. M., *op. cit.,* pp. 109–118. More adequate is KRÅSKOVIČ, B., *Die Psychologie der Kollektivitäten,* Vukovar, 1915; MOEDE, W., *op. cit.* For the ancient theories in this field see *Rivista Italiana di Sociologia* for 1900, 1901, where are published the papers of BIANCHI, "Il charattere di razza"; DE ROBERTIS, R., "Intorno alla concezione della psicologia sociale"; ALIMENA, "Per la storia della psicologie colletiva," *Archivio di Psicologia collettiva,* May, 1900; ORANO, *Psicologia sociale,* Bari, 1920.

Take further L. Ward's hypothesis of the *replacement of the blind character of natural evolution by a conative and teleological progress in the course of time*. As far as this theory, and a similar theory of Professor L. T. Hobhouse, claim that in the course of time man's behavior becomes more and more rationalistic and the social processes tend to be more and more controlled by the conscientious volitions of human beings, the theory is far from being proved. It appeals to us and appears convincing, and yet, when carefully tested, it must be recognized as being at least questionable. Modern man in some respects is certainly more rationalistic than primitive man; but in other respects we are likely to be a prey of blind forces in a greater degree than the peoples of the past and ancient societies.

In a similar way, it would be possible to indicate other questionable features in the discussed theories, but a lack of space does not permit our doing it. By these remarks I shall finish a general criticism of the theories. The above remarks are sufficient to show their weak points.[84] These shortcomings we shall meet again in the discussion of the theories which deal with the social rôle of religion, *mores,* law, arts, public opinion, and other psycho-social factors. (See the next chapter.)

G. *Conclusion on the Introspectivist Interpretations.*—The preceding criticism of these theories has been adverse as far as these theories try to intrude upon the field of the trans-subjective phenomena which cannot be studied with the methods of these theories; and also as far as the theories claim to make of the psychical agency a causative agency of trans-subjective phenomena. This, however, does not mean that the introspective theories are value-

---

By the way, it should be noted that several years before Tarde, N. K. Mikhailovsky published his *Heroes and Crowd,* and other works, in which he more accurately than Tarde set forth the theory of imitation-suggestion. The theory itself is very old. In the works of Confucius and Plato we already find a clear description of the phenomena and practical utilization of imitation for the sake of education.

[84] The pretensions of the theories which claim to view the desire, or the interests, or the wishes as the "sociological atoms" or the "sociological electrons" or the "ultimate elements of social phenomena," and to view their dynamics as "the simplest modes of motion" are mere pretensions. Being an imitation of the "social physics" of the seventeenth century, these pretensions are altogether unwarranted. To talk about them as "the simplest modes of motion which we can trace in the conduct of the human being" is to say something similar to: "A walk to the moon is the simplest walk after lunch."

less. On the contrary, they are very valuable, inasmuch as they describe *the inner psychical experience and meaning of psycho-social phenomena.* This realm is as valuable for us as the world of trans-subjective facts, and, within this realm, the introspective psychological theories are likely to be the only method of their study. This means that they may have a great cognitive value. Likewise, the dynamics of the psychical experience of a man or a group could be properly described only with the methods and terminology of the introspective theories. At any rate, they are necessary and unavoidable for its knowledge. Even when we study some trans-subjective phenomena, for instance a writing, a book, speech-reactions, paintings, music, ceremonies, and other "symbolical" stimuli and reactions, we must be introspectivists to understand their meaning and, to some extent, even their relationship. All this means that the introspective description of the inner experience in its terms of desires, wishes, and so forth, or, according to Charles H. Cooley, "the dramatic knowledge," [85] may have a great cognitive value.

But *suum quique.* We must remain behaviorists regarding the causation, classification, and description of trans-subjective phenomena, and "introspectivists" in the interpretation of purely inner experience and meaning of the psycho-social value. The intrusion of either of the parties into the field of the other one is scientifically fruitless.

Finally, *we may try to study a parallelism in the dynamics of both series, but without claiming to make one series the cause or the effect of the other.* This task consists in a description of the changes within either of the fields which parallel the changes within the other. Naturally, each series must be described in its own terminology. Helmholtz's classical study has shown that such a description is possible;—a thing which from a trans-subjective standpoint is the number of vibrations of the air-waves of a certain length in a unit of time, from an inner standpoint is perceived as a sound of a certain tune. A change in the quantity and quality of food consumed is paralleled by certain changes

---

[85] Compare the above with COOLEY, CHARLES H., "The Roots of Social Knowledge," *American Journal of Sociology*, Vol. XXXII, pp. 59–80; PETRAJITZSKY, LEO, *Introduction to the Theory of Law*. Part I, *passim*.

in the processes of perception, attention, emotion, imagination, association, and so on. What, from a behaviorist standpoint, is described as a certain change in the movement of our muscles and secretion of glands, from the inner standpoint is described as "lust," or "fear," or "jealousy." Such a "two-sided" picture of the psycho-social phenomena is richer in its cognitive value than "the one-sided picture."

But again, in a description of "each" side we must remain either a behaviorist or an introspectivist. We must avoid a behaviorist description of the inner side, and an introspectivist description of the trans-subjective phenomena. From this stand·point the discussed theories are somewhat unsatisfactory because, being introspectivist in their nature, they are constructed along the line of the "scientific tools" used for a study of the trans-subjective facts. Like them they are "mechanical"; like them they pretend to be quantitative; and like them they try to classify their objects into a few classes and to manipulate their units as a chemist or physicist manipulates atoms, electrons, or their trans-subjective units. Such an imitation being quite useless, at the same time robs the theories of what might be their original value. It makes of them "the units of weight" destined to measure a distance. As a result of such an imitation, they lose a great deal as an introspective description of the inner side of socio-psychic phenomena. They are colorless, dull, and, for an understanding of the inner world of a man, or group, or an epoch, give incomparably less than a good novel, historical narrative, "case-study," romance, biography, or even a talented social philosophy which, like Keyserling's *The Travel Diary of a Philosopher* or O. Spengler's work, or the works of Carlyle, Leontieff, Danilevsky, and many others, do not imitate the natural sciences in their description of the "mind and spirit of an epoch or society" and are "honestly and genuinely introspective." Approaching the psychic world from the inner side and describing it in "introspective terms," such novels, biographies, histories, and social philosophies give an incomparably deeper insight into the "mind of a culture" than all these "stiff theories" of wishes and desires and other "social atoms" in which there is nothing left after a careful scrutiny of the wish, desire, or sentiment, and which represent a kind of "a material psychic" or "mechanical spirit." [86]   Being incongruous in their logical nature, such theories do not add much either to the understanding of the mechanics of trans-subjective things, or to the quite heterogeneous dynamics of the inner phenomena.   Such is the fate of all logically incongruous theories. [87]

In order to be free from these defects, the theories must be honestly introspective.   Only a freshman or a poor instructor in sociology may be afraid of the word, "introspection," and think of it as "an outworn source of all scientific evils."   If they learn a little they will see that this "outworn instrument" is absolutely indispensable for a study of inner experience. [88]   Being honestly introspective, the theories will forsake imitating the logical structure of the generalizations from sciences of trans-subjective phenomena.   They must quit also the mechanistic and quantitative character of these sciences.   It is beyond their competence and purposes.   Neither can they meddle with the problem of the causation of the trans-subjective phenomena, but instead, it is their business to describe the inner world of a man, group, or epoch; it is their obligation to show us, not in statistical tables and causal formulas, but in an introspective description, "the inner picture of a criminal," "the case of revolutionary psychology," the psychological type of a king, ruler, priest, captain of industry, "Protestant," "Buddhist," "the psychological style of the Renaissance," or of the "Age of Pericles," or "the mentality of the Western society in the twentieth century."   Furthermore, it is their business to describe the *meaning* of psycho-social values.   These tasks

[86] Compare from this standpoint, for instance, the excellent summaries of concrete cases of various "unadjusted girls" or "Polish immigrants" as they are depicted in their "introspective" letters and in the "introspective comments" of W. Thomas and F. Znaniecki, with the places in the books where the authors introduce their theory of the wishes and try to describe the behavior of the same people in the concepts of their theory.   In my opinion, the works of the second type do not add any tangible value to an understanding of the situation in each case.

[87] This does not mean that the above works are valueless.   On the contrary, they are very valuable, but just because the authors do not follow their own theories criticized here.

[88] See the quite appropriate remarks of Professor Cooley about this point, in *The Roots of Social Knowledge*, pp. 65 ff.; Petrajitzsky's theory of a combined method of an introspective and behaviorist observation, *Introduction*, part I; SOROKIN, *System of Sociology*, Vol. I, pp. 50–76.

are as important as the tasks of the behavioristic, quantitative, and "objective" study of social phenomena.

These indications are enough to see the limits and functions of both types of psychological interpretation of social life.[89]

[89] Compare COOLEY, CHARLES H., *"The Roots," passim;* SPRANGER, E., *Lebens-formen,* Halle, 1922; WEBER, MAX, "Uber einige Kategorien der verstehenden Soziologie," *Logos,* IV, 1913; "Die 'Objektivitat' sozialwissenschaftlicher und sozialpolitischer Erkenntnis," *Archiv für Sozialwissenschaft und Sozialpolitik,* Vol. XIX, 1904; JASPERS, K., *Allgemeine Psychopathologie,* Berlin, 1913; KLÜVER, H., "M. Weber's 'Ideal Type' in Psychology," *Journal of Philosophy,* Vol. XXIII, pp. 29–35; SPANN, O., *op. cit.,* pp. 1–22. Everybody who is familiar with the *"Verstehende Soziologie,"* or the *"Verstehende Psychologie,"* developed in the works of Max Weber, Spranger, Jaspers, partly even in the works of the *Gestalt Psychologie,* may see that the above of my statements which repeat what I said in my *Systema Soziologii* are in harmony with these strong currents within contemporary sociology and psychology.

CHAPTER XII

PSYCHO-SOCIOLOGISTIC THEORIES OF RELIGION MORES, LAW, PUBLIC OPINION, ARTS, AND OTHER CULTURAL PHENOMENA AS FACTORS

IN THIS chapter we must briefly survey those sociological theories which try to interpret social phenomena as a function of various cultural forces, like religion, law, or arts. In so far as these "variables" are psycho-social phenomena, the corresponding theories belong to the sociologistic as well as to the psychological school. For this reason they may be styled as psycho-sociologistic theories. Any sociologist knows that their number is enormous. The impossibility of surveying all of the theories in a general work like this is evident. Therefore I am going to proceed in the following way. I shall take one group of the theories, for instance those which study the social rôle of belief and religion, and after surveying the principal theories in this field I shall attempt to show to what extent they are valid, and what are their difficulties and weak points. Their shortcomings in essentials are the same as those of the other theories of cultural factors. For this reason, after an analysis of this group of theories, the other ones may only be mentioned. A few examples and remarks will be sufficient to show in what way they are valid and in what way they are questionable. This way of handling the immensely numerous theories of cultural factors appears to me the most plausible under the circumstances. In so far as these theories are psychological, their analysis will substantiate the statements laid down in the preceding chapter about the psychological school. Let us now glance at the interpretations of social phenomena in terms of beliefs and religion.

I. BELIEFS, MAGIC, MYTHS, SUPERSTITIONS, IDEOLOGIES AND RELIGION AS A FACTOR

I. GENERAL REMARKS

I am going to survey the principal theories which try to show the rôle of beliefs and of religion generally, especially in the dynamics of social phenomena. By "beliefs" I understand the totality of judgments which are either beyond the competence of science, or are inaccurate in a scientific sense, or are not proved scientifically. All judgments which are non-scientific are beliefs, whatever their contents may be. There is no need to say that in the "mental luggage" of every one such judgments compose a considerable part. They often assume a pseudo-scientific character and are not easily detected. What are the social functions of such beliefs? Do they play any part in determining social phenomena? If they do, what is it, and what correlations are established between the beliefs and the other components of social life? Such are the problems to be answered by the works to be discussed in this chapter. Among numerous and valuable studies devoted to these problems, only those will be taken here which attempt to answer the above questions. All theological theories with a claim that the history of the universe and humanity is controlled by Providence, God, or any other mystical power, also must be excluded because they are beyond the competence of science and we cannot either prove or disprove them.[1] Such are the limitations set forth by the nature of the subject. The literature devoted to the study of the above problems is enormous, and

---

[1] Among such theological ideologies, beginning with St. Augustine's wonderful *The City of God*, and ending with the brilliant ideologies of the providential control of human history set forth by J. de Maistre and De Bonald, there are the most ingenious, enchanting, and impressive "philosophies of history." Each of us may or may not believe in them, but since they are beyond the competence of science, we cannot discuss them. Only as far as these philosophies lay down, beyond their basic hypothesis, a series of theories which are within the competence of science, may they be discussed and analyzed. In these "non-transcendental" parts they often contain the most valuable scientific observations, statements, and hypotheses. For instance J. de Maistre's *Considérations sur la France* and *Les soirées de Saint-Petersbourg* or De Bonald's *Théorie du pouvoir politique et religieux dans les société civile* (1796), or Leontieff's *Bysantinism and Slavinism* (1883, Russ.), contain in their "empirical" parts more sociology than a dozen sociological textbooks taken together. In those parts such works are naturally within the competence of sociologists, and should be studied by them.

it is beyond the power of a single man to summarize them. However, the principal types of these studies are sufficiently well represented by relatively few works. Let us turn to their survey.

A. *Predecessors.*—The theory that belief, especially a magical or religious belief, is the most efficient factor in human destiny is possibly the oldest form of social theory. It permeates practically all the most ancient sources of human thought known to us. It is manifested in the very facts of religion or magic found among the most primitive groups. It is the motto of almost all of the *Sacred Books of the East,* the *Odyssey, Iliad,* the *Bible,* and other similar sources. Later on, from St. Augustine and the Church Fathers to St. Thomas Aquinas, Machiavelli, Marsilio of Padua, Campanella, J. Bodin, Boussuet, Voltaire, J. Rousseau, Saint-Simon, A. Comte, and H. Spencer have recognized the rôle of beliefs in some degree.[2] August Comte even made it a basic factor, and constructed his "theory of the three stages" on the basis of the character of religion. Since that time social thinkers have formulated a multitude of various theories in this field. Among those who have tried to study the rôle of beliefs, magic, and religion more or less factually, and have attempted to set forth some generalizations in this field, the most conspicuous are the theories of F. de Coulanges, B. Kidd, G. Le Bon, Charles Ellwood, E. A. Ross, G. Sorel, É. Durkheim, J. Frazer, and finally, of Max Weber.

B. *F. de Coulanges' Theory* (1830-1889).—Being one of the most prominent French historians of the ancient world and of mediæval history, Fustel de Coulanges laid down his sociological theory of religion in his classical book, *The Ancient City.* It represents an attempt "to show upon what principles and by what

---

[2] Even the anti-religious thinkers have recognized religion as an efficient factor at least in the sense of Machiavelli or Marsilio of Padua. "Religion is always necessary for the maintenance of civilization. . . The sagacious politician will always respect religion even if he has no belief in it . . . because through inculcating it even by craft much valour has been roused for the defense of the country," MACHIAVELLI, *Discourses,* Bk. I, Chaps. XI–XII. For Marsilio of Padua its function consists in a "police job" of intimidating and discovering secret crimes and their perpetrators. Because governmental control is not sufficient, a "legislator has therefore imagined a God from whom nothing is concealed and who commands the observance of the Law under penalties." A priest helps the police and court through his intimidation "by the fear of Hell." As we see, even this type of "theories" does not deny the rôle of religion as a factor.

rules Greek and Roman society was governed,"[3] and what factors were responsible for the evolution or changes in their social and political organization in the course of time. The author's theory may be seen from the following quotations.

The cause which produces the changes must be powerful, and must be found in man himself. If the laws of human association are no longer the same as in antiquity, it is because there has been a change in man. There is, in fact, a part of the human being which is modified from age to age; this is our intelligence. It is always in movement; almost always progressing; and on this account our institutions and our laws are subject to change. Man has not, in our day, the way of thinking that he had twenty-five centuries ago; and this is why he is no longer governed as he was governed then.[4]

Thus F. de Coulanges contends that ideas generally are the cause of social changes and the primary factor of social phenomena. Further he specifies more definitely what sort of ideas he has in view.

The history of Greece and Rome is a witness and an example of the intimate relation which always exists between men's ideas and their social state. Examine the institutions of the ancients without thinking of their religious notions, and you find them obscure, whimsical, and inexplicable . . . But by the side of these institutions place the religious ideas of those times, and the facts at once become clear, and their explanation is no longer doubtful. If, on going back to the first ages of this race,—that is to say, to the time when its institutions were founded,—we observe the idea which it had of human existence, of life, of death, of a second life, and of the divine principle, we perceive a close relation between these opinions and the ancient rules of private law; between the rites which spring from these opinions and their political institutions. A comparison of beliefs and laws shows that a primitive religion constituted the Greek and Roman family, established marriage and paternal authority, fixed the order of relationship, and consecrated the right of property, and the right of inheritance. The same religion, after having enlarged and extended the family, formed a still larger association, the city, and reigned in that as it had reigned in the family.

[3] I use the English translation by SMALL, W., *The Ancient City*, p. 9, Boston, 1900.
[4] *Ibid.*, p. 11.

From it came all institutions, as well as all the private laws, of the ancients . . . But, in the course of time, this ancient religion became modified or effaced, and private law and political institutions were modified with it.[5]

F. de Coulanges shows that the most ancient religion of the Greeks and the Romans was the worship of their dead ancestors, and this had for its principal symbol the sacred fire. Further, he very conspicuously demonstrates how these ideas determined the character of the ancient family, the laws of marriage, divorce, the inequality of son and daughter, the forms of kinship, the right of property, the character of authority, the right of succession, and all the essential characteristics of ancient society.[6] In a second period of the history of these peoples there came another type of ancient religion — a deification of physical nature in the form of Zeus, Athene, Juno and so forth. This religion grew at the cost of the former family-religion. "The morality of this new religion was different. It was not confined to teaching men family duties. As this second religion continued to develop, society must have enlarged." As a result the whole social and political structure of these societies was changed also. The city was formed, and the government, the magistracy, the laws, the institutions, the social classes changed. A series of reforms and revolutions took place.[7]

The final conclusions of the elaborate theory of the author are as follows:

The ancient society had been established by an old religion whose principal dogma was that every god protected exclusively a single family or a single city, and existed only for that. This religion has produced laws. The relations among men were all regulated, not by the principles of natural equity, but by the dogmas of this religion, and with a view to the requirements of its worship. In the social system of the ancients, religion was absolute master; the state was a religious community, the king a pontiff, the magistrate a priest, and the law a sacred formula; patriotism was piety, and exile, excommunication; individual liberty was unknown, [and so on]. But little by little, society became modified. Changes took place in

---

[5] *Ibid.*, pp. 11-12. [6] *Ibid.*, pp. 49-153. [7] *Ibid.*, pp. 154-469.

the government and in the laws *at the same time* as in religious ideas [note this.] . . . law and politics began to be a little more independent. *It was because men ceased to have religious beliefs.* [Note this formulation.]

Later on came Christianity, which introduced new ideas, and through them it again radically modified ancient society, creating a new one with a new form of social organization.[8] F. de Coulanges concludes:

We have written the history of a belief. It was established, and human society was constituted. It was modified, and society underwent a series of revolutions. It disappeared, and society changed its character. Such was the law of ancient times.[9]

The theory is so clear that there is no need to interpret it. Before criticizing it let us glance at other theories of the social rôle of religion.

C. *Charles A. Ellwood's Theory.*—To essentially similar conclusions about the social functions of religion came Professor Charles Ellwood [10] in the process of an analysis of the present crisis of religion and civilization.

Today we are in the midst of a religious revolution, which is going on so quietly that many do not notice it, although it is a greater and more fundamental revolution than any since the early years of the Christian era.

This crisis is due to a change in our ideas and values due to the progress of science.[11] Such a crisis in ideas and religion will be followed, and is indeed being followed, by a corresponding change in human behavior and in social institutions, because religion has always been one of the most important instruments in the social control of man and society. If this great controlling factor is weakened, there is a danger of man's retrogression to primitive and anti-social forms of behavior, of the regress and decay of civilization, and of a return to social and moral paganism. The

---

[8] *Ibid.*, pp. 519 ff.   [9] *Ibid.*, p. 529.
[10] Born in 1873. Author of a series of valuable works: *Sociology and Modern Social Problems, Sociology in Its Psychological Aspects; Introduction to Social Psychology; The Psychology of Human Society.*
[11] ELLWOOD, CH. A., *The Reconstruction of Religion*, pp. 1-11, N. Y., 1922.

symptoms of such a regress, due to the crisis of Christianity, are already present, according to the author. A glorification of physical force and struggle in popular ideologies like that of Nietzsche; the World War; an increase of sensual hedonism and egotism; disorganization of the family, and increase of divorce; "free love"; an increase of venereal diseases; a rising tide of mysticism, polytheism, atheism, and materialism; an increase of the belief in violence and social struggle, and many other facts of today are, in the first place, a result of this religious crisis.[12] The author proceeds to show the determining rôle of religion in regard to various non-religious social phenomena. Psychologically, religion is a power which sometimes may efficiently control human behavior and physiological processes. The examples of the ascetics and martyrs show this. It gives a maximum of vital energy. "What reason does for ideas, religion does for the feelings." Through its projection of the essential values of human personality and of human society into the universe as a whole, it consecrates human life, bridles purely egotistical impulses, and facilitates man's socialization. "It harmonizes man on the side of will and emotions with his world." It is one of the most efficient means of social control. It stimulates social habits and checks anti-social tendencies. It gives to the whole society a conception of its own sacred value. The same is true in regard to social institutions, law, and order. "A religionless social world would be a social world of uncertainties, destitute of enthusiasm and of vision, reduced to the dead level of individual expediency." Therefore it is natural that any progress of a people would be manifest in a progress of their religion, while the decay of a civilization would be preceded by that of religion. "The death of religion would accordingly mean the death of all higher civilization."[13] Even if an individual may be moral without being religious, a whole society cannot be moral without it.

After this general summary of the social functions of religion, the author proceeds to analyze the character of today's crisis of

[12] *Ibid.*, pp. 14–26. See also his "Religion and Social Control," *Scientific Monthly*, Oct., 1918. Similar opinions have been expressed by many other authors. See KIDD, B., *The Science of Power*, first part; HAYES, E. C., *Sociology and Ethics;* HOBHOUSE, L. T., *Morals in Evolution*, N. Y., 1915; ROSS, E. A., *Social Control*, 1920, Chaps. XII–XVI.

[13] *Ibid.*, Chaps. I–III

Christianity, and outlines the direction in which the religion must be reconstructed in order to serve successfully its important social functions.[14] We need not follow this part of the author's plan. It is but the practical conclusion of his theoretical statements.

D. *É. Durkheim's Theory.*—We have already seen the essentials of Durkheim's theory of religion. Being the product of a society, and concentrating "the social" in its brightest and best form, religion has served as a powerful means for the creation, expansion, and increase of solidarity among its members. From this standpoint its rôle has been great and quite positive.

Religious beliefs rest upon a specific experience whose demonstrative value is, in one sense, not one bit inferior to that of scientific experiments, though different from them.[15]

Nearly all the great social institutions have been born in religion . . . The fundamental categories of thought, and consequently of science, are of religious order. Up until a relatively advanced moment of evolution, moral and legal rules have been indistinguishable from ritual prescriptions. The religious life is the eminent form and the concentrated expression of the whole collective life. If religion has given birth to all that is essential in society, it is because the idea of society is the soul of religion.

[From this standpoint] the believer who has communicated with his god is not merely a man who sees new truths of which the unbeliever is ignorant; he is a man who is *stronger*. He feels within him more force, either to endure the trials of existence, or to conquer them. . . . Thus there is something eternal in religion which is destined to survive all the particular symbols in which religious thought has successively enveloped itself. There can be no society which does not feel the need of upholding and reaffirming at regular intervals the collective sentiments and the collective ideas which make its unity and its personality.[16]

E. *G. Le Bon's Theory* (1841–   ).—With a different flavor, but also quite definitely, Le Bon states the great efficiency of beliefs. The essence of his theory is as follows. Man is not a

---

[14] *Ibid.*, Chaps. IV–XI.
[15] DURKHEIM, *Elementary Forms of Religious Life*, p. 417; comp. JAMES, W., *The Varieties of Religious Experience*, pp. 20 ff.
[16] *Ibid.*, pp. 416–427.

logical creature. He is apt to believe the most illogical and unreasonable things if they correspond to his emotions and feelings. As soon as a belief enters man's mind, reason becomes incapable of controlling it. Any criticism becomes impotent in such a case. Therefore the historical rôle of reason and logic has been rather moderate. The real factors in life and history have been beliefs. They are unavoidable. They have always composed the essential part of human mental luggage. Up to this time humanity could not have lived without beliefs, and it cannot avoid it in the future. A certain God and religion may be overthrown, but only to be replaced by a new form of God and beliefs. Their place has never been vacant and is not going to be vacant in the future. Hence any change in the beliefs of a people is followed by a great change in their whole social life. In this sense beliefs have been one of the most powerful factors of human history.[17]

F. J. G. Frazer's Theory (1854–   ).—Much more factual and definite are the conclusions to which this eminent investigator of primitive society and human beliefs has come in his study of the social rôle of beliefs and superstitions. These conclusions are: first, that beliefs are efficient factors of human behavior and social control; and second, that all in all the rôle of superstitions has been rather beneficial. This is Frazer's own summary of his study.

To sum up this review of the influence which superstition has exercised on the growth of institutions, I think I have shown, or at least made probable:

> I. That among certain races and at certain times superstition has strengthened the respect for government, especially monarchical government, and has thereby contributed to the security of its enjoyment:
>
> II. That among certain races and at certain times superstition has strengthened the respect for private property and has thereby contributed to the security of its enjoyment:
>
> III. That among certain races and at certain times superstition has strengthened the respect for marriage and has thereby contributed to a stricter observance of the rules of sexual morality both among the married and unmarried:

[17] Le Bon, G., *Psychology of Socialism*, Chaps. I, III, and *passim*.

IV. That among certain races and at certain times superstition has strengthened the respect for human life and has thereby contributed to the security of its enjoyment.[18]

G. C. Bouglé's Theory (1870–).—C. Bouglé, in his study of the India caste régime, has come to the conclusion that without the religious factor neither the origin nor the long existence of the caste-system are comprehensible. Neither the economic theory of Niesfeld, nor the familial theory of Senart, nor the racial theories of several authors, satisfactorily explain the origin of the caste system. Although possibly playing some part, these factors could not have produced the system if it were not for the interference of the religious factor. It originated the first law in the form of a religious *fas*. It promoted the isolation of various racial groups and made any mixture of races an unforgivable sin. It gave consecration to such a separation, and turned the former family sacrifice into something sacred. As the rules and the rites of sacrifices grew more and more complicated, more and more necessary became a special technical education for their performance. Hence the increase in the power of the Brahman caste; and hence their isolation from other groups, and from one another. In the course of time this formerly only relative specialization of various groups became more and more rigid, became hereditary, and finally was fixed forever under the influence of

[18] FRAZER, J. G., *Psyche's Task, A Discourse Concerning the Influence of Superstition on the Growth of Institutions*, 2d ed., London, 1913, p. 154. See here the facts on which these conclusions are based. If not in its evaluative part, then at least in the part which states the efficiency of beliefs and superstitions in controlling human behavior and relationship among the primitive societies, Frazer's theory has been corroborated and supported by many field-studies. As an example of such works I may mention: MALINOWSKI, B., *Argonauts of the Western Pacific*, London, 1922; JAMES, E. O., *Primitive Ritual and Belief*, London, 1917; CODRINGTON, R., *The Melanesians*, Oxford, 1891; HAUER, L. W., *Die Religion, ihr Werden, ihr Sinn, ihre Wahrheit*, Bd. I, *Das religiöse Erlebnis auf den unteren Stufen*, Stuttgart, 1925. See further the courses in anthropology and in primitive society by Kroeber, R. Lowie, W. Wallis, W. Rivers, and others; WESTERMARCK, W., *The Origin and Development of the Moral Ideas*, Vol. I. Especially valuable from the discussed standpoint is E. D. STARBUCK'S *The Psychology of Religion*, N. Y., 1903. In the way of a quantitative study the author reaches the conclusion that religion helps the adult to realize the need of helping others and to adapt the adolescent's budding self into the social organism which is "fixed in its ways and relentless in its demands." *Ibid.*, p. 195. See also LEUBA, JAMES H., *The Belief in God and Immortality*, Boston, 1916.

the Brahman priests.[19]   In this briefly outlined theory we have an attempt to correlate religion with a political and social system.

H. *E. A. Ross', G. Sorel's, W. G. Sumner and A. G. Keller's Statements.*—Very concisely and clearly E. A. Ross and G. Sorel have stressed the specific point of the influence of beliefs, legends, and myths on human psychology and social processes. Professor E. A. Ross [20] in his *Social Control* outlined in a systematic form the influence of various cultural agencies — belief, religion, law, arts, science, and so on—upon human behavior and social processes.   With typical inspiration, and in his shining style, he stressed that man's conduct may be and is controlled by illusion. A belief—regardless of whether it is right or not—if it is believed, is a real force which determines human actions. Religion has been one of the forces which has conditioned social processes.[21]   Sorel's point is that the framing of a future course of action or events is efficient, and determines greatly their objective course, even when such a framing is quite wrong from an objective standpoint. The same is true in regard to various myths and legends.

Experience shows that the framing of a future, in some indeterminate way, may, when it is done in a certain way, be very effective, and have very few inconveniences. This happens when the anticipations of the future take the form of those myths, which enclose with them all the strongest inclinations of a people, of a party, or of a class, inclinations which recur to the mind with the insistence of instincts in all the circumstances of life; and which give an aspect of complete reality to the hopes of immediate action by which men can reform their desires, passions, and mental activity. The truth of this may be shown by numerous examples. The first Christians expected the return of Christ and the total ruin of the pagan world, with the inauguration of the kingdom of the saints, at the end of the first generation. The catastrophe did not come to pass, but Christian thought profited so greatly from the apocalyptic myth that certain contemporary scholars maintain that the whole preaching

[19] See BOUGLÉ, C., *Essais sur le régime des castes*, Paris, 1908.

[20] Born in 1866. One of the founders of American sociology. Author of several valuable works: *Foundations of Sociology; Social Control; Social Psychology; Principles of Sociology.* The "American Tarde"—such is a short summary of Ross as a sociologist.

[21] See Ross, E. A., *Social Control*, Chap. XXIII.

of Christ referred solely to this one point. The hopes which Luther and Calvin had formed of the religious exaltation of Europe were by no means realised. Must we for that reason deny the immense result which came from their dreams of Christian renovation? It must be admitted that the real developments of the Revolution did not in any way resemble the enchanting pictures which created the enthusiasm of its first adepts; but without those pictures, would the Revolution have been victorious. In our own times Mazzini pursued what the wiseacres of his time called a mad chimera but it can no longer be denied that, without Mazzini, Italy would never have become a great power.[22]

Thus myths as myth, and belief as a mere belief, determine the course of events.

I. *Benjamin Kidd's Theory* (1858-1916).—B. Kidd attempted to give possibly one of the most general theories of the social functions of belief and religion. The essentials of Kidd's hypothesis are as follows: The primary factor in the evolution of all organisms has been the struggle for existence. Through it the superior organisms have been surviving at the cost of the inferior ones. Any step in evolution has cost an enormous price in the extermination and elimination of a great many lives. Man also evolved through the factor of the struggle for existence. His victory over other animals was due particularly to reason or intellect which he developed in the process of this inexorable struggle. As among other animals, any progress within mankind itself has cost an enormous price. In order that a few individuals or a few groups could progress, a great many other individuals or groups have had to sacrifice themselves. If, however, only this factor were responsible for human progress, a great many phenomena would have become incomprehensible. Indeed, if the law of a struggle for life, which is fought with the egotistical weapon of intellect, were the only factor of human progress, then most intellectual and egotistical social groups should have always survived at the cost of the less intellectual ones. Then a pitiless struggle would have been welcomed among human beings and the law of an absolute egotism would have reigned supreme. But

[22] SOREL, G., *Reflections on Violence*, pp. 133 ff., N. Y., 1912. See also MALINOWSKI, B., *Myth in Primitive Psychology*, N. Y., 1926; SUMNER and KELLER, *op. cit.*, pp. 1465-1467; TODD, A. J., *op. cit.*, Chap. XXIX.

progress itself should have been stopped to avoid this terrible cost, because, from the purely egotistical standpoint, there could not be any rational motive for continuing a progress which required an incessant sacrifice of individuals in favor of a group, and of a great many groups in favor of a few. Neither of these expectations has been realized. A great many peoples with brilliant brain-capacity, for instance the Greeks, decayed while some other people with an inferior intellectual capacity have survived. Even our own civilization has been ascending not so much through our intellectual superiority, which is certainly not higher than that of many extinct civilizations, but through another factor. In the second place, in our social life we do not preach the command of absolute egotism, but the opposite command of an unlimited altruism and sacrifice of one's interests and lives in favor of his fellow men. We have charitable and philanthropic institutions, and so on. Finally, in spite of the direct interests of men to stop progress, they do not stop it, but continue to pay an enormous price for it incessantly.

All these phenomena represent the paradox of progress. They evidently cannot be accounted for through human intellect only, which in its essence is egotistical, or even through the struggle for existence led by egotistical reason. Since the above facts are unquestionable, we must admit besides egotistical reason and the struggle for existence some other factor as being responsible for the social progress of man, for incessant sacrifices of individuals in favor of a group and of the groups in favor of mankind, for our altruism, charity, philanthropy, and finally, for the very fact of the survival of many groups which are not more superior intellectually than many extinct groups.[23]

This factor is religion, as

a form of belief, providing an ultra-rational sanction for that large class of conduct in the individual where his interests and the interests of the social organism are antagonistic, and by which the former are rendered subordinate to the latter in the general interests of the evolution which the race is undergoing . . . No form of belief is capable of functioning as a religion in the evolution of society which does not provide an ultra-rational sanction for the social conduct

[23] KIDD., B., *Social Evolution*, pp. 66–72, 106–107, 305–306, N. Y., 1894.

of the individual . . . A rational religion is a scientific impossibility, representing from the nature of the case an inherent contradiction of terms.[24]

Such is Kidd's answer. This means that human social evolution has been due not only, and not even so much, to egotistical reason as to ultra-rational faith or religion. Its rôle has been increasing more and more. It is responsible for all the altruistic actions among human beings. It is the force which urges individuals to sacrifice for the group; and the group, for the whole of mankind. The stronger it is the more social are the groups, and the more chances they have to survive. This explains why some intellectually superior but religiously weak societies perished, while some other groups which were less brilliant intellectually, but stronger socially or religiously, have survived. Finally, religion is responsible for man's non-revolt against progress, and for his continuing to pay its terrible price. "The intellect, of course, continues to be a most important factor in enabling the system to which the individual belongs to maintain its place in the rivalry of life; but it is no longer the prime factor." [25]

J. Max Weber's Sociology of Religion.[26]—*The Fundamental Problem of His Study.* The three large volumes devoted by M. Weber to the sociology of religion [27] represent possibly one of the most valuable contributions in this field made in the twen-

---

[24] *Ibid.*, pp. 108–116. Compare this with Ellwood's and Durkheim's "*rational religion.*"

[25] *Ibid.*, pp. 306–307. See about Kidd's theory, GIDDINGS, F., *Studies in the Theory of Human Society*, pp. 9–11; LICHTENBERGER, J., *op. cit.*, pp. 287–291; KOVALEVSKY, M., *Contemporary Sociologists*, pp. 210–222; BARTH, P., *op. cit.*, pp. 425 ff.

[26] Died in 1920. Professor of economics at various German universities. Besides *Religionssoziologie*, Weber's principal works are: *Wirtschaftsgeschichte*, 2d ed., 1924; *Gesammelte Aufsätze zur Wissenschaftslehre*, 1922; *Wirtschaft und Gesellschaft*, Grundriss der Sozial-ökonomik, III, 1921–22; *Gesammelte Aufsätze zur sozial- und Wirtschaftsgeschichte*, Tübingen, 1924. These works made M. Weber possibly one of the most outstanding economists and sociologists of the present time. About M. Weber's works see WALTER, A., "Weber, M., als Soziologe," *Jahrbuch für Soziologie*, Vol. II; VON SCHELTING, A., "Die logische Theorie der histor. Kulturwissenschaft von M. Weber," etc., *Archiv für Sozialwissenschaft*, Vol. XLIX, Heft 3; a series of papers published in two volumes in memory of M. Weber: *Erinnerungsgabe für Max Weber*, München und Leipzig, 1923, 2 vols.; HONIGSHEIM, P., "Max Weber als Soziologe," *Kölner Vierteljahrshefte für Soziologie*, I. Jahrgang, I. Hefte, 1921; WEBER, M., *Max Weber: Ein Lebensbild*.

[27] WEBER, MAX, *Gesammelte Aufsätze zur Religionssoziologie*, I, II, III, Tübingen, 1922–23; further in references it will be indicated *Religionssoziologie*.

tieth century. Though these volumes are a collection of his papers published in the period from 1904 to the moment of his death, and though the whole work is unfinished, nevertheless these volumes, together with some other works of the author, give a sufficiently systematic and clear idea of M. Weber's theory in this field. The principal topic of the work is an analysis of the relationship between religion and economic phenomena. This topic is, however, taken on such a large scale and with such an extraordinary erudition, that the work represents not only a sociology of religion but of all culture. Again, contrary to a great many works in this field, it is based on immense factual material which makes it especially valuable. I shall omit here Max Weber's specific methodology and terminology and somewhat simplify his too complicated "technique" of analysis, without, however, disfiguring his principles. The fundamental problem of his study is probably to ascertain just what the relationship between economic and religious phenomena is. Is it a one-sided conditioning of religious phenomena by economic ones, as is contended by the economic interpretation of history; or it is a conditioning of economic phenomena by the religious ones; or are both of these phenomena mutually interdependent? If they are mutually interdependent upon each other, and each of them upon other categories of factors, then how is it possible to find out that the religious factor is efficient; and if it is efficient, what are its real effects on economic phenomena and on the whole cultural life and social organization of a society? Such is the fundamental problem the solution of which is attempted by Max Weber.

Methodological Principles. His answer to the above questions may be outlined as follows: First, religious and economic phenomena are mutually dependent. Any one-sided interpretation of one of them as a mere function of another is wrong. Wrong therefore is the theory of the economic interpretation of history; and wrong also is the opposite theory which would view the economic phenomena as a mere function of the religious factors. They are interdependent, and each of them is influenced by a series of other conditions. But methodologically it is possible to take one of these factors as "a variable" and to find its specific effects in a certain field, in this case, in the field of economic phenomena. Such is the starting point of Max Weber. He takes the religious factor as a variable and tries to disclose its influence on the economic and on other social phenomena.[28] Thus Max Weber is a pluralist and "a functionalist" in the sense which I outlined in the chapters about Pareto and the economic interpretation of history.

What Components of Religion Are Taken for a Study of the Effects of Religion on Economic Phenomena? Having taken the religious factor as a methodological variable, Max Weber takes "the economic ethics of a religion" (*Wirtschaftsethik*) to find the influence of religion on economic life. By the "economic ethics of religion" he means not so much the various theological dogmas of religion, as the totality of *"the practical forms of conduct"* required and urged by a religion in regard to its members. He acknowledges that the economic ethics of every religion is the result of various factors; but among them there is the factor of religion also. As a study of all the factors of "economic ethics" would lead to infinity, and is impossible factually, one must take "economic ethics" as an essentially religious product, and through a study of its effects find the effects of religion generally. Such a task may be realized when an investigator studies the economic effects of religious ethics on the life of those social groups which strongly influence its character and are influenced by it.[29] Limiting in this way his task, Weber takes the *"Wirtschaftsethik"* of

[28] See WEBER, MAX, *op. cit.*, Vol. I, pp. 12, 21–22, 37–38, 82, 183, 233–237; WEBER, MAX, *Wirtschaftsgeschichte*, pp. 16, 238, 308–315, München und Leipzig, 1924. "Any explanation (of a typical social phenomena) must in the first place take into consideration the economic conditions. But also it must not overlook the reverse causal relationship, because a rational technique and rational law, as well as an economic rationalism, in their origin are dependent on the capacity and predisposition of men to a certain kind of a practical manner of living (*Lebensführung*). Where the former meet the obstacles of this psychical (*seelische*) kind, there the development of an economically rational organization finds the strongest obstacles. To the most important factors of the manner of living belong, especially in the past, the magical and the religious powers, and the ethical ideas of duty (*Pflichtvorstellungen*) based on them." A religion and *"Eine Wirtschaftsethik ist keine einfache 'Funktion' wirtschaftlicher Organisationsformen, ebensowenig wie sie umgekehrt diese eindeutig aus sich herausprägt. Keine Wirtschaftsethik ist jemals nur religiös determiniert gewesen. Sie besitz selbstverständlich ein im höchsten Mass durch wirtschaftsgeographische und geschichtliche Gegebenheiten bestimmtes Mass von reiner Eigengesetzlichkeit gegenüber allen durch religiöse oder andere (in diesem Sinn) 'innerliche' Momente bedingten Einstellungen des Menschen zur Welt."* *Religionssoziologie*, Vol. I, pp. 12, 238.

[29] *Religionssoziologie*, Vol. I, pp. 238 ff.

the six world religions: Confucianism, Hinduism, Buddhism, Christianity, Islam, and Judaism, and studies the character of the *Wirtschaftsethik* of each of them, with its effects on the economic organization and life of the peoples who belong to one of these religions.[30]   In this way he tries to correlate religion with economics.   We naturally cannot follow here Weber's long and elaborate analysis of the effects of each of these religions.   However tempting such a task may be, space does not permit doing it. Therefore I shall take only one example to illustrate Max Weber's method of analysis and conclusions.   Adding to this his own summary of the fundamental influences of other religions, we shall have an idea of the work of Max Weber.   As an example, I shall take the relationship between modern capitalism and Protestantism, which was especially well studied by the author.

Modern Capitalism and Protestantism.[31]   Though various elements of what is styled a "capitalistic economy" have been found in the past and in many non-European societies, modern Western capitalism is a recent and specific phenomenon.   The typical characteristics of "the spirit of the modern capitalism" (*"Der Geist des Kapitalismus"*) are: a rationally organized and managed economic enterprise based on exact scientific principles, and private property; the production for a market; the production for masses and through masses; the production for money; and the maximum of enthusiasm, ethos, and efficiency in work which requires the complete devotion of a man to his calling, vocation, or business.   Such a devotion is accompanied by viewing vocational work as a self-goal, as a principal function of everybody's life; accordingly, work is not regarded as something incidental in a modern capitalistic society, but as something for which man exists, which is his principal life-vocation, and which imposes on him the most important obligations to serve his vocation or calling earnestly, devotedly, and "religiously."   This "vocational ethics" is one of the most conspicuous traits of the spirit of modern capitalism.   Consequently, men are estimated and paid according to the efficiency of their work.   Those who are poor in their voca-

[30] In the published three volumes, a factual study is made of Protestantism, Confucianism, Taoism, Hinduism, Buddhism, and Judaism.
[31] R. H. Tawney's *Religion and the Rise of Capitalism*, N. Y., 1926, is but a mere recapitulation of M. Weber's theory.

tion go down; and those who are good go up; capitalistic society rates a man in first place as a worker, whatever may be his work or vocation. To these traits there must be added: rationalism, utilitarianism, stimulation of initiative and inventiveness by all possible means, on the one hand; and on the other, the greatest repulsion to "traditionalism," to everything which is inefficient, and obsolete, existing only through inertia, or to anything which is superstitious, irrational, or imperfect from the standpoint of the existing more perfect and rational methods.[32] Such are the typical — the ideally typical — characteristics of modern capitalism.[33] In these traits it differs radically from other forms of ancient or mediæval capitalism, and represents a specific modern phenomenon of Western society.

In order that such an economic organization may be possible, we must have human beings with a definite psychology, conduct, and corresponding social conditions. It is clear that among quite idle, superstitious, inefficient, and irrational people, such a system of economic organization is impossible. It became possible only when men began to have "a certain psychology" and conduct, and when there were given the conditions of: (a) rational capital accounting and business-management; (b) appropriation of all the means of production; (c) rational technique of production; (d) rational law; (e) free labor; and (f) commercialization and marketing of the products of labor.[34]

As to the psychology and conduct which are necessary for the existence of such a system, they are ideally exemplified by one of the builders and early representatives of the spirit of modern capitalism, Benjamin Franklin, in his own conduct and in his *Advice to a Young Tradesman* and *Necessary Hints to those that*

---

[32] *Religionssoziologie*, Vol. I, pp. 17–63; *Wirtschaftsgeschichte*, pp. 238 ff., 308 ff.

[33] In this we have an illustration of M. Weber's methodological theory of the "ideal type." The "ideal type" is a concrete, but at the same time a general image of studied social phenomena, in which must be summarized the specific characteristics of the phenomenon in its most conspicuous, even in an exaggerated form, to make quite clear the specificity of the phenomenon. An ideal type is not an "average" of the phenomenon, but a conspicuous stressing of its specific traits. The outlined "spirit of modern capitalism" is an example of one of the "ideal types" of Max Weber. From the above we see that his "spirit of modern capitalism" is not an image of the average business-organization, or of the psychology of the average business man or working-man, but an image of an ideal business organization, an ideal captain of industry, or working-man.

[34] *Wirtschaftsgeschichte*, pp. 237–239.

would be Rich. Here again the method of the "ideal type" is applied by Max Weber, "Time is money," "Credit is money," "Money grows money," "Honesty is the best policy," "Careful accounting is necessary for any business," "And orderly conduct and honesty, diligence, efficiency, truth, sincerity and integrity are necessary for success in any field and in the field of business, too." These and similar recipes given by Franklin and carried on methodically by him in his own activity,[35] are the psychological characteristics without which, at least in some degree, modern capitalism would have been impossible.[36] Since it has appeared and exists, evidently such a psychology and conduct have been inculcated to some extent into the masses of Western society.

Now the problem to be solved is just what forces have been responsible for such a transformation of human beings, and for their behavior and psychology. Weber answers: *Modern Western capitalism has been originated by the Protestant religion and its "Wirtschaftsethik." The spirit of modern capitalism is that of Protestantism, of its rules of conduct and practical ethics.* Before modern capitalism appeared, it had been perceived, cultivated, and prepared in the realm of the Protestant religion. The spirit of capitalism appeared before capitalism itself. This is, Weber remarks, an example of how an economic organization is preceded and conditioned by the ideological factors.[37]

What are the proofs of such contention? They are numerous. In the first place, Weber, by a painstaking analysis of the teachings of Luther, Calvin, and of a great many other Protestant teachers, shows that the spirit of Protestantism in its practical everyday ethics was identical to the above spirit of modern capitalism. Protestantism set forth a rationalization of human life on a large scale; it gave an immense ethical value to a worldly vocation and calling; it consecrated labor, and began to regard an orderly, honest, and enthusiastic performance of man's vocational work as his sacred duty; and through its preaching that the salvation of man consisted primarily in an orderly and rational living,

[35] See especially Franklin's *Autobiography.*
[36] *Religionssoziologie*, Vol. I, pp. 30–34, 63 ff.
[37] *Ibid.*, pp. 38–39.

it averted man from a purely "ascetic ideal" and turned him to more worldly but religious duties. Protestantism also inspired honest money-making as a sinless activity. In brief, the *Geist des Kapitalismus* is essentially the *Geist* of Protestantism. In the second place, the validity of Weber's answer is also supported by the fact that since the Reformation the economically leading countries have been the Protestant countries (Holland, England, America and so on), while the Roman Catholic or the non-Protestant countries have been far behind. The explanation of this is at hand. The Protestant economic ethics educated and trained its members to a capitalistic economy. The spirit of Protestantism has been an inculcation of the habits and forms of activity necessary for a successful building and management of modern capitalistic enterprises. In the third place, the validity of the hypothesis is shown also by the statistical data which show that in Germany the Protestant population is better off economically, and their children attend in greater per cent the practical and business schools than do the non-Protestant part of the population and their children. Max Weber perceives the possibility of an opposite explanation of these facts. This hypothesis is as follows: England, Holland, and some other countries have been economically better off not because they accepted Protestantism; but they accepted it because they were economically better off. Protestantism was accepted by the wealthier families for the reason of their being wealthy. Such is the opposite hypothesis. It is, however, wrong, says Weber, because there were a number of poor and persecuted Protestant sects in the Roman Catholic countries, the Huguenots in France, the Protestants in Austria, and Quakers of England, and so on; and yet all of them became famous by their successful industries, by their prosperous management of business, and by their leading rôle in the field of economic activities. Even in the countries where Roman Catholics reigned supreme, and where the previously well-to-do classes were Roman Catholics, they were outdistanced by the Protestants of those countries, who were very often recruited from the poorer classes. These and similar facts show the fallacy of the hypothesis and the validity of that of Max Weber. In this way, step by step he follows the Calvinistic, the Pietatic, the Methodist, and other Protestant varieties, and shows that his correlation is supported by a study of all these Protestant peoples in Germany, England, Holland, and America.[38] Such are the essentials of Max Weber's theory of the origin of modern capitalism from Protestantism. The above of course gives only a skeleton of Weber's careful and painstakingly factual argumentation in favor of his hypothesis, but the skeleton gives a sufficient idea of the character of the author's theory and method.

In a similar way, Weber analyzes the *Wirtshaftsethik* of Confucianism, Taoism, Hinduism, Buddhism, and finally of Judaism.[39] The economic and everyday life ethics of each of these world religions have been such as to shape the corresponding economic and social organization exactly in the form in which they have existed among the peoples of each of these religions. Their "traditionalism" and spirit are quite different from "the spirit of modern capitalism," which has been responsible for the undevelopment of capitalism in those countries.[40] The following quotation sums up the essentials of Weber's theory of the influence of the religious factor on the economic organization and phenomena of a society.

For a realization of modern capitalism, there has been necessary "a rational long-time existing enterprise, a rational bookkeeping, a rational technique, a rational law; and, besides a rational frame of mind (*Gesinnung*), a rationalized manner of living, and a rational economic enthusiasm (*Wirtschaftsethos*). At the beginning of all ethics and the corresponding economic relationships, traditionalism has everywhere reigned supreme in the form of a sacredness of tradition, and in a sticking to the economic ways and economic methods of the forefathers. Traditionalism exists in abundance even up to the present day." Rooted in the earliest ethics and economic methods, traditionalism may be reinforced through two special conditions: when it happens to

[38] *Ibid.*, Vol. I, pp. 17–30, 63–236, especially 162, 190–195, 202–206.

[39] *Ibid.*, Vol. I (Chinese religions); Vol. II (Hinduism and Buddhism); Vol. III (Judaism) and its economic ethics.

[40] See the summary of the Confucianist and the Taoist economic effects, Vol. I, pp. 524–528; the summary of the economic effects of the Buddhist and the Hindu religions, Vol. II, pp. 367 ff.; a short resumé of the economic effects of all world religions is given in Weber's *Wirtschaftsgeschichte*, pp. 302–315.

be in harmony with the vested interests of some social groups, and through the magical stereotyping of human actions, which makes man follow by intimidation the path of traditionalism.

"These traditional obstacles cannot be broken through a mere desire for profit (*Erwerbstrieb*). The idea that our rationalistic and capitalistic epoch has a stronger gainful impulse than other epochs is childish. A representative of modern capitalism is not driven by a stronger gainful motive than a dealer of the East." Similarly, an increase in a population is not sufficient to break the chain of traditional folkways. China shows this clearly. There has always been only one way to break it, and that is by the *appearance of great rational prophets*. Not always, but often, such prophets, being "legalized" by miracles and other "proofs," have succeeded in breaking the chains of traditionalism, driving away its magical enchantment, and through this, creating the foundations of modern economic organization, technique, and capitalism. "In China such prophets failed to appear. When they happened to come, they came from outside like Lao-tse and Taoism." In India, on the contrary, such prophets appeared and laid the path for liberation from the chains of traditionalism. But, unfortunately, they were the prophets of the Hindu type who, like Buddha, though calling for a liberation from traditions, saw rational freedom only in the field of a purely spiritual meditation and thinking (Nirvana), neglecting completely the empirical everyday life. As a result, their rationalizing prophecy and teaching could influence only a narrow group of thinkers. For the large masses they were too delicate to be understood and assimilated. For them Buddhism has meant only a primitive magical method of getting salvation. For this reason, prophecy failed to inspire rationalism in the masses of the Indian population, leaving their economic activity in its traditional frame. Contrary to these religions, Judaism and Christianity exerted an immense influence on the masses and their activity, because these religions were ever the "plebeian mass-religions." It is true that there also was a struggle between "the intellectual aristocracy" (the gnostics) and the "intellectual plebs." The former tried to transform religion into a refined philosophical system, while the latter held the simplified forms of teaching which were accessible to the minds of the masses. The struggle luckily was solved in the form of a dualism. The intellectual aristocracy could isolate themselves into the monastery and deserts, and meditate there, leading the rational form of life. The intellectual plebs, however, were given the possibility of carrying on their worldly life, and of performing their duties as laymen without the obligations of the religious aristocracy of the monks and ascetics. Hence the difference of degree in the rationalization of the manner of living of these two Christian strata. The mediæval monk was the first living man who in the Middle Ages, methodically and with rational means tried to achieve his goal—Heaven. Only for him was there a watch-ringing, his time alone was methodically divided into hours. The economic organization of the monasteries was also a rational organization, methodically planned, computed, measured, and managed. But these monastery limits of life-rationalization were too narrow; the life of the masses remained outside it. Then came Protestantism, which, in its own way, expanded life-rationalization over the masses, thus creating the foundations of modern capitalism. Protestantism was exclusively responsible for its creation.[41] At the present moment these religious roots of modern capitalism are dead. The early religious enthusiasm and religious conception of the world are lost. This means that a stage in the development of modern capitalism is over. With the death of its religious roots, it must be changed also.[42] Such are the prin-

---

[41] Contrary to Sombart, who holds that modern capitalism was created principally by the Jews, Weber shows that this is a wrong theory. Though Judaism early overcame the obstacles of traditionalism, and, like Christianity, became inimical to magic, nevertheless, the specific situation of the Jewish people during the Middle Ages, their isolation from the Christians, the absence of the *jus connubium*, and their situation of a "pariah-people," made any rational and creative economic achievement impossible for them. If they participated somewhat in economic activity through money-lending and so on, this was not modern rational capitalism, but a degenerated "pariah-capitalism." "A rational capitalist was exclusively Christian, and only on the basis of Christianity thinkable." Outside of the pariah-capitalism, the economic ethics of the Talmud became conspicuously traditional and unprogressive. "The repellence of a pious Jew from any novelty is as great as that of a native of a primitive society with magical traditions." Only in modern times did the Jewish enterprisers begin to play a rôle in the field of capitalism. *Wirtschaftsgeschichte*, pp. 305–308; *Religionssoziologie*, Vol. III, *passim*.

[42] WEBER, M., *Wirtschaftsgeschichte*, pp. 302–315.

ciples of Weber's sociology of religion, and his theory of the religious determining of economic phenomena. With this we may end our survey of these theories and turn to their criticism.

K. *Criticism.*—I. A serious criticism of these theories is greatly handicapped by the very nature of the concepts with which they operate. In spite of the fact that some of the theories give a definition of religion, it remains somewhat vague. Therefore neither the authors nor the readers know exactly what they are dealing with and talking about. For instance, shall we understand by religion or magic only some system of ideas and other psychical experiences, or shall we include also the trans-subjective phenomena of rituals, ceremonies, forms of religious behavior, and all the physical compulsion and punishing coercion with which they are often backed? If one takes only religious ideas and psychical experience, one has to show exactly how and in what way they, in their pure form, are efficient. This in conditioning the trans-subjective social phenomena has practically never been done by these authors. All these theories include *mores,* rules of conduct, rites, interests, ceremonies and almost all laws, customs, and ethical prescriptions in their "religious factor." In other words, it represents an unanalyzed mixture of trans-subjective and psychic phenomena. Such a broad understanding of the "religious factor" makes much easier the task of demonstrating its efficiency, but it also has a great disadvantage. It is this. Since such a "religious factor" represents "a hodgepodge" filled with the forms of behavior, rites, ceremonies, "economic ethics," laws and ethical norms, "interests," and even with physical compulsion and repressive coercion, it factually embraces almost all psychic and a great many physical factors. It ceases to be "a religious" factor in fact; and becomes a mere factor covering a multitude of the trans-subjective factors and psychical experiences, vague and mosaical in its very nature. If, therefore, the authors succeed in showing its efficiency, it is not the efficiency of "the pure factor of religion," "magic," or "belief" as a psychical experience, but that of a series of various physical and "cultural" agencies. With no less reason such a factor could be styled "speech-reactional," "physical," "coercive," "ethical," "juridical," or a factor of the *"mores."* In fact many sociologists called them these names. In this way the theories prove much less and much more than they intend to prove. Such is their first general shortcoming. It vitiates them in their nature. It makes it absolutely impossible for them to reach any clear and convincing evidence of the causative influence of religion, as a psychical force, on the dynamics of trans-subjective phenomena. The reason for this was indicated clearly in the preceding chapter. It consists in a mingling of the trans-subjective and psychic categories, and in making either of them the cause or the effect of the other. As a result, we have a causal chain of trans-subjective phenomena all the time disconnected by psychic agencies, and described partly in objective, partly in introspective, terms. Since the "religious factor" represents a mysterious box filled with numerous trans-subjective stimuli-like speech-reactions, bodily movements in rituals, by stimuli of songs, music, paintings, dances, statues, buildings, "religious" objects, other men and their behavior-patterns, the actions of physical punishment, coercion, imprisonment, various chemicals used in the ceremonies, etc., and by numerous psychical experiences like "ideas," images, emotions, sentiments, volitions, etc.; we are lost in the multitudinal complexity of the factors united under the name of "religion," and we do not know which of these stimuli is really effective, even if it is proved that the "religious factor" is generally influential. Thus we see here in a concrete form the general shortcomings of the psychic theories discussed in the preceding chapter. In order to show how great are the difficulties to be overcome in obtaining any certain conclusion about the rôle of beliefs, religion, or ideals, I shall take an incomparably simpler case. It will show more clearly the shortcoming of these theories.

In order to find whether or not "it is possible to inculcate ideals and attitudes powerful enough to dominate human purposes and conduct," Dr. P. F. Voelker took four experimental groups of Boy Scouts, and two control groups of other children,—all of them having about the same intelligence, and home and neighborhood environment. The inculcated ideal was that of trustworthiness. Through various methods, the puzzle test, lost-article test, the overstatement test, the let-me-help-you test, and others, the groups were tested in trustworthiness at the beginning of the training. After that the experimental groups B, C, J, K, were trained in trustworthiness with the usual methods of Boy Scout training during approximately three months, while the control groups E and I were not trained. At the end of the training the experimental and the control groups were tested again. The essential results are shown in the following table.[43]

In the first test various groups made the following points in trustworthiness.

Group	Character	Amount of Training	Average Points	Rank
A........	Private school	None	59.5	7
B........	Boy Scouts	Just organized	60.5	6
C........	Boy Scouts	Just organized	58.1	8
D........	Boy Scouts	Six months	80.4	2
E........	Private school	None	75.0	4
F........	Private school	Four months	62.2	5
G........	Camp Fire girls	None	78.2	3
H........	Boy Scouts	Two years	82.3	1
I........	Public school	None	56.8	9
J........	Boy Scouts	Just organized	42.1	11
K........	Boy Scouts	Just organized	53.4	10

The table shows only a slight correlation of trustworthiness with training.

After the training of the four experimental groups, the changes in the trustworthiness of these and the non-trained two groups happened to be as follows:

Experimental group B showed a gain of 13.5 points in trustworthiness
"   "   C   "   " " " 9.9   "   "   "
"   "   I   "   " " " 15.0 "   "   "
"   "   K   " " loss " 10.2   "   "   "
Control group E showed a loss of 7.6 points in trustworthiness
"   "   J   "   " " " 10.2 "   "   "

[43] VOELKER, P. F., *The Function of Ideals and Attitudes in Social Education*, pp. 99, 115–118, 120–126, and *passim*, N. Y., 1921.

I regard these results as much less convincing than the author thinks, especially when we take into consideration that in the second test in the groups B and C the worst boys were dropped, which naturally led to a rise in the points of these groups. But even granting that the training was efficient, can we say that the changes in the trans-subjective behavior were due to "ideals" as a psychical experience? This is just what could not be inferred from the study. The changes were due to a bunch of various factors styled by the name of "training": to the patterns of conduct conveyed through speech-reactions, to the reactions and actions of the leaders of the Boy Scout groups and other Boy Scouts, to the repetition of an inculcated pattern of behavior, to various trans-subjective incentives and interstimulation, to an overt menace to exclude the dishonest boys from the group, and so forth. In brief, there were operating numerous and various trans-subjective stimuli,[44] and just exactly what the efficiency of "the ideals" and what was meant by them—a pattern of behavior conveyed through words, or something else—the study does not and cannot answer. If the situation is so indefinite in this relatively simple case, how much more indefinite it must be in the problem of the influence of a religion on the masses and complex social processes. In this case we certainly do not know what we are talking about. Neither the agency whose influence we try to measure, the phenomena on which we try to trace the influence of "the religion," nor the criteria of the measurement are known.

[44] This is more clearly shown by E. D. Starbuck's table of the causes of the religious conversion of 1011 men and 254 women studied by him. The "causes" are as follows:

Cause	Per Cent
Fear of Death or Hell	14
Other Self-Regarding Motives	6
Altruistic Motives	5
Moral Ideal	17
Remorse	16
Response to Teaching	10
Imitation and Example	13
Social Pressure and Urging	19
Total	100

Op. cit., p. 52. Thus the act of a religious conversion is a function of many variables, among which the last three groups are overtly trans-subjective, while the first five groups are in part, at least, trans-subjective too, as a result of "experience" received from others.

Therefore the theories cannot give even a remotely certain answer. All their statements are but vague and dogmatic assumptions. So much for this point.

II. Even granting, however, that together with the authors we know what we are dealing with and talking about, we can still see a very serious "flaw" in all the theories. F. de Coulanges assures us that the whole dynamics of Greek and Roman history was but the result of the dynamics of religious beliefs. They changed, and as a consequence, the social and political institutions changed also. Such is a summary of his theory. But does he prove his contention? Does he really show that the causal sequence was such that in the first place there was a change in religious ideas, and after this came the changes in the institutions? Does he demonstrate that the opposite sequence, or a simultaneity of the changes did not happen? No, he does not give even a scintilla of such a demonstration. More than that, if the reader rereads the above quotations from his work, especially the lines which I have put in italics, we may see that F. de Coulanges in one place says that law and politics began to change "because men ceased to have religious beliefs," while in another place he claims that "changes took place in government and in laws at the same time as in religious ideas." This is a conspicuous illustration of F. de Coulanges' dogmatic assumption, of the inconsistency of his thought, and of the lack of demonstration in his thesis. All that his brilliant book proves is only that changes in one field of social phenomena are concomitant with changes in other fields. No more. But which of these changes is the cause, and which is the effect? This is not demonstrated at all in his work. Taking its factual side, one may say together with Ed. Meyer: "Religion is not a source (*Wurzel*) of mores, but only an expression and manifestation of the social life of human beings," or together with W. G. Sumner:[45] "Religion comes out of the mores and is controlled by them," but *mores* (and institutions) do not come out of religion, nor are they controlled by it, as we are assured by the above authors. Moreover, even granting that F. de Coulanges

---

[45] SUMNER, W. G., "Religion and the Mores," *American Journal of Sociology*, Vol. XV, p. 591. Later on we shall see that the above objection may be made also against Sumner's *mores* factor. He treats it just as the criticized authors treat their religious factor.

is right in his contention, he does not answer at all the question: if all social institutions change under the influence of the changes in religion, how then and why does religion itself change? If such an answer had been attempted, it would at once have shown the fallacy of the theory, which is similar to that of the one-sided economic interpretation of social processes. (See the chapter on the economic school.)

The above may also be said of the theories of Ellwood, Le Bon, Sorel, Ross, Frazer, and others. As far as they try to show that, in the causal relationship between the religious and the other phenomena, the religion, belief, or magic is the cause and other phenomena are the effects, their proofs are inadequate. For instance, does Professor Ellwood demonstrate that in the alleged parallelism of the decay of religion and of civilization, the decay of religion is the cause for the decay of civilization instead of a mere expression or symptom of it or of other operative forces? No, his arguments do not prove such a contention. This may be seen even in his own book. At one place he interprets the present crisis of religion as a mere symptom of the general social crisis of to-day,[46] and at another place, the social crisis as a result of the crisis of religion.[47] He does not give any conclusive proof that the modern reversion to paganism, to unmorality, to brute force, and so on, is the result of the religious crisis, as he claims, implicitly and explicitly. With no less reason one may reverse the causal relation and say that to-day's religious crisis is the result of an increase in paganism, brute compulsion, war, disintegration of family, and so on. The net result of his study is that a series of social phenomena undergo a change together or simultaneously, but which is the cause, and which is the result, his study fails to show. We may agree with Ross, Le Bon, Sorel, or Frazer, that beliefs, myths, or superstitions may *appear* as effective factors in human behavior and social processes when they are accepted, objectivized in overt actions, backed by a physical coercion and compulsion and permeated by emotions, instincts, feelings, volitions and interests. This, however, is not sufficient

---

[46] "All the institutions of the modern world may be said to be at the present time in the melting pot, being tested in the crucible of fiery criticism," and so on. *The Reconstruction of Religion*, p. 14.

[47] *Ibid.*, pp. 15 ff., and *passim*.

to demonstrate their contention. In the process of history millions of various beliefs, superstitions, and myths have been originated; yet we know well that the majority of them have not been followed by the masses. They have fallen flat, and have not found any response from the people. This means that beliefs or myths, as mere beliefs, are not sufficient to grasp the "human soul"; and that there are some other conditions which must be present to make them acceptable and influential. Pareto may be right in saying that beliefs and myths are only derivations of some other operative forces. These forces determine whether a belief is accepted or not, the ideologies being only a kind of a cloak for these operative forces. The cloak, since it is accepted and objectivized, is certainly not impotent and counts for something, but it is inaccurate to ascribe to it the whole power of these operative forces hidden beneath the "cloak" of beliefs or superstitions. The same may be said of religious dogmas generally. Guignebert has shown in his excellent monograph that "the beliefs or dogmas of religion are only an ideological mani- festation of the emotions and feeling of man." It is quite unim- portant as to whether they are logical, reasonable, and rational, or irrational and absurd. What is important is that they suit corresponding "emotions and drives." If they suit and beautify them they will be accepted, and *vice versa*. "This [emotional] faith does not care for logic in dogmas and beliefs." "It would accept any belief or dogma which is suited to its appetite." [48] From this standpoint St. Augustine's paradox: *Credo quia ab- surdum* (I believe because it is absurd) is typical of the attitude possessed by a man with such a faith. [49] For these reasons it is not sufficient to show that some of the accepted myths, beliefs, and dogmas seem to have been "effective." To show their effec- tiveness, the authors have to take an idea in its pure form and demonstrate with it the accuracy of their theory. Contrariwise, their analysis remains "superficial" and their conclusion uncon- vincing.

[48] See GUIGNEBERT, *L'évolution des dogmes, passim* and pp. 143 ff., Paris, 1910.
[49] Comp. SOROKIN, *The Sociology of Revolution*, Chaps. III, IV, XV; LIPPMANN, W., *Public Opinion, passim;* LOWELL, *op. cit., passim;* SUMNER, *Folkways, passim,* and "Religion and Mores"; see also Pareto's theory, and the literature indicated there.

In a somewhat better condition is the theory of Max Weber. Since he takes the religious factor only as a methodological variable, he avoids much of the above objection. Nevertheless, Weber very often slips from his "functional" standpoint into that of one-sided "causation." In this case he also makes the above mistake. Furthermore, his very concept of the *Wirtschaftsethik* does not entitle him to regard its effects as that of religion alone or even as its principal effects. According to Weber's own statement, "no *Wirtschaftsethik* has ever been determined by religion only." It is a function of geographical, historical, and other physical and psychological facts. The religious factor is only one, among many factors of the *Wirtschaftsethik*.

Zu den Determinanten der Wirtschaftsethik gehört als eine— wohlbemerkt: nur eine—auch die religiöse Bestimmtheit der Lebensführung. Diese selbst aber ist natürlich wiederum innerhalb gegebener geographischer, politischer, sozialer, nationaler Grenzen durch ökonomische and politische momente tief beeinflusst.[50]

This shows that the *Wirtschaftsethik* (X) is in no way a product of the religious factor only (A), and that neither Weber nor we know what is its relative importance among the other factors (B, C, D, E, F,) which shape it. For this reason granting that Weber's analysis of the effects of the *Wirtschaftsethik* on economic life is accurate, we in no way can ascribe these effects to religion (A) only because the factor of the *Wirtschaftsethik* is a complex embodiment of numerous and various factors (B, C, D, E, F,) which shape it. In a schematical way this may be expressed as follows:

X (*Wirtschaftsethik*) = f((A) (religion) + B + C + D + E + F, ...)
X exerts such and such effects on the economic phenomena. These effects will be not only the effects of A, but + B + C + D + E + F, . . .

In other words, if Weber's conclusions concerning the effects of the *Wirtschaftsethik* were true, he would have proven only that a series of factors: A, B, C, D, E, F, . . . exert such and such effects on the economic life, but in no way could he be

[50] WEBER, M., *Religionssoziologie*, Vol. I, pp. 238–239.

thought to have proved that these effects are that of religion (of A) as Weber often states, or that the religious factor is the most important among these, A, B, C, D, E, F, ... Even more, Weber's analysis does not show even tentatively what the share of the religious factor is in molding the *Wirtschaftsethik,* and correspondingly, its share in conditioning the effects of the *Wirtschaftsethik* in the field of economic phenomena. Thus, after M. Weber's work we are as ignorant about the degree of efficiency in the religious factor as we were before. In this respect, Weber's work has the same shortcomings as these theories.

III. Side by side with these fundamental "flaws" of the theories which considerably invalidate their scientific value — but not their practical utility — there are numerous factual assumptions which are either vague or at least questionable. For instance, Hobhouse and Ellwood [51] claim that a decay of religion is followed by a decay of civilization, and that "the death of religion would mean the death of all higher civilization." Frankly, I find such a statement vague. I do not find a single example of an absolute decay of religion. All I know is that the decay of one religion is followed by the ascent of another. For instance, in ancient Rome about the end of the second century B.C., there appeared a decay of the former religion; but side by side with it we see the expansion and progress of various oriental religions, and finally of Christianity. In Europe, about the end of the fourteenth century, the Roman Catholic religion began to show some symptoms of decay, but it was followed by a growth of various sects, and finally by the triumph of Protestantism. The same may be said of all other cases of "decay" in religions. When one religious system is dying, another is coming in its place. If such is the real situation, then the above statement appears "empty" in essence. If the statement means a relative weakening of a religion, it must show how this could be measured. Only after such measurement may the explanation have some significance. If we take it as an approximate judgment, the situation is no better. For instance, since the end of the second century A.D., in the

---

[51] ELLWOOD, *The Reconstruction,* pp. 60–64; "Religion and Social Control," pp. 335 ff.; HOBHOUSE, L. T., *Social Evolution and Political Theory,* p. 128.

history of Rome "from the intellectual and spiritual point of view the main phenomenon is the decline of ancient civilization, of the city civilization of the Greco-Roman world." Science, literature, philosophy, and so on began to become more primitive, elementary, less fine and creative.[52] According to the statement criticized, this must be paralleled by an increase of irreligion. Was it paralleled in fact? This is quite doubtful. It was paralleled rather by an increase but not by a decrease of another religious mentality in various forms.

It was the mentality of the lower classes, based exclusively on religion and not only indifferent but hostile to the intellectual achievements of the higher classes. This new attitude of mind gradually dominated the upper classes, or at least the larger part of them. It was revealed by the spread among them of the various mystic religions, partly Oriental, partly Greek. The climax was reached in the triumph of Christianity.[53]

Thus the Roman Empire's decay, which is usually thought to show the decay of a civilization through the decay of religion, testifies rather against such an assumption. Gobineau already indicated that there are many cases when a society or even a civilization declined in the midst of a strong religious spirit of the people. Tyre, Carthage, and Judea are examples.[54] These remarks are enough to show the insufficiency of such a statement. Perhaps it is accurate potentially, but this possible accuracy must be shown by a systematic scientific verification which is not given at all in the presentation of these theories.

Let us take another example. B. Kidd, E. Durkheim, and many others state that the fundamental social function of religion has been the creation and expansion of solidarity (Durkheim), and that practically all the altruistic actions of individuals and groups, and the whole process of the liberation of the masses from slavery and bondage, has been due to religion (B. Kidd). Can these propositions meet successfully a scientific test? I am

---

[52] ROSTOVTZEFF, M., *op. cit.*, p. 479.

[53] *Ibid.*, pp. 479–480; see also ANGUS, S., *The Mystery-Religions and Christianity*, pp. 4–5, N. Y., 1925; LEGGE, F., *Forerunners and Rivals of Christianity*, Vol. I, p. xlix, Cambridge, 1915; AUST, E., *Die Religion der Römer*, p. 107, Münster, 1899.

[54] See GOBINEAU, *op. cit.*, Vol. I, pp. 21–22.

afraid they cannot. Judging, as these theories do, on the bases of the surface of the phenomena, one may obviously see that religion in some cases serves as an instrument of solidarity; but in other cases as an instrument of mutual animosity, warfare, and struggle (persecution and torturing of the peoples of a different religion, their spoliation, religious wars, religious antagonisms, conflicts, and so forth). Therefore it seems to be inaccurate to stress one side and to forget the other. Kidd's statement may be valid in regard to some of the historical cases, but it is fallacious in regard to others. For instance, it seems to be safe to say that the India caste system and a complete disfranchisement of the lower castes appeared and has been existing with the support of religion. Mohammedanism and Judaism, in the period of their expansion, have made thousands of slaves from the vanquished peoples. Even Christianity is not free from the same traits. If, on the one hand, Saint Paul and the Church Fathers condemned slavery and disfranchisement of the masses, on the other, they preached: "Servant be obedient unto them that . . . are your masters, with fear and trembling," and it is rather hard to say whether Christianity's rôle has been greater in a liberation of the masses from slavery and bondage or in supporting these institutions. Whether a thing is good or bad does not concern us. What is important here are the real facts, and these do not permit us to say that Kidd's statement is valid. It is at least one-sided.

No more valid is his assumption that science and the intellect are purely egotistical agencies, or that super-rational beliefs have been increasing in the course of history. I do not belong to those enthusiasts of science who believe that science is always altruistic, and that any scientific progress leads to a progress of sociality and altruism. However, Kidd's statement is no less fallacious than the statements of these enthusiasts of science. Neither of these two opposite statements appears to be accurate. Neither do I belong to those who expect that within a few days the "irrationalism" of human beings shall disappear, and that "rationalism" will grow in the course of history. But if I fail to see this, it does not give me any serious reason for finding Kidd's opposite statement accurate. Both opinions belong to the field of the unverified assumptions whose truth or fallacy is yet to be ascertained. Furthermore, Kidd's starting points are rather questionable. In the chapter about the Darwinistic school I have indicated that the concept of the struggle for existence is somewhat vague. If it has been a factor in the evolution of organisms, it has not been the only factor. Side by side with it has been operating the factor of mutual aid or solidarity. It was operating as early as the factor of the struggle for existence. Therefore it is fallacious to say that the "progress" of organisms has been due to the struggle for existence only, as is claimed by Kidd. Since mutual aid has existed among plant and animal organisms, this means that such actions are possible without religion because the assumption of religion among plants and animals would be childish. This means that mutual aid is as general a phenomenon of life as the struggle for existence. Therefore the acts of solidarity, sacrifice, and mutual aid among humanity could be satisfactorily explained as a manifestation of the same biological factor within human beings. This means that Kidd's fundamental assumption that all altruistic actions are due to religion, and that without it, there would be none, is rather fallacious. Since such actions are possible and may be satisfactorily explained without religion, the whole theory of Kidd about the social rôle of religion loses its ground and becomes unconvincing.

Let us now turn to the factual side of M. Weber's theory. It is also questionable on several points. He claims that only Christianity, and partly Judaism, have been inimical to traditionalism, to magic, and to superstition; and that their practical ethics alone have been rational and have promoted a rationalization of life. "Outside of Judaism, Christianity, and two or three oriental sects, there has been no religion with an obvious animosity towards magic" (and traditionalism).[55] Through this, as we saw, Weber explains why modern capitalism has been developed within the Christian world, and why it has failed within the countries of other world-religions. I am afraid such a statement is questionable. I do not see why Confucianism with its evident contempt of supernaturalism and mysticism, its openly agnostic attitude toward the existence of supernatural beings, its extraordinary "practical" character, its balanced common sense,

[55] WEBER, *Wirtschaftsgeschichte*, p. 307.

and, finally, with its systematic and rational theory of the education of man,[56] should be declared more superstitious and less inimical toward magic than Christianity or Judaism. Together with many a competent investigator of Confucianism, I am inclined to regard it as one of the most "positive" and the least magical, mystical, and superstitious religions in the world.[57] Therefore in no way can I agree with Weber's statement. It is true that Confucianism stresses "traditionalism," but only in the sense of a prudent and harmonious policy of sound conservatism. In this respect it is no more "traditional" than Judaism or Christianity. Finally, the whole system of Confucianism is a consistent theory of a pragmatic and balanced rationalization of social life, free from any mysticism and magic.[58] Thus Weber's discussed presumption is at least questionable. In so far as it is so, all his conclusions concerning the religious origin of modern capitalism and the causes responsible for the existing economic régimes in each of the countries of the principal world religions become questionable. In a similar way, one can seriously question other "typological" characteristics of Weber. Being quite complex and fluctuating, Weber's "ideal types" of each of the world religions and of their *Wirtschaftsethik,* even his concepts of "rationalism" and "traditionalism," are at least vague and questionable as adequate explanations of reality. Finally, a series of facts directly contradicts his theory. Since the second half of the nineteenth century in Japan, there has not been any conspicuous change in the religion of the population. Japan has not become

[56] "To search for what is mysterious, and to practice marvelous arts in order to be mentioned with honour in future ages—this is what I do not do." This is one of Confucius' mottoes. Another is given by him in his answer to the question about human fate after death: "When you do not know about life how can you know about death?"

[57] Read *The Texts of Confucianism* published in *The Sacred Books of the East,* Vols. III, XXVII, XXVIII; see also LEGGE, J., *The Life and Teaching of Confucius,* London, 1895, pp. 100 ff., Ch. XV, and *passim;* LEGGE, J., *The Life and Works of Mencius,* Philadelphia, 1875; CHANG, CHEN HUAN, *The Economic Principles of Confucius and His School,* N. Y., 1911.

[58] If Weber finds the organization of life in mediæval monasteries rational, I wonder why he fails to see that in the field of a purely economic organization of society, China has tried the most various rational systems beginning with various forms of socialism and state-socialism, and ending with the régime of private property. See CHANG, CHEN HUAN, *op. cit., passim;* LEE, MABEL PING-HUA, *The Economic History of China, passim,* N. Y., 1921.

either Christian or Jewish. In its religion it has remained essentially the same as it was before the second half of the nineteenth century; yet the country has made a miraculous progress in the way of a "rationalization" of its economic, social, political, and cultural life. "The traditionalist and the magical" religion of the majority of Japan's population evidently did not hinder at all the most successful development of modern capitalism. According to Weber, this is impossible, in the midst of such a religion. Furthermore, his statement that the Protestants everywhere and always are economically better off than the members of other religions is likely to be far from being universal in space and time phenomena. His statistical data are rather scarce and concern almost exclusively Baden in Germany. It is impossible to make any universal generalization on the basis of such fragmentary and limited statistical material.

Space does not permit me to go into an analysis of many of the other factual statements of Weber.[59]   The above, however, may be sufficient to show that Weber's theory is highly vulnerable in its fundamental and secondary points. It is far from being unquestionable and perfect as we are told by some of Weber's followers.

The above is sufficient to show that all these sociologies of religion are still speculative and unsatisfactory. No one gives to us a really scientific analysis of "the rôle of religion." No one supplies us with a severely verified correlation between well-defined religious and non-religious social phenomena.

This does not mean that they do not possess at least a part of truth. It is highly probable that they do. How great this part is remains to be found. The theories themselves do not give any certain basis for solving the problem. It is up to the future student, first, to forsake the existing half-speculative method of these theories; second, to define clearly and scientifically their "factor of religion"; and, third, to plunge into a scrupulous sifting of the truth from "the rubbish" in the field by a careful statistical, historical, and even experimental analysis of the corresponding facts.[60]

[59] See BRENTANO, L., *Der Wirtschaftende Mensch in der Geschichte*, Leipzig, 1923.
[60] Something in the way of a statistical study of the correlations between religious and non-religious phenomena is already being done. We even have some

2. SOCIAL RÔLE OF FOLKWAYS, MORES, AND CUSTOMS

The "flaws" of the above theories of the social rôle of religion may be found also in the theories which stress the importance of folkways, *mores,* and customs as factors. Long ago their importance was discovered and used for practical purposes. This is evident in the Confucianist applied sociology, which is built principally on the decisive importance of folkways, styled there "path," and "rules of propriety," or "ceremonial usages."

The rules of propriety serve as instruments to form men's characters, and they are therefore prepared on a great scale. Being so, the value of them is very high. They remove from a man all perversity and increase what is beautiful in his nature. [They] secure the display of righteousness . . . showing the people all the normal virtues. . . . Their path may not be left for an instant. If it could be left it would not be the path. . . . The rules of propriety and ceremonial usages should be most carefully considered.[61]

Tacitus' *Quid leges sine moribus!* and hundreds of similar statements of ancient and more modern thinkers who have stressed the conditioning rôle of the *mores,* traditions, and customs are further examples. More recently a series of sociologists have developed the same idea in a detailed form. As examples of this may serve H. Spencer's theory of "Ceremonial Government"; [62]

---

quantitative data and some hypothetical conclusions made on their basis. Such are, for instance, the tentative correlations: between certain religions and divorce (G. von Mayr, Bosco, Oettingen, Lichtenberger and others); between certain religions and suicide (Durkheim, von Mayr, and others); between a certain religion, criminality, and types of criminality (von Mayr, G. Aschaffenburg, Lombroso, P. R. Radosavljevich, and others); between a certain religion and marriage and birth rates (M. Tougan-Baranovsky, J. Wolff, and others); between certain religions and the economic status (M. Weber, B. Shell, M. Offenbacher, C. A. Hanna, and others); between certain religions and the character of *mores* (W. G. Sumner and others); between religion and certain characteristics of ethics and political and social institutions. It is possible to say with a reasonable degree of certainty that some of these correlations are "fictitious," being a mere coincidence of a parallel or of an opposite fluctuation of the figures due to the fragmentary and limited-in-time-and-space character of the data studied. Some of them, however, are likely to be functional correlations. Continuing this type of study with all the necessary precautions, we may gradually come to more and more valid conclusions, free from the defects of these theories. In spite of the great interest of this kind of study, space does not permit me to enter here into further analysis. It is the proper object of a special monograph.

[61] *Li-Ki,* VII: 3; VIII: 15, 1; I: 62–63.
[62] See SPENCER, H., *Principles of Sociology,* Part IV, "Ceremonial Institutions."

M. Kovalevsky's theory of the origin and the interrelation between "custom and law"; [63] Waxweiler's formula of social adaptation; [64] E. A. Ross's brilliant generalizations in this field; [65] E. Westermarck's theory of the origin and rôle of moral rules; [66] and finally, W. G. Sumner's work. [67]

A brief analysis of Sumner's [68] theory of the folkways and *mores* is enough to show the shortcomings of all these theories. Its essence is as follows: "The folkways are habits of the individual, and customs of the society which arise from efforts to satisfy needs." As "the first task of life is to live, men begin with acts, not with thought." By the trial and error method of various ways of doing, the best and the fittest under the conditions are selected. They are repeated. The repetition "produces habit in the individual and custom in the group." Thus "folkways as a rule are made unconsciously." After their appearance, "they become regulative for succeeding generations, and take on the character of a social force. They arise no one knows whence or how. They grow as if by the play of internal life energy. They can be modified, but only to a limited extent by the purposeful efforts of men. In time they lose power, decline, and die or are transformed. While they are in vigor they very largely control individual and social undertakings, and they produce and nourish ideas of world philosophy and life policy." "When the elements of truth and right are developed into doc-

---

[63] KOVALEVSKY, M., *Coutume contemporaine et loi ancienne*, in Russian, published in 1886, and his *Origin of the Permitted and Unpermitted Actions*, Russ., and in *Revue int. de soc.*, 1891–2.

[64] Waxweiler's formula of the origin of the *mores* and successive stages of social adaptation runs as follows: In a group of interacting individuals, many actions are performed; the best ways of acting are repeated; repeated actions become customs; when customs become conscious they turn into a juridical rule; a totality of such rules pertaining to one field of activity composes a social institution; and a totality of such institutions composes the social organization of the group. In a shortened way the scheme is expressed in the formula: "action-repetition,—habit,—custom,—rule,—institution-organization." See WAXWEILER, E., "Avant-propos," in *Bulletin Mensuel* of the Solvay Institute of Sociology, 1910, No. 1.

[65] Ross., E., *Social Control*, Chaps. XI, XIX, XV, and *passim*.

[66] WESTERMARCK, E., *The Origin and Development of the Moral Ideas*, 1906, Vol. I, Chaps. I–XIII and *passim*.

[67] SUMNER, W. G., *Folkways*, 1906. See also KELLER, A., *Societal Evolution*, 1915.

[68] Born in 1840, died in 1910. Author of many valuable works in economics, political science, and sociology.

trines of welfare, the folkways are raised to another plane. Then we call them mores." The folkways and the *mores* "are a directive force." "Institutions and laws are produced out of mores." "World philosophy, life policy, right, rights, and morality are all products of the folkways." "They pervade and control the ways of thinking in all the exigencies of life, returning from the world of abstractions to the world of action to give guidance and to win revivification." [69]

Such is the essence of Sumner's theory in which he recapitulated more systematically what had been said by E. Burke, Savigny, Puchta, H. Spencer, H. Taine, E. Renan, Kovalevsky, Makarewicz and other historians of custom, law, and moral rules. We may agree that the theory states correctly the origin, variation, selective character, societal nature, growth, and decay of the folkways and *mores;* [70] but quite different is the situation in that part of the doctrine which claims a great controlling power for the folkways and *mores,* and tries to make them a basic factor of social processes. Is this part sufficiently proved? Is the very meaning of the claim itself clear? I am afraid it is not. Since the folkways and *mores* "are the ways of doing things which are common in a society" (*Folkways,* pp. 34, 61), to say that they determine human behavior, means no more than a tautology: "the ways of doing things determine the ways of doing things," or X determines X. Sumner himself seems to have felt the unsatisfactory character of his basic statement, and many times has tried to indicate the forces which are responsible for the powerfulness of the folkways. In some places he mentions "the interests" (pp. 1-2), as such a force lying behind the folkways; in some places, "the first task of life is to live"; in some others, the "four great motives of human actions: hunger, sex passion, vanity, and fear" (p. 22); in some others, "pain and pleasure," and so on. If the above tautological statement is unsatisfactory, this interpretation of the powerfulness of the folkways as a shrine,

---

[69] Sumner, W. G., *Folkways,* pp. 1, 2, 25, 26, 34, 39, 44, 61, 66–67, and *passim.* See also Keller, A., *op. cit.,* Chaps. III, L, and *passim.*

[70] Though even there several points are dark; for instance, the selective character of the folkways. Sumner, Keller, and Kovalevsky also, have to admit that "there are folkways which are positively harmful." Sumner, *op. cit.,* p. 26. Such exceptions testify that the selection is not always good, or that sometimes there is no selection.

or an embodiment of "interests, hunger, sex passion, vanity, and fear, pleasure," and many other forces makes of them a factor of exclusively complex and vague character, in which the specificity of the folkways and *mores* as a factor is lost in a sea of various trans-subjective, physical, biological, "introspective" social and psychical forces. The "variable" becomes indefinite and as broad as "the factor of life"; being such, it does not give any possibility of establishing any definite correlation with other phenomena, or of clearly describing its functions in life. As a result, statements like this: "institutions and laws, life policy and philosophy, right and rights are determined by the folkways" become "empty." Thus we have either a tautological "the ways of doing determine the ways of doing," or an indefinite statement which claims that interests, plus pleasure and pain, plus hunger, plus sex passion, plus vanity, plus many other drives and things exert an influence on human behavior and social processes. Certainly so. But what about the influence of the folkways, as a specific factor differing from these forces? What is its influence? Which are its correlations with certain other phenomena? The answer is not given by the theory. Furthermore, it is enough to modify slightly my other objections against the "religious" theories to see that they may be set forth against the theory of the *mores* too. This task I leave to the reader. The above allusions are sufficient to show in which points Sumner's and other similar theories are imperfect. Let us now turn to the theories which try to analyze the social rôle of such a "variable" as law and morality.

3. Social Functions of Law

Among numerous and various psychological theories of law [71] and its social rôle, possibly the most elaborate is the theory of

---

[71] See their excellent survey and criticism in PETRAJITZSKY, L., *Essays in Philosophy of Law*, Russ.; *Theory of Law and Morals*, Vol. II, 1909, Russ. See also JHERING, R., *The Struggle for Law;* CRUET, *La vie du droit et l'impuissance des lois*, Paris, 1908; EHRLICH, E., *Grundlagen der Soziologie des Rechts*, München, 1913; JERUSALEM, F. W., *Soziologie des Rechts*, 1925; ROSS, E., *Social Control*, Chap. XI; PARK, R., and BURGESS, E., *Introduction*, Chap. XII; SOROKIN, P., *Theory of Law*, Russ., 1920; COMMONS, J., *Legal Foundations of Capitalism*, N. Y., 1924; STAMMLER, R., *Wirtschaft und Recht; Theorie der Rechtswissenschaft;* KANTOROWICZ, H., "Der Aufbau der Soziologie," IV, part, Die Rechtssoziologie, in

Professor L. I. Petrajitzsky. In its essence it is as follows: Law is neither "official nor state orders" which are only a variety of the more general phenomena of law; nor are they the obligatory rules of conduct enacted by the state officials because a state and the state authorities presuppose the existence of law without which their very existence would be impossible or unlawful. Neither is law the expression of a general will of the people, because in the past and in the present there have existed many laws enacted without any consultation with the majority of the people. Nor are laws to be found in codes, because, physically, codes are but paper with some figures in the form of letters. *Law is a specific psychical experience.* Outside of the human mind it does not exist as law, but only as a symbol of law which, without a corresponding psychical experience, is incomprehensible and represents a mere combination of various physical phenomena. Psychologically law-experience is composed of a specific emotion, which is simultaneously passive and active, and of an idea of certain patterns of action (rules and conduct). This latter element consists of the ideas of (a) a subject who is entitled to be given what he has a right to demand; (b) of the subject of an obligation who is obliged or bound to do his duty; (c) of the idea of what is to be done by the subject of the right; and (d) what, by the subject of the obligation; plus several other "ideational images." In other words, psychologically the phenomena of law are composed of an emotion plus the above ideas of the subjects of the right and the duty, and of their corresponding forms of conduct. Emotional elements give to law-experience its force, and dynamics; "ideational" elements define the patterns of conduct to which the law-emotion is urging. Such a psychological composition of law manifests itself in our feeling of the law-rules of conduct as "obligatory" or two-sided. On the one hand they assign to the subject of a duty the obligation to perform it; on the other, they entitle the subject of the right to require or demand a satisfaction of his right. By this two-sidedness the phenomenon of law differs from that of morals. Moral rules of conduct only command to do such and such things,

---

Errinnerungsgabe für M. Weber, Vol. I; Todd, A. J., *op. cit.,* Chap. XXIV; Pound R., *Introduction to the Philosophy of Law,* 1922.

for instance, to give one's wealth to a poor man; but they do not ascribe to this poor man the right to demand the wealth of the other. They are one-sided, only imperative; while the law-rules are two-sided, imperative-attributive. Being such, they naturally are felt as "binding" or "obligatory." Thus, according to Professor Petrajitzsky, law is imperative-attributive psychical experience, composed of specific emotion plus an idea of a certain pattern of behavior of the subjects of right and obligation. Such is the psychical essence of the phenomena of law. Any psychical experience which has the above characteristics is a phenomenon of law regardless of the concrete character of the rules of conduct. Even a band of brigands has its own law, as far as its members have the above experience. There are many varieties of law. The two principal ones are the official law enacted by the state officials, and the unofficial law, which may very often be contradictory to the official law, and sometimes may break it.[72]

Guided by the above conception of law, Petrajitzsky very clearly depicted the influence of law on human behavior and law's social functions. *Law's influence on human behavior, and through it, on social phenomena is manifested in three principal forms: (a) in a definite motivation of human behavior; (b) in its shaping through repetition of the forms of conduct required by law; (c) in the physical coercion to follow the forms of conduct indicated by law.* As a motivating force, law urges us to do our duty; it gives us the power to demand what we are entitled to by law; it makes us fight for our rights when they are transgressed and it urges a subject to a sense of the obligation to do his duty. Without the law-factor we would do nothing unpleasant or hard; we would not dare to require service of other men if we were not entitled to it by law; we would not have the energy to oppose a strong man or to fight for our rights in case of their transgression.

In brief, without law as a motivating factor, our behavior

---

[72] The above is only a poor skeleton of an extraordinarily logical and deep psychological theory of law developed in detail by Petrajitzsky, in his *Introduction to the Theory of Law*, and *Theory of Law*, Vols. I and I!. Contrary to many philosophical theorizers of law, the author made a minute analysis of the codes of the constitutional, civil, administrative, criminal, and processual law from the standpoint of his theory, and he has most successfully shown how easily his conceptions "work" in their analysis and interpretation.

would be quite different. Law is an energy which puts the human machinery into motion and controls its movement. The influence of law, however, goes further. Actions performed at the beginning under the influence of law as a motivating agency, become, after many repetitions, habits, and begin to be performed as quite habitual actions. In this way law influences human behavior still more profoundly. Finally, when certain forms of conduct required by law are not fulfilled, or when certain forms of actions prohibited by law are fulfilled, the law manifests itself as a physical power, and through coercion, compulsion, punishment and execution, forces "the offenders" to follow its requirements, or it imposes upon them a compulsory rigid form of conduct in prison, or it eliminates them from the field of life. In the last case it operates as an agency of social selection and elimination of "the unfit." Such are the three principal forms of law's influence on human behavior. Taken together they exert an enormous amount of pressure on human beings; they give to their behavior a quite definite shape; they greatly change the population through selection and elimination; and through all this, they shape social institutions and processes.

The social functions of law are two: *distributive and organizational.* Being in its essence an emotional idea which distributes rights and duties among human beings, law determines all the essential forms of human relationship; prescribes *suum quique,* distributes rights and duties among the members of a group; and, in brief, operates as a distributive agency. It definitely indicates to everybody what, when, where, and in regard to whom he has to act. As far as rights and duties are social values, their distribution by law means the distribution of all social values, among the members of a society including the economic ones. In this function the social rôle of law is enormous. It is the force which shapes the whole social organization; the political constitution, economic institutions, social classes, and so forth. Official "laws," courts and judges are nothing but instruments for the realization of the distributive function of law. Its *organizational function* is the other side of the distributive function. In order that the distribution of rights and duties may be efficient, there must be some power or authority through which the distribution is enforced and protected. On this basis appeared the government, or power, the state, and the law agents; legislatures, courts, judges, police and so on. Authority is nothing but a creation of law. The power of a government is but the power of law; that is, the power of a conviction which attributes to the corresponding persons the rights of governing, and to the subjects, the duty of obedience. Giving to the various classes of people and authorities different rights and duties, law creates a hierarchy of the authorities, organizing the social, economic,[73] and political institutions of a society. From these statements it follows that there must be a close correlation between the character of the law-convictions of a group and its social and political organization. The former being changed, the latter will be changed also. Such is the essence of Petrajitzsky's theory of law as a psycho-social factor.

In the opinion of the writer the theory is logical, elegant, and valid, as far as the law-convictions are taken as a given variable. Certain law-convictions like the *mores* being given, they influence human behavior in the above three forms and perform the distributive and organizational functions. But is this enough, and will we penetrate far enough into the wilderness of the dynamics of trans-subjective social phenomena with these propositions? I am afraid we shall not. Indeed, in the first place the theory has all the difficulties of the above theories as an explanation of the influence of psychic experience on overt action. Furthermore, it tells us that human beings tend to behave in accordance with the forms of convictions which they have in regard to behavior and relationship. But why do they have any particular law-convictions? Why do some individuals and groups have one form of law-convictions, while other individuals and groups have often the opposite ones? Why do the law-convictions of the same individual or group often change in the course of time? Why, in a complex society, in spite of the heterogeneity of the law-convictions among its members and classes, do only certain

[73] Professor John Commons, in his *Legal Foundations of Capitalism*, in his own way has demonstrated a similar idea and has backed it by an enormous mass of materials.

forms of these convictions become "the official law," while other ones are often suppressed and persecuted?

Furthermore, there have been set forth millions of forms of conduct and many constitutions like the French constitutions of 1791, 1793, 1795, 1814, 1830 which should have been followed. And yet, these and many similar constitutions remained on paper only, and only some of these patterns of conduct became "the law-convictions" of a certain group at a certain time. The majority of would-be-law patterns of behavior could not be inculcated, and were without effect.[74] We may agree that the power of a government consists in the power of the law-convictions of its subjects, who attribute to the government the right of governing, and to themselves, the duty of obedience. But why do they do it? And why do they often obey a government which they style as "rotten," and why, out of the thousands of the would-be rulers, do only a few candidates become rulers in fact? It is enough to put these questions to see that the theory does not answer them. Like the theory of the *mores* it is true in the contention that men tend to behave and to shape their social institutions in accordance with their convictions of what ought to be the forms of conduct and relationship. But this is near to a tautology. To be a real explanation the theory must answer all the above questions which it does not. If it tried to do so, it would be obliged to turn elsewhere to explain why these factors are such and such in a given case but not in others; why they change; why they are different among various groups; why among these different convictions only certain ones become "the enforced official law"; and so on. In this case the law-factor appears principally as a mere channel through which numerous non-law forces find their aggregate outlet, and whose aggregate power is what determines the form of the power of the law-factor. As a result, the proper power of the pure law-factor remains unknown. At the same time, an undifferentiated complex of various factors, united under the name of the law-factor, makes their analysis, or the establishment of a correlation, exceedingly difficult, and dooms us to go around in a world of vague uncertainty. In other words, we have here the same "flaw"

---

[74] See about this a sharp criticism in CRUET, *op. cit.*, pp. 1–10, 336 and *passim.*

which was indicated above in the criticism of the religious and the *mores* theory.

4. Public Opinion and Propaganda, as Factors

During the last few years several studies have been published devoted to the analysis of what is styled "public opinion,"—its nature, factors, mechanism of formation, accuracy, and influence.[75] The studies have clarified our knowledge of the phenomena to a considerable degree. They have also given us a deeper insight into the nature and influence of various instruments which aid in the formation of public opinion,—such as the newspapers, press, propaganda, and so forth.[76] Have they clarified the problem of these influences on the dynamics of social events? Can we say now exactly what is the influence of these agencies? The question must be answered rather negatively. We still know little in this field. On the one hand, several authors assure us with conspicuous talent that "the way in which the world is imagined determines at any particular moment what men will do"; that "the picture of our environment which we have in our heads," regardless of its accuracy when compared with the real world, determines our behavior; and that these "pseudo-environments, men's interior representations of the world, are the determining elements in thought, feeling, and action."[77] Having shown further that these "pictures in our heads" are greatly

---

[75] See especially LIPPMANN, W., *Public Opinion*, N. Y., 1922; *Phantom Public*, N. Y., 1926; TÖNNIES, F., *Kritik der öffentlichen Meinung*, Berlin, 1922; LOWELL, L., *op. cit.*; *Public Opinion and Popular Government*, N. Y., 1913; HAYES, E. C., "The Formation of Public Opinion," *Journal Applied Sociology*, September-October, 1925; DICEY, A. V., *Law and Public Opinion in England*, 1905; WALLAS, G., *The Great Society*, N. Y., 1914; BAUER, W., *Die öffentliche Meinung und ihre geschichtlichen Grundlagen*, Tübingen, 1914; TODD, A. J., *op. cit.*, Chap. XXV; and the quoted works of Pareto, J. Bryce, Ostrogorski, G. Mosca, and R. Michels.

[76] YARROS, V. S., "The Press and Public Opinion," *American Journal of Sociology*, 1899; PARK, R., "The Natural History of the Newspaper," *ibid.*, November, 1923; LEUPP, F. E., "The Waning Power of the Press," *Atlantic Monthly*, February, 1910; LUNDBERG, G., "The Newspaper and Public Opinion," *Social Forces*, June, 1926; SALMON, L. M., *The Newspaper and the Historian*, N. Y., 1923; IRWIN, W., "The American Newspaper," *Collier's*, XLVI and XLVII, 1911; SCOTT, W. D., *The Psychology of Advertising*, 1916; BELLOC, HILAIRE, *The Present Position and Power of the Press*, London, A. Allen and Unwin, Ltd.; SCOTT-JAMES, R. A., *Influence of the Press*, London, 1913. See other bibliography in these works.

[77] LIPPMANN, WALTER, *Public Opinion*, pp. 25-30.

disfigured by artificial censorships, the limitations of social contact, the comparatively meager time available in each day for paying attention to public affairs, the vested interests, the fragmentary character of newspaper information, the intentional distortion of the truth, and other factors, these authors come to the conclusion that "the pictures in our heads" are fallacious, inadequate, and wrong; and that for this reason a competent public opinion can scarcely exist. Consequently, various interindividual and intergroup misunderstandings and social conflicts are almost unavoidable.[78] If indeed we admit that "the world's picture in our head" determines our behavior as efficiently as a real world, and that these pictures are greatly dependent upon the above agencies, and especially upon the newspapers, then it seems logical to conclude that the newspapers "create great men out of next to nothing, and destroy the reputation of men truly fit for leadership, decide questions of war and peace, carry elections, overawe and coerce politicians, rulers, and courts, and when they are virtually unanimous, nothing can withstand them" (Yarros, *op. cit.*, p. 32). In this case the popular belief in the great efficiency of propaganda and in the omnipotence of the capitalist or communist groups, which control the press, seems to be unreservedly right.

Nevertheless, a little closer study of the facts makes the theory very questionable. All the objections against the above theories of psychic factors may be set forth against this theory. In its essence it is a variety of the old belief in the omnipotent rôle of ideas. At the present moment the belief can scarcely be sustained. If the theory is right, we should expect that in Soviet Russia, where during the last few years the press and all information has been absolutely monopolized by the communists who have fed the people exclusively with what they have wanted to give them, these and the communist ideology should be exclusively popular. As a matter of fact, the ideology is discredited among the Russian population probably more and certainly no less, than in any other country. This evidently contradicts the theory. G. Lundberg's study leads to the same conclusion. He compared the attitude of several newspapers in several important

[78] *Ibid.*, pp. 30–32, and *passim*.

political issues,—the city manager plan, presidential elections, and
so on, with how their regular readers voted on these issues. If
the hypothesis of the influential rôle of newspapers on their
readers' attitudes had been true, we should have expected the
existence of a close correlation between the attitude of the paper
and that of its regular readers. As a matter of fact, Lundberg's
study did not find any tangible correlation. *The Times* had a
vigorous position against the city-manager plan. Of its readers,
42 per cent voted in favor, and 52 per cent, against the plan. *The
Post-Intelligence* and *The Star* favored the plan. Of the *Post*
readers 50 per cent, and of the *Star* readers only 35 per cent,
voted in accordance with the stand of the papers. Similar are
the results in other political issues.[79]

In spite of the claim that the dominant public opinion in England determines the course of legislation, A. V. Dicey shows
especially clearly that public opinion itself "arises from the occur-
rence of the circumstances," and is determined "by external—
one might almost say by accidental conditions." This, and the
facts given by him, show clearly that public opinion itself is a
kind of a weathercock which is turned by any change in the wind,
but which in itself has little influence to change the wind. These
and similar studies testify against the theory of the exclusive
influence of newspapers and propaganda, as a factor in human
behavior and social processes.[80] They show also that the statements of W. Lippmann about the decisive rôle of "the wrong
pictures in our heads" is considerably exaggerated. His theory,
being pushed to its conclusion, leads to the conviction that men
live mainly in, and react principally to, a pseudo-environment,
having almost no chances of being in contact with the real world.
This psycho-social solipsism obviously cannot be accepted, because if it were true, mankind would have already ceased to exist
for the simple reason that under a dominantly inadequate reaction

---

[79] LUNDBERG, *op. cit.*, pp. 710–711.

[80] For these reasons C. A. Ellwood's criticism of the exaggerated belief in an
influence of propaganda and Park's statement that the press rather reflects than
makes public opinion, seem to be nearer to the truth than the criticized theory.
See ELLWOOD, C. A., "Tolerance," *Publications of the American Sociological
Society*, Vol. XIX, pp. 10–11. In my *Sociology of Revolution*, I have tried to
show also how changeable are ideas, and how closely they depend upon deeper
factors.

to the real environment, no maintenance of life would have been, in a long course of time, possible. If mankind still exists, evidently human beings have been living to a considerable degree in a real world rather than in a Plato-Lippmann's den, and have reacted principally to the real environment, rather than to the shadows of the pseudo-environment which they see from the bottom of the den.[81] These indications are sufficient indeed to show that we still know little about the exact social influence of propaganda, news, opinions, ideas, and "public opinion" in their pure forms. Like the above theories of religion, *mores*, and laws, these theories have the same flaw. The truth seems to lie somewhere between those who believe in the omnipotence of the discussed factors, in their objectivized form, and those who deny their efficiency. But even this conclusion must still be tested.

5. OTHER CULTURAL AGENCIES

After the above it is unnecessary to analyze the various theories of the social rôle of arts, morality, fashions, and other cultural agencies. It is safe to say that in their trans-subjective form they play some part in social control, but just how great it is, the existing theories do not answer.[82] At best they show only in what forms each of these agencies influences social life or certain phenomena. But what the coefficient of the influence is, and whether the influence is due to the particular factor itself, or to other

[81] There is another doubtful point in Lippmann's theory, namely, his belief that the more truth men obtain in their information about human affairs, the more beneficial will be its rôle. In spite of the popularity of such a rationalist opinion, one may doubt it. If every man or group knew exactly what other men really have in mind and what is really happening in the world, the animosity, hatred, war, and conflicts would scarcely be decreased. If many present conflicts due to an imaginary animosity would have disappeared in this case, other ones, due to a knowledge of the hidden animosity unknown now, would have taken their place. The net balance of such an omniscient information in regard to conflicts would probably be near what we have now, when a part of our environment is a pseudo-environment. See LIPPMANN, *op. cit.*, Part VIII. Compare PASCAL, B., *Thoughts*, Section V, p. 294, Harvard Classics, Vol. XLVIII.

[82] See for instance about the rôle of the arts, GUYAU, M., *L'art au point de vue sociologique, passim* and pp. 378–384, Paris, 1895; ROSS, E., *Social Control*, Chap. XX; BUSHEE, *op. cit.*, Chap. XXIX; BUCHER, K., *Arbeit und Rhythmus*, Leipzig, 1902; LEDERER, E., "Aufgaben einer Kultursoziologie," *Erinnerungsgabe für M. Weber*, Vol. II; COMBARIEU, J., *La musique et le magic*, Paris, 1908; VON VOGT, O., *Art and Religion*, New Haven, 1921; ELLIS, H., "The Philosophy of Dancing," *Atlantic Monthly*, 1914. Much better is DISERENS, CH. M. *The Influence of Music on Behavior*, 1926

forces for which the factor is a mere shrine or channel, the theories do not answer. As a rule they do not even attempt to make such a discrimination. More than that, under various names they often count the same "force" many times. When one reads attentively the existing discussions about the rôle of belief, opinion, ceremony, law, arts, religion, morals, and so on, he may easily discover that under the names of these various agencies there are, to a great extent, identical "forces." In this way the same agency is counted several times. The theories identify what is different, and separate what is identical. One must not be surprised, therefore, that the theories are vague and have not given us any valid correlation.[83] In this field our scientific knowledge is especially small, making particularly great our need of beginning to study these phenomena more carefully with a strict separation of the trans-subjective from the psychic variables, and with a clear definition of the studied factors. Otherwise, we are doomed to wander amidst the existing dim half-true, half-false speculations.

6. General Conclusion

The last two chapters give a sufficient idea about the character of the psychological school,—its branches, varieties, pluses, and

[83] From this standpoint there are some preferences for a different approach to the problem of social control used by Professor F. E. Lumley in his *Means of Social Control*, N. Y., 1925. Instead of the traditional subdivision of the agencies of social control into science, religion, arts, and so on, he classifies them according to the nature of the actions through which individuals are influenced by other individuals. As a result we have: rewards, praise, flattery, persuasion, advertising, propaganda, gossip, satire, laughter, calling names, threats, and punishments, as means of social control. A similar approach has been used by the writer in his *Crime and Punishment, Service and Reward*, Russ., 1914. All these means of control are used by religious, scientific, judicial, æsthetic, moral, educational and other agencies of social control. As a result, when the agencies are classified in the above traditional way the same "force" enters under different names in the rôle of arts, religion, *mores*, and so on. This greatly vitiates the whole theory. Meanwhile, by proceeding in the way of Lumley we avoid such a false duplication or triplication of the same means under various names; we may make all means of control trans-subjective; we can observe them, and obtain more accurate data on their influence, and a more valid sociological correlation. Generally speaking, the traditional division of social phenomena into law, arts, science, religion and so forth must be abandoned in sociology. Being important from a practical point of view,—just as "vegetables," or "game," are important practically, scientifically these subdivisions cannot be sustained. Botanists and zoölogists have already ceased to classify "vegetables" and "game" as a plant or animal species. We sociologists still operate with such "classes" of social phenomena.

minuses. Being certainly valuable the school should be remodeled greatly along the suggested lines in order to get rid of its present shortcomings, which greatly vitiate all its achievements. Instead of the present mixed half-behavioristic and half-introspective theories, we must have the pure behavioristic and the pure introspectivist types of the psychological interpretation of social phenomena. Such a reform made, it is reasonable to expect that both of them would contribute more than the present dim theories.

CHAPTER XIII

OTHER PSYCHO–SOCIOLOGISTIC STUDIES OF THE COR-
RELATION BETWEEN VARIOUS PSYCHO–SOCIAL
PHENOMENA AND THEIR DYNAMICS

B E S I D E S the general and special sociologistic and psychological theories, there are numerous studies devoted to an analysis of
the functional relationship between two or more specified components of psycho-social phenomena. As a rule these studies
do not pretend to give an all-explaining interpretation of social
life. All that they claim is to show that such and such a correlation exists between such and such studied phenomena. In
spite of this modesty, they are highly valuable because of their
factual, quantitative, and experimental character. Being such,
they contribute to the science of sociology no less than the broad
philosophical generalizations. Until these generalizations are
verified through such special studies, their accuracy remains unknown. The data of these researches accumulating, they more
and more compose the foundation of a real inductive sociology.
For the last few decades the progress of sociology has been due
principally to this type of study. They already are of such importance that no future writer of a general treatise in sociology
can ignore them if he does not want to be behind the times. For
these reasons it is necessary at least to mention briefly the principal groups of such studies. Part of them I have already used in
the above criticism of various schools. Samples of other studies
will be surveyed in this chapter.

I. STUDIES OF A CORRELATION BETWEEN FAMILY OR HOME, AND
OTHER SOCIAL PHENOMENA

Among these special studies, a conspicuous place belongs to
those which analyze correlations between various components of
the family home, and other social phenomena. Of such researches, the first group is composed of studies which measure

the influence of family and home environment, as variables, on the personality and behavior of the people who come from them. All in all, the studies corroborate the contention of Confucius, the Le Play school, and that of Charles H. Cooley, that the family and the home environment are very important factors in molding human personality. Different investigators have taken various components of the family and home environment: the economic status of the family, the characters of the parents, their occupation, their morality, their relationship, cleanliness of the home, the number of the books in the home, the character of home furniture, and so on. Having graded the families and homes according to one or several of these criteria, they have studied the correlations between these conditions and health, juvenile delinquency, criminality, suicide, insanity, feeble-mindedness, intelligence, genius, school and business success, and other personality traits of the people who have come from these families. Almost all of these studies have discovered the existence of various tangible correlations. As a rule, the families and homes which have a better economic status, better home environment, honest and intelligent parents, and good relationship between them, yield a greater portion of children with better health, superior intelligence, those successful in their school and business curriculum, and a greater number of geniuses and men of talent; and, at the same time, a smaller proportion of the feeble-minded, insane, the young delinquent, criminals, prostitutes, and other socially inadequate individuals, than do the families and homes which are poor, dirty, and unattractive, whose parents are biologically defective, ignorant, bad-tempered, drunkards, divorced, deserted, dead, immoral or criminal; and whose relationship is far from being good. In brief, on the basis of these studies, the existence of these and similar correlations seems to be certain, and quite tangible, though not perfect. It goes without saying that what in these correlations is due to family and home and what to heredity, the studies cannot exactly answer. Probably both of these factors are responsible.[1]

---

[1] Of an enormous literature, see the following representative studies of the correlations between the family and delinquency and moral deficiency: WILLIAMS, J. H., "The Whittier Scale for Grading Home Conditions," *Journal of*

In addition, several other studies have shown that practically all the important social characteristics of an individual, such as religion, language, *mores*, habits, beliefs, and even his economic status and occupation, are determined principally by the family.

Delinquency, Vol. I, pp. 273–286; "The Intelligence of the Delinquent Boy," *ibid.*, Mono. No. 1, 1919; BRECKENRIDGE, S., and ABBOTT, E., *The Delinquent Child and the Home*, N. Y., 1912; FERNALD, M., HAYES, M., and DAWLEY, A., *A Study of Women Delinquents in N. Y. State*, N. Y., 1920; HEALY, W., *The Individual Delinquent*, Boston, 1915; JOHNSON, E., "The Relations of the Conduct Difficulties of a Group of Public School Boys," etc., *Journal of Delinquency*, Nov., 1921; SHILDER, E. H., "Family Disintegration and the Delinquent Boy," *Journal of Criminal Law*, Jan., 1918; GERNET, M. N., *Criminal Children* (Russian), Moscow, 1909; DRUCKER, S., and HEXTER, M. B., *Children Astray*, Cambridge, 1923; BURT, C., *The Young Delinquent*, N. Y., 1925; TAFT, J., "The Effect of an Unsatisfactory Mother-Daughter Relationship," *The Family*, March, 1926. See a good summary of these studies in SUTHERLAND, E., *Criminology*, Chaps. VII–VIII; GILLIN, J., *Criminology and Penology*, Chap. XI, 1926; BURGESS, E., "Topical Summaries of Current Literature, The Family," *American Journal of Sociology*, July, 1926. The following studies are representative of a demonstration of the correlations between the family and the intelligence, school success, genius, integrity of personality, and so on: TERMAN, L., *Genetic Studies of Genius*, 1925, Vol. I; O'BRIEN, F., *The High School Failures*, N. Y., 1919; KELLY, A. M., and LIDBETTER, E. J., "A Comparative Inquiry of the Heredity and Social Conditions," etc., *Eugenic Review*, Vol. XIII; BOOK, W. F., *The Intelligence of High School Seniors*, N. Y., 1922; ISSERLIS, L., "The Relation between Home Conditions and the Intelligence of School Children," London, 1923; DUFF, J., and THOMSON, G. H., "The Social and Geographic Distribution of Intelligence in Northumberland," *British Journal of Psychology*, Vol. XIV; PINTNER, R., *Intelligence Testing*, N. Y., 1923; HOLLEY, CHARLES E., *The Relationship between Persistence in School and Home Conditions*, Chicago, 1916; WAPLES, D., "Indexing the Qualifications of Different Social Groups," *The School Review*, 1924; BURDGE, H., *Our Boys*, N. Y., 1921; COUNTS, G. S., *The Selective Character of American Secondary Education*, Chicago, 1922; ELLIS, H., *A Study of British Genius*, London, 1904; ODIN, A., *Le genèuse des grands hommes*, Paris, 1895; DE CANDOLLE, A., *Histoire des sciences et des savants*, Genève, 1885; MAAS, F., "Ueber die Herkunftsbedingungen der Geistigen Führer," *Archiv für Sozialwissenschaft*, 1916; CATTELL, J. McKEEN, *American Men of Science*, 3d ed.; CLARKE, E., *American Men of Letters*, N. Y., 1916; DAVIES, G. R., "A Statistical Study of the Influence of Environment," *Quarterly Journal of University of North Dakota*, Vol. IV; SOROKIN, P., "American Millionaires," *Journal of Social Forces*, May, 1925; "Monarchs and Rulers," *ibid.*, 1925–26; WOODS, F. A., *op. cit.*; HUNTINGTON, *op. cit.* See other sources and summary in SOROKIN, *Social Mobility*, Chaps. X–XII; HOLLINGWORTH, L. T., *Gifted Children*, N. Y., 1926. The quoted studies of N. Paton and L. Findlay, A. B. Hill, and E. Elderton, have shown that the health of the mother and the mother's care of the children is the most important factor in the children's health and behavior. H. Hartshorne's and M. A. May's study has shown also that the children, in their knowledge of right and wrong, show the greatest likeness to that of their parents, the coefficient of the correlation being .545, while the coefficient of the correlation in the likeness to children's friends is only .353; to club leaders .137; to their teachers .028 and .002. "Testing the knowledge of Right and Wrong," *Religious Education*, Vol. XXI, p. 545.

As a rule, the majority of men formerly had the same religion, native language, *mores,* economic status, and occupation which their parents had. The closeness of the correlation in these fields varies from time to time, from society to society, and it is greater in the field of language, for instance, than in the field of occupation. Nevertheless, the correlations remain tangible even within modern Western society.[2]

The second group of the studies has disclosed many correlations between such family conditions as being married, single, divorced, or widowed, and duration of life, criminality, suicide, insanity, and pauperism. Almost all the studies with few exceptions, show that the married have a lower per cent of insanity, criminality, suicide, and pauperism, and have a longer duration of life than the unmarried, or, especially the divorced of the same sex, age group, and social status.[3]

The third group of studies has tried to show the factors which influence a modification of various family characteristics. Contrary to the above investigations, these studies take a certain family characteristic as a function and endeavor to find its variables. Many studies of this type have already been mentioned in the preceding paragraphs of the book. Of other studies we have several valuable contributions to the problem of the factors responsible for an increase or decrease of divorce and desertion. These studies have shown that occupation, industrial changes, economic status, religion, social and racial heterogeneity of husband and wife, the number of children, social mobility, the character of the laws of marriage and divorce, war, and several other factors determine the movement of divorce and separation.[4]

---

[2] See especially VON MAYR, G., *Die Gesetzmässigkeit im Gesellschaftsleben,* München, 1877, *passim.* About the fluctuation of these correlations in time and space see SOROKIN, *Social Mobility,* Chaps. VII, IX, XVI–XIX. See there the bibliography.

[3] See the data and the literature in VON MAYR, G., *Statistik und Gesellschaftslehre,* Vols. II, III; OETTINGEN, A., *op. cit.;* LEVASSEUR, E., *La population française,* Vols. I, II; OGBURN, W. F., "The Relationship of Marital Condition to Death, Crime, Insanity. and Pauperism," *XVI⁰ session de l'Institut International de Statistique,* Roma, 1926.

[4] Besides the quoted works of von Mayr, Levasseur, and Oettingen, see LICHTENBERGER, J. P., *Divorce,* N. Y., 1909; WILLCOX, W., *The Divorce Problem,* N. Y., 1891; JACQUART, C., *Le divorce et la séparation de corps,* Bruxelles, 1909; United States Bureau of the Census, *Marriage and Divorce,* 1867–1906, 2 vols., Washington, 1908–09; BOSCO, A., *I divorzi e le separazioni personali dei conjugi,*

The next group is composed of researches which analyze the factors responsible for a choice in marriage, or for preferential and assortative mating in men. As far as the studies show, neither the theory that "the opposite poles attract" nor the theory of *similia similibus curantur* seem to be correct in their extreme forms. As a general rule, the similarity of the mates in stature, age, color, race, nationality, and in social, occupational, religious, economic, cultural, and other respects, facilitates marriage choice, and is a preferential factor. But the rule knows several exceptions which make necessary a further study of the phenomena.[5]

The next group of studies has endeavored to discover the factors responsible for determining the sex of individuals. The problem still remains more or less certainly unsolved.[6]

A large number of the studies deal with the factors which determine the fluctuation of the birth rate in time and space, as well as with that of the different fecundity of various social classes. The principal works of this type have been mentioned in the preceding chapters.

Without mentioning other researches dealing with the corre-

Roma, 1908; BERTILLON, J., *Étude demographique du divorce*, Paris, 1883; BOCKH, R., "Statistik der Ehescheidungen in der Stadt Berlin in den Jahren 1885 bis 1894," *Bulletin de l'Institut International de Statistique*, tome XI, pp. 251–281; YVERNES, M., "Les divorces et les separations de corps en France depuis 1884," *Journal de la Société de Statistique de Paris*, 1908; SAVORGNAN, F., "Nuzialità e fecundità delle case sovrane d'Europa," *Metron*, Vol. III, No. 2; SOROKIN, P., "Influence of the World War upon Divorces," *Journal Applied Sociology*, Nov., Dec., 1925; OGBURN, W., "Factors Affecting the Marital Conditions of the Population," *Proceedings Amer. Sociol. Soc.*, Vol. XV, 1923; EUBANK, E., *A Study of Family Desertion*, Chicago, 1916; COLCORD, J., *Broken Homes*, N. Y., 1919; SHERMAN, C., "Racial Factor in Desertion," *The Family*, Vol. III, 1922–23; THOMAS, W. I., and ZNANIECKI, F., *The Polish Peasants in Europe and America*, 4 vols., Boston, 1918–20.

[5] FAY, E. A., *Marriages of the Deaf in America*, Washington, 1898; PEARSON, K., *Grammar of Science*, 2nd ed., pp. 431–437; SAVORGNAN, F., *La scelta matrimoniale*, Ferrara, 1924; BENINI, *Principi di demografia*, 1901; CHESSA, F., *La trasmissione ereditaria delle professioni*, Torino, 1912; JENKS, A. E., "Ethnic Census in Minneapolis," *Am. Journal Soc.*, Vol. XVII; HARRIS, J. A., "Assortative Mating in Men," *Scientific Monthly*, April, 1912; LUTZ, F. E., "Assortative Mating in Man," *Science*, N. S., 1905; DRACHSLER, J., *Intermarriage in N. Y. City*, N. Y., 1921; MARVIN, D., "Occupational Propinquity as a Factor in Marriage Selection," *American Statistical Assn.*, Vol. XVI, pp. 131–151; WEATHERLY, W. G., "Race and Marriage," *American Journal of Sociology*, Vol. XV; "Assortative Mating in Man: A Coöperative Study," *Biometrika*, Vol. II, pp. 481–498.

[6] See the literature and brilliant analysis in GINI, C., *Il sesso dal punto di vista statistico, Le leggi della produzione dei sessi*, 1908; see also VON MAYR, *op. cit.*, Vol. II.

lations between the family and other social phenomena, the above is sufficient to show the intensive work which has been going on in this field. The data obtained already permit us to a considerable degree to build an inductive theory of "family sociology."

2. STUDIES OF THE CORRELATION BETWEEN THE CHARACTER OF
A NEIGHBORHOOD AND OTHER SOCIAL PHENOMENA

The second category of the studies is represented by careful investigations of *the influence of a neighborhood* on man's physical, mental, and moral characteristics. They have also yielded many data which indicate the kind and the character of the correlation between the neighborhood and a man's behavior. Studies of Charles Booth, B. S. Rowntree, R. D. McKenzie, J. Williams, E. W. Burgess, R. A. Woods, W. J. Thomas,[7] and other investigators, have thrown a great deal of light on the effects of the neighborhood on man's traits, behavior, and psychology. Now we are reasonably certain that among the many factors which shape a personality, the agency of the neighborhood in which a man was born and reared must be taken into consideration. Otherwise, one of the effective factors is likely to be overlooked.

3. STUDIES OF THE INFLUENCES OF OCCUPATION, AND
OCCUPATIONAL CORRELATIONS

Side by side with these works which, like Durkheim's *De la division du travail social,* try to analyze the general influences of the division of labor, we have now numerous factual studies which give accurate data about the effects of occupation on man's physical, vital, mental, and moral nature. The studies are so

[7] ROWNTREE, B. S., *Poverty,* London, 1901; BOOTH, CHARLES, *Life and Labour of the People in London,* all volumes; McKENZIE, R. D., *The Neighborhood,* Chicago, 1923; WILLIAMS, J. H., "A Scale for Grading Neighborhood Conditions," *Whittier State School,* Bull. No. 5, 1917; CHAPIN, F. S., "A Quantitative Scale for Measuring the Home, etc.," *Journal of Educational Psychology,* Feb., 1928; BURGESS, E. W., "Juvenile Delinquency in a Small City," *Journal of Criminal Law,* Jan., 1916; GOLDMARK, P., *West Side Studies,* Boston, 1898; WOODS, R. A., *The City Wilderness;* THOMAS, W. I., *The Unadjusted Girl,* Boston, 1923; ADDAMS, J., *The Spirit of Youth and the City Streets,* N. Y., 1909; SIMKHOVITCH, M. K., *The City Worker's World in America,* N. Y., 1917; WOODS, R., "The Neighborhood in Social Reconstruction," *American Journal of Sociology,* Vol. XIX.

numerous that it is impossible to give here even a very abbreviated list of the corresponding works. Instead, it is better to indicate a few sources in which the greater part of such researches have been already summed up. *Krankheit und Soziale Lage,* edited by Professors M. Mosse and G. Tugendreich, (München, 1913) and *Handbuch der Sozialen Hygiene und der Gesundheitsfursorge,* five volumes, edited by Professors A. Gottstein, A. Schlossman, and Dr. L. Teleky (Berlin, 1926-27), give a summary of a great many studies of the biological effec's of occupation on the human body and health. In my *Social Mobility* [8] I have summed up the principal works and correlations between the character of the occupational groups and their physical, vital, and intellectual properties.[9] Numerous studies in this field have made certain the enormous influence of this social condition on man, his behavior, and through that, on social processes. Neither individual conduct and psychology, nor group behavior and characteristics, nor social antagonisms and solidarity, nor processes of social reconstruction and revolution, nor almost any important social change or irregularity, can be accounted for satisfactorily without the occupational factor. Besides, the studies have disclosed a series of correlations between the nature of occupational groups and their bodily, vital, and mental characteristics. If we classify the occupational classes beginning with the unskilled occupations, passing to semi-skilled, skilled, clerical, and the semi-business class, and ending with the big business and qualified professional groups, we may see that as we proceed from the unskilled to the qualified professionals, the stature, weight, health,

[8] Chaps. VI, X–XII, XIII, XVII.

[9] Out of the immense literature, I shall mention only a few studies of the various "occupational" types of social group: WILLIAMS, J. M., *Our Rural Heritage,* N. Y., 1925; *The Expansion of Rural Life,* N. Y., 1926; GROVES, E., *Rural Mind and Social Welfare,* Chicago; HERMES, G., *Die geistige Gestalt des Marxistischen Arbeiters und die Arbeiterbildungsfrage,* Tübingen, 1926; LURÝE, *Sostav proletariata* (Composition of the Proletariat), Russian, 1918; BLÁHA, ARNOŠT, *Sociologie sedlaka a delnika,* Prague, 1925; RUHLE, OTTO, *Die Seele des proletarischen Kindes,* Dresden, 1925; several exclusively valuable volumes of the *Deutsche Verein für Sozialpolitik, Auslese und Anpassung der Arbeiterschaft,* Vols. CXXXIII–CXXXV; SOMBART, W., *Der Bourgeois;* TAUSSIG, F. M., *Inventors and Money-Makers,* N. Y., 1915; BAUER, A., *Les classes sociales,* Paris, 1902. See also *Revue international de sociologie* for 1900–1903, where a series of discussions concerning this point is given; also VEBLEN, T., *The Theory of the Leisure Class.* See other literature in the indicated books of Mosse and Tugendreich and Sorokin. See also the next paragraph.

duration of life and the size of head are increasing; while fertility, on the contrary, decreases.   Intelligence again increases. There is a considerable overlapping, and some exceptions to the rule; nevertheless they do not annul the correlation.[10]

4. STUDIES OF THE EFFECTS OF URBAN AND RURAL ENVIRONMENT

During the last few decades numerous and valuable studies of the complex effects of city and country environment have been published.   At the present moment we already have the fundamental division of sociology into the rural and urban branches. The studies disclosed a series of the most conspicuous differences in physical traits, vital processes, mentality, criminality and *mores* between the people of the country and the city, correlated with various components of these two environments, their predominant occupations and their selections.   The investigations have contributed a great deal to our knowledge of the "social mystery." The energetic work which goes on in these fields promises to contribute still more to the science of sociology.[11]

5. STUDIES OF PSYCHO-SOCIAL TYPES OF INDIVIDUALS AND GROUPS, AND THE CORRELATIONS BETWEEN THE PSYCHOLOGICAL TRAITS AND SOCIAL AFFILIATIONS OF INDIVIDUALS

We have already mentioned several kinds of studies which try to depict the psycho-social types of individuals and social groups.

[10] See the literature and the data in *Social Mobility*, Chaps. X–XII.

[11] The literature is already enormous.   See the data and the bibliography in the following representative courses on rural sociology: GILLETTE, J. M., *Rural Sociology*, N. Y., 1925; VOGT, P. L., *Introduction to Rural Sociology*, N. Y., 1920; TAYLOR, C., *Rural Sociology*, N. Y., 1926; PHELAN, J., *Reading in Rural Sociology;* GALPIN, CHARLES J., *Rural Life*, N. Y., 1918; STEINER, J. F., *Community Organization*, N. Y., 1925; SIMS, N. L., *The Rural Community*, N. Y., 1920; McCLENAHAN, B. A., *Organizing the Community*, N. Y., 1922.

A careful bibliography of urban sociology is given in PARK, R., and BURGESS, E., *The City*, Chicago, 1925; in BURGESS, E., *Urban Community*, Chicago, 1926. See also WEBER, A. F., *The Growth of Cities in the Nineteenth Century*, N. Y., 1899; THURNWALD, R., "Stadt und Land im Lebensprozess der Rasse," *Archiv für Rassen und Gesellschafts Biologie*, 1904; KOHLBRÜGGE, J. H. F., "Stadt und Land als biologische Umwelt," *Archiv für Rassen und Gesellschafts Biologie*, 1909; KUCZYNSKY, R., *Der Zug nach der Stadt*, Stuttgart, 1897.   Besides, see the data and the literature in the quoted works of von Mayr, Oettingen, and Levasseur. An exhaustive and severely critical monograph in the field is now being prepared by the writer and C. Zimmerman.

Such, for instance, are the patriarchal, particularist, and state-communist types of personality and people, as set forth by the Le Play school. Another example of this typological sociology is given in the above works which try to picture *the occupational or class types* of a farmer, proletarian, banker, priest, scholar, physician, and so on. The third variety of the typological sociology is represented by the works which describe the *national* psycho-social types. The works of Emile Boutmy, H. Münsterberg, A. Fouillée, A. De Tocqueville, and James Bryce [12] are good samples of this variety. The works of this kind are numerous, but a great part of them are either one-sided or superficial.

The fourth variety of sociological typology is represented by various theories of the *cultural types of personality and groups.* Possibly the most serious attempt to clarify the concept of the "ideal social type" and to develop the method of the "ideal type" as a specific method in an investigation of social problems, has been made by Max Weber. We saw something of it in his analysis of the "ideal types" of capitalism, Protestantism, Confucianism, and so on.[13] It was used, however, long ago, and used well. At the present moment we have many samples of cultural typologies of various kinds. Such, for instance, are the eight types of cultures set forth by O. Spengler, a theory which in this, as well as in many other respects, is in fact an independent recapitulation of what was developed in 1869 by Danilevsky.[14] Another variety of this "cultural typology" is represented by numerous works of various historians and sociologists, who have tried to make a classification of cultures or societies. The theories are so numerous that there is no possibility of giving

[12] See BOUTMY, E., *Essai d'une psychologie politique du peuple anglais au XIX* siècle, Paris, 1901, English translation, N. Y., 1904; *Eléments d'une psychologie politique du peuple Américan*, Paris, 1902; MÜNSTERBERG, H., *The Americans;* FOUILLÉE, A., *Psychologie du peuple français*, 2d ed., 1898; *Esquisse psychologique des peuples européens*, 2d ed., Paris, 1903; DE TOCQUEVILLE, A., *Democracy in America;* BRYCE, JAMES, *The American Commonwealth*, 1891. See also the mentioned works of E. Demolins, P. Rousieurs, H. de Tourville, and F. Le Play.

[13] See WEBER, M., *Gesammelte Aüfsätze zur Wissenschaftslehre*, pp. 190 ff., 1922; WALTER, ANDREAS, "Max Weber als Soziologe," *Jahrbuch für Soziologie*, Bd. II, 1926; KLÜVER, H. M., "Weber's 'Ideal Type' in Psychology," *Journal of Philosophy*, Vol. XXIII.

[14] See SPENGLER, O., *op. cit.*, Vol. I, *passim.* Compare DANILEVSKY, *Russia and Europe* (in Russian), 2nd ed., 1871. See SCHWARTZ, M., *Spengler and Danilevsky* (in Russian), *Sovremennia Zapiski*, Vol. XVIII, pp. 436–456.

even their mere enumeration.[15] It is enough to say that in historical, political, sociological, economic, and other cultural sciences, the method of the "ideal type" or simply, typology, is widely practiced and seems to be unavoidable. When an historian talks of "the Greek city-society," "feudal," "caste," or "modern society," he uses this method. When an economist classifies economic organization into the "capitalist" and the "socialist" systems, or into a system of "natural economy," "money economy," "credit economy," and so on, he applies the same method. The same may be said of the anthropological classification of races, of "democratic and autocratic types" of society, and so forth. Being unavoidable and useful, the method is, however, often used unsatisfactorily and results in a distorted classification, and a quite one-sided characterization of the corresponding "type" of cultural phenomena. In order to give positive results, the method requires a great deal of knowledge of the subject, an ability to grasp the typical traits in the multitude of the concrete characteristics, and a talent for a well-balanced synthesis of these traits. Only great minds and talents use it with good results.

The fifth variety of psycho-social typology is given in the theories which may be styled as *"the formal typologies of individuality."* E. Spranger's classification of the "ideal types" of man may serve as an example. He discriminates between the ideal types of the theoretical man, the economic man, the æsthetic man, the social man, the man of power, and the religious man.[16]

The sixth variety of the classification of the types of human personality is represented by numerous *psycho-analytical and psycho-sociological* theories. They try to classify individuals not so much on the basis of their "ideologies," "speech-reactions,"

---

[15] See a survey and analysis of the principal theories of the sociologists in SOROKIN, P., *Systema Soziologii,* Vol. II, pp. 306–346; STEINMETZ, S. R., "Classification des types sociaux et catalogue des peuples," *L'année sociologique,* Vol. III; SOMLÓ, F., *Zur Gründung einer beschreibenden Soziologie,* Berlin-Leipzig, 1909; MAZZARELLA, *op. cit., passim;* KAREEFF, N., *Historical Typology* (in Russian).

[16] See SPRANGER, E., *Lebensformen,* Halle, 1922; see other samples in *Die Typen der Weltanschauung und ihre Ausbildung in den metaphysischen Systemen,* Weltanschauung, herausgegeben von M. Frischeisen-Kohler, Berlin, 1922; KLÜVER, H., "Problem of Type in 'Cultural Science' Psychology," *Journal of Philosophy,* Vol. XXII, pp. 225–234.

and the character of their opinions as on the basis of their temperament, emotionality, reactibility, and other somewhat deeper characteristics. Accordingly, the types are regarded as "universal" and "eternal" and found amidst various societies and at various periods. Pareto's types of the *"rentieri"* and the *"speculatori"* is one sample of such classifications. C. G. Jung's, and other psychologists' classifications of individuals into the introvert and extravert types [17] are other examples. L. Klages' classification of temperaments according to the formula $\dfrac{T \text{ (drive)}}{W \text{ (resistance)}} = R$ (reactibility) [18] is a third sample. The still more complex classification of E. Kretschmer into the schizothymic and cyclothymic types,[19] or the typologies of personality set forth by E. R. Jaensch, H. Rorschach, G. Ewald, A. Kronfeld, and K. Jasper are further samples of this variety.[20] Though the majority of these psychological typologies are very old, nevertheless, modern theories try to base their classifications on the data of experimental study and exact measurement. If their present form is far from being unquestionable, they at least promise to be fruitful and scientifically significant.

In connection with these psychological classifications of the types of human personality, it is necessary to mention some studies which try to analyze some more overt social groups in the terms of these classifications. We saw above that this was done by Pareto, who correlated his type of the *"speculatori"* with certain societies and social processes (Athens, democracies, etc.), while the type of the *"rentieri"* was correlated with other societies (Rome) and processes. Men similar ideologically may belong to opposite types, from the standpoint of their dominant "residues," and *vice versa*. Such is the conclusion of Pareto. A similar idea lies at the basis of several studies of such social types as the radical, the reactionary, the conservative, and so on. Outwardly these types of personality seem to be opposite, be-

---

[17] JUNG, C. G., *Psychological Types*, 1923.

[18] KLAGES, L., *Principien der Characterologie*, Leipzig, 1920.

[19] KRETSCHMER, E., *Körperbau und Character*, Berlin, 1922.

[20] See a good survey of the theories and their analysis in KLÜVER, HEINRICH, "An Analysis of Recent Works on the Problem of Psychological Types," *The Journal of Nervous and Mental Disease*, Vol. LXII, pp. 561–596. See there a good bibliography.

cause their aspirations and ideologies are opposite. But are they different from the standpoint of their emotionality, reactibility, intelligence, extra- and introversion, and other deeper traits? And if they are different, in exactly what consists the difference? H. T. Moore's and F. A. Allport's studies may serve as an example of the experimental or quantitative attack of the problem. Professor Moore (1886–) studied about 350 radical and conservative students from this standpoint. The principal results of his elaborate study show that neither of the groups differs from each other either in intelligence, emotional stability, or any general superiority and inferiority. The principal differences are "innate," and consist in such specific factors as "greater speed of reactions among the radicals, and their ease in breaking habits; and their readiness to make snap judgments and independence (of opinion) in the face of majority influence. The last of these differences is the most clearly indicated." [21] Somewhat similar is F. A. Allport's and D. A. Hartman's study. They studied the psychological differences of radicals and reactionaries, and the differences between these groups and a group of the moderates. The first result of the study was to show that the extreme groups were more similar to each other than to the moderates. This supports the opinion of Pareto that the difference in ideology is rather superficial, and does not hinder an essential similarity between radicals and reactionaries in their deeper psychological traits. The study showed further that both extreme groups have a much greater certainty in their opinion than the moderates. The next difference between the groups is that religion plays a vital part in the radical group, while "the reactionary group is lowest in its interest in religion," the moderates occupying the intermediary position. Further, both extreme groups rate themselves as distinctly less rapid in talking and walking, and less emotional and more self-reliant in their opinions than are the moderates. The radical group rates itself as the least expansive, the conservative group being the most expansive, and the reactionary intermediary. As to a regard

[21] MOORE, H. T., "Innate Factors in Radicalism and Conservatism," *Journal of Abnormal and Social Psychology*, Vol. XX, 1925–6, pp. 234–244. See there the method of the study and the quantitative data.

for the opinions of others the moderates and reactionaries are less sensitive to the approval of others than the radicals. As to the degree of insight, and self-estimation, the reactionaries have the least degree of insight and the highest self-estimation; the next place in this respect belongs to the radicals, and the moderates occupy the intermediary position. Furthermore, the reactionary group is more scientifically minded, snobbish, cynical, and mechanistic in its ideology; while the radicals are more idealistic, religious, moralistic, and meliorative in their attitudes.[22]

One scarcely can think that the differences found in these two studies are really certain. Their data are somewhat contradictory.[23] Their method, which is based on the data of speech-reactions, can scarcely yield reliable and accurate results. The character of the curves of the second study is much more complex and indefinite than the above conclusions of the authors. The conclusion of Professor Moore about the "innate factors" in radicalism and conservatism appears to go beyond the data given to support it. In brief, the conclusions may be taken only as very tentative, as properly say the authors themselves. Yet the studies are interesting and valuable as the first steps toward a quantitative and factual study of the discussed and similar phenomena.

6. STUDIES IN A CORRELATION OF LEADERSHIP AND INTELLIGENCE WITH A NUMBER OF SOCIAL GROUPS PARTICIPATED IN AND WITH A SOCIAL SHIFTING

We know that De Roberty, Durkheim, Simmel, and Bouglé have contended that there had to be a positive correlation between the mental and leadership capacity of an individual and the number of groups participated in by him. However, they have not supplied sufficient factual material to corroborate their

---

[22] ALLPORT, FLOYD A., and HARTMAN, D. A., "The Measurement and Motivation of Atypical Opinion in a Certain Group," *The American Political Science Review*, Vol. XIX, pp. 735–760.

[23] Somewhat discordant also are the results obtained by S. A. Rice, Wolfe, G. Lundberg. See RICE, S. A., *op. cit.;* WOLFE, *Conservatism, Radicalism, and Scientific Method*, Chap. VII; LUNDBERG, G., "The Demographic and Economic Basis of Polit. Radicalism and Conservatism," *Amer. Journ. of Soc.*, Vol. XXXII, pp. 719–732.

statement. At the present moment, we already have some factual studies in this field. Professor F. S. Chapin's (1888–) studies may serve as representative of this purpose. Having studied 250 students, and having compared their extra-curricular activities with their academic grades and physical condition, he found a tangible positive correlation between these three series. "The upper 50, or most active students (connected with a great number of groups and more intensively participating in their activity) are also highest in average academic grade and in physical condition." The correlation between the extra-curricular activities and the academic grades is 0.402, which is quite a tangible, though not perfect, correlation.[24] O. M. Mehus, in a study of 500 University of Minnesota students, reaches similar results. Thus, these findings corroborate the contention of earlier sociologists. The writer's study of 1,400 labor leaders of America and Europe has also shown that the group of the big leaders are affiliated with a greater number of social groups than the group of the small leaders. This confirms Professor Chapin's finding. (See Sorokin and others, *Leaders of Labor and Radical Movements*.) Whether such a correlation is the result of the influence of the participation in the groups, or the participation itself and high intelligence are a result of the innate ability of the individuals, these studies do not answer. However this may be, still further studies of this type would seem to be necessary to test the extent to which the correlation is universal and permanent.

Another correlation between intelligence and leadership, on the one hand, and social mobility of the individuals, on the other, should be mentioned. Understanding by mobility any change in the habitation or social position of an individual, it is possible to claim that the mentioned phenomena are correlated within a certain limit. The writer's and Professor C. Zimmerman's studies of the leaders of American farmers, and the writer's study of labor leaders, have shown that the territorial shifting of the leaders is greater than that of the common population. The per cent of leaders who live in other states or countries than that of

[24] CHAPIN, F. S., "Measuring the Volume of Social Stimuli: A Study in Social Psychology," *Social Forces*, March, 1926; "Extra-Curricular Activities of College Students, A Study in College Leadership," *School and Society*, Feb., 1926; "Leadership and Group Activity," *Journal Applied Sociology*, January, 1924.

their birth seems to be higher than that of the common people.[25] The same is true of the notables in *Who's Who in America* and seems to be true of prominent men generally. A similar correlation is shown by a rough historical comparison of the periods of intensive social mobility and the periods of a relatively less intensive mobility with the number of the men of genius born in these periods. The facts tend to show that, within a certain limit, the periods of upheavals and high mobility are marked by a more abundant crop of men of genius, and by a more intensive progress of inventions and mental achievement.[26] Professor Carl Murchison has also found that among the criminals studied, those criminals who came from the regions far more distant than the criminals from the nearer places, have a conspicuously higher intelligence than the "home-criminals." R. Livi indicated that the upper classes of Italian population are more mobile than the lower classes.[27] Several other facts suggest the same correlation. If we take into consideration that the more mobile individuals are likely to participate in a greater number of groups than the less mobile ones, the two discussed correlations mutually support each other. However, the correlations seem to be limited and cease to exist after a certain degree of mobility. Even in this limited sense they are still tentative and need to be tested further. It is clear also that the studies cannot yet answer whether leadership and higher intelligence are the result of participation in many groups and of greater mobility, or whether the participation itself is the result of an innate characteristic of the corresponding individuals, although Chapin's recent study, "The Measurement of Sociality" (*Journal of Applied Sociology,* Feb., 1928) bears on this very important point.

7. STUDIES OF CONDITIONS WHICH FACILITATE INTERINDIVIDUAL AND INTERGROUP SYMPATHY AND REPELLENCE

We saw that, according to E. Durkheim and G. Simmel, a

[25] See SOROKIN, P., and ZIMMERMAN, C., "Leaders of Farmers of the United States," *Social Forces,* March, 1928; SOROKIN, P., and others, "Leaders of Labor and Radical Movements in the United States and Europe," *American Journal of Sociology,* 1927; "Leadership and Geogr. Mobility," J. APPL. SOC., Vol. XII.

[26] See SOROKIN, *Social Mobility,* Chap. XXI.

[27] MURCHISON, C., *Criminal Intelligence,* 1926, pp. 44–57; LIVI, R., *Antropometria Militare,* pp. 46–51, 87–91, and *passim,* Roma, 1896.

division of labor and increase of social dissimilarity of individuals lead from a "mechanical" to an "organic solidarity." They and their followers are inclined to think that such an increase of heterogeneity facilitates generally an increase of solidarity. An opposite theory was set forth by Franklin Henry Giddings.[28] He coined the expression, "the consciousness of kind," and claimed first, that "like-mindedness" or similarity of individuals is a necessary condition for the conversion of a mere gregariousness into a society; and second, that it is a factor facilitating an increase of solidarity or positive liking in the relationship of the individuals.[29] In this sense his theory is opposite to that of Durkheim, Simmel, Bouglé, and others, being similar to that of F. Tönnies. Though the problem is still little studied, the truth seems to be principally on the side of Professor Giddings. His later factual studies in this field have shown that similarities in taste, ideas, beliefs, manners, and morals "unmistakably" facilitate the relationship of liking, sympathy, and solidarity among the individuals and groups, while the dissimilarities in this field tend to produce the relationship of repellence or antipathy.[30] A great many other sociologists have discussed the phenomena of social antagonism and solidarity. At the present moment we already have several quantitative studies of the factors of these phenomena. The studies of Professor E. Bogardus should be mentioned as representative in this field.[31] Using the quantitative

---

[28] Born in 1855. Pioneer of the American and world sociology. Author of many valuable works in sociology, especially in the methodology of sociological investigation. In his later works he developed his valuable theory of "the pluralistic behavior." Principal works of Giddings are: *The Principles of Sociology*, 3d ed., 1896; *Elements of Sociology*, 1900; *Readings in Descriptive and Historical Sociology*, 1906; *Inductive Sociology*, 1901; *Studies in the Theory of Human Society*, 1922; *The Scientific Study of Human Society*, 1924. About Giddings see KOVALEVSKY, M., *Contemporary Sociologists*, Chap. II; BARTH, P., *op. cit.*, pp. 446 ff.; SQUILLACE, F., *op. cit.*, pp. 381 ff.; GILLIN, J. L., in H. W. ODUM's *American Masters of Social Science*, pp. 191–231, N. Y., 1927; and a great many articles and practically the majority of the textbooks in sociology.

[29] GIDDINGS, F., *Studies in the Theory of Human Society, passim* and pp. 164 ff. and Chap. XV.

[30] GIDDINGS, F., *The Scientific Study of Human Society*, pp. 122 ff.

[31] See a series of the articles of E. Bogardus on "Social Distance" in the *Journal of Applied Sociology*, 1925, 1926, 1927. See also his "Social Distance in the City," *Proceedings of the American Sociological Society*, Vol. XX. The only thing to which I may object is the term of "Social Distance" given to these studies. In my opinion, the term of "sociology of friendliness and antagonism"

and the case methods he has disclosed, first, the complexity of the phenomena; second, a series of factors responsible for the creation of either sympathetic or antagonistic relationship; third, the mechanism for the development of these attitudes; and fourth, the possibility of converting one attitude into another through a corresponding modification of the stimuli. In this way a step has been made toward a better understanding of these phenomena.

8. STUDIES OF THE FLUCTUATIONS, RHYTHMS, AND CYCLES OF SOCIAL PROCESSES

For the last few decades in few fields have sociological investigations been so intensive as in the field of a study of various aspects of social dynamics. One of the aspects of such a study has been the character of the fluctuations and rhythms in the field of various social processes. Let us briefly survey today's situation of this problem.

Social thought of the second half of the nineteenth century has been marked by a *linear* conception of social and historical change. The majority of sociologists, economists, and philosophers of history have been busy principally in formulating "the laws of historical evolution" and in discovering "the historical tendencies and trends." Since Auguste Comte's "law of the three stages," which represents a conspicuous example of the linear conception, dozens of similar "laws" and "tendencies" have been offered by many sociologists, historians, economists and social philosophers. In their theories the social process has been depicted as something drifting toward a definite goal. The process of history has been outlined as a kind of college course: all peoples start with the same historical class of freshmen (*e.g.,* Comte's "theological stage"); later on, all pass into the stage of the sophomore (Comte's "metaphysical stage"); and, having passed through the class of the juniors, all societies are graduated with "the stage of positivism" or "socialism" or "anarchy" or "democracy" or "degeneration" or what not. In this way the linear conception has assumed the character of an eschatological interpretation of a social and historical process.

---

more properly describes the object of Bogardus' studies. See also DELEVSKY, J., *Social Antagonisms,* 1910 (Russian), French edition, in 1923.

It is not my purpose to characterize or to criticize here all the varieties of this linear conception. After the criticisms of it by F. Boas, W. H. Rivers, A. Goldenweiser, C. Wissler, R. H. Lowie, and others, there is no need to prove the contention that almost all such "laws" happened to be "pseudo-laws" and "successive stages" of a mere fiction.[32] The domination of this conception since the second half of the nineteenth century has led sociologists to neglect another,—the cyclical conception of social change and historical process. Having been busy with a discovery of "the historical tendencies" they naturally could not pay much attention to cycles, rhythms, and repetitions in social change. If I am not mistaken, at the present moment we are at the turning point of social thought in this field. Changes in social life for the last few decades; a failure of the eschatological conception of history and that of the attempts to discover *the* "historical trends"; a better knowledge of many social phenomena; discoveries of many brilliant civilizations of the past; these and many other factors, are responsible for the fact that social thought seems to begin again to pay a somewhat greater attention to the repetitions, rhythms, and cycles in social and historical processes. The great success of Bergson's conception of a goalless creative evolution in modern philosophy; the substitution of the term "social change" for that of "social evolution" in sociology; a more and more attentive study of business cycles, fluctuations, oscillations in economics and social sciences; the extraordinary success of O. Spengler's *Der Untergang des Abendlandes* with its cyclical conception of history;—all these phenomena are only a few symptoms among many others which indicate the mentioned turn of contemporary social thought.

Under such conditions it may be timely to outline briefly the principal cyclical conceptions of the historical process given in contemporary sociology. Both the linear and the cyclical conceptions are by no means new discoveries. They were set forth long ago, and have been running throughout the history of human

---

[32] See a very good survey of the problem and the literature in GOLDENWEISER, A., "Cultural Anthropology," in *The History and Prospects of the Social Science*, pp. 221–232, N. Y., 1925.

thought.[33] For the sake of brevity I will not characterize separately the very numerous attempts made in the nineteenth and the twentieth centuries to prove the existence of cycles in various fields of social life, but will give only a concise summary of them in the form of a table which will indicate, in the first place, the character of a cycle; in the second place, the social field in which it is observed; and in the third place, the authors who have indicated or discovered it. Proceeding in this way, I will include all cycles, regardless of whether they are given by the authors as the cycles which in their totality tend to lead to a definite goal (linear theory of cycles), or whether they do not have any steady and perpetual trend (non-linear theory of cycles). In giving the contemporary theories of social cycles I naturally do not take any responsibility for their scientific accuracy and validity. Since the cycles may be *periodic,* that is, repeated regularly in a definite span of time, and *non-periodic,* which take place in an indefinite and varying span of time, therefore it is convenient to divide all attempts to establish the existence of the cycles into these two groups and to give them separately. We will begin with the periodical cycles.

PERIODIC CYCLES

Time-Span of the Cycles	The Character of a Social Process Whose Change Is Supposed to Be Cyclical		Authors and Works
24 hours	*Deaths and suicides:*	In each 24 hours, the maximum number of death and suicide cases happens from 6–7 A.M. and from 7–10 P.M.; the minimum from about 12–2 P.M.	Guerry, Durkheim, Millard[34]
7 days	*Work and leisure:*	Six weekdays and Sunday	

[33] See SOROKIN, "A Survey of the Cyclical Conceptions of Social and Historical Process," *Social Forces*, September, 1927; see also an excellent analysis of the concept of "cycle" by W. Mitchell, in *Business Annals*, N. Y., 1926; see further "Report of Conference on Cycles," *The Geographical Review, Special Supplement*, October, 1923.

[34] DURKHEIM, E., *Le suicide*, Paris, 1912; COLONEL MILLARD, "Essai de physique social et de construction historique," *Revue International de sociologie*, February, 1917.

Time-Span of the Cycles	The Character of a Social Process Whose Change Is Supposed to Be Cyclical		Authors and Works
1 year (seasonal fluctuations)	*Births:*	For many European countries the maximum of births happens in the months from January to April; the minimum, in November and December, and in June, July and August.	Many authors, among them Villermé, Quetelet, Oettingen, G. von Mayr, Levasseur and others[35]
	Deaths:	For many European countries the maximum falls in the months from January to April; the minimum in the summer and the fall. In the countries with a warm climate, there is an increase of deaths during the hot summer months.	Many authors[36]
	Suicides:	The maximum in May, June, July; the minimum in November–February (for the European countries)	A. Wagner, Morselli, Bodio, Masaryk, Krose and many others[37]
	Crimes:	In Europe the crimes against the person have their maximum in the summer, the minimum in the winter; the crimes against property have their maximum in the winter, the minimum in the summer. In the tropical	Guerry, Quetelet, Oettingen, Ferri, E. Levasseur, Lombroso, Kurella, E. G. Dexter, and many others[38]

[35] See VILLERMÉ, "De la distribution par mois des conceptions," etc., *Annales d'hygiene*, Vol. V, 1831; QUETELET, A., *Physique social*, Vol. I, 1869, pp. 104 *et seq.;* OETTINGEN, *Moralstatistik*, 1882; VON MAYR, G., *Statistik und Gesellschaftslehre*, 1897, Vol. II, pp. 169 *et seq.;* LEVASSEUR, *La population française*, Vol. II, 1891, pp. 20 *et seq.*

[36] See the quoted works of Quetelet, Oettingen, von Mayr, Levasseur, and other statisticians.

[37] WAGNER, A., *Die Gesetzmässigkeit in den scheinbar willkürlichen Handlungen*, etc., Teil I, Hamburg, 1864, pp. 128 *et seq.;* MORSELLI, *Der Selbstmord*, Leipzig. 1881, p. 72 *et seq.;* MASARYK, T. G., *Der Selbstmord*, 1887, pp. 7 *et seq.;* VON MAYR, G., *Statistik und Gesellschaftslehre*, Vol. III, 1917, pp. 281–291; the quoted works of Durkheim, Oettingen, Levasseur, and Quetelet.

[38] See the quoted statistical works, DEXTER, E., *Weather Influences*, N. Y., 1904; FERRI, E., *Das Verbrechen in seiner Abhängigkeit v. d. Temperaturwechsel*, 1882.

Time-Span of the Cycles	The Character of a Social Process Whose Change Is Supposed to Be Cyclical		Authors and Works
		countries the cycles are almost reversed.	
		Furthermore, seasonal fluctuations have been noticed by various investigators in the phenomena of dependency, labor demands and unemployment, in the movement of different illnesses, in business, and in labor turnover. It is apparent that such phenomena as seasonal fluctuations of the principal forms of economic activities of the population, especially in the agricultural countries; fluctuations in seasonal buying and selling of different objects necessary in one season of the year and not necessary in another; repetition from year to year of the seasons of teaching and vacation; repetition from year to year of definite days of holidays (Christmas, Thanksgiving Day, etc.); these and many similar phenomena show pretty regular periodic cycles within one year.	
3½ and 4 years	*Business cycles:*	Fluctuation of the periods of increase and depression	Juglar, J. Kitchin, and Lescure[39]
	Births:	In France each fourth year, since 1815 to 1878 shows an abnormally low birth rate. Since 1875 up to 1905 the cycles continue to exist in somewhat modified forms.	Col. Millard[40]
		In the life of the great men (Alexander the Great, J. Caesar, Napoleon I, Bismarck, Cromwell and some others) every fourth year was a conspicuous turning	Millard[41]

[39] KITCHIN, J., "Cycles and Trends in Economic Factors," *Review of Econ. Statistics,* Jan., 1923; LESCURE, J., *Les crises générales et periodiques des surproductions,* Paris, 1907.

[40] MILLARD, *op. cit.,* pp. 71–72.

[41] MILLARD, *op. cit.,* pp. 71–72.

Time-Span of the Cycles	The Character of a Social Process Whose Change Is Supposed to Be Cyclical		Authors and Works
		point in their career. The same is true in regard to the course of the great revolutions and social upheavals.	
5 years	*Number of births of prominent men of letters in France:*	Since 1475, 42 times (out of 70) each five years of abundant births of the men of letters has been superseded by a five-year period of comparative infrequency of their births. In regard to the most prominent men of letters such cycles took place 51 times out of 69 five-year periods.	A. Odin[42]
7, 8 and 11 years	*Business cycles*		Tugan-Baranovsky, Sombart, W. M. Persons, A. Aftalion, H. L. Moore, W. Mitchell and others[43]
	Phenomena correlated with business cycles: unemployment, divorces, poor relief, marriages, births, deaths, suicides, crimes, religious revival		Tugan-Baranovsky, Ogburn, Thomas, Hexter and others[44]
15–16 years	*Political life:*	Within every sixteen years there are considerable changes in po-	Justin, Dromel[45]

[42] ODIN, A., *Génèse des grands hommes*, Vol. I, pp. 424–426, Paris, 1895.

[43] TUGAN-BARANOVSKY, M., *Les crises industrielles en Angleterre;* AFTALION, A., *Les crises periodiques de surproduction*, Paris, 1913; MOORE, H. L., *Economic Cycles*, 1913; *Generating Economic Cycles*, 1923; MITCHELL, W., *Business Cycles;* ROBERTSON, *A Study of Industrial Fluctuation.*

[44] OGBURN, W. F., "The Influence of Business Cycle on Certain Social Conditions," *Journal of American Statistical Assn.*, 1922; HEXTER, M. B., *Social Consequences of Business Cycles*, 1925; THOMAS, D. S., *Social Aspects of the Business Cycle*, 1925. See further, BONGER, W. A., *Criminality and Economic Conditions* 1916; VAN KAN, J., *Les causes économiques de la criminalité*, Paris, 1903; TUGAN-BARANOVSKY, *op. cit.*

[45] DROMEL, J., *La loi des révolutions.*

Time-Span of the Cycles	The Character of a Social Process Whose Change Is Supposed to Be Cyclical		Authors and Works
		litical opinions and in government.	
30–33 years	*Births:*	Thirty-year cycles in the movement of the births in France	Millard[46]
	Epidemics:	Cholera	
	Death:	Movement in Finland, Sweden, Norway	
	Business cycles		Moore[47]
	Dominating literary movements and schools:	Within thirty or thirty-three years they change, superseding each other.	Millard[48]
	Dominating political parties and governmental policy:	Great many different social phenomena have the cycle of 30–33 years. This span of time is a natural unit of historical period.	G. Ferrari, O. Lorenz, K. Joël[49]
48–60 years	*Business cycles:*	Many social phenomena correlated with these large business cycles; the first rushing period of business cycle is followed by social upheavals, wars, revolutions, and other social and political changes.	N. Kondratieff, A. Spiethoff, Moore[50]

[46] MILLARD, *op. cit.*

[47] MOORE, *Economic Cycles.*

[48] MILLARD, *op. cit.*

[49] LORENZ, O., *Die Geschichtswissenschaft in Hauptrichtungen und Aufgaben,* Berlin, 1886, pp. 299 *et seq.; Leopold von Ranke,* 1891, pp. 143–276; JOËL, K., "Der seculare Rhythmus der Geschichte," *Jahrbuch für Soziologie,* B. I, pp. 137–165; FERRARI, G., *Teoria die periodici politici,* Milano, 1874.

[50] KONDRATIEFF, N., *Great Cycles of Conjuncture* (Russian), *Voprosy Konjunctury,* Vol. I, Part I, pp. 28–79, 1925; SPIETHOFF, A., "Krisen," *Handwörterbuch der Staatswiss,* 4th ed.; MOORE, *Generating Economic Cycles.*

Time-Span of the Cycles	The Character of a Social Process Whose Change Is Supposed to Be Cyclical		Authors and Works
100 years	A great many historical processes run through a one-hundred-year cycle, as a "natural" historical period. Great social upheavals like the French Revolution and Napoleonic Wars, the World War, and present revolutions, Renaissance and Reformation happen in a period of about one hundred years.		O. Lorenz, K. Joël, A. Bartels, Fr. Kummer[51]
200 years	*Fluctuation of birth and death rate*[52]		
300 years	*Great changes:*	The beginning and end of many dynasties and social, religious, and political institutions; appearance, development and decline of literary and ideological systems.	O. Lorenz, K. Joël, W. Scherer[53]
500 years	*Approximate period for the growth and decline of some cultures and States* (Persia, Greece), or a period designating a whole era in the history of states which exist twice, thrice, or four times 500 years (Rome, France, England).		Millard[54]
600, 1200 and 1800 years	Some fundamental historical processes run their whole course within 600, or 1200, or 1800 years. Epoch-making events mark the end of each of these periods.		O. Lorenz, K. Joël, W. Scherer[55]
1330 years	*The period of a great revolution in the change of civilization*		W. Petrie[56]

[51] Same as footnote No. 49 above.

[52] BROWNLEE, D. J., "The History of the Birth and Death Rates in England and Wales," *Public Health*, June-July, 1916. See Beveridge's criticism in BEVERIDGE, W., "The Fall of Fertility among European Races," *Economics*, 1925.

[53] SCHERER, W., *Geschichte der Deutschen Literatur*, Introduction and Chaps. I, II.

[54] MILLARD, *op. cit.*

[55] LORENZ, O., *op. cit.;* JOËL, K., *op. cit.;* SCHERER, W., *op. cit.*

[56] PETRIE, W. M. F, *The Revolutions of Civilizations*, 1911, pp. 84 *et seq.*

I will not continue this list of the attempts to establish the existence of a periodic cycle in social and historical processes. The above gives an approximate idea of the variety of periodicity according to different authors. Let us now proceed to the non-periodical cycles.

NON-PERIODICAL CYCLES

Side by side with periodic cycles many authors have indicated the existence of cycles, or oscillations, which repeat themselves without any definite periodicity, but, nevertheless, cyclically. Here are samples of such theories:

The invention cycle: An incline, a plateau, and decline. (Mikhailovsky, Tarde, E. Bogardus, F. S. Chapin, W. F. Ogburn, and many others) [57]

Social process cycle: 1—Imitation; 2—opposition, as a collision of two different waves of imitation; 3—adaptation-invention. (Tarde and many others) [58]

Cycles in an increase and decrease of economic prosperity: Economic, political, and occupational stratification; vertical mobility or circulation. (V. Pareto, W. Mitchell, P. Sorokin) [59]

Social institution cycle: Appearance, growth, disintegration. (F. S. Chapin, W. Ogburn) [60]

Cycles in the sphere of ideologies, belief, religions, political opinions, fashions, etc.: incline, plateau, decline. (V. Pareto, Guignebert) [61]

Rhythm of the spiritual and materialistic civilizations: (Their alternation) (Weber) [62]

Rhythm in the growth of population: The period of a rapid increase of population is superseded by a period of a slow increase and *vice versa.* (Verhulst, Schmoller, R. Pearl, G. U. Yule) [63]

[57] MIKHAILOVSKY, N., *Heroes and Mob* (Russian); TARDE, G., *The Laws of Imitation;* BOGARDUS, E., *Fundamentals of Social Psychology,* pp. 401–402; CHAPIN, F. S., "A Theory of Synchronous Culture Cycles," *Journal of Social Forces,* 1925, p. 599; OGBURN, W., *Social Change.*
[58] TARDE, *Social Laws, passim.*
[59] SOROKIN, *Social Mobility;* MITCHELL, WESLEY, *Business Annals,* N. Y., 1926.
[60] CHAPIN, F. S., *op. cit.;* OGBURN, W., *Social Change.*
[61] PARETO, V., *Trattato di Sociologia Generale,* Vols. I, II, 1916; GUIGNEBERT, *L'évolution des dogmes,* 1910.
[62] WEBER, *Le rhythme du progrès,* Paris, 1913.
[63] PEARL, R., *op. cit.;* VERHULST, *op. cit.;* YULE, *op. cit.*

Rhythm in the distribution of national income: Alternation of periods of a concentration of wealth and a more equal distribution of wealth. (G. Schmoller, V. Pareto, P. Sorokin) [64]

Rhythm of the periods of prosperity and impoverishment in the life of a nation. (D'Avenel, Pareto, Sorokin, and many others) [65]

Cycle in the life of a nation or culture: Appearance, growth, decline. (K. Leontieff, Danilevsky, V. de Lapouge, C. Gini, O. Ammon, O. Spengler) [66]

Rhythm of an expansion and decrease of state interference: (G. Hansen, H. Spencer, P. Sorokin and many others) [67]

Cycles in historical self-realization of the world spirit or logos: Thesis, antithesis and synthesis. (Hegel)

Eternal rhythm of transformation of substance into energy and energy into substance. (G. LeBon) [68]

Rhythm of "the critical" and dynamic periods in history and that of the "organic" or static periods. (Saint Simon, Pareto, E. A. Ross, P. Lavrov) [69]

Cycle in the course of revolution: Period of "liberation" and that of "restraint." (P. Sorokin) [70]

Cycle in rise and degeneration of aristocracy. (P. Jacoby and others) [71]

The world history is an eternal repetition of the same cycles. (F. Nietzsche) [72]

The above is enough to give an idea of the great variety of dif-

[64] SCHMOLLER, "Die Einkommensverteilung in alter und neuer Zeit," *Bull. de l'Inst. Int. de Statist.*, Vol. IX.

[65] D'AVENEL, G., *Le paysan et l'ouvrier; La fortune privée.*

[66] DANILEVSKY, *Russia and Europe* (Russian); SPENGLER, O., *Der Untergang des Abendlandes;* DE LAPOUGE, V., *Les sélections sociales;* AMMON, O., *Die Gesellschaftsordnung und ihre natürlichen Grundlagen,* 1895.

[67] HANSEN, G., *Die drei Bevölkerungsstufen,* 1889; SPENCER, H., *Principles of Sociology,* Vol. II, Chap. XVII; SOROKIN, P., "Influence of Inanition on Social Organization and Ideology," *Ekonomist* (Russian), 1922.

[68] LeBon, G., *L'évolution de la matière.*

[69] SAINT-SIMON, *Letters of an Inhabitant of Geneva to his Contemporaries;* PARETO, *op. cit.;* Ross, E. A., *Principles of Sociology;* LAVROV, P., *Zadatchi Ponimania Istorii,* 1903.

[70] SOROKIN, P., *The Sociology of Revolution.*

[71] JACOBY, P., *Études sur la séléction chèz l'homme,* 1904.

[72] NIETZSCHE, F., *Also Sprach Zarathustra.*

ferent rhythms and cycles which have been indicated by different authors.[73]

All varieties of the above theories of the cyclical conception of historical and social changes may be conveniently summed up in the following scheme:

Theories of cyclical conception of historical and social change
- Theory of linear or spiral cycles which tend toward a definite goal
  - Periodic
    - Progressive
    - Regressive
  - Non-periodic
    - Progressive
    - Regressive
- Theory of ever-repeating identical cycles
- Theory of cycles and rhythms which are neither identical nor tending toward a definite goal
  - Periodic (many of the above theories)
  - Non-periodic (majority of the above theories)

It is not my intention to discuss here all the above theories and the many complicated problems connected with the conception of the historical process generally, and that of the linear and cyclical conceptions of evolution. I have discussed these problems elsewhere.[74] What I desire to do here is to put dogmatically several statements which, in my opinion, may contend for scientific validity. These statements are as follows:

1. The existence of ever-repeating identical cycles, whether in the evolution of the whole world or in the history of mankind is

---

[73] See also VIERKANDT, A., *Die Stetigkeit in Kulturwandel*, Leipzig, 1908.

[74] SOROKIN, "The Fundamental Problems of the Theory of Progress," *New Ideas in Sociology*, Vol. III (Russian); "The Concepts of Evolution and Progress," *The Psycholog. Review* (Russian), Sept., 1911; "The Theory of Social Factors," *In Memory of M. Kovalevsky* (Russian), 1917. See RICKERT, H., *Die Grenzen d. Naturwissenschaftlichen Begriffsbildung;* WINDELBAND, W., *Die Praeludien*, Vol. II, 1911; XÉNOPOL, A. D., *La théorie de l'histoire*, 1908; SIMMEL, G., *Die Probleme der Geschichtsphilosophie*, 1907; *Hauptprobleme der Philosophie;* LAPPO-DANI-LEVSKY, A., *Methodology of History*, Vol. I (Russian); EULENBURG, FRANZ, Sind "Historische Gesetze" moglich, *Eringnerungsgabe für Max Weber*, Vol. I; CROCE, BENEDETTO, *Zur Theorie und Geschichte des Historiographie*, Tübingen, 1915; BERNHEIM, *Lehrbuch der Historischen Methode*, Leipzig, 1914; BERR, H., *La synthèse en histoire*, Paris, 1911; the quoted works of E. Mach, P. Duhem, A. Cournot, A. Tschuproff.

not proved.   Therefore the corresponding theories of the identical cycles are likely to be scientifically in error.[75]

2. The existence of a definite, steady, and eternal trend in historical and social changes is not proved either.   All attempts to establish the existence of a definite historical tendency, as permanent and eternal, have failed.   Among hundreds of such tendencies, formulated by various authors, I do not know of a single one which, after a careful scientific scrutiny, could be said to have scientific validity.   It is certain that there may be some temporary "secular trends" and "tendencies," but many of them have happened to be only a part of a long-time cycle, and there is no guaranty that all such tendencies would not share the same fate.   Even such an apparently undoubted tendency as an increase of human population on this planet may be a long-time parabola —at least, the natural sciences which predict the future cooling of the sun seem to suggest this conclusion.   Parallel to the cooling of the sun the amount of life on the earth has to decrease; consequently, the human population has to decrease also.   G. Tarde in his *Utopia* has very conspicuously depicted this process.   V. de Lapouge has outlined it in scientific terms.[76]   For this reason, all "linear" and "eschatological" theories of evolution and historical process seem to be only speculations rather than scientific conceptions.   As to the theories of progress or regress, since they are "judgments of evaluation" they are doomed, because of this very fact, to be subjective and, according to their logical nature, they never can be scientific statements.   "Science always speaks in the indicative mood, and never in the imperative, as the ethical statements and the judgments of evaluation do," says H. Poincaré quite properly.   In so far, the theories of progress, with their evaluation of what is good and what is bad, what is progressive and what is not, may express only the subjective tastes of their authors and nothing more.[77]   If sociology is

[75] See the quoted works of Windelband, Rikkert, Xénopol, Simmel, Eulenburg and others.

[76] See DE LAPOUGE, V., *Les sélections sociales*, Chap. XV

[77] See the writer's indicated works.   See also SOROKIN, "Is Ethics a Normative Science and is a Normative Science Logically Possible?" *Pysch. Review* (Russian), 1914; PARETO, V., *Trattato di sociologia generale*, Vols. I, II; POINCARÉ, "Science and Ethics," in his *Dernières Pensées;* HUSSERL, E., *Logische Untersuchungen,* Vol. I (Russian translation), pp. 33–34; SIGWART, *Die Logik* (Russian translation), Vol. I, p. 425.

going to be a science, it must get rid of such judgments of evaluation.[78]

3. The existence of a periodicity in the cycles of various social processes is still questionable and needs to be tested further.[79]

4. From the above it follows that it is possible to speak only of a "temporary and relative" trend or "tendency," which, being a trend during a comparatively short period of time, may be superseded by an opposite trend or tendency, and in this way finally may happen to be a part of a long-time cycle.

5. From the above it follows that we scarcely may admit the existence of identical cycles in history or in social change. Every social cycle or social rhythm seems to be only similar to, or only approximately identical to, another in the same field of social change. This means that we may speak only of the relative and approximately similar social or historical cycles.

6. From this position of sociological relativism, a study of the cyclical or rhythmical repetitions of social phenomena is, at the present moment, one of the most important tasks of sociology. It should be promoted by all means because, in the first place, only where a cyclical or rhythmical repetition of social phenomena exists, may we grasp its causal or functional interrelations and formulate "sociological laws." Without repetition there is no possibility of making any valid generalization. Without such generalizations the very *raison d'être* of sociology, as a generalizing science, disappears. In the second place, the field of the repeated, or cyclical, or rhythmical phenomena is more convenient for a study of correlative dependence and interdependence with different social processes. The most valuable scientific conclusions have been obtained in just this way. In the third place,

---

[78] From this standpoint Pareto's pitiless criticism of all evaluating theories in sociology is quite valid. However, in a purely conditional sense, with an explicit declaration in the conventionality of a certain ideal of progress, it is possible to discuss and measure scientifically whether a society is approaching or going away from such an ideal in the course of time. Samples of such a study are given by NICEFORO, A., *Les indices numeriques de la civilisation et du progrès*, Paris, 1921; WILLCOX, W., "A Statistician's Idea of Progress," *International Journal of Ethics*, 1913; TÖNNIES, F., "Richtlinien für das Studium des Forschritts und der Soziale Entwicklung," *Jahrbuch für Soziologie*, Vol. I, 1925, pp. 166–221. See the theories of progress in TODD, A. J., *Theories of Social Progress*, N. Y., 1918. There is a good bibliography in PARK and BURGESS, *Introduction*, Chap. XIV.

[79] See my *Social Mobility*, Chaps. III–VI.

the field of the repeated social phenomena seems to be one of the most convenient for a quantitative study, which is the final purpose of any generalizing science.   If in this way we may obtain only an approximately true generalization this must not trouble us; we still know so little about the "mysterious" world of social events that any approximate real knowledge is of great value. If, among these attempts to establish the existence of cycles in social life, there are some childish theories, this does not vitiate many other theories which compose the comparatively valid generalizations of social science.   Studying more and more different repeated social phenomena, we approach more and more to a solution of the great sociological problem: what in the incessantly changing process of history is relatively permanent, and what is quite temporary; what is relatively universal, and what is purely local; what relations between two or more phenomena are incidental, and which are really causal.   In this way, sociology may more and more transform itself into this real *"Scienza Nuova"* of which the great Vico dreamed, and which he tried to establish.

Such, in brief, are the reasons which urge us to pay a greater attention to the cyclical, rhythmical, and repeated phenomena in social life and history, than has been paid in the last century.[80]

9. STUDIES OF THE VELOCITY OF CHANGE OF VARIOUS PARTS OF CULTURE, AND THE CLOSENESS OF A CORRELATION BETWEEN THEM

The next group of studies in social dynamics is represented by the investigations which try to find how close the correlation is between various components of "culture" in the process of its change.   Does a change of one of these components at once and necessarily lead to a change of other components?   If it does, do these other components change in only one direction, or are there several alternative possibilities?   Which of these components usually takes the lead or is the "starter" in a social change, and which are led and follow the "starters"?   What is the velocity of the change in various fields of social processes? Such are the principal problems of this group of studies.

[80] The writer hopes to publish in the near future a special monograph devoted to the problems discussed in this paragraph.

W. F. Ogburn's (1886–   ) *Social Change* and F. S. Chapin's "Theory of Synchronous Culture Cycles" try to answer these questions. In essentials, their similar conclusions are as follows: What is styled "culture" is in a permanent process of change. However, various parts of a culture do not change simultaneously. Some parts of it, especially material culture, may change, while other parts, especially non-material culture, forms of social organization, religion, arts, and *mores,* may remain, at least for a time, unchanged. This means that the correlation between various components of culture is not so close as to lead to the simultaneity of a change in all its parts. This results in cultural lags, and disharmony between various parts of material and non-material culture. For instance, through the industrial revolution, the material culture of modern Western society has changed enormously during the last hundred years. Meanwhile, our family institution and other social and political forms of organization still remain in the form which was well adapted to the material culture preceding the industrial revolution, but is ill-fitted to the material culture of to-day. This non-material part of culture has lagged. Hence, a disharmony between these parts and social maladjustment is the result. Furthermore, the authors show that the change of culture becomes more and more rapid in the course of time. In this they recapitulate the "law of acceleration" formulated by Novicow.[81] Both authors ask which part of culture—the material or the non-material—usually leads in the process of a culture change, and which usually lags. Their answer is that, though there are cases where the non-material part of culture changes somewhat earlier in time than the material one, as a general rule, the changes in material culture precede and lead to the changes in the other part of culture. Besides, the changes in material culture exert a stronger influence on the non-material culture than that of the latter on the former. In this way they come to a conclusion somewhat similar to the economic interpretation of history. The principal arguments in favor of this answer are that, first, the changes in material culture are relatively more rapid in time than those in non-material

[81] NOVICOW, J., *Les luttes entre sociétés humaines*, Paris, 1896, chapter on "Loi de l'acceleration."

culture; that they come first; that material culture is markedly cumulative while the non-material is not so markedly cumulative; that a new invention in material culture diffuses more rapidly and is adopted more quickly than an invention in the field of non-material culture; and that finally, the changes in material culture influence culture's non-material part more effectively than the changes in the latter influence material culture. Such is the essence of this elaborated theory.[82]

As we see, the theory is a mild form of an economic interpretation of history. Which part of it is valid and which is questionable? It seems to be true that various parts of culture do not change simultaneously. In other words, the correlation between various parts is not quite close. We have seen this in all the preceding parts of this book. For this reason, a discrepancy between, and a maladjustment of, various components of a culture complex seems indeed to exist. This part of the theory is valid, but its other part, which claims that "material culture is a source of modern social change" or a "starter," has many of the above indicated shortcomings of the economic interpretation. In the first place, it is uncertain as to whether the changes in material culture require a shorter period of time than those in non-material culture. The methods of production in the form of agriculture existed in mediæval Europe for centuries without any serious change. However, religious beliefs, *mores*, political organization, social organization, forms of marriage, customs, poetry, schools of painting, styles of architecture, and other forms of non-material culture changed many times. Change in the political sympathy of a population seems to belong to the non-material culture. According to my computation, in England it underwent a change on an average of every two and a half years; in France, in each nine months. (See *Social Mobility*, Chap. XVI.) According to E. Bogardus' study, the average duration of various fads rarely exceeds one year. The rapidity of the change of various "fashions" and "tastes" in literature, arts, music, dances, and ideologies of the present society is well

---

[82] OGBURN, *op. cit.*, Part IV, especially pp. 268–280; CHAPIN, *op. cit.*, *passim* and pp. 596–601. See also WISSLER, CLARK, "Aboriginal Maize Culture as a Typical Culture Complex," *American Journal of Sociology*, March, 1916, p. 661.

known.   I wonder if such a rapid change in these and other fields of non-material culture could be confronted by as rapid changes in material culture, and in the first place, in industry.   It is true that for the last century industry has undergone a rapid change, but it is doubtful whether it has been more rapid than many changes in non-material culture.   We know also some periods in the past which were marked by stagnation in material culture, while the religious attitude of the people changed very rapidly.   Such, for instance, were the first centuries of the appearance and diffusion of Buddhism, Mohammedanism, Christianity, and Protestantism.   Furthermore, there seems to be some truth in the theory of L. Weber that there are periods marked by intensive innovations in material technique, and periods marked by innovations in the non-material culture of a society.[83] For this reason the proposition of the authors is still questionable. The above briefly enumerated periodicity of various social processes also shows that the shortest periods do not belong to the changes in material culture only; they are given in other fields of culture, too.   These brief allusions, which could be substantiated seriously, must show that the question is quite complex, and needs to be studied more carefully before any definite answer can be given.

Questionable also to me is the contention that the change in material culture commonly precedes that in its non-material part. The reason for this doubting is given by W. Ogburn himself.

Concerning the question of whether in modern times the initiation of the vast cultural changes lies more largely with the material culture or with the non-material culture, it should be recalled that there are a great many changes occurring in the material culture because of inventions—(*op. cit.,* p. 269).

I subscribe with both my hands to this statement.   It means that the changes in the material culture are greatly determined by inventions.   Inventions are an embodiment of human thought and knowledge, and are dependent on the general state of science. Knowledge, thought, and science, as I understand, belong to non-

[83] See WEBER, L., *Le rhythme du progrès, passim,* Paris, 1913.

material culture. *Ergo*: the conclusion is rather in accordance with the opposite theory of De Roberty than with the author's theory. I attentively read Professors Ogburn's and Chapin's analysis of the problem, and looked for a method whereby they would reconcile their contention with the rôle of knowledge and science, but I failed to find in their works any systematic answer to the question. If science is a part of non-material culture, and if, as a rule, a scientific study and thought precedes a materialization of this thought in almost all the inventions, it is hard to agree with the contention that changes in the material culture precede those in the non-material one. If we add to this that at a great many periods the scientific thought of a society used to have at its disposal a series of already elaborated plans for the reconstruction of the material and the non-material culture of society, (a primitive "steam engine" was discovered more than a thousand years ago) and that, owing to the resistance of material and non-material culture, a realization of the plans which had already been born in the realm of thought used to lag for dozens and even hundreds of years,[84] one would comprehend the questionable character of the statement.

In a similar way I question the contention that inventions in material culture spread more rapidly than inventions in non-material culture. I think the question has been studied too little to justify a definite answer in the field. I wonder whether the radio, the automobile, or the ideas of communism have spread more rapidly in the last few years?[85] I wonder also whether "jazz," the Charleston, or the bathtub have been diffused more rapidly for this period? I am sure that in Russia for the same period the pattern-behavior of a sex-freedom has been spreading more rapidly and successfully than tractors or gas stoves. In the past, the rapidity of the diffusion of many world religions, or many mediæval psychical epidemics, or the idea of the Crusades, or hundreds of similar non-material innovations have

[84] For instance, modern science has an excellent plan for a construction of "Garden-cities"; yet the resistance of the existing cities and material culture does not permit the realization of it.

[85] The degree of diffusion of a cultural trait—material and non-material— should be measured by the number of people who adopt and use it, rather than by the size of a geographical area.

scarcely been slower than that of the more or less substantial innovations in material culture. In brief, the problem seems to be still open, and needs to be studied further.

Doubtful also is the statement that material culture is more cumulative than non-material. If science, human experience, and knowledge are a non-material culture, then certainly the non-material culture is cumulative. Each new generation does not start anew with its own experience, but with the gathered experience of all previous generations which has been accumulating in the course of time. This is evident. The same may even be said of beliefs, arts, music, literature, and other forms of non-material culture. Neither the *Iliad,* Mahabharata, Plato's philosophy, the Buddhist religion, Beethoven's symphonies, nor Rembrandt's pictures are lost. We have them, and we enjoy them. Without such a non-material value created by previous generations, our non-material wealth would be very poor. On the other hand, the disappearance of a culture-trait has happened not only with non-material cultural values, but with material too. W. H. R. Rivers and W. J. Perry have shown this clearly in regard to primitive groups. The history of human culture supplies the facts in regard to more complex society.[86]

Finally, all the preceding chapters have shown that "non-material" innovations influence very strongly the material ones. Weber's theory is especially important in this respect. Before our eyes we have an example of how great is the importance of a non-material innovation such as Marx's theory. The communist plan of social reconstruction has been largely responsible for the destruction and paralysis of the whole economic life of Russia.

Space does not permit me to go into a more detailed criticism of these propositions. However, the above remarks may show that these problems are not solved as yet. It is to the credit of the authors that they put them in a clear and scientific way for further study.

---

[86] PERRY, W. J., "The Disappearance of Culture," *The Eugenic Review*, July, 1924, pp. 104–113; RIVERS, W. H. R., "The Loss of Useful Arts," *Westermarck Anniversary Volume*, 1912.

10. STUDIES IN MIGRATION, DIFFUSION, AND MOBILITY OF CUL-
TURAL OBJECTS, FEATURES, VALUES AND INDIVIDUALS

As we have seen, the term "social dynamics, mechanics, and social physiology" had been invented long ago. Their purpose was to be a study of the "motions" or processes going on within a social group or a culture complex. Although perhaps something in this field was gained from a purely qualitative standpoint, very little was done from a purely quantitative point of view. Treatises published on the subject talked more of the social physiology or mechanics than really studied social processes. Only recently there appeared the first attempts at real study of the dynamics of social processes or of social change. The first variety of this is given in the works of the so-called "diffusionists" in cultural anthropology. Their contribution to sociology has consisted not only in their decisive criticism of the "linear concept of evolution," and not so much in a setting forth of interesting but doubtful broad hypotheses, as in their careful study of the area, the alteration, the routes, the velocity, the obstacles, and the favorable conditions of the migration or diffusion of a definite and tangible cultural feature, beginning with a pot or design, or stone collars, and ending with a definite rite, ceremony, myth, or belief. Studying carefully these phenomena they started what may be styled a scientific study of the social circulation and diffusion of cultural features. A real knowledge of these phenomena is as important for sociology as a knowledge of the circulation of blood in an animal organism for physiology. The works of F. Graebner and his pupils, W. H. R. Rivers, Elliot Smith, W. J. Perry, Franz Boas, R. H. Lowie, A. L. Kroeber, A. Goldenweiser, C. Wissler, and of many others, have already given a great deal in this field.[87] They have set forth an example to

[87] See GRAEBNER, F., *Methode der Ethnologie*, Heidelberg, 1911; BOAS, F., "Evolution or Diffusion," *Am. Anthropologist*, July-September, 1924; WISSLER, C., *The Relation of Nature to Man in Aboriginal America*, N. Y., 1926; LOWIE, R. H., *Primitive Society;* MACKENZIE, D. A., *The Migration of Symbols*, N. Y., 1926; GOLDENWEISER, A., *Early Civilization;* see other literature in GOLDENWEISER, A., "Diffusionism and the American School of Historical Ethnology," *American Journal of Sociology*, July, 1925; BARNES, H. E., *New History and Social Studies*, Chap. IV; WALLIS, W., *An Introduction to Anthropology*, 1926, Chap. XXXIX; *Ethnologica*, a special journal edited by F. Graebner. See also OGBURN, W., *Social Change*, Part III; and VIERKANDT, A., *Stetigkeit im Kulturwandel;*

be followed by an intensive study of migration and diffusion of various cultural traits within the present complex society. An accumulation of accurate and quantitative data about these phenomena would permit us to construct an inductive theory of social circulation, migration, diffusion, fading, modification, combination and disassociation of the components of culture, and through that, the "dynamics" of culture complexes.

The second group of studies in social dynamics deals with the phenomena of territorial migration, shifting, segregation, and concentration of individuals. They were started much earlier. Being done principally by statisticians, they have already yielded many valuable results free from any speculation. As a variety of this type of study may be mentioned that of migration from the country to the city, and *vice versa*. The investigation of the dynamic processes in the social mobility of cultural traits and individuals, however, did not stop with the above phenomena. A series of sociologists, like V. Pareto, G. Sensini, O. Ammon, M. Kolabinska, and many others, began to study the social circulation of individuals from one occupational, religious, economic, political, and other social position to another, and from one social stratum to another. In this way, step by step, the field of "social physiology" has been broadened, and at the present moment we are at the beginning of the first attempts to construct a general, but factual theory of social mobility. One of such attempts has been made by the writer in his *Social Mobility*. Concentrating his attention principally on the vertical mobility of individuals, he has tried to give an account of what has been done in this field, and what are the factors, the forms, the fluctuations, the mechanism, and the effects of social mobility, especially in its vertical form. The reader had best go to this book for detailed information, but it may be proper here to outline briefly the principal conclusions of the study. In its essentials they are as follows:

Conception of Social Mobility and Its Forms.—By social mobility I understand any transition of an individual or social

WILLEY, M. M., and HERSKOVITS, M. J., "Psychology and Culture," *Psychological Bulletin*, Vol. XXIV, 1927. The school has, however, many doubtful premises and questionable generalizations. Part of its weak points is well outlined in *L'année sociologique*, 1923–24, pp. 310–318, 324–330.

object or value—anything that has been created or modified by human activity—from one social position to another. There are two principal types of social mobility, *horizontal* and *vertical*. By horizontal social mobility or shifting, I mean the transition of an individual or social object from one social group to another situated on the same level. Transitions of individuals, as from the Baptist to the Methodist religious group, from one citizenship to another, from one family (as a husband or wife) to another by divorce and remarriage, from one factory to another in the same occupational status, are all instances of social mobility. So too are transitions of social objects, the radio, automobile, fashion, communism, Darwin's theory, within the same social stratum, as from Iowa to California, or from any one place to another. In all these cases, "shifting" may take place without any noticeable change in the social position of an individual or social object in the vertical direction. By vertical social mobility I mean the relations involved in a transition of an individual (or a social object) from one social stratum to another. According to the direction of the transition there are two types of vertical social mobility : *ascending and descending,* or *social climbing and social sinking.* According to the nature of the stratification, there are ascending and descending currents of economic, political and occupational mobility, not to mention other less important types.

The situation is summed up in the scheme shown on page 750.

Immobile and Mobile Types of Stratified Societies.—Theoretically, there may be a stratified society in which the vertical social mobility is nil. This means that within it there is no ascending or descending, no circulation of its members; that every individual is forever attached to the social stratum in which he was born. Such a type of stratification may be styled as absolutely closed, rigid, impenetrable, or immobile. The opposite theoretical type of inner structure of stratification is that in which the vertical mobility is very intensive and general; here the membranes between the strata are very thin and have the largest holes to pass from one floor to another. Such a type of social stratification may be styled open, plastic, penetrable, or mobile. Between these two extreme types there may be many middle or intermediary types of stratification.

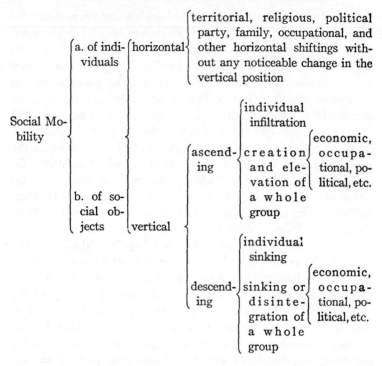

Some Results of a Study of the Vertical Mobility.—*Propositions Concerning the Fluctuation of the Velocity and Generality of Vertical Mobility in Space and Time.*—1. There has scarcely been any society whose strata were absolutely closed, or in which vertical mobility in its economic, political, occupational, and other forms was not present.

2. There has never existed a society in which its vertical mobility has been absolutely free and in which the transition from one social stratum to another has had no resistance.

3. The intensiveness and generality of vertical mobility varies from society to society (fluctuation in space) and within the same society from time to time.

4. In the fluctuation of vertical mobility in time there seems to be no definite perpetual trend toward either an increase or a decrease of the intensiveness and generality of mobility. All trends seem to have been only temporary, being superseded by the

opposite ones in a longer period of time. This is proposed as valid for the history of a country, for that of a large social body, and, finally, for the history of mankind.

5. The nineteenth and the twentieth centuries in the history of the Western societies have been periods of highest mobility in its occupational, economic, and political forms. However, in the past there have been periods of an equal and, perhaps, even greater mobility.

Propositions Concerning the Channels and the Machinery which Controls the Vertical Mobility of Individuals.—1. The most common channels through which vertical shifting of individuals goes on are the series of social institutions like: the army, church, school, political parties, and different occupational institutions. They play the rôle of "elevators" through which people go "up" and "down."

2. With the exception of periods of anarchy, vertical mobility of individuals and their placement at different social strata is controlled by a complex machinery of social testing, selection and distribution of individuals within the society. This machinery is composed of social institutions of the family, church and school, which test the general intelligence and character of individuals, and of different occupational institutions which re-test the results of the family, church and school testing, and especially test the specific ability of individuals necessary for a successful performance of definite occupational functions. This "testing and selective" rôle of these institutions is no less important than their "educational and training" rôle. From this it follows that the population of different social strata is selective.

Propositions Concerning the Effects of Mobility.—1. In the field of racial composition of a society: Under the condition of lower procreation of the upper strata an intensive vertical mobility leads to wasting of the best population of society. It is probable that in a long period of time this wasting may lead to a racial depletion of the population. This is the price paid by a mobile society for its rapid progress.

2. In the field of human behavior and psychology: An intensive vertical mobility facilitates an increase of the plasticity and versatility of behavior, open-mindedness, mental strain, in-

tellectual progress, and progress of discoveries and inventions. On the other hand, it facilitates an increase of mental diseases, superficiality, insensitiveness of nervous system, scepticism, cynicism, and "idiosyncrasies"; it also diminishes intimacy in interrelations of individuals, increases their social isolation and loneliness, favors an increase of suicide, hunting for sensual pleasure and restlessness; finally, mobility facilitates disintegration of morals.

3. In the field of social processes and organization: Mobility, under some conditions, facilitates a better and more adequate social distribution of individuals among different social strata, economic prosperity and social progress. The effects of mobility on social stability are very complex, partly positive, partly negative; all in all, rather negative. Its influence upon longevity and continuity of culture complex is negative also. It facilitates atomization and diffusion of solidarity and antagonisms, increase of individualism followed by a vague cosmopolitanism and collectivism.

Such are the most general conclusions reached. They, however, are tentative only. In spite of the author's desire to base his conclusions only on factual materials, the data were often lacking. Therefore, the propositions need to be tested by future studies in the field.

11. STUDIES OF SUDDEN, CATACLYSMIC, REVOLUTIONARY, AND CATASTROPHIC CHANGES

The last group of the studies of social dynamics deals with the phenomena of a sudden and spasmodic social change. The first variety of these works deals with sudden "mutations" of cultural features generally.[88] Their principal object is a study of the factors of, and the regularities in, the dynamics of inventions, as a principal form of such innovations. The above mentioned works dealing with men of genius have contributed a great deal to the elucidation of the problem. Furthermore, the studies of W. Ogburn, Charles Cooley, W. Ostwald, A. E. Tanner, R. Thurnwald, Engelmeyer, F. Taussig, C. L. Morgan, G. Tarde,

---

[88] See PETRIE, W. M. F., *The Revolutions of Civilization*, London, 1912; TEGGART, F. J., *Theory of History*, 1925; PERRY, W. J., *The Growth of Civilization*; PAULHAN. FR., *Les transformations social des sentiments*, Paris, 1920.

T. Ribot, V. Pareto, and others have indicated many social conditions important from this standpoint.[89]

The next variety of studies is a factual study of the social changes called forth by a catastrophe like an inundation, earthquake, cyclone, or other cosmic phenomena. S. H. Prince's monograph represents a good sample of this type of investigation. Like a naturalist or a geologist he observed and analyzed the effects of the Halifax disaster (explosion) on various sides of social life, behavior, activity, and organization of the Halifax community.[90]   A continuation of similar studies promises a great deal for the inductive knowledge of the character of such catastrophic changes.

The third variety of the studies deals principally with what is known as political or social revolution.   Among many works of this class, especially important are the contributions of H. Taine, G. LeBon, A. Bauer, Galeot, Charles A. Ellwood, R. Pöhlmann, G. Richard, I. King, L. von Wiese, G. Landauer, L. P. Edwards, A. Vierkandt, and the writer.[91]

[89] See OGBURN, W., and THOMAS, D., "Are Inventions Inevitable?" *Political Science Quarterly*, March, 1922; COOLEY, CHARLES, "Genius, Fame, and the Comparison of Races," *Annals of Amer. Academy Political and Social Sciences*, 1897; ENGELMEYER, *A Theory of Creation*, Teoria Tvorchestva (Russia); TAUSSIG, F., *Inventors and Money-Makers*; OSTWALD, W., *Grosse Männer*, Leipzig, 1909; TANNER, A. E., "Certain Social Aspects of Invention," *Amer. Journal of Psychology*, 1915; MORGAN, C. L., *Emergent Evolution*, London, 1923; RIBOT, T., *Essay on the Creative Imagination*, Chicago, 1906; BALDWIN, M., *Social and Ethical Interpretations*, part II, N. Y., 1897; GOWIN, E. B., *The Executive and His Control of Men*, N. Y., 1915; THURNWALD, R., "Führerschaft und Siebung," *Ztschjt. für Völker Psychologie und Soziologie*, March, 1926.

[90] PRINCE, S. H., *Catastrophe and Social Change*, N. Y., 1920.

[91] One of the deepest analyses of the phenomena of revolution still remains in H. Taine's classical work: *Les origines de la France contemporaine*, translated into English: *The French Revolution*, N. Y., 1878–85; LE BON, G., *The Psychology of Revolution*, N. Y., 1913; PÖHLMANN, R., *Geschichte d. Antik. Communismus*; BAUER, A., *Essai sur les révolutions*, Paris, 1908; ELLWOOD, CHARLES A., "A Psychological Theory of Revolutions," *American Journal of Sociology*, XI, 1905–06; *The Psychology of Human Society*, N. Y., 1925, Chap. VIII; RICHARD, G., "Les crises sociales et les conditions de la criminalité," *L'année soc.*, 1899; VIERKANDT, A., "Zur Theorie der Revolution," *Schmoller's Jahrbuch f. Gesetzgebung*, 46 Jahrgang, Heft 2, 1922; GALEOT, *La psychologie révolutionaire*, Paris, 1923; VON WIESE, L.,'s, and several other studies in *Verhandlungen des Dritten Deutschen Sociologentage*, Tübingen, 1923; LANDAUER, G., *Die Revolution*, Frankfurt, 1907; FREIMARK, H., *Die Revolution*, etc., München, 1921; KING, I., "The Influence of the Form of Social Change upon the Emotional Life of a People," *American Journal of Sociology*, Vol. IX; EDWARDS, L. P., "Mechanics of Revolution," *St. Stephen's College Bulletin*, May, 1923; LEDERER, E., *Einige Gedanken zur Sociologie der Revolution*, 1918; SOROKIN, P., *The Sociology of Revolution*, 1925; TOLLER,

As a result of the studies at the present moment we know a great deal about the phenomena of revolution, and what is especially important, we know several regularities and "eternal components," which, in a degree, are found in all revolutions and compose their "eternal" skeleton. In their totality, the studies enumerated above under the paragraph numbers 7, 8, 9, 10 and 11 are a great contribution to our knowledge of social dynamics. They do not unravel all its mysteries, but none the less they represent a considerable progress toward a better and more objective acquaintance with social processes and their relationship.

12. BEGINNING OF THE STAGE OF EXPERIMENTAL SOCIOLOGY

Though in the above the term "experimental" has been used in an application to several studies, nevertheless they are experimental only in a broad sense of the term. Purely "experimental" studies in which all the relevant conditions are under the control of an investigator and are created by him have been very few in sociology. Meanwhile, in so far as sociology is a nomographic science, and tries to formulate functional or causal laws, it needs an experimental method in a narrow sense of the term no less than any other nomographic science. Hence, sooner or later, sociology has to begin to work "experimentally." A series of quite comprehensible conditions makes an application of this method to the study of social phenomena difficult, often impossible. None the less, there are many problems which seem to be possible to be studied experimentally. As an example of such pioneer experimental attempts may be mentioned here the investigations of P. F. Voelker, F. Allport, G. S. Gates, A. Mayer, E. Meumann, quoted in Chapter VIII, and the studies of E. B. Hurlock, M. Parten, M. Walker, and the writer carried on at the University of Minnesota.[92]   These studies are to be regarded as the first

---

E., *Masse Mensch*, Potsdam, 1921; LOMBROSO, C., *Le crime politique et les révolutions*, Paris, 1922.   Besides, still extraordinarily valuable are DE MAISTRE, J., *Considérations sur la France; Théorie des revolutions par l'auteur de l'ésprit de l'histoire*, Paris, 1817, 4 volumes; not to mention the wonderful analysis of revolution by Plato, Aristotle, Machiavelli, Guicciardini, J. Bodin, T. Hobbes and other classical authors.

[92] See for instance, HURLOCK, E. B., "The Value of Praise and Reproof," *Archives of Psychology*, Vol. XI, No. 71; SOROKIN, P., "An Experimental Study of the Effects of Collective and Individual, Equal and Unequal Remuneration and Pure Competition on the Efficiency of the Work," *Kölner Vierteljahrshefte*

weak steps toward a really experimental sociology.   It is highly probable that these attempts in a better and better form will be made more and more often until sociology, at least in some parts, will become a really experimental science.   Anyhow, things seem to be drifting that way.

13. CONCLUSION ABOUT SPECIAL STUDIES

Space does not permit us to continue a further enumeration of other special studies.   The above, however, shows that at the present moment we already have a considerable number of them.   They suggest that the stage of speculation in sociology is passing away.   If general theories, as hypotheses, were necessary to start special and more accurate investigations, the general hypotheses themselves may now be judged on the basis of the special studies. As they have been accumulating, they have begun to exert more and more influence on the general theories themselves.   This means that a real progress of sociology as a science has been going on principally in the form of these special studies.   I do not hesitate to prophesy that, such studies being continued, within a few decades we shall have textbooks in sociology as different from the existing ones as the biological treatises before Lamarck and Darwin are different from the present courses in biology.

Being grateful to our predecessors for their suggestive hypotheses and tentative generalizations, we, nevertheless, must devote ourselves not to a pondering upon generalities, but to the special, factual, and especially experimental studies, of social problems.

14. GENERAL CONCLUSION ABOUT THE SOCIOLOGISTIC AND PSYCHOLOGICAL SCHOOLS

We have passed a long way in our analysis of the general theories of the sociologistic and psychological schools, their branches, and special studies.   It is time to give a general conclusion about the schools.   It is brief.   There is no doubt that they have contributed greatly to the science of sociology.   There is no doubt also that they have an unquestionable right to existence.

ür Soziologie, Bund *V*, Heft *I*, 1927.   Further studies of the writer and of several graduate fellows who work under his guidance (A. Anderson, M. Tanquist), will be published some time in the future.

There is no doubt that a continuation of the studies along the lines of their principles promises a rich harvest, but in so far as they pretend to have a monopoly on the scientific study of social phenomena, and in so far as they try to regard the processes of history as an equation with one unknown, their claims are not justified and ought to be rejected.

CHAPTER XIV

CONCLUSION: RETROSPECT AND PROSPECT

It is time to finish our walk over the field of sociology. We have crossed it from border to border in various directions. It is certain that we have not studied its secondary features as attentively as perhaps we should have. It is certain also that we could not study in detail the character of the small sociological houses built by individual sociologists. Nevertheless, we have explored the most important features of the field sufficiently well to have an approximately accurate idea about its present situation. Let us briefly sum up our impressions.

First, the field is divided into many areas with different methods of cultivation of sociological knowledge. Consequently, the knowledge itself grows in an elementary and somewhat anarchical way. The whole field reminds one of a half-wild national forest rather than a carefully planned garden. Shall we regret such a situation? The answer is that some improvement in the general planning for the whole field is probably desirable. Nevertheless, the planning and standardizing must not be overdone. An artificial standardization in sociology is especially dangerous. It may lead to a degeneration of real sociological knowledge into dry and lifeless scholastics. The complex nature of social phenomena makes rather necessary a variety of the approaches and methods of study. Attacking them with various methods and from various scientifically sound standpoints we have more chances to know them than by attacking with only one standardized method and from one standardized standpoint. Some sociologists are worried about the lack of such a uniform standard, and some non-sociologists often indicate this feature as an evidence that there is no such science as sociology. We must not be troubled much with these worries and criticisms. If the critics know something about the non-sociological cultural sciences like law, economics, history, political science, psychology, and so on, they must recognize that these disciplines are approximately in the same state of wilderness in which sociology is placed. Only those of these "scholars" who do not know their specialty beyond a couple of textbooks, or beyond their own block in the whole field of these sciences, can believe that they are standardized and well "combed." As a matter of fact, each of these sciences is in about the same state of "wilderness" as sociology. Therefore we may advise the critics that they would be better silent in this respect. *Medice cura te ipsum* we can say to them. So much about this point.

The second conspicuous feature of the explored field is that it is rich with "sterile flowers" and "weeds." Speculative discussions about what sociology is; what it ought to be; what culture is; whether society is a bio-organic, psycho-organic, super-organic, or mechanic system; whether culture is a psychical or non-psychical phenomenon; what the difference is between cultural, social, psycho-social and psychological phenomena; what progress is; what the relationship of society and the individual is; and so forth and so on are examples of what is styled "sterile flowers" in sociology. Many sociological works have factually consisted in a mere speculation over these and similar problems and have not gone further. They have taken the "antechamber" of sociology for its whole building. Besides, even these introductory problems have been often outlined in the vaguest and the most unsatisfactory way. Shall we wonder that such "sociologies" have not given us any real knowledge of social phenomena, except a lot of somewhat indefinite words piled one upon another? Shall we be surprised that after reading such "sociologies" many people of thoughtful mind should have assumed a negative attitude toward such a "science"? They are right as far as this "word-piling" is concerned. They rightly say: "Instead of a long and tedious reasoning of what sociology is, show it in fact." "Instead of a discussion over how sociology ought to be built, build it." "Instead of 'flapping' around the introductory problems of the science, give us something certain; show us your causal formulas, and give us a single real analysis of the phenomena." They seem to be right in their criticism, 'as far as these "sterile flowers" of sociology are concerned.

Now come the "weeds." Their first variety is represented by "the preaching and evaluating judgments" in the field. Many a "sociological" work in its bulk is but a book of prescriptions of what is good and what is bad, what ought to be done, and what ought to be avoided, what is progress, and what is regress, what reforms are to be made to save "the world" from its evils, and so on. As this preaching job does not require any serious study of the facts, a great many incompetent persons have pretended to be omniscient doctors who know how the world is to be saved, and give their "prescriptions" about war eradication, birth-control, labor organization, the sex and race problem, and so forth. In this way, all kinds of nonsense have been styled, published, circulated, and taught as "sociology." Every idler has pretended to be a sociologist. Shall we wonder that this again has discredited sociology greatly? In view of the heterogeneity of scientific and evaluative judgments, and in view of the radical difference between a study of the facts as they are and moralizing on what they ought to be, it is rather evident that this "weed" should be eradicated from the field of scientific sociology and planted where it belongs.

Other "weeds" are different, but also harmful. An insufficient study of the facts in time and space; a mania for generalizing a certain conclusion far beyond the factual basis on which it is built; an ignorance of the theories and studies made by others and in preceding times; a failure to make from a certain hypothesis all the important conclusions and to verify them as to whether they are corroborated in space and time; a failure to test an invented hypothesis seriously—such are some of these "weeds." Shall we wonder that even the best theories in sociology are fallacious to a certain extent? A slight attempt to test them shows at once that either their factual analysis is wrong, or that their generalization is overdrawn, or that a purely fictitious correlation is accepted for a real one, or that the conclusion is one-sided. Under such conditions, it would naturally be expected that sociology would remind one of a "museum of scientifically pathological theories," as Professor Petrajitzsky rightly says. The reading of this book has shown this. It is needless to say that these "weeds" must be eradicated, too.

This criticism does not mean, however, that in this field we have found only sterile flowers and weeds. By no means. We have seen in each district a considerable number of potentially strong trees, fine plants and beautiful flowers. I say "potentially" because they are considerably overgrown by the weeds and sterile flowers that need to be cleared away from them. This being done, they may be the pride of every scientific gardener. In so far as this, sociology is not only going to be a science, but already *is* one; but only within the mentioned limits. In order to broaden these limits, we must evidently avoid a repetition of the above mistakes. This is the task of the younger and the future generations of sociologists.

Finally, one inference is to be made from the above survey. There are a great many theories devoted to a discussion of what sociology is and what is its subject-matter. It is not my intention to enter into a discussion of the problem. My intention is to indicate that instead of a speculation over the problem, many an author would have done better by studying the development of sociological theories for the last fifty years. Such study shows something very instructive in this respect. In the first place it shows that several definitions of sociology are in contradiction with the real movement of sociological studies. For instance, if we must accept the definition of the formal school, almost all the above studies would have to be excluded from sociology. What would remain would represent something so insignificant that it scarcely would deserve the name of a sociology or any other science. With a corresponding change, this may be said of some other definitions of sociology. In the second place, the development of sociology begins to show more and more clearly what its subject-matter is. It seems to be a study, first, of the *relationship and correlations between various classes of social phenomena, (correlations between economic and religious; family and moral; juridical and economic; mobility and political phenomena and so on); second, that between the social and the non-social (geographic, biological, etc.,) phenomena; third, the study of the general characteristics common to all classes of social phe-*

nomena. All the surveyed schools are busy with either the establishment of correlations between various classes of social phenomena or between the social and the non-social phenomena, or with an elaboration of the formulas which describe their most general features.[1] Whether a sociologist likes this or not, such seems to have been the real subject-matter of sociological theories. More than that, this subject-matter becomes more and more clear as we proceed from the beginning to the end of the period studied. It is not my purpose to develop and substantiate this conception of sociology and its subject-matter. I have done it elsewhere. Through indicating the above fact I want only to draw the attention of the sociologist to what has been the real subject-matter of sociological theories. This may prevent many a wild speculation over the problem and may be useful for those who are inclined to study this type of topic. In addition, I shall observe only that this conception agrees with the best definitions of sociology, though differently worded, and with the nature of really existing sociology. Being a mere inference from the survey, it is less speculative and more inductive than many other definitions; and therefore, it is likely to be more accurate than many other definitions set forth by various authors. Sociology has been, is, and either will be a science of the general characteristics of all classes of social phenomena, with the relationships and correlations between them; or there will be no sociology.

[1] It is easy to understand that both components of the subject-matter of sociology are logically inseparable. Where we have to study N classes of phenomena there logically should be $N + 1$ classes of sciences. Each of N special sciences studies the characteristics of its special class of phenomena; the additional $N + 1$ science would study the characteristics common to all N classes. Two fundamental classes of organisms, plants and animals, require the existence of botany, which studies the specific characteristics of plant-organisims; zoology, which deals with animal organisms; and general biology, which studies the characteristics common to both classes of organisms and their relationship. Likewise if social phenomena are classified into the classes: $a, b, c, d, \ldots n$, each class being studied by a special social science (economics, political science, law, etc.), besides N special sciences there should be an $N + 1$ science which would study the general characteristics common to all N classes of social phenomena and the relationship or correlation between them. Such is the logical reason for an existence of sociology in the defined sense. And such has really been the subject-matter of sociological theories for the period studied. See a brilliant analysis of the above in PETRAJITZSKY, LEO, *Introduction to the Theory of Law and Morals*, pp. 80–81; *vide* also SOROKIN, P., *Systema soziologii*, Vol. I, pp. 30–36.

INDEX OF NAMES

GENERAL INDEX

harper ✦ torchbooks

HUMANITIES AND SOCIAL SCIENCES

American Studies: General

THOMAS C. COCHRAN: The Inner Revolution. *Essays on the Social Sciences in History* TB/1140

EDWARD S. CORWIN: American Constitutional History. *Essays edited by Alpheus T. Mason and Gerald Garvey* △ TB/1136

CARL N. DEGLER, Ed.: Pivotal Interpretations of American History TB/1240, TB/1241

A. HUNTER DUPREE: Science in the Federal Government: *A History of Policies and Activities to 1940* TB/573

A. S. EISENSTADT, Ed.: The Craft of American History: *Recent Essays in American Historical Writing*
Vol. I TB/1255; Vol. II TB/1256

CHARLOTTE P. GILMAN: Women and Economics: *A Study of the Economic Relation between Men and Women as a Factor in Social Evolution.* ‡ *Ed. with an Introduction by Carl N. Degler* TB/3073

OSCAR HANDLIN, Ed.: This Was America: *As Recorded by European Travelers in the Eighteenth, Nineteenth and Twentieth Centuries. Illus.* TB/1119

MARCUS LEE HANSEN: The Atlantic Migration: 1607-1860. *Edited by Arthur M. Schlesinger* TB/1052

MARCUS LEE HANSEN: The Immigrant in American History. TB/1120

JOHN HIGHAM, Ed.: The Reconstruction of American History △ TB/1068

ROBERT H. JACKSON: The Supreme Court in the American System of Government TB/1106

JOHN F. KENNEDY: A Nation of Immigrants. △ *Illus.* TB/1118

LEONARD W. LEVY, Ed.: American Constitutional Law: *Historical Essays* TB/1285

RALPH BARTON PERRY: Puritanism and Democracy TB/1138

ARNOLD ROSE: The Negro in America TB/3048

MAURICE R. STEIN: The Eclipse of Community. *An Interpretation of American Studies* TB/1128

W. LLOYD WARNER and Associates: Democracy in Jonesville: *A Study in Quality and Inequality* ¶ TB/1129

W. LLOYD WARNER: Social Class in America: *The Evaluation of Status* TB/1013

American Studies: Colonial

BERNARD BAILYN, Ed.: Apologia of Robert Keayne: *Self-Portrait of a Puritan Merchant* TB/1201

BERNARD BAILYN: The New England Merchants in the Seventeenth Century TB/1149

JOSEPH CHARLES: The Origins of the American Party System TB/1049

LAWRENCE HENRY GIPSON: The Coming of the Revolution: 1763-1775. † *Illus.* TB/3007

LEONARD W. LEVY: Freedom of Speech and Press in Early American History: *Legacy of Suppression* TB/1109

PERRY MILLER: Errand Into the Wilderness TB/1139

PERRY MILLER & T. H. JOHNSON, Eds.: The Puritans: *A Sourcebook of Their Writings*
Vol. I TB/1093; Vol. II TB/1094

EDMUND S. MORGAN, Ed.: The Diary of Michael Wigglesworth, 1653-1657: *The Conscience of a Puritan* TB/1228

EDMUND S. MORGAN: The Puritan Family: *Religion and Domestic Relations in Seventeenth-Century New England* TB/1227

RICHARD B. MORRIS: Government and Labor in Early America TB/1244

KENNETH B. MURDOCK: Literature and Theology in Colonial New England TB/99

WALLACE NOTESTEIN: The English People on the Eve of Colonization: 1603-1630. † *Illus.* TB/3006

LOUIS B. WRIGHT: The Cultural Life of the American Colonies: 1607-1763. † *Illus.* TB/3005

American Studies: From the Revolution to 1860

JOHN R. ALDEN: The American Revolution: 1775-1783. † *Illus.* TB/3011

MAX BELOFF, Ed.: The Debate on the American Revolution, 1761-1783: *A Sourcebook* △ TB/1225

RAY A. BILLINGTON: The Far Western Frontier: 1830-1860. † *Illus.* TB/3012

W. R. BROCK: An American Crisis: *Congress and Reconstruction, 1865-67* ° △ TB/1283

EDMUND BURKE: On the American Revolution: *Selected Speeches and Letters.* ‡ *Edited by Elliott Robert Barkan* TB/3068

WHITNEY R. CROSS: The Burned-Over District: *The Social and Intellectual History of Enthusiastic Religion in Western New York, 1800-1850* △ TB/1242

GEORGE DANGERFIELD: The Awakening of American Nationalism: 1815-1828. † *Illus.* TB/3061

CLEMENT EATON: The Freedom-of-Thought Struggle in the Old South. *Revised and Enlarged. Illus.* TB/1150

CLEMENT EATON: The Growth of Southern Civilization: 1790-1860. † *Illus.* TB/3040

LOUIS FILLER: The Crusade Against Slavery: 1830-1860. † *Illus.* TB/3029

DIXON RYAN FOX: The Decline of Aristocracy in the Politics of New York: 1801-1840. ‡ *Edited by Robert V. Remini* TB/3064

FELIX GILBERT: The Beginnings of American Foreign Policy: *To the Farewell Address* TB/1200

FRANCIS GRIERSON: The Valley of Shadows: *The Coming of the Civil War in Lincoln's Midwest: A Contemporary Account* TB/1246

---

† The New American Nation Series, edited by Henry Steele Commager and Richard B. Morris.

‡ American Perspectives series, edited by Bernard Wishy and William E. Leuchtenburg.

* The Rise of Modern Europe series, edited by William L. Langer.

¶ Researches in the Social, Cultural, and Behavioral Sciences, edited by Benjamin Nelson.

§ The Library of Religion and Culture, edited by Benjamin Nelson.

Σ Harper Modern Science Series, edited by James R. Newman.

° Not for sale in Canada.

△ Not for sale in the U. K.

FRANCIS J. GRUND: Aristocracy in America: *Social Class in the Formative Years of the New Nation* TB/1001
ALEXANDER HAMILTON: The Reports of Alexander Hamilton. ‡ *Edited by Jacob E. Cooke* TB/3060
THOMAS JEFFERSON: Notes on the State of Virginia. ‡ *Edited by Thomas P. Abernethy* TB/3052
JAMES MADISON: The Forging of American Federalism: *Selected Writings of James Madison. Edited by Saul K. Padover* TB/1226
BERNARD MAYO: Myths and Men: *Patrick Henry, George Washington, Thomas Jefferson* TB/1108
JOHN C. MILLER: Alexander Hamilton and the Growth of the New Nation TB/3057
RICHARD B. MORRIS, Ed.: The Era of the American Revolution TB/1180
R. B. NYE: The Cultural Life of the New Nation: 1776-1801. † *Illus.* TB/3026
FRANCIS S. PHILBRICK: The Rise of the West, 1754-1830. † *Illus.* TB/3067
TIMOTHY L. SMITH: Revivalism and Social Reform: *American Protestantism on the Eve of the Civil War* TB/1229
FRANK THISTLETHWAITE: America and the Atlantic Community: *Anglo-American Aspects, 1790-1850* TB/1107
ALBION W. TOURGÉE: A Fool's Errand. ‡ *Ed. by George Fredrickson* TB/3074
A. F. TYLER: Freedom's Ferment: *Phases of American Social History from the Revolution to the Outbreak of the Civil War. 31 illus.* TB/1074
GLYNDON G. VAN DEUSEN: The Jacksonian Era: 1828-1848. † *Illus.* TB/3028
LOUIS B. WRIGHT: Culture on the Moving Frontier TB/1053

American Studies: The Civil War to 1900

THOMAS C. COCHRAN & WILLIAM MILLER: The Age of Enterprise: *A Social History of Industrial America* TB/1054
W. A. DUNNING: Essays on the Civil War and Reconstruction. *Introduction by David Donald* TB/1181
W. A. DUNNING: Reconstruction, Political and Economic: 1865-1877 TB/1073
HAROLD U. FAULKNER: Politics, Reform and Expansion: 1890-1900. † *Illus.* TB/3020
HELEN HUNT JACKSON: A Century of Dishonor: *The Early Crusade for Indian Reform. ‡ Edited by Andrew F. Rolle* TB/3063
ALBERT D. KIRWAN: Revolt of the Rednecks: *Mississippi Politics, 1876-1925* TB/1199
ROBERT GREEN MC CLOSKEY: American Conservatism in the Age of Enterprise: 1865-1910 TB/1137
ARTHUR MANN: Yankee Reformers in the Urban Age: *Social Reform in Boston, 1880-1900* TB/1247
WHITELAW REID: After the War: *A Tour of the Southern States, 1865-1866. ‡ Edited by C. Vann Woodward* TB/3066
CHARLES H. SHINN: Mining Camps: *A Study in American Frontier Government. ‡ Edited by Rodman W. Paul* TB/3062
VERNON LANE WHARTON: The Negro in Mississippi: 1865-1890 TB/1178

American Studies: 1900 to the Present

RAY STANNARD BAKER: Following the Color Line: *American Negro Citizenship in Progressive Era. ‡ Illus. Edited by Dewey W. Grantham, Jr.* TB/3053
RANDOLPH S. BOURNE: War and the Intellectuals: *Collected Essays, 1915-1919. ‡ Edited by Carl Resek* TB/3043
A. RUSSELL BUCHANAN: The United States and World War II. † *Illus.* Vol. I TB/3044; Vol. II TB/3045
ABRAHAM CAHAN: The Rise of David Levinsky: *a documentary novel of social mobility in early twentieth century America. Intro. by John Higham* TB/1028
THOMAS C. COCHRAN: The American Business System: *A Historical Perspective, 1900-1955* TB/1080

FOSTER RHEA DULLES: America's Rise to World Power: 1898-1954. † *Illus.* TB/3021
JOHN D. HICKS: Republican Ascendancy: 1921-1933. † *Illus.* TB/3041
SIDNEY HOOK: Reason, Social Myths, and Democracy TB/1237
ROBERT HUNTER: Poverty: *Social Conscience in the Progressive Era. ‡ Edited by Peter d'A. Jones* TB/3065
WILLIAM L. LANGER & S. EVERETT GLEASON: The Challenge to Isolation: *The World Crisis of 1937-1940 and American Foreign Policy* Vol. I TB/3054; Vol. II TB/3055
WILLIAM E. LEUCHTENBURG: Franklin D. Roosevelt and the New Deal: 1932-1940. † *Illus.* TB/3025
ARTHUR S. LINK: Woodrow Wilson and the Progressive Era: 1910-1917. † *Illus.* TB/3023
GEORGE E. MOWRY: The Era of Theodore Roosevelt and the Birth of Modern America: 1900-1912. † *Illus.* TB/3022
RUSSEL B. NYE: Midwestern Progressive Politics: *A Historical Study of Its Origins and Development, 1870-1958* TB/1202
WILLIAM PRESTON, JR.: Aliens and Dissenters: *Federal Suppression of Radicals, 1903-1933* TB/1287
WALTER RAUSCHENBUSCH: Christianity and the Social Crisis. ‡ *Edited by Robert D. Cross* TB/3059
JACOB RIIS: The Making of an American. ‡ *Edited by Roy Lubove* TB/3070
PHILIP SELZNICK: TVA and the Grass Roots: *A Study in the Sociology of Formal Organization* TB/1230
IDA M. TARBELL: The History of the Standard Oil Company: *Briefer Version. ‡ Edited by David M. Chalmers* TB/3071
GEORGE B. TINDALL, Ed.: A Populist Reader ‡ TB/3069
TWELVE SOUTHERNERS: I'll Take My Stand: *The South and the Agrarian Tradition. Intro. by Louis D. Rubin, Jr., Biographical Essays by Virginia Rock* TB/1072
WALTER E. WEYL: The New Democracy: *An Essay on Certain Political Tendencies in the United States. ‡ Edited by Charles B. Forcey* TB/3042

Anthropology

JACQUES BARZUN: Race: *A Study in Superstition. Revised Edition* TB/1172
JOSEPH B. CASAGRANDE, Ed.: In the Company of Man: *Twenty Portraits of Anthropological Informants. Illus.* TB/3047
W. E. LE GROS CLARK: The Antecedents of Man: *Intro. to Evolution of the Primates. º ∆ Illus.* TB/559
CORA DU BOIS: The People of Alor. *New Preface by the author. Illus.* Vol. I TB/1042; Vol. II TB/1043
RAYMOND FIRTH, Ed.: Man and Culture: *An Evaluation of the Work of Bronislaw Malinowski* ¶ º ∆ TB/1133
DAVID LANDY: Tropical Childhood: *Cultural Transmission and Learning in a Puerto Rican Village* ¶ TB/1235
L. S. B. LEAKEY: Adam's Ancestors: *The Evolution of Man and His Culture. ∆ Illus.* TB/1019
ROBERT H. LOWIE: Primitive Society. *Introduction by Fred Eggan* TB/1056
EDWARD BURNETT TYLOR: The Origins of Culture. *Part I of "Primitive Culture." § Intro. by Paul Radin* TB/33
EDWARD BURNETT TYLOR: Religion in Primitive Culture. *Part II of "Primitive Culture." § Intro. by Paul Radin* TB/34
W. LLOYD WARNER: A Black Civilization: *A Study of an Australian Tribe. ¶ Illus.* TB/3056

Art and Art History

WALTER LOWRIE: Art in the Early Church. *Revised Edition. 452 illus.* TB/124
EMILE MÂLE: The Gothic Image: *Religious Art in France of the Thirteenth Century. § ∆ 190 illus.* TB/44

W. O. HASSALL, Ed.: Medieval England: *As Viewed by Contemporaries* △ TB/1205

DENYS HAY: Europe: The Emergence of an Idea TB/1275

DENYS HAY: The Medieval Centuries ○ △ TB/1192

J. M. HUSSEY: The Byzantine World △ TB/1057

ROBERT LATOUCHE: The Birth of Western Economy: *Economic Aspects of the Dark Ages.* ○ △ *Intro. by Philip Grierson* TB/1290

FERDINAND LOT: The End of the Ancient World and the Beginnings of the Middle Ages. *Introduction by Glanville Downey* TB/1044

G. MOLLAT: The Popes at Avignon: 1305-1378 △ TB/308

CHARLES PETIT-DUTAILLIS: The Feudal Monarchy in France and England: *From the Tenth to the Thirteenth Century* ○ △ TB/1165

HENRI PIRENNE: Early Democracies in the Low Countries: *Urban Society and Political Conflict in the Middle Ages and the Renaissance. Introduction by John H. Mundy* TB/1110

STEVEN RUNCIMAN: A History of the Crusades. △
Volume I: *The First Crusade and the Foundation of the Kingdom of Jerusalem. Illus.* TB/1143
Volume II: *The Kingdom of Jerusalem and the Frankish East, 1100-1187. Illus.* TB/1243

FERDINAND SCHEVILL: Siena: *The History of a Medieval Commune. Intro. by William M. Bowsky* TB/1164

SULPICIUS SEVERUS et al.: The Western Fathers: *Being the Lives of Martin of Tours, Ambrose, Augustine of Hippo, Honoratus of Arles and Germanus of Auxerre.* △ *Edited and trans. by F. O. Hoare* TB/309

HENRY OSBORN TAYLOR: The Classical Heritage of the Middle Ages. *Foreword and Biblio. by Kenneth M. Setton* TB/1117

F. VAN DER MEER: Augustine The Bishop: *Church and Society at the Dawn of the Middle Ages* △ TB/304

J. M. WALLACE-HADRILL: The Barbarian West: *The Early Middle Ages, A.D. 400-1000* △ TB/1061

History: Renaissance & Reformation

JACOB BURCKHARDT: The Civilization of the Renaissance in Italy. △ *Intro. by Benjamin Nelson & Charles Trinkaus. Illus.* Vol. I TB/40; Vol. II TB/41

JOHN CALVIN & JACOPO SADOLETO: A Reformation Debate. *Edited by John C. Olin* TB/1239

ERNST CASSIRER: The Individual and the Cosmos in Renaissance Philosophy. △ *Translated with an Introduction by Mario Domandi* TB/1097

FEDERICO CHABOD: Machiavelli and the Renaissance △ TB/1193

EDWARD P. CHEYNEY: The Dawn of a New Era, 1250-1453. * *Illus.* TB/3002

G. CONSTANT: The Reformation in England: *The English Schism, Henry VIII, 1509-1547* △ TB/314

R. TREVOR DAVIES: The Golden Century of Spain, 1501-1621 ○ △ TB/1194

G. R. ELTON: Reformation Europe, 1517-1559 ○ △ TB/1270

DESIDERIUS ERASMUS: Christian Humanism and the Reformation: *Selected Writings. Edited and translated by John C. Olin* TB/1166

WALLACE K. FERGUSON et al.: Facets of the Renaissance TB/1098

WALLACE K. FERGUSON et al.: The Renaissance: *Six Essays. Illus.* TB/1084

JOHN NEVILLE FIGGIS: The Divine Right of Kings. *Introduction by G. R. Elton* TB/1191

JOHN NEVILLE FIGGIS: Political Thought from Gerson to Grotius: *1414-1625: Seven Studies. Introduction by Garrett Mattingly* TB/1032

MYRON P. GILMORE: The World of Humanism, 1453-1517. * *Illus.* TB/3003

FRANCESCO GUICCIARDINI: Maxims and Reflections of a Renaissance Statesman (Ricordi). *Trans. by Mario Domandi. Intro. by Nicolai Rubinstein* TB/1160

J. H. HEXTER: More's Utopia: *The Biography of an Idea. New Epilogue by the Author* TB/1195

HAJO HOLBORN: Ulrich von Hutten and the German Reformation TB/1238

JOHAN HUIZINGA: Erasmus and the Age of Reformation. △ *Illus.* TB/19

JOEL HURSTFIELD, Ed.: The Reformation Crisis △ TB/1267

ULRICH VON HUTTEN et al.: On the Eve of the Reformation: "Letters of Obscure Men." *Introduction by Hajo Holborn* TB/1124

PAUL O. KRISTELLER: Renaissance Thought: *The Classic, Scholastic, and Humanist Strains* TB/1048

PAUL O. KRISTELLER: Renaissance Thought II: *Papers on Humanism and the Arts* TB/1163

NICCOLÒ MACHIAVELLI: History of Florence and of the Affairs of Italy: *from the earliest times to the death of Lorenzo the Magnificent. Introduction by Felix Gilbert* △ TB/1027

ALFRED VON MARTIN: Sociology of the Renaissance. *Introduction by Wallace K. Ferguson* TB/1099

GARRETT MATTINGLY et al.: Renaissance Profiles. △ *Edited by J. H. Plumb* TB/1162

MILLARD MEISS: Painting in Florence and Siena after the Black Death: *The Arts, Religion and Society in the Mid-Fourteenth Century.* △ *169 illus.* TB/1148

J. E. NEALE: The Age of Catherine de Medici ○ △ TB/1085

ERWIN PANOFSKY: Studies in Iconology: *Humanistic Themes in the Art of the Renaissance.* △ *180 illustrations* TB/1077

J. H. PARRY: The Establishment of the European Hegemony: *1415-1715: Trade and Exploration in the Age of the Renaissance* △ TB/1045

J. H. PLUMB: The Italian Renaissance: *A Concise Survey of Its History and Culture* △ TB/1161

A. F. POLLARD: Henry VIII. ○ △ *Introduction by A. G. Dickens* TB/1249

A. F. POLLARD: Wolsey. ○ △ *Introduction by A. G. Dickens* TB/1248

CECIL ROTH: The Jews in the Renaissance. *Illus.* TB/834

A. L. ROWSE: The Expansion of Elizabethan England. ○ △ *Illus.* TB/1220

GORDON RUPP: Luther's Progress to the Diet of Worms ○ △ TB/120

FERDINAND SCHEVILL: The Medici. *Illus.* TB/1010

FERDINAND SCHEVILL: Medieval and Renaissance Florence. *Illus.* Volume I: *Medieval Florence* TB/1090
Volume II: *The Coming of Humanism and the Age of the Medici* TB/1091

G. M. TREVELYAN: England in the Age of Wycliffe, 1368-1520 ○ △ TB/1112

VESPASIANO: Renaissance Princes, Popes, and Prelates: *The Vespasiano Memoirs: Lives of Illustrious Men of the XVth Century. Intro. by Myron P. Gilmore* TB/1111

History: Modern European

FREDERICK B. ARTZ: Reaction and Revolution, 1815-1832. * *Illus.* TB/3034

MAX BELOFF: The Age of Absolutism, 1660-1815 △ TB/1062

ROBERT C. BINKLEY: Realism and Nationalism, 1852-1871. * *Illus.* TB/3038

ASA BRIGGS: The Making of Modern England, 1784-1867: *The Age of Improvement* ○ △ TB/1203

CRANE BRINTON: A Decade of Revolution, 1789-1799. * *Illus.* TB/3018

D. W. BROGAN: The Development of Modern France. ○ △
Volume I: *From the Fall of the Empire to the Dreyfus Affair* TB/1184
Volume II: *The Shadow of War, World War I, Between the Two Wars. New Introduction by the Author* TB/1185

J. BRONOWSKI & BRUCE MAZLISH: The Western Intellectual Tradition: *From Leonardo to Hegel* △ TB/3001

GEOFFREY BRUUN: Europe and the French Imperium, 1799-1814. * *Illus.* TB/3033

ALAN BULLOCK: Hitler, A Study in Tyranny. ○ △ *Illus.* TB/1123

4

Intellectual History & History of Ideas

5

PHILIP P. WIENER: Evolution and the Founders of Pragmatism. △ *Foreword by John Dewey* TB/1212
BASIL WILLEY: Nineteenth Century Studies: *Coleridge to Matthew Arnold* º △ TB/1261
BASIL WILLEY: More Nineteenth Century Studies: *A Group of Honest Doubters* º △ TB/1262

Literature, Poetry, The Novel & Criticism

JAMES BAIRD: Ishmael: *The Art of Melville in the Contexts of International Primitivism* TB/1023
JACQUES BARZUN: The House of Intellect △ TB/1051
W. J. BATE: From Classic to Romantic: *Premises of Taste in Eighteenth Century England* TB/1036
RACHEL BESPALOFF: On the Iliad TB/2006
R. P. BLACKMUR et al.: Lectures in Criticism. *Introduction by Huntington Cairns* TB/2003
JAMES BOSWELL: The Life of Dr. Johnson & The Journal of a Tour to the Hebrides with Samuel Johnson LL.D.: *Selections.* º △ *Edited by F. V. Morley. Illus. by Ernest Shepard* TB/1254
ABRAHAM CAHAN: The Rise of David Levinsky: *a documentary novel of social mobility in early twentieth century America. Intro. by John Higham* TB/1028
ERNST R. CURTIUS: European Literature and the Latin Middle Ages △ TB/2015
GEORGE ELIOT: Daniel Deronda: *a novel. Introduction by F. R. Leavis* TB/1039
ADOLF ERMAN, Ed.: The Ancient Egyptians: *A Sourcebook of Their Writings. New Material and Introduction by William Kelly Simpson* TB/1233
ÉTIENNE GILSON: Dante and Philosophy TB/1089
ALFRED HARBAGE: As They Liked It: *A Study of Shakespeare's Moral Artistry* TB/1035
STANLEY R. HOPPER, Ed: Spiritual Problems in Contemporary Literature § TB/21
A. R. HUMPHREYS: The Augustan World: *Society, Thought and Letters in 18th Century England* º △ TB/1105
ALDOUS HUXLEY: Antic Hay & The Giaconda Smile. º △ *Introduction by Martin Green* TB/3503
ALDOUS HUXLEY: Brave New World & Brave New World Revisited. º △ *Introduction by Martin Green* TB/3501
HENRY JAMES: The Tragic Muse: *a novel. Introduction by Leon Edel* TB/1017
ARNOLD KETTLE: An Introduction to the English Novel. △
Volume I: *Defoe to George Eliot* TB/1011
Volume II: *Henry James to the Present* TB/1012
RICHMOND LATTIMORE: The Poetry of Greek Tragedy △ TB/1257
J. B. LEISHMAN: The Monarch of Wit: *An Analytical and Comparative Study of the Poetry of John Donne* º △ TB/1258
J. B. LEISHMAN: Themes and Variations in Shakespeare's Sonnets º △ TB/1259
ROGER SHERMAN LOOMIS: The Development of Arthurian Romance △ TB/1167
JOHN STUART MILL: On Bentham and Coleridge. △ *Introduction by F. R. Leavis* TB/1070
KENNETH B. MURDOCK: Literature and Theology in Colonial New England TB/99
SAMUEL PEPYS: The Diary of Samuel Pepys. º *Edited by O. F. Morshead. Illus. by Ernest Shepard* TB/1007
ST.-JOHN PERSE: Seamarks TB/2002
V. DE S. PINTO: Crisis in English Poetry, 1880-1940 º △ TB/1260
GEORGE SANTAYANA: Interpretations of Poetry and Religion § TB/9
C. K. STEAD: The New Poetic: *Yeats to Eliot* △ TB/1263
HEINRICH STRAUMANN: American Literature in the Twentieth Century. △ *Third Edition, Revised* TB/1168
PAGET TOYNBEE: Dante Alighieri: *His Life and Works. Edited with Intro. by Charles S. Singleton* TB/1206
DOROTHY VAN GHENT: The English Novel: *Form and Function* TB/1050
E. B. WHITE: One Man's Meat. *Introduction by Walter Blair* TB/3505

BASIL WILLEY: Nineteenth Century Studies: *Coleridge to Matthew Arnold* △ TB/1261
BASIL WILLEY: More Nineteenth Century Studies: *A Group of Honest Doubters* º △ TB/1262
RAYMOND WILLIAMS: Culture and Society, 1780-1950 º △ TB/1252
RAYMOND WILLIAMS: The Long Revolution. º △ *Revised Edition* TB/1253
MORTON DAUWEN ZABEL, Editor: Literary Opinion in America Vol. I TB/3013; Vol. II TB/3014

Myth, Symbol & Folklore

JOSEPH CAMPBELL, Editor: Pagan and Christian Mysteries *Illus.* TB/2013
MIRCEA ELIADE: Cosmos and History: *The Myth of the Eternal Return* § △ TB/2050
MIRCEA ELIADE: Rites and Symbols of Initiation: *The Mysteries of Birth and Rebirth* § △ TB/1236
THEODOR H. GASTER: Thespis: *Ritual, Myth and Drama in the Ancient Near East* △ TB/1281
C. G. JUNG & C. KERÉNYI: Essays on a Science of Mythology: *The Myths of the Divine Child and the Divine Maiden* TB/2014
DORA & ERWIN PANOFSKY: Pandora's Box: *The Changing Aspects of a Mythical Symbol.* △ *Revised edition. Illus.* TB/2021
ERWIN PANOFSKY: Studies in Iconology: *Humanistic Themes in the Art of the Renaissance.* △ *180 illustrations* TB/1077
JEAN SEZNEC: The Survival of the Pagan Gods: *The Mythological Tradition and its Place in Renaissance Humanism and Art.* △ *108 illustrations* TB/2004
HELLMUT WILHELM: Change: *Eight Lectures on the I Ching* △ TB/2019
HEINRICH ZIMMER: Myths and Symbols in Indian Art and Civilization. △ *70 illustrations* TB/2005

Philosophy

G. E. M. ANSCOMBE: An Introduction to Wittgenstein's Tractatus. º △ *Second Edition, Revised* TB/1210
HENRI BERGSON: Time and Free Will: *An Essay on the Immediate Data of Consciousness* º △ TB/1021
H. J. BLACKHAM: Six Existentialist Thinkers: *Kierkegaard, Nietzsche, Jaspers, Marcel, Heidegger, Sartre* º △ TB/1002
CRANE BRINTON: Nietzsche. *New Preface, Bibliography and Epilogue by the Author* TB/1197
MARTIN BUBER: The Knowledge of Man. △ *Ed. with an Intro. by Maurice Friedman. Trans. by Maurice Friedman and Ronald Gregor Smith* TB/135
ERNST CASSIRER: The Individual and the Cosmos in Renaissance Philosophy. △ *Translated with an Introduction by Mario Domandi* TB/1097
ERNST CASSIRER: Rousseau, Kant and Goethe. *Introduction by Peter Gay* TB/1092
FREDERICK COPLESTON: Medieval Philosophy º △ TB/376
F. M. CORNFORD: Principium Sapientiae: *A Study of the Origins of Greek Philosophical Thought. Edited by W. K. C. Guthrie* TB/1213
F. M. CORNFORD: From Religion to Philosophy: *A Study in the Origins of Western Speculation* § TB/20
WILFRID DESAN: The Tragic Finale: *An Essay on the Philosophy of Jean-Paul Sartre* TB/1030
A. P. D'ENTRÈVES: Natural Law: *An Historical Survey* △ TB/1223
MARVIN FARBER: The Aims of Phenomenology: *The Motives, Methods, and Impact of Husserl's Thought* TB/1291
HERBERT FINGARETTE: The Self in Transformation: *Psychoanalysis, Philosophy and the Life of the Spirit* ¶ TB/1177
PAUL FRIEDLÄNDER: Plato: *An Introduction* △ TB/2017
ÉTIENNE GILSON: Dante and Philosophy TB/1089
WILLIAM CHASE GREENE: Moira: *Fate, Good, and Evil in Greek Thought* TB/1104

ERICH NEUMANN: Amor and Psyche: *The Psychic Development of the Feminine* △ TB/2012
ERICH NEUMANN: The Archetypal World of Henry Moore. △ 107 illus. TB/2020
ERICH NEUMANN: The Origins and History of Consciousness △ Vol. I Illus. TB/2007; Vol. II TB/2008
C. P. OBERNDORF: A History of Psychoanalysis in America TB/1147
RALPH BARTON PERRY: The Thought and Character of William James: *Briefer Version* TB/1156
JEAN PIAGET, BÄRBEL INHELDER, & ALINA SZEMINSKA: The Child's Conception of Geometry ○ △ TB/1146
JOHN H. SCHAAR: Escape from Authority: *The Perspectives of Erich Fromm* TB/1155
MUZAFER SHERIF: The Psychology of Social Norms TB/3072

Sociology

JACQUES BARZUN: Race: *A Study in Superstition. Revised Edition* TB/1172
BERNARD BERELSON, Ed.: The Behavioral Sciences Today TB/1127
ABRAHAM CAHAN: The Rise of David Levinsky: *A documentary novel of social mobility in early twentieth century America. Intro. by John Higham* TB/1028
THOMAS C. COCHRAN: The Inner Revolution: *Essays on the Social Sciences in History* TB/1140
ALLISON DAVIS & JOHN DOLLARD: Children of Bondage: *The Personality Development of Negro Youth in the Urban South* ¶ TB/3049
ST. CLAIR DRAKE & HORACE R. CAYTON: Black Metropolis: *A Study of Negro Life in a Northern City. △ Revised and Enlarged. Intro. by Everett C. Hughes*
Vol. I TB/1086; Vol. II TB/1087
EMILE DURKHEIM et al.: Essays on Sociology and Philosophy: *With Analyses of Durkheim's Life and Work.* ¶ *Edited by Kurt H. Wolff* TB/1151
LEON FESTINGER, HENRY W. RIECKEN & STANLEY SCHACHTER: When Prophecy Fails: *A Social and Psychological Account of a Modern Group that Predicted the Destruction of the World* ¶ TB/1132
ALVIN W. GOULDNER: Wildcat Strike: *A Study in Worker-Management Relationships* ¶ TB/1176
FRANCIS J. GRUND: Aristocracy in America: *Social Class in the Formative Years of the New Nation* △ TB/1001
KURT LEWIN: Field Theory in Social Science: *Selected Theoretical Papers.* ¶ △ *Edited with a Foreword by Dorwin Cartwright* TB/1135
R. M. MAC IVER: Social Causation TB/1153
ROBERT K. MERTON, LEONARD BROOM, LEONARD S. COTTRELL, JR., Editors: Sociology Today: *Problems and Prospects* ¶ Vol. I TB/1173; Vol. II TB/1174
ROBERTO MICHELS: First Lectures in Political Sociology. *Edited by Alfred de Grazia* ¶ ○ TB/1224
BARRINGTON MOORE, JR.: Political Power and Social Theory: *Seven Studies* ¶ TB/1221
BARRINGTON MOORE, JR.: Soviet Politics—The Dilemma of Power: *The Role of Ideas in Social Change* ¶ TB/1222
TALCOTT PARSONS & EDWARD A. SHILS, Editors: Toward a General Theory of Action: *Theoretical Foundations for the Social Sciences* TB/1083
JOHN H. ROHRER & MUNRO S. EDMONDSON, Eds.: The Eighth Generation Grows Up: *Cultures and Personalities of New Orleans Negroes* ¶ TB/3050
ARNOLD ROSE: The Negro in America: *The Condensed Version of Gunnar Myrdal's An American Dilemma* TB/3048
KURT SAMUELSSON: Religion and Economic Action: *A Critique of Max Weber's The Protestant Ethic and the Spirit of Capitalism.* ¶ ○ *Trans. by E. G. French. Ed. with Intro. by D. C. Coleman* TB/1131
PHILIP SELZNICK: TVA and the Grass Roots: *A Study in the Sociology of Formal Organization* TB/1230
GEORG SIMMEL et al.: Essays on Sociology, Philosophy, and Aesthetics. ¶ *Edited by Kurt H. Wolff* TB/1234

HERBERT SIMON: The Shape of Automation: *For Men and Management* △ TB/1245
PITIRIM A. SOROKIN: Contemporary Sociological Theories. *Through the First Quarter of the 20th Century* TB/3046
MAURICE R. STEIN: The Eclipse of Community: *An Interpretation of American Studies* TB/1128
FERDINAND TÖNNIES: Community and Society: *Gemeinschaft und Gesellschaft. Translated and edited by Charles P. Loomis* TB/1116
W. LLOYD WARNER & Associates: Democracy in Jonesville: *A Study in Quality and Inequality* TB/1129
W. LLOYD WARNER: Social Class in America: *The Evaluation of Status* TB/1013

RELIGION

Ancient & Classical

J. H. BREASTED: Development of Religion and Thought in Ancient Egypt. *Intro. by John A. Wilson* TB/57
HENRI FRANKFORT: Ancient Egyptian Religion: *An Interpretation* TB/77
G. RACHEL LEVY: Religious Conceptions of the Stone Age and their Influence upon European Thought. △ *Illus. Introduction by Henri Frankfort* TB/106
MARTIN P. NILSSON: Greek Folk Religion. *Foreword by Arthur Darby Nock* TB/78
ALEXANDRE PIANKOFF: The Shrines of Tut-Ankh-Amon. △ *Edited by N. Rambova. 117 illus.* TB/2011
ERWIN ROHDE: Psyche: *The Cult of Souls and Belief in Immortality Among the Greeks.* △ *Intro. by W. K. C. Guthrie* Vol. I TB/140; Vol. II TB/141
H. J. ROSE: Religion in Greece and Rome △ TB/55

Biblical Thought & Literature

W. F. ALBRIGHT: The Biblical Period from Abraham to Ezra TB/102
C. K. BARRETT, Ed.: The New Testament Background: *Selected Documents* △ TB/86
C. H. DODD: The Authority of the Bible △ TB/43
M. S. ENSLIN: Christian Beginnings △ TB/5
M. S. ENSLIN: The Literature of the Christian Movement △ TB/6
JOHN GRAY: Archaeology and the Old Testament World. △ *Illus.* TB/127
JAMES MUILENBURG: The Way of Israel: *Biblical Faith and Ethics* △ TB/133
H. H. ROWLEY: The Growth of the Old Testament △ TB/107
GEORGE ADAM SMITH: The Historical Geography of the Holy Land. ○ △ *Revised and reset* TB/138
D. WINTON THOMAS, Ed.: Documents from Old Testament Times △ TB/85

The Judaic Tradition

LEO BAECK: Judaism and Christianity. *Trans. with Intro. by Walter Kaufmann* JP/23
SALO W. BARON: Modern Nationalism and Religion JP/18
MARTIN BUBER: Eclipse of God: *Studies in the Relation Between Religion and Philosophy* △ TB/12
MARTIN BUBER: For the Sake of Heaven TB/801
MARTIN BUBER: Hasidism and Modern Man. △ *Ed. and Trans. by Maurice Friedman* TB/839
MARTIN BUBER: The Knowledge of Man. △ *Edited with an Introduction by Maurice Friedman. Translated by Maurice Friedman and Ronald Gregor Smith* TB/135
MARTIN BUBER: Moses: *The Revelation and the Covenant* △ TB/837
MARTIN BUBER: The Origin and Meaning of Hasidism △ TB/835
MARTIN BUBER: Pointing the Way. △ *Introduction by Maurice S. Friedman* TB/103
MARTIN BUBER: The Prophetic Faith TB/73
MARTIN BUBER: Two Types of Faith: *the interpenetration of Judaism and Christianity* ○ △ TB/75

8